"Cher alme" :
Texts of Anglo-Norman Piety

Medieval and Renaissance Texts and Studies

Volume 385

French of England Translation Series (FRETS)

Occasional Publication Series

Volume 1

"Cher alme" : Texts of Anglo-Norman Piety

Edited by
Tony Hunt

Translated by
Jane Bliss

with an Introduction by
Henrietta Leyser

ACMRS
(Arizona Center for Medieval and Renaissance Studies)
Tempe, Arizona
2010

Published with the assistance of Fordham University.

Published by ACMRS (Arizona Center for Medieval and Renaissance Studies)
Tempe, Arizona

Library of Congress Cataloging-in-Publication Data

"Cher alme" : texts of Anglo-Norman piety / edited by Tony Hunt ; translated by Jane Bliss ; with an introduction by Henrietta Leyser.
p. cm. -- (Medieval and Renaissance texts and studies ; v. 385) (The French of England translation series (FRETS) ; Occasional publication series ; v. 1)
English and Anglo-Norman.
Includes bibliographical references and indexes.
ISBN 978-0-86698-433-1 (alk. paper)
1. Spiritual life--Catholic Church--Early works to 1800. 2. Christian life--Early works to 1800. I. Hunt, Tony. II. Bliss, Jane. III. Leyser, Henrietta.
BX2350.3C435 2010
248.4'82420902--dc22

2010013233

Cover Art:
A hooded Franciscan friar hears the confession of a nun, who is kneeling on the other side of a table or altar.
A scene from the lower margin of an image taken from the Luttrell Psalter, Psalm 37.
Originally published/produced in England [East Anglia]; circa 1325–1335.
Shelfmark/Page: Add. 42130, f.74

This book is made to last. It is set in Junicode using LyX and XeLaTex, smyth-sewn and printed on acid-free paper to library specifications.
Printed in the United States of America.

Table of Contents

III The Passion

IV Private Prayers

V Vices and Confession

VI Virtues and Rewards

Series Editors' Preface

We are pleased to offer as the first Occasional Publication in the French of England Translation Series (FRETS) *"Cher alme": Texts of Anglo-Norman Piety*, an important collection of hitherto unedited and untranslated works of Anglo-Norman doctrine and devotion. Any notion that Anglo-Norman works of piety lack interest — as has been their undeserved reputation — is thoroughly refuted here in the excellent presentation by the team of Henrietta Leyser, Tony Hunt, and Jane Bliss, in a volume that is a first of its kind.

Cher alme fills a long-standing void in our knowledge of the English Middle Ages, for making sense of the period requires an understanding of the French of England as the pre-eminent language of pastoral and devotional works from the twelfth century onwards. In turn, these French texts furnish the necessary context for fully appreciating medieval English religious writings, which developed alongside their francophone counterparts.

The texts presented here are grouped thematically so as to provide a range of pastoral and devotional works, from doctrinal instruction to prayers and devotions, confessional precepts and practices, guides to good lives and last things. This is a volume which delights as well as informs: again and again, moving and vivid glimpses of medieval beliefs, hopes, and fears leap to the eye. Tony Hunt's editions will be essential to scholars who want to read these works in their original language, and they will be welcomed by those who have keenly awaited their publication, noted as forthcoming in *Anglo-Norman Literature: A Guide to Texts and Manuscripts* by Ruth Dean, with Maureen B. M. Boulton (ANTS OPS 3, 1999). At the same time, Henrietta Leyser's introduction and Jane Bliss' translations ensure that readers new to the field can also discover its fascination.

FRETS itself is designed to make more readily available the works composed in French in medieval England over the twelfth to fifteenth centuries. There exist many excellent editions produced by the Anglo-Norman Text Society: FRETS presents annotated translations, with introductions, that refer back to the principal ANTS editions. But in the still under-studied field of the French of England, with nearly a thousand literary texts and a vast corpus in documentary, administrative, and occupational insular French, there remain many unedited texts or texts that have not been re-edited since their first nineteenth-century editions. Our Occasional Publication series is designed to help fill this need as occasion and opportunity offer.

Thelma Fenster
Jocelyn Wogan-Browne

Preface

This volume presents a selection of material from a variety of religious writings, of which many were listed as "forthcoming" in Dean and Boulton, *Anglo-Norman Literature.* The texts are edited by Tony Hunt and translated by Jane Bliss; Henrietta Leyser has provided an Introduction; typesetting is the work of Quentin Miller. We aim to present the texts thematically rather than generically: beginning with the Tenets of the Faith (1 & 2), continuing through Marian and Passion texts (3–7), we include Prayers (8 & 9), then texts on Vices and Confession (10–13), with the last three pieces (14–16) about Virtues and Rewards.

Acknowledgements

We take this opportunity to thank the following colleagues and friends, for permission to cite their unpublished work, or for their advice and comments: Catherine Batt, Julia Boffey, Maureen Boulton, Clive Brooks, Victoria Condie, Margaret Connolly, Linda Gowans, Douglas Gray, Cecilia Hatt, Margaret Healy-Varley, Julia Hofman, Richard Howard, Peter Jackson, Andrew Kay, Matthew Kilburn, Conrad Leyser, Leslie MacCoull, Martin Maw, Nicholas Orme, Natasha Romanova, Richard Sharpe, Lesley Smith, Eric Southworth, Robert Sturges, Timea Szell, Julia Szirmai, David Trotter, Benedicta Ward, Nicholas Watson. We thank our series editors, Thelma Fenster and Jocelyn Wogan-Browne, for their meticulous work on our text; in addition, we are grateful to numerous college and library staff, who have helped in so many ways.

Abbreviations

AND *Anglo-Norman Dictionary*
ANTS Anglo-Norman Text Society
AV Authorized Version (Bible)
AW *Ancrene Wisse*
BL British Library
BLR *The Bodleian Library Record*
BNF Bibliothèque Nationale Française
BVV *The Book of Vices and Virtues*[1]
CCSL Corpus Christianorum Series Latina
D&B Dean and Boulton, *Anglo-Norman Literature*
EETS Early English Text Society (OS = Original Series)
FM *Fasciculus Morum*
GL *Golden Legend*[2]
JEH *Journal of Ecclesiastical History*
Lumere *La Lumere as Lais*
LV Latin Vulgate (Bible)[3]
MÆ *Medium Ævum*
MERP *Middle English Religious Prose*
MLR *Modern Language Review*
MHRA Modern Humanities Research Association
Neuphil. Mitt. *Neuphilologische Mitteilungen*
ODCC *Oxford Dictionary of the Christian Church*
ODNB *Oxford Dictionary of National Biography*
ODS *Oxford Dictionary of Saints*
PL *Patrologia Latina*
SATF Société des Anciens Textes Français

[1] One of the 14th-century Middle English translations of the 13th-century *Somme* by Lorens d'Orléans. An account of the *Somme le Roi* (which is unedited) may be found in Langlois 1928, vol. 4, pp. 123–98.

[2] Jacobus de Voragine, trans. Ryan; the Latin version (*Legenda Aurea*, ed. Maggioni) may also be consulted.

[3] Citations are from *Biblia Sacra Vulgatæ Editionis*, Paris 1702; we used `vulsearch.sourceforge.net/vulgate.pdf` as a concordance.

Bible Books

An asterisk denotes a book in the Vulgate which, in *AV*, is found only in the Apocrypha. The following books are cited without abbreviation: Job, (the Gospel of) John, Jonah, Judges, (the second book of) Kings, (the Gospel of) Luke, (the Gospel of) Mark, (the first Epistle of) Peter, Wisdom (**AV*, in Apocrypha). Bible books are indexed by their English titles (Vulgate titles are easily found on facing pages in our text below).

Acts The Acts of the Apostles

Apoc. The Apocalypse (Revelation in *AV*)

Cant. Canticum Canticorum (Song of Solomon in *AV*)

II Chron. II Chronicles (II Paralip. in *LV*)

Col. Epistle to the Colossians

I and II Cor. Epistles to the Corinthians

Dan. Daniel

Deut. Deuteronomy

Eccles. Ecclesiastes

Ecclus. Ecclesiasticus (or, the Book of Sirach)*

Ep. ad Titum Epistle to Titus (Titus)

Ephes. Epistle to the Ephesians

Ex. Exodus

Ez. Ezechiel

Gal. Epistle to the Galatians

Gen. Genesis

Hab. Habakkuk

Is. Isaiah

Jac. The Epistle of James (in *LV*)

James The Epistle of James

Jer. Jeremiah

Lam. Lamentations

Lev. Leviticus

I Macc. Maccabees (in *AV* Apocrypha)*

Mal. Malachi

Matt. Matthew

Mic. Micah

Num. Numbers
II Paralip. Paralipomenon Secundus (II Chron. in *AV*)
Ps. Psalm(s)
Prov. Proverbs
I Reg. Regum Primus (I Sam. in *AV*)
IV Reg. Regum Quartus (II Kings in *AV*)
Rev. Revelation (Apocalypse in *LV*)
Rom. Epistle to the Romans
I Sam. Samuel
Sap. Sapientia (Wisdom)*
Song Song of Solomon (Canticum Canticorum in *LV*)
II Thess. Epistle to the Thessalonians
Titus (Epistle entitled simply "Titus" in *AV*)
Tob. Tobit*

General Introduction

Cher alme qe ceste escrit lirez . . .[1]

From Christianity's earliest days in Anglo-Saxon England, its converts could expect instruction in their new faith in their own tongue. Bede (c. 673–735), monk of Jarrow in Northumbria and author of the *Ecclesiastical History of the English People*, famously records the miraculous tale of the Northumbrian cowherd Caedmon, to whom was granted the gift of song so that he could put into vernacular verse "the whole course of sacred history," beginning with the creation of the world, covering the teaching of both the Old and the New Testament, and telling of "the horrors of the pains of hell and the joys of the heavenly kingdom."[2] Caedmon's supposed output (even his existence) is now viewed sceptically by literary scholars,[3] but there can be no doubt of Bede's own attachment to Anglo-Saxon sacred verse or of his commitment to vernacular instruction: on his deathbed he is depicted as anxiously finishing his translation of the opening chapters of the Gospel of Saint John.[4] In the following century, King Alfred (d. 899) vigorously revived this vernacular tradition, persuaded as he was that the Viking attacks on his kingdom were a verdict on the godlessness of a people deprived of the learning they needed for the development of Christian virtue.[5] Such anxieties surfaced again under the pressure of the further Viking attacks that so ominously occurred around the year 1000. In such testing times the need to teach the laity to know and understand the fundamental beliefs of their faith became ever more urgent. Aelfric, abbot of Evesham (d. 1010), and Wulfstan, archbishop

---

[1] This phrase, which inspired our title, is found in the last of our texts (Purgatory, p. 410 below).

[2] *Bede's History* (ed. and trans. Colgrave and Mynors), bk. iv. chap. 24, p. 419.

[3] See, for example, the analysis of Bede's Caedmon in Lerer 1991 (pp. 42–48).

[4] Bede's last hours are described by Cuthbert, later Abbot of Wearmouth, in a letter to a certain Cuthwin in *Bede's History* (ed. and trans. Colgrave and Mynors), p. 583. Cf. Bede's insistence on the importance of teaching the laity, as well as monks or clerics who do not know Latin, both the Creed and the Lord's Prayer in the vernacular; see his *Epistola ad Ecgbertum*, ed. Plummer, p. 409.

[5] See Alfred's Preface, in *Alfred the Great* (trans. Keynes and Lapidge, p. 125). The tradition that King Alfred was himself a translator has recently been reviewed with considerable scepticism (Godden 2007). But supposing Alfred to have been a patron rather than a scholar king does not detract from the importance attached at his court to the vernacular, a tradition upheld in the tenth century by Aethelwold, bishop of Winchester (d. 984): "it certainly cannot matter by what language a man is acquired and drawn to the true faith, so long as he comes to God." *Councils and Synods*, vol. 1, 151–52 (quoted in Giandrea 2007, p. 92).

of York (d. 1023), have both left us with plentiful evidence of an impassioned and determined effort to provide vernacular instruction to lay congregations through preaching and through prayer. According to Wulfstan, it was essential that all who wanted to receive the Eucharist, to have a Christian burial, or to undertake the duties of a godparent, must know both the Lord's Prayer (the *Pater Noster*) and the Creed; parents meanwhile were to teach these texts to their children just as soon as they knew how to speak.[6] Even if the ideal would have been for these texts to be known in Latin, Anglo-Saxon remained a well-favoured second-best.[7]

In 1066, some forty years after the death of Archbishop Wulfstan, William Duke of Normandy conquered England. William never managed to master the language of his new kingdom; nor, it may be imagined, did many of his followers.[8] Nonetheless, anecdotal evidence survives to suggest that during the course of the following century England became a country in which a significant number of the newcomers had learnt English while at the same time many of the native-born now knew Anglo-Norman (the French of England). Despite this, the languages were not given parity of status, so that for several centuries it was French that was the prestige vernacular, whereas English by contrast could be seen as the language of "lowe men."[9]

Despite the inferior status which the English language began to acquire in 1066, it still at that time embodied a corpus of literature without parallel in the Anglo-Norman world. The reaction of the invaders was impressive: during the twelfth century, authors worked zealously to redress this situation and scribes found ready employment as Old French began to establish itself as a literary language. The originally Norman *Song of Roland* and the *Life of Alexis* were among the notable *chansons* now committed to parchment, fresh Lives of saints were composed, and Latin and Anglo-Saxon works translated into the

[6] Wulfstan, *Homilies*, ed. Bethurum: Homily 8c, pp. 181–83.

[7] An explanation for the unusually prominent use of vernacular in England is provided in Remley 1996: "... it should be recalled that the issues surrounding the use of the vernacular in England differed fundamentally from those arising in the continental churches, especially in Francia and other territories in which a pre-Romance dialect was spoken. Whereas Latin texts were entirely incomprehensible to converts whose only language was Old English, they could often be read successfully to European audiences simply by introducing a change of inflection" (p. 58).

[8] For William's attempt to learn English see Orderic Vitalis, *The Ecclesiastical History*, II, pp. 256–57.

[9] For the use of this term, see Turville-Petre 1996 (pp. 17–18); for a recent overview of the evidence on languages after the Conquest see Thomas 2003, esp. chap. 9.

newly-valued vernacular.[10] What was still lacking was anything comparable to the pastoral literature of the late Anglo-Saxon world. However, the intense interest shown in just such issues during the late twelfth century among the masters of the schools of Paris (an interest which bore fruit in the decrees of the Fourth Lateran Council of 1215) helped to remedy this, and in the thirteenth century a wealth of texts written in the French of England began to appear. It is hoped that those presented in this volume will throw light on the very considerable Anglo-Norman contribution to this pastoral revolution.[11]

The introductory sections that follow will correspond as far as possible with the order of the texts in this book, grouped together under five headings.

Tenets of the Faith: The *Dialogue* and the *Lord's Prayer*

Innocent III's summons to the Fourth Lateran Council of 1215 was answered by over four hundred bishops, together with twice as many abbots and deans. To this impressively large audience, Innocent presented a programme based on a newly inclusive vision of the church.[12] Salvation was no longer reserved only for an elect band of Christians, but was now proclaimed to be within the reach of all: "not only virgins and the continent but also married persons find favour with God by right faith and good actions and deserve to attain eternal blessedness."[13] Such salvation depended on regular reception of the sacraments and on "the nourishment of God's word."[14] The teaching of correct doctrine was therefore essential, and bishops were urged to appoint men who were "powerful in word and deed" to help them fulfil the task.[15] Behind this measure lay Innocent's acute fear of heresy and of the threat it posed to his church. In order both to establish and to secure the tenets of orthodoxy, the Pope therefore opened the Lateran Council with a resounding statement of correct faith aimed at rebutting all dualist tendencies and erroneous views on the Trinity, and with a firm condemnation of "... all heretics, whatever names they may go under. They have different faces indeed but their tails

[10] On this topic see esp. Short 1992 and Howlett 1996.

[11] For the importance of this contribution see Watson and Wogan-Browne 2004; note in particular the comment: "Anglo-Norman pastoral writing deserves to be recognised as the principal medium in which the formation of the self and the politics of access to vernacular texts were thought and experienced" (pp. 41–42). For a recent overview of vernacular theology in this period, see a collection of articles in *English Language Notes* 44 (2006).

[12] For the influence of Paris intellectuals, including Langton, on the background to Lateran IV, see Baldwin 1970, esp. chap. 16.

[13] *Decrees*, ed. Tanner, chap. 1, p. 231.

[14] Ibid. chap. 10, p. 239.

[15] Ibid. (p. 239).

are tied together ....”[16] To continue the fight against heresy, metropolitan churches across Europe were to hire theologians “to teach scripture to priests and others and especially to instruct them in matters which are recognised as pertaining to the care of souls,”[17] this being seen now as the “supreme art” (*ars artium*).[18] It was a task which demanded sustained recruitment of able men, and indeed the success of Innocent’s measures came to depend heavily on the contribution made by the preaching and teaching, in the various vernaculars of the countries to which they went, of both the Augustinian canons and of the two new orders of friars Innocent had himself had licensed — the Franciscans in 1209 and the Dominicans in 1216. The *Dialogue of Father and Son*, with which this anthology opens, was very probably written for use as a teaching text by one such friar, even though provision for the spiritual needs of any child remained primarily the responsibility of parents, a point the *Dialogue* itself is at pains to stress.

The *Dialogue* poses a number of complex theological problems (for example, on the nature of the Eucharist) before moving on to consider the Day of Judgement and the horrors of Hell. The interest in the Eucharist may be seen as a reminder that these texts, albeit designed for the laity, did not avoid complex doctrinal issues, and that although the Fourth Lateran Council had insisted on the real presence of Christ’s Body and Blood in the Eucharist (provided the bread and wine had been consecrated by a properly-ordained priest) it had not attempted to answer the question of how the transformation was effected. Some degree of debate here was legitimate,[19] but other tenets of the faith required unconditional assent: thus all Christians must know and adhere to the Apostles’ Creed and the Lord’s Prayer. The requirements — already familiar in Anglo-Saxon England — were to be repeated again and again in the later Middle Ages, particularly after Lateran IV.[20] Not only were they repeated, they were also regularly explicated. Here we will look firstly at the presentation of the Creed in the *Dialogue* and next at the *Pater Noster* as it came to be expounded by Adam of Exeter.

First, the Creed: a template for the analysis of the Creed was laid down in Anglo-Norman England by Richard Wetheringsett of Leicester (fl. c. 1200–c. 1230) immediately after Lateran IV. Richard’s work on the Creed forms part of his manual for priests “who rule well” (his *Summa Qui Bene Pre-*

[16] Ibid. chap. 3, p. 233.
[17] Ibid. chap. 11, p. 240.
[18] Ibid. chap. 27, p. 248.
[19] For the complexity of the debate, see Macy 1994.
[20] See Tanner and Watson 2006.

sunt), a book that continued to be used throughout the Middle Ages.[21] The notion that at Pentecost the Apostles had composed the Creed dates already from the fourth century; new in the twelfth century was the creation of a list of twelve articles of faith, closely associated with the tenets of the Creed but including (as in the *Dialogue*) the seven sacraments. The dissemination of this idea owes much to the influence of Richard's teacher, William de Montibus, Chancellor of Lincoln Cathedral (d. 1213).[22] William had been a student at the schools of Paris during those years when the "think-tank" behind Lateran IV was assembled there, and the importance he attached to the teaching of the Creed may date already from this period. The Apostles' Creed, according to William, "contains in brief compass the Trinitarian, indeed the catholic faith. The creed was given to us that we all, clerics as well as lay people, might confess our faith each day."[23] But faith was not expected to be unquestioning or blind. Philosophers, whether from monastic cloisters (like Saint Anselm) or from university classrooms (like Thomas Aquinas), were eloquent on the nature of faith. For Anselm, following Isaiah 7:9, faith promoted understanding: "I believe so that I may understand."[24] For Aquinas, writing in a very different milieu, God can be known by faith and his existence proved through the exercise of reason and revelation.[25] The author of the *Dialogue*, as he in turn grapples with the relationship between faith, belief, and reason, may not always be very exact in the use of his terminology, but it is clear from his arguments that he was well versed in current debates.

The interest of the *Dialogue* in numbers is indebted both to the new passion of university teachers for schematisation and to a long-standing belief in their meaning. For any medieval Christian, numbers had both symbolic and mnemonic value; God himself when he created the world had *ordered all things in measure and number and weight* (Wisdom 11:20). But the significance of numbers could vary: 3, for example, stood both for the Trinity and for the theological virtues of Faith, Hope, and Charity; 4 both for the cardinal virtues of Justice, Prudence, Fortitude, and Temperance, and for the Evange-

---

[21] For the importance and influence of Richard Wetheringsett's *Summa* see esp. Goering 1992 (*William de Montibus*, pp. 86–95).

[22] For William de Montibus, see ibid. esp. chap. 3, "The Literature of Pastoral Care," pp. 59–99.

[23] William's Sermon no. 129, quoted in ibid. p. 20; for the Latin text, see ibid. p. 561.

[24] See Dialogue (p. 43, note 18) below. Anselm of Canterbury (1033–1109); his *Opera*, ed. Schmitt, I:100; trans. Ward, chap. 1, p. 244.

[25] Thomas Aquinas (c. 1225–1274); for an introduction to his theology see Pelikan, *The Christian Tradition*, vol. III, pp. 268–93.

lists. 3 added to 4 equalled the number of the gifts of the Holy Spirit but, when multiplied, the number of the Apostles. To William de Montibus 12 seemed so useful a number that in one of his best-known teaching manuals, the *Numerale*, the last three of the twelve sections of the work enumerate the 12 articles of faith, the 12 hours of the day, and finally the 12 prerogatives of the Virgin.[26] The work was hugely popular, albeit not definitive. Although the author of the *Dialogue*, like William, bases his 12 articles of the faith on the Apostles' Creed, there was another school of thought, also associated with the schools of Lincoln, which took into account not only the Apostles' Creed but also the more complex Nicene Creed (named after the Council of Nicaea in 323) and the somewhat later Athanasian Creed from which were derived not 12 but 14 articles of faith (7 concerned with the Trinity, and 7 with the Incarnation).[27] Yet, despite the endorsement of these 14 articles of faith by John Pecham, archbishop of Canterbury, in his decree of 1281, *Ignorantia Sacerdotum* (The Ignorance of Priests),[28] it is clear from the *Dialogue* that the earlier tradition of 12 articles based on the Apostles' Creed remained strong, possibly for the sake of pedagogical simplicity, given that the Apostles' Creed was sufficiently short that everyone (in theory) could, and indeed should, be able to learn it by heart.

For seven uneasy years before Lateran IV, from 1207 to 1214, the English Church had suffered from the interdict imposed on the country as the result of the refusal of King John (d. 1216) to accept Stephen Langton (d. 1228) as his archbishop of Canterbury.[29] Langton was known as a progressive scholar and luminary of the schools of Paris, so that the lifting of the interdict in 1214 immediately energised the battered English church, thus making it particularly receptive to Innocent's initiative and programme. Bishops returning from Lateran IV had barely alighted from their ships before undertaking measures designed not only with the priesthood in mind but also with the body of the faithful, aimed at spreading to them knowledge of the tenets of the faith and encouraging devout practice at parish level. Throughout the thirteenth century such concern continued. Pastoral instructions are extant for the sees of Salisbury, Coventry and Lichfield, Lincoln, Worcester, and

[26] For William's *Numerale* see Goering 1992, pp. 226–260.

[27] The standard work on the history of the development of the creeds remains Kelly 1972.

[28] The biography, Douie 1952, has not yet been surpassed; though Benjamin Thompson's entry on Pecham in *ODNB* should now be consulted [article 21745, accessed 8 April 2009] for an overview and for recent bibliography.

[29] For Langton, see Christopher Holdsworth, "Langton, Stephen (c. 1150–1228)," *ODNB* [article 16044, accessed 8 April 2009].

Durham. Archbishop Pecham's Constitutions of 1281 (mentioned above), issued for the whole of the southern province, were somewhat more elaborate and demanding than a number of the earlier decrees, but they were not in any sense a new departure. To these episcopal works must be added learned treatises such as the work of the Oxford-trained theologian and canon lawyer William of Pagula (d. 1332?) entitled *Oculus Sacerdotis* (The Eye of the Priest), which ranged from confessional practice and morality to matters of belief.[30]

The *Oculus Sacerdotis* was highly influential: over fifty manuscripts survive. But it goes without saying that if the ideals of Lateran IV were to be fully implemented, even the most accessible of Latin treatises and admonitions to the clergy would never be enough: what was wanted were works in the vernacular and enough committed priests, preachers, and writers to whom the laity would listen and whom they could understand; it is precisely here that the role of the Dominicans and the Franciscans proved vital. Both Franciscans and Dominicans had been founded as pastoral orders. The Dominicans were the *domini canes*, the hounds of the Lord (in contrast therefore to the dumb dogs of Isaiah 56:10 which never barked), while the Franciscans were bound by their rule of 1223 to preach (with episcopal permission) in ways which would be "of benefit and for the edification of the people, announcing to them virtues and vices, punishment and glory."[31]

Dominicans had arrived in England already in 1221, closely followed three years later by a group of nine Franciscans. By then the Dominicans already had houses in Oxford and London; within months of their arrival the Franciscans had had even greater success and were established in four influential centres (Canterbury, London, Oxford, Northampton). Within ten years, the number of Franciscan houses had risen to twenty-two. Initially the Dominicans were the more learned of the two orders, whereas Franciscan appeal was based on the simplicity in which they aimed to live and the poverty of which they made a virtue — their first recruit, in England, was allegedly afraid he might die

[30] For the texts of the episcopal decrees, see *Councils & Synods* (ed. Powicke and Cheney, vol. II). Pantin 1955 considers the legacy of the thirteenth century (pp. 1–9) and gives a valuable introduction to fourteenth-century sources, including the *Oculus Sacerdotis* (pp. 196–202). *Pastors and the Care of Souls*, ed. Shinners and Dohar, provides a useful anthology of texts in translation, including the statutes for Lincoln of 1239 and an extract from the *Oculus Sacerdotis*.

[31] For a recent translation of the 1223 rule see *Francis of Assisi*, ed. Armstrong, Hellman, and Short; the quotation comes from this edition (chap. ix, p. 105). It is worth noting that this injunction is used as the opening sentence of the handbook for preachers written by an English Franciscan in the fourteenth century; see *FM*, p. 33.

from cold and it was only the warmth of his brethren "huddling against him in the way that pigs do" that saved his life.[32] Nonetheless it was not long before both orders became widely influential within university circles, and at court as well as among the laity. Notable early recruits included Adam of Exeter (d. c. 1233, known also as Adam Rufus) to whom is attributed the *Pater Noster* in this volume, a friar who like a number of his order (including Saint Francis himself) took his mission to save souls to include not just backsliding Christians but also the Saracens occupying the Holy Land. Adam died before he was able to fulfil his ambition, but his zeal for Muslim souls comes across in his treatise.

Adam of Exeter was an intimate friend of Robert Grosseteste, bishop of Lincoln (c. 1175–1253). Robert Grosseteste by any standards must count as one of the towering figures of thirteenth-century religious and intellectual life in both his roles: at Oxford, where he became lector to the Franciscan school, and at Lincoln as its bishop. To Grosseteste, the saving of souls was "the absolutely overriding art," a task not to be entrusted to careerists but rather "to those who understand the Gospel of Christ as set forth in the Old and New Testament";[33] this meant, in effect, Dominicans and Franciscans. Both Grosseteste and the friars were deeply concerned by the possible approach of the Last Days. To the friars the rapid and unexpected advance into Europe of the Mongols in 1241 lent credibility to earlier prophecies that suggested the world might end in the mid-thirteenth century, a view Grosseteste was ready to share, since to him the political machinations at the papal curia of his day could only forebode evil. Hence the anguished cry of another Franciscan, Adam Marsh, at one point a close associate of Adam of Exeter's, in one of his letters to Grosseteste: "The last of the perilous times … are now upon us … no one doubts that Satan is already loosed or shortly to be released …. In a word, all things are pervaded and ravaged by the instruments of hell's torments."[34]

Apocalyptic anxieties added urgency to the business of saving souls. From the early days of the Church, knowledge of the Lord's Prayer had been seen as fundamental for salvation. The Gospels themselves provided two versions of the prayer (Matthew 6:9–13 and Luke 11:2–4), but the seven petitions of Matthew's version, as opposed to the five of Luke's, gave added scope for hep-

[32] Thomas of Eccleston, *The Coming of the Friars Minor*, trans. Salter, p. 18.

[33] See "Robert Grosseteste at the Papal Curia," ed. Gieben, p. 365. For a discussion of the text (and the translation used here) see Southern 1986, pp. 280–81 (for current work on Grossteste, see `www.grosseteste.com`).

[34] Ep. 90, *The Letters of Adam Marsh*, ed. and trans. Lawrence, p. 231.

tamerologies, the seven-ness of things so beloved by medieval theologians, and it was this version which ultimately prevailed. Thus for Robert Grosseteste and his circle the 7 petitions could be aligned with the 7 deadly sins; the 7 virtues; the 7 sacraments, and the 7 gifts of the Holy Spirit. The prayer itself was seen as made up of two parts: the first three petitions concerned with God, the last four with the needs of man. Attempts to make sure that the laity both knew and understood the Prayer ranged from yearly examinations (advocated by Grosseteste) to the production of Pater Noster plays. None of these has survived, but it seems certain that they had a pedagogical function.[35]

Marian Devotion

A growing sense of devotion to Mary, the Mother of God, is amply demonstrated in the high Middle Ages by the adoption of the Hail Mary as a prayer, in conjunction with the Creed and the *Pater Noster*, that everyone should know. The prayer, composed of the salutation (the Annunciation) given by the Angel Gabriel to Mary (Luke 1:28), together with the greeting to Mary of her cousin Elisabeth (Luke 1:42), was possibly known already in Anglo-Saxon England; in the twelfth century it became current; by the thirteenth century it was (or should have been) on the lips of all Christians. Across Europe the sternly regal figure of Mary of the earlier Middle Ages was replaced now by the image of the compassionate mother: a woman whom even the most hardened sinners could confidently approach, and in whose continually elaborated story all could in some measure share.[36]

The collection of holy stories known as the Golden Legend (*Legenda Aurea*) that began to circulate in England in the thirteenth century gave wide currency to many of the legends that had long been told concerning the Virgin's life.[37] Already, from the second century, the exiguous information provided by the Gospels about Mary had been supplemented by a number of apocryphal stories which by their very nature added as much confusion as they did clarity to the supposed events surrounding both Mary's life and her death. Controversies focused, for example, on whether Mary had been born free from Original Sin and on the nature of her death: her soul, it could be conceded, had been taken up — "assumed" — immediately to heaven, but had it been re-united with her body and if so when? Such theological quandaries

[35] See Johnston 1975, and Duffy 1992 (pp. 53–68); and *Þe Pater Noster of Richard Ermyte*, ed. Aarts, esp. chap. VI.

[36] A comprehensive study of changing forms of devotion to the Virgin can be found in Rubin 2009.

[37] For a recent study of the *Golden Legend* see Reames 1985.

did nothing to prevent the establishment at Rome, already by the end of the seventh century, of four Marian feasts: the Purification (2nd February), when Mary was brought to the Temple for the ritual cleansing that followed childbirth; the Annunciation (25th March); the Assumption (15th August); and the Birthday (8th September). By 900 these feasts were regularly observed in England, and sermons in the vernacular were composed for their celebration. In addition, in about 1030 two further Marian feasts, otherwise not recognized in Western Europe, came to be celebrated in England: the Feast of the Presentation of Mary (November 21st), when Mary's parents, Joachim and Anna, are said to have brought her as a young girl to serve in the Temple; and the feast of her Conception (8th December).[38] This particularly English veneration of Mary did not go unchallenged by the Norman conquerors (Lanfranc, archbishop of Canterbury, for example, seems to have rejected both of these latter feasts), but English devotion to the Virgin nonetheless developed apace. It is to England that must be traced the origins of those collections of stories of the miracles of the Virgin that were to become so popular across Europe throughout the Middle Ages;[39] it is in England that a replica of the Virgin's house was built (at Walsingham under her instructions) long before anything of the kind was to be found at Loreto in Italy;[40] it is in England that devotion to Mary's mother Anna first becomes pronounced;[41] and it is Aelred, the Cistercian abbot of Rievaulx (c. 1110–1167), who is the earliest writer to suggest how a devout Christian (in this case his sister who was living as a recluse) might imagine herself as actually present at the nativity: "Accompany the Mother as she makes her way to Bethlehem. Take shelter in the inn with her, be present and help her as she gives birth …."[42]

The development of empathetic bonds between Christians, the Virgin, and through her with her Son during his life on earth, was fostered in the later Middle Ages through a number of different channels. From the twelfth century onwards the terrible grief of the Virgin as she stood at the foot of the Cross came to be represented both in dramatised versions of her lament (*planctus*) and in those paintings and sculpture of the scene at the crucifix-

[38] For Anglo-Saxon Marian feasts, see Clayton 1990.

[39] See Southern 1958.

[40] See Dickinson 1956.

[41] For the cult of St Anne in England see Ashley and Sheingorn 1990.

[42] Aelred of Rievaulx, *De Institutione*, ed. Hoste and Talbot (cap. 29, p. 663); the quotation is from Aelred's *Rule of Life*, trans. Macpherson, p. 81.

ion known as the *Pietà*.[43] Highly-wrought Franciscan preaching and poetry encouraged such fervent and widespread devotion to Mary and to the humanity of Christ that the gap between the observances of laymen and women and their monastic counterparts rapidly narrowed.[44] It became fashionable to own Books of Hours.[45] These elaborately illuminated prayer books, based on the Little Office of the Virgin, made provision for laymen and women to pattern their prayer life on the canonical hours of the day observed by monks and friars.[46] The eightfold division of each day traditionally opened with contemplation of an Annunciation scene accompanied by appropriate prayers, psalms, and readings, and ended with the Assumption of the Virgin into heaven; an accompanying cycle might start with Christ's agony in the Garden and close with his burial. Such division of the day into a Gospel chronology did not, of course, depend on the possession of a luxury book. Anyone might adopt such a routine, and indeed even before the first actual Book of Hours had been produced, it looks as if the small community of women recluses for whom the *Ancrene Wisse* was composed was following a similar timetable.[47] These women may also have been pioneers in the way they recited clusters of the Hail Mary, for they are instructed to say fifty, divided into sets of ten. Did such women have rosaries to help them keep count? We cannot tell, although it is worth noting that in the eleventh century Lady Godiva (Godgifu) of Coventry, at the point of death, is said to have had a "circlet of gems hung round the statue of St Mary. She had sewn them on a string, so that by touching each one in turn as she started her prayers, she could be sure to complete the full number."[48]

Lady Godiva's bequest of her beads to the statue of the Virgin is a useful reminder of the importance of "props" in late medieval religion. Monastic communities might, sometimes, be austere in their furnishings (such at least was the ideal put forward by the Cistercian abbot Saint Bernard),[49] but this

[43] See Part Two (*Maria Compatiens*) of Fulton 2002, esp. pp. 215–17. For the *Planctus*, see Dronke 1988. For the *Pietà*, see Woolf 1968, pp. 392–94.

[44] Fleming 1977 remains an essential introduction to Franciscan influence on vernacular literature and piety.

[45] See Duffy 2006.

[46] These are: Nocturns, Matins or Lauds, Prime, Tierce, Sext, Nones, Vespers, Compline (the first two of these were often conflated, giving seven Hours instead of eight).

[47] See Millett 2000; Duffy points out that despite the injunctions found in *AW* to say the Hours at the correct time, in practice they were often run together (Duffy 2008, p. 97).

[48] William of Malmesbury, *Gesta Pontificum*, ed. and trans. Winterbottom, I, pp. 471–73.

[49] Bernard of Clairvaux (c. 1090–1153); for his views on art in churches, see Rudolph 1990.

brand of simplicity was never expected of those still living in the world; nor indeed would even the most ascetic of churchmen have ever suggested depriving the Christian year of its sense of theatre and of performance. Even before the staging of the first miracle play, emperors had ridden donkeys on Palm Sunday, and monks had impersonated the Three Marys looking for Christ on that first Easter Sunday.[50] But the drama of the Christian story was not limited to feast days and holy days: it belonged to every day. Even those with no fine books to help them pray, and with no beads to leave to any statue of the Virgin, could be present imaginatively — and constantly — both at the moment of Christ's birth and at his death, and every woman and man could find ways in which to efface the time that had since passed. Kings could be lavish (Henry III, for example, demonstrated his very fervent devotion by making rich gifts to Our Lady at Walsingham — he gave her a gold crown and many thousands of candles),[51] but it cost nothing, beyond spiritual and emotional energy, to kneel fifteen times before the statue of Mary that any parishioner could expect to find in the Lady Chapel of their local church, in celebration of the Virgin and her fifteen joys.[52]

Numbers, as we have seen, mattered in medieval pastoral theology. What then was the significance of 15? One answer must be that fifteen was the number of the so-called Gradual Psalms (Psalms 119–33) which Mary is imagined as reciting as she climbed the steps to the Temple in Jerusalem where (according to the Apocryphal Gospels) she had spent her childhood.[53] Sometimes Mary's 15 Joys were matched by 15 Sorrows. Fifteen was not, however, the only number chosen for this form of devotion, and while 5 Joys are found both in the *Ancrene Wisse* and in *Sir Gawain and the Green Knight*, another common pairing was of 7 Joys and 7 Sorrows as below:

Annunciation — the prophecy of Simeon
Nativity — the flight into Egypt
Adoration of the Magi — the loss of Jesus in the Temple
Resurrection — the meeting of Christ and the Virgin on the way
Ascension — the Crucifixion
Pentecost — the descent from the Cross
Coronation of the Virgin — the burial of Jesus

---

[50] Here Hardison 1965 remains valuable.

[51] For his devotion to Mary, see Vincent 2004.

[52] See p. 150 below.

[53] See p. 135, note 5, in Young Mary below.

For the most part Mary's joys and sorrows have a scriptural basis, but the case for her Coronation and her Queenship lies in the later debates: these were prompted by the paradox that behind the seemingly simple human story of a baby born in poverty in a manger lay questions of enormous theological complexity. Mary was not only Christ's Mother, she was also believed to be God's Bride. Necessarily, therefore, once her earthly life was over, and she had been assumed into heaven, Mary was imagined to have taken her rightful and regal place beside God her spouse. This concept of Mary's sovereignty had been developed early in the Middle Ages, but from the twelfth century onwards it had gained in importance. An influential advocate in England was Eadmer of Canterbury (c. 1060–c. 1126). His explanation brings out the force of the idea:

> Just as God, who made all things by his power, is Father and Lord of all things, so Blessed Mary, who repaired all things by her merits, is Mother and Mistress of all. For God is Lord of all because he established each thing in its own nature by his command, while Mary is Mistress of all because she re-established them in their original inborn dignity by the grace she merited. And just as God generated from his own substance his Son, through whom he gave all things their origin, so Mary gave birth from her own flesh to him who restored all things to the beauty of their creation.[54]

As Queen of Heaven, Mary was identified both with the Bride of the Song of Songs and with the woman clothed with the sun of Revelation 12:1: *And there appeared a great wonder in heaven; a woman clothed with the sun, and the moon under her feet, and upon her head a crown of twelve stars.* The early twelfth-century depiction, on one of the capitals of Reading Abbey, of the coronation of Mary by Christ himself is the earliest known representation of this scene, and as such is a striking testimony to the appeal in Anglo-Norman England of the newly shaped concept of Mary's regality.[55]

Private Prayer

Mary, as Queen of Heaven, was the advocate of sinners; it was in this role, as the prayers in this volume show, that the whole company of angels in attendance on their Queen had their part to play. The role of angels in Christian

[54] Eadmer, *De Excellentia* cap. xi, *PL* 159:578AB; trans. Gambero, in *Mary in the Middle Ages*, p. 120.

[55] See Zarnecki 1950.

history is complicated. On the one hand, it was certain that everyone had a guardian angel whose job it was to provide support and guidance to the designated soul.[56] On the other hand, some angels were bad and untrustworthy. Although references in the Old Testament to the fallen angels who had rebelled against God are somewhat enigmatic, the Jewish apocryphal *Book of Enoch* provides a more detailed tale as to why humans should be wary in their dealings with these creatures, whose seduction of women had led to the birth of a race of monstrous giants. An understandable anxiety then, about distinguishing between "good" and "bad" angels, accounts for the attempts to draw up a list of vetted angels and to organise them into some sort of order. The result was the establishment of a hierarchy of angels with Seraphim, Cherubim, and Thrones coming at the top; followed by Virtues, Principalities, and Powers; and in third place Dominations, Archangels, and Angels. Unless they were needed on earth, the role of angels was to contemplate God and to worship him in song, but they could always be depended upon (so Honorius of Autun tells us) "when necessary ... to come down to help, particularly when they are called upon by prayers,"[57] and in the hands of Archbishop Pecham each order of angels suggested exemplary qualities of service.[58] Repeatedly the Church attempted to limit the number of archangels to those mentioned by name in the Bible (Michael, Gabriel, and Raphael), but as the Harley prayers testify,[59] rival angels continued to have their adherents, and there seems to have been little the church could do except attempt to monitor inappropriate use of their supposed powers.[60]

Orthodox prayer included the practice of the saying of Psalms as laid out in Books of Hours (mentioned above). In this volume the extracts from a Harley manuscript include a meditation on the Passion of Christ structured around the Hours, which gives a flavour of the emotions considered appropriate to this form of devotion (even if it omits some relevant Psalms and, unusually, starts with the bedtime office of Compline). Very different in character are a number of the other prayers copied into this manuscript. Here, a much greater emphasis is placed on the magical power of prayer and the apotropaic value of observing certain customs, whether by reciting psalms, fasting, or

[56] For guardian angels see Keck 1998, pp. 161–65.

[57] Honorius of Autun, *Elucidarium* bk. ii, cap. 28, *PL* 172:1154; quoted in Mayr-Harting 1998, p. 17.

[58] See Pecham's treatise, the *Jerarchie*, discussed in Wogan-Browne 2005.

[59] In Chapter 8, below.

[60] For one such attempt, see the reference to Charlemagne's *Admonitio Generalis* of 789 discussed in Mayr-Harting 1998 (p. 12).

by the lighting of candles. These are not random acts, but rather highly ritualised activities. The number of candles has been carefully chosen to have meaningful associations, while the Psalms mentioned include Psalm 90, which at least as early as the fifth century had been used as an amulet on account of the refuge offered by its opening verse: *Lord, thou hast been our dwelling place in all generations.*[61] In prayer, the Christian man or woman certainly praised God, as did the angels, but just as importantly, and with their help, he or she fought off the Devil.[62]

"He" or "she": the attentive reader will notice that more than one text in this volume anticipates a female or at least a mixed audience. This need cause no surprise. It is a well-accepted paradox of the Middle Ages that while on the one hand a strong current of misogyny runs throughout much of the extant literature, on the other hand women appear regularly as the spiritual counsellors of men and as figures endowed with considerable religious authority and even influence. Among the aristocracy (both within and beyond religious communities) it is women who had the time, the resources, and the inclination to set themselves up as patrons of religious literature, sharing books, and writing or commissioning new work.[63] Significantly, because very few women knew Latin, such work tended to be in the vernacular, so that the corpus written in the French of England is considerable. Noteworthy are the links Bishop Grosseteste forged with a number of aristocratic women. His *Chasteau d'Amour*, a highly influential work of pastoral theology, is likely to have been written for a noblewoman; certainly it became a favoured text among the reading circles patronised by Anglo-Norman women.[64]

The hugely influential relationship between women and the vernacular should not, however, allow us to forget the exceptions, notably those prayers written in Latin by Saint Anselm for a number of his women friends, including Adelaide, daughter of William the Conqueror, and Matilda of Tuscany. These writings have a particular importance in the history of private prayer because of their emotive quality and because they include Anselm's instructions on how to pray. His prayers are not to be read in a hurry or to be said by rote. Thus Matilda is expressly told that the prayers Anselm is sending her "are arranged so that by reading them the mind may be stirred up either to the

[61] Ps. 89 in *LV.* See Skemer 2006, pp. 84–89.

[62] As discussed in Flint 1991, esp. pp. 157–72.

[63] For a comprehensive survey, that examines women both as readers and as patrons, see Green 2007.

[64] See also Wogan-Browne 2005a.

love or fear of God, or to a consideration of both; so they should not be read cursorily or quickly, but little by little, with attention and deep meditation."[65]

Sin and Confession

The most quoted decree by far of the Lateran Council of 1215 must be Chapter 21. This is the decree which enjoined on all Christians beyond "the age of discernment" the duty of confessing their sins at least once a year to their own priest, and of undertaking whatever penances he thought fit to impose. The priest in turn was to act like a skilled doctor. He must take into account the circumstances both of the sinner and the sin and then choose the most appropriate remedy. And he must at all costs respect the penitent's confidentiality.

Behind Chapter 21 lay many a debate thrashed out in the Paris circles which had acted as the seedbed for Lateran IV. Confidentiality was a fine ideal, but what about confessions, such as those to flagrant adultery or open murder, which it was not felt could or should be kept secret? In what way, and to what extent, should sins against God be differentiated from sins against one's neighbour or against the Church? Every service of Mass included a general confession — what, beyond this, might be required? Robert of Flamborough, an Englishman living in Paris in the early twelfth century and himself the author of a confessor's handbook (c. 1208–1215, which he dedicated to the bishop of Salisbury), described three different and additional confessional scenarios:

> Some penance is solemn, some public, some private. Solemn is that which is done on Ash Wednesday, when the penitents are expelled from church, with solemnity, in ashes and sackcloth .... Public and non-solemn is that which is done before the church without the above mentioned solemnity, like pilgrimage. Private is that which is done ... privately before a priest. No one except a bishop, or someone acting on his authority, imposes solemn penance .... A simple priest may enjoin public penance, as well as private, and at any time.[66]

Lateran IV chapter 21 is then clearly concerned not with all kinds of penance but specifically with private penance, now to be newly managed and in need

[65] St Anselm's relations with women have been studied in Vaughn 2002; the letter to Matilda cited here comes from the translation by Ward, in *The Prayers of Saint Anselm*, p. 90 (Latin text in Anselm's *Opera*, ed. Schmitt, III, p. 4).

[66] Robert's *Liber poenitentialis*, ed. Firth (bk. v, cap. 236, p. 205); quoted in Mansfield 1995, p. 29 (and note 30 for the Latin text).

of close attention in respect both of its theology and its practice, since the circumstance of every sin and the motives of each sinner had to be carefully scrutinised. Three separate but interdependent elements were involved: contrition (or compunction), confession, and penance. The penitential system henceforth became much more elaborate, so that now a trained work-force was needed to make sure every confession was adequately heard with all details being properly considered, and an appropriate penance assigned (duties that tended to fall most heavily on the friars).[67] A sustained programme of education for both priests and laity alike was therefore essential. Reference has been made already to the flurry of episcopal legislation in England that followed Lateran IV; but those decrees could be only part of the picture. Before long, guides for confessors and their penitents were appearing, often in both French and English versions, with the same speed (relatively speaking) as self-help books today, so that by the fifteenth century the translator of the *Orologium Sapientiae* could complain "there are so many books and treatises on the virtues and vices of divers doctrines that any man's life, which is so short, would end before he could either study or read them."[68]

One of the first of the new-style Penitentials to appear in England was composed by Thomas of Chobham, a teacher in the Paris schools before returning (after the lifting of the Interdict) to a post as vice-dean of Salisbury Cathedral. Thomas will have been party to the intricate debates that preceded Lateran IV, so the opening words of his Penitential have particular force: "We shall pass over the subtle theoretical questions concerning penance and instead pursue with great diligence what practical knowledge and behaviour is necessary to priests in hearing confessions and imposing penance."[69]

The "practical knowledge" Thomas considers necessary begins with an explanation of the nature and the importance of the Seven Deadly Sins, a topic later found in all confessors' manuals. These sins have a long history in Christian theology.[70] They appear most usually (as in this volume) in the order given to them by Pope Gregory the Great (c. 540–604): pride, envy, wrath, sloth, covetousness or avarice, gluttony, and lastly lechery. Strictly speaking the sins are not "deadly" at all; rather, they are "capital": serious, therefore, but not enough in themselves to warrant damnation, but at some point in the fourteenth century they became known as deadly and this is

[67] For a reminder of the role that public penance nonetheless continued to play after 1215, see Mansfield 1995, *passim*.

[68] See Wenzel 1967 (quoted at p. 69).

[69] Thomas' *Summa Confessorum*, ed. Broomfield, p. 3.

[70] For what follows, see esp. Bloomfield 1967.

the usage that prevailed. A further shift is the change in the meaning of "sloth." The word used by Gregory is *tristitia* (literally "sadness"), a word he felt was sufficiently encompassing to include the eighth deadly sin, named by the earlier monastic writer Cassian, of *accidia* (probably best translated as depression). The question must be: in what ways did medieval writers understand the two meanings implicit in Gregory's definition?

A number of theologians (Grosseteste included) solved the problem by differentiating between "laziness of the soul ... an inner grief of the mind," and "idleness of the body ... when the body shrinks from holy works." "Laziness of the soul" was necessarily harder to combat than "idleness of the body," so that it may come as no surprise that Thomas of Chobham in his Penitential went to some lengths to stress the practical implications of *accidia. Accidia*, according to Thomas, was the worst of sins because it discouraged good works: "through tedium and weariness it deprives a man of his good works with which he might merit eternal life." By the fourteenth century this notion, that *accidia* was no more than a form of laziness, had become firmly entrenched. Paradoxically, then, the mission of Lateran IV to extend the use of the confessional and to make it sensitive to the particular circumstances of each sin and sinner led in practice to certain psychological simplifications, as demonstrated by the use in sermons of those three stock-character enemies of the Christian Soul: Hardheart, who resisted contrition; Stopmouth, who stood in the way of a full confession; and Closepurse, who did what he could to prevent the fulfilling of any penance.[71] Nonetheless, even allowing for the shortcomings in the system, it is evident from the texts in this volume that the confessional (along with sermons, plays, and wall-paintings) provided one of the means by which the laity might be taught not only about which of the seven deadly sins they might have committed but also about the full content of Archbishop Pecham's syllabus. This was: the Creed (as discussed above); the Ten Commandments, or Decalogue, said to have been given by God to Moses on Mount Sinai in Exodus 20; the two evangelical precepts of Matthew 22:35–40; the seven works of mercy (Matthew 25:31–46, to which was added the burial of the dead, from the Book of Tobit 1:17–19); the seven principal virtues (made up of the three theological virtues of Faith, Hope, and Charity allied with the four cardinal virtues of Prudence, Justice, Temperance, and Fortitude); and lastly the seven sacraments: baptism, confirmation, penance,

[71] For these three characters, see the anonymous sermon for Ash Wednesday in *Preaching*, trans. Wenzel, p. 94 and note 13.

the Eucharist, extreme unction, holy orders, and marriage.[72] But this instruction was never an end in itself. Underpinning it lay an insistence on God's mercy and of his love for mankind. Behind the admonitory character of our texts lies the consoling message that, provided he was truly contrite, a sinner could yet be saved even without priestly help. A formal confession was never essential. What mattered ultimately was the penitent's state of heart: "contrition is the heart's confession."[73]

Punishments and Rewards

Inseparable from Lateran IV chapter 21 is the history of the development of the doctrine of Purgatory: the explanation of how Christians could make themselves fit for heaven and compensate for the penances they themselves or their kin had failed to fulfil. In 1981, Jacques Le Goff opened up a debate which continues to this day by arguing that Purgatory, the place where sins could indeed be purged, did not come into existence as a fixed place until the 1160s when the noun *Purgatorium* first appeared, and that a "third place," distinct from heaven and hell, was only then ushered in a properly defined form into the economy of salvation.[74] Though this thesis remains hotly debated, there is general agreement that ideas about Purgatory did indeed change and develop during the later twelfth century and that this change both reflected and promoted a greater willingness on the part of the Church to acknowledge the possibility that salvation was within the reach of every Christian.[75]

In the first instance, the notion of Purgatory provided an answer to the question of what happened to each soul between the individual judgement meted out at death and the Last Judgement at the end of time. Visions and miracles provided sufficient evidence to make it seem that while the truly bad would go to hell, the truly good were able to go straight to heaven. Such saints had of course to wait until the Last Trump before being re-united with their bodies, but from the moment of their leaving this world they could enjoy the Beatific Vision as promised in Mark 5:8 (Pope John XXII argued otherwise, but his ideas had short-lived currency), and through their intercessions they

[72] For a succinct but important statement on the long-term effects of Lateran IV chap. 21, see Boyle 1985. Note also the suggestion in Wogan-Browne 2005a (p. 88, note 12), that Pecham may have based his syllabus on the *Speculum Ecclesie* of Archbishop Edmund of Canterbury (d. 1240). The *Speculum*, translated as the *Mirour de Seinte Eglyse* and also translated into English, was a very influential work.

[73] See Chapter 12 (p. 301), below.

[74] Le Goff 1981 (and trans. Goldhammer).

[75] See esp. Edwards 1985; and McGuire 1989.

could give help to those on earth who called to them. But what was the fate of everyone else?

It was generally recognized that most men are neither outstandingly good but nor are they outrageously wicked; rather they veer somewhere between the two. A just God had of necessity to make appropriate provision for these souls. A number of visions suggested that a four-fold division provided the solution. The vision of Ailsi recorded in the early twelfth century by his grandson, Peter of Cornwall, lends credence to this view. Ailsi sees a field "in which rest the souls of the blessed in utmost quiet and joy." The field is clearly not heaven, but it can be recognised as a paradise, the home seemingly of the "nearly good" who have already been purged of minor sins.[76] Other visions suggest separate locations for particular groups — the Cistercians, for example, appear from one account to have had their own destination where both Saint Benedict and the Virgin Mary were on hand to provide solace, even though it was a place of torture and where one reprobate (who had deserted the order) was "from the soles of his feet to the top of his head . . . completely on fire."[77]

Medieval readers of the texts in this volume might well have been familiar with the account of Purgatory given by Marie de France in her widely circulated poem, *Espurgatoire Seint Patriz*, recounting the visit of a certain knight to the Otherworld and of the horrors (as well as the joys of Paradise) he witnessed there.[78] Marie's poem reminds its readers and listeners how the masses, prayers, and donations of the living can help the sufferings of the dead. Such a belief was of course widespread across Christendom, and it is somewhat strange that on so important a topic our volume is silent; our two penultimate texts, moreover, emphasise traditional monastic values rather than the pastoral concerns of the wider community with which Lateran IV was so concerned. The final text of our volume, however, speaks loudly and clearly to all. Although the fires of hell will have been familiar to many through the paintings on their church walls of lurid dooms, even such fires will have seemed wan in comparison with the horrors of the "hot steamy fog of hell" as presented in this vision of the Last Days. Despite the focus of God's love for his creation as presented elsewhere in this volume, in the last resort the choice was indeed stark: perfect joy or eternal damnation. There would in the end be no middle way.

---

[76] Peter's "The Vision of Ailsi," ed. and trans. Sharpe, pp. 34–35.

[77] See McGuire 1989 (p. 77), where he quotes from a Paris manuscript. Benedict (c. 480–c. 550) wrote a Rule for the Benedictine order.

[78] Marie's *Saint Patrick's Purgatory*, ed. and trans. Curley.

Treatment of Text and Editorial Conventions

D&B numbers and titles are provided in a footnote to each chapter-heading. In texts, the conventional distinction between vocalic and consonantal i/j, u/v, and on occasion when the scribe fails to do so, between c and t, has been adhered to. Disambiguating accents and punctuation are editorial. It has not seemed desirable to standardize capitalization; each (con)text demands its own treatment. No attempt has been made to emend or advertise rare forms. In texts, square brackets indicate material that has been added to the manuscript, at the discretion of the editor; paragraphs may be added for the convenience of readers.

The translation aims to be as literal as is consistent with modern English prose, to allow readers to study the Anglo-Norman on the facing page. The generalizing masculine pronoun in French has usually been translated as "he or she," or "they," except where a male is clearly indicated (in the *Dialogue*, for example).

Biblical quotations which appear in Latin will have *LV* references supplied; the *AV* will appear correspondingly in the translation (index entries will be to *AV* only). Bible quotations paraphrased into French will be identified on the translated page.[79] This arrangement also demonstrates just how free many writers were in their translation of Bible passages;[80] it will readily be understood, therefore, that we have not always been able to locate biblical references. If the writer's Latin does not correspond closely with the Vulgate then no concordance can help us. Furthermore, when the Latin is not given at all we can find references only by general Bible knowledge, and with the help of luck. The above-mentioned difficulties apply equally to quotations from Church Fathers and so forth, especially Augustine (of Hippo, 354–430, who is frequently cited in our texts).[81] Quotations from named authorities have been identified wherever possible, in footnotes. Many writers used compilations, of *Sententiae* or florilegia, and these possible secondary sources have

[79] Psalm numbers, which differ between the two Bibles, will be identified in both (although indexed as *AV*).

[80] See Heinzer 2008 (esp. p. 45): medieval writings are literally paved with allusions to the Psalter; these are not so much quotations as part of an "intertextual dialogue," because writers knew many biblical texts (especially the Psalter) almost by heart.

[81] Many passages attributed to Augustine may in fact be from Pseudo-Augustine texts (see Sturges, "Pseudo-Augustinian Writings"; we are grateful to the author for supplying us with a copy), if not paraphrased or mis-attributed altogether. See, for example, Aarts' Introduction to the Middle English *Pater Noster*, p. lxxxiii: he has been unable to trace five passages attributed to St Augustine, two of which appear in our Anglo-Norman text.

not been identified.[82] For example, we traced a quotation from "Augustine" to the very popular *Liber Scintillarum*, where it is ascribed to Basil; however, editions of the *Liber* give no note on Basil or any other Fathers cited in its text.[83]

Primary sources are identified by short title in footnotes, giving edition or translation (or both) as appropriate; all works cited are listed with full details at the end of the book.

[82] See, for example, the Introduction to *FM*, p. 27.

[83] For Defensor's *Liber*, see MacCoull 2002. For medieval writers' habit of paraphrasing their "quotations," see for example *MERP*, p. 62, note to ll. 31–32: "it was common to offer a free development of a biblical passage"; see also Trotter 1987 (p. 259).

Part I

The Tenets of the Faith

Chapter 1

Dialogue of Father and Son[1]

Introduction

This Dialogue is found only in Cambridge, Emmanuel College, MS 106 (I.4.31) (s.xiv^{m}), ff.119r–142r.

The Dialogue is related to a long didactic tradition of texts assembling instructions by a father to his son(s) or by a mother to her daughter(s).[2] More closely, it is part of a constellation of texts in French to which Paul Meyer first drew attention.[3] The dialogue exists both as the second part of an abbreviated Bible history and as a free-standing piece. Listing twelve manuscripts, Meyer noted the version contained in BNF, MS fr. 25408, a manuscript written in England and dated (on f.106v) to 1267, which contains both the "abrégé d'histoire sainte" and the Dialogue. Two of the three excerpts he prints from BNF, MS fr. 1546 match very closely corresponding passages in the Dialogue printed below, in which there is an initial discussion of baptism, followed by a number of questions about salvation. This leads into an explanation of faith and an exposition of the Creed, in which each article is attributed to an apostle. The Dialogue culminates, under the rubric "Chanson des angles" (*Gloria in excelsis Deo. Et in terra pax hominibus bone voluntatis*),[4] in a passage celebrating the Nativity, which had been signalled at the start where the father mentions Christ coming into the world "en temps que ore est." Meyer's pioneering piece was augmented by the study of Charles Langlois,[5] who provided an analysis of the version in BNF, MS fr. 25408, as well as a number of hypotheses about the genesis of the two-part text. From this summary it is obvious that there are many correspondences as well as divergences between the two manuscripts, including changes in the order of contents. A manuscript unknown to Langlois which contains both the Bible history and the Dialogue, though the latter is incomplete, is Oxford, Bodleian Library, MS Fairfax 24 (s.xiv^{m}), ff.21r–48v and ff.48v–61v ("Ci parole comment le devin e[n]seigne son enfant").

[1] D&B 633, prose (and cf. 632).

[2] See *The Good Wife*, ed. Mustanoja, pp. 31ff. A recent edition by George Shuttleton may be found online (`www.lib.rochester.edu/camelot/TEAMS/sgas4int.htm`).

[3] Meyer 1899, pp. 258–61.

[4] Luke 2:14.

[5] Langlois 1928, vol. 4, pp. 47–65; see p. 60 for the author's probable familiarity with the *Elucidarium* of Honorius of Autun.

The Dialogue stands alone in Cambridge, Emmanuel College, MS 106 (I.4.31) (s.xiv^{m}), ff.119r–142r. An edition of this interesting manuscript, which includes no fewer than twenty-three Anglo-Norman homiletic and devotional texts,[6] along with some English texts,[7] was planned by J. P. Strachey for the Anglo-Norman Text Society, in the belief that the manuscript served as a kind of vade-mecum for a teaching friar, but the edition never came to fruition. The Dialogue is preceded by a text of instructions comparable to the *Enseignements Trebor* of Robert of Ho (Hoo), as it is in BNF, MS fr. 25408. In his edition of *The Good Wife taught her Daughter*, Mustanoja described the Cambridge MS as being written c. 1350, by an Anglo-Norman scribe in an attractive Gothic bookhand which extends throughout the whole volume except for the last item, a fragment of the Gospel of Nicodemus written in a current hand.[8] He argues cautiously for its production "in the ancient diocese of Worcester, and probably in one of the areas which now form part of Warwickshire, Oxfordshire, or Gloucestershire."[9]

[6] These include one of the versions of Mary's Lament presented in this volume.
[7] See Salminen 1940.
[8] Mustanoja, *The Good Wife*, p. 92.
[9] Ibid. p. 102.

Text

[Le pere] [f.119r] Beau fiz, mult ad Dieu feet pur totes genz par sa grand curtesie en diverse maneres, et noméments a nous crestiens a qui il ad doné sa grace de venir en ceste siecle en temps que ore est quant toutz les sacramentz de seinte Eglise sunt si prestementes ordinés a doner a nous pur nostre salvation. Car auncienement ne soleit nul estre baptizé tanqu'il fut en age que il eust sens et discretions et seust enquere ceo que il [ne] saveit et respondre a ceo que hom li demandeit. Et lors esteit custume que bein enseignout chescun, ainz qu'il fu baptizé, les poinz de la creance et quant il saveit ceo que il deveit crere et dire et fere come crestien, lores aprimes si se fesoit baptizer et responeit pur sei.

E itel estoit seint Martin quant il dona soen mauntel al povere dount il vit Jesu Crist vestu la nuit aprés par avision. Il n'ert pas unquore baptizé, mes il ert enseigné de la creance. Mes ore est autrement, car seint Eglise esgarda que plusurs morirent sodeinement einz tiele age et esteient dampné pur ceo [f.119v] q'il furent mort sanz baptesme, si establi l'em, ceo que ore est, q'il fuissent baptizé en enfance.

Et pur ceo que l'Escripture dit : *Qui crediderit et baptizatus fuerit, salvus erit* [Mark 16:16], ceo est a dire "Qui crera et seit baptizé, il serra sauf", ore puet l'em ver q'il [ne] covient de estre sauf sanz deus choses, creance et baptesme, ou le uaillant, car nul ne puet estre sauf par baptesme s'il n'ad creance, ne pur creance sanz baptesme ou le vaillant, si com est martire. Et de teus trovoms nous multz que furent martirizé pur Jesu Crist einz que il eussent leiser d'estre baptizé. Et pur ceo deit l'em saver que lui enfant qui sunt baptizé et ne unt pas creance, pur ceo q'il ne sevont rien, si il morirent einz age, il serront sauf en la fei et en la creance de lur parentz.

Et de ceo troeve l'em en le Evangile plusurs ensamples que par la creance de autri puetz l'em avoir garison et pardon de ses pecchez. L'em troeve en le Evangile que gent apporterunt un paralitiqe devant Jesu Crist, et Jesu Crist [f.120r] esgarda la creance de eus que le porterent et pus dist al malade "Tes pecchez tei sunt pardonez" et si le garri. En un autre Evangile refu une pucele garie par la creance de sa mere. De teus ensamples purreit l'em assetz dire si ne fust pur la demorance.

Translation

[Father] Dear son, God has done much for all mankind, through his sovereign grace, in so many ways. And especially for us Christians, to whom he has granted his grace by coming into this world, at the present time, when all the sacraments of Holy Church are prepared and ready to be given to us for our salvation. For in the old days nobody used to be baptized until he was old enough to have sense and discretion, and knew how to ask what he did not know and to answer what anybody asked him. Then, it was the custom for each to be properly taught the articles of the faith before receiving baptism; when he knew what he ought to believe and say and do as a Christian, he immediately sought baptism and answered for himself.

This is how it was with Saint Martin, when he gave his cloak to the poor man, and the next night in a vision he saw Jesus Christ wearing it. He had not yet been baptized, but he was instructed in the faith.[1] But nowadays matters are different, for Holy Church observed that many people were dying suddenly, before reaching that age, and were damned because they died unchristened. And so it was established, as is now the case, that people should be baptized as infants.

This is because Scripture says *He that believeth and is baptized shall be saved*, which means that whoever will believe and be christened will be safe. Now you can see that you cannot be sure of salvation without two things: faith, and baptism or its equivalent; for baptism can save nobody unless he has faith, nor faith without baptism, or its equivalent which is martyrdom. Among those we find many who were martyred for Jesus Christ before they had time to be baptized. And so one must understand that children who are baptized and, because they know nothing, have no faith; if these die before growing up they will be safe in the faith and the belief of their (god)parents.

We find many examples of this in the Gospels, how one is able to receive healing and pardon for their sins through the faith of another. In the Gospels, we find that people brought a cripple before Jesus Christ, and Jesus could see the faith of those who carried him, and said to the sick man "Your sins are forgiven" and thus healed him.[2] In another Gospel, again, a maiden was cured because of her mother's faith.[3] I could tell you many such examples, but it would delay us too long.

---

[1] The *Life* of Martin of Tours (c. 316–400), by Sulpicius Severus, was widely disseminated throughout Western Europe. See also *GL* II:292–300.

[2] Matt. 9:2, and see Mark 2:3–5.

[3] Mark 7:25–30.

Les parens sunt auxi come plegges, que cil qu'il[i] receivent en baptesme crera a dreit quant il serra en age qu'il deive saver quei est bien et quei est mal. Entretant se deivent les parent contin[u]er com plegges et somondre le e enseigner de la creance, car s'il remeint en fole creance par lur defaute que il n'aient fet vers lui ceo que a eus partient, il le comperunt mult cher al jour de jugement e s'il ne serra pas quites. Car puis que il est venutz en dreit age, s'il veut estre sauf, il covient q'il eit verrai creance.

Et ceo contient treis choses : que il creie de queor, et que il le die de bouche, et que il le monstre par overaigne. Issi le dist seint Poul : *Corde creditur ad justiciam, ore autem confessio fit ad salutem* [Rom. 10:10]. Et seint Jakes dit : *Fides si non habet opera, mortua est* [Jac. 2:17], c'est a dire que [f.120v] 'Creance sanz overaigne est morte chose.' Et seint Poul dit que tiels i ad : *confitentur se nosce deum, factis autem negant* [Ep. ad Titum 1:16], coe est a dire 'Il reconoissent Deu par bouche, mes il le reneient par oevere.' Et aillors dist seint Poul *Ignorans ignorabitur* [cf. I Cor. 14:38], ceo est a dire 'Cil qui Deu mesconust, Deu mesconuist.' E pur ceo, beau fiz, apernetz de conustre Deu a dreit solom l'aprise de[ii] seinte Eglise.

Le fiz Beau pere, volunters. Mes mult me mervaille de une chose que jeo oi de vous et de ceo que jeo vous dirrai. Vous deistes que celui que Deu mesconust, Deu lui mesconustra al jour de jugement. Et autresi redit le Evangile que Deu dirra a ceus i averont : *Nescio vos* [Matt. 25:12], c'est a dire 'Jeo ne vous conu pas.' Coment purra ceo estre que Deu [qui] tuit siet et tuit conuist conoisse les uns et mesconust les autres ? Et si il les conust et il lur dist 'Jeo ne vous conois pas', dounque dirra il mensunge, et coment porra ceo dire li Deus qui unques ne menti ?

Le pere A ceo respond jeo, beau fiz, que la seinte Escripture ad diverses maneres [f.121r] de parler que l'em ne poet pas saver legierement sanz aprendre de mestre ou sanz grant usage, car par usage le puet l'em savoir. Dunt seint Gregorie dit un ensample. Quant l'em veit un home primerement, l'em puet conuistre sa chiere, mes l'em ne puet pas conuistre soen queor, mes tant puetz home raunter un autre q'il conustra soen corage a pou de parole, veire tiel houre serra sanz parler. Autresi n'entent pas chescon les Escriptures sitost come il les veit, mes tant les puet il haunter qu'il les entendra si il est sotil et pardevant.

[i] MS qui. [ii] MS du.

Parents are as it were guarantors, that the one they received in baptism will believe correctly when he is old enough to know what is right and what is wrong. Meanwhile, the parents must continue as guarantors, and counsel him, and teach him of the faith, for if he retains foolish beliefs through their fault, because they failed to do their duty to him, if he is not absolved they shall pay dearly for it at the Day of Judgement. For once he has come of age he must, if he wishes to be saved, have true faith.

And this comprises three things: let him believe it in his heart, let him speak it with his mouth, let him show it in his works. Thus says Saint Paul: *For with the heart man believeth unto righteousness, and with the mouth confession is made unto salvation.* And Saint James says: *Even so faith, if it hath not works, is dead, being alone.* This means: "Faith without works is a dead thing." And Saint Paul says that there are some who *profess that they know God; but in works they deny him.* This means: "They recognize God by their speech, but they deny him by their deeds." Elsewhere, Saint Paul says: *But if any man be ignorant, let him be ignorant*, meaning "He who knows not God is not known of God." And so, dear son, learn to know God aright, according to what Holy Church teaches you.

Son Gladly, dear father. But I wonder very much about something I have heard from you, and that I shall tell you: you said that whoever does not know God, God shall not know him at the Day of Judgement. And similarly, the Gospel tells how God shall say to those who are there *I know you not*, that is: "I do not know you." How can it be that God, who knows and understands everything, can know some and not know others? And if he does know them but says to them "I do not know you," then he will be telling a lie, and how shall the God who has never lied say that?

Father I shall answer, dear son, that Holy Scripture has divers ways of speaking, so that one cannot understand easily without learning from a master, or without a great deal of practice; for with practice one can understand. Saint Gregory gives an example of this: when first one meets a man, one can look into his face but one cannot look into his heart; but then, one man can keep company with another for so long that he can know his heart without many words — even, in time, with no words at all. So it is that not everybody understands Scripture as soon as he sees it, but he can make himself so familiar with it that he will understand, if he is subtle and enquiring.

L'Escripture parle sovent par semblance ausi com l'em dit d'un home felon, 'c'est un chen', et de un home pesant 'c'est une vache', e nepurquant cil que ceo dist et ceus que l'escoutent sevent et veient apertement qe cil ne est chien ne vache et si n'est ceo pas mensonge que cil dit solum ceo que il entent. Car autretant vaut cele parole cum s'il disoit 'cil semble chien de felonie' et 'vache de pesantie'. Autresi dirra Dieu a ceus[i] 'jeo ne vous conois mie' noun pas pur ceo que il ne les conuist, mes pur [f.121v] ceo que il se fra vers eus come vers estranges, car ja ové ses amys et ses privees ne en son pais n'en sa compaignie ne mettront le pié, einz irront en enfern od les diables qui furent lur aqueinte en ceste siecle.

Le fiz De ceste question jeo me tieng bien paié, mes vous avietz dist une parole que me esbaist mult et espounte, car vous dites que cil irrunt en enfern qui peccherunt par noun-savance, et coment fera ceo Dieu qui est fontaigne de pité et de misericorde ? Car a un enfant pardoune l'em une folie q'il dit ou fet pur ceo q'il le fet par noun-savance, et ne tient l'em pas a sens home de metre son sen a sen d'enfant ne de coroucier sei de parole d'enfant. Autresi m'est il avis que Deu que est debonere sur tote rien ne devereit pas prendre vengance de chose que est fet ou dit par noun-savoir, et meesmement mort pardurable semble trop cruele chose et trop cruele vengance pur tiele pecché.

Le pere Une bone question et forte me as demandé et que mult est bone [f.122r] a savoir. Ore entendez bien et jeo t'en respondrai. Il sunt troi maneres de noun-savans : li un ne sevent pas ceo que lur covient saver a estre sauf, ne il ne le volunt aprendre, car il n'ent volunt oir parler ; de ceus dit David le prophete : *Verba oris eius iniquitas et dolus : noluit intelligere ut bene ageret* [Ps. 35:4], c'est a dire que 'Ses paroles sunt iniquitez et tricherie, car il ne volt aprendre pur bien fere.' Icés ne serrunt pas acounté al jugement pur noun-savance, mes pur despisanz, car il despistrent a aprendre a bien fere et a bien vivre, et pur ceo si serront il dampnez pur duble pecché ; l'un serra qu'il ne voudront mie aprendre de vivre a dreit, l'autre q'il firent mal.

L[i] autre sunt noun-savantz en tiele manere que qui lur aprendreit, il l'orreint volunters. Et qui ne lur offre, il ne s'enpurchacent pas.

---

[i] MS c. et iavera.

Scripture often speaks in metaphors, as one says of a bad man "he is a dog," or of a heavy man "he is a cow," and nevertheless the speaker and the listener know and see quite clearly that here is neither dog nor cow; it is surely no lie if he speaks according to what he means. The words are as if he said "this looks like a dog of wickedness," or "a cow of heaviness." Thus it is that God shall say to those people "I do not know you," not because he doesn't know them but because he will behave to them as to strangers. Never shall they set foot in his kingdom or his company, nor among his friends and intimates; rather, they shall go to hell with the devils who were their associates in this world.

Son On this question, I declare myself well satisfied. But you said something that really astounds and frightens me: you said that those who sin through ignorance will go to hell. How shall God, the fount of pity and mercy, do that? After all, we forgive a child the folly it says or does, because it does so out of ignorance; we think it unreasonable for a man to expect his own reason in the reasoning of a child, or to be angry at the words of a child. And so it seems to me that God, who is fair-minded above all things, ought not to take vengeance for anything that is said or done through ignorance; especially, eternal damnation seems too cruel a thing, too cruel a vengeance, for such a sin.

Father You have asked me a good question, and a difficult one, which is very profitable to know about. So listen well, and I shall answer it for you. There are three kinds of ignorant people. Some do not know what they need to know to be saved, and nor do they wish to learn, for they do not wish to hear it spoken about. Of these, the prophet David says: *The words of his mouth are iniquity and deceit: he hath left off to be wise, and to do good.*[4] This means that "his words are iniquity and treachery, for he does not wish to learn how to do good." At the Judgement, these shall not be accused of ignorance but of contempt. For they were too contemptuous to learn how to do good and to live well, so they shall be damned for double sin: one is that they would not learn to live righteously, the other that they did harm.

The second kind are ignorant in such a way that to whomsoever would teach them, they would willingly listen. But they do not seek it of those who do not offer it.

---

[4] Ps. 36:3 in *AV.*

Iteuz resont digne d'estre dampné si Deus n'en a pité, car il eusent suffrete du pain et de dras il n'entendissent pas tant qe l'em lur apportast, einz meissent grand peine a gainer ceo que mester lur fust. Et [f.122v] autretant come l'alme vaut meuz del cors, autretant duissent il plus laborer a conquere la vie de l'alme des queus le prophete parle et dit : *Sapientes sunt ut faciant mala, bene autem facere nescierunt* [Jer. 4:22], c'est a dire, 'Il sunt sages de mal fere, mes de bien il ne sevont rien.' A teus genz reproche Jesu en le Evangile q'il sevent bien quant il deit fere bele temps ou leid, mes il ne sevent pas ceo que apartient a lur sauvement.

Li tiercz sunt bien appellez noun-savanz, car il sunt si nice et si bestial que qui lur dirreit rien, il ne l'entendreint pas des teus choses ja q'il n'ount mie tant de reson en eus. Iceo n'est pas pecché quant il ne pount plus fere, mes ceo est de la penance del pecché Adam. Car si le pecché Adam ne fust, nous fuissoms tuz sages et des totes bones teches. E icés ne ount garde al jugement de chose q'il eient [fet] ou dit par itele noun-savance.

Le fiz Mult me avez bien dit. Ore vei[i] jeo bien que il me covient aprendre ou jeo la comperai. Jeo solai lesser de apprendre pur ceo que m'ert [f.123r] avis qui que plus sciet plus ad [a] respondre, mes jeo vei que cele reson ne me puet mes valer, par quei jeo vodrei apprendre ceo que mei puet plus profiter.

[L]e pere Yl te covient tut avant saver quei est crere. Quider de la creance et crere et saver sunt treis choses. Cil qui quide ne se fet certain de rien. Cil qui sciet, il est certain de ceo qu'il sciet. Crere, ceo est entre deus, plus que quider, meins que saver. Saver puet l'em en deus maneres, par reson et par esprove, sicome quant tu veis le solail, dunque ses tu bien q'il est jor, et quant tu sentes le fu, dunque ses tu bien q'il [est] chaud, c'est saver par esprove. Saver par reson est : 'Si li reis est a Paris, dunque n'est il mie a Estaumpes ; s'il est sein, dunque n'est il mie malade ; si il est sages, dunque n'est il pas fol.'

[i] MS viei.

These too deserve damnation unless God takes pity on them, for even if they lacked food and clothing they would pay no heed unless somebody brought it for them, rather than going to the trouble of procuring what they needed. And just as the soul is worth more than the body, so much the harder they should work to win the life of the soul; of these the Prophet speaks, saying: *They are wise to do evil, but to do good they have no knowledge.* This means, "they are clever at doing bad things, but they know nothing about doing good." Jesus reproaches such people in the Gospel, saying that they know when the weather is going to be fair or foul but they do not know anything pertaining to their salvation.[5]

The third kind are well named the ignorant, because they are so stupid and brutish that whatever anybody may say to them they can never understand such things, because they have not enough sense in them. It is not sin, that they can do no more, but it is punishment for the sin of Adam. Were it not for Adam's sin, we should all be wise and have every good quality. These people give no thought to the judgement, of what they did or said through ignorance.

Son What you have said is very good. Now I see that I must learn, or I shall pay dearly. I was slacking in my study, because it seemed to me that the more one knows the more one has to answer for. But I see that I can no longer use this reasoning, because I want to learn whatever will be of most benefit to me.

Father You ought to learn, first of all, what it means to have faith. Believing by faith, believing, and knowing, are three things. Whoever believes, is not certain of anything. Whoever knows is certain of what he knows. Faith is between these two: more than believing and less than knowing. You can know in one of two ways: by reason and by experience; as when you see the sun, you know it is daytime, and when you feel the fire, you know it is hot — this is knowing by experience. Knowing by reason is: "If the King is in Paris, then he is not at Etampes;[6] if he is in good health, then he is not ill; if he is wise, then he is not stupid."[7]

---

[5] Matt. 16:1–4.

[6] Etampes is in the north-east of the Beauce region, between Chartres and Orléans; there was a royal palace there.

[7] Cf. *BVV*, p. 101: a similar example demonstrates how we know that Our Father is in Heaven. "When I say the king is at London, I am saying the king is the king and that he is at London ..." (my translation). Unfortunately the notes give no ultimate sources, but the French is provided for comparison: "quant ie di. le roy est a paris / je di deux choses ..."; we may assume this to be a standard teaching example.

C'est saver par reson, car reson ne puet consenter que un home seit ensemble sein et malade, fol et sage, ci et la a une fez. Et qui issi set, si home la posast de diverses choses, tutz jours savereit ceo q'il set et de cel saver ne deit il attendre ne geiter nulle [f.123v] autre loer de Deu, car il le sciet par reson ou par esprove. Mes de ceo que l'em creit dunt l'em ne puet pas trover reson plenerement et ou l'en consente a Deu pur estre obedient a lui, de ceo rendra Deu a home louer.

Et pur ceo te di jeo que si tu seuses certeinement que Deu fust si que tu le eusses veu as oilz, il n'i afereit point de louer. Et nequedent sachetz que celui que bien creit, [creit] com si il le saveit, fors de tant que il ne l'ad pas esprové, car s'il l'ust esprové, ja puis n'en devereit aver louer, car ceo ne serreit mie crere mes saver. Ore sachez dunques q'il covient, a estre sauf, tut avant ferme creance et verrai. Il covient que sa creance seit ferme, q'il ne la guerpisse pur mort ne pur vie nient plus que ne firent li martir que miez vodreient morir que guerpir lur creance soulement de la bouche. Il covient qu'il seit verrai, et s'il te membre que jeo dis, il n'ad mie verrai creance s'il n'ad treis choses : que ceo q'il creit de queor, que il le die de bouche quant mestier est, et puis que il le mette en overaigne. L'em deit preme[f.124r]rement saver et crere fermement que un Deus est, le Pere et le Fiz et li seint Espirit.

Le fiz Vous mei dites que jeo dei crere que un Deus est et vous me nometz treis pur un. Coment puet ceo estre ?

Le pere Beau fiz, membre tei que jeo dis que si jeo mostrase pleneremententes la reson coment ces treis choses sunt un, ceo ne serreit pas crere, mes savoir. Et lores attendrietz tu louer pur nient. Mes il n'i avera pas defaute si grande de reson que l'em ne puisse aschun point trover, car Deu ad issi sa creance atempré que li bons i troevent aschune chose ou il se pount apower et li maveis aschune chose ou il se puissent abouter. Car ne sunt pas dignes que Deu les deive receivre od les soens. Et pur ceo que la creance Deu est une partie aperte et une partie coverte dit seinte Eglise en une livre que Salomon fist que l'em apelle *Cantica ca[n]ticorum* : *Dilectus meus stat post parietem respiciens per fenestras* [Cant. 2:9], c'est a dire 'Moun Amy derere la parei est mussé et geytant par les fenestres.' Il n'est [f.124v] pas del tuit covert ne de[l] tuit descovert.

This is knowing by reason, for reason cannot allow a man to be well and sick, wise and stupid, here and there, at the same time. Whoever knows in this way, if one were to ask him about various things he would always know what he knows; in this knowledge he should not expect or wait for any further counsel from God, for he knows it by reason or by experience. But for what a man believes — what he cannot fully find any reason for, what he consents to in order to be obedient to God — then God will give him counsel about it.

So I tell you this: if you knew for certain that God was exactly as you had seen him with your own eyes, then there would be no need for counsel. Nevertheless, understand that whoever believes, [believes] as though he knew it beyond anything he had experienced; for had he experienced it he would need no further counsel, for it would be not belief but knowledge.[8] Now understand that, to be saved, firm and true faith is necessary before all things. This faith must be firm; one must not leave hold of it for death nor for life, no more than did the martyrs who preferred to die rather than deny their faith even by mouth. And it must be true — remember that I said this: there is no true faith without three things, that is what you believe in your heart, what you say with your mouth when need is, and then how you put it into practice. One must first of all know and believe steadfastly that there is One God: Father, Son, and Holy Spirit.

Son You tell me that I must believe there is one God, and then you name Three for this One. How can that be?

Father Dear son, remember I said that if I showed you clearly how these three things are one, then it would be not belief but knowledge. And then you would seek counsel for nothing. But there is not so great a lack of reason that one can find nothing to grasp, for God has so ordained his faith that good people can find something to lean on, and bad people something to object to. For they are not worthy that God should receive them as his own. And because faith in God is in part open and in part hidden, so Holy Church says, in a book Solomon made called the Song of Songs: *My beloved . . . standeth behind our wall, he looketh forth at the windows, shewing himself through the lattice.* This means "My love is hidden behind the wall and watches through the windows." He is not completely hidden nor completely revealed.

---

[8] Cf. the Middle English *Pater* (p. 23, ll. 5–6; note on p. 106), a similar passage on the nature of belief is credited by the editor to Hugh of St Victor's *De Sacramentis*. See, further, the *Lumere* (I:176), where the context is a discussion of Faith, Hope, and Charity, and Augustine is cited; see note to vv. 5801ff (III:112).

Autresi tei die jeo la creance Deu n'est pas si coverte del tut que l'em ne puisse trover aschune chose de reson. Ne ele n'est pas si descoverte del tuit que l'em la puisse tote prover par reson si que les malveis assetz i troevent ou abouter come firent li Jeu qui esgarderent que Jesu Crist beveit et mangeit et dormi et suffri mort et lur fu avis que si il fust Deu, si come il diseit, il ne pout pas ceo fere, car Deu ne pout pas morir. Et issi le mescrustrent. Ne ele ne est mie si coverte que l'em n'i troefse aschune point de reson si que les bons il troevent ou apouer come firent cil que se crestienerent pur l'amur de li pur ceo qu'il esgarderent que il resuscitout les mortz et garisout les forsenés, les sours, les muetz, les meseaus et que il saula cink mille homes de cink pains et de deus pessons si que demorent illeoques .xii. corbeaus de relef. Si esgarderent que ceo ne poit estre fet si par Deu noun. Sur ceo crurent ceo q'il diseit et issi crurent que il estoit Deu.

Autresi te di [f.125r] jeo bien que l'em ne puet pas dire de tut reson, mes pur ceo que ceo n'est mie del tuit saunz reson. Ore ente[n]g ceo que jeo dirrai. Tu demandes coment ceo puet estre que ceus treis persones, le Pere, le Fiz, le seint Espirit seient un Deu. Le soleil ad en sei treis choses : chalur, clarté et substance, que sunt diverses, que l'une puet estre conu sanz l'autre. Car un home qui goute ne veit puet sentir le chalur du solail. Qui le demaundreit 'quei sentetz vous ?', si il diseit 'jeo senk le soleil', il ne mentireit pas. Un autre, s'il veit la rai du solail en une mesun, si il diseit 'jeo vei le solail', il ne mentireit pas. Le tiercz, si il gardout vers le ciel, celi purreit dire sanz faille 'jeo vei[i] le solail'. Et nequedent ceo que l'un veit ne veit pas l'autre et ceo que ceus veient ne veit pas cil, ne ne sent pas, qui est esvoegle qui rien ne veit. Et si est ceo verité aperte que ces treis choses ne sont pas treis solails, mes un. Autresi te di jeo que ces treis persones ne sont pas treis Deus mes un. Si ne te di jeo pas que il soit issi del tuit del solail come de Deu. Kar [f.125v] il n'est riens qui de[l] tut semble a Deu. Mes pur ceo le te di que tu ne deis pas trop merveiller coment ces treis choses sont un Deu. Quant tu veies autre ciel en choses corporeus il covient[ii] que tu demandes crere, ne mie saver. Car ceo [est] le plus haute secré de tote la creance.

[i] MS veie. [ii] MS corporeus et i. c. ceo que.

And so I say to you that divine faith is not so completely hidden that one can find nothing of it by reason. Nor is it so completely open that one can prove it completely by reason; so wicked people can find enough objections. Thus did the Jews, who saw that Jesus Christ drank and ate and slept, and suffered death; it was their opinion that were he God he could not do that, for God cannot die. So, they did not believe in him. Nor is faith so obscure that one can find no foothold in fact, as good people find to hold to; witness those who became Christians for love of him, seeing that he raised the dead and cured the mad, the deaf, the dumb, and the leprous — and that he fed five thousand people with five loaves and two fishes, so well that there were twelve baskets full of food left over. They saw that this could not have been done except by God. With this, they believed what he said, and so they believed that he was God.

Now I tell you that if you cannot prove everything by reason this is not to say that it is all without reason. Listen to what I shall say: you ask how it can be that these three Persons, Father and Son and Holy Spirit, can be one God. Of itself the sun has three things: heat, light, and substance — which are all different, because one of them can be experienced without another. A man who can see absolutely nothing is able to feel the sun's heat. If you ask him "What can you feel?" and he says "I can feel the sun," then he will not be lying. Another, seeing a ray of sunshine in a house, will say "I see the sun" and not be lying. A third, looking skywards, can say with truth "I see the sun." Nevertheless, what one sees is not what another sees; nor can he who is blind, and sees nothing, see or feel what the others feel. But it is obviously true that these three things are not three suns but one.[9] Likewise, I tell you that these three Persons are not three Gods but one.[10] But I don't mean to say that the sun is exactly like God, for nothing exists that is exactly like God. But I tell you so that you won't wonder how three things can be one God. When you see another heaven in corporeal things, it is fitting that you ask to believe, not to know. This is the highest of all the secrets of faith.

---

[9] The father draws a clear distinction between a ray of sunshine and the visible orb. This idea of the Trinity, and the discussion below about how the Father does not precede the Son, is very reminiscent of passages on light in Grosseteste's *Hexaëmeron* (see ed. Dales and Gieben, pp. 220–24: Part 8, caps. 3 & 4; *On the Six Days*, trans. Martin, pp. 224–28). However, a comparable passage in the *Lumere* (III:70, note to vv. 711–1076) is likely to be based on Honorius' *Elucidarium*. For Grosseteste and the *Lumere*, see Hessenauer 1995 (the argument goes back to the fourth-century Cappadocian Fathers).

[10] Cf. Love's *Mirror* (p. 23), which makes no attempt to explain the Trinity.

Ne unques home tant ne fu bien de Dieu que ceste secré seust plenerement tanque après la mort. Seint Poul que fu ravi si que al tierce ciel dist : *Videmus quasi per speculum in enigmate et ex parte videmus* [...] *et ex parte prophetamus* [I Cor. 13:12 & 9], c'est a dire 'Nous veoms de Deu com en un miroir, noun pas apertement, et si come nous veoms en partie, en parlom.' Nous que sumes en terre orde, soillé en fens de pecché, que poum nous ver, quant saint Poul qui fu de si bone vie et porté par li seint Esperit si que al tierz ciel ne veit rien de Deu fors par divinaille ? Ore n'i ad dunques plus fors que nous devoms crere que le Pere, le Fiz et li seint Espirit sont un Deu. Et autresi come la clarté de solail n'est pas la chalur ne la chalur n'est pas la substance et nequedent ces treis choses ne sont pas treis solails, mes [f.126r] un, autresi te di jeo la persone del Pere n'est pas cele del Fiz ne cel de[l] Fiz n'est pas cele del seint Espirit, et nequedent ces ne sunt pas treis Deus mes un Deus. Et pur ceo n'est pas le solail de treis pieces si il ad en sei treis choses, ne Deu n'est pas pur ceo de treis pieces ne de treis parties pur ceo treis persones. *Deus non est corpus nec corporis habet similitudinem*, n'il n'ad mie forme de home si come quident plusors fous, car espirit n'ad pas forme de home, et si ne te merveille pas que l'Escripture dist que Deus fist home a sa ymage. Ceo n'est pas dit pur le corps, mes pur les spiritz, que ad en sei reson et entendement come Deu. Ceo n'ad nule chose certene fors homme. Unquore deis tu crere que l'une de ces treis persones n'est meillur ne greignor ne plus puissant ne plus sachant ne que l'une fu umques einz que l'autre. Car ces treis sunt un Deu que unques ne commencera ne jamés ne finera, car il fu touz jours et touz jours serra et ceo signifie ceo que Ysaie le prophete vit. Il vit que deus angles coverirent la face Deu de lor eles et les piez autresi. Le chef et les [f.126v] piés signifient le commencement et la fin. Iceus deus choses sunt si covertes en Deu que nul ne puet ver ne l[e] commencement ne la fin. Car il n'i ad point, einz fu tout jours et serra.

Li fiz Deus merveilles m'avetz counté : que l'une des persones fu autresi tost come l'autre, et coment pust estre ausi tost come l'autre et coment pust estre ausi tost le Fiz com le Pere ?

Never was there a man so favoured by God that he knew the secret fully, until after his death. Saint Paul, who was rapt into the third heaven, said *For now we see through a glass, darkly ... we know in part, and we prophesy in part.* This means: "We see God as if in a mirror, not openly; and as we know in part so do we speak of it in part." We who are in this filthy earth, soiled with the ordure of sin, what can we see when Saint Paul, who was of such holy life and was borne by the Holy Spirit to the third heaven, could only see God enigmatically? Therefore there is nothing more important to believe than that the Father, Son, and Holy Spirit are one God. Just as the sun's light is not the heat, nor the heat its substance, and nevertheless these three things are not three suns but one, so I tell you that the person of the Father is not the Son's, nor is the Son's that of the Holy Spirit, and nevertheless they are not three Gods but One.[11] Because the sun is not three pieces for being made up of three things, so I tell you therefore God is not three pieces or three parts being these three Persons. "God is not body, nor has he the likeness of a body." Nor has he the form of a man, as some fools believe; for the spirit is not human in form, and do not be surprised that Scripture says God made mankind in his image.[12] This does not mean in body, but in spirit, which has reason and understanding as God has. Certainly, no other creature but mankind has this. Further, you must believe that no one of these three Persons is better or greater, more powerful or wise, nor that any one existed before another. These three are one God who has no beginning and no end, for he was ever, and ever shall be. This is the meaning of what the prophet Isaiah saw. He saw that two angels covered the face of God with their wings, and his feet likewise.[13] The head and the feet signify the beginning and the end. These two things are hidden of God, that none may see either beginning or end. For there is none; he has been for all time, and so shall be.

Son You have told me two marvels: that one of the Persons existed as soon as the others — but how can one be as soon as another, how can the Son exist as soon as the Father does?

---

[11] Combinations such as this, making up a ternary group to help explain the Trinity, are not uncommon and may be derived in part from Augustine. See Alan of Lille's *Anticlaudianus*, pp. 164–65 (and note 28), and Augustine's *De Symbolo ad Catechumenos Sermo alius* cap. ix (*PL* 40:658).

[12] Gen. 1:26.

[13] Is. 6:1–2; neither the Vulgate nor the Authorized Version actually says that the angel covers the Lord's face and feet with his wings; for this reading by other medieval commentators, see Carruthers and Ziolkowski 2002 (pp. 83–102).

L'autre si est que vous dites que Deu n'ad pas forme de home et puis si redites que Ysaie le vit en forme de home fors q'il aveit le chief et les piés covertes. L'Escripture redit que meinte foiz apparurent li angle en forme de home et si sunt il espiritz et vous deistes que Deu n'ad pas forme de home, car espirit n'ad nule forme.

Le pere Issi parole que si siet. Tu dis ceo que tu as veu en la generation charnel, q'il covient que le Piere seit avant que le Fiz, mes il n'est pas issi des espirituels choses come des corporels. Il fet bon ver la lumere del solail, c'est le jour, car par la lumere savom nous ou nous devom aler. Mes qui velt esgarder vers le ciel et ver la lumere dunt il nest, qui plus regarde et plus si blohist. Autresi di jeo il fet bon [f.127r] crere que le Fiz Deu est Deu. Mes qui veut saver coment il nasqui, qui plus pense, plust s'ebahist. Mes puis que tu ne te poetz tenir de teus choses enquerer, jeo t'en responderai : Tu poetz ver que la clarté nest de soleil et si ses tu bien que autresi tost fu la clarté come le solail. Et nequident si nest la clarté du solail. Ore nes[t]-se pas merveille dunque si autresi tost fu li Fiz com li Pere.

Tu te merveilles de ceo que Deu n'ad pas forme de home, car il est espiriz que n'ad nule forme. Et de ceo que jeo dis aprés que Ysaie l'aveit veu en forme de home, a ceo te respon jeo que Deu apparuist a qe q'il voet et en tiel forme come il voet, as uns en une manere, as autres en autre, car nuls nel vit umques par avision, nus nel puet vere en ceste mortiel vie apertement si come il est, si come jeo tei vei. Moises fu bien de lui, ceo dit l'Escripture, que il parlout a lui face a face si come home fet a soen veisin et si[i] nel puez il pas veer apertement e si l'en priast il et dit 'si tu mei eimes, moustrét moi ta chiere' et Deu li respondi que nules que vive en ceste [f.127v] siecle nel puet ver. Unquore dis tu que angle apparurent en forme de home et jeo te respon que li angles sunt espiritz et que il ne pount estre veu de nulle home mortiel tant com il soient en lur propre nature. Mes quant il volent apparer, il pernent forme de home et funt corps del heir et la robe dount il sunt vestu ceo semble [...] car nent plus ne unt corps que robe. Et ceo siet l'em bien q'il n'ad en ciel nule[ii] terriene chose, dont vendreit ne seie ne leine dont la robe fu teissue, taillé et cosue.

---

[i] MS sil. [ii] MS n. ciel.

The other is, you say God has not human form and then say Isaiah saw him in the form of a man, except that his head and feet were covered. Scripture for its part says that many times angels appear in human form and that they are spirits; and you said God has not human form, for spirit has no form.

Father [Scripture] speaks rightly; you say what you have seen concerning fleshly generation, that it is necessary for the Father to precede the Son, but it is not so with spiritual things as it is with corporeal. It is good to see the sun's light, that is the day, for we know by the light where we are going. But whoever wants to look skywards, towards the light whence he is born, the more he looks the more he is blinded. Likewise, I tell you it is right to believe that the Son of God is God. But if you want to know how he was born, the more you think about it the more bewildered you will become. But, since you cannot help asking about such things, I shall answer you. You can see that the light is born from the sun, and similarly you know that the light has existed as long as the sun has. And yet the light is indeed born from the sun. So it is no wonder then, that the Son was just as soon as the Father was.[14]

You are wondering how it is, that God has not human form, for he is spirit which has no form. And concerning what I said next, that Isaiah saw him in human form, I reply to that: God appears to whom he pleases, and in whatever form he pleases; in this way to some and in that way to others. None has ever seen him but in a vision, none in this mortal life can see him as he is, as I can see you. Moses was favoured by him, as Scripture says, and talked with him face to face as one does with a neighbour, and yet he could not see him openly. He begged him, saying "If thou lovest me, show me thy face,"[15] and God replied to him that none living in this world might see him. And again, you say that angels appeared in human form, and I answer you that angels are spirits and cannot be seen by any mortal man when they are in their natural shape. But when they wish to appear they take a man's form and make bodies out of air, and the robes they wear seem . . . ,[16] for they have no more body than dress. We know there is no earthly matter in heaven, nor could any silk or wool come there for robes to be woven, cut, and sewn from.

---

[14] See p. 37, note 9, above. See also Alan of Lille's *Anticlaudianus* (p. 165), where a ray of sunlight is characterized as coeternal with its source.

[15] See Ex. 33:11–23; verse 13 reads . . . *shew me now thy way*, but in *LV* the prayer is *ostende mihi faciem tuam* (thy face).

[16] Gap in MS.

Et quant ceo est que il volent apparer, il semblent mielz et plus beal que il pregnent cors de home et figure, car il venunt parler as homes et nequedent il unt esté veu en autre forme.

Le fiz Jeo m'acorde bien a ceo que vous dites.

Le pere Unquore deis crere que le Fiz Dieu prist humanité en la virgine Marie pur reindre Adam des peines d'enfern, et ceus que de lui isserent, et que pur ceo suffri il mort en croiz et descendi en enfern et demora illeoques quarante oures, c'est[i] a dire deques al tierce jour [f.128r] et en osta ceus que il vout et resuscita au tiercz jour et apparust a ses amis et fust quaraunte jours en terre. Et puis mounta en ciel en char et en os ou il est unquore et serra si que atant q'il vendra al jugement et que nous releverom ausi en corps et en alme encountre cel jugement aprés ceo que nous serrom departi de ceste siecle. Et si dois crere que quant il nasqui de la Virgine que autre fu il en ciel come devaunt, et quant il suffri mort, la deité ne morust pas mes la humanité et que il fu ensemble verrei Deu et verrei homme. *Nam sicut anima rationalis et caro etc.*, car autresi come homme est de deus choses, c'est de cors et de alme, et nequedent ces deus choses ne sunt pas deus, mes un, et c'est un home, autresi ces treis choses, Deuz et corps et home, furent ensemble une persone.

Le fiz Merveilles me dites et jeo crei bien si come vous m'avetz enseigné q'il covient crere, ne mie saver, la reson de chescune chose, mes nequedent si vous me moustretz une petit de raison et de avisement, jeo en serroie plus aese.

Le pere Issi deis tu dire. Il covient [f.128v] miauz crere que entendre si come dist lui prophete : *Si non credideritis non intelligeris*, c'est a dire 'si vous ne creez, vous n'entendriez mie.' Et Salamon dist *Intellexi quod omnium operum Dei nemo potest invenire rationem ; Quanto magis laborabit, tanto minus inveniet* [Eccles. 8:17], c'est a dire 'ceo ai entendu que nul ne porreit trover reson de quanque Deu fet, et tant plus se peinereit[ii] home, e meins la trovereit.' Mes nequedent ceo que purrai trover, tei dirrai jeo. Si jeo pense ore que vousisse estre reis, tu ne savereis pas cele pensee et si jeo escrivai en parchemin devant tei issi, 'jeo pense que jeo voudrei estre reys', donques purretz vous dire verre[i]ment 'jeo vei vostre pensé.'

[L]e fiz Oÿl[iii] sanz faille.

---

[i] MS ceste. [ii] MS pernereit. [iii] MS Eyl.

And when they want to appear, they look better and more beautiful, taking human body and form, for they come to speak with men; nevertheless they have been seen in other forms.

Son I accept what you are saying.

Father Further, you must believe that the Son of God took human form through the Virgin Mary to redeem Adam, and those descended from him, from the pains of hell; therefore he suffered death by the Cross and descended into hell and stayed there forty hours, that is until the third day, and he brought out those he wanted and rose from death on the third day, and showed himself to his friends, and he was on earth for forty days. Then he ascended to heaven, in his flesh and blood, where he is still and shall be until he comes to Judgement, and after that we shall be taken out of this world. And you must believe that when he was born of the Virgin he was different from when he was in heaven before, and when he suffered death it was not his Godhead that died but his manhood, and that he was at once truly God and truly man. "For just as reasonable soul, and flesh, etc."[17] For just as man is two things — that is body and spirit, and yet these two things are not two but one, a man — likewise these three things, God and body and man, were together in one Person.

Son You tell me marvellous things, and I believe as you have taught me: to believe, and not to know, the reason for each thing. But still, if you can show me a little reason and explanation I shall be easier in my mind.

Father So you ought to say. It is better for you to believe than to understand, as the Prophet says:[18] "If you do not believe, you will understand nothing." And Solomon says: *Then I beheld all the work of God, that a man cannot find out the work that is done under the sun: because though a man labour to seek it out, yet shall he not find it.* This means "I have understood this: that none can find reason for whatever God does, and the more trouble one takes, the less one can find." And yet I will tell you what I can find. If I were to think now that I should like to be king, you would not know that thought; but if I were to write on parchment before you, like this: "I think I should like to be king," then you could truly say "I see your thought."

Son Yes, indeed.

---

[17] Cf. the Athanasian Creed.

[18] Is. 7:9: *If ye will not believe, surely ye shall not be established* [*non permanebitis*]. See Anselm's *Opera*, ed. Schmitt, I, p. 100; and trans. Ward, chap. 1, p. 244. See also p. 5, note 24, above.

Le pere Veire. Nepurquant icele mesme pensee serreit autresi en mon queor come ert avant que fu escrite ne umques pur ceo s'enparti ne pou ne grand, et si tu depesces et defacies cele escripture, [n']averaies tu pur ceo empiré ma pensee ne osté la de moen queor. Nanyl. Par autretiel semblaunce te di jeo que Deu ne puet estre veu en sa deité nent plus [f.129r] que la pensé en le queor. Mes quant il prist humanité, lors puet il estre veu, ne pur ceo ne fu il pas meins en ciel ové soen Pere que devant. Autresi come la pensee quant il prist le corps de l'escripture, c'est[i] quant ele fu escrite, pout estre veuue ne pur ceo ne fu ele pas meins en queor que devant. Et quant Jesu Crist suffri mort, la deité ne fu de rien empiré nent plus que la pensé del queor fu quant tu effaças l'escripture. Mes ceo fu la humanité que morust, non pas la deité, autresi come ceo fu l'escripture que fu effacié, non pas la pensee del quor. Ore ne te merveille pas dunque si Deu pout issi fere, car il fet quanque q'il voet et rien [n']est mervelle que il face, car nient plus ne lui couste[ii] a fere les grandz choses que les petites, car rien ne li cust.

Le fiz Paié m'avetz. Mes ore me redites pur quele raison fumes nous rains de la mort d'enfern, si com vous dites, par la mort Jesu Crist plus que par un autre.

Le pere Quant home peccha, Deu se parti de lui. Le Deable prist home et lui mist en sa prison d'enfern issi qu'il ne poet sanz Deu jammés estre [f.129v] delivrez. Et quant Jesu Crist fust neez, il esteit verrai Deu et verrai home et le Deable ne saveit mie coment il vint en le siecle ; si le tempta, mes il ne trova en lui ne avant ne aprés rien de sa dreiture. Et puis il mist Judas[iii] en queor que il le traist, ceo dist l'Evangile, et entisa les Jués que il le occisent et Jesu Crist suffri ceo voluntiers, quar pur ceo ert il venuz. Mes par la dreite jugement quant le Deable mist main a Jesu Crist ou il n'out nulle dreit, il deservi a perdre ceo ou il out dreit. Donques perdi ceo q'il out de dreiture en home, si rien i out, par le claim q'il clama plus haut que dreiture ne fust.

Le fiz Que deit ceo dunques que touz ceus del munde que sunt baptizé ne sunt sauf ?

Le pere Pur ceo que Jesu Crist ne suffri mort fors pur ceus que le Deable voudreit[iv] lesser et convertir sei a lui, il ne lour fet pas force, car Dieu fist home et lui dona tiel dignеté et tiel poesté qu'il feist le quel que il voudreit sanz force ou bien ou mal.

---

[i] MS ceste. [ii] MS coustent. [iii] MS mist a J. [iv] MS voudreient.

Father True. And yet this same thought would be in my heart just as it was before it was written, nor would it have ever left there at all for that reason. If you tear up and deface that writing, you will not thereby harm my thought, nor efface it from my heart. Not at all. By a similar figure I tell you that God cannot be seen in his Godhead any more than thought can be seen in the heart. But when he became man, then he could be seen; but he was not consequently any less in heaven with his Father than before. Like the thought that was embodied in writing, that is, when it was written, it can be seen but is not consequently any less in the heart than before. And when Jesus Christ suffered death, the Godhead was not harmed at all, any more than the heart's thought was when you rubbed out the writing. It was the humanity that died, not the deity; as it was the writing that disappeared, not the heart's thought. Do not be surprised, then, that God can do this, for he does whatever he wishes and it is no surprise that he does it. It costs him no more trouble to do great things than little things, for it costs him nothing.

Son You have reassured me. But now, tell me why it is we were redeemed from hell, as you said, by the death of Jesus Christ rather than by another.

Father When man sinned, God left him. The Devil took mankind and put him in his prison of hell, so that without God he can never be delivered. When Jesus Christ was born, he was true God and true man, and the Devil did not understand how he had come into the world. He tempted him, but could find nothing in him, before or after, to give him any power over him. And then he put it into Judas' heart to betray him, as the Gospel says, and provoked the Jews into killing him; Jesus Christ suffered it willingly, for this is why he had come. But because the Devil laid hands on Jesus Christ when he had no right to do so, he rightly deserved to lose what he did have the right to. So he lost whatever power, if any, he rightly had over man, by his attempt to take higher things than he had any right to.[19]

Son What does this mean, then, that not everybody in the world who is baptized is saved?

Father Because Jesus Christ suffered death only for those who wished to leave the Devil and convert to him; he does not force them, for God made man and gave him the dignity and capacity to do whatever he wants, good or bad.

---

[19] Cf. *Preaching*, trans. Wenzel, p. 98.

Le fiz Jeo ai entendu. L'Escripture dist que Jesu se livera [f.130r] a mort pur nous : *Tradidit semetipsum pro nobis* [Gal. 1:4], et si redit il que Judas le livera a mort a les Jués a qui il le vendi, *tradidit eum principibus sacerdotum*, dunque fist Judas ceo que Deu fist et ceo que Deu voleit. Quele pecché fist il donques ?

Le pere Il fist pecché grand. Car il le fist par mal entention com par coveitise et par treson, ceo que Deu fist par charité et par amour que il aveit devers nous. Et issi poez ver que trop est male chose a fere rien en male entente.

Le pere[i] Vous devez crere le sacrament que le prestre feet sur le auter, si est le verrei corps Deu, et que il ne puet par bounté del chapelain de rien estre amendé ne par sa maveisté [de] nulle rien estre empiré. Tu veis que plusurs le receivunt et chescun le resceit tout, dont[ii] ceo ne sunt mie, pur ceo, cent corps ne deus centz que cent homes ou deus centz receivent, mes un. Autresi come qui dirreit une parole oiantz mil homes, chescun l'orreit tote, et ceo ne serreint pas mil paroles mes une. Et si tu esgardeies en[iii] cent mirours ensemble, si verreis tu en chescun toun ymage. Pur ceo ne serreis tu pas cent [f.130v] homes, mes un. Et si tu bruseis un mireor en pieces, tu verras tun ymage en chescune piece. Autresi, di jeo, si tu veisses le sacrament departir en pieces, tu deis crere que il est tut en chescune piece.

Jeo te voille unquore dire une reson de tote la creance ensemble et paier tei en gros si jeo puis. Le Deable dist que il voleit estre pere a Deu ; ceo fust si grand pecché que pur ceo fu il tresbuché du ciel. Jesu Crist dit q'il estoit Deu et pur ceo li occistrent les Jués, mes encontre ceo il fesoit tant des miracles que l'em siet ben que il ne puissent estre fet si par Deu non. Dunque siet l'em bien q'il diseit verité. Et il diseit q'il esteit Dieu.

[i] The copyist may have omitted something here. There is a considerable break in the sense: a jump from Judas' sin to the sacrament on the altar. A question missing, from the son, would explain the repetition of "Le Pere." See Langlois 1928, pp. 58–59, for a clue about what might be missing. [ii] MS ne dont. [iii] MS un.

Son I understand. Scripture says that Jesus delivered himself up to death for us — *Who gave himself for our sins* — and then it says Judas delivered him up to death, to the Jews to whom he had sold him: "he betrayed him to the high priests."[20] Judas did what God did and what God wanted, so what was his sin?[21]

Father He committed a very grave sin. For he did it with evil intent, by avarice and by treason; God did it by charity, out of the love he had for us. So you can see how terrible it is to do anything with evil intent.

Father[22] You are to believe in the sacrament made by the priest on the altar, which is the true Body of God; it cannot be improved by the goodness of the chaplain, nor spoiled by his wickedness, in any way. You see that many receive it, and each one receives it whole. But this does not mean a hundred or two hundred Bodies received by a hundred or two hundred people: but just one Body. Likewise, when somebody says a word in the hearing of a thousand people, each one hears it but there will not be a thousand words: just one. And if you looked into a hundred mirrors at once you would see your reflection in each one; nevertheless you would not be a hundred men. If you broke one mirror into pieces, you would see your reflection in each piece. Likewise I say, if you were to see the sacrament divided into pieces you must believe that it is complete in each piece.[23]

Further, I want to give you an explanation for the whole faith, completely, and satisfy you entirely if I can. The Devil said he [Lucifer] wanted to be equal to God; this was such a terrible sin that he was thrown out of heaven for it. Jesus Christ said he was God, and the Jews killed him for it. But in return, he performed so many miracles it is clear they could not have been done except by God. So we know that he spoke the truth, and he said he was God.

---

[20] For this phrase (in Latin opposite), see e.g. Matt. 27:3. The copyist has abbreviated the verse from Galatians.

[21] Cf. *Lumere* (I:158–59), where the context of the passage is a discussion of the Passion and Redemption; the source is broadly Peter Lombard's *Sentences* (see III:106, note to vv. 4979–5286). Peter (c. 1100–1160) was known as "The Master of Sentences."

[22] At least one question from the son is missing here; see note opposite.

[23] It was common to explain this aspect of transubstantiation by the figure of a broken mirror: see, first, *Lumere* vv. 9704ff, and note at p. 143 in vol. III. Cf. also Aquinas, *Summa Theologiæ* (IIIa q. 76; in Blackfriars ed., vol. 58, pp. 102–3), where the image is used to explain the unity of the sacrament. At pp. 100–1 (ibid.), Augustine is cited on this subject, though without the mirror image.

Dunques est ceo veirs q'il est Deus et dunque devom nous crere en lui et crere tut ceo qu'il dist. Et il dist et enseigna ceste creaunce que te ai dite, dunques fet ele a crere sanz dotance.

Unquore dirra[i] jeo un autre reson. Le siecle se converti a Deu par simple gentz innocens. Et si il eust esté converti par sages gentz, l'em pout dire que il eussent la gent desceu par lour sens. Et si il fu converti par force de gentz, l'em pout dire que ceo eust esté par force. Pur [f.131r] ceo eslust Deu a ses disciples povre gentz et nice et foles des sens del siecle qui erent povere peccheurs en Galilee. Et quant il aloient par terre precher ceste lei, li riche home en aveient tiel eschar que tiel rascaille de poeple les osout areiner de lur creaunce q'il aveient changé. Et li sages hommes del siecle en aveient eschar que tiel rascaille osout parler encontre eus de tiele chose. A ceo q'il disoient tiel chose ert contre raison de nature, car c'est contre nature que femme seit puscele puis que ele ad enfaunt. Ceo reest contre nature que Deus seit mort com fust Jesu Crist, encontre nature que puis que home est mort q'il vive en terre.

Pur iteles choses en aveit l'em eschar et les batoit l'en et tormentoit et fesoit l'em tote la hounte et le mal qu'em poeit purpenser. L'en lor ardeit a fers chaus les membres genitals et au femmes botout les fers chaus es secrés[i] pardesus et les menout l'em toutz nuz et fesoit l'em tote la hounte e le mal qu'em pout et ils toutz jours disoient le bien. Et Deu fesoit grandz miracles pur eus veantz [f.131v] touz quant l'em les donout as urs et as lions a manger et as autres bestes et les bestes que erent devant ceo come esragés et que soleient la gent manger s'ageneloient devaunt eus et devenoient si deboneres come aigneus. L'em les mettoit en plum et en piz et en oille boillant et ceo freidisseit come glace. L'em lé mettout en feu et le feu ne lur fesoit ja mal.

Lors se purpe[n]soient sages home que devant ces en avoient eschar et disoient en queors ces homes deient verreiment tiele chose qui ne puet estre solum le curs et la raison de nature. Mes nous veom qu'il funt autresi ceus vertuz que sunt contre. Ces choses qu'il dient et qu'il funt, ne pount avenir fors par celi qui est sur nature et qui en fet quanque il voet. Cest Deu dunques funt il bien a crere, car autretiel sunt il come il dient. Issi se convertirent li sage home et deveneient crestien et ceo n'ert pas merveille.

[i] MS isecres.

Therefore it is true that he is God, so we must believe him and believe everything he says. He spoke and taught the faith that I have told you, so it must be believed without any doubt.

Here is another reason: the world was converted to God by simple and innocent people. Had it been converted by wise men, one could say they would have deceived people by their cleverness. Had it been converted by men's strength, one could say it would have been by force. This is why God chose poor and foolish men as his disciples: simple in worldly knowledge, poor fishermen from Galilee.[24] And when they went about the land preaching this Law, the rich men were scornful of it because such common folk dared to address them about their law, that they had changed. And the wise men of the world were scornful that such common folk dared speak against them about such things. On these subjects, they said certain things which were against nature, for it is against nature that a woman can be a virgin after she has had a baby. And it is against nature that God could be dead as Jesus Christ was, and against nature that once a man is dead he can be alive on earth.

They were despised for these things; they were beaten and tortured and put to all the pain and shame that could be imagined. They scorched their genital organs with hot iron, and the women had hot iron thrust into their private under-parts, and they paraded them naked and did them all the pain and shame they could — and they never ceased to preach goodness. And God wrought great miracles for them, in the sight of all, when they were given to bears and lions and other beasts to be eaten. These beasts, which were used to eating people and raged at them like mad things, kneeled down before them and became tame as lambs. They were plunged into lead and pitch and boiling oil, and it cooled down like ice. These men and women were thrown into fire, and the fire did them no harm.

Then the wise men who scorned them began to reflect, and say in their hearts that these men spoke truly about such things as could not be true according to the right course of nature. But we can see that they likewise had powers that were not according to nature: the things they said and did could not come to pass unless through him who is above nature and can do whatever he wishes. So they were able to convince them that this was God, for they are just as they said. Thus the wise men were converted and became Christians, and this is not to be wondered at.

---

[24] Augustine is fond of reminding us that God did not elect an orator or a senator, but a fisherman. See Auerbach 1965, p. 43; the chapter (*Sermo Humilis*, pp. 25–66) deals with rhetoric and preaching.

Si un home diseit qil feroit une [asne] voler, jeo le tendrei pur fol. Mes si il fesoit le asne parler oiant moi, pur quei nel crerei q'il l'asne ferroit [f.132r] voler quant jeo verrai qu'il avereit fet ausi forte chose ou plus ? Ore en i aveit de ceus qui erent plus dure et disoient que ceo fesoient il par enchauntement, mes quant il les aveint occis, lors virent il plus des miracles que devant, si se purpensoient puis que cil [qui] est mort, ne feit il mie enchauntement et les os des autres martirs qui pieça sunt mortz ne savent rien d'enchauntement et si vei jeo q'il funt grand miracles. Issi se convertirent ceus que avant nel voleient crere.

Jeo ne te voil pas chose dire que seit trop fort a entendre, car ausi com l'em norist l'enfant de let et com plus crest en age, solum ceo enforce l'em[i] ses viandes si com dist seint Poul : *Tanquam parvulis*[ii] *in Cristo lac potum dedi vobis non escam* [I Cor. 3:1–2], car qui dorreit a l'enfaunt a mangier croustes et chars de boef et vin a beivre, il le tuereit. Autresi doit l'em enseigner des choses que a Deu apartienent [a] home solum ceo qu'il ad reson et entendement, car l'em li porreit tiel chose dire, s'il ne l'entendist, que plus tost le freit mescrere et issi le occireit l'om en alme.

Le fiz [f.132v] Deu qui est dreiturel sur tote rien, coment doune il si largement ses biens terriens a les mauveis come a les bons ?

Le pere Deu doune bien a home en tere tiel hour pur attrere lui a s'amour et a soen service si come il fist jadis au poeple de Israel a qui il dona la terre de promission pur ceo q'il tenissent bien sa lei. Issi le dit David : *Dedit illis regiones gentium et labores populorum possiderunt ut custodiant justificationes eius et leges eius requirant* [Ps. 104:44–45]. Lors se deit home purpenser 'pur ceo m'ad Deu doné de soen bien en ceste siecle que jeo face bien soen service', car pur ceo sunt les serganz le rey a bel harneys qu'il soient prest a servir le rey en toutz pointz. Et cil que tiel richesce ad ne la deit pas tenir pur soen, einz deit dire 'Deu m'ad feet despenser de sa chose et jeo la dei despendre en soen servise et doner a sa povere gent que sount de sa meiné.' Issi fist David le roy : il ne acountoust pas la richesse pur soen, tut fust il riche et puissant, mes diseit q'il esteit povre et mendif : *Quoniam mendicus et pauper sum ego* [Ps. 39:18]. [f.133r] Deu redoune a home bien en terre pur sei aquiter vers lui del tuit.

---

[i] MS enforcent. [ii] MS *parvulus*.

If a man said he could make a donkey fly, I should think him mad. But if he made the donkey speak in my hearing, why should I not believe he could make it fly when I had seen him do something as difficult or even more so? Now, there were some who were harsher, and said they did these things by sorcery, but after they had killed them they saw even more miracles than before; then they realised that if a man is dead he can do no sorcery. The bones of other martyrs who died long ago know nothing of sorcery, yet I can see that they perform great miracles. Thus those, who did not wish to believe before, were converted.

I don't want to tell you anything that is too hard to understand; as one feeds a child on milk, and as it grows up one feeds it stronger meat accordingly — as Saint Paul says: … *even as unto babes in Christ. I have fed you with milk, and not with meat.* Anybody who gave a child bread-crusts and beef to eat, and wine to drink, would kill it. Likewise, you must teach a person things concerning God according to his reason and understanding; if you told him such things that he does not understand, you would make him disbelieve and thus you would kill his soul.

Son God who is righteous in all things, how is it that he gives his earthly goods as generously to the wicked as to the good?

Father God indeed gives such fortune to man on earth, to draw him to his love and his service, as he once did to the people of Israel, to whom he gave the Promised Land so that they would keep his laws well. This is what David says: *And gave them the lands of the heathen: and they inherited the labour of the people; That they might observe his statutes, and keep his laws.*[25] So one must reflect "this is why God has given me of his goods in this world, so that I may perform his service well." This is why the king's servants are finely equipped, so that they may be ready to serve the king in every way. Whoever has riches must not look on them as his own, but say "God has given me his goods to spend, and I must spend them in his service, and give to his poor people who are among his followers." Thus spoke King David: he counted not his riches as his own, although he was rich and powerful, but said he was poor and beggarly: *For I am poor and needy* ….[26] God gives goods to man on earth to requite himself to everything.

[25] Ps. 105:44–45 in *AV.*

[26] Ps. 40:17 in *AV.*

Car il i ad[i] assetz de ceus que unt fet bien et mal, mes il ount fet tant de mal et poi de bien q'il ne deivent pas aver la joie du ciel, ci lour rend Deu en ceo siecle lur louer tant de bien come il unt fet ou deservi et s'aquite devers eus q'il lur deit rien aprés la mort, einz vont en enferns.

De ceo troeve l'em en escrit que un[ii] heremite ert que aveit un sergant. Cil sergant ala un jour a une vile et vist que l'em portout en bere a mult grand honur et sollempneté un home que aveit esté tenuz mauveis, riches, avers et orgoillous. Quant il revint a l'heremite, il trova que bestes l'aveint mangé. Il se abaï de ceste aveinture trop fierement et pensa 'cil riches home que ad fet tut le mal en sa vie ad eu tuit le bien et tut le honur et en sa vie et en sa mort, et cist que ad fet taunt de bien et travaillé soen corps en vines et autres labours si est mort en tel manere, il est fols qui ne prent les delices de ceste siecle si comme il veignent, car Deu ne sei entremet de nos fetz ne ne guerdone nul [f.133v] home soen travail. Jeo returnerai al siecle et viverai desornemés a mon talent.' Il returna, et si come il alout une voiz lui dist qu'il ne sei desconfortast mie, 'car il n'est nulle home si mauvais que ne face aschun bien ne nule si bon qu'il ne face aschun mal. Li riches home aveit honur et ayse pur tant de bien come il aveit fet et ceste dereine honur ert la parpaie. Ore avera il mes toutz jours dolur et peine encontre li heremites. Par ceste dereigne anguisse fu il tut espurgé de tant de mal come il out fet en tote sa vie. Ore serra mes toutz jours en joie.' Quant cil oï ceo, si s'esjoï[iii] et returna a l'he[r]mitage et fust puis seint home.

Un autre est que Deu dist en le Evangile de un riche home que richement se vesteit et pesseit. Un povre malade qui aveit a noun Lazre ert devant sa porte et volunters mangast des mices que chaierent de la table au riche home. Il ert nul que lui donat. Li riches home morust et deables l'enporterent en le feu de enfern ; li povre morust et li angles le porterent el [f.134r] sein Abraham. Li riches home le vist et pria a seint Abraham que cele lazre moillast soen dei en l'eawe et le degustast sur sa langue que il ardeit tut en la flame de enfern. Mes ceo ne lui voleit Abraham graunter, einz respoundi : 'Membre tei que tu aveis bien en ta vie et le lazre out mal. Ore est luier changé, car tu as mal et il le bien.'

Pur ceo, beau fiz, te doit il souvenir tote le temps que tu te sentiras a ayse aver grant pour que Deu se quite ver tei et que tu eies al jour de jugement ceo respounse ou le vaillant.

---

[i] MS il l i ad. [ii] MS une. [iii] MS sei joï.

For there are many people who have done good and evil, but they have done so much evil and so little good that they are not entitled to heavenly joy. So God gives them their reward on earth for as much good as they have done or deserved, so that he owes them nothing after death: they go to hell.

We find a story about this in a book, that there was a hermit who had a servant. This servant went into town one day and saw carried on a bier, with great honour and solemnity, a man who had been regarded as wicked, rich, avaricious, and arrogant. When he came home to the hermit, he found that wild beasts had eaten him. He was utterly horrified at this turn of events, and thought "that rich man who did so much evil in his life had all goods and honour in his life and in his death; and this one, who did so much good and wore out his body in the vineyard and at other labours, has died in this way. A fool is he who does not take the delights of the world as they come, for God does not concern himself with our deeds nor reward any man for his works. I shall return to the world and from now on live as I please." He turned away, and as he went a voice spoke, telling him not to be troubled, "for there is no man so wicked that he does no good at all, nor any man so good that he does no evil. The rich man had honour and luxury for as much good as he had done, and the last honour was the final payment. From now on he will have pain and torment for ever, unlike the hermit. By this final torment he was completely purged of all the evil he had done in all his life. Now he will be in joy for ever." When the man heard this, he rejoiced and went back to the hermitage and became a holy man.[27]

Another story is the one God tells in the Gospel,[28] about a rich man who dressed and ate luxuriously. There was a poor sick man named Lazarus before his gate, who would eagerly have eaten up the crumbs that fell from the rich man's table. Nobody gave him anything. The rich man died, and the devils took him away to the fires of hell. And the poor man died, and angels carried him to the bosom of Abraham. The rich man saw him, and prayed to Saint Abraham to let Lazarus dip his finger in water so he, who was all burning in the fires of hell, could taste it on his tongue. But Abraham did not wish to grant this, replying "Remember that you had good fortune, and Lazarus bad, on earth. Now your fortunes are reversed: you have the bad and he the good."

Therefore, dear son, you must remember all the time when you are feeling comfortable, to be afraid lest God requite you, and at the Day of Judgement you hear that answer, or something like it.

---

[27] For analogues to this story, see Tubach 1969, 223, p. 24.

[28] Luke 16:19–21.

Le fiz Ore voudrai jeo savoir pur quei mal eschet si communement ausi bien a les bons com a les maveis.

Le pere Deu doune tribulation a gent pur .v. choses. L'une est pur ceo que Deu seit glorifié quant il les en delivre si come de seint Lazre qui morust et que Deu resuscita et lores fust Deu glorifié de cele miracle et Jesu Crist aveit dist einz qu'il morust que sa maladie ert pur la glorie Deu. Li apostles virent un autre foiz un home que unques n'aveit veu [f.134v] goute et demaunderunt a Jesu Crist quiel pecché il aveit feet ne soen pere ne sa mere pur quei il ert nee sanz veue. Et Jesu lur respondi que ceo n'ert pas pur pecché que il ne eus eussent feet, mes pur ceo que la vertu Deu appariust en lui, et lores si le garri.

La secunde chose est pur estre esprové, si com avient que l'em fiert d'une martel sur une piere que ad a noun diamant que l'em ad mise sur l'enclume et si il puet tenir sanz depesser, lors sciet l'em bien que c'est verrei diamant. Issi fut Job esprové, car il out moud des tribulations, mes il fut si fort en Deu et si pacient, qu'il fu bien prové que il ert verrai Deu amant. Il n'out mie iceles dolurs pur pecché que il eust feet, si come il dist *Non peccavi et in amaritudinibus moratur oculus meus* [Job 17:2], c'est a dire 'Jeo n'ai pas feet le pecché pur quei jeo su en amaritume.' Et de ceo lui porte bien temoigne Deu qui dist au Diable *Considerasti servum meum Job quod non sit ei similis in terra,* [*vir*] *simplex* [*et*] *rectus timens Dominum* [...] *Tu autem commovisti me adversus eum, ut affligerem eum frustra* [Job 2:3], c'est a dire 'As tu veu Job mon [f.135r] sergant qui est si bon qu'il n'ad soen piere en terre et tu m'as esmu a fere lui mal sanz forfet.'

La tierce chose est non pas pur pecché que l'em ad feet mes que l'em ne face. Ausi come l'en lie un desveé non pas pur le mal qu'il ad unquore fet mes qu'il ne face. Des teus par aveinture ad il assez dount Deus n'ad cure q'il soient riches, qu'il ne soient luxurious et orgoillous. Et itiel fust seint Poul qu'il suffri un torment qu'il ne se orgoillist des grand biens que Deu lui aveit fet. Issi le dit il meismes : *Ne magnitudo revelacionum extollat me, datus est michi* [...] *angelus Sathane, ut me colaphizet* [II Cor. 12:7].

Son Now I should like to know why bad things happen so commonly, as well to the good as to the wicked.

Father God sends trouble to people for five reasons. One is so that God may be glorified when he delivers them from it, as with Saint Lazarus who died and God revived him. Then God was glorified for this miracle; and Jesus Christ had said before he died that his sickness was for the glory of God.[29] Another time, the apostles saw a man who had never been able to see a thing, and asked Jesus Christ what sin he had done, or his father and mother had done, that he had been born sightless. And Jesus answered that it was for no sin that he or they had done, but so that the power of God should be manifest in him, and then he cured him.[30]

The second reason is for being tested, as when one strikes the stone called diamond with a hammer, having placed it on the anvil. If it can endure without smashing, then one can be sure it is a real diamond. Thus Job was tested, for he had many tribulations, but he was so patient and so strong in the Lord that he was proved to be a true lover of God.[31] He did not endure these sufferings for any sin he had done, for as he said: *Are there not mockers with me? and doth not mine eye continue in their provocation?*[32] This means: "I have not committed the sin for which I am in bitterness." Of this, God himself bears witness when he says to the Devil: *Hast thou considered my servant Job, that there is none like him in the earth, a perfect and an upright man, one that feareth God ... thou movedst me against him, to destroy him without cause.* This means: "Have you seen my servant Job, who is so good that he has no equal on earth, and you have made me hurt him, without any crime."

The third reason is not for sin that one has done, but so that one shall not do it: just as we tie up a madman, not for the damage he has already done but to stop him doing any. There are many such, and God does not care that they are rich so long as they do not revel in luxury or pride. It was thus with Saint Paul, who suffered torment to prevent him being proud about the great benefits God had given him. He said himself: *And lest I should be exalted above measure through the abundance of the revelations, there was given to me a thorn in the flesh, the messenger of Satan to buffet me.*

---

29 John 11:1–44.

30 John 9:1–7.

31 Here is an untranslatable play on words: Di - amant, Deu - amant. For the importance of puns in medieval thought, see e.g. Batt 2007.

32 This verse, in *AV*, does not match *LV* (cf. the Douai version: "I have not sinned, and my eye abideth in bitterness"); Job complains at being punished for a sin he did not commit.

La quarte chose est quant Deu doune home mal pur chastiement et pur penance des mals qu'il ad fet ausi come le pere qui chaustie soen enfaunt si come est escrite en le Evangile : *Ego quos amo, arguo et castigo* [Apoc. 3:19], c'est a dire 'Ceus que jeo aime, repren jeo et chastie', et ausi come l'em met le fer en le feu et puis si l'em bate pur houstier le roille come l'em bate le grein pur sevrer en la paille si qu'il seit bien net a metre en le garner soen seignur. C'est une des [f.135v] grenior bountés que Deu fet a home quant il en ceste siecle lui encharge sa penance, car le feu de purgatoire est si anguissuse que nul ne le savereit esmer et cele d'enfer passe tuit et est sanz fin. Mes ceo ne sevent pas cil que groucent le flael Dampnedeu. S'il seussent esmer la centisme partie de ces dolurs, il les soffrisent od bele chere et od pacience tutes les mals que lur puissent avenir et que l'em lor poetz fere. Ne ja ne haissent ceus que mal lor font, einz les amassent. Autresi com l'em aime le sergeant al mire qui aporte le poison amere qi lui maladies deit beivre pur sancté et cil fet de soen prou soen grand damage qui grouce del flael Deu. Car Deu aime celi q'il chastie et mult deit aver grand pour cil que est en pecché et n'a nul mesestance, car c'est signe que Deu l'ad guerpi. Ausi come le mire lerra garir li malade quant il est certain de sa mort.

La quinte manere pur quei home ad mal fet trop a doter. Ceo sunt cil qui en ceste siecle unt fet tant de mal qu'il deivent aver mal qu'il ont ci [qui] est autresi come erres de lur [f.136r] marchaundie dount la parpaie serra en enfern. Issi avint il de Antiocho epiphane que tant tormenta le poeple de Israel. Et autresi de Herodes que occist les innocens et qu'il fust trop cruel. Il morirent ambedeus [de] dolerouses maladies et en teuz plenté de dolur devant la mort. De teus ad il en ceste siecle que suffrent[i] grantz dolurs et grandz miseises et sunt toutz jours en lour pecchez et nel voillent lesser, car nule penitence ne vaut a celi qui soen pecché ne let nent plus que ne fet la medicine a la plaie tant come le fer ou le venim i seit.

[i] MS saeffrent.

The fourth thing is when God sends ill fortune to man as a chastisement, a penance for the wickedness he has done, like the father who chastises his child; as it is written in the Gospel: *As many as I love, I rebuke and chasten.* This means: "I reprimand and chastise those I love."[33] So we put the iron in the fire and then beat it to get the rust off, as we beat the grain to separate it from the straw, so that it shall be clean enough to put into the lord's granary. It is one of God's greatest bounties to man, that he gives us penance in this world, for the fire of Purgatory is so agonizing that none can imagine it, and that of Hell surpasses it and is everlasting. But those who complain about the scourge of God do not realise this. If they could imagine a hundredth part of those pains, they would endure patiently and cheerfully all the ill fortune that could come to them and that anybody could do to them. Nor would they ever hate those who do them evil, but they would love them. Likewise, as we love the doctor's assistant, who brings the bitter potion that the sick must drink to be cured. He who complains about the scourge of God is turning a benefit into a very great disadvantage. For God loves whom he chastises, and whoever is in a state of sin ought to be very fearful if no affliction comes to him, for that is a sign that God has abandoned him; just as the doctor leaves off treating the sick man when he is certain of his death.

The fifth reason why mankind has misfortune is very much to be feared. These are the people who have done so much evil that they deserve the ill fortune they have here, and it is like an advance payment for their dealings, which guarantees a full retribution in hell. This happened to King Antioch who so tormented the people of Israel.[34] And likewise to Herod, who killed the innocent children with such cruelty.[35] They both died of painful illnesses, and were in great agony before their death. There are those who suffer great pain and misery in this world, and remain in their sin, not wishing to abandon it; for no penitence can help one who will not abandon his sin, any more than medicine can help the wound while the iron,[36] or the poison, is still in it.

---

[33] "Gospel" has its medieval meaning of the whole New Testament.

[34] This is Antiochus IV (c. 215–163 BCE), surnamed *Epiphanes* (a royal title); see I Maccabees, chapters 1–6 (in the *AV* Apocrypha).

[35] Herod I killed the Holy Innocents (Matt. 2:16). His son (Herod II) killed John the Baptist, and tried Jesus (Luke 23:6–15). This reference is actually to his grandson Herod III (who killed James the Greater; Acts 12:2), who died *eaten of worms* (Acts 12:21–23).

[36] This refers to a wound where the weapon that made it has broken, leaving a piece of metal in the body. See *BVV*, p. 241; it is explained that prayer is useless from a wicked heart, just as salve is useless if the iron is still in the flesh.

Le fiz Jeo ai entendu que Deu ne fist unques chose que bon ne fust. Et ceo temoine l'Escripture que dist *Vidit Deus cuncta que fecerat et erant valde bona* [Gen. 1:31], c'est a dire 'Deus esgarda quanque il out fet et vit que tut ert mult bon.' Ki fist dunques puces et muches et crepaus et colures et totes autres mals vermins ? Jeo oï dire meinte foiz que le Deable les fist.

Le piere Beau fiz, Deu tei tiegne en bone creance. Ces sunt fables des vieus que tu me dis. Il fet grand pecché que de tiele chose [f.136v] les escoute et greignor que les escreit. Ore enten tei si il est nule creature que Deu ne criast. E si il est creature que Deu ne creast, dunques ad il un autre creatur ; si il est plus de un creatur,[i] dunques est il plus de un Deus. Qui ceo creit il est pys de un Gieu et pys que un paen. Car lé paen, quei que il creussent jadis, il creient ore qu'il n'est qu'un Deu qui fist ciel et terre et quanque leinz est, espirituele chose et corporele. Mes entendetz, unquore est le Diable de qui l'em seit[ii] ben que Deus le fist et si est il mout mauveis et enginor de maveistés. Mes il ert bon et beaus quant Deu le fist, mes il s'empeira pur soen pecché et par soen orgoil. Ausi erent iceles bestes bones quant Deu les fist, mes il sunt empirés par le pecché Adam. Eles furent fetes totes pur soen prou, mes il deservi pur soen pecché que eles lui fuissent mal. Autresi avient il que tieles honorent mie home tant come il est bien du rei que puis lui font mal et honte quant il est mellé au rei si lui reis lour commaunde. L'Escripture dist que Deu dist a Adam quant il [f.137r] out pecché : *Maledicta terra in opere tuo et pro peccato tuo spinas et tribulos germinabit tibi* [Gen. 3:17–18], c'est a dire 'Maudite soit la terre, pur ton pecché ele te portera espines et chardons.' Autresi puet l'em savoir que les autres choses empirerent pur le pecché Adam come la terre. Deu avoit issi establi que totes choses de la terre obeissent a Adam et Adam obeist[iii] a lui. Et quant Adam ne fust obeissant a Deu, il deservi que rien ne fust obeissant a lui. Mes qui est misericors l'en lessa une partie et l'autre lui tolli, si que totes les membres de l'home ne sunt pas obeissant a lui, einz i a tiel membre qui ne lui obeist mie tiel houre est, c'est itiel member dount la gendrure est feet. A signifiance que tut cil que sunt engendré sunt corrumpu par icele pecché et pur ceo voleit Deu que la circumcision fust fete en tiel membre plus qu'en un autre. En teu manere les creatures que furent fetes obeissantz devindrent contrarians et que furent fetes bones devindrent mauveis par le pecché Adam.

[i] MS creature. [ii] MS iset. [iii] MS obeiat.

Son I have heard that God never did anything that was not good. Scripture proves this where it says: *And God saw every thing that he had made, and, behold, it was very good.* That is: "God looked at all he had done, and he saw that everything was very good." So who made fleas and flies, toads and snakes, and all the other horrible vermin? I have often heard that the Devil made them.

Father Dear son, God keep you in good faith. These are old folks' tales you are telling me. Whoever listens to such things commits a grave sin, and worse who believes them. Now listen, there is no creature that God did not create. If there is a creature that God did not create, then it must have a different creator. So if there is more than one Creator, therefore there is more than one God. Whoever believes this is worse than a Jew and worse then a pagan. For the pagans, whatever they believed before, now believe that there is but one God who made heaven and earth and everything that is spiritual and corporeal therein. And now listen, there is also the Devil, of whom it is well known that God made him; he is very evil, and he is the instigator of wickedness. But he [Lucifer] was good and beautiful when God made him, and he ruined himself by his sin and his pride.[37] So were these animals good when God made them, but they were ruined by Adam's sin. They were all made for his benefit, but for his sin he deserved that they should harm him. Likewise it happens that they do not honour a man when he is in the King's favour, and later they hurt him, because he has fallen out with the King and the King orders them to. Scripture says that God told Adam after he had sinned: *Cursed is the ground for thy sake … Thorns also and thistles shall it bring forth to thee.* That is "Let the earth be cursed for your sin; it will bear briers and thistles for you." Likewise it is we can see that other things were spoiled because of Adam's sin, as the earth was. God had arranged for all things on earth to obey Adam, and Adam to obey him; and when Adam disobeyed God he deserved that nothing should obey him. But being merciful God left one thing while taking away another, so if a man's members are not obedient to him, there is yet one member that is obedient only at certain times, that is the member of generation. This means that all Adam's descendants are corrupted by that sin, and this is why God wishes circumcision to be carried out on this member and not on another. In the same way, beasts that were created to be obedient rose up in opposition; those that were made good became bad by the sin of Adam.

[37] See Is. 14:12ff.

Issi tolli Deu a home par son pecché [f.137v] la seignorie que il li out doné et a ceus que serront dampnez en enfern la toudra il issi del tut q'il ne troverent nule creature que ne lor face mal ne feu ne eawe ne autre chose si come dist l'Escripture : *Pugnabit pro Deo universus orbis terrarum contra insensatos* [Sap. 5:21], c'est a dire que toutes creatures se combaterunt por Deu contre les mal senés.

Le fiz En quel manere lerrai jeo mon pecché, ou pur l'amour de Deu ou pur doute de Deu ou pur pour d'enfern ?

Le pere Cil qui lest soen pecché pur l'amur de Deu il prent le plus haute point et le meillor q'il poeit aver de lesser soen pecché, car le seint dist que amur est coverture des toutz vertus et paremplement des toutz bien fetz et par bien amer pus tu rendre a Deu quanque vous lui devetz et a toun proeme ensement, et ceus sunt les deus commaundementz dont tote la lei depend. De autre part, la chose que est bien amé chescun home ad pour de perdre. Et pur ceo si tu ne lesses toun pecchié pur doute de Deu, c'est a dire pur pour de perdre Deu ausi avant com pur pour [f.138r] d'enfern, tu n'es pas digne de aver la joie du ciel ové Deu, car doute d'enfern delivre home de peine et amur et doute de Deu attrait a home grant merite en ciel et joie sanz fin.

Le fiz Coment fust ceste creance avant dite ordiné et par qui establie quant ele ne fu mie tenuz en le temps que Jesu Crist ala sur terre ?

Le pere Quant Jesu Crist ala sur terre, il precha ceste creance, mes la gentz ne furent mie si sage ne ne aveient tant de grace que il le puissent pleinement entendre. Et pur ceo quant Jesu Crist s'em parti hors de ceste siecle et mounta en ciel veiant ses disciples, il les commaunda [de] demurer ensemble tanq'il lur enveiast li seint Espirit et quant il les out vestu del seint Espirit ceus que furent avant si rud[e] et si nice q'il ne savoient nule manere de lettrure devindrent si sages qu'il saveient respoundre a totes les choses que home lur voleit demaunder et parler tote manere [de] languages q'il ne aveient umkes apris et lors les duze apostles par la grace et la vertu del seint Espirit feseient duze chapitres en les queus tute nostre dreite creance pleinement est [f.138v] contenuz.

So for his sin God took away from man the mastery he had given him, and from those who shall be damned in hell he shall likewise take it utterly away, so they shall find no creature that will not harm them, not fire nor water nor any other thing, as Scripture says: *And the world shall fight with him against the unwise.*[38] This means that all creatures shall fight for God against those mad people.

Son How shall I abandon my sins: for love of God, for fear of God, or for fear of hell?

Father He who abandons sin for the love of God takes the highest way and the best he can have, to leave off his sin. For the Saint says that love surpasses all the virtues, and especially all good deeds,[39] and by loving well you may render to God everything you owe him, and to your neighbour as well, and these are the two commandments on which all the Law depends. On the other hand, everybody fears to lose what they love very much. Therefore if you do not leave your sin for fear of God: that is, for fear of losing God as much as for fear of hell, you are not worthy to have the joy of heaven with God. Fear of hell frees a man from punishment, and love and fear of God bring a man merit in heaven and joy without end.

Son How was this faith you spoke of ordained, and by whom established, if it was not held in the days when Jesus Christ walked on the earth?

Father When Jesus Christ was on earth he preached this faith, but the people were not wise enough, nor did they have enough grace to understand fully. So when Jesus Christ left this world and went up to heaven in the sight of his disciples, he commanded them to stay together until he should send them the Holy Spirit. When he had clothed them with the Holy Spirit, then they, so rough and simple before as to be completely illiterate, became so wise they were able to answer everything anybody wished to ask them, and they could speak all manner of languages they had never learned before.[40] Then the twelve apostles, by the grace and power of the Holy Spirit, made twelve Articles, in which are contained the whole of our Creed.

---

[38] Wisdom (in the Apocrypha) 5:20; the verse is numbered differently from the Latin version.

[39] Cf. I Cor. 13:1–8.

[40] The reference is to Pentecost; see Acts 2:1–4.

Et commensunt en tiel manere : *Credo in deum patrem omnipotentem creatorem celi et terre*, c'est a dire 'Jeo crei en Deu le Pere tuit-puissant, creyour de ciel et de terre.' Ceste chapitre fist seint Pere et partient especialment a Deu le Pere.

Le secunde chapitre : 'Jeo crei en Jesu Crist le Fiz Deu u meinet nostre Seignur.' Cest article fist seint Jon le Evangeliste et partient especialment au Deu le Fiz com a sa deité et en ceste article devom crere q'il est Deus en totes choses owel a soen piere sauf que la persone est autre que la persone soen piere.

La tierce article partient a sa humanité de quei il est dit que il est conceu del seint Espirit et nee de la virgine Marie, c'est a entendre que il fu conceu en la virgine Marie par la grace et la vertu del seint Espirit et nient par generation de home charnel et que il fust nee de lui sanz blemisement de soen pucelage et que ele fust seinte virgine en le enfantier et devant l'enfantier et après le enfantier et toutz jours issi remeindra. Ceste article fist seint Jake, frere seint Jon.

Le quarte chapitre partient a sa passion qe il suffri desoutz [f.139r] Pounce Pilate qui esteit paen et juge en Jerusalem en cel temps de par les Romeins et desoutz ceo juges par la requeste des Gieus fust Jesu Crist dampné a tort e mis en croiz et morust et puis seveli. Ceste chapitre fist seint Andreu.

Le quinte chapitre est q'il descendist en enfern après sa mort a deliverer et a hors prendre touz les almes que en la drete foi furent mort en esperance de sa venu pur eus deliverer et ne mie a deliverer les maveis que furent mortz en lur pecchez, car ceus sunt dampnez sanz nule fin. Ceste chapitre [fist] seint Phelippe et le mist en la creance.

Le syme chapitre partient a sa resurrection, ceo est a dire coment il resuscita le tierce jor de mort en vie et sei moustra a ses disciples et prova sa resurrection en multz des maneres par quaraunte jours. Ceste chapitre fist seint Thomas et le mist en la creance.

Le setime chapitre partient a sa ascencion coment a la carantime jour aprés sa resurrection quant il aveit mangié et beu apertement devant ses disciples, puis mounta en ciel [f.139v] devant euz toutz et seist a destre soen piere. Ceste chapitre fist seint Bartholomeu et le mist en la creance.

It begins like this: *I believe in God the Father Almighty, Maker of heaven and earth.* That is: "I believe in God, the all-powerful Father, who made heaven and earth." Saint Peter made this article, which pertains especially to God the Father.

The second article: "I believe in Jesus Christ, the Son of God in whom dwells Our Lord." This article was made by John the Evangelist, and pertains especially to God the Son, as to his Godhead, and we must believe in this article that he is God equally with his Father in all things, except that his Person is other than the Person of his Father.

The third article belongs to his human nature, concerning which it says he was conceived by the Holy Ghost and born of the Virgin Mary. This means he was conceived in the Virgin Mary by the power and grace of the Holy Ghost, and not by intercourse with mortal man, and that he was born from her without any staining of her virginity; that she was a holy virgin in childbirth, both before and after childbirth, and shall remain so for ever. This article was made by Saint James, brother of Saint John.

The fourth article pertains to his Passion, that he suffered under Pontius Pilate, who was a pagan judge for the Romans at that time in Jerusalem. Under this judge, at the Jews' request, Jesus Christ was wrongly condemned and put on the Cross; he died, and then was buried. This article was made by Saint Andrew.

The fifth article is that he descended into hell after his death, to release and bring out all the souls of those who died in the faith and hope of his Coming, to deliver them but not to deliver the wicked who died in their sins, for those are damned for ever. Saint Philip made this article, and placed it in the Creed.

The sixth article pertains to the Resurrection, that is, how he rose again to life on the third day after death, and showed himself to his disciples and proved his resurrection in many ways for forty days. Saint Thomas made this article and placed it in the Creed.

The seventh article pertains to his Ascension, how on the fortieth day after his resurrection, when he had eaten and drunk openly in the presence of his disciples and then ascended into heaven before them all, and sat at the right hand of his Father. Saint Bartholomew made this article and placed it in the Creed.

Le utime chapitre partient a[l] jour de jugement coment il vendra pur jugier les mortz et les vifs, les bons et les mals, et rendra a chescun solum ceo q'il ad deservi en ceste vie. Ceste article fist seint Mathié et le mist en la creance.

Le novime et les treis suiant partienent al seint Espirit en tiel manere : 'Jeo crei en le seint Espirit', ceo est a entendre que il est Deu owel ové le Fiz et ové le Pere, de qui il sunt touz estreit par vertu de grace, et que il [est] un meismes Deu et une meime chose owel au Pere et au Fiz sauve que sa persone est autre que la persone del Pere ou la persone del Fiz. Ceste chapitre fist seint Jake frere seint Symond et seint Jude si le mist en la creance.

Le dime article si est 'Jeo crei en seint Eglise et en la compaignie et a l'assemblé de touz seintz et de totes seintes', ceo est a entendre en la compaignie de tutz ceus que unt esté ou que serrunt mort en la [f.140r] dreite creance del commencement del munde deques al fin et en esperance de estre sauvé par la venue Jesu Crist. En ceste chapitre sunt entendutz les seet sacramentz de seint Eglise, c'est a saver baptesme, confirmacion, le sacrament del corps nostre Seignor en le auter, ordre du chapelain et de clerk, esposailles, seinte confession, et la dreiner est unction que est la dreiner sacrament. Cest chapitre fist seint Symond et le mist en la creaunce.

Le unsime chapitre est 'Jeo crei remission des pecchez que Deu doune as totes gentz que sunt de lur mesfés verraiement repentauntz par vertu des sacramentz que sunt ordinés en seint Eglise.' Ceste chapitre fist seint Jude et le mist en la creance.

Le duzime article est 'Jeo crei resurrection de char de home et vie pardurable sanz fin', c'est a entendre la joie de Paradis que Deu durra a ceus que le deservunt par dreite creance et bons oevres, et la peine sanz fin a ceus que serrunt dampnés. Ceste article serra entenduz que chescun home et chescune femme, seiunt il bons ou maveis, [f.140v] serrunt contre le jour de jugement resuscitez de mort en vie en meime le corps que il vesquirent einz en terre et receiverunt lur jugement en corps et en alme solum ceo que il unt en corps et en alme deservi en ceste vie. Et pur ceo serrunt [les] bons mis en joie en corps et en alme et les mauveis dampnés en corps et en alme.

The eighth article pertains to Judgement Day, and how he will come to judge the quick and the dead, the good and the bad, and will render to each accordingly as each has deserved in this life. Saint Matthew made this article and placed it in the Creed.

The ninth, and the three following it,[41] pertain to the Holy Spirit as follows: "I believe in the Holy Ghost," that is to say, he is God equally with the Son and with the Father, from whom they all issue by the power of grace, and that he is even one God and one Being equal with the Father and the Son — except that his Person is other than the Person of the Father and the Person of the Son. This article was made by Saint James,[42] brother of Saint Simon and Saint Jude, and he placed it in the Creed.

The tenth article is "I believe in the Holy Church and in the company and assembly of all saints, men and women"; that is to say, in the company of all those who have been, or will die, in true faith, from the beginning unto the end of the world, and in the hope of salvation in the Coming of Jesus Christ. In this article are understood the seven sacraments of Holy Church, that is: baptism, confirmation, the sacrament of the Body of Our Lord at the altar, the ordination of chaplains and clergy, matrimony, holy confession, and finally the unction which is the last sacrament. Saint Simon made this article, and placed it in the Creed.

The eleventh article is "I believe in the remission of sins which God grants to all people who are truly repentant of their misdeeds, by virtue of the sacraments ordained in Holy Church." Saint Jude made this article and placed it in the Creed.

The twelfth article is "I believe in the resurrection of the body, and the life everlasting." That means, the joy of Paradise that God shall give those who deserve it by true faith and good works, and everlasting torment to those who shall be damned. This article is to be understood, that every man and woman, be they good or bad, shall be raised up from death to life for the Day of Judgement, in the body they once inhabited here on earth, and shall receive their judgement, body and soul, according to what they have deserved, body and soul, in this life.

---

[41] It is not clear what is meant by "les treis suiant," because the next article (number 10) is not about the Holy Ghost — it may be because of the "Three Persons" explanation appended. Cf. *BVV*, p. 8, for a similar passage at the ninth article.

[42] Saint James the Less; see *ODS* pp. 251 (brother of the Lord), & 271 (Jude as one of the brethren of the Lord); and see below, p. 155, for Mary's family.

La creaunce de la fey. Ceo est verra[i]ement la creance par qei seinte Eglise creist et conuist Deu. Qui ceste cr[e]ance a, si ad bone creance et si il fait[i] bon oevre, par [quei] il seit iceles que Deu voille regarder vers son bon fait le bien que il avera fait serra receu devaunt Deu. Et si li serra estuez desques al jour grant bosoigne si il ne forfeit entre si et la.

Seignurs, ceste creance [que] seinte Eglise ad en Deu est fundement et commencement des touz biens, car, si com dist li apostle, sanz lui ne puet nul home a Deu plere. Ceste devoms tenir et amer et garder que vous ne maumettét les biens que en vous sunt, par nulle mescreance ne par sorceries ne par charmes ne par nule autres choses que sunt contrarie [f.141r] a creance de seinte Eglise, car certeinement cil que sunt crestien [et] creient en Deu et funt les sorceries, cil maumettunt et destruent del tut en tut la seinte crestienté et la seinte creance que en eus fu. Et pur ceo dist li apostle a tele manere [de] gent : *Dies inquid observans et tempora et annos ad facienda opera nostra. Timeo ne et frustra laboraverim in vobis* [Gal. 4:10–11]. Ore oyez, seignurs, mettez la seinte creaunce que est fundement des touz biens en vos queors et en tiele manere que vous la puissez garder fermement et seurement et establement et desus edifier les vertuz et les bons oevres *et crescere in habitaculum in spiritu sancto* [Ephes. 2:21–22].

Chanson des angles *Gloria in excelsis Deo. Et in terra pax hominibus bone voluntatis* [Luke 2:14]. Nous lisoms en le Evangile Deu que nostre Sire Deu nasqui de ma dame seinte Marie en Bethleem, si furent pasturs delez al jour d'ui, sicom aveient premis ancienement par les prophetes. Et come il fu neez en Bethleem, si furent pasturs delez la nuit de la cité que voleint garder lur uailles, si vint ignelepas un angele a eus. Et la clarté Deu [f.141v] resplendi sur eus, si urent pour grant et merveilluse. 'N'avez mie pour,' dist li angles, 'jeo vous aporte une message de une grant joye que est a tute le munde, quar nez est hui lui salveres del munde en la cite de Bethleem qui est Christus dominus. Et si le troveretz a teles enseignes que vous le troveretz envolupé de une drapeletz gisant en une mangere.' Quant li angele out ceo dit, si se justa a lui grant host des autres angles qui comencerunt a chaunter *Gloria in excelsis Deo*. 'Glorifié seit en ciel en haut et en terre pais a home de bone volunté.' Ici entendetz queus est le fruit de la parole et de tute chose de homme.

[i] MS faite.

The Creed of Faith. This, truly, is the Creed whereby Holy Church believes in, and knows, God. Whoever holds this Creed, he has good faith, and if he does good works, then by these may God be pleased to behold his good work; the good that he does may be accepted before God. And it shall be reserved to him until that Day of greatest need; unless he loses it between here and there!

My lords,[43] this faith that Holy Church holds in God is the foundation and beginning of all good things for, as the Apostle says, no man may please God who has it not. We must hold it fast and love it, and keep watch that you do not misuse the good that is in you by any unbelief, nor by sorcery or charms or any other things that are contrary to the Creed of Holy Church. For surely those Christians who, believing in God, practise sorcery, they abuse and utterly destroy the holy Christianity and the holy faith that was in them. And so the Apostle says to such people: *Ye observe days, and months, and times, and years. I am afraid of you, lest I have bestowed upon you labour in vain.*[44] Now listen, my lords, place in your hearts the holy Creed that is foundation of all virtues, in such a way that you are able to keep it firmly and securely and reliably, and build virtue and good works upon it, and grow ... *for an habitation of God through the Spirit.*

The Angels' Song *Glory to God in the highest, and on earth peace, good will toward men.* We read in the Gospel of God that our Lord God was born of my lady Saint Mary in Bethlehem. There were shepherds nearby that day, as had been promised of old by the prophets. And when he was born in Bethlehem, the shepherds were there, near the city at night, meaning to look after their sheep, and an angel suddenly appeared to them. And the glory of God shone upon them, and they were terribly afraid. "Do not be frightened," said the angel, "I bring to you a message of great joy which is for all the world, for today in the city of Bethlehem is born the Saviour of the world, who is Christ the Lord. You will find him by certain signs: you will find him wrapped in a little cloth and lying in a manger." When the angel had said this, a great host of other angels came close to him and began to sing "Glory be to him on high, and in earth peace to men of good will."[45] Here, understand what is the fruit of these words, and of all human things.

---

[43] "Seignurs" — the speaker now addresses a plural audience, and the father/son format has disappeared.

[44] The previous chapter, Galatians 3, may be the passage cited above, that none may please God who has not the faith (*fides*).

[45] Note that the Gospel phrase in English reads: *good will toward men* (Luke 2:14).

Ici poetz oir que cil unt pais a Deu et bien de lui qui unt bone volunté, et cil qui unt male volunté a autri si sunt severez de Deu, ja ne facent il plus mes la male volunté, kar si volunté seit male ou bone, si ert cunté pur oevre a celui que l'a. Ore poeiz oir que male volunté deseivre home de Deu et la bone lui ajuste. Dunque [qui] voudra avoir pais en Deu, si eit bone volunté de bien faire, si face bien ataunt [f.142r] com il puet, si conquera la joie pardurable. Et entre Deu et homme aveit esté longe descorde si grant que jusque al Fiz Deu que a cele jour que hui est nasqui de la Virgine Marie n'estoit home ne feme ne alme que entrast en la glorie. Et si tost com le Fiz Deu nasqui fust faite pais entre Deu et home. Li pastor com il oirent iceo, si parlerunt ensemble que il irrunt en Bethleem et alerent si troverent nostre Seignur cum li angeles lur avoit dit, si returnerent leez et joüs loaunt Dompnedeu de ceo que il avoient trové la chose si com li angle lur aveit dist. Bone gent, despisoms celes choses que Deu despit et amouns celes choses que il aime, creom le par bone volunté, par bone ovre, si averums pais en terre et sa glorie en ciel. *Quod nobis praestare dignetur qui vivit in secula seculorum.*

Here you may hear that they who have good will have peace towards God and good from him, and those who have ill-will to others are separated from God; let them no longer have ill-will, for desire, be it good or evil, shall be counted among the deeds of whoever has it. Now you may hear that evil desire separates man from God, and good desire brings him close. So whoever wishes for peace with God, let him have good will to do good; let him do good as best he can, so he shall earn everlasting joy. And between God and man there had long been strife so great that until the Son of God was this day born of the Virgin Mary there was no man or woman — no soul — who ever came into glory. And as soon as the Son of God was born, then peace was made between God and man. The shepherds, when they heard this, said to one another that they would go to Bethlehem, and they found Our Lord as the angel had said, and they returned happy and joyful, praising the Lord God because they had found just what the angel had told them. Good people, let us despise those things that God despises, and love those things that he loves; let us believe in him through good will and good works, and we shall have peace on earth and his glory in heaven. "Which may he who lives for ever and ever deign to grant us."

Chapter 2

Pater Noster[1]

Introduction

Adam of Exeter's Commentary on the Pater Noster appears in several manuscripts. This edition is based on Cambridge, Pembroke College, MS 112 (s.xiii^{ex}), ff.71r–92r; this manuscript may be from Reading. There are four other manuscripts. No source for the work has been identified; Adam's work is exceptional for its length and detail. It is uncertain whether he wrote anything else.[2] Little is known of him; he may in fact have been from Oxford: manuscript readings of his name vary, some call him "de Oxonia"; "de Exonia" for Oxford is not unknown "even in English manuscripts of the thirteenth century."[3]

The commentary is of interest for several reasons, not least because it was originally addressed to a female religious and her companions. This feature, however, results in a rather curious translated version: the Cambridge copy presented here has been partially corrected for a male addressee. It would be misleading to standardize the text — this is, after all, a version that somebody owned, used, and read. The footnotes show how often "chere mere" and similar phrases have been erased, and the text is presented as it is. Why would Adam be writing for a woman? It is known that many writers addressed their works to women, and it may be that this was to ensure a wide audience among those who could not read Latin, both men and women. Legge quotes Walter Map, who lamented the fact that his friend Gerald of Wales refused to write in French "for the unworthy reason that he would have enjoyed a wider public had he so condescended."[4] Adam and others, including Grosseteste, seem to have been taking advantage of the perceived illiteracy of women: looking beyond their first readers, they aimed to feed a growing demand for personal devotional material. The fact that this Pater Noster was then re-copied for male readers bears out such a view.[5]

---

1 D&B 846, prose, general heading "Pater Noster." Tony Hunt has pointed out that nos. 845 and 846 are the same work (see his review in *MÆ*, p. 343).

2 Both Legge and Emden maintain the attribution of the Commentary to this Adam (d.c. 1235): see Legge 1950 (pp. 82–84), and Legge 1963 (pp. 226–27); Emden 1957, 660B.

3 Thomson 1940, p. 89.

4 Legge 1950, p. 126.

5 See also *The Idea of the Vernacular*, ed. Wogan-Browne *et al.*, pp. 73–74 (notes to *Speculum Devotorum*) and p. 159 (notes to Capgrave's Prologue to his *Life of St Gilbert*).

There is no mention of insular French commentaries in Siegfried Heinimann's study of medieval translations of the Lord's Prayer into the Romance languages,[6] and no general study of expositions of the Prayer in the twelfth and thirteenth centuries.[7] Scholars wishing to investigate Adam of Exeter's work are thus at a severe disadvantage. Of the vast number of Latin commentaries on the Pater Noster — Bloomfield *et al.* list the incipits of over a thousand[8] — all but a handful remain unprinted.[9] The commentary by Richard of St Victor which forms Pt. II, Lib. XI, caps. v–xiii of the *Liber Exceptionum*[10] was perhaps one of the best known and was used by Maurice of Sully in the exposition which is prefixed to his collection of homilies,[11] but whether the French text of the homiletic works is really the responsibility of Maurice, as Robson believed, or that of a successor, has not so far been determined.[12] An extensive, but apparently uninfluential, commentary on the Pater Noster is found in Robert of Bridlington's *Colloquium*.[13] So far as vernacular treatments are concerned, most contain little or no expository material.[14] There is a modest expository element in the virtuoso Anglo-Norman versified Pater Noster in Oxford, Bodleian Library, MS Bodley 57 f.91r,[15] and an elementary exegesis in the *Mirour de Seinte Eglyse*,[16] but there is nothing in print so far which can be shown to represent a source of the Anglo-Norman commentary attributed to Adam of Exeter.

However, Adam's Pater Noster became the source for a later English text, much of which consists of a careful translation of the earlier work: *Þe Pater*

[6] Heinimann 1988. On the earliest Old French prose translations see Heinimann 1989.

[7] For the later period see Adam 1976; for the evidence of Christian art see Behm 1994.

[8] Bloomfield 1979, pp. 567–686 (nos. 801–9261).

[9] Some idea of the traditional elements can be gained from works by Tertullian (*PL* 1:1149C–96B), Ambrose (*PL* 16:450A–54B), Augustine (*PL* 38:377–86, 393–400, 400–2), Rabanus (*PL* 107:817; 112:188–89), Honorius (*PL* 172:819D–23A), Abelard (*PL* 178:489A–95D), Geoffrey Babion (*PL* 162:1305B–9C), Peter Comestor (*PL* 198:1564D–65B), Bernard of Clairvaux (*PL* 183:181C–83C), Geoffrey of Auxerre (*PL* 185:617C–20C), Anon. (*PL* 217:897C–906C), and Hugo Rothomagensis (*PL* 192:1330C–34B).

[10] See Richard's *Liber Exceptionum*, ed. Chatillon, pp. 447–57.

[11] See Robson 1952, pp. 83–87 (text) & 38–40. There is a prayer by Maurice (d. 1196) in Harley Prayers, below.

[12] See Zink 1976, pp. 34 & 173–80.

[13] See *Bridlington Dialogue*, pp. 79–94.

[14] See *Pater Noster* (in *Grundriss* pp. 23–25: twenty-four versions in verse and prose), and Långfors 1912.

[15] See Hunt 1995.

[16] See Wilshere's edition, pp. 46–54.

Noster of Richard Ermyte, a late Middle English exposition of the Lord's Prayer (ed. Aarts). It is similarly addressed to a woman: in this case, "his dere sistir in God."[17]

Adam of Exeter is normally identified with the Adam Rufus to whom Robert Grosseteste addressed the letter "Rogavit me dulciflua dileccio tua . . . ," a letter which actually comprises two treatises: the early *De forma prima omnium*, and the *De intelligenciis*.[18] In Eccleston's *De adventu fratrum minorum in Angliam* Adam appears as Ada de Exonia (var. Oxonia).[19] Grosseteste, in one of his letters (*Ep.* 18), consoles the friars for the departure of Adam de Oxonia on a journey to preach to the Saracens before his entry to the order on 25th January, 1229. He was *socius* of Master Adam Marsh, whom he persuaded to join the order.[20] He himself joined the order with the express purpose of travelling to the East; he was dispatched by Pope Gregory IX, although he died before reaching his destination. He was apparently dead by 1235, and may have died at Barletta in Apuleia on his outward journey.

* * * * * * * * * * *

The commentary on the Pater Noster is found in five manuscripts,[21] with two quite distinct families, CP and DL:

C = Cambridge, Pembroke College, MS 112 (s.xiii^{ex}), ff.71r–92r. The manuscript measures 193 x 143 mm, the writing block 130 x 82 mm, and includes a text of Part 1 of Nequam's *Corrogationes Promethei* (ff.53r–70r), the *Assumption Nostre Dame ki fu revelee a une nonein* (ff.93r–95v) which is an Anglo-Norman verse translation of chapters 31 and 32 of Bk. 2 of the Visions of Elizabeth of Schönau (referred to

[17] We are grateful to Nicholas Watson, who recognized (and subsequently confirmed) the relationship between the texts, on the occasion of a talk by Jane Bliss and Henrietta Leyser: "'Dear Mother': A Pater Noster of the Thirteenth Century," at "The French of England: Linguistic Accommodation and Cultural Hybridity, c. 1100–c. 1500" (University of York, July 2008). We also thank Margaret Healy-Varley for showing us a draft of her work (forthcoming), which details how far the Middle English author has translated directly from the Anglo-Norman.

[18] See Thomson 1940, pp. 98–99 & 104–5.

[19] See Little's edition, p. 16.

[20] See Douie 1940, pp. 81–97 (esp. p. 85), and Cantini 1948. The library of the Franciscan convent at Reading records "Adam de Marisco de decem preceptis," see *The Friars' Libraries*, ed. Humphreys, p. 233 (F 10 28). Adam Marsh, who may have come from Somerset, is reputed to have written a number of biblical commentaries, but none survives. On books and Oxford Greyfriars, see Rouse and Mynors 1991 (*Registrum*, pp. cxxvii–cxlviii).

[21] See D&B 846 (and 845).

as "Ysabel"),[22] and a number of religious treatises in various hands of the twelfth and thirteenth centuries.[23] The manuscript may be from Reading.

D = Dublin, Trinity College, MS 374 (D.1.29) (s.xiii²), ff.43va–54va (the manuscript is largely unfoliated). The exposition appears as part of a larger compilation, as in L (see below). D and L are extremely close. They omit the Latin of each prayer, also certain references to "beau frere" etc., and they lack the opening and final paragraphs. But there are no different readings, only slight differences due to the copyists. The description of the manuscript by Mario Esposito does not adequately identify the contents.[24] Ff.1ra–30vb contain an Insular version of portions of Herman de Valenciennes' *Histoire de la Bible* which is not recorded in Ina Spiele's edition.[25] The poem which follows on ff.30vb–35ra ("Queor ke tut volt si ke rens ne faille") has been edited by F. J. Tanquerey, "Exhortation à l'amour divin: poème du XIIIe siècle," pp. 321–54. The series of meditations on ff.35ra–43va has not been studied, though the incipits of certain prayers contained in ff.35ra–37vb are recorded by K. V. Sinclair.[26] Sinclair did not recognize Adam of Exeter's "Exposition," which is embodied in a confessional manual (see below, p. 294). Ff.54va–58va contain a treatise on the three things (compunction, confession, and satisfaction) necessary for penance, whilst ff.58va–67ra transmit a narrative account of the Passion in octosyllabic couplets, the opening of which is also found in MS Lambeth 182 (see below). It is followed on ff.67ra–69va by a meditation on the Cross, also in octosyllabic couplets, and on ff.69va–73vb by a treatise on the virtues of preserving chastity, renouncing property, and maintaining silence.[27] On ff.74ra–76vb are a set of lamentations of the Virgin, apparently based on a Latin original sometimes attributed to Augustine or Bernard.[28]

L = London, Lambeth Palace Library, MS 182 (s.xiii²), ff.189rb–201vb.[29] The fourth section of this manuscript consists of a num-

[22] See *Poem on the Assumption*, ed. Strachey, pp. 13–26; Dean 1944, and Dean 1937.

[23] See James 1905, pp. 108–9.

[24] Esposito 1914, pp. 191–92.

[25] Herman, *Li Romanz de Dieu.*

[26] Sinclair 1979, and Sinclair 1982.

[27] Our Chapter 14, below.

[28] Our Chapter 6, below.

[29] See James 1930, pp. 285–86, who does not identify the work of Adam.

ber of devotional works in French including: ff.201vb–202rb, a short treatise on penance ("A fere penance sunt treis choses bosoignables . . ."), also contained in Dublin, Trinity College, MS 374 (D.1.29), ff.54va–58va; ff.202rb–202va, the decalogue ("Les dis comandemenz de la lei que Deu dona a Moyses"); ff.202va–203va, the seven deadly sins ("Les set vices principaus sunt icés"); ff.203va–206rb, confession ("A confession de ben fere"). These form a confessional manual which is found in a number of manuscripts (see below, p. 294). On f.206va/b is the beginning of a narrative poem in octosyllabic couplets ("Ci faz un poi de mencion / e Jesu e de sa passion / e de la sue douce Mere / ki est joie singulere") which is found complete in Dublin, Trinity College, MS 374 (D.1.29), ff.58va–67ra.

P = Paris, BNF, MS fr. 19525 (anc. 2560, Saint-Germain 1856) (s.xiii^{2}), ff.72va–82vb. The manuscript, the work of two scribes, measures 225 x 155mm and comprises 202 folios written in England towards the end of the thirteenth century representing a significant collection of Anglo-Norman works.[30] Paul Meyer pointed out that it contained a number of items included in London, BL, MS Egerton 2710.[31]

Pa = Paris, BNF, MS fr. 6276 (s.xiii/xiv), ff.127rb–132rb. Ff.3r–127ra are taken up by the so-called *Compileison* which constitutes the Anglo-Norman version of the *Ancrene Riwle*.[32] There are 130 folios proper, which conclude with the Pater Noster, enclosed in two sheets of a treatise in Latin (ff.1–2 and ff.133–134).

Adam's commentary is of a fairly elementary nature. One striking feature is that it was at first addressed to a female religious (and through her to "vus femmes de religion"), but most of the references to a female addressee in the Cambridge copy have been erased and replaced with male forms of address.[33] In the older Paris MS, on the other hand, the addressee is exclusively addressed as a male; indeed the commentary begins with the title "A son treschier frere" and opens "Mun cher frere . . . ," altering the reference to "vus femmes de religion" to "hommes de religiun." In the Cambridge copy the following relics of the original addressee(s) are found: the first of two references to "rei

[30] See *La Vie de Saint Laurent* (ed. Russell), pp. 1–3.

[31] Meyer 1889.

[32] See *The French Text* (ed. Trethewey, description of MS on pp. xiv–xv), and Appendix below.

[33] As we shall see, James is wrong to say "The name of the person or persons addressed has been erased wherever it occurs" (James 1905, p. 109).

coroné" is accompanied by an erasure which reveals that the original reading was "reine coronee": the third paragraph of the text contains, still visible under an erasure, "tres cher[e] [me]re," which has then been altered to "trescher beau sire" (Paris "treschier frere"); later the phrase "ma chere mere" is clearly visible beneath the barring which marks deletion, and again later the reading "ma chere mere" is replaced by "beau sire," "ma treschere mere" is deleted, as is also "ma tresdu[ce mere]." In this introductory section, the older Paris MS furnishes the following forms of address: "mon chier frere," "[mon] biau frere," "bel tresduz frere," "mon tresduz frere." The younger Paris MS begins with the greeting "Ses treschers frers e suers saluz e pees" and eliminates most references to those being addressed; indeed, it generally replaces "vus" with "nus" and first person plural forms.

In the exegesis of the first petition, the reviser of the Cambridge copy has failed to clear "ma chere mere" on two occasions (see below p. 96), and there are two erasures. In the second petition the reviser has left "reine coronee del ciel" (see below p. 100), where the older Paris text has substituted "rei del ciel," and also "reine del ceil" (P "rei") (see below p. 104). In one place (see below p. 102) "tresdoce mere" has been deleted by barring and replaced with "biau sire." There are seven straightforward erasures. A final case of imperfect revision is the leaving of "vile" and "despite" in their feminine forms, where the Paris copy has masculine forms.

In Petition 3 there are four erasures ("ma chere mere" and "ma doce mere" are still visible), the last of which corresponds to the reading "vus homes de religion" in the older Paris MS. In Petition 4 "ma doce mere" and "bele mere" are left uncorrected, "querante" is on two occasions inflected for the feminine (see below p. 112) and there are two further erasures. In Petition 5 there is another instance of "ma doce mere" deleted by barring and replaced with "beau sire" (P "mon duz frere") and similarly "bele mere" replaced by "beau sire." In one place "bele doce mere" has been left unaltered (P substitutes "beau duz frere"). In the sixth petition there are two instances of both "vencu" and "tempté" displaying signs of erasure of a feminine -e, whilst "cheitive" remains feminine (P "chaitif"). There is also an erasure. In the seventh petition there are three erasures over which has been written "beau sire," and in the concluding paragraph another erasure. There were, then, in the Cambridge text forty-three allusions to the addressee, in the Paris (Pa) text forty-five.

The Dublin and Lambeth MSS contain twenty-eight references to an addressee, consistently called "b(e)au frere," once "mun tresduz frere," once "tresduz frere." Internal references are consonant with the idea of a male addressee.

The text below is based on MS C, corrected from P (where they bear on the destination of the text). The readings of DL are given extensively, but not exhaustively. Pa is cited sparingly.

Text

[f.71r] ***Le Exposiciun meistre Adam de Eccestre sur la Pater Nostre***

[Preface] Suvent avient ke amur crest par conisance, kar ço ke nul ne seit ne purra legerement amer.[i] Dunc sachez ke home taunt cume il entent e veit plus de la verité e del ben, taunt plus l'eime e plus en a joie. Por ce sunt gent de religiunt ki clers sunt mot a eise quant il entendent les paroles k'il dient en lur oreisuns. E vus femmes[ii] de religion avez a la fiez en ce defaute quant vus n'entendez pas ceo ke vus dites en vos oreisuns. Nel di pas par ceo ke vus n'eez autant joie e devociun en vos oreisuns cume les clers, einz crei vereiment ke vos en eez autant u plus, kar joie espirital ne vent pas de saver, ainz fet[iii] d'amer nostre tresduz Seignor Jesu Crist. Einz le di pur ceo ke, quant vos preez nostre tresduz Seignor Jesu Crist, mot vodriez volentiers entendre en vostre quer ceo ke vus dites de buche pur la amur ke vos avez a nostre tresduz Seignor a ki vus parlez. Por ceo pensaue [mon chier frere, P][iv] ke jo par la grace nostre Seignor vus espounderei la [f.71v] Pater Noster solum mun fieble sen e solum ceo ke Deus le me dune, kar ceo est la especiale oreisun ke nostre tresduz Seignor Jesu Crist nos ensigna a dire. En cest oreisun a set preeres e je vos ai escrist [frere, P] sor chescune preere ceo ke jo i entenc solonc le sen ke Deu m'a doné. E jo vus pri pur Deu ke vus nel despisez pas, tut nel puissez vos pas entendre a la premor, kar si vos le lisez sovent, vos l'entendrez bein,[v] e tant plus le lirrez e meus l'entendrez. E pur l'amur nostre tresduz Seignur Jesu Crist eforce[z] vos de mettre en la amur de vostre quer ceo ke vus i troverez, kar il n'i a si verité non, e le Saint Espirit vos alume le quer a entendre e amer la verité. Amen.

[General Introduction] Nostre Pere qui es en ceus, toun nun seit saintifié, avegne tun regné, la toue volenté seit fete en tere come en ceus. Donez a nus hui[vi] *nostre pain de chescun jor e relessez a noz nostre dette,*[vii] sicome noz relessoms a nos dettors, e ne nos ameine mie en temptation, mes delivre nos de mal, Amen — c'est a dire, 'issi seit il'.

---

[i] The rubric, preceded by a paragraph mark, is written in red at the top of the page. P has no rubric other than the title 'A son treschier frere', Pa has *Oratio dominica*. Heading, and text from 'Suvent' to 'Dunc', written (in larger letters) in red. It does not appear in P which begins 'Mun cher frere, sachez', nor Pa which has 'Mes treschers frers e suers [sachez]'. [ii] P 'hommes'; Pa 'lai gent'. [iii] Final 't' is written in red over expuncted 'z'. [iv] Erasure in MS. Pa 'mun treschere frere'. [v] The second letter is apparently expuncted, though I have retained it, since 'bein' is attested elsewhere in the text, whereas 'bin' is not. [vi] MS hom. [vii] DL 'nos dettes'.

Translation

The Exposition of Master Adam of Exeter on the Pater Noster

[Preface] It often happens that love grows on acquaintance, for one who knows nothing cannot easily love. So you must see that the more a man understands and sees truth and goodness, the more he loves and rejoices in it. This is why religious, who are educated, are very pleased when they understand the words they speak in their prayers. And you religious women sometimes have this shortcoming, that you do not understand what you say in your prayers. By this I do not mean that you have less joy and devotion in your prayers than the clerks have; I truly believe you have as much or more, for spiritual joy does not come from knowledge, but rather from loving our dear Lord Jesus Christ. Rather, I say this because when you pray to Our Lord Jesus Christ, you earnestly wish to understand in your hearts what you are saying with your lips,[1] for the love you feel for our dear Lord whom you are speaking to. Therefore [my dear brother], I thought I would expound, by the grace of Our Lord, the Pater Noster for you — according to my feeble wit and the help God gives me — for it is the special prayer that our sweet Lord Jesus Christ taught us to say.[2] In this prayer there are seven petitions, and I have written for you [brother,] on each petition what I understand about it, according to the wit God has given me. And I beg you for God's sake not to hold it in contempt, even if you do not understand it at first, for if you read it often you will understand it well; the more you read it the better you will understand it. And for the love of our dear Lord Jesus Christ, strive to take what you find here into the love of your heart, for there is nothing but truth in it. And may the Holy Spirit kindle your heart to understand and love the truth. Amen.

[General Introduction] Our Father, which art in Heaven, hallowed be thy name, thy Kingdom come, thy will be done on earth as it is in Heaven. Give us this day our daily bread, and forgive us our trespasses as we forgive those who have trespassed against us. And lead us not into tempation, but deliver us from evil, Amen — that is, "So be it."

[1] Cf. Edmund's *Mirour*, ed. Wilshere, p. 54, vv. 139ff.

[2] See Matt. 6:9–13.

Nostre Seignor Jesu Crist nos ensegne en l'evangelie a fere tel oreisun. Pur [f.72r] ceo vousisse jo [mon chier frere, P][i] ke vos seusez a comencement quei est oreisun e puis entendisez les parties de cest oreisun. Oreisun ne est fors desir de alme ové certeine esparance. 'Ke ceo avegne' : en cest esperance nos met nostre Seignor Jesu Crist quant il nos[ii] enseigne apeler Deu 'Nostre[iii] Pere qui es en ceus'. Kar en celui deit l'em aver certaine esparance qui poet e veut toz les bens doner[iv] ke nostre alme seit desirrer e plus d'asez. La volenté est signifiee [par] cest mot 'Nostre Pere'[v] e le poer par cest mot 'qui es en ceus'. Kar si Deu se veout apeler nostre Pere, donc nos fet il asaver k'il nos eime come ses fiz e ke il noz veut les beins doner dont nos avum mester. E sachez [beal frere, P][vi] ke si totes les amurs[vii] ke unkes pere ne mere charneus eurent vers lur enfaunt fusent joint en un amor e icel amor fust encore multipliee taunt come quoer de home seust penser, ne poreit ele pas encore de rien atteindre a l'amor ke Deus nostre Pere ha vers nos neis la ou nos emes ses enemis. E ceo verrum noz bien par la grace Deu se nos veum en quele [f.72v] manere il est nostre Pere e quei il a fat pur nos.

Sachez dunc [mon biau frere, P][viii] quant Deus fist totes creatures de neent, nos ne lisom ke il feist nule creature a sa semblance fors home. Por ceo est il Deu e creatur as atres choses[ix] del monde, mes n'est pas lour pere. Mes a nos est il par la sue tresdouce misericorde Deu e creatour e pere pur ceo ke nostre alme est fete a la semblance del Pere e del Fiz e del Saint Esperit qui sunt un Deu e treis persones. E totes les autres choses de cest mund a il fet a nos servir tant come nos voudrum demorer[x] en la sue amur cume ses fiz. Mes sitost come nos lesom la sue amur pur la amur de la char ou d'akune autre creature, nos perdum la seignorie de cest munde e devenoms serfs a une vile creature la ou nus esteiom si frouns[xi] cum fiz del rei celestial[xii] e seignors de tut le munde. A las! quel doleros chaunge ci a. Qui l'entendist [bel, tresduz frere, P],[xiii] a[xiv] ci grant amur quant Deus ki fu senz comencement e est senz nule chaunge e serra senz fin, qui est si trespusant e si tressage e si tresbon ke quer de home nel poez penser, en ki est vie e joie par[f.73r]durable, nos degna fere a sa semblance, si ke nous feusoms ses fiz. Kar il vus peust lesser aver esté un poi de tere dount vos fustes[xv] fete ou il vus peust aver fet une best[e].

---

[i] Erasure in MS. DLPa omit reference to the addressee. [ii] DL 'vus'. [iii] DL 'vostre pere'. [iv] DL 'tenir'. [v] DL omit 'Nostre … mot'. [vi] Erasure in MS. DLPa omit reference to the addressee. [vii] MS amures. [viii] Erasure in MS. DLPa omit reference to the addressee. [ix] Pa 'bestes'. [x] DL 'd. en son servise e en'. [xi] DLPPa 'francs'. [xii] P 'celestre'. [xiii] Erasure in MS. DL 'bau frere'. [xiv] DL 'nad', Pa 'ia mult nus mustra'. [xv] DL 'nus pust … nus sumes', Pa 'poet aver lessé ester un poi'.

Our Lord Jesus Christ teaches us in the Gospel to say this prayer. Therefore I would have you know from the beginning what prayer is [my dear brother,] and then to understand the parts of this prayer. Prayer is simply the desire of the soul, together with certain hope. "Let thy Kingdom come": Our Lord Jesus Christ gives us this hope when he teaches us to call God "Our Father which art in Heaven." For we ought to have certain hope in him who can and will grant us all the good things our hearts can desire and more besides. The will is signified by this word "Our Father," and the power by this word "which art in Heaven." For if God desires to be called our Father, so he makes known to us that he loves us as his children and he wants to give us the good things we need. And know this [dear brother]: if all the loves that ever human father and mother had for their child were joined into one love, and this love were further multiplied as much as the heart of man could imagine, still it could be nowhere near as great as the love God our Father has for us — even when we love his enemies. And we shall see this clearly, by the grace of God, if we consider in what ways he is our Father and what he has done for us.

Know then [dear brother,] that when God made all creatures from nothing, we do not read that he made any creature in his own likeness except man. So he is God and Creator to other things in the world, but he is not their Father. But to us he is, by his tender mercy, God and Creator and Father — because our soul is made in likeness of the Father and the Son and the Holy Spirit who are one God and three Persons. And he has made all other things in this world to serve us as long as we wish to dwell in his love as his children. But as soon as we forsake his love for love of the flesh or of any other creature, we lose the kingdom of this world and become slaves to a vile thing, whereas we were so free as children of the celestial King and lords of all the earth. Alas! What a doleful change it is! Who understands this [most beloved brother,] has great love here on earth, because God — who was without beginning, and is unchanging, and shall be without end, who is so very powerful, wise, and good that no man's heart can conceive of it, and who is life and joy everlasting — deigned to make us in his likeness, so that we might be his children. For he could have left you as the lump of earth from which you were made,[3] or he could have created you as a beast.

[3] Other MSS have "we" here.

Si morissez[i] dunc ensemblement cors e alme quant il vus fist home e dona alme a la sue beneite[ii] semblance por estre rei coroné[iii] del cel e vivre en la sue tresgrant joie pardurablement.

Il[iv] n'i a nul si dur quer ki ne se amollireit a amer Deu de tot poer e neis fundereit tut de joie se il pensast veraiment de ceste tresgrant grace ke nostre tresduz Pere Deus nus a fet sur autres creatures. E encore fist il plus par la sue tresgrant misericorde, kar quant nos par nostre tresdolerus peché partimes[v] de Deu nostre tresduz Pere e devenimes sers al deble, il par la sue tresgrant[vi] misericorde envea sun cher fiz, qui est un Deu ové lui, en tere pur prendre sanc e char de la tresduce Virgine saint[e] Marie e le fist en teu manere en estat de serf, sofrit tresgrant poverté e vieuté[vii] e tresangessoses peines qui unkes peché n'avet fet. E puis le livera il a la plus vile mort ke home [f.73v] seust penser pur delivrer nos cheitifs hors de la tresdolerose prison au deable[viii] e pur fere nos revenir a la cort del cel dount nos serroms reis coronez si nos siums la volenté a icel doz Seignor ki pur nos deigna morir en la croiz cum un larrun.

Trescher beau sire,[ix] ore avez veu deus choses en quei Deus nos a mostré k'il est nostre Pere e k'il nos aime come ses fiz neis la u nos eimes encontre lui. La premere chose est k'il nos cria a sa semblance, e la secunde k'il nos recria par sa trespiteose[x] mort quant il devint home pur nos. De la premere chose li est home tenu a amer e servir de tot [son] poer. E quei li fra dunc home pur la secunde chose ? Kar si jo par fine deité dei amer[xi] Deu nostre Pere e loer e servir de tute m'alme e de tot mun quer en tot tens pur ceo k'il me fist de nient e me dona alme a la soue semblance, sicome il fu comandé en la veu lei einz ke Deu fust home pur nos, quei li porrai jo ore fere quant il pur mei dolerus pechere[xii] se abessa taunt ke il devint home e se dona a mei quant il par la sue tresdouce misericorde vout pur mei murir de la plus angessose e la plus vile mort [f.74r] ke unkes fust pensee ? Ne sai quei jo purrai ci dire. Kar si jo vesquise cent mil aunz[xiii] e puse donc chescun jor murir de ausi dure mort pur lui come il sofri pur mei, encore ne sereit ceo rien envers ceo ke il nos dona quant il qui est verrei fiz Deu e Deu dona sei meimes a nos, qui esteioms par la ordure de peché[xiv] descendu el puis de enfern e en despit de Deu servimes al deable.

---

[i] DL 'morissum', Pa has a blank. [ii] P 'debonaire'. [iii] Erasures in the MS indicate that, in conformity with the original addressee, the words read 'reine coronee', as in DL. [iv] There is a paragraph mark here and in the right-hand margin, where there has been added *amor dei*. [v] DL 'vus par vostre ... partistes ... vostre ... devenistes'. [vi] MS gnat. [vii] Pa 'meinte honte'. [viii] DL 'd'enfern'. [ix] 'beau sire' is a superscript addition above a deletion and partial erasure which can be read as 'tres cher[e] me[re]'. P has 'Treschier frere', but there is nothing in DLPa. [x] L 'trespreciuse'. [xi] P 'a. e servir'. [xii] DL 'chaitif'. [xiii] DL 'cent anz'. [xiv] DL 'de nos pechez'.

So you would have died, both body and soul; but rather, he made you man and gave soul to his blessed likeness, to be crowned king of heaven and to live in his great joy for ever.

There is no heart so hard that it would not soften by loving God with all its strength, and even dissolve utterly in rapture, if it fully realised this grace so great, that our beloved Father God made us above all other creatures. And yet he did still more, in his great mercy: when we were separated from God our dear Father by our miserable sin and became servants of the Devil, by his mercy he sent his dear Son, who is One God with him, to earth to become incarnate through the most gentle Virgin Saint Mary. And he made him to be of servant's estate, to suffer poverty and vileness and most terrible torments — he who never committed any sin. And then he consigned him to the cruellest death that could be imagined, to deliver us wretches out of the Devil's miserable prison and to bring us back to the Court of Heaven, through which we shall be crowned kings if we follow the will of that sweet Lord who deigned to die for us like a thief on the Cross.

Beloved sir, now you have seen two things by which God shows us that he is our Father and that he loves us as his children, even when we love contrary to him. The first thing is that he created us in his likeness; the second, that he re-created us by his piteous death when he became man for us. By the first, man is bound to love and serve him with all his power. And what then shall man do for him, because of the second? For if I, by the power of true divinity, ought to love God our Father, and love and serve him with all my soul and all my heart unceasingly because he made me and gave me a soul in his likeness, as it was commanded in the Old Law before God became man for us, what can I do now — when for me, a miserable sinner, he humbled himself so much he became man and gave himself to me, when in his gentle mercy he was willing to die, for me, the most agonizing and wretched death that could ever be imagined? I know not what to say. For if I lived a hundred thousand years, and every day could die as hard a death for him as he suffered for me, still it would be nothing to what he gave us when he, true Son of God, gave himself to us who by filth of sin had gone down into the pit of Hell and served the Devil in despite of God.

E coment li rendrom nos dunc icest tresriche dun k'il nos dona ? Jo vus enseignerai [biau frere, P][i] si Deu plest. Nostre Pere ne demande de nos autre retor fors ke nos reconessoms nostre fieblesce e nostre cheitivité. E donc serrom nos en amertume [de] penaunce[ii] e crioms[iii] a lui merci, k'il nus sauve pur le sen saintime[iv] nun, kar de nous ne vent nul bein dunt nos li peusom rens rendre. E c'est ceo ke Davi dit : *Quid retribuam domino pro omnibus que retribuit michi ? Calicem salutaris accipiam et nomen domini invocabo* [Ps. 115:12–13] ; ceo est a dire, 'Ke rendra[i] jo a Deu pur totes les choses k'il m'a doné ? Jo prendrai le hanap de salu e apelerai le nun Deu.' Le hanap de salu, c'est le hanap dunt Jesu [f.74v] Crist but, ce[v] est amertume de penaunce, e celui en totes ses pensees apele le nun Deu k'il verreiement reconoist ke de sei n'a ren fors dolur e peché. E[vi] sachez [mon chier frere, P][vii] ke si en vos a verité, taunt come plus vus done Deu grace, taunt plus vus [vus] conoistrez come a feble e a cheitive[viii] e plus li demaunderez. Issi fu il de nostre tresduce Dame,[ix] kar ele out plus de grace ke nul home ki nasqui de home e de femme e pur ceo se tint ele plus petite e plus basse ke nul autre home[x] [e plus cria merci ke nul altre home, P][xi] e plus resçut ke nul autre home[xii] quant le verrei Fiz Deu descendi en sa char.

Ore veez aprés [mon chier frere, P][xiii] pur quei nostre Seignor nus ensegne en la evangile a dire 'nostre Pere' e ne[xiv] mie 'mon Pere', kar par ceo vus veut il ensegner ke vus devez recuillir toz homes en vos preeres, kar toz sunt vos[xv] freres, e crestiens e mescreans, des l'ore ke tot avez un pere. E ke vus peusez ceste chose par la grace Deu clerement veer, metez bone entente a ceo ke jo vous dirrai. Icelui apelez vus vostre frere charnel[xvi] ki a sa char de meimes le pere charnel de ki vus avez la vostre. Donc devez bein tenir a frere celui [f.75r] qui a sa alme de meimes le pere celestial de ki vus avez la vostre e d'autele nature e de meimes la semblance. Kar ausi fist Deus la sue alme en la semblance de la Trinité come la vostre e nos deusom ceste fraternité plus amer e cherir ke cele ke vent de la char. De autant come l'alme est plus noble ke la char e d'eutant cum Deu nostre Pere del ciel est plus noble e plus a amer ke nostre pere charnel, si feisom nos si nos veisoms ausi cler de l'oel espirital come nos veum de l'oel charnel.

---

[i] Erasure in MS. DL 'bau frere'. [ii] MS amærtume (in which the 'a' of the æ ligature is expuncted and 'penaunee' with penultimate letter expuncted). Pa has 'amur de p.' [iii] DL 'crieroms'. [iv] MS saineime. [v] MS cee. DL 'le salu', Pa 'ce est amur de p.' [vi] MS A. [vii] Erasure in MS. DL 'bau frere'. [viii] DLP have 'chaitif' in accordance with the change of addressee. [ix] DL 'n. d. sainte marie'. [x] DLPa 'ou femme'. [xi] DL 'e plus cria merci e plus r.' [xii] DLPa 'ou femme'. [xiii] Erasure in MS. DL 'bau frere'. [xiv] MS en. [xv] DLP 'nos'. [xvi] MS c. de ki vus (which has been expuncted).

And how then can we repay him for this rich gift that he gave us? I shall tell you, if it please God. Our Father asks of us no return, but that we acknowledge our frailty and our wretchedness. So we shall be in bitterness of penance and beg him for mercy, that he may save us by his holy Name, for from ourselves comes no good by which we can repay him in any way. And this is what David says: *What shall I render unto the Lord for all his benefits toward me? I will take the cup of salvation, and call upon the name of the Lord.*[4] This means "How shall I repay God for all the things he has given me? I shall take the cup of salvation and call upon the Name of God." The cup of salvation is the cup from which Jesus Christ drank, that is bitterness of penance; and he calls on the name of God in all his thoughts, that he may truly acknowledge that there is nothing but pain and sin in himself. And know this [my dear brother]: if there is truth in you, then the more grace God gives you the more you will know yourself to be frail and wretched, and the more you will ask of him. Thus it was with our precious Lady, for she had more grace than any creature born of man and woman; and so she held herself to be smaller and lower than any other [and begged more for mercy than any other], and she received more than any other when the true Son of God came down into her flesh.

Now [my dear brother,] see in what follows why Our Lord teaches us in the Gospel to say "Our Father" and not "My Father." By this he wants to teach you that you must include all men in your prayers; for they are all your brothers, both Christians and unbelievers, since you all have one Father. And that you might see this matter clearly, by the grace of God, pay close attention to what I shall tell you. You call him your fleshly brother, who takes his flesh from the same natural father you take yours from. So, you should consider him your brother who receives his soul from the same celestial Father that you receive yours from: the same nature, and the same likeness. For God made his soul also, in likeness of the Trinity, just as he did yours, and we ought to love and cherish this brotherliness more than that which comes from the flesh. For just as the soul is more noble than the flesh, and as God our Heavenly Father is more noble and more worthy to be loved than our natural father, so shall we do right if we see as clearly with our spiritual eye as with our bodily eye.

---

[4] Ps. 116:12–13 in *AV.* The printed *Vulgate* has Psalm 115 beginning at v. 10, so that the passage in question is at 12–13. Online versions begin the psalm at v. 1, so the passage appears as vv. 3–4.

Mes por ceo ke nous ne veum fors de l'oel charnel come bestes, n'avum nus conesaunce ne amur fors de la fraternité ke vent de la char porie. Ne ne pensom pas ke l'alme un Sarazin ki est crié a la semblance Deu, come la m[e]ie, fu rechatee[i] par la mort al verei fiz Deu ausi avant come la meie. A las! quele dolerose chose nos a si avuglé en l'alme? Jo vus dirai. Ren ne poet l'alme esvogler fors amur de akune temporele chose ki prent fin. Pur ceo cuvent il a home totes ses propre[s] volentés lesser si il veut parfitement conoistre e amer ceste tresamiable frater[f.75v]nité dount nos avom parlé. Pur ceo sunt gent ke unt guerpi le mond e propre volenté apelé freres e soers,[ii] ne mie ke il ne fueissent avaunt freres e soers, tot nel seusent il mie, mes quant il unt tot guerpi pur la amur Deu, dunt aprimes reconoisent il ke tot sunt freres e soers. Ceo poez vus veer par une esample ke jo vus dirrai.

Deus freres charneus taunt come plus amerunt richeces, taunt meins[iii] se entreameront e sovent veez ke l'un desire la mort a l'autre pur aver le eritage. E se il amasent autant poverrté, le un soferreit volenters la mort pur la sauvatiun de l'autre. E ceo nus mostra ben nostre tresduz Seignor Jesu Crist, ki en sei meimes nos dona premerement esample de poverté e de humilité e ne coveita mie [nostre mort por aver, DLPPa] nostre eritage come fet le riche home, einz mist sei meimes a la mort pur fere a nus aver le soen eritage. Ore dira acuns [mon frere, P][iv] ke tote gent ne poent pas venir a ceste perfection ne veer si clerement en espirite ke toz seom freres. Pur ceo parlerai ore un pou plus apertement de ceste fraternité e vus demaunt en ceste manere le queil [f.76r] amez vus vostre frere charnel pur ço ke il est de meimes la char dunt vus estes u pur ço ke il ad la char figuree en semblance de homme e ad le alme cum vus avez. Pur la premere chose ne poet ce pas estre, kar dunc amer[i]ez voz une pece de la char vostre pere si ele en fust trenchee, e ceo serreit deiverie a dire! Donc est ce pur ceo k'il a la char formee come vos. Ore vous demaunt ki li forma la char,[v] vous,[vi] ou vostre pere charnel, ou Deu vostre Pere del Cel? Ici vous covent respondere ke Deus le fit e ne mie home, kar si home le peust fere, i feist ses enfanz[vii] beaus e bons e masles quant il vousist. Donc ne vous est vostre frere charnel neent plus precein ke un autre, fors de tant ke vous dui avez d'un pere charnel le comencement de vostre char, ki est un pou de ordure trespulente. Kar quant ki i a en cors ou en alme de bonté ou de beauté vent de nostre Pere Deu del Ceil, ki nos est pere pardurable sanz fin.[viii]

[i] DL 'e fu achaté de la m.' [ii] MS sores (with expunction marks under 'r' and 'e'). DL omit 'soers'. [iii] P has 'mielz', which destroys the sense and is doubtless due to a misreading 'meius'. [iv] MS ma chere mere (deleted by a bar). DL 'Ore ne poent mie tute gent v.' [v] A letter has been erased after 'r'. [vi] DL omit. [vii] MS en femmes. [viii] DLPPa 'pere oelement a tuz'.

But because we see only with our bodily eye, like beasts, we have neither knowledge nor love beyond the brotherliness that comes from foulness of the flesh. Nor do we think that the soul of a Saracen, which is created in God's likeness as mine is, was redeemed by the death of the true Son of God too, as mine was.[5] Alas, what wretched thing has so blinded us in our soul? I shall tell you. Nothing can blind the soul except love for some finite worldly thing. Therefore it behoves a man to forsake all his own desires if he wants to know and love perfectly this very lovable brotherhood of which we have spoken. People who have abandoned the world and their own will are therefore called brothers and sisters. Not that they were not brothers and sisters before — though they knew it not — but when they abandoned everything for the love of God, then they first recognized that they were all brothers and sisters. You can see this by an example that I shall tell you.

The more two natural brothers love riches, the less they love each other, and you often see that one desires the death of the other so as to get the inheritance. But if they loved poverty as much, then the one would willingly suffer death for the salvation of the other. And our dear Lord Jesus Christ showed us this, who first gave us an example, in himself, of poverty and humility and did not covet [our death so as to have] our inheritance as the rich man does, but rather surrendered himself to death so that we might gain his own inheritance. Now somebody will say [my brother,] that not everybody can reach such perfection, nor see so clearly in the spirit that we are all brothers. So I shall now speak rather more explicitly about this brotherhood, and ask you which of you loves your natural brother because he is of the same flesh as you are, or because his body is made in the likeness of man and he has a soul as you have. It cannot be the first reason, for then you would love a piece of your father's flesh if it were cut from him. It would be madness to say that! So, it is because his body is formed as yours is. Now I shall ask who made his body: you? or your natural father? or God your Father in Heaven? Here you will rightly say that God made it, and not a man. For if a man could do so, he would make his children fair, good, and male, as he wished. So, your natural brother is no closer to you than any other, excepting only that you two received from a natural father the beginning of your body, which is a piece of putrid filth. For any goodness and beauty in our body comes from our Father, God in Heaven, who is our Father world without end.

[5] For Adam's missionary journey, see pp. 8 & 73 above; for Saracens, cf. *BVV*, p. 100.

A las ! quele dolur e queu vilté ke nos esmes liez[i] a nostre frere charnel en si grant amur por un poi de sanc porri ke nus avom d'un pere charnel e ne fesom force des autres ki ount figure de home come nos, ne mie de pere charnel, mes de nostre Pere Deu del Ciel, de ki il unt come nos alme, ki est la plus noble creature [f.76v] ki seit criee, kar ele est la plus preceine a Deu par nature por ceo ke ele est criee a sa semblance.

Ore desirrei, beau sire,[ii] ke nos cestes choses recevisoms[iii] en amur tresfermement por la amor Deu nostre Pere del Ciel qui nos devom amer sur tote ren, ke si tost come nos veisom u oisom parler ou pensisom ke a akun home fust malveis,[iv] qui k'il unkes fust,[v] tantost feusom esmeu en nostre cuer e pensisoms a doz[vi] Deu : A[vii] cestui feiste[s] vous de une orde tere cors e semblance de home, come a mei, [e li donastes alme a vostre semblance come a mei, DLP] e le rechatastes de enfer par vostre trespiteose mort,[viii] come mei. E quant ke nos avom de bonté, pur quei home deit estre amé, tot l'avoum de voz trestdoz Pere.[ix] Icestui est mun frere, icestui dei jo amer come mei, tot seit il mescreant ou autre pecheur, kar en pou d'ore l'avrez fet bon quant vos plerra, come vous feistes la gloriose Magdaleine e saint Pol.[x]

Ore avez veu [mon chier frere, P],[xi] coment nostre Seignor nos mostre sa tresdoce volenté k'il a vers nos par ceo k'il nos fet apeler sei nostre Pere. Ore saverez aprés par la soue grace coment il nos mostre soen poer par ceo ke il se fet apeler del Cel, tot seit il en cel e en tere e par tot. Kar il est issi ke les choses ki sunt en terre, sicome herbes e arbres [f.77r] [e] bestes e homes, envellisent e morent e anentissent ou tost ou tart. E en terre faut a la fiez le dreit cours de nature, sicome femme, ki par dreit cuors de nature ne deust enfaunter fors al novime meis, enfaunte a la fiez plus tost, a la fiez plus tart, e enfaunte a la feiz enfaunt senz pez ou senz mainz, a la feiz a plus mainz ou a plus deiz ki ne deust aver par nature. Mes en Cel n'avent nule manere de coruption ne nule faute de nature, kar enkore i sont meimes les esteiles e en autel manere come il furent jadis e ausi est le cours de la lune cume il fu todis[xii] e leve le solail chescun matin en orient come il sout fere, ne ce ne poet faillir jeske a la fin del munde. E une autre chose i a il, ke le poer del Ciel e des esteiles est sor toz les poers ki sunt en tere.

---

[i] DLP 'alié'. [ii] 'beau sire' is written above 'ma chere mere' which has been deleted by a bar. P has 'mon chier frere', DL 'bau frere'. [iii] PPa 'retenissoms'. [iv] 'fust malveis' is a superscript insertion by the hand of the text. P has 'come nus veisom de aucum home ki k'il unkes fust, tant tost fuissom', DL 'p. de aucun home qui ke il unke fust, tant tost fussum'. [v] Pa 'f. ke fust choez en pecché ke t. f.' [vi] DLP 'dire'. [vii] DLP omit 'A'. [viii] DL 'tresprescius sanc'. [ix] DL 'p. h. deit e. a. tut l'amur de vus'. [x] DL omit 'e saint Pol'. [xi] MS ma treschere mere (deleted by a bar). DL 'bau frere'. [xii] P 'jadis'.

Alas! What wretchedness, what vileness, that we should be bound to our natural brother with such great love because of a drop of corrupt blood that we have from a natural father! And we have no care for others who are formed as men just as we are: not by a fleshly father but by our Father God in Heaven, from whom they have a soul just as we have, which is the noblest created thing in all creation, for it is the closest to God by its nature, being created in his own likeness.

Now, dear sir, I would wish us to receive these things most steadfastly in love, for the sake of God our Heavenly Father whom we ought to love above all things; that as soon as we see or hear, speak or think, evil to any man, whoever he may be, then let us be moved in heart and think of our dear Lord: "You made body and human likeness from a filthy bit of earth, for this man as for me [and gave him a soul in your likeness, as to me], and you redeemed him, like me, from hell by your pitiful death. And whatever goodness we have, for which a man should be loved, we have it all from you, dearest Father. This man is my brother, I must love him as myself even though he be an unbeliever or other sinner. For in an instant you could make him good, whenever it pleases you, as you did the glorious Magdalene and Saint Paul."

Now [my dear brother,] you have seen how Our Lord shows his gentle disposition towards us, because he makes us call him Our Father. Now, you shall know presently by his grace how he shows us his power, because he calls himself Heavenly, although he is in heaven and earth and everywhere. For it is thus: things that are on earth, such as plants and trees and beasts and men, grow old and die and come to nothing sooner or later. And on earth sometimes the proper course of nature fails: as with a woman, who by the proper course of nature should not give birth except in the ninth month; sometimes she gives birth sooner, sometimes later. Sometimes she has a child without feet or hands, or it has more hands or fingers than it ought naturally to have. But in Heaven there is no sort of defilement, and no fault of nature. For even the stars are the same as they used to be, and the course of the moon is as it has ever been, and the sun rises every morning in the east as it always does; nor can this fail until the end of the world. And another thing: the power of Heaven and of the stars is above all the powers on earth.

Donc nos mustre nostre Sire Deu, quant il se fist[i] apeler 'Pere qui est en Ceus', ke sen poer ne poez faillir a nul foer e ke sen poer est sur toz poers. A ! tresglorios Deu, de quele cheitiveté aven[t] ce ke home n'a en vos trescertaine esperance, quant vos par vostre tresgrant bonté volez a home fere toz les bens k'il seit [f.77v] desirer, e plus d'asez, e quant ke vous volez, si poez vos fere e fetes, kar vostre poer est sur tote ren e ne poet faillir. [Mon tresduz frere, DLP][ii] metez ces moz ne mie en vostre escren,[iii] mes en la amur de vostre cuer, sicome fist nostre tresduce Dame, kar quantt k'ele oi ou vit de son cher[iv] fiz mist ele en son cuer tres fermement. E donc porrez vous orer a dreit afiance e avrez quant ke vus demaundrez senz nule faute[v] si vous demandez ben, kar ceo dist Nostre Seignor Jesu Crist en la evangelie : *Petite et accipietis* [John 16:24], 'Priez[vi] e rec[e]vrez.'

[Petition 1] [Mon tresduz frere, P][vii] la premer oreison ke nostre tresdoz Seignor Jesu Crist nos ensegne a fere est ceste : 'Nostre Pere del Cel, ton noun seit saintifié.' Ore nos[viii] covent il premerement veer par la grace Deu quel est le noun Deu. E puis ke ce seit a dire 'ton noun seit saintifié', ore porreit akun demaunder 'Ha Deus autre noun ke Pere ?' Vous devez saver ke oïl, kar ausi come le noun de vostre pere charnel n'est pas pere — kar issi ne l'apelent mie autre gent, einz est Richart[ix] ou Robert par quei autre gent le conoisent — ausi vos ai je dit avant ke Deu n'est pere a nule creature fors a home ; por ceo a il autre nun par unt il est coneu en totes creatures[x] e par unt totes creatures le cleiment e loent e prechent, e icest noun [f.78r] si est bounté, sicome dist Sainte Escripture. E ceo poez vos veer par reison, kar noun de home si ad deus proprietez : le une si est ke noun se espaunt en plusors lius[xi] e l'autre si est ki en toz lius conoisent[xii] la persone par le noun. Issi est il de Deu, kar la soue bonté se espaunt e[n] totes creatures e en cel e en tere, kar il par sa bonté fist totes creatures de neent, e per meimes la[xiii] bonté le[s] sostent il, ke eles ne dechecent en neent, e les ordeine chescune a s[a] propre fin. Ore poez donc veer ke la bonté nostre Seignor est espoundue ben comunement e c'est ben reison, kar autrement ne serreit ce mie bonté si ele ne fust comune.

---

[i] P 'fait', DL 'ki se fet a'. [ii] MS ma tres duc (with 'e mere' erased). [iii] DL omit 'ne . . . escren', Pa 'en lui enclos'. [iv] MS chere. [v] DL 'faille', Pa 'defaute'. [vi] DL 'c'est a dire "Requerez e" '. [vii] MS ma trescher (with 'e mere' erased). DL 'bau frere'. [viii] DL 'vus'. [ix] Pa 'Johan'. [x] MS c. il. [xi] MS plusors la gent suis. [xii] DLP 'conoist em', Pa 'c. la gent'. [xiii] DL 'sa'.

So our Lord God shows us, when he named himself "Father which art in Heaven," that his power cannot fail in any way; his power is above all powers. Ah, most glorious God! What wretchedness it is, that man has not that certain hope in you, when by your great goodness you wish to give man all the good things he can desire, and even more; whatever you wish you can and do do it, for your power is over all things and cannot fail. [Dearest brother], do not put these words away in your coffer, but into the love of your heart; this is what our precious Lady did: all she heard and saw about her dear Son she put away steadfastly in her heart.[6] And thus you may pray with true faith, and you will have whatever you ask for, nothing lacking, if you ask well; for Our Lord Jesus Christ said in the Gospel: *ask, and ye shall receive*; "Pray, and receive."

[Petition 1] [My dear brother], the first petition our dear Lord Jesus Christ teaches us to pray is this: "Our Father, which art in Heaven, hallowed be thy name." Now it behoves us, first, to see by God's grace what the name of God is. And since "hallowed be thy name" is to be said, then one might ask "Has God any other name but Father?" You should know that the answer is yes, for just as the name of your natural father is not "Father" — because other people do not call him that, rather, it is as Richard or Robert that he is known to other people — so, as I said before, God is Father to no other creature but man. Therefore he has another name by which he is known to all creatures; by which all creatures call him, and glorify and praise him. And this name is Goodness, as Holy Scripture says.[7] And you can see this by reasoning, for a man's name has two properties: one is that a name spreads into many places, and the other is that everywhere the person is known by the name.[8] So it is with God, for his goodness spreads among all creatures both in Heaven and on earth, for in his goodness he made all creatures from nothing; and by the same goodness he sustains them so they do not fall, and he ordains to each its proper end. Now you can see that the goodness of Our Lord is spread widely, and this is right, for it would not be goodness unless it were in common.

---

[6] See Luke 2:19 & 51.

[7] Cf. Augustine, *Confessions*, 10.vi (II:87–91).

[8] Compare the passage in Chrétien's *Conte du Graal* (ed. Busby), where the nameless hero's mother explains "Par le sornon connoist on l'ome" (v. 562. A variant is "par le non"). See also Morawski 1925, *Proverbes*, 1100 (dated 1350–1400) & 198 (13th century).

De autre part nos ne poum pas Deu veer en sa divinité,[i] mes nos le coneisom par sa bonté ke nos veom e aparcevom[ii] en chescune creature, kar chescune creature nos preeche e c[r]ie ke Deus est bon, kar si Deu vousist, ren ne serreit. Donc si tost come la creature est, si[iii] vos dit ele, si voz l'en[tendez],[iv] '[Deu] par sa *bonté* me fist de neent.' E la creature ne dist mie[v] 'Deu par sa *poesté* me fist de neen[t], ne par son *saver* solement',[vi] kar il ne fet mie quant ke il set fere ne quant k'il poet, tot seit il issi ki il face totes choses [f.78v] par sen poer e par sen saver, mes il fet quanc'il veut[vii] par sa bone volenté e[viii] sa volenté est sa bonté. Ore poez donc veer ke bonté est le propre nun Dampnedeu par ces deus proprietez de nun. A las ! come vile chose e dolerose est pecheur, kar chescune creature, neis cel ki parler ne poez, louue totdis sun creatur e dit totdis k'il est tresbon. E home pecheor a ki nostre Seignor[ix] a doné plus ke a nule autre creature vient encontre nostre Seignor e lui[x] tout sun dreit nun e done le noun Deu a une vile creature, kar kaunt home eslit par sa propre volenté acune chose encontre Deu, si k'il passereit un[xi] des comandemenz Deu plus tost k'il n'eust[xii] sa volenté de cele chose, iceste volenté est mortel[xiii] peché e icest home eime plus cele chose ke Deu. Donc dist il en sen cuer ke cele chose est mellore ke Deu, kar home ne eime fors ce k'il prise e ce k'il eime plus prise il plus. A las ! A las ! cheitif doleros, ja n'a nule creature bonté ne valur fors de Deu, ne vos, las pechere, ki ke vos seez, n'avriez pas alme dunt vos peusez ren amer plus ke une pere si nostre tresdoz Segnor ne la vous euest donee. E quant vos deprisés Deu, vos deprisés vos meimes, kar voz n'avez nul pris fors de lui ki [f.79r] semblance vus portez.

Ore avez veu ke le noun Deu est la sue tresgrant bonté qui est espaundue en chescune creature e chescune creature loe Deu par cest noun totdis taunt come ele dure. Ausi deust home tant come il dure loer e amer la bonté nostre Seignor e[n] totes creatures de cest monde, sicome dist David :[xiv] *A solis ortu usque ad occasum laudabile nomen domini* [Ps. 112:3]. L'entente de cestes paroles est 'Ke home del comencement de sa vie jeske a la fin deit loer le noun Dampnedeu' ; ce est a saver, sa bonté[xv] en totes les creatures de cest munde.

[i] P 'deité'. [ii] DL 'conussum'. [iii] DL 'ne vus d.' [iv] In the MS there is a blank with no apparent signs of an erasure. [v] L omits. [vi] DL 'e si ne mist mie tut son saver'. [vii] DL omit 'par … veut'. [viii] MS e par. DL 'e par sa bonté'. [ix] P 'a ki Deu a doné'. [x] MS le. [xi] MS une. DL 'un des dis c.' [xii] DL 'pus qu'il i met la v.', Pa 'plus tost k'il mist'. [xiii] MS mortele. [xiv] P 'seint davi'. [xv] MS b. est en.

On the other hand, we cannot see God in his divinity, but know him by his goodness, that we can see and perceive in every creature, for every creature speaks and calls to us that God is good, for if God so willed, then nothing would exist. So as soon as the creature exists, it says to you, could you but hear it: "God by his *goodness* made me from nothing." And the creature does not say "God by his *power* made me from nothing, nor just by his *wisdom*." For he never does as much as he knows how to or is able to do, even though he does all things by his power and wisdom, but he does all that he wants to do by his good will, and his will is his goodness. Now you can see that Goodness is the proper name of the Lord God, according to these two properties of the name. Alas! How vile and miserable a thing is a sinner: every creature praises its Creator unceasingly, even one that cannot speak, saying unceasingly that he is truly good. And sinful man, to whom Our Lord has given more than to any other creature, goes against Our Lord and takes away his proper name and gives the name of God to a worthless creature, for when man by his own will chooses anything against God — so that he would break one of God's commandments sooner than not have his will of that thing — that will is mortal sin and he loves that thing more than God. Then he says in his heart: this thing is better than God, for man loves only what he values, and what he loves more he values more. Alas! Alas, miserable wretch! No creature ever has goodness and value except from God; nor you, poor sinner, whoever you are — you would have no soul with which to love anything more than a stone if Our Lord had not given you one. And when you scorn God you scorn yourself, for you have no value except from him whose likeness you bear.

Now you have seen that the name of God is his very great Goodness, which is spread into every creature, and every creature praises God by this name as long as it lives. Thus ought man, as long as he lives, to praise and love Our Lord's goodness in all the creaures of this world, as David says: *From the rising of the sun unto the going down of the same the Lord's name is to be praised.*[9] The meaning of these words is: "From the beginning of his life, unto the end, man must praise the name of the Lord God"; that is to say, his goodness in all the creatures of this world.

[9] Ps. 113:3 in *AV*.

Mes por ce ke nous par nostre cheitiveté fallom trop sovenz de ceste loenge quant nos come cheitifs avogles prisom plus la bonté de la creature ke la bonté Deu, pur ceo cuvent il preer Deu nostre Pere ke le sen noun seit saintifié, c'est a dire, ke la sue bonté seit confermé en nous,[i] kar en sai est ele tote confermee e en totes creatures fors en home, kar nule creature ne se poez torner ore endreit[ii] de ben a mal fors home, kar les bons angles sont confermé en ben e les maveis en mal. E donc ert la bonté Deu confermé en nos cuers quant nos parfitement [f.79v] amerom Deu ki est [le] soverein ben sur tute ren. E quant il avendra ke ausi come nule creature n'est ren fors par la bonté Damnedeu, ke nos en meimes[iii] la manere en nule creature ne en nos meimes ne en autres ren n'amom[iv] fors la bonté Dampnedeu, e si le noun Deu fust en tele manere confermé en nos, donc avriom nos gangné treis precioses choses.

L'une est ke nos de nule ren ki seit ne nos corescериom fors de peché sol, kar tote ren fors peché avent par la bone volenté[v] nostre Seignor. Dont si vus estes corescee ne dolente, ou pur maledie de cors ou por perte d'aver ou por mort de ami ou pur nule tribulation ki puisse avenir a vous ou de vos ou de ami ke vos ees,[vi] sachez ke le noun Deu n'est pas confermé en vostre cuer.

La autre chose est ke nos ne querrom en nule ren[vii] de ceste munde for le onor nostre Pere del Ciel e[viii] tendrom nos meimes en grant despit e en grant vilté. E sachez ke celui ki quert en tere ki seit amé e prisé fors taunt cume afert a l'enor Deu, il n'eime pas le ben Deu, mes le sen. Iteus sunt ces ki mot se esjoissent quant Deus a mis en eus[ix] akun ben come science ou ver[f.80r]tu ou akune autre grace e ne se esjoissent mie de l'autri ben, einz en unt envie. E por ceo lur avent il par dreit jugement k'il perdent le ben ke Deu lur aveit doné, kar ben ne poet estre ben s'il ne seit comun a toz. Donc si tost come vos desirez[x] ke le ben ke Deus vos[xi] a doné seit a vos[xii] solement, vos fetes[xiii] de vostre[xiv] ben mal. E taunt come plus saverez desirer le ben en autri por mot eshaucer le noum Dampnedeu, taunt plus en avrez deu[xv] ben, ausi come un tisun[xvi] enflambé taunt come il plus jette sa clarté as choses ki sunt entur lui, tant plus en a, e taunt plus come meins en jette, taunt meins en a,[xvii] e quant il ren ne jette de clarté, ren nen a.

[i] MS vous. [ii] MS trover e ore en deit. [iii] MS emimes, DL 'ameine'. [iv] DLPa 'n'avun'. [v] MS velenté. [vi] DL 'a vus ou a nul de voz amiz que vus eez'. [vii] DL 'q. ne [en, D] nule chose ren'. [viii] P 'einz'. [ix] DL 'q. il unt en eus'. [x] DL 'nus desirum'. [xi] DL 'nus'. [xii] DL 'nus'. [xiii] DL 'nus fesum'. [xiv] DL 'nostre'. [xv] P 'de'. DL omit 'deu ben'. [xvi] DL 'vertisun'. [xvii] DL omit 'e taunt … meins en a'.

But because we through our wretchedness fail too often in this praise, when we like blind wretches prize the goodness of the creature above the goodness of God, it behoves us therefore to pray to God our Father that his name be hallowed. That is, that his goodness may be confirmed in us. For in itself it is fully established, and in all creatures but man, for man is the only creature now capable of turning from good to evil; the good angels are established in their goodness, and the bad angels in their wickedness. And so the goodness of God will be established in our hearts when we perfectly love God who is the sovereign good over all things. And when it comes to pass, that as all creatures are nothing without the goodness of the Lord God, that we likewise love nothing in any creature — in ourselves nor in others — except the goodness of the Lord God, and if likewise the name of God is established in us, then we shall have gained three precious things.

One is that we should be angered at nothing whatsoever save only sin, for all things but sin come through the good will of Our Lord. So if you are angry or sorrowful, either through bodily illness or for loss of goods, for a friend's death or any other tribulation that could happen to you or from you or through any friend that you have, know that the name of God is not established in your heart.

The second thing is that we should seek for nothing in this world except the honour of our Heavenly Father, and hold ourselves in great despite and disgust. And know that whoever seeks to be loved and valued on earth, without giving thought to the honour of God, does not love God's good but his own. These are they who rejoice greatly that God has instilled some good in them, like knowledge or virtue or any other grace, but do not rejoice in others' good; they even envy it. Therefore it happens quite rightly that they lose the good God gave them, for nothing can be good unless it is common to all. So when you wish the good that God gave you to be yours alone, you make evil of your good. And as you learn how to desire good in others so as better to exalt the name of the Lord God, so much more good will you have: like a flaming brand, the more it sheds brightness on the things around it the more things there are, and the less it sheds the fewer there are, and when it sheds no brightness then there are none.

E sachez, ma chere mere,[i] ki veut son ben aproprier a sei e k'il ne fuist mie comun, il veut ke Deu ne seit mie comun, donc veut il ke Deu ne seit mie Deu, kar il ne poet estre Deu se il ne seit comun.[ii] E Jesu Crist pur la soue misericorde ki si comunement espoundi sen sanc por toz vos[iii] defende de singulere amor.

La terce chose est ke si le noun Deu est issi saintifié en vous, vous loerez[iv] Deu en totes vos ovres, en manjaunt, en dormaunt,[v] e en quanke vos orrez[vi] e verrez. Ma chere mere,[vii] icestes choses ne [f.80v] poent pas estre ci parfites, kar en ceste mortele vie ne poum nos pas aver amor si tresordenee, mes isci devom nos sur totes choses desirer ke nos l'eom quant Deu plera e devom comencer a destrure les choses ki la desturbent.[viii] E Deus la nos doinst si comencer ci ke ele nus seit parfete en la vie pardurable ou nul desturber n'avera.

Ore avez veu[ix] [mon chier frere, P][x] ke le noun Deu est en la sue bonté par ki il est conneuue en totes creatures, kar nos nel poum pas veer en sa deité.[xi] Enkore poez vous plus avant[xii] e autrement entendre ke le noun [Deu] est Jesu Crist, kar nul home ne pot conuistre Deu en sa deité ne veer, mes quant il prist sanc e char de la tresdoce Virge Nostre Dame sainte Marie e devint home por nos chetifs par la soue tresgrant misericorde, donc le purent[xiii] toz veer e conoistre Deu e home. Pur ce est ce ben dit ke Jesu Crist, le fiz la tresgloriose Pucele, est vereiment le noun Deu. Ore preom donc nostre Pere del Cel ke le sen nun ki est nostre tresdoz Seignor Jesu Crist seit confermé en nos cuers,[xiv] c'est a dire, ke tote nostre amur seit ferme en Jesu Crist ki toz les bens nus fist e fet e fra par sa misericorde e totes les peines sofri por nos. Icest nun fu ben confermé [f.81r] el cuer saint Ignace ki respondi al tirant k'il ne pout a nul foer reneer Jesu Crist, kar il fu[xv] escrit en sen cuer. E le tirant, quant il li out fet[xvi] sacher le cuer,[xvii] si trova il escrit el quer par lettres d'or 'Jesu est m'amor.'[xviii] A ! doz Jesu Crist ! si vous feusez ben confermé en nos cuers, come nos ameriom mot poverté e meseise e vilté, s'il ne fust por el fors por vous resembler ! Tresdoz Deu de misericorde, vos veistes ben ke Lucifer vout estre semblable a vos e il ne pout ceo desirer sain peché. Por ce chaï il en[xix] enfer. Autresi Adam e Eve voleient come Deu saver ben e mal, e ne peurent ce desirer k'il fusent semblable a Deu sen peché.

---

[i] Not erased or expuncted as elsewhere. P has 'mon chier frere', DL 'beau frere'. [ii] DL omit 'comun … comun'. [iii] DLP 'nus'. [iv] DL 'nus lorrum', Pa 'loerrum'. [v] DL 'en bevant e en d.' [vi] DL 'overerez', Pa 'nus overum'. [vii] Again, not erased or expuncted as elsewhere. P has 'mon chier frere', DL 'Bau frere'. [viii] MS destrurent. [ix] DL 'oï'. [x] Erasure in MS. DL 'bau frere'. [xi] L 'sa dreit'. [xii] MS a avant. [xiii] DL 'porrum', P 'purreient', Pa 'poeint'. [xiv] MS cures. [xv] DL 'out'. [xvi] Final 't' is written above an expuncted 'r'. DL 'e le t. fist s.' [xvii] DLP add 'hors del ventre'. [xviii] DL omit 'est'. [xix] MS en en.

And know, my dear mother, that whoever wants to keep his good to himself, so that it is not in common, wants God not to be in common; so he wants God not to be God, for what is not in common cannot be God. And Jesus Christ in his mercy, who offered his blood for all so communally, forbids you such private love.

The third thing is that if the name of God is thus hallowed in you, you will praise God in all your doings: eating, sleeping, and when you hear and see. My dear mother, these things cannot be accomplished here, for in this mortal life we cannot have such well-governed love. But we should desire above all things to have it when it shall please God, and we should begin by destroying the things that trouble it. And God grant that we can begin love here so that it will be perfect in us in eternal life where no trouble can touch it.

Now [my dear brother,] you have seen that the name of God is in his goodness, by which he is known in all creatures, for we cannot see him in his godhead.[10] Further, you can understand more and differently that the name of God is Jesus Christ, for no man can know or see God in his godhead. But when he took blood and flesh from the gentle Virgin Our Lady Saint Mary and became man for us wretches by his great mercy, then all could see and know God and man. Therefore it is well said that Jesus Christ, Son of the most glorious Maiden, is truly the name of God. Now let us pray our Heavenly Father that his Name, that is our dear Lord Jesus Christ, may be established in our hearts; that is, that all our love may be steadfast in Jesus Christ, who did and does and will do all good things for us in his mercy, and who suffered all pains for us. This name was well established in the heart of Saint Ignatius, who answered the tyrant that he could in no wise deny Jesus Christ — it was written on his heart. And the tyrant, when he had the heart torn out, found written there in gold letters "Jesu is my love."[11] Ah, dearest Jesus Christ! If you were well established in our hearts, how greatly we would love poverty and discomfort and low estate, if for nothing else but to be like you! Sweet God of mercy, you saw that Lucifer wanted to be your equal, and he could not desire that without sin. For this he fell down into Hell. Similarly, Adam and Eve wanted to know good and evil, like God, and could not desire this — to be like God — without sin.

---

[10] See Dialogue (pp. 36–43, above), which contains a discussion of just how much of God a mortal can see.

[11] Ignatius of Antioch, bishop, was martyred under Trajan c. 107. He is widely quoted in England in the Middle Ages; see *GL* I:140–43. Adam has expanded the inscription: in the *Legend* it is simply "Jesus Christ" written on the heart.

Pur ce chaïrent il en peché e furent jeté hors de Paraïs. E vos, par la vostre tresdoz misericorde, feistes vos meimes povre e vil en tere por home, k'il puist ben e[i] saintement desirer a estre semblable a vous. Mes ore i a mult poi[ii] ki[iii] desirent poverté e vilté pur resembler vos, tresdoz Jesu Crist. Ben vodriom resembler vos en vos eneurs[iv] por estre anoré[v] come vous estes. Mes nos n'avum talent d'estre vil e povre e despit en tere come vos fustes pur nous. A las! doleros cheitifs! Donc nus[vi] vendra il a regner ové lui el Cel en tote [f.81v] sa gloire, si[vii] nus ke sumus tere e ordure e vil pecheros ne volum sofrir en tere poverté ne meseise e vilté ové lui, ki taunt en sofri pur nos pechez? Sachez [mon chier frere, P],[viii] ki ne poez sofrir ke l'em li meface e mesdie e ke l'en le despise, le noun Deu, c'est Jesu Crist, ne seit[ix] confermé en son cuer. Deu nostre Pere del Ceil conferme en nous sa bonté e son cher Fiz ke nous en tele manere le pussom ci amer e loer[x] en totes ses creatures e en sen cher Fiz,[xi] ki nos die al jor de jugement 'Venez[xii] le[s] beneiz fiz mun Pere', kar si le beneit noun nostre Pere del Cel est ci confermé en nos[xiii] cuers, nos serrom[xiv] al grant jugement apelé ses cher fiz beneiz.

[Petition 2] La secunde preere[xv] ke vos devez fere [mon chier frere, P][xvi] est ceste : *Adveniat regnum tuum* ; c'est a dire, 'Avegne toun regné'. Le regné Deu poez estre entendu en treis[xvii] maneres. Kar chescun home deit estre le regné Deu. Ce poez vos veer legerement, kar regné ne est autre chose ke tere sevree d'autre qui a motes cités e un rei ki les governe par sa justise. [Mun dolz frere, P][xviii] vostre cors est ceste tere[xix] e les cinc sens de vostre cors sunt le[s] ci[n]c cités, e les ovres ki issent e entrent par vostre veue e oie e le [f.82r] sentir del nes e gust e tast sunt la gent[xx] de ces cités. La reison de vostre alme qui juge entre[xxi] ben e mal est la justice e Deu vostre Pere est le rei. E idonc aprimes estes vous le regné Deu quant vostre reison, ki deit justiser vos cinc sens, n'a autre rei ne autre governor fors Deu. E si tost come ele veit nul ovre ne pensee[xxii] ki seit encontre la volenté le rei, tauntost come bone justice le defet e destrut, e les ovres e les pensees ki pleisent al rei meintent e multiplie a tot sen poer. E quant vostre reison en ceste guise sieut en toz ses jugement[s] la volenté son rei, ki est Rei del Cel, donc est ele franche e dame de tote la tere, des cités e de la gent, c'est a saver, de la char e de[s] sens, des ovres, des pensees.

---

[i] MS a. [ii] MS poie (with final letter expuncted). [iii] MS kil. [iv] DL 'oeveres'. [v] L omits 'anoré'. [vi] PPa 'vus'. [vii] DL 'kaunt'. [viii] Erasure in MS. DL 'bau frere'. [ix] DLP 'n'est pas'. [x] P 'ci beneistre e tutes'. [xi] DL omit 'Fiz ... Fiz'. [xii] DL 'devenez'. [xiii] DL 'voz'. [xiv] DL 'vus serrez'. [xv] In the left-hand margin is written in dry point 'la secunde prere'. [xvi] Erasure in MS. [xvii] P 'dous'. [xviii] Erasure in MS. DL 'bau frere'. [xix] DL 'rei'. [xx] DL 'les sens'. [xxi] MS entere. [xxii] Pa 'pecché'.

Thus they fell into sin and were thrown out of Paradise. And you, by your gentle mercy, made yourself poor and low on earth for man, so that he could in virtue and holiness desire to be like you. But now there are too few who desire poverty and lowliness in order to be like you, dear Jesus Christ. We would much rather be like you in your honour, to be honoured as you are. But we have no desire to be low and poor and despised on earth as you were for us. Alas, miserable wretches! Thus, how can we come to reign with him in Heaven in all his glory, if we who are earth and ordure and filthy sinners do not want to suffer poverty and discomfort and low estate on earth with him, who suffered so much for our sins? Know that whoever cannot bear to be mistreated and insulted and despised, the name of God — that is Jesus Christ — is not established in his heart. God our Heavenly Father confirm us in his bounty, and his dear Son, so that he will say to us on the Day of Judgement "Come, blessed children of my Father."[12] For if the blessed name of Our Father in Heaven is established here in our hearts, we shall be called his dear blessed children at the Great Judgement.

[Petition 2] The second petition you must make is this [my dear brother]: *Adveniat regnum tuum*, meaning "Thy Kingdom come." The kingdom of God may be understood in three ways: for every man ought to be the kingdom of God. You can see this easily, for a kingdom is nothing but land, separated from other land, that has many cities and a king who governs them through his judges. [Dearest brother], your body is this land, and the five senses of your body are its five cities, and the events that go out and in by your sight and hearing, and the sensations of your nose and taste and touch, are the people of these cities. Your soul's reason, that distinguishes between good and evil, is the judge; God your Father is the king. And so you are close to the kingdom of God when your reason, which ought to control your five senses, has no other king or governor but God. Like a good judge, as soon as it sees any deed or thought against the king's will, it will immediately undo and destroy it; it will maintain and multiply the deeds and thoughts that are pleasing to the king with all its might. And when your reason so follows the will of its king, who is the King of Heaven, in all its judgements, then it is free and mistress over all the land, its cities and its people; that is, over the flesh and the senses, deeds and thoughts.

[12] Matt. 25:34.

E si vos en iteu manere justicez vos meimes en terre, vos serrez por vostre bon servise aprés ceste vie reine coronee del cel.[i] Mes de ce vos donez guarde, ke le rei celestial e le rei terien ne sont pas de une manere, kar le rei terien ne poez pas veer la volenté d'ome, le rei del cel veit ben la volenté e pur ceo li un juge par les ovres e nostre Seignor par la volenté. E pur ce vus pri jo [mon chier frere, P][ii] ke sur tote ren vos aforcés a bone volenté, [f.82v] quei ke seit des ovres, ke vostre reison puisse dreitement juger solonc la volenté le Rei del Ceil e si ma reison consent[iii] en akun delit ki vegne de akun de[s] cinc sens ou ki en acune manere seit ancontre la volenté le Rei, tauntost li covent chaïr de sa segnorie e de sa justiserie e devenir serve plus vile e plus chative ke nule creature. A las ! A las ! Quel doel quant home lest de sun einzdegré[iv] la gregnor franchise de cest monde por devenir le plus vil serf del monde !

En autre manere poez entendre [mon treschier frere, P][v] ke Saint' Eglise ci en terre est le reaume Dampnedeu, kar la pape en ad la sovereine main[vi] desoz le rei, e les chardonaus e les eveskes e les arcediakes sont come contes e veskuntes e ballivs[vii] a governer le pople. E Jesu Crist est le chef e le rei de Saint' Eglise. E si nos pensisom e entendissom de verei cuer come icest rei descendi del Cel e devint home en la gloriose Pucele e puis mena si povre[viii] vie e si angoisose e au derein sofri la tresanguisuse mort de la croiz por delivrer nos almes de mort, les queles almes il a baillé as prelas de Sainte Eglise a guarder e a pestre,[ix] mot deusom aver grant pité en noz cuers quant nos veisom akun prelat plus mettre cure e amor a l'aver ke as almes guarder, kar il est mauveis pastur ki lest ses ouuales [f.83r] devorer a lous, kar il ne quert fors k'il eit le leit e[x] la leine. E iteus prelaz destruent le reaume Jesu Crist e despisent ses comaundemenz por la dolerose coveeitise de cest monde. E por ceo deusez vous preer de tot cuer ke vostre Pere del Cel feist les prelaz de Seinte Eglise teus k'il guvernassent sen people, ke sen reaume ne fust destrut. A ! las ! Quel doel si le rei de Engletere[xi] m'eust ballé une soue amie k'il mout amast a guarder e jo la veise defoler[xii] de ribaut en ma guarde ![xiii] Mout en serreie dolent, mes ke ele ne me feust mie bailee.[xiv] E cel traitre de prelaz ne se deudra mie quant il verra le deable estrangler e defoler ne mie une alme, mes plusurs ke Jesu Crist li a baillé en guarde come ses trescheres amies[xv] pur ki il sofri peine e mort en la croiz.

---

[i] The reviser who has erased references to female addressees has forgotten to alter the phrase. Cf. P which has 'rei del ciel'; and cf. p. 104, below. [ii] MS ma treschere mere (erased). [iii] DLP 'se c.' [iv] DL 'endreit'. [v] Erasure in MS. DL 'bau frere'. [vi] DLPPa 'la s. justice'. [vii] MS baslius. [viii] MS poivre. [ix] Pa 'a prestres'. [x] MS a. [xi] In the right-hand margin is written *similitudo*. [xii] DL 'defuler', P 'defulé'. [xiii] MS en maen gaurde. [xiv] DLPPa 'Mult en avereie grant doel si avereient autres en ki guarde ele ne fust mie' (P 'baillé'). [xv] DL 'ses chers amis', Pa 'ses treschers amis'.

And if you govern yourself in this way on earth, you shall for your good service be crowned queen in heaven after this life. But pay attention to this, that the celestial king and the earthly king are of different kinds. The earthly king cannot see the will of man; the heavenly king can see it well. So the one judges by deeds, and the other, Our Lord, judges by disposition. And so I urge you, [my dear brother,] strive to be of good will in all things, whatever the deeds may be, so that your reason may judge rightly according to the will of the Heavenly King. And if my reason consents to any pleasure that comes by way of the five senses, or which is in any way against the King's will, then it ought to fall from its lordship and office and become a slave more vile and wretched than any other creature. Alas! Alas! What sorrow, when a man of his own accord leaves the greatest freedom of the world to become the basest slave of the world!

In another way, [my dear brother,] understand that Holy Church here on earth is the kingdom of the Lord God; for the Pope has the sovereign hand below the King, and the cardinals and bishops and archdeacons are like counts and viscounts and bailiffs to govern the people. And Jesus Christ is the head, and the king of Holy Church. And if we think and understand truly in our hearts how this king came down from Heaven and became man in the glorious Maiden, and then led such a poor and painful life, and at last suffered a most agonizing death on the Cross to deliver our souls from death — those souls he entrusted to the prelates of Holy Church to keep and to feed — we should feel so much pity in our hearts when we see any prelate having more care and affection for possessions than for guarding souls. He is a bad shepherd who lets his sheep be devoured by wolves, for he seeks only to have the milk and the wool. Such prelates destroy the kingdom of Jesus Christ, and despise his commandments for the wretched covetousness of this world. Therefore you must pray fervently to your Father in Heaven, to make the prelates of Holy Church govern the people well, so that his kingdom shall not be destroyed. Alas! What sorrow, if the King of England had entrusted me with a friend he greatly loved, and I saw her corrupted by a lecher while in my care! I should be in despair — but she ought never to have been entrusted to me. And this traitor prelate will not mourn the least bit when he sees the Devil strangling and debauching not just one soul but many: those that Jesus Christ entrusted to his care as his dear friends, for whom he suffered pain and death on the Cross.

Priez, beau sire,[i] pur le regné Deu ki est Saint' Eglise k'il par sa misericorde meintegne toz les membrez ki sont seins[ii] e guarise ces ki sunt malades par peché mortel e reingne[iii] ces ki en sont severez par escomunication, e ces ki deusent estre membrez e onkes n'en furent por lor mescreantise face membrez de Saint' Eglise por la soue trespiteose mort k'il sofri por eus ausi ben come por nous.

En la terce manere devez prier ke le reaume vostre Pere del Cel avegne, icelui [f.83v] reaume ki serra quant tote Saint' Eglise vendra[iv] el Cel aprés le jor del jugement. E ce deusom nos sor tote ren desirer, kar la avrom nos la grant joie pardurable[v] ke nul home mortel ne poet penser e donc regnera Deus utreement en nos, kar nos ne desirom ren la fors la volenté al Rei del Cel. E avrom sens fin quancke nos saverom[vi] penser de joie e de delit en alme e en cors e serrom tot esseur ke jamés ne nos faudra. E sachez [mon chier frere, P][vii] ke en ceste mortele vie ne serra ja le regné Deu parfet en nos[viii] en[ix] itele manere ke toz noz senz e noz amors e nos ovres[x] seint del tot solonc la volenté Deu, kar totes hores contredit la char, mes nekedent totes feiz la deit en constreindre a servir a l'espirite ou bon gre ou mau gre, k'ele au dereint ne seit fors partie de la grant glorie la ou ele serra ausi lusaunte[xi] come le solail e donc serra tot parfitement e[n] totes choses un desir de cors e de alme senz nul contredit. E enkore i a il plus defautes en nos, kar tot fust la char consentaunt a l'espirit, la grant defaute de saver ki est en nos nos destorbe a amer totes choses solonc la volenté Deu, kar nos ne savon quele est sa volenté en motes choses. [Mon chier frere, P][xii] icest saver n'est pas apris par clergie, einz est par humilité, kar si vos reconessez vereiment ke de vos n'avez nul ben ne nul saver e priez Deu ki est fonteine de saver ki vos doinst entendement [f.84r] a reconoistre la souue volenté, sachez ke le Saint Espirit par sa tresgrant misericorde decendra en vos e vos enluminera de sa grace e ensegnera a estendre[xiii] vostre amur[xiv] solonc la soue volenté. E tant plus despirez vous meimes e plus vos tendrez a cheitive[xv] e a nient, taunt plus receverez sen e saver de la grace del Saint Espirit, autresi come vos veez d'un vessel ke quant il est parfont, il recevera mot euue.[xvi]

---

[i] Inserted after barring of 'tresdoce mere' before 'priez'. DP have 'Tresduz frere priez', L 'duz frere priez'. [ii] DL 'leinz'. [iii] DL 'remeigne le' (D 'el') 'cors de sainte esglise'. P has 'reiungne' written above 'remenge', which is followed by 'al cors de sainte iglise'; Pa has 'remeigne'. [iv] DL 'v. communement'. [v] MS pardurarable. DL omit 'avrom … rei el cel'. [vi] MS sarierom. [vii] Erasure in MS. DL 'bau frere'. [viii] P 'vus'. [ix] MS en en. [x] DL 'pensees'. [xi] DL 'set fiez plus l. que'. [xii] Erasure in MS. DL 'bau frere'. [xiii] DL 'destreindre', Pa 'entendre'. [xiv] Pa 'nostre feblesce'. [xv] 'cheitif' in the other MSS in accordance with the change of addressee. [xvi] DL 'ewe e tant cum serra plus parfund tant plus tendra ewe', P 'parfunt tant plus tendra ewe', Pa 'receit le plus de l'eawe e tant cum plus serra parfund tant plus receivra'.

Pray, dear sir, for the Kingdom of God which is Holy Church; that by his mercy he will preserve all those members that are healthy, cure those that are sick, and lead back those that have been severed by excommunication. And those who ought to be members but never have been because of their unbelief, make them members of Holy Church by that most piteous death he suffered for them as well as for us.

Thirdly, you must pray for your Heavenly Father's Kingdom to come: the Kingdom that shall be when all Holy Church comes to Heaven after the Day of Judgement. We should desire this above all things, for there we shall have that great everlasting joy that no mortal can imagine. And then God will reign in us in another way, because there we shall desire nothing but the will of the Heavenly Father. And we shall have as much as we can conceive of joy and delight, body and soul, without end, and we shall be assured it will never fail us. And understand [my dear brother]: in this mortal life the Kingdom of God will never be perfect so that all our senses and loves and deeds are completely in accord with God's will, for the flesh contradicts all the time. But nevertheless one must constrain it all the time, to serve the spirit whether it will or no, lest it fail at last to be part of the great glory there: where it will be shining like the sun. So, there will be perfectly, in all things, one desire in body and soul without any contradiction. And there are yet more faults in us: even when our flesh consents to the spirit, our great lack of wisdom prevents us from loving all things in accordance with God's will, for we do not know what his will is, in many things. This wisdom is not learned by study, but by humility: if you acknowledge truly that of yourself you have no goodness and no wisdom, [my dear brother,] and you pray God the fount of wisdom to give you understanding to know his will, be assured that the Holy Spirit by his great mercy will come down into you and illumine you with his grace and teach you to stretch out your love according to his will. And the more you despise yourself and the more you hold yourself to be a wretch and a nothing, the more you will receive sense and wisdom from the Holy Spirit, just as you see that a vessel, when it is deep, can hold a lot of water.

Pur ceo fu nostre tresdoce Dame Saint' Marie trépleine de grace e de saver, kar ele fu la plus umble femme ki onkes nasquid de mere e ki plus se tint petite e vile e neent, ne mie por ceo k'ele eust peché, la tresnette pucele, mes por ceo k'ele n'aveit nul ben de sai. E de ce ke ele aveit plus de saver ke nule autre fu ele outreement dame de sai, si k'ele pout e sout e vout par la vertu del Saint Espirit governer[i] toz ses sens e totes ses volentez a la volenté Deu. E pur ceo est ele reine sur tote la court del Ceil, kar ele en terre passa toz les autres par humilité e plus out de saver a governer sei come tresbone reine. De ceste humilité nous[ii] doinst Deus partir par sa misericorde, ke nos peussom cele grace receivre dount nos seom sages a governer ci nos volentés solonc la volenté Deu. Kar si issi le fesom, nos serrom reis coronez del cel totdiz taunt come Deus est Deus. [A ! mon treschier frere, P][iii] pensez dellore[iv] k'il vos[v] est [f.84v] si grant delit d'aver ci en tere une petite orete acune chose ke vos ben amez, come il vous serra tresgrant delit d'estre reine[vi] del Ceil senz fin ou vous n'averez mie une sole chose ke vos ben amerez, enz averez Deu Pere e Fiz e Saint Espirit e tote la ren del monde en quei home se porra deliter. Mes a ceste hautesce[vii] ne porrez vos avenir si vos ne vos tegnez vil(e) e despit(e)[viii] par vereie humilité, si ke Deus peusse en vos regner.

[Petition 3] La terce preere[ix] [mon cher frere, P][x] est *Fiat voluntas tua sicut in celo et in terra*, c'est a dire, 'La tou[e] volenté seit fete en tere sicome ele est fete a[s] ceus', c'est a dire, ke nous homes taunt come nos esmes en cest mortele vie façom la volenté nostre Pere dé ceus, sicome font li angle del Cel. E ce devom nos desirer de tot quer, kar Lucifer ki fu si tresbeaus,[xi] si tost come il guerpi[xii] la volenté Nostre Segnor e sewi sa propre volenté, devint il si tresled e si treshidos ke cel e tere le despitrent e le jeterent de sei jeske al puis d'enfern. Ausi fu il d'Adam e de Eve en Pareis, kar tant come il furent obeissant a la volenté Nostre Segnor, furent il segnors de tot le monde. Il furent si sein ke jamés ne lor covenist morir e se tost come il seuuierent[xiii] lur propre volenté, devindrent il cheitifs e servs al Diable.

[i] MS governor. DL omit. [ii] MS vous. [iii] Erasure in MS. DL 'bau frere'. [iv] The scribe seems to have confused 'delors' and 'desore'. P has 'de hore', DL 'del hure', Pa 'del oure'. [v] MS nos. [vi] The reviser has failed to note this reflection of the original female addressee. P, consistently, has 'rei'. DL read 'rei en ciel' here, Pa has 'reis coronez del ciel' (cf. p. 100 above). [vii] DL 'joie'. [viii] The feminine endings reflect the original addressee. DLPPa have 'vil' and 'despit'. [ix] In the left-hand margin is written in drypoint 'la terce prere'. [x] Erasure in MS. DL 'bau frere'. [xi] MS beues (with superscript insertion of 'a' and expunction of the second 'e'). [xii] MS guerps. [xiii] P 'siwirent'.

Therefore our dear Lady Saint Mary was filled full of grace and wisdom, for she was the humblest woman ever born of mother; and further, she held herself to be little and low and nothing. Not because she had sinned, that cleanest of maidens, but because she had no virtue of herself. And because she had more wisdom than all others, she was also mistress of herself; she could, would, and knew how to govern all her senses and all her will, by the virtue of the Holy Spirit, to God's will. Therefore she is Queen in all the court of Heaven, for on earth she surpassed all others in humility, and had more wisdom to govern herself like the best of queens. God in his mercy give us a share of this humility, so we may receive this grace: to be wise in governing ourselves here on earth according to God's will. For if we do this, we shall be crowned kings of Heaven for ever, just as God is God. [Ah, dearest brother], now think what joy it is to have here on earth, for a little space, something that you love very much. How great a joy will it be to be queen of Heaven for ever, where you will have not just one thing you love very much: you will have God the Father, the Son, and the Holy Spirit, and all those things that people of the world could take pleasure in. But you cannot come to this high estate unless you hold yourself low and despicable with true humility, so that God may reign in you.

[Petition 3] The third petition [my dear brother,] is *Fiat voluntas tua sicut in celo et in terra*, that is: "Thy will be done in earth as it is in Heaven." It means that we men, as long as we are in this mortal life, must do the will of our Father in Heaven, just as the angels of Heaven do. And we must desire this whole-heartedly, for Lucifer — who was so beautiful[13] — as soon as he abandoned Our Lord's will and followed his own he became so very ugly and hideous that heaven and earth despised him and threw him away from them, right down into the pit of Hell. Thus it was with Adam and Eve in Paradise, for as long as they were obedient to Our Lord's will they were lords of the whole world. They were so healthy that they were never going to die, and as soon as they followed their own will they became miserable and slaves of the Devil.

[13] See Is. 14:12ff.

E morir lor covint en tere aprés cest dolerose vie e puis entrer en enfern e enkore i alissom[i] nos por cel peché [f.85r] en enfer, ne fust ke le verrei Fiz Deu nostre tresdoz Segnor Jesu Crist nos eust rechaté par sa tresgrant misericorde quant il vout pur nos soffrir mort.[ii] Enkore est il issi, ke home ne poet nul ben fere ki li tort a salu de alme fors en tant come il siwt la volenté Deu, e toz les pechés comencent de ce ke home souet[iii] e eime sa propre volenté. Ore sachez donc ke taunt come vostre desir est a la volenté Deu, vos est[es] joint(e)[iv] en une volenté e en un espirit a lui, ki est vie pardurable e joie pardurable, en ki toz le[s] desirs ke quer de home set penser sont acompliz [e] plus. E si vos siueuz[v] vostre propre volenté e guerpissez la soue, vos vos sevrez de la vie [de] joie e de la vie pardurable. Donc Deus vus defende [mon duz frere, P],[vi] vos poez ben veer reison pur quei vos devez seivre la volenté nostre Segnor e despire la vostre, kar Deu nostre Pere poez totes choses e set quanke[vii] mester vos est a salu d'alme e de cors e vos eime plus ke vus meimes ne ferés e est si curios de vostre salu come s'il n'eust allors ren a fere. E por ce deveus[viii] de tot quer aforcer vus a siure la soue volenté e a despire [la] vostre, kar vos meimes ne poez ren[ix] ke de vos vegne fors peché ne ne savez quei mester vos est ne n'amez ce ke amer deusez.

E deus avantages vus avendrunt si issi ordenez vostre volenté par la grace Deu. L'une si est ke jamés [f.85v] coroscé ne dolant ne serrez for de sol peché, kar totes les choses ki avenent en tere sont solonc la volenté Deu fors peché sol [e] por ceo serreus[x] mervelles joios de totes les choses ke avenent fors de peché sol si vos amez la volenté Deu.[xi] E sachez si vous vos corescés de ren, enitant [siuez] vos vostre volenté, e taunt [plus] siurez vostre propre volenté, taunt plus avrez coroz e meseise. E ces ke plus despisent sei meimes e le monde plus unt joie en cest munde.[xii] L'autre avantage est ke si vos ne desirez fors la volenté Deu, vos serrez [sire][xiii] de totes les possessions de cest munde. Kar idonc aprimes est home segnor de sa chose quant il en poet fere ce k'il veut e quant la chose va del tot a sa volenté. En tele manere n'est nul riche home segnor de ceo[xiv] k'il a, kar il poet morir ou la chose poet perir ou autre la poet tolir ou il la poet vendre.[xv] E donc aprés[xvi] n'en porra il pas fere sa volenté.

---

[i] DL 'serium', Pa 'alaissum'. [ii] Erased are the words 'ma chere mere'. DLPPa have no addressee here. [iii] MS souent, P 'siwt', Pa 'siuent'. DL omit. [iv] 'joint' in the other MSS in accordance with change of addressee. [v] DLP 'siwez'. [vi] Erased in the MS are the words 'ma doce mere'. [vii] MS quanle. [viii] P 'devels'. [ix] DL 'r. quider'. [x] DL 'serirez'. [xi] DL 'avez la v. d. en vus'. [xii] DL 'el ciel'. [xiii] Blank in MS. DL have 'dame'. [xiv] DL 'nul h. r. de ceo'. [xv] DL omit 'ou … vendre'. [xvi] MS apris.

And they had to die on earth after that painful life, and then enter Hell. And we too would go to Hell because of that sin, were it not that the true Son of God, our dear Lord Jesus Christ, redeemed us by his great mercy when he sought death on our account. Yet it is so, that man can do nothing good towards the salvation of his soul except insofar as he follows God's will, and the beginning of all sins is that man follows and loves his own will. Understand: as much as your desire is to God's will, you are joined in one will and one spirit with him who is life and joy everlasting, in whom all desires the heart can imagine — and more — are accomplished. And if you follow your own will and forsake his, then you cut yourself off from the life of joy and from life everlasting. So, God help you, [dearest brother,] you can see good reason why you must follow Our Lord's will and despise your own, for God our Father can do all things, and knows when you have need of salvation for your soul and body. He loves you more than you do yourself, and is as anxious for your salvation as if he had nothing else to do. And so you must whole-heartedly make yourself follow his will and despise your own. For nothing comes of you yourself but sin, nor do you know what you need, nor do you love what you ought to love.

And two advantages will come to you, if you rule your will by the grace of God. One is that you will never be angry or sorrowful for anything but sin alone, for all the things that happen on earth — but sin alone — are according to the will of God. So you will be marvellously joyful for everything — but sin alone — that happens, if you love God's will. And know that if you get angry about anything, you are following your will: the more you go on following your own will, the more you will feel anger and unease. And those who most despise themselves and the world will have the most joy in this world. The second advantage is that if you desire nothing but God's will, you will be master or mistress[14] of all the world's possessions. For a man is close to mastery of his own when he can do what he wants with it, and when all goes entirely to his liking. Hence no rich man is master of what he has, for he may die or the thing may perish, or another may take it from him or he may sell it. And then he cannot do what he wants with it.

[14] "sire" has been supplied (as elsewhere), in accordance with the practice of this scribe, to fill the blank in the MS at this point. Other mss have "dame."

Mes quant le home a tot guerpi pur amur Deu,[i] k'il ren ne desire fors la volenté Deu, [idonc][ii] aprimes corent totes les choses del monde a sa volenté e grant joie a d[e][iii] totes choses, quei ke avegne, fors de [sul] peché. Kar il poet donckes en totes aventures la volenté veer Deu k'il taunt eime. E sachez ke[iv] d'autant[v] come ci guerpirez plus vostre propre volenté por la volenté Deu, d'autaunt vus dorra Deu plus [de][vi] joie [f.86r] de sei meimes e acomplira vostre volenté pardurablement. E ki despit la volenté Deu e sueit la suue, il li toudra pardurablement la sue propre volenté, ke jamés sen fin ren n'avra de ce k'il desire. De ce nus[vii] defende Deus par sa pité. Icest estat afert especiaument a [vus homes, P][viii] de religion. Kar por ceo estes vos sevrez del secle, ke vous peusez meuz restreindre vostre veu[e] e vostre launge e vos autre sen[s][ix] e ke en tele manere peusez recore[x] a vos meimes e quere[xi] dedenz vostre quor quele seit la volenté vostre Segnor en totes choses, ke vos ren ne amés ne ne desirez fors ce ke vos quidez ke seit a sa volenté. E si issi le fetez, vos receverez en ceste vie si tresgrant joie ke nul ne savereiz dire fors celui ki l'a esprové e sentu, e avrez aprés la mort vie pardurable sicome nostre Seignor le dit en la [e]vvangile. Si aut[r]ement le fetes, vos le comperez a mult chere derreez.[xii]

[Petition 4] La quarte preere[xiii] est *Panem nostrum cotidianum da nobis hodie*, c'est a dire, 'Le nostre pain k'il covent chescun jor aver donez nos oui.' Icest poet en entendre en deus meneres : ow del pain donc[xiv] le cors est sustenu une petite hore ow del pain donc l'alme est sustenue a toz jorz e le cors ensement. Icestui est le verrei pain ki done vie pardurable a[xv] ces ki le manjuent. Si nos demaundom icest pain ki est la grace Deu e le desi[f.86v]rom de fin quer, il le nos dorra e de l'autre ensement, sicome il meimes pramet en la evvangile : 'E priét primez le regné Deu e asez avrez de temporeus choses.' Ore entendét,[xvi] ma doce mere,[xvii] ke cors de home e de bestes dechet totes hores par l'ardor[xviii] e par la corruptiun ki est dedenz la cors s'il ne seit susteneu par norrisement de viande. E quant il a defaute de norissement, donc a il feim, si il est sein de cors, e desire a manger. Mes si il est malade, il avent sovent ke por la maladie ne poet il sentir sa defaute ne ne desire point a manger.

---

[i] DL 'g. amur de sei'. [ii] A blank without signs of an erasure. [iii] A letter has been erased after 'd'. [iv] Followed by an erasure. [v] MS dauatant. [vi] Erasure in MS. DL omit 'de'. [vii] DL 'vus'. [viii] Erasure in MS. DLPa 'gent de r.' [ix] Followed by erasure. [x] Followed by erasure of two letters. P has 'retorner', DL 'recoverer'. [xi] P 'que rien d.' [xii] P 'chieres dereies', DL 'deres'. [xiii] In the left-hand margin is written in drypoint 'la quarte prere'. [xiv] Followed by 'l'alme est' which has been expuncted. [xv] MS e. [xvi] In the left-hand margin is written in drypoint *similitudo*. [xvii] The reviser has omitted to remove this indication of the original addressee. P, consistently, has 'mon duz frere', DL 'bau frere'. [xviii] DL 's'ordure', Pa 'l'ordure'.

But when the man has forsaken everything for God's love, he desires nothing but God's will. And next, all things in the world hasten to his will and he has great joy in all things, whatever happens, except only sin. For in everything that happens he can see the will of God whom he loves so much. And know that as much as you forsake your own will here for the will of God, so much more will God of himself give you joy, and fulfil your will for ever. And whoever despises God's will and follows his own, God will take away his own will from him for ever, so that he will never, ever, have what he desires. God in his mercy defend us from this! The matter concerns you religious men and women especially: for why else are you shut away from the world? So that you can better restrain your eyes and your tongue, and your other senses, so that you may look into yourselves and seek in your heart for what the Lord's will is in all things; so, you may love and desire nothing but what you believe will be according to his will. And if you do this you will receive in this life such great joy, that none could speak of it except him who had experienced and felt it, and you will have after death the life everlasting as Our Lord says in the Gospel.[15] If you do otherwise, you will pay a very dear price for it.

[Petition 4] The fourth petition is *Panem nostrum cotidianum da nobis hodie*, that is: "The bread which it is proper for us to have every day, give us today." One may understand this in two ways:[16] either the bread that sustains our body for a little time, or the bread that sustains the soul for ever — and the body as well. The latter is the true bread that gives everlasting life to those who eat it. If we ask for this bread that is God's grace, and wish for it with a pure heart, he will give it to us, and the other as well, as he himself promises in the Gospel: "And pray first for the Kingdom of God and you shall have your fill of temporal things."[17] Now understand, my sweet mother, that the body of a man, and of beasts, is decaying all the time because of the heat and the foulness that is within it, if it is not sustained by the nourishment of food. When nourishment is lacking then he is hungry, if he is healthy, and wants to eat. But if he is ill, then often, because of the illness, he does not feel the lack and does not want to eat.

---

[15] See e.g. John 10:28.

[16] See *Pater Noster*, ed. Aarts, p. 40 and note to ll. 11–12 (on p. 109): "A material interpretation of the bread is found in the work of most exegetes."

[17] Matt. 6:33.

Autresi est il en alme, kar Jesu Crist est la vie de l'alme, e la grace del Saint Espirit est le pain par ki l'alme est sustenue en sa tresdelitose vie ki est Jesu Crist. E por ce ke [l']alme en cest dolerose vie est jointe a la char, ele dechez totdis e se remue de sa vie ki est Jesu Crist par la corruption de la char si ele ne seit sustenue par le pain ki est la grace del Saint Espirit. E por ceo covent il, ne mie une sole feiz mes totes hores, desirer de tot cuer e demander cest pain, kar quele hore ke le norisement de cest pain faut a l'alme, ele dechet erraument de sa vie gloriose jeske a la tresdolerose mort. Ore veét ben [mon duz frere, P][i] por quei cest pain est ben apelé 'de chescun jor', kar nos en avum chescun jor tresgrant mester. Mes [f.87r] quant alme est [si] tresmalade par peché, ke ele est tot enmortie, donc n'a ele poin de faim ne[ii] desir de manger cest pain, einz refuse icestui[iii] pain dunt les angles sunt sustenuz e se delite en celui qui est pouture al Diable, c'est a dire, au delit de la char e a la vanité del monde. E desoz ces deliz ki ne durent fors poi de hore est covert le ameçon[iv] al Diable ki treit l'alme jeske a la mort pardurable.

[Mon chier frere, P],[v] ore vus aprenderai[vi] coment vos ne perderez[vii] [ja] par la grace Deu la tresdelitose feim e le tresdoz desir de cest gloriose pain. Ne vos delitez mie en chose ki prent fin, e senz faille vus avrez delit de celui pain ki ne prent fin. Ore dirreit akun, fort serrét de lesser le solat de totes creatures[viii] e je vos di ke non est, kar le delit de chose ki prent fin termine en dolor, kar taunt come le delit est gregnor, taunt est la fin plus dolerose. E ki ben se[ix] reguardast il ne querreit ja solaz en chose ki prent fin. D'autre part, il est propre nature de home k'il se delite[x] en sa chose e ne mie en l'autri, mes en ceo ki suen est, e sac[hez][xi] ke ren n'est a dreit vostre ki vos poet estre tolé maugré le vostre.[xii] Celes sunt totes choses ki pernent fin. Donc ne se deit home deliter en nule ren ki prent fin, kar n'est pas sa chose. Mes la grace Deu, si vos l'avez,[xiii] nul home ne la vus poet tolir maugré vostre, ne Deus ne veut. Donc jamés ne la perderez si vos meimes ne la guerpi[sez].[xiv] Por [f.87v] ce l'apelum nos ben nostre pain, kar a nul for perdre nel poum si nos meimes ne volum, e por ce deussum nos cestui[xv] desirer e en lui deliter, kar il est vereiment nostre e n'a nul delit ne solaz en creature ke en lui ne seit. E enkore plus ke nul home mortel ne sache penser, icestui[xvi] pain poez vous trover dedenz vous si vous retreez[xvii] vous senz de forains deliz.

---

[i] Erasure in MS. [ii] MS ne ne. [iii] MS icestii. [iv] Pa 'e ceo l'enticement'. [v] Erasure in MS. DL 'bau frere'. [vi] In the right-hand margin is written in drypoint *similitudo inter panem et panem.* [vii] MS peiserez. [viii] MS crea creatures. [ix] DL 'ço', Pa 'ceo'. [x] DLP 'd. e quert solaz, Pa 'd. querge solaz'. [xi] Erasure in MS. DLP 'e rien n'est', Pa has 'e rien est'. [xii] PPa have 'nostre', 'nus' and 'nostre'. [xiii] DL 'l'avez desservi'. [xiv] There is an erasure in the MS. [xv] MS cestii. [xvi] MS cestii. [xvii] MS retieez.

Thus it is with the soul, for Jesus Christ is the life of the soul, and the grace of the Holy Spirit is the bread by which the soul is sustained in its most delicious life that is Jesus Christ. And because the soul in this sorrowful life is joined to the flesh, it decays all the time and moves away from its life, Jesus Christ, because of the foulness of the flesh, if it is not sustained by the bread that is the grace of the Holy Spirit. And that is why it behoves us, not just once but all the time, to desire and ask for this bread whole-heartedly, for in the same hour that this bread's nourishment fails the soul, then it quickly falls from its glorious life straight to a most sorrowful death. Now see [dearest brother,] why this bread is well named "daily," for we have great need of it every day. But when the soul is so very sick through sin that it is paralyzed, then it feels no hunger nor desire to eat this bread. So it refuses this bread upon which the angels are fed,[18] and delights in the Devil's filth — that is to say, in pleasure of the flesh and vanity of the world. And under these delights, that last no more than a little while, is hidden the Devil's hook that drags the soul to everlasting death.[19]

Now I shall teach you, [my dear brother,] by the grace of God, how you will never lose that delicious hunger and sweet desire for this glorious bread. Never take delight in things that come to an end, and you will not fail to have delight in the bread that never comes to an end. Now you might say it is hard to give up what is the pleasure of all created things, but I tell you it is not so, for the pleasure of finite things ends in pain: the greater the delight the more painful the ending. Whoever looks well at himself will never seek pleasure in any finite thing. On the other hand, it is the proper nature of man to delight in his things and not in another's, in what is his own; understand that nothing is rightfully yours which can be taken from you against your will. Those are all things that come to an end. Therefore man must not delight in a thing that comes to an end, for it is not his thing. But nobody can take the grace of God from you against your will, if you have it, unless God wills it. So you will never lose it unless you yourself abandon it. So it is well named "our bread," for we can by no means lose it unless we ourselves want to, and so we must desire it and delight in it because it is truly ours; and there can be no delight or pleasure in any creature, where this bread is not. And even more than any mortal man can imagine, you may find this bread inside yourself if you remove your senses from external delights.

[18] See Ps. 78:25 (in *AV*).

[19] For the Devil's hook, see Hab. 1:15; cf. *FM*, p. 697.

E si le poez trover en chescune creature si vus estes se sage e si querante[i] com sont les es ki trovent le mel sor chescune flur de ceste monde, kar il sont si sages k'il ne demorent mie sor la flor pur reguerder la beauté ne por sentir l'odor ne por manger la flor,[ii] si ele est saverose, ne ne eschivent pas la flur, si ele est lede ou pullente ou amere, einz descendent sur la flur, quele ke ele seit, ne mie pur la flur, mes por le mel ke lei trovent, kar quele ke l'erbe seit, le [mel est mult] doz.[iii] Il i a autre manere de mosche e de verms ki manjue la foille e la flor, kar il ne sevent pas trover le mel. Autel est il de vos, bele mere,[iv] ke si vous estes sage e ben querante[v] come le e, vos troverez en chescune flur de ceste munde le mel, c'est a dire en chescune creature porre[z] vous sentir e trover la tresgrant largesce e la tresgrant bonté Deu nostre Pere, kar il fist totes choses ne mie pur nul bosoing, mes par [sa] sole bone volenté. Mes sachez, quant vostre amur se repose sur la [f.88r] creature, ou por la beauté ou por la richesce ou por akun delit k'ele i trove ki prent fin e ne se estent mie outre a la tresgrant amur nostre Segnor, ki est mostree en chescune creature, vos a icel hore perdez le tresdoz mel celestial e mangez la amere foile[vi] ki pert doce a ces ki n'ont point tasté del mel. Di ! cest glorious mel fu la mere Deu, nostre tresdoce Dame pleine, kar ele se tint si a petite, k'ele ren ne vout user de sa propre volenté, mes del tot outreement sewi la volenté Deu e ele en nul tens ne en sei meimes ne en autre creature ren ne desira fors l'enor e la bonté sen Creatur. E por ce k'ele de tot quer desirra icest glorious pain fu ele digne de aver le pain tot entier, kar ele fu [si] famelose e isi croese[vii] par humilité ke nule partie[viii] del pain ne la poet esauler devant ce k'ele out tot quant ele conceut le verrei fiz Deu, nostre[ix] tresdoz Segnor Jesu Crist.

[Petition 5] Aprés ce vent la quinte preere :[x] *Et dimitte nobis debita nostra sicut et nos dimittimus debitoribus nostris*, c'est a dire, 'Relessez nos nos deites, sicome nos relessom a nos detors.' Ceste preere mont[e] a taunt : 'Deu, nostre Pere, relessez nos nos pechez ke nos avom fet acontre Voz, sicome nos pardonom a ces ke unt peché encontre nos.' Ore entendez, beau sire,[xi] a ce ke Deus nos ensegnera[xii] a dire.

[i] Another relic of the original female addressee. LP have 'querant', D 'querante'. [ii] DL 'foille'. [iii] Erasure in MS between 'le' and 'doz'. [iv] Again, the reviser forgot to clear a reference to the original addressee. P has 'beal frere', DL 'bau frere'. [v] DLPPa 'querant', consistently adjusting to the new addressee. [vi] MS folle. [vii] DL 'e desiruse', Pa 'curiuse'. [viii] DL 'pece'. [ix] MS vostre. [x] In the left-hand margin is written in drypoint 'la quinte prere'. [xi] Written above 'ma doce mere' which has been deleted by a bar. P has 'mon duz frere', DL 'bau frere'. [xii] DL 'vus enseignerai'.

And if you are able to find it in all creatures, then you are as wise and persistent as the bees that find honey in every flower of this earth, for they are so wise that they never linger on a flower to behold its beauty or smell its scent, nor to eat the flower if it is tasty; nor do they avoid the flower if it is ugly or smelly or bitter. But they come down to the flower, whatever it is, not for the flower itself but for the honey they find there. For whatever the plant is, the honey is very sweet.[20] There are other kinds of fly and worm that eat the flower and the leaf, for they do not know how to find the honey. So it is with you, dearest mother: if you are wise and a good seeker like the bee, you will find the honey in every flower on this earth. That is to say, in every creature you will be able to feel and find the great generosity and goodness of God our Father, for he made all things — not out of necessity but solely through his good will. But know that when your love is set upon the creature, whether for beauty or riches, or for any delight it perceives that is mortal and does not stretch out to the great love of Our Lord that is revealed in all creatures, at that moment you lose the sweet celestial honey and you eat the bitter leaf that appears sweet to those who have never tasted honey. O God! This glorious honey was the Mother of God, our sweetest Lady, for she held herself to be so small that she wanted to exercise nothing of her own will, but she followed God's will completely in everything. And never, not in herself nor in any other creature, did she desire anything but the honour and goodness of her Creator. And because she whole-heartedly desired this glorious bread she was worthy to receive the Whole Bread, for she was so famished and hollowed out by humility that no portion of bread could sate her, until she received all of it when she conceived the true Son of God, our blessed lord Jesus Christ.

[Petition 5] After this comes the fifth petition, *Et dimitte nobis debita nostra sicut et nos dimittimus debitoribus nostris*, that is: "Release us from our debts, just as we release our debtors." The prayer amounts to this: "God our Father, release us from our sins that we have committed against you, just as we forgive those who have sinned against us." Now listen, dear sir, to what God will teach us to say.

[20] We have been unable to find a direct source for Adam's image of the bee gathering the good in others to make the honey that is spiritual bread. In Aldhelm's treatise *De Virginitate*, presented to Barking Abbey (c. 675), the nuns are encouraged to be hungry like the bees and fill themselves with the "booty of scriptural gathering" (Aldhelm, *The Prose Works*, pp. 61–63). This notion resembles the idea developed here, but is unlikely to be Adam's source. For a comprehensive discussion of bee imagery in a number of medieval contexts, see Griffiths 2007, pp. 91–107.

I pert al comencement ke peché ne seit mie dette envers Deu, mes toz les benz ke nos avom sont deite envers lui, kar les bens avom nos de soun prest e de [f.88v] son don.[i] E les maus venent de nos meimes e por ceo sont il nostre propre chatel. A ceste chose devez respondre ke ren ke nos eom n'est deite envers Deu fors peché sol.[ii]

Ore veez la manere coment.[iii] Si jo sui serjaunt un riche home e il me eit baillé ses deners a despendre en son servise, si jo les despent a sa volenté, jo ne sui pas de taunt sun detor. Mes si jo prenc les deners ke jo deusse despendre en son servise e les met allors a la moie volenté e ne mie a la sowe, de ce li su ge verreiment dettor. En tele manere vos di ge ke Deus nos a ballé motes graces pur despendre les a sa volenté. E quant vos les[iv] despendez a sa volenté,[v] vos li estes tenu a graces rendre e ne mie a deite. Mes si vos nule rien turnez a vostre volenté encontre la volenté Deu, de ço li deveus respondre come de dette. A las ! A las ! taunt avreit chescun de nos grant hunte de fere une deslauté encontre la volenté sen segnor ou sen ami,[vi] e n'avon pas honte de fere desleauté a Deu, ki nos fist de neent e rechata de soen cher sanc e nos a doné tot kanke nos avom de ben ! E si ne poum nul mal fere k'il ne veit tot.[vii] Mes sour totes ces choses m'est il avis ke la miseri[cor]de Deu nos deust mervelles de peché retrere, kar kant il est si tresdeboneire ke ja taunt ne taunt sovent n'avrom peché si nos en dreite repentance le preom merci, il nos pardura tantost ne il ne quert plus par sa tresgrant doçor fors ke nos nos repentom de fin quer. A ! Deus ! coment ose nul fere encontre la volenté a si tresdoz Segnor ? [f.89r] Iceste doçor nos mostra ben nostre Segnor quant il vout ke nos preissom pardom de nos pechez envers lui ausi come nus pardonom a ces ki unt peché encontre nos. Kar nul home ja taunt ne nos mesface ne pecche d'asez taunt encontre nus come nos fesom encontre Deu. Kar sicome dist saint Austin : 'Si jo me curruz[viii] de chose ke mon prosme face encontre mei, il n'est pas cause de mon curruz,[ix] en[z] sui jo meimes. E pur ceo deusse jo prendre venjance de mei meimes e ne[x] mie de lui.' E veez la reison pur quei, beau sire.[xi] Si ci fust un fort champion e un petit fieble garson le asausist, ben veez k'il ne porreit duree aver encontre le champion.

[i] Pa 'n'avum mie de soen don, mes de prest'. [ii] Pa 'ci poez entendre ke de tutes les choses ke nus avum, eimes endettés envers Deu fors de pecché sul.' [iii] In the left-hand margin is written in drypoint *similitudo*. [iv] MS ules (with barring of the first letter). [v] 'a sa volenté' has been inserted in the left-hand margin. DLP has 'q. v. si les d.' [vi] P 'tant a verite chescun de nus grant honte serreit une d. e. la v.' [vii] P 'kil nel veit'. [viii] Written above 'corroz'. [ix] Written above 'corroz'. [x] Written above 've' deleted by barring. [xi] Written above 'bele mere' which has been deleted by a bar. P has 'beau frere'. DL omit reference to the addressee.

It may seem at first that sin is no debt towards God, though all the good we have is owed to him: we have good things because he supplies and gives them to us, and evils come from us, ourselves, and therefore they are our own belongings. To this, you must answer that nothing we have is owed to God excepting only sin.

Now look, it is this way: if I am the servant of a rich man and he has handed over his money to me to spend in his service, if I spend it according to his will I am not in debt to him for it. But if I take the money that I ought to spend in his service and lay it out elsewhere, at my pleasure and not at his, I am indeed in his debt for it.[21] In this manner, I say to you, God has entrusted many talents to us, to spend according to his will. And when you spend them so, then you are deemed to have returned them to him and not to be in debt. But if you divert anything to your own purpose, against God's purpose, you will have to answer for that as for a debt. Alas! Alas! How ashamed any one of us would feel, to do such disloyalty against the will of our lord or our friend, and would not be ashamed to act disloyally to God, who made us from nothing and gave us everything good that we have! And further, we can do no evil thing but he sees it all. But above all things I believe that the mercy of God does marvellously to draw us back from sin: he is so very gentle that as soon as, as often as, we sin and with righteous repentance beg his mercy, he forgives us straight away; nor does he ask more, he is so very merciful, than that we repent with pure heart. Ah God! How does anybody dare to go against the will of such a gentle Lord? Our Lord shows his gentleness to us when he wants us to beg forgiveness for our sins against him, as we forgive those who have sinned against us. For nobody ever commits so much sin or misdeed against us as we do against God. For, as Saint Augustine says, "If I am angered at something my neighbour does against me, he is not the cause of my anger. It is I myself. Therefore I ought to be revenged upon myself and not upon him." And look at the reason why, dear sir: if there were a strong champion and a feeble little boy assaulted him, you can see the boy could not last long against the champion.

[21] The example of the servant with his master's money is found also in "Treatise on Job" (ed. Taguchi, p. 181). The corresponding passage is headed, as ours is, by the petition *Dimitte nobis*; the idea is an extension of the Parable of the Talents (Matt. 25:14–30), as is suggested in the next sentence here.

Si le champion de sun einzdegré se lessat chaer a tere desoz le garson, si ke le garson le defulast e crevast les euz, [ceo] feist a reter[i] premerement al chanpion. Autresi est il parde[ça], kar alme de home passe totes autres creatures ke vos poez veer de vigor e de nobleté, si ke nule ren de cest monde ne la poet blecer si ele meimes ne s'abesse[ii] a terre por estre defolee. Issi est il : quant l'en nos mesfet ou mesdit, tenez vostre alme en haut ové Deu, come afert a sa nature, e ja ne vos coroscerez ; e grant[iii] vilté fetes quant vos la lessés chaer a la longaine[iv] pur estre defolee de checune ordure. Bele doce mere,[v] pur nostre Segnor Jesu Crist ki tant sofri pur vos, sovegne vos de cez moz, ke vos peusez akune chose sofrir[vi] pur lui.[vii]

[Petition 6] [L]a[viii] sime preere[ix] si est cest : *Et ne nos inducas in temptationem*, c'est [f.89v] a dire, 'Ne nos parmenez[x] mie en temptation.' E ne devez pas preer ke vous ne seez pas tempté, mes ke vous ne seez vencu[xi] par temptation. Kar saint Jake[xii] nos ensegne ke nos devom aver mervelles grant joie quant nos chaom en diverses temptations. Kar autresi come l'or est purgé par le feu e le chevaler en dure bataille prové a bon,[xiii] autresi est home purgé par temptation e esprové a bon, si il ne se lesse veintre. Donc porrez vos aver espeir de grant vertu quant vos estes mot tempté,[xiv] kar saint Agustin dist ke la perfection de chescune vertu est par ceo ke home est mot troblé par temptation ki est contrarie. Kar autresi come vos veez ke quant un home veut ficher un pel en tere ben ferme,[xv] il fert d'on mail sor le pel treis feit ou quatre e quant le pel ne descent nent plus, donc fert il le pel a destre e a senestre pur alargir la fosse, ki le peusse ficher plus parfont e puis[xvi] fert sur le pel e derechef a destre e a senestre, e puis a drein le bat en tere, e donc serra le pel d'asez plus ferm fiché en tere k'il ne serreit si il n'eust esté point esloché, fors feru dreit aval, ausi fet nostre Segnor, kar quant il veut[xvii] k'un home seit tres ben ferme en akune vertu, donc le loche il a destre e a senestre pur ficher la vertu plus ferme en son quor. Eez donc grant joie quant nule temptation vos vent. Jo ne di pas ke vous seez pur ceo dolent quant ele ne vos vent mie, kar Deus la vous enverra si il veit ke mester vos [f.90r] seit.

---

[i] P 'areiter'. [ii] Pa 'e chet a t.' [iii] MS quant. [iv] P 'v. l'abeissez p.', DL 'la lessez leidement estre d.' [v] The reviser has once more failed to clear the reference to the original addressee. P has 'beau duz frere', DL 'bau frere'. [vi] MS sofrrr. [vii] Pa 'lui ki tute dolur suffri pur nus'. [viii] A red initial has been effaced. [ix] In the left-hand margin is written in drypoint 'la sime prere' and in the right-hand margin *sexta*. [x] DL 'amenez'. [xi] A final 'e' has been erased in accordance with the clearing of indications of the original addressee. [xii] DL 'Jacob'. [xiii] In the left-hand margin has been written in drypoint 'semblance'. [xiv] A final 'e' has been erased. [xv] In the left-hand margin has been written in drypoint 'semblance'. Pa has 't. pur ester b. f.' [xvi] MS plus puis. [xvii] DL 'veit'.

If the champion of his own accord lets himself fall to the ground under the boy, and if the boy trampled him and poked his eyes out, then the champion would be primarily to blame. Likewise, in this: the soul of man surpasses all other creatures you can see, for vigour and nobility: nothing in this world can wound it unless it lowers itself to the earth to be trampled. Thus it is: when anybody does or says anything bad to us, keep your soul up on high with God, as is proper for it, and never become angry; you do a very vile thing when you let it fall into the sewer to be defiled by every foulness. Dear mother, for Our Lord Jesus Christ's sake who suffered so much for us, remember these words so that you may be able to suffer something for him.

[Petition 6] The sixth petition is this: *Et ne nos inducas in temptationem*, that is to say: "Do not lead us into temptation." You must not pray not to be tempted, but pray not to be overcome by temptation.[22] For Saint James teaches us we ought to feel marvellous great joy when we fall into many temptations.[23] As gold is purified by the fire and the knight is proved good in harsh battle, so a man is purified by temptation and proved good if he does not let himself be overcome. You may hope to achieve great virtue when you are much tempted, for Saint Augustine said that the perfection of each virtue is because a man is much troubled by a hostile temptation. For you see, when somebody wants to fix a post into very firm ground, he strikes the post with a maul three or four times. When the post will go down no further, then he strikes the post to the right and to the left to enlarge the hole, so he can thrust it in deeper, then he bangs on the post once more, to right and left, then he hammers it straight down into the earth. Then the post will be more firmly fixed in the earth than if it had not been knocked sideways instead of hammered straight down. So Our Lord does, for when he wants a man to be very firm in any virtue, then he hammers him to the right and to the left to fix the virtue more firmly in his heart.[24] Have great joy, then, when any temptation comes to you. I am not saying you should therefore be sorrowful if none comes at all, for God will send it you when he sees you have need of it.

---

[22] See I Cor. 10:13.

[23] James 1:2.

[24] Cf. *BVV*, p. 114: St Bernard says that when the tempter smites us on the back with his hammer, he is forging crowns of joy for us. In this passage, God employs the devil, as tempter, to assay his new knights (cf. *PL* 183:858).

Mes priez li ke il[i] vous sofre a estre tempté,[ii] ne vous soefre a estre vencu,[iii] mes vous doinst vertu a rester a la temptation. E si vos volez aver vertu de rester, reconessez de verrei quer ke vos meimes n'avez poi[n]t de vertu fors grant enfermeté e peché e dolor e ke[iv] en Deu e de Deu est tote vostre vertu. E afiez vos de tot quer en la misericorde nostre Segnor, e tant plus vos tendrez a fieble e a cheitive,[v] taunt plus avrez force de Deu a rester as essauz del deable e del monde e de la char. Tele fu nostre tresdoze Dame, kar por ce ke ele [se] tint si petit[e] de sai fu ele pleine de la vertu Deu ke nule manere de angoisse ne la pout veintre. E sachez [beau frere, P][vi] ke ceste manere de humilité ne vaut mie solement encontre temptation, einz vaut a purger peché e a monte[r] en charité plus ke nule penance de cors, kar quant home reguarde sa ordure e sa febleté de cors e de alme, molt en a gregnor dolor a quer k'il n'avreit de nule penaunce de cors. E de autre part penaunce de cors fet sovent monter alme en orgoil, mes quant home reconuist sa cheitiveté,[vii] ce le fra totdis homble. E sachez ke si vos eez ceste humilité, tote autre penaunce vos semblera legere.

[Petition 7] [L]a[viii] setime preere[ix] est *Sed libera nos a malo*, c'est[x] a dire, 'Delivrez nos de mal.' En ces paroles deveus[xi] preer ke Deu vus delivre de mal de peché e de mal de peine.[xii] E[n] ceste preere devez requellir especiament lez al[f.90v]mes de purgatorie, ke Deu[xiii] par sa merci les oste de peine. Beau sire,[xiv] si vous volés veer les maus ke home sofre en ceste siecle e les meseises, pernez guarde[xv] de l'estat de home einz ke il eust peché, kar autrement ne verrez vos pas les defautes nent plus ke si un enfant mesel fust né en une chartre[xvi] e ne fust hunkes issu hors de la chartre ne n'eust veu home sein ; il quedereit estre en bon estat de home. Mes se il eust veu un home sein e la clarté del solail, donc dirreit[xvii] il k'il fust chaitif e malades.

[i] MS reads 'li ke' followed by an erasure and 'il ke'. P has 'p. li kil ke v.' [ii] A final 'e' has been erased to conceal the originally female addressee. DL omit 'vous … tempté'. [iii] Again a final 'e' has been erased. [iv] DL 'e regeiz que de Deu'. [v] The reviser has failed, unlike DLP, to clear the feminine ending. [vi] Erasure in MS. The word 'mere' is still legible. [vii] Followed by an erasure. [viii] A red initial has been effaced. [ix] In the left-hand margin there is written in drypoint 'la setime prere' and in the right-hand margin *septima*. [x] MS ceste. [xi] P 'develz'. [xii] MS mal e de peine. P 'de mal p. e de m. de p.', DL 'male peine'. [xiii] Followed by blank in MS. [xiv] Written over an erasure. DLP have 'beau frere'. [xv] MS grace. [xvi] Followed by 'de une femme mesele' deleted by a bar. The reading is retained in P. [xvii] MS dureit.

But beg him that he will suffer you to be tempted: that he will not suffer you to be overcome, but will give you strength to resist the temptation. And if you want the strength to resist, acknowledge with true heart that you yourself have no power except great infirmity and sin and pain, and that in God and from God is all your strength. And trust yourself whole-heartedly to Our Lord's mercy: the more you hold yourself to be feeble and wretched, the more you will have strength from God to resist the assaults of the Devil, the world, and the flesh.[25] Such was our glorious Lady: because she held herself to be so little in herself she was so full of God's virtue that no kind of anguish could overcome her. And know [dear brother,] that this kind of humility is valuable not only against temptation, it is also valuable to purge sin and increase charity more than any bodily penance, for when man looks at his filthiness and frailness of body and soul, he has much greater anguish than he would from any bodily penance. For another thing, bodily penance often makes the soul rise up in pride, but when a man recognizes his wretchedness that always makes him humble. And know that if you have this humility, all other penance will seem light to you.

[Petition 7] The seventh petition is *Sed libera nos a malo*, that is: "Deliver us from evil." In these words you must pray that God will deliver you from the evils of sin and of pain. In this prayer you must beg especially for souls in Purgatory, that God in his mercy will bring them out of punishment. Dear sir, if you want to see the evils that man suffers in this world, and the discomforts, take care to look at the estate of man before he has sinned, for otherwise you will not see the faults, any more than if a leper child had been born in prison and had never been out of the prison nor seen a healthy man; he would think himself in a good human condition.[26] But if he saw a healthy man, and the light of the sun, then he would say that he was wretched and sick.

[25] See Wenzel 1967a; and *Le Besant de Dieu* (ed. Ruelle), pp. 56ff.

[26] See Gregory, *Dialogues* (ed. de Vogüé, trans. Antin), where a child born in prison is told of the outside world by his mother (3:IV, 1:3; the editor's footnote remarks on the analogy with Plato).

Sachez donc ke si home n'eust peché, il avereit la char nette de tote manere de ordure e de totes maladies, ne ne morreit ja ne n'amaladireit[i] ne n'afieblireit par nule vellesce ;[ii] il avreit les delicios mangers, les fruz des arbres, e de ce ne prendereit[iii] il ne trop[iv] ne trop petit,[v] einz savreit la dreite mesure cum ben convendreit a sa nature. Il avreit la veue e le oie e les autre[s] sens si tresclers e si trespleins de vie, k'il porreit sens nule peine tot par sei conquere totes les clergies de cest monde. E en chescune chose[vi] k'il verreit ou sentireit, lorreit[vii] il e amereit Dampnedeu. Sa reison e sa volenté serreit totes orres jointe a son Creator la ou tote la joie est e la char serreit obeisante a la reison sanz nule difficulté.[viii] Ore poez veer come nos defaillom dolerosement en totes ces choses [e tut ne seez vus pas mesel, se vostre frere l'est, vus le devez acointer a vostre peine, car ausi le poez vus estre, e sur tutes les autres choses P],[ix] i a il une chose ke[x] mervel[f.91r]les plus greve, ke nul home, ja ne seit il si bon, ne poez estre eseur s'il est en charité ou[xi] nun, kar totes les ovres k'il fet poet il fere par orgoil. Por ceo dist Job, ki fu le plus saint home ki feust en tere, k'il aveit poür de totes ses overagnes. E Dampnedeu par sa merci nos[xii] doinst ceste poür.

Ore, beau sire,[xiii] cestes peines vous covent sofrir en ceste vie mau gré ou bon gré. E si vus les recordez sovent e les sofrez a bone volenté, vos serrez umble e cresterez en l'amur nostre Segnor de jor en jor e il vos deliveira de ces maus e de[s] autres ke vus avez deservi par aventure. E ki ne veut cest fere, il soffra les peines ci maugré son e allors ensement, dont Deus nos[xiv] defende par sa pitié. A las ! coment poet home estre essuer en cest siecle kaunt il si legerement poet chaïr en peché, ja si prodome ne seit ! E si legerement poet avenir k'il morge taunt come il est en peché e dont va il en enfer as pein[e]s pardurables, dont Deus nos defende e la souue gloriose Mere, nostre doce Dame sainte Marie, amen.[xv] Mes, beau syre,[xvi] ices peines d'enfer sunt si tresgrant ke quor de ome ne les poet penser, kar la mendre peine d'enfer est gregnor ke totes celes ke unkes furent pensees en ceste monde, kar chescune peine, ja si petite ne seit, taunt plus dure, taunt est gregnore.

---

[i] The letters 'ma' are a superscript insertion, as is the third 'a' which is written above an expuncted 'e'. P has 'n'enmaladireit', DL 'n'enleidireit', Pa 'ne la lederait'. [ii] P 'feblesce'. [iii] The final letters 'it' are written above expuncted 'z'. [iv] MS torp. [v] The words 'trop petit' are written above 'meimes' which has been deleted by a bar. P reads 'ne meins', Pa 'memes'. [vi] The words 'chescune chose' are written above 'kaun' which has been deleted by a bar. DLPPa read 'e en quant k'il'. [vii] PPa 'loereit', D 'horreit', L 'horeit'. [viii] DLPPa 'cuntredit'. [ix] DL omit 'frere'. [x] MS kil. [xi] MS vo. [xii] DL 'vus'. [xiii] Written over an erasure. DLP have 'beau frere'. [xiv] DL 'vus'. [xv] Pa ends here. [xvi] Written over an erasure. P has 'mun chier frere'.

Know then that if man had not sinned, he would have flesh clean of all kinds of filth and of all illnesses, would not die, nor sicken, nor ever become enfeebled with age. He would have delicious food, the fruit of the trees, and he would take neither too much nor too little, for he would know the right measure proper to his nature. He would have such clear and lively sight and hearing, and the other senses, that he could effortlessly master all the arts and sciences of the world by himself. And in everything he saw or felt he would praise and love the Lord God. His reason and his will would always be joined to his Creator, where all joy is, and his flesh would be obedient to reason without any difficulty. Now you can see how we fail lamentably in all these things. [And even if you are not a miserable wretch, if your brother is you must be at pains to tell him, or you will be one also. And above all else] there is one thing that is most especially troubling: that no man, be he never so good, can be sure whether he is in charity or not. For all the deeds he does may have been done in pride. Therefore Job, the holiest man who ever was on earth, said he was afraid of all his deeds.[27]

May God in his mercy give us this fear. Now, dear sir, you must bear these pains in this life whether you will or no. And if you bear them in mind often and in good will, you will be humble and grow in the love of Our Lord day by day and he will deliver you from these pains and from others that you may have deserved. And he who does not wish to do this shall suffer these pains against his will and more besides — which God forbid, by his pity. Alas! How can a man be certain in this world, when he can so easily fall into sin, however worthy a man he is! And it can so easily happen that he dies while he is in sin, and so goes to Hell and to everlasting torment, from which God and his glorious Mother, our precious Lady Saint Mary, defend us, Amen. But, my dear brother, these torments of Hell are so great that the heart of man cannot imagine them, for the least of Hell's torments is greater than all that could be imagined in this world, for each torment however small it is, is greater the longer it goes on.

[27] Job 9:28.

E quant ele [f.91v] dure senez[i] fin, ele est si graunt ke nule fin n'en est. D'autre part ele est si graunt en sei la mendre peine de enfer, ke nul home ne la poet dire. Kar nent plus n'est le nostre feu envers le feu d'enfer ke le feu depeint en la pareie envers le feu ki art devant nus. E de celes peines i a taunt ke nul home n'ent seit le nombre.[ii] Ki la serra, il avra faim e seif sanz nule esparance de relegement[iii] e chaut e freit l'un aprés l'autre si grant ke home mortel ne poet dire. Illoc serront les tenebres si espesses ke l'en les porra taster, si k'il ren n'i verra fors les hidos visages[iv] as diables ne n'orra fors le cri doleros ne [ne] sentira del nes fors la tresorde puor de la longaine[v] de enfer. Les serpens e les autres verms le perceront[vi] parmi le quer e il ne se porra defendre, kar il n'avra pas force de mover son mendre[vii] dei fors quant diables le moveront. E kaunt il avra ploré autantes lermes com il i a gotes en la mer, tot serra a recomencer, kar les gotes de la mer unt acune fin, mes les soues lermes sunt senz fin e il totdis serra en moriaunt,[viii] ke ja ne porra parmorir. Celui donc ki eime e desire solaz e delit del secle u de la char prenge sei guarde k'il ne vegne la, kar la n'avra il ren de ce k'il desire, mes taunt le desira plus, taunt meins en avera e kanc k'il het la trovera e il harra totes les choses [f.92r] k'i sunt e Deu meimes harra il pardurablement de ki veue il sarra sevré senz fin, e de la doce compaignie des sainz ki avront le cors ausi lusant come le solail e si entres[ix] e si sains ke nule peine ne les porra grever e avront Deu en lor quor senz fin. La nos meint Deu par sa misericorde.[x]

[Mon cher frere, P] jo n'ai pas escrit icés peines por vos, kar vous ne eschivez[xi] mie peché por poür de peine, mes por la amur nostre tresdoz Seignor Jesu Crist.

---

[i] DLP 'sanz'. [ii] P 'ne les siet numbrer'. [iii] DL 'allegement'. [iv] P 'ymages'. [v] For the second time replaced in DL ('del fosse'). [vi] MS percerent. [vii] P 'petit'. [viii] MS emoraiunt. [ix] DLP 'ent(i)ers'. [x] There is an erasure extending from the end of one line to the beginning of the next. DL end here. [xi] P 'eschiwe'.

And when it goes on for ever, it is so great as to be never-ending. Again, the least torment is so great in itself that no man can tell of it. For our own fire is no more, compared with the fire of Hell, than a fire painted on the wall is to the fire burning here in the hearth.[28] And there are so many of these torments, no man knows the number of them. Whoever is there, he will feel hunger and thirst without any hope of relief, and cold and heat one after the other, greater than mortal man can tell. There will be shadows so thick he can feel them,[29] and he will see nothing but the hideous faces of devils; he will hear nothing but screams of pain, and smell with his nose nothing but the disgusting stink of the sewer of Hell. Serpents and other worms will bite through his heart and he will be unable to defend himself, for he will have no power to move his smallest finger except when devils move it for him. And when he has wept as many tears as there are drops in the sea, it will all begin again, for the drops of the sea are finite and his tears are infinite; he will always be dying, who can never be completely dead. Therefore whoever loves and desires pleasure and delight of the world or the flesh, let him take care not to come there, for he shall have nothing of what he desires there: the more he desires the less he shall have. Whatever he hates he shall find there, and he shall hate all the things that are there. He shall hate God himself for ever, from whose sight he shall be severed for ever, and from the sweet company of saints whose bodies shall be as shining as the sun, so whole and sound that no pain can ever hurt them, and who shall have God in their hearts for ever. May God in his mercy lead us to them there.

[My dear brother], I have not written of these torments for you,[30] because it is not from fear of punishment that you avoid sin, but for the love of our sweet Lord Jesus Christ.

---

[28] See "Treatise on Job," ed. Taguchi (pp. 214–15: notes to 892–94, 894–97), where this metaphor is attributed to Augustine (a passage from Pseudo-Augustine is cited). The accompanying statement, that Hell's torment is greater than anything imaginable in this life, is likewise attributed (both notes refer to *FM*; in which see p. 113, where the passage about painted fire is not attributed), but no Augustinian or pseudo-Augustinian source has been located. See also Sturges (p. 21, note 81 above); and in On Penance (p. 303) below.

[29] The image comes ultimately from Ex. 10:21: the Plagues of Egypt include a darkness … *even darkness which may be felt.*

[30] Cf. *Ancrene Wisse*: the addressee is not in need of certain parts of the advice: "I write much for others that in no way touches you, my dear sisters" (Part II; ed. Hasenfratz p. 97, and trans. Savage and Watson p. 67). This is just one of several such remarks in the Middle English text. Compare, too, this passage on the torments of Hell with the Purgatory (Chapter 16 below). Although it is common for texts of this kind to be addressed to a woman in the first instance, here the writer is explicitly looking beyond her to a wider audience.

Einz le ai fet por autres en ki main iço escrit vendera, ki seveaus non s'il ne velent[i] por amor, si lerront il por poür le mal a fere. Eissi comenceront il a amer Jesu Crist nostre tresdoz Segnor, le Fiz a l[a] treglorios[e] Pucele, nostre tresdoce Dame, ssainte Marie.

[i] P 'volent'.

But I have done it for others, into whose hands this writing will come. At least if they cannot avoid doing evil because of love, they will do so because of fear. Thus they will begin to love Jesus Christ our dear Lord, Son of the most glorious Maiden, our precious Lady Saint Mary.

Part II

Marian Texts

Chapter 3

Young Mary[1]

Introduction

This Anglo-Norman version of an apocryphal "Birth of Jesus" is taken from Oxford, Bodleian Library, MS Bodley 82 (s.xiv^{m}), ff.58r–72v. It lacks the beginning of the story, but this can be supplied from the Gospel of Pseudo-Matthew (see below), or from one of the four Continental manuscripts. It deals mainly with the birth and youth of Mary, breaking off at the Nativity and the arrival of Zedemer and Salome. The piece is narrative in style, with much dialogue; there is no hint who the audience might be.

The account is based on the "Historia de nativitate Mariae et de infantia salvatoris," otherwise known as the Gospel of Pseudo-Matthew. This apocryphal text makes considerable use of the Protevangelium (the Book of James) and the Gospel of Thomas. It is a Latin compilation (8th or 9th century; the earliest manuscript is 11th century), popular in the later medieval period. The account of Mary's birth entered the *Legenda Aurea* of Jacobus de Voragine.[2]

In M. R. James, *The Apocryphal New Testament*, pp. 38–49, the Gospel of Pseudo-Matthew (based on the Book of James, which in turn is based on the Protevangelium) offers supplementary details corresponding to features in MS Bodley 82.[3] Analysis of the Gospel of Pseudo-Matthew is on pp. 73–79; its first seventeen chapters show use of the Protevangelium. For example, on pp. 73ff we have the following details: five months absence of Joachim, Anna throwing herself on her bed for a day and a night; the detail that she would have dedicated her child to the temple, the summoning of her maid, reproaches directed to her maid for not coming to her.[4]

The Anglo-Norman translation is acephalous, and commences at Chapter 2, ending abruptly in the middle of chap. 13 (pp. 81–85). At this point the translator abandons pure narrative, and delivers a paean of praise to the Virgin Mother.

---

[1] D&B 645r (p. 358), prose.

[2] See *GL* II:149–58.

[3] See also the replacement of James, by Elliott.

[4] For the Latin text see *Codex* (ed. Thilo, pp. cv–cxvii, & 339–400); and the edition of Giles (*Codex Apocryphus*, pt. 1), pp. 66–89; the latter is the edition from which page-references in the notes below are drawn.

Text

[chap. II] *Factum est autem, ut in diebus festis inter eos qui offerebant incensum Domino, staret Joachim portans munera sua in conspectu Domini. Et accedens ad eum scriba templi Domini nomine Ruben ait ad eum, 'Non licet tibi inter sacrificia Dei consistere, quia non benedixit tibi Deus, ut daret tibi germen in Israel.*[i]

[f.58r][ii] '... estre entre les sacrifices Deu pur ço ke Deu ne tei benesquit tant ke il donast engendrure de Israel.' [I,4] Puis ke il aveit dist tant de hounte devaunt le pople, si departi Joachim del temple tendrement plurant e ne returna mie a sa mesun, mes ala a ses bestes e mena ové luy sa possession entre les montaynes en leynteine tere, issi ke sa femme Anna par cink moys ren de luy ne poet oir. Dunt ele en plurant dist a nostre Seinur : 'Sire, Deu de Israel, tresfort, pur ço ke vus ne mey dunastes fiz ne file, pur quey avez guerpi mun barun e le me avez tollu ? E ja sunt sink meys passés ke jo mon baron [f.58v] ne vy e ne say, s'il seit mort, u ke jo use fet sa sepulture ?' E tut en plurant entra en un chambre de sa meson e chaït en oreysons priant a Deu. [III,1] E aprés se leva de ses oreysons, si comensa a lever les oyls a nostre Seynur e vit le ny de un moysson en une arbre de une lorere e leva un voiz ové gemissement, si dist : 'A ! Sire, Deu tut-pussant, ky avez doné fiz a tote creature, a bestes, a jumens, a serpens, a pessons, a oyseuz, e s'esent sur lur fiz[iii] a tey sul reng graces, pur ço que vus avez ordiné, sicum vus voylez, en tele manere, ke moy soul avez hors clos de le doun de ta benigneté. Sire, vus conu mun quor, ke jo me regeisse aver vué dé le comencement [f.59r] ke jo fu esposé, ke si vus mey ussét doné fiz ou file, jo le usse offert a tey e[n] tun seynte temple ové dons.' [IV,1] E puis ke ele en itele manere dit out, sudeynement luy apparut l'aungel nostre Seynur, si ly dist : 'Anna, ne vos dotez mie, kar en le cunseil Deu est le frut ke de tey isra e [ke de tey] nee sera, [e] ert en anunciacion a tuz sieclys dequez en la fin.' Quant le angele sele chose out dist, tantot de ses oylz evanist. E ele tauntost fu esponte de la vision e de la parole, entra sa chambre e se just en sun lyst cum morte e tut le jour e tute la nuyt fu en oreysun e en grant dute. Aprés ço apella a luy une pucele ke luy servy e dist a luy : 'Vus m'avez wuu [f.59v] en ma vidueté decewe e en grant anguisse mise e ne volez a mei entrer ?'

[i] p. 67, 12–18. [ii] B82 begins here after the loss of a folio. [iii] MS f. e a tey.

Translation

[chap. II] [And so it happened, that on the feast-days, among those who offered incense to God, Joachim stood bearing his gifts in the presence of the Lord. And a scribe of God's temple by the name of Ruben came to him and said, "It is not lawful for you to stand among the sacrifices of God, because God has not blessed you by giving you seed for Israel.]

"... to be among the sacrifices to God, because God did not bless you when he gave offspring to Israel." Because [Ruben] had said so much shame before the people, Joachim went away from the temple weeping piteously, and did not go back to his house; he went to his cattle and took his possessions[1] into the mountains in a distant region, so that his wife Anna could get no tidings of him for five months. Then she wept and said to Our Lord, "Lord God of Israel, Almighty, why have you given me neither son nor daughter; why have you forsaken my husband and taken him away from me? And now five months have passed since I saw my husband, and I do not know whether he is dead or whether I should have his sepulchre made." And all in tears she went into a room of her house and fell down in prayer, praying to God. And then she rose from her prayers, and began to raise her eyes to Our Lord, and saw a sparrow's nest in a laurel tree; she lifted up her voice and wailing said, "Ah, Lord, all-powerful God, who has given children to all creatures — to cattle and mares, to serpents and fish, to birds — who rejoice in their offspring; I give thanks to you alone, because you have ordained in your pleasure that I alone am shut out from the gifts of your bounty. Lord, I revealed my heart, which I confess to have dedicated since the beginning of my marriage, that if you had given me a son or a daughter, I should have offered it to you in your holy temple with gifts." And when she had spoken in this way, suddenly the angel of Our Lord appeared to her and said, "Anna, do not be afraid, for in the counsel of God is the fruit that shall come forth from you, and be born of you; and it shall be the admiration[2] of all the ages, even unto the end of the world." When the angel had said this, immediately he vanished from her sight. And she was so frightened by the vision and by the words that she went straight to her chamber and lay on her bed like a dead thing, and all day and all night remained in prayer and in great fear. After that, she called one of her serving-maidens and said to her, "You saw me in my widowhood, all betrayed and cast into great anguish, and you do not want to come in to me?"

---

[1] In the Latin, *pastores* (p. 67).

[2] "anunciacion" (*admirationem*, p. 68).

Dunt ele en grundilant respondi e dist : 'Si Deu ad fors clos tun ventre e tey e ad tollu tun baron e ke puge mes ?' E quant Anna oyt cele parole, suspira de parfund e o grant cri plurut.

[chap. III] En cel tens apparut un juvencel a Johachym entre les montaynes, u il pesseit ses berbis, e dit a ly : 'Pur quey ne returnées a ta femme ?' E Joachim respondi e dist : 'Jo l'ay ou par vint anz, e ore pur ço ke Deu ne mey vout doner de luy fiz ne file, su jo issu del temple Deu od grant hounte. Puz ky jo su degeté une feze en despit, a quey returneray rere a luy ? Jo serray od mes owailes tant [f.60r] cum Deu mey vodra doner la vye, e par les meyns mes enfans volunters dorray e restoray a poveres, vidues, orphans e as autres dunt avez Deu lur partie[?].' Quant il out cele chose dist, respondi cel juvencel e dist : 'Je su le angel Deu, ky me suy apparu a ta femme plurante e priante, e l'ay conforté. E sachez luy de tei aver conceue une file qe tu a tun departir de luy ne saverés e ele serra en le temple Deu e le seint Espirit reposera en luy, e ele sera benete sur tutes seintes femmes, en tele manere, que nule puse dire ky tele eit esté devan luy, ne jamés avendra aprés, ne serra en cete siecle. Pur la quele chose descendez del montayne e returnez a ta femme e vus le troverez eant en ventre tele chose de quey vus rendrez graces a nostre Seynur. E la semence de luy serra beneyt[i] [f.60v] e ele serra benete e mere de beneyson pardurable serra clamé.' E Joachim le aora e dist : 'Si jo ay trové grace devant vus, seez un poy en mun tabernacle e donez ta benysun a moy tun serjant.' E l'aungel ly dit : 'Ne diez mie sergant, mez serf, ke nus sumus serganz un sul seynur, kar mun manger e mon bevere ne put estre vu des homes mortels, e pur ço ne me devez prier de entrer tun tabernacle. Mes ce ke vos voliez aver a mey doné, offrés a Deu en sacrifice.' Dunc prist Joachim un aygnel sanz tecche e dist a l'angel : 'Je ne serray mye si osee de offrir sacrifise a Deu, si cum comandement ne mey dounast le poer de offrer [...'.][ii]

[f.61r] ['...] nos enemis. La mere est fet barayne e ad engendrure grant en Israel. E purquey me voylunt defendre mes enemis ? Mun Seynur les ad turné de moy e mey ad doné joye pardurable.'

[i] MS beneyi. [ii] Folios missing, covering p. 69, 27 to p. 71, 19.

Then she sullenly replied, saying, "If God has closed your belly and has taken away your husband then what could I do?" And when Anna heard these words, she sighed deeply and with a great cry burst into tears.

[chap. III] At this time a young man appeared to Joachim in the mountains where he pastured his sheep, and said to him, "Why do you not go back to your wife?" And Joachim answered him, saying, "I have had her for twenty years, and now because God does not want to give me a son or daughter I came away from God's temple in great shame. Since I have once been thrown into contempt, why should I return to her again? I shall stay with my sheep for as long as God wishes to give me life. By the hands of my children I will gladly give and restore their share to the poor, to widows, to orphans and to others [. . .]."[3] When he had said this, the young man answered him, saying, "I am the angel of God, who appeared to your weeping, praying wife and comforted her. And know that she has conceived a daughter of you, that you knew nothing of when you left; she will be in God's temple and the Holy Ghost will rest in her. And she will be blessed above all holy women, so blessed that nobody can say there was ever such a one before her, nor will ever come again, nor ever be in this world. Because of this thing, go now down the mountain and return to your wife, and you will find there is something in her womb that will make you give thanks to Our Lord. And her seed shall be blessed, and she known as the mother of eternal blessings." And Joachim worshipped him and said, "If I have found favour with you, sit awhile in my tent and give your blessing to me, your servant." And the angel said to him, "Do not say servant, but serf; for we are all servants of one Lord alone. My food and my drink cannot be seen by mortal men, and therefore you may not ask me to enter your tent. But what you wanted to give me, offer that as a sacrifice to God." Then Joachim took a spotless lamb, and said to the angel, "I would not dare to offer a sacrifice to God, had you not by your command given me the power to offer . . . ."

[leaves missing here — chapters IV and V. What follows must be the end of chap. V]

". . . our enemies. The mother is made barren, and there are many offspring in Israel.[4] And why do my enemies wish to hinder me? My Lord has turned them from me, and given me everlasting joy."

[3] The French text is obscure at this point.

[4] Perhaps a reference to Luke 23:29.

[chap. VI] Tut le pople aveit merveyle de Marie, pur ço ke kant ele fu de treys anz, surement ala. E si parfitement se tint en le longes nostre Seynur, ke tus furunt grantment enbaïz ke la virent, kar il ne quidereyent mie ke ele fust enfant, mes come grande e ja [a]sez auns[i] acomplie, ne sesent Deu prier. E la face de luy fu ja resplendisant sicum la neif, ke a peyne garder sun vult poyerent, e tut jours fut en bons overaynes. En totes choses ke les aunciens femmes ne poerent fere, ele en sa tendre age mise ne sessout parempler. [f.61v] Ceste rule establit ele a luy, ke del matin dekes a houre de noune deserit a l'overaygne de tistre. De noune derichef ne se departereit de ses oreysons dekes le angel luy apareit, de ky main ele reseust[ii] sa viande, issi ke meuz e meuz se profitereit en le amur Deu. Au drein, ové les eynees virgines esteit enseyné en les loynges Deu, ço est a saver en vigilies nul premereine esteit trové de luy, nule plus humble, nule plus coynte en lé dices dé prophecyes David, nule plus aprise en le saver Deu, nule plus gracius en charité, ne plus clere en chasteté de cors e de pensé, ne plus parfite en tute manere de vertu, kar ele esteit si estable en tuz vertuz e si nunchangable, ke checun jour [f.62r] crust de muz en mouz. Unkes nul ne le oït maldire, unkys nul curucé ne le vit.[iii] Checune parole esteit si pleyn de grace, ke tut fu pure verité kanc ke de sa bouche isseit. Tuz jours fu assiduele en ses oreysons e en la ley Deu. E tut jours esteit ententive entur ses compaynouns, ke akune ne pecchat en une parole, ne eshausçat sa voys en risee, ne ke acune en tort ou en orgoil encuntre sun pere ou sa mere fust. E ele ne cessa[iv] de Deu prier, ke ele fust[v] ocupé de loer nostre Seynur pur la salvacion de alcun u de alcune ; si alcun le saluast, ele respondereit par la salu[t]acion *Deo gracias* ! Checun jour fu ele saule de la viande ke ele resceut de l'angel e la viaunde [f.62v] ke ele resceust dé veskes departi ele as poveres. Sovenerement esteyent weu les angels ové luy e parlerent oveke luy e cum a lur trechere amye s'abeserunt e se humilierunt a luy. Si acun des malades la tuchat, meimes le houre returnerent sein e sauf a sa mesun.

[i] MS amys (*quasi iam plena annorum*). [ii] MS reuseust. [iii] MS avoyt (*vidit*). [iv] MS els ne cessacent. [v] MS prier e ke ele ne f.

[chap. VI] All the people wondered at Mary, because when she was three years old she could walk confidently. And she performed so admirably the praises of Our Lord, that all were dumbfounded who saw her.[5] For they would never believe she was an infant, but grown up and already of mature years; they never cease their prayers to God. And her skin was always shining like the snow, so that they could hardly look at her face; and she was always busy with good works. Everything the old women could not do, she, still in her tender years, never failed to achieve. She established this rule for herself: from the morning until the hour of noon she carried out the work of weaving.[6] From noon onwards, she never left her prayers until the angel appeared to her, from whose hand she received her food. Thus she grew more and more in the love of God. Lastly, with the older virgins, she was instructed in the Divine Offices — that is to say, in the vigils none was superior to her; none was more humble, nor more knowledgeable about the sayings of the prophecies of David; none was more learned in God's law, nor more gracious in charity. She was brighter in her chastity of body and thought, and more perfect in all manner of virtues; for she was so stable in all virtues and so steadfast, that every day she grew better and better. Nobody ever heard her speak evil, nor ever saw her angry. Every word was so full of grace, so that everything that came from her mouth was pure truth. Every day she was assiduous in her prayers and in studying God's law. And every day she was attentive to her companions, that no one of them should sin by a single word, nor raise her voice in laughter, nor act wrongfully or proudly against her father or mother. And she never ceased praying to God, so that she was constantly praising Our Lord for the salvation of this person or that; she would reply to anybody greeting her with the greeting "God be praised!" Every day she was filled full with the food she received from the angel; the food she received from the priests she distributed to the poor. Above all, the angels were seen with her; they talked with her and, as to their adored mistress,[7] they bowed down and humbled themselves to her. If any of the sick touched her, they returned home that same hour both whole and sound.

---

[5] See General Introduction, p. 12 above, for the Gradual Psalms, which were said to have been recited on the steps of the Temple in Jerusalem; Mary was able, at the age of three, to climb them by herself, saying the correct psalm for each step (*gradus*).

[6] The account of Mary's daily routine is attributed to Jerome; see *GL* II:153, and *PL* 30:300–1 (see also Love's *Mirror*, p. 21 and note).

[7] For angels as friends to virgins, because related to them, see *Preaching*, trans. Wenzel, p. 170.

[chap. VII] Dunc i out en le temple un esveske, Abiachar par noun, ky offrit grant douns as esveskes, qu'il ly grantassent que sun fiz la poust reseyvere e a marier. E Marie lur descendist e dist : 'Ço ne pust estre ke jo houme conuse ou sey conu de home.' Dunc respundirent les esveskes e ses parenz e diseyent a luy : 'Deus est honuré e ahuré des filz, sicum il fu del pople de Israel.' Seint Marie lur respondist : [f.63r] 'Deus est primes e principalement eloé en chasteté, kar devant Abel nul ne fu trové dreitturels en tuz e celuy pur sa offrende plut a Deu, pur ço ke l'autre luy desplut, e par ço fust il mauveysement ossiz. E il receut deus corounes, une par sa offrende, e l'autre par sa virgineté, pur ço ke il ne ressut unkes polliciun en sa char. E ausi Helye le prophete, pur ço ke il gardat sa char en virginité, fu il pris sus en char. E cest chose a[i] ge apris en le temple Deu, [dés l'en]faunce, ke virgine est chere a Deu. Pur ço ay jo establi en mon quer ke jamés home ne conustray charnelement.'

[chap. VIII] Aprés ço quant ele fu de quaturze anz, aveint que les[i] phariseus diseyunt ja pur custome que femme en le temple Deu ne pout demorer. E troverent teil conseil entre eus, [f.63v] qu'il veyerient envoyer pur luy, par tuz les lignes de Israel, que tuz assemblereyunt le tierz jour en le temple Deu. Quant tut le pople fu assemblé, dunt se leva Abyakar le veske e munta les plus haut grez, qu'il fust oï de tut le pouple. E fit[ii] fere grant silence e dist : 'Oeez, les fiz Israel, e escutez de vos orayles mes paroles. De icele tens ke Salomon edifia cel temple furent cyeins virgines filies de reys e de prophetis e de sovereynes pretris e des eveskes e grant e merveyluyses esteyent. E quant il veindreyent a tel age, ke eles puent barons resceyvere, volunters les resceyverent e suyrent l'ordre e la manere de cels ke esteyent avant eles e plurent a Dampnedeu.[iii] Ore est trové de Marie un novel ordre a Deu, que sey ad promis [f.64r] en virginité servir Dampnedeu. Dunt il mey est avis, ke de nostre demande de Deu e de sa response saver puroms e conustre a ky ele deist estre bayllye en garde.' Dunt plut sel parole a[iv] tute la synagoge e fu sort geté des pretres sur les duze lignes de Israel, e chaït le sort sur Judam. E pus diseynt les princes ke seluy ke fust sanz femme venit l'eindemain e portast[v] sa verge. Avint issi ke Joseph, ke fust eymé des autres, porta sa verge entre les autres.

---

[i] MS leus. [ii] MS sit. [iii] MS plurent e a D. [iv] MS e. [v] MS porstat.

[chap. VII] There was then in the temple a high priest, Abiachar by name, who offered rich presents to the other priests, to grant that his son might take Mary and marry her. And she came down to them and said, "It cannot be, that I should know a man or be known by a man." Then the priests and her parents answered, saying, "God is honoured and adored by sons, as he was by the people of Israel." Saint Mary replied to them: "God is first, and above all, praised by chastity, for before Abel none was found to be righteous in all things; he pleased God by his offering — for the other [Cain] displeased him — and for this he was wickedly killed.[8] And he received two crowns: one for his offering, and the other for his virginity, for there was never any pollution in his flesh. And also Elijah the prophet: because he kept his flesh in chastity he was taken up to Heaven in the flesh.[9] And I learned this in God's temple, ever since I was a child, that a virgin is beloved of God. Therefore I am set in my heart, that never shall I know a man carnally."[10]

[chap. VIII] After that, when she was was fourteen, it came about that the Pharisees were saying, as was customary, that women could not stay in the temple. Having taken counsel among themselves, they sent for her, and for all the tribes of Israel — by the third day they must all be assembled in the temple of God. When all the people were gathered, Abiachar the priest rose, and mounted to the highest of the steps, to be heard by all the people. He ordered complete silence, and said, "Hear, O sons of Israel, and lend your ears to my words. From the time when Solomon built this temple, virgins have lived in it. Daughters of kings and prophets, of priests and chief priests — they were great and marvellous. And when they were of an age to take husbands, they took them willingly, and they followed the order and the way of those who went before them and were pleasing to the Lord God. But now Mary has found a new rule of God — she has promised herself to serve the Lord God in virginity. And so it seems to me, that we may put our question to God and know his answer; to know into whose keeping she should be delivered." These words pleased the whole synagogue, and lots were cast by the priests over the twelve tribes of Israel, and the lot fell upon the tribe of Judah. And then the princes said that any man who was without a wife should come next day and bring his staff. So it was that Joseph, who was beloved of the others, carried his staff among them.

---

[8] See Gen. 4:1–16.

[9] *AV*, II Kings 2:1–12; *LV*, IV Reg. 2:1–12.

[10] For Mary's vow of virginity, see e.g. *Preaching*, trans. Wenzel, p. 172.

Quant il aveyent tuz baylé a le esveske lur verges, il offrit sacrifise a Deu, e en priant dist e demanda nostre Seynur. [Nostre Seynur] respundi e dist a luy : 'Metés tuz les verges dedens le seintuarie e seint illooc tut la nut. E matyn kant il vendrunt, [f.64v] comandez ke checun preingne sa verge. E de une des verges istra une columbe e volera a cel, e en ky mein la verge tendue avera doné cel signe, a luy seit baylé Marie a garder.' Lautre jour aprés vindrent plus surement trestuz, e aprés le offrende fete de l'encens si entra le eveske le seintuarie e porta avant les verges. Quant il aveyt baylé les verges desques a treis mil e de nul des verges issit la columbe, dunc se fubla Abiachar le esveske de sa vesture pontifical a dusze seins e entre le seintuarie e ad sacrificé a Deu. E en urant luy apparust l'aungel e dist : 'Ceo est ceste petite verge ke vus acuntastes pur nent e vus le meistis ceste oveke les autres. Quant vus averez ceste verge avant portés e le eyét doné, [f.65r] en cele appara le signe dunt jo parlay a tey.' E cele verge esteit a Joseph, e il esteit simple en habite, pur ço ke il esteit veuz ; e ke il ne fust contreit de receyvere Marie, il ne voleit mie requere sa verge. E cum il esteit umbles e derein, Abiachar cria a haute vois a li e dist : 'Venez e receyvez ta verge, pur ço ke tu l'atendes.' E Joseph se duta pur ço ke le sovereyn eveske le aveit apellé a grant cri. Vint demeintenaunt e tendit sa mein, si reseut sa verge, e tantost de la verge issit une columbe plus blanche de neif e tresbele, e vola lungement utre le temple e persa les cels. E cum le soverein eveske luy dist 'Receyvez luy, pur ço ke tu sul [es] elu [f.65v] de tuz les autres de Deu a luy garder', dunt prist il aurer e prier e a vergoyn dire : 'Je su veils e de grant age. Pur quey mey baylés cele enfant ?' Abiachar le veske le respondi e dist : 'Remembrez vus, Joseph, coment Dathan e Abyron perierent pur ço ke il ne voleyent fere le comandement Deu : tut issi avendra a tey si tu eis en despit ço ke est comandé a tey de Deu.' E Joseph luy dist : 'Jo ne ay pas en despit la volunté Deu, si je puse conutre seirtenement si la volunté Deu issut ou nun.[i] Pur ço seyent donez a luy acunes virgines de[ii] ses compaines ové lesqueles endemeynteres s'aforce de vivre.' Derechief Abyachar le eveske ly dist :[iii] [f.66r] 'E tut le munde serra par tey enluminé.'

[i] p. 75, 28: *quis eam possit habere ex filiis meis conjugem.* [ii] MS des. [iii] Folios missing, covering p. 75, 31 to p. 76, 21.

When they had all given their staves to the chief priest, he offered a sacrifice to God; praying, he questioned Our Lord. And Our Lord gave answer, saying to him, "Put all the staves into the sanctuary and the holy place, for the whole night. In the morning when they come, order each to take back his staff. And from one of the staves shall come forth a dove and fly into the heavens; the man who holds the staff which gave this sign, into his keeping shall Mary be given." The next day, after they had all arrived without fail, and after the offering of incense had been made, the priest entered the sanctuary and brought out the staves. When he had handed back three thousand staves, and no dove came from any of them, then Abiachar the priest put on his pontifical robe with the twelve signs, and entered the sanctuary and sacrificed to God. As he prayed, the angel appeared and said, "It is this little staff that you overlooked; put it with the others. When you have brought this staff out and given it back, then the sign I told you of will appear in it." And this staff belonged to Joseph; he was simple in his dress, because he was old. So that he would not be obliged to take Mary, he did not want to take his staff. Being humble, he was right at the back, so Abiachar called to him in a loud voice, saying, "Come and take your staff, for you are waiting for it." And Joseph was afraid, because the chief priest had called him so loudly. He came forward now and held out his hand, and received his staff. And with that the most beautiful dove, whiter than snow, came out of the staff and flew far beyond the temple to pierce the heavens. And when the chief priest said to him, "Take her, for you alone among all others have been chosen by God to have her in your care," then he began to beg and pray, saying shamefastly, "I am old, and of great age. Why give this child to me?" Abiachar the chief priest answered him, saying, "Remember, Joseph, how Dathan and Abiram perished because they would not do God's commandment.[11] Thus it will happen to you, if you scorn what is commanded of God." And Joseph said to him, "I do not scorn the will of God, if I could only know for certain whether God's will is thus, or not. Therefore let her be given some of her virgin companions, to live with her in the meantime." And straight away Abiachar the priest said ... [fols. missing, including most of chap. IX, which ends thus] "... And all the world shall be illumined by you."

[11] See Num. 16.

E memes le jour cum ele comensa overer purpre de[i] ses meyns entra a luy un juvencel, de ky la bealté ne pout estre conté, e a la vue de luy comensa a duter e a trembler. Dunt le juvencel luy dist : 'Ne vus dotez, Marie, kar vus conceyverez un rey e enfanterez, ky comendera ne mie soulement en tere, mes en ciel, e regnera en le secle de tuz cecles, Amen.'

[chap. X] E cum cest chose fu feit, Joseph esteit ocupé de overaygne en Capharnaun, car il esteit fevere de fust, e la demora noef moys. Quant il fu returné a sa meysun, trova Marie enceynte e comensa tut a trembler e, en grant anguisse mys, cria e dist : 'A ! Sire Deu, receyvez mun espirit, kar meuz [f.66v] vaut a moy morer ky vivere.' E les virgines ky esteyent ové Marie luy distrent : 'Nus savum ben ky unkes home nel tuchat. E nus ben savom qe ele est virgine enter e nient soylé, kar ele est en garde de Deu e checun jour ad esté en oreysons assiduelement. Les angeles Deu parlerent ové luy. Ele ad ressu checun jour sa viande de la meyn de l'aungel. Coment pout cest estre ke acun pecché seit dedens luy ? Car si vus voylez, nus vus demoustrums nostre suspecion : nule home ne le ad fest enseynte for le angel Deu.' Joseph dist : 'A quey fere me decevez, ke jo dusse creyre a vus, ke l'aungel Deu le ust enceynte ? Bien pout estre, [f.67r] ke acun[ii] fu joint a luy en furme de l'aungel, ke luy descevereyt.' E quant il aveit ço dist, plurut tendrement e dist : 'En quele manere m'en irray al temple Deu ? A quele face veray jo les prestres Deu ? Quey me est a fere ?' Quant il aveit ço dist, il pensa privément de lesser le de tut.

[chap. XI] En la noit suiant aprés, cum il out enpensé de fuir e de sei musser de ele, en cele nuyt meymes luy aparust le angel en somoil e dist a luy : 'Joseph, le fiz David, ne vus dotét mye, receyvez Marie ta femme, car ço ke ele ad conçu en ventre est del Seint Espirit. E ele enfauntera un fiz e il serra apellé Jesus, car il savera sun pople de tuz lur pecchez.' E Joseph se leva e rendi graces a sun Deu e parla a Marie e as virgines, [f.67v] ke esteyent ové luy, e cunta la vision k'il out wou, e il se conforte de Marie e dist : 'Jo ay pecché, car jo avoye suspecion en tey.'

---

[i] MS des. [ii] MS acun ke fu.

And that same day, as she started working at the fine cloth with her hands, a young man [the Angel Gabriel][12] came in to her, whose beauty could never be described; at the sight of him she began to fear and tremble. Then the young man said to her: "Fear not, Mary, for you shall conceive a King and give birth to him, who shall reign not only in earth but in Heaven, and shall reign in the world for ever and ever, Amen."

[chap. X] And when this thing happened, Joseph was busy with work in Capernaum, for he was skilled in wood-working, and he stayed there nine months. When he returned to his house, he found Mary pregnant and he began to tremble all over in the greatest anguish: he cried out, saying, "Ah! Lord God, receive my spirit, for it would be better for me to die than to live." And the virgins who were with Mary said to him, "We know that no man ever touched her. And we know that she is perfectly virgin and not soiled at all, for she is in God's keeping and has been busy at her prayers every day. God's angels talked with her. Every day she received her food from the hand of the angel. How can any sin be in her? If you wish it, we can tell you what we suspect: no man but the angel of God has made her pregnant." Joseph said, "Why do you deceive me, that I should believe the angel of God made her pregnant? It could be that somebody fornicated with her, in the shape of an angel, who deceived her." And when he had said that, he wept bitterly and said, "How can I now go into the temple of God? How can I face the priests of God? What am I going to do?" When he had said this, he thought to himself that he would simply abandon everything.

[chap. XI] During the following night, as he thought of running away and hiding from her, that same night the angel appeared to him in his sleep and said, "Joseph, son of David, do not be afraid; take back Mary your wife, for what she has conceived in her womb is from the Holy Spirit. She shall give birth to a son, and his name shall be Jesus, for he shall save his people from all their sins." And Joseph arose and gave thanks to his God.[13] He spoke to Mary and to the virgins who were with her, telling of the vision he had seen; he took comfort from Mary, and said, "I have sinned, for I suspected you."

---

[12] See Luke 1:11–27 for the angel's name (the same that visited Zacharius earlier in the chapter).

[13] This passage follows Matt. 1:19–24, in which the angel is not named.

[chap. XII] Aprés ceo, issi la novele e vint hors ke Marie fu enceynte. Dunt Joseph fu pris dé ministris del temple e mené a l'eveske, e il le comença a turner a hounte ensemblement a tuz les prestres, e dist : 'A quey fetes vus de ceyte virgine ces noeces ky les angeles Deu norirent el temple sicum columbe, ke unkes homme ne voilet ver, e bien fu aprise en la ley Deu ? E si vus ne l'ussez fet violence, onkore durast ele en estat.' Joseph comença afermer que unkes nel tucha [f.68r] e l'eveske Abiachar luy dist : 'Je vus jure par le nun Deu, ke ore[i] te fray bevere de le ewe ke est apellé la potatiun Deu, e tant tot apparot tun pecché.' Dunt fu ensemble tut la multitudine del peuple Israel, ke ne put estre anumbré. Marie esteit amené al temple. E ses parens e ses cosinis plururent e diseyent a luy : 'Regeissez as prestres tun peché, ke tu esteis sicum columbe en le temple Deu e receustes viande de la meyn le angel.'

Joseph esteit tantost apellé al seint auter e le ewe avant-dite ly fu doné, ke fu de tele vertu, ke si homme ou femme l'ust gusté e fust de mensu[n]ge trové,[ii] e set feze out l'auter envirouné, Deus demustreit signe en sa face, dunt il [f.68v] sereit ateynt. Quant il out beu cele potaciun e surement out le auter envituné, nulle signe apparust en luy. Dunc comencerunt tuz les prestres e les ministris de le pouple a justifier luy e diseyent : 'Beneit seiez tu, qe nule culpe est trové en tey.' E dunc appellerent Marie e diseyent a luy : 'Quele excusacion purras tu trover ? Ou ké greynur signe aperge en tey que[iii] ceo que tun ventre ad mustré ? Cele chose sulement requerum de tey, ke tu regeis ses ke ceo est, k'y t'ad deceu, kar nus savumus ben ke Joseph ne ad culpe de cele chose. Meuz vaut ke ta confession demustre ta vie ke la vengance e la ire Deu doune signe a demoustrer ta malice [f.69r] devant tote le pople.' Dunt dist Marie saunz nule dute : 'Si en mey seit acun polliciun u akun pecché, u akun covetise de incontinence u de nunchasteté feust unkes en moy, jo pri a Deu qe ço seit demustré devant tote le pople, ke jo pouse estre ensaumple a[iv] tuz menturs.' Ele sey approcha a l'auter hardiement, e beust le ewe de potaciun, set feze envirunant le auter, e ele esteit trové sanz culpe. E cum tut le pople estut enbaÿ e virent que ele aveit conçu en sun ventre e signe nule apparust en sa face, comencerunt a parler diversis paroles entre eus. Les uns diseyent ke ço fu seinté, les autres par malice e male conscience la acuserunt. Dunc vit Marie [f.69v] la suspecion del pople ke ele ne fu purgé enterement.

---

[i] MS ke ore ke ore. [ii] Giles, p. 78, 24, has *si gustasset homo metuens* (*The Apocryphal Gospels*, trans. Cowper, p. 47: 'when anyone who had told a lie had tasted'). The difference is presumably explained by variant readings in the Latin editions. [iii] MS ca. [iv] MS de.

[chap. XII] After this, the news came out and spread abroad that Mary was pregnant. Then Joseph was taken up by the ministers of the temple and led before the chief priest. He began to chide him shamefully, saying, "What is this marriage you have done to this virgin, whom the angels of God fed like a dove in the temple, who never wanted to see a man, and who was so learned in God's law? If you had not done her violence, she would be even now in that condition." Joseph began to swear he had never touched her, and the priest Abiachar said to him, "I declare in God's name I shall now make you drink the water that is called God's Potion, and your sin will immediately become apparent." Then all the multitude of the people of Israel assembled, so many they could not be counted. Mary was led to the temple. Her parents and cousins wept, saying to her, "Confess your sin to the priests, that you were like a dove in God's temple and received food from an angel's hand."

Joseph was called to the holy altar forthwith, and the said water was given to him. It had the property that if a man or woman tasted it and was found to be lying, and went seven times round the altar, God would show by a sign on their face that they were tainted. When he had drunk the potion and had safely done the circuit of the altar, no sign appeared on him. Then all the priests and ministers of the people began to render him justice, saying, "You are blessed, for no guilt is found in you." And then they called Mary, and said to her, "What excuse can you invent? What better sign could appear in you than what your belly shows? We ask only this of you, that you confess who it is that has deceived you. For we now know for certain that Joseph has no guilt in this matter. It would be best for you if your confession shows forth your deeds, that the vengeance and wrath of God may give a sign to show your wickedness before all the people." Then Mary said fearlessly, "If there is any pollution or sin in me, or if any desire for incontinence or unchastity was ever in me, I pray God that it may be shown forth before all the people, so that I may be an example to all liars." She came forward to the altar boldly, and drank the potion water, went round the altar seven times . . . and she was found to be without guilt. Because all the people were astonished, and saw she had conceived in her womb and that no sign appeared on her face, they began to say all manner of things among themselves. Some said she was holy; others accused her through malice and ill will. Then Mary saw the people's suspicion that she was not fully purged.

Tuz oyaunz, [a] clere vois dist : 'Deu le seit, en la regardure ky jo suy esteant, ke unkes conisanse de homme charnele ne aveye, ne ay eu purpos de aver, ke jo establi ma pensé en ço dé enfaunce, e ceste chose ay vouwé a mon Deu, ky jeo puse parmeindre entere en chasteté, a luy qui me crea, e en luy je mey afy e a luy soul, tant cum jo viveray, sanz nul manere de pollucion me tendray.' Dunc comencerunt tuz a douter Deu, e beyserunt Marie e prierent pardun de lur mauveys suspeciun. E tut le pouple, prestres e virgines, a grant joye la menerent deques a sa mesun.[i]

[chap. XIII] Cel fet fu fet del provost de Syre.[ii] Il covent ke Josep[h] alast [f.70r] ové Marie en Bethleem, pur ce ke il steit de Bethleem, e ausi Marie de la lignee Juda e de la mesun e del pays David. E cum il alerent vers Bethleem en la veye, dunt dist Marie a Joseph : 'Jo vey deus poples devant moy, le un plurant e l'autre joye fesaunt.' Joseph le respondi e dist : 'Seez en pes e tenez vus suz le jumente e ne parlez mie trop paroles ne folies.' Dunc lur apparust un bel enfant, ke esteit vestu de blaunk vestement e resplendisant, e dit a Joseph : 'Pur quey deistes trop de paroles e veynes dé deus pouples dé queus vus oyates Marie dire ? Kar ele vit le pople dé Jués en plorant pur ço ke il departist de sun Deu, e la pople dé payns en joyant pur ço ke il approcha a nostre Seynur, e aprochera, sicum [f.70v] il ad pramis a nos peres, e dist dans Habraham, dans Ysaac,[iii] dans[iv] Jacob. Le tens est ja venu ke en le semence[v] Habraam la beniçon seit doné a tute gens.' E cum le angel out dist cele chose, [envanist encoste Betlehem] ;[vi] il comanda sa jumente ester pur ço ke le tens esteit venu ke ele deust enfanter. E il comanda ke Marie descendist e entrat une mesun desuz tere just la veye ou hunkes lumere ne entra, mes tuz jours fu tenebruse. A l'entrer Marie comença le luy a resplendir taunt cum solail i fust, comença demoustrer fudrez, e cum ce fust la sime hore de jour e al dreyn la lumere Deuz enlumina le liu, issi ke de jour ne de noit ne il fayllout la lumere devyne. E la enfanta [f.71r] Marie sun fiz, car l[i] aungel environunerent l'enfaunt nee e aorerent en disant : 'Glorie seit en haut a Deu e en tere pes a homes de bone volunté.' E Joseph esteit ja alé pur quere une femme de estre pres de Marie. E quant il revint, trova ja l'enfant né. Dunc dist Joseph a Marie : 'Je vous ay amené deus femmes ky esteunt issi dehors e ne poent entrer pur la grant lumere ke est ceynz, e sunt apellé Zedemer e Salomee.'

---

[i] Omits *clamantes et dicentes ei, 'Sit nomen Domini benedictum, qui manifestabit sanctitatem tuam universae plebi Israel'* (p. 79, 31–33). [ii] Omits *Factum est autem post aliquantum tempus, ut fieret professio ex edicto Caesaris Augusti, ut proficisceretur unusquisque in patriam suam* (p. 79, 35–80, 2). 'Cel fet' refers to *Hec professio.* [iii] MS dans de Y. [iv] In all three cases of 'dans', MS has d˜s. [v] MS le seinte H. [vi] (Not in Protevangelium); MS Betlehlem.

In the hearing of all, in a clear voice she said, "God knows this, seeing the condition I am in, that I have never known a man carnally; nor have I ever intended to do so. For I set my heart on it as a child and I promised it to my God, that I could remain wholly chaste for him who created me. And I give to him and only him my troth, as long as I shall live, keeping myself from any kind of pollution." Then they all began to fear God, and they kissed Mary and asked pardon for their evil suspicions. And all the people, the priests, and the virgins, led her with great joy to her house.

[chap. XIII] This edict was made by the provost of Syria.[14] Joseph was required to go with Mary to Bethlehem, because he was from there — and so did Mary, of the tribe of Judah and of the house and the land of David. And on the road as they went towards Bethlehem Mary said to Joseph, "I see two peoples before me, one weeping and the other rejoicing." Joseph answered her, saying, "Calm yourself, and sit still on the mare. Don't say such foolish words." Then there appeared to them a beautiful child who was robed in white and shining garments, and said to Joseph, "Why are you saying such foolish words about the two peoples you heard Mary speak of? For she saw the race of the Jews weeping because they were going away from their God, and the race of the pagans rejoicing because they were approaching Our Lord — and shall approach, as he promised to our fathers, and says through Abraham, Isaac, and Jacob. The time has now come, that in the seed of Abraham blessing shall be given to all people." And when the angel had said this, [she began to faint, just near Bethlehem]. He ordered her mare to stop, because the time had come for her to be delivered. And he told her to get down and go into a house under the ground, beside the road, where no light ever entered so it was always filled with shadows. With Mary's entrance, the place began to shine as if the sun had come in, bright as lightning. And as if it were the sixth hour of the day, the light of God brightened the place throughout, so that neither by day nor by night did the divine light fail. And there Mary gave birth to her son, and the angels surrounded the new-born child and worshipped, saying, "Glory to God in the highest, and on earth peace to all men of good will." And Joseph had departed to find a woman to be with Mary. And when he returned, he found the child already born. Then Joseph said to Mary, "I have brought you two women, who were standing outside but could not enter because of the great light that is in here, and their names are Zedemer and Salome."

---

[14] See note opposite; for the edict, see Luke 2:1–2.

Marie oist cete chose, ke plein esteit de sen[i] e de saver e Jesu Crist dedens luy. Pur ço la vertu de Deu e tuz les tresors de sen e de saver dedenz Marie. Ceste se cit ne mie sulement a peez, mes al chef nostre Seynur [f.71v] de oyer la parole Deu. Cest garda tuz les paroles des angeles, des pasturus, des reys e les porta en sun quor. Nul home gusta taunt de dulçure de Deu cum ceste. Ele esteit enbu del delit e de la plentivuse de nostre Seynur. E n'e[st] mie mervelle, kar envers luy e dedens luy esteit la funtayne de vie e de laquele funtayne ert la perfection de l'une vie e de l'autre. Cele esteit ocupé sicome Marcha entour plusurs choses e ele se delitout entur une chose sicum Marie. Pur ço une chose est nessessarie, plusurs choses s'en irront, une chose remeyndra. Ele fist la partie Marthe singuler e ele esleut la tresbone partie Marie, mes la partie Marthe luy est tollu, kar ele ne est [f.72r] ja ententive de server le sicome enfaunt, kar lé ordres des angels le serunt sicum a Seynur e ele ne serra ja desturbé come ele fu fuyant ové luy en Egypte de la Herode. Pur ço ke il est munté en cel e Heroudes est aval en enfern de sa face e ele ne serra ja desturbé entur plusurs choses ke les Jous firunt a sun fiz, pur ço ke tote choses sunt subjet a luy. Le fiz Marie ne serra ja turmenté des Jués ne des chivalers ne occis. Pur ço ke Crist est levé de mort e ja ne mora, la mort n'avera jammés seynurie de luy, pur ço ke la partie Marthe luy est tollu, mes a sun ben, pur ço ke la partye Marie est doné a ly que jamés ne serra de luy tollu, kar ele est enhauscé sur tote la companie des angels, sun desir ja fet en bien e ele veit Deu [f.72v] face a face, sicum il est, ele se joye ové sun fiz saun fin. Cele partie ne serra jamés tollu de ly, de quele partie nous sumus parceners e seroms par ses meritis e par ses prieres e par la grace sun fiz nostre Seynur, Jesu Crist, qui vit e regne ové Deu Pere en unité del Seint Espirit, *per infinita seculorum secula*. Amen.

---

[i] MS sein.

Mary heard these words,[15] who was full of wisdom and knowledge, and Jesus Christ within her. Therefore the power of God and all the treasures of wisdom and knowledge are within Mary. She sat not only at the feet of Our Lord, but by his head, so as to hear the word of God. She kept all the words of the angels, of the shepherds, of the kings, and bore them in her heart.[16] No man ever tasted such sweetness from God as this woman did. She was imbued with joy and with the abundance of Our Lord. And this is no wonder, for around her and within her was the fountain of life, and that fountain shall be the perfection of this life and of the other. She was busy, like Martha, with many things; and she delighted in one thing, like Mary.[17] For one thing is necessary; many will pass away, and one will remain. She did Martha's especial part, and she chose the best part: that of Mary. But Martha's part is taken from her, because she is not minded to serve him like a baby, for the companies of angels will be minded [to serve him] as their Lord, and she shall never again be troubled as she was when she took flight with him from Herod into Egypt. For he went up to Heaven, and Herod is below in Hell, shut out from the sight of his countenance, and she will never more be troubled by the many things the Jews did to her son, because all things are subject to him. The son of Mary will never again be tormented by Jews or soldiers, nor killed. Because Christ is risen from death, and will never die, death will never have dominion over him.[18] Therefore Martha's part is taken from her, but for good, because Mary's part is given to her and will never be taken from her. For she is exalted above the whole company of angels, her desire is ever fulfilled, and she sees God face to face, as he is; she rejoices with her Son for ever. This part will never be taken from her; we are partners in this part, and shall be by her virtues and by her prayers and by the grace of her son Our Lord Jesus Christ, who lives and reigns with God the Father, one with the Holy Spirit, "for ever world without end." Amen.

---

[15] Now the poet abandons the Pseudo-Matthew gospel to embark on a paean to Mary.
[16] Luke 2:19.
[17] For Mary and Martha, sisters of Lazarus, see Luke 10:38–42.
[18] Rom. 6:9.

Chapter 4

Thirteen Joys[1]

Introduction

The following text is found in Oxford, Bodleian Library, MS Bodley 82 (s.xiv^{m}), ff.33r–36v. This meditation on Mary's Joys is probably of Continental composition originally; each prayer or meditation is quite short, and each begins with an address to Our Lady differing slightly from one to the next.[2] Although devotion to the Virgin was in fact shared by men and women, clues in our text indicate that this was a woman's prayer (the speaker calls herself "perdue"). Fifteen Joys are clearly intended, but there are only thirteen here (Nativity and Ascension are missing). Texts of this type may contain between five and twenty Joys: see "Marian devotion" in the General Introduction, above; and see our Harley Prayers for a prayer by five Joys (p. 247, below). In Love's *Mirror* (p. 29), Mary's Five Joys are matched with her five sovereign Virtues: meekness, chastity, faith, hope, and charity. All the events are from the New Testament, except the Assumption.[3]

[1] D&B 766, prose, general heading "Les Quinze Joies Nostre Dame."

[2] Mary is repeatedly addressed as "duce," meaning "sweet," though this word can also be translated more freely ("gentle," "lovely," "dear," etc.); see Carruthers 2006.

[3] See James, *Apocryphal New Testament* (p. 194), and the Assumption text in this volume.

Text

[f.33r] Duce Dame de misericorde, mere de pité, funtayne de tuz bienz, qe portas Jesu Crist nef [moys][i] en vos precius flancs e qui le letates de vos duce mameles, bele treysduce Dame, priez le vostre chere Fiz, qu'il voille aver pité e merci de moy e qu'il me voylle enseygner e me doint en tele manere vivere [f.33v] e en siecle ky jo puse venir a sa misericorde e en la fin a verray confession e verray repentance de tuz les pecchez ky je unkys fiz, e me doint sun beynete cors receyvere al profit de m'alme e quant ele departera de mun cors, qu'il la voylle reseyvere. E ensi luy priez, bel tresduce Dame, e je mey ageneleray quinze feze devant vostre ymage en le honur e en la remembrance des quinze joyes ky vus eustes de vostre chere fiz en terre.

Bele tresduce Dame de Paradis, pur icele g[ra]nt joye ke vus eustes [f.34r] quant ly seint Angel Gabriel vus aporta la novele ke ly salvers de tut le mounde vendroit en vus, duce Dame, priez luy qu'il voylle ouster de moy quanque luy desplet e ke voylle vener en moun quer [e le seint] Espirit uelement.

Tresduce Dame, seinte Marie, pur icele grant joye que vus eustes quant vus alastes en la mountayne visiter seinte Elysabez, vostre cosine, e ele dist ke vus esteyez benete sur totes femmes e ke le frut de vostre ventre esteyt benete, duce Dame, priez luy que sele beneit frut me voylle resayrir.

Tresduce Dame, seinte Marie, pur icele grant joye [f.34v] ke vus eustes kaunt vus sentites mover en vos precius flancs, duce Dame, priez ly ky il voille esmovir moun quer a luy serveir, amer e a honurer.

Tresduce Dame, seint Marie, pur icele grant joye ke vus eustes kant ly pastors vus troverent e vostre duce enfant, duce Dame, priez ly ke jo le pouse trover en totes mes tribulacions e angusses.

Tresduc[e] [D]ame, virgine pucele, pur icele grant joye qe vus eustes quant luy troys roys vindrent offrer a vostre duce enfant or, mirre e encens e il les resçut, duce Dame, priez luy que il voyle reseyveire ma[ii] [f.35r] oreysun e qu'il eit pité de moy.

Tresduce Dame, seynte Marie, pur icele grant joye que vus eustes quant vus offritis al temple vostre cher enfant e seint Symeon le resçut entre ses meyns, duce Dame, priez luy ky il voylle reseyvere m'alme quant ele departera de mon cors.

Tresduce Dame de Paradis, pur icele grant joye ke vus eustes quant vus eustes perdu vostre duz enfant e vus le retrovates entre leus Jués en Jerusalem, duce Dame, priez ly ke sy jo soy perdue par defaute de mé pechez, ke jo leus pousse trover par ses seinte merites.

---

[i] Inserted in a post-medieval hand. [ii] MS ma ma.

Translation

Sweet Lady of mercy, mother of pity, fountain of all virtues, who carried Jesus Christ nine months in your precious womb and suckled him from your sweet breasts, precious Lady, pray your dear Son to have pity and mercy on me; that he will teach me, and grant me so to live in the world that I may come to his mercy, and at last to true confession and true repentance of all the sins I have ever done, and grant me to receive his blessed Body for the good of my soul, and that he will receive my soul when it departs from my body. And pray him thus, dear Lady, and I will kneel fifteen times before your statue in honour and memory of the fifteen joys you had of your dear Son on earth.

Lovely sweet Lady of Paradise, for the great joy you had when the holy angel Gabriel brought you the news that the Saviour of all the world would come into you; dear Lady, pray him to take from me all that displeases him, and to come into my heart, together with the Holy Spirit.

Sweet Saint Mary, for that great joy you had when you went into the mountains to see your cousin Saint Elisabeth, and she said you were blessed above all women, and the fruit of your womb was blessed — dear Lady, pray him that that blessed fruit will receive me.

Sweetest Lady, Saint Mary, for the great joy you had when you felt the movement in your precious womb, gracious Lady, beg him to move my heart to serve, love, and honour him.[1]

Sweetest Lady, Saint Mary, for that great joy you felt when the shepherds found you and your darling baby, Lady, pray him that in all my anguish and tribulation I may find him.

Sweetest Lady, virgin maiden, for the great joy you had when the three kings came to offer your sweet child gold, myrrh, and incense and he accepted them; gentle Lady, beg him that he will accept my prayer and have pity on me.

Sweetest Lady, Saint Mary, for the great joy you had when you offered your beloved child in the temple, and Saint Simeon took him in his hands; blessed Lady, entreat him to take my soul when it leaves my body.

Sweetest Lady of Paradise, for that great joy you felt when you had lost your beloved child, and you found him again among the Jews in Jerusalem; precious Lady, pray him that if I am lost in the guilt of my sins, that I may find him by his holy virtues.

[1] Normally, the Joy of the Nativity would come next.

Tresduce Dame, seint Marie, pur icele grant joye ke vus eustes quant [f.35v] vus somous e as noeces de seym Archedeclin e vostre duce Fiz muta le ewe en vin, duce Dame, priez luy qu'il voyle mover la maveysté de mon quer e de mon cors e moy doyne joye pardurable.

[T]resduce Dame, virgine e pucele, pur icel grant joye ke vus eustes de votre duce Fiz [quant] replenit sink mil homes de sink payns de orge e deus pessons, duce Dame, priez luy ke il mey voyle governer mes cink sens.

Tresduce Dame, virgine pucele, por icel grant joye ke vus eustes quant vostre duce Fiz resçut passion e mort pur nus en la croys, duce Dame, priez luy pur la mort k'il suffri [f.36r] pur nus, [qu'il] mey voyle deliverer de la mort de enfern, e les dolurs e les peynes k'il suffri moy seyent escu encountre les tribulacion[s] de ceste munde al legement de m'alme.

Tresduce Dame, mere Deu, pur icel grant joye ke vus eustes quant vostre duce Fiz resuscita de mort en vie sur le jor de Paskes, duce Dame, priez luy ky jo pouse en tel manere resusciter al tremblable jor de jugement, ke je le peusce ver e salvement de m'alme.

Tresduce Dame, seint Marie, pur icele grant joye qe vus eustes al jor de Pentecoste quant vostre duz Fiz envoya le Seint Espirit a ses deciples e il les lumina [e] enbrasa, duce Dame, priez luy ky il enlumine moy a luy[i] [f.36v] server e amer e conustre e honurer.

Tresduce dame, pur icele grant joye ke vus eustes le jor de vostre Assumpcion quant vostre duz Fiz vus enporta en ciel e vus asist a la destre e le vus corouna sur totes autres, duce Dame, priez a luy pur icele joye que vus eustes adunc pur moy e pur tuz peccheurs e pur totes pecheresses dunt il volt estre depriez, qu'il par sa digne pousance eyent poer e desir de lur pechés amender e pur tuz ceus e pur totes celes ke sunt en bone vie e en bon fey ke Deu les teynge dekes a la fin e pur les trespas ke il unt fet, qu'il eyent merci e repos.

[i] MS mon a luy a luy s.

Sweetest Lady, Saint Mary, for that great joy you had when you were invited to the wedding of Saint Archedeclin,[2] and your dear Son changed water into wine; entreat him that he will change the wickedness of my heart and body, and give me everlasting joy.

Sweetest Lady, virgin and maiden, by the great joy you felt in your dear Son when he filled five thousand people with five barley loaves and two fishes; Lady, beg him to govern my five senses for me.

Sweetest Lady, virgin maid, for that great joy you had when your gentle Son received passion and death for us on the Cross; dear Lady, beg him by the death he suffered for us that he will deliver me from the death of Hell, and may the torments and pains he suffered be my shield against the tribulations of this world, for the relief of my soul.

Sweetest Lady, mother of God, for that great joy you felt when your beloved Son arose from death to life on Easter Day; precious Lady, entreat him that I may likewise arise on the dreadful Day of Judgement: that I may see it, in my soul's salvation.[3]

Sweetest Lady, Saint Mary, for the great joy you had on the day of Pentecost when your beloved Son sent the Holy Spirit to his disciples, and illumined them and set them on fire; dear Lady, beg him to illumine my soul to serve and love him, to know and honour him.

Sweetest Lady, for that great joy you felt on the day of your Assumption, when your dear Son took you away to Heaven and seated you on his right hand and crowned you above all others; by that joy you had then, pray to him for me and for all sinners — men and women whose prayers he would want to hear, that by his worthy might they will wish and desire to amend their sins — and for all those men and women who are in good life and good faith, that God will keep them to the end, and in spite of the sins they have done they may have mercy and peace.

---

[2] See John 2:8–9. The *architriclinus* was steward of the wedding feast. This title was erroneously taken as a name, a) of the steward or b) of the bridegroom at Cana; because this occasion was so holy, the figure was taken to be a saint (see Trotter 1987).

[3] Normally, the Joy of Christ's Ascension would come next.

Chapter 5

Assumption[1]

Introduction

The Assumption text presented here is from Oxford, University Coll. MS 100 (s.xiii^{m}), ff.100ra–109va.[2] There are eight Anglo-Norman manuscripts. Attributed to Wace by Dean and Boulton, and Continental in composition (probably before 1155), the poem survives in a score of manuscripts. The evidence for Wace's authorship is strong but not conclusive. If he did write it, it may have been before his *Brut* — perhaps to promote the Feast of the Immaculate Conception; this would date it to 1130–40. The Assumption material is largely based on the "Liber de transitu beatae Mariae virginis" (Pseudo-Melito).[3] Ashford's edition (*The Conception Nostre Dame*) takes the Tours MS[4] as base with variants from the others. The poem, as edited here, corresponds to lines 1128 to the end in Ashford's edition, and begins with a sketch of Mary's family (summarized in the figure opposite).[5]

The poem has a personal tone: the writer frequently uses phrases like "parlerum," "voil conter," "sicum vus avez oi dire." A number of Bible stories are referred to, and Peter says the psalm *In Exitu* (vv. 471–72) — this is not translated, so it appears that the audience is expected to be familiar with it, as with the untranslated phrase at v. 234. The poem ends with an affirmation of faith ("si nul demande ke jo crei . . .") in the Virgin's purity, and in her Assumption.

[1] D&B 489, verse, entitled "La Conception Notre Dame by Wace."

[2] See Meyer 1906.

[3] See James, *Apocryphal New Testament* (pp. 209 ff), and Wace's *Conception* (ed. Ashford), for further details about other apocryphal sources. See also the version in *GL*, II:77–97.

[4] Tours, Bibl. Munic., MS 927 (Marmoutier 237). The Oxford MS was known to Ashford, and is listed as his "MS O."

[5] See *GL*: for the family, II:150; for James the Greater, II:3; James the Less, I:270; Simon and Jude, II:260 (see also the entries for these in *ODS*).

Mary's Family

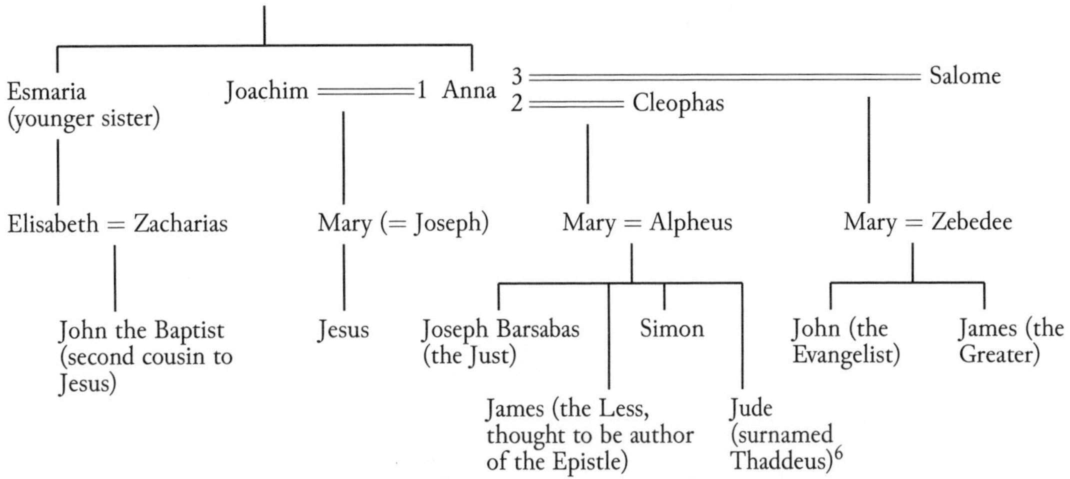

[6] See text below, p. 165, where James is said to be "son of Thaddeus"; "son" is probably an error for "brother."

Text

[f.100ra]
[P]arlerum a la Deu aïe
Com(ent) Nostre Dame issi de
(ceste) vie
Quant Deu la fist al ciel munter.
Mais primerement voil conter
Un petit de sun parenté
Dunt maint[e] gent avunt duté.
Une sorur out seint' Anna
Kë out a nun Esmaria.
Elizabeth fud de lui nee
K'a Zacharie fud donee.[i]
Dë eus dous fud cil Johans né[ii]
Ki Baptistes fud apelé,
Ki le baptesme començat
E Jhesu Crist [pus] baptizat.
[f.100rb]
Seint' Anna fud la soer ainzne[e],[iii]
Treis feiz fut [ele] marie[e]
De lui furent treis filles neies
Ke Maries sunt apeleies.
Treis soru[r]s furent d'une mere,[iv]
Mais chescune out par sei sun
pere.
Joachim fud li primer sire,
Sicum vus avez oï dire,
Li secund out nun Cleophas,[v]
E li terz out nun Salomeas.
Joachim fud pere Marie
Ki nus restorra nostre vie.
Quant Joachim fu devïez
E de cest secle [fu] passez,
Ceo lui loërent si ami
K'Anna pre[ï]st autre mari.[vi]
[f.100va]
Par le los ke sages li fist
Cleophas, un prodome, prist.
De ces dous fu Marie nee
Kë ad Alpheüm fu donee.
De lui out dous fiz Alpheüs,
Ceo fud Joseph e Jacobus.
Cil Jacobus apostres fu,
[E] frerë apelét Jesu.
Frere dist [l'em] par parenté,
Auques le resemblout de hé,[vii]
[Mult] le resemblout de façun,[viii]
Si fud de grant religïun.
Ceo dist sa vie k'il vesqui
Mult seintement tant k'il fini.
Unques ne but cisre ne vin,
Tuz si drapel furent de lin.[ix]
Unques de nule vesteüre
Ke fust de leine në out cure.
Në out cure de char manger,[x]
[f.100vb]
Ne cessout pas de Deu prier.
Tant fut li sains en genuilluns
E tant priad a aureisuns
K'il out la char crue mult grant[xi]
Desur les dous genuus devant.
Cil Jakes vit la Passïun
La u esteit en oreisun.[xii]
En Jherusalem fut occis,
Si s'en alat en Paraïs.
[A]gna pus la mort Cleophas
Refud done[e] a Solomeas.

[i] MS Ke a. [ii] MS nee. [v] MS secunde out a nun. [vi] MS Ke Anna. [vii] MS hee. [ix] MS Trestuz. [x] MS chare. [xi] MS creu. [xii] MS u il esteit.

Translation

1 Let us speak, with God's help, about how Our Lady[1] went out of this life when God took her up to Heaven.

4 But first I want to tell a little of her family, which many people have wondered about. Saint Anna had a sister whose name was Esmaria.

9 Elisabeth was born of her, who was given to Zacharias. From these two was born that John who was called Baptist, who began the practice of baptism, and baptised Jesus Christ. Saint Anna was the elder sister; she was married three times.

17 From her were born three daughters, who were called Mary. Three sisters were from one mother. But each had her own father. Joachim was the first father, whom you have heard tell of. The second was named Cleophas, and the third was named Salome.

25 Joachim was the father of Mary, who restored life to us. When Joachim had died and passed from this world, Anna's friends advised this: that she should take another husband. Following their wise advice she took Cleophas, a worthy man.

33 Of these two Mary was born, who was given to Alpheus. By him, Alpheus, she had two sons, Joseph and James.

37 This James was an apostle and he called Jesus brother. They were known as brothers by parentage. He was not close to him in age, but he resembled him very much in manner.[2] He was very religious. His *Life* says he lived in a very holy fashion, to the end.

45 He never drank cider or wine. All his clothes were of linen; he never cared to wear any garment that was of wool. Nor did he care to eat meat. He never ceased praying to God.

51 The saint was on his knees so much, and he was at prayer so much, that he had great patches of raw flesh on his knees at the front. This James saw the Passion, there where he was in prayer. He was killed in Jerusalem, and then went to Paradise.

59 Then after Cleophas' death Anna was given anew, to Salome.

---

[1] "Nostre Dame" is not in Ashford's text, but is supplied by the writer because the text of this version begins here: A "Coment eissi de ceste vie" (v. 1130).

[2] See *GL* I.270: this resemblance explains why Judas had to identify Jesus, at his arrest, by kissing him.

D'eus dous fust une fille ne[e][i]
Ke Marie fud apelee.
Si fud dune[ë] a Zebee,
Un prodome de Galilee.
De lui furent né dous baruns,
Le greinnur Jamë apeluns,
Ki Herodes fist martirer,[ii]
Le chef a une feiz trencher.
[f.101ra]
Li autre frere, le puisnez,
Fut par nun Johan apelét.
Jeo ne di pas Johan Baptiste,[iii]
Ainz di Johans Evangeliste.
Cestui amat plus Jhesu Crist
Ke nul autre ke li servist,[iv]
Pur ceo l'ama meïme[me]nt
Kë il vesqui virginaument,
Pur ço l'out en greinnur cherté[v]
Kë il guarda virginité.
Quant pur nostre redemptïun
Suffri Jhesu Crist passïun
E pur nos pecchez fu dampnez
E en la seint[e] croiz posez,
Li apostres se departirent,
De dreit[e] poür le guerpirent,
Ne remist nul fors seint Johan
Ke vit le travail e le han,
Les peines e les [grans] dolurs,
[f.101rb]
Ke Deu suffri pur peccheürs.
Quant en la crois fu li Sauvere,
Dejuste la croiz vit sa mere
E Johan avoc k'il amat,
L'un[e] a l'autre [si] comandat
A meintenir e a guarder
E a servir e a amer,
K'ele fuist mere e il fust fiz.[vi]
Cil firent ben sulunc ses dis,
Cil ki esteit nevou [fiz] devint
E pur mere leument la tent,
Al nevou fud l'autre livre[e],
Curteise fu cele asemblee,
Kar virgine a virgine comanda
E virgine virgine aconpaingna.[vii]
Curteisement pere apelat[viii]
Quant virgine a virgine comanda.
Deu mult par est ben[e]ürez,
Seit hom, seit femme, bor fu nez!
[f.101va]
Qui set virginité guarder
Ben peot as angles resembler.
Qui ceste bunté ad perdue,
Puis ne pot estre a nul rendue.
Ja puis ne serra recovre[e]
K'ele ert une feit vïole[e].[ix]
Ben deit l'em del perdre guarder
Ke l'em ne pot pas recovrer.
Autres vertuz, autres buntez[x]
Puet recovrer ki volt asez.
Ki guerpi ad humilité
Guarde honur, si avrat bunté.[xi]
Ki de ben est venu a vice
E de largesce en avarice,
De ço se poet il ben retraire
Së il encontre volt ben faire.

[i] MS De eus. [ii] MS martirizer. [iii] MS abaptiste. [iv] MS nul des autres. [v] MS chereté. [vi] MS Ke ele. [vii] MS v. a v. acoipaingna. [viii] MS le pere. [ix] MS Ke ele. [x] MS v. e a. b. [xi] MS g. ben h.

61 Of these two was born a daughter who was named Mary. She was given to Zebedee, a worthy man of Galilee. Of her were born two good men: the greater of them we call James, whom Herod had martyred — he had his head cut off.

69 The other brother, the younger, was called John by name. I'm not talking of John the Baptist, but of John the Evangelist.[3] Jesus Christ loved this one more than any other who served him, and this is why he loved him especially: because he lived virginally. Therefore he held him in greater affection, because he kept his virginity.

79 When for our redemption Jesus Christ suffered death, and was condemned for our sins and placed on the holy Cross, the apostles went away. In downright terror they forsook him; none remained but Saint John, who saw the travail and the suffering, the pains and the great torments, that God endured for sinners.

89 When the Saviour was on the Cross, he saw before the Cross his mother and John, whom he loved, with her. He commended the one to the other, to keep and guard, to serve and love, she to be the mother and he the son.

96 They did as he said: he who had been nephew became [son] and loyally treated her as mother. And she was given to the nephew; this was a noble arrangement, for virgin was commended to virgin, and virgin accompanied virgin. The Father spoke nobly when he commended virgin to virgin.

105 He is very blessed of God: whether man or woman, happy they were born! He who is able to keep his virginity is like the angels. Whoever has lost this virtue, never again can it be restored to anybody. Never can it be recovered, when it has once been reft away. One should guard well against losing what one cannot recover. Other virtues, other good things, one can recover if one wants to badly enough.

117 Whoever has forsaken humility, let him keep honour and he will regain virtue. Whoever has fallen from virtue to vice, and from generosity to avarice, he may be able to draw back if he truly wants to struggle against it.

3 In the Middle Ages John the Evangelist was often considered to be identical with John the Divine, author of the Book of Revelation.

Ki ad guerpi sa vertu,[i]
Reprenge la sicum ainz fud.
Virginité n'ad autrement,
[Del recovrer est puis nient]
Virginité ne put hum mie[ii]
[f.101vb]
Recovrer pus k'ele est honie.[iii]
Ceste guarda seint Johan ben,
Ne la voleit perdre pur rien.
Pur ces vertuz l'out Deu si cheres
K'il l'en fist sun privé chamberes,
E sa mere a lui comanda
E en la fin mult l'honura,[iv]
Kar al terme k'il finir dust,
Nostre Sire li aparust,[v]
Si li dist : 'Vein t'en, mis amis,[vi]
A tes freres en Paraïs.'
En suen sepulcre vis entra
E ses compangnuns salua,
E a covrir se comanda,
Issi dist l'em k[ë] il fina.
[Q]uant l'em vout le cors regarder
K'en quidout en terre trover,[vii]
Ne trovat nun si manne nun,
[f.102ra]
Ço nus reconte sa lesçun.
Manne resemble par blancheur,
Novele neif u blanche flur.
Cist Johan dunt jeo vus di,
Sicum Jhesus l'out establi
Out en guarde e en conpaignie
Nostre Dame seint[e] Marie.
[E] quant li apostres precherent
E par le mund Deu anuncerent[viii]
E il urent issi sorti
Ke trestuz furent departi,
Johans a sa dame ostel prist
Dejuste le munt Olivete la mist
Ovoc gent de sun parenté
Ke mult l'urent en grant cherté.
Virgines od sei plusurs aveit
K'ele nurri et ensegneit.[ix]
L'an secund aprés la Passiun[x]
Ert Nostre Dame en sa maisun,
[f.102rb]
Sule [e] en dolur privément,
Si prist a plorer tendrement
Pur amur e pur desirer
De sun fiz k'el out [si tres]cher.[xi]
E [si] se mist en genillun[xii]
E puis dist [il] cest' ureisun :
'[M]ut vosisse, si Deu pl[e]üst,
Ke Deus ore me receüst.
Forment desire ke la fuisse
U [jeo] mun [cher] fiz veër puisse.
Beau Sire e Reis regarde mai,[xiii]
Fei que jeo puisse estre ovoc tei
La u tu es en Paraïs
Ke tu pramis a tes amis.'
A ço ke la dame plurout
Pur sun fiz que tant desirout
Es vus l'angle Nostre Seignur[xiv]
Od merveilluse resplendur.[xv]
Devant lui vint si li donat
[f.102va]
Un raim de palme k'il portat,[xvi]

---

[i] MS vertuz. [ii] MS num mie. [iii] MS ke ele. [iv] MS le honura. [v] MS aparuit. [vi] MS veint te amis. [vii] MS Ke l'en. [viii] MS anuncirent. [ix] MS Ke ele. [x] MS secunde. [xi] MS chere. [xii] MS genisun. [xiii] MS sire e sire r. [xiv] MS le angle. [xv] MS resplendisur. [xvi] MS ke il.

123 Whoever has forsaken his virtue, let him take to it again as before. Virginity is not like this [there is no recovering of it afterwards].[4] Nobody can ever regain virginity once it has been shamed.

129 Saint John kept this well; he did not want to lose it for anything. For these virtues God held him so dear that he made him his best friend and commended his mother to him, and honoured him greatly at the end.

135 For when it was time for him to die Our Lord appeared to him and said to him, "Come away, my friend, to your brothers in Paradise." He entered his grave alive, and greeted his companions; he asked them to cover him. Thus, they say, he ended his life.

145 When they wanted to look at the body they thought they would find in the earth, they found nothing but manna: this is what the legend tells us. Manna, in its whiteness, is like new snow or white flour.[5]

151 This John I'm telling you of, just as Jesus had arranged it, had Our Lady Saint Mary in his ward and his company. And when the apostles preached and proclaimed God throughout the world, and they had gone forth and all departed, John took a lodging for his Lady.

160 He placed her near to the Mount of Olives, with people of their family who held her in great affection. She had a number of virgins with her, whom she tended and taught.

165 The second year after the Passion, Our Lady was in her house; alone, and in private sorrow, she began to weep tenderly for love and longing for her Son whom she held so dear. She went down on her knees and then said this prayer:

173 "If it pleased God, I would so dearly like God to receive me now. I desire so much to be there, where I can see my dear Son. Fair Lord and King, look at me. Make it so I can be with you, there where you are in Paradise, as you have promised to your friends."

181 As the Lady wept for her Son whom she so desired, behold, the angel of Our Lord, in marvellous splendour, came before her and gave her a branch of palm that he carried.

---

[4] Blank in MS; the line is imported from Ashford (v. 1256).

[5] For the manna found in John's grave, etc., see e.g. his legend in *The Early South English Legendary* (ed. Horstmann).

Pus [li] dist il : 'De Paraïs
T'at Deu cest raim [ici] tramis.
De cest secle trepasseras,
D'hui al tierz jor al ciel serras.[i]
Tis fiz t'atent od ses archangles,
Od ses vertuz e od ses angles.
Devant ta bere fai porter
Le raim kë il t'a fait doner.'
[Q]uant la Virgine ad le raim eu,
A l'anglë ad tost respundu :
'Jhesu puisse jeo gracïer
E ceo te prie e ceo requere
K'ici seient od mei le jor[ii]
Tuz li apostres mun Seignur.'
Encontre ço li angles dist :
'Par la vertu de Jhesu Crist
Serrunt ici tuz asemblé
Sicum vus l'avez demandé.'
[f.102vb]
[Q]uant li angles out si parlé
E le raim de sa main livré
E il fu de la chambre issu,
La Dame ad ses meillurs dras vestus,
Pus est de la meisun turne[e]
E al munt d'Olivete alee.[iii]
S'ureisun la reïne i fist,[iv]
A Dampnedeu parla si dist :[v]
'Deu glorïables, reis benigne,
Unkes nul jor tant ne fui digne[vi]
Ke tu en mei descendre deusses
Si tu de mei merci n'en eusses.
E nequedent ben ai guardé
Le tresor que tu m'as doné.[vii]
Tei depri, Rei de Majesté,
Ke nule enfernale poësté
Ne puisse ferë annuisance
Ne n'ait vers mai nule pussance.
Recoil mei en ta compaignie
[f.103ra]
Od tei en pardurable vie
U set cent angles chescun jor
Trenblent devant tei de poür.
Ben deit hom estre esponté
Ki de tere est fait e furmé,
Ki n'ad de ben ne de bunté
Fors tant cum tu l'en as doné.
T[res]tut le ben k'il ad receu
Ad il de ta largescë eu.
Deus es e as beneïçon
In secula seculorum.'
[Q]uant la Dame out fait s'ureisun,[viii]
Si s'en repeire a sa maisun.[ix]
Dunc apelé [ad] ses veisins
E ses amis e ses cosins
Si lur dist : 'Vus ki estes ci,
Oez e creez ço que vus di.
De cest secle turner m'en dai[x]
[f.103rb]
E Deus me deit mener od sei.
Pur ceo vus di que vus veillez
Deci que pres ma fin veez.
Sachez ke quant hom deit murrir
E l'alme deit del cors issir,
Dous angles entur sei descendent[xi]
Mult ententif ke l'alme atendent.
Li uns est del ciel descenduz,
Li autre d'enfern [est] venuz.
Chescun en vout l'almë atraire,
Mes lur veie est forment contraire :

[i] MS De hui. [ii] MS Ke ici. [iii] MS de Olivete. [iv] MS Sa u. [v] MS si li d. [vi] MS nule. [vii] MS me as d. [ix] MS reperire. [x] MS ceste.

187 Then he said to her, "From Paradise God has sent this branch [here] to you. You shall pass away from this world: on the third day from today you shall be in Heaven. Your Son awaits you with his Archangels, with his Virtues,[6] and with his Angels. The branch that he has given you, let it be carried before your bier."

195 When the Virgin had received the branch, she quickly replied to the angel: "Let me give thanks to Jesus,[7] and I ask and beg of you that all the apostles of my Lord may be there with me that day."

201 To this, the angel said: "By the power of Jesus Christ they shall all be gathered here, as you have asked."

205 When the angel had said this, and delivered the branch from his hand, and had gone out of the chamber, the Lady put on her best clothes. Then she went away from the house, and went to the Mount of Olives. There the Queen made her prayer and spoke to the Lord God, saying:

213 "Glorious God, kindly King, never once would I have been worthy enough for you to come down into me, unless you had had mercy on me. Nevertheless I have kept the treasure well, that you gave me. I pray you, King of Majesty, that no infernal power may do me any harm, nor have any power over me. Receive me into your company, with you in everlasting life, where seven hundred angels every day tremble in awe before you.

227 "Man may well be in terror: he who is made and formed of earth, and who has neither good nor virtue except as much as you have given him. All the good he receives, he has had through your generosity. You are God, and have blessings, world without end."

235 When the Lady had made her prayer, she returned to her house. Then she called her neighbours, and her friends and cousins, and said to them:

239 "You who are here, hear and believe what I tell you. I am going to leave this world, and God is going to lead me with him. Therefore I say this to you: watch now until you see me near my end.

245 "Know that when somebody is to die, and the soul to go forth from the body, two angels come down around them. They wait very intently for the soul. One is from Heaven, the other comes from Hell. Each wants to take the soul, but their way is very different:

---

6 For the Orders of Angels, see General Introduction, p. 14 above.

7 Some manuscripts add two and even four lines here (Ashford's critical apparatus, note to vv. 1327–29).

Kar sulunc ço ke l'alme ad fait,
Aneire est recunté senz pleit.
Mes de mei ne seit pas dutance
Ke nule maligne puissance
Me puisse faire desturber
Ne vers mei poüst aprocher.'
[L]a Dame esteit a sun ostel
U parlout de ceo e dë el.[i]
[f.103va]
Seint Johan ki a guarder l'out
En Ephese iert u il prechout.
Par un dimaine tirce esteit
Quant il al pople sermoneit.
E Deus un terremot[e] fist
E un[e] nue vint k'il prist
De terre e d'eloc le levat,
En Josaphat l'en aportat,
A l'ostel ou la dame fu.
Quant Nostre Dame [si] l'ad veu
E il fud aprismé a lui,
'Fiz Johan,' dist elë a lui,
'Pur amur Deu ore te pri
Ke tu aies en remenbrance,
Ne metez pas en ublïance,
Les paroles que Deu parla
Quant il mei a tei comanda,
Car al terz jur desseverat[ii]
L'alme de mei, si s'en irrat.
[f.103vb]
Mais lui Jeüs unt purparlé
E de ço lur cunseil fermé,
K'aprés ma mort f[e]runt arder[iii]
Mun cors, s'il le pöunt aver.[iv]
Pur sul iço ke jeo portai
E ke jeo mun fiz aletai
Jhesu Crist [ki est] mun Sauveur
Kë il tienent pur sudoitur.'
Dunc va la Dame en sun recoi,
Seint Johan meinë ovoc soi[v]
Si lui mustra un vestement[vi]
A sun ensepelisement.
'Johan,' dist ele, 'tien ces dras
Dunt ensepelir me f[e]ras.'[vii]
Puis lui mustra le raim k'el out
Ke luminarie grant jetout,[viii]
Si li ruva faire porter
Devant la bere a l'enterer.
'Dame,' dist il, 'jo ne puis mie
[f.104ra]
Tel mester feire sanz aïe.
Ne puis sul faire tel mester
Ne tuen sepulcre aparailler
Si li apostre od mei ne sunt[ix]
Ki ta sepulture f[e]runt.'
Endementres ke si parlout
E les apostres remenbrout,
Es vus les apostres venuz
E d'une nue descenduz.
[C]ele nue les assemblat,
De plusurs lius les amenat
U il i erent pur precher
E la lei Deu annuncïer.
Si vus volez, d'icés baruns
Si purrez ben oïr les nuns :
Peres, Johans, Jakes, Andreu,
L'autre Jakes, le fiz Taddeu,[x]
Bartholomeu, Philip, Thomas.

[i] MS U ele p. [ii] MS terce. [iii] MS Ke apres. [iv] MS si il . . . avere. [v] MS sei. [vi] MS une. [vii] MS ensepelire me fras. [viii] MS mult grant. [ix] MS apostres. [x] MS Li autre.

253 "For, depending on what the soul has done, it is all recounted forthwith, without discussion. But for me let there be no doubt — let no malign power be able to trouble me, nor be able to approach me."

259 The Lady was at her lodging, where she spoke of this and of other things. Saint John, who was her guardian, was in Ephesus where he was preaching. It was on a Sunday, at the hour of Tierce, that he was teaching the people.

265 And God made an earthquake, and a cloud came that took him up off the ground and lifted him from that place and brought him to Josaphat, to the lodging where the Lady was. When Our Lady saw him and he approached her, she said to him:

272 "John, my son, I now pray you for the love of God to remember, and not to forget,[8] the words God spoke when he commended me to you. For in three days my soul will depart from me and go hence. But the Jews have plotted and decided on their plan in this matter: after my death they will have my body burned, if they can get it, only because I bore and suckled my Son, Jesus Christ [who is] my Saviour, whom they hold to be a false prophet."

287 Then the Lady went to a private place, leading Saint John with her. She showed him a vesture for her burial. "John," she said, "take this robe that you are to bury me in."

293 Then she showed him the branch she had, that gave forth great light, and begged him to have it carried to the burial in front of the bier.

297 "Lady," he said, "I cannot do this business without help. A task such as this I cannot do alone, nor prepare your sepulchre, if the apostles who will make ready your sepulchre are not with me."

303 While he was speaking, and remembering the apostles, lo! they arrived, coming down in a cloud. This cloud had gathered them and brought them from several places where they had been to preach and announce the Word of God.

311 If you want to hear the names of these good men, you shall: Peter, John, James, Andrew, the other James son of Thaddeus,[9] Bartholomew, Philip, Thomas, and Simon.

[8] The copyist has made three lines out of two; see Ashford, 'Johanz, dist ele, ore te pri' (v. 1400).

[9] This is very probably James (the Less): one of his brothers, Jude, was also known as Thaddeus, and the writer may have put "son" for "brother" by mistake; see above, p. 155 and note 6.

[E] Simun ; le mauveis Judas
[f.104rb]
Fut mis hors de la conpaignie
Pur ço k'il fist la felunie.[i]
Mathïas fu en sun liu mis[ii]
Ki par sort fu eslu e pris.
[Q]uant devant l'ostel venu furent
La u la Dame ert se conurent,[iii]
Conurent sei, ben s'entrevirent,
S'entrebeiserent, joie firent.[iv]
A merveilluse chose tindrent
K'en tel manere s'entrevi[nd]rent,[v]
E si ne sevent l'acheisun
Pur quei [il] vindrent ne par hund.
Dunc seint Johan est fors issuz
De la maisun, si [le]s ad veuz,
[f.104va]
Ensemble les ad saluez,
Pus les ad a l'ostel menez.
[Q]uant li barun [ded]einz entrerent,
Nostre Dame si saluerent :
'Li tres haut Rei vus beneïe,'
'E vus,' ço dist seinte Marie,
'Or me dites cumfaitement[vi]
Estes venuz tant sudaiment.'
Seint Johan [li] respunt primer :[vii]
'En Ephese estei pur precher,
Od mei aveit grant assemble[e]
E grant pople de la cuntree,
Quant une nue iloc me prist,
D'entr'eus m'emblat e ci me mist.'[viii]
Chescuns li redist ensement
De quel terre il vint e coment.[ix]
'Deu', dist ele, 'seit mercïez
Ke vus tuz ad ci assemblez
[f.104vb]
A faire mun confortement
Encontre mun trespassement.
Mais or, seignurs, vellir devuns[x]
E estre tuz en ureisuns
Desci k'al jur que Deu vendra,
M'alme del cors departira.'
Quant il urent tuz otrïé
E desquë al tierz jur veillé
E en afflictïons esté,
Dampnedeu preé e loué,
Al tiers jur endreit la terce ure
Un tel sumul lur cur[u]t sure
Ne n'out nul en la meisun
Ke ne dormist, si apostre nun.
Li apostres pas ne dormirent
Ne treis virgines kë iloc furent.
Quant li autres sunt endormi,
Jhesu Crist entr'eus descendi,[xi]
Ensemble od lui out grant clarté
[f.105ra]
E de ses angles grant plenté,
Ki tuz chantent par grant duçur[xii]
E louen[t] Deu nostre Seignur,
Nel vus puis pas conter ne dire.
Issi parla bien nostre Sire :

[i] MS ke il. [ii] MS fu en eus en. [iii] MS si se c. [iv] MS grant joie. [v] MS Ke en tele. [vi] MS Ore. [ix] MS quele. [x] MS ore. [xi] MS entre eus. [xii] MS chanterent.

316 The wicked Judas was excluded from the company because he committed treason. Matthias was put into his place; he was chosen by lot and accepted.

321 When they had arrived before the lodging where the Lady was, and knew and recognized one another, they looked at one another and kissed and made great joy. They thought it a marvellous thing that they had all come together so; they did not know the reason why they had come, nor how.

329 Then Saint John came out of the house and saw them, and greeted them all and led them into the lodging. When the good men went in they greeted Our Lady:

335 "May the Most High God bless you." "And you," said Saint Mary. "Now tell me how it is you have arrived so suddenly."

339 Saint John replied first: "I was in Ephesus to preach. With me there was a great assembly, and many people of the region, when a cloud took me up there, hiding me from them, and brought me here." Each one told her, likewise, what region he had come from and how.

347 "God be thanked," she said, "that he has assembled you all here, to comfort me at my passing. But now, lords, we must all watch and stay in prayer from now until the day that God will come and separate my soul from my body."

355 When they had all agreed, they watched and were sorely troubled until the third day, praying and praising God; on the third day, about the third hour, such a sleep descended on them that there was nobody in the house not asleep except the apostles.

363 The apostles did not sleep, neither did three virgins who were there. When the others were asleep, Jesus Christ came down among them.

367 With him was a great light, and a great number of his angels, all singing most sweetly and praising God our Lord — I can neither tell you nor speak of it. Thus said Our Lord:

'[M]arie, gemme precïuse,
Virgine seintisme, mere, espuse,
Vien t'en en pardurable vie,
Evangeline conpaignie.
Jo sui ti fiz e sui tun pere,
Tu es ma fille, si es ma mere.
Ben est dreit[ure], e jeo l'otrei,
Ke tu seez ensemble od mei.
Tu me portas e me nuriz,
Si me lettas e mei servis.
Quant jeo pur le [munde] sauver
Degnai en terre converser,
Unkes ne poi femme trover
Fors tei u jeo deüsse entrer.
[f.105rb]
Car recet [e] ostel me fus,[i]
[Mult] volunters [tu] me receus,
Desore serras benure[e],
Reïne del ciel corune[e].
Jeo sui rais, tu serras reïne,
Bunté serrat a tei acline.
La poüsté d'aider avras[ii]
A tuz iceis ke tu voldras.'
Quant Nostre Dame l'out oï,
Jus a la tere s'estendi.
Ureisun fist mut humblement
E pria Deu Omnipotent :
'Deu, ki eslire me dignas
E ton secroi me comandas
Sicum tu sez ke jo t'amai[iii]
E tuen commandement gardai,
E tut ço fis ke tu vousis,[iv]
M'alme receif en Paraïs.'
[Q]uant ele out s'ureisun finee,[v]
[f.105va]
Idunc arere s'est turne[e].
Dunc est l'alme del cors issue
E Jhesu Crist l'ad [bien] receue.
A seint Michael la comandat
[E sainz Michael bien la garda]
E seint Gabriel odvoc lu,[vi]
Ço sunt li maistre angle Deu.
Li angles vunt entur chantant
E mult ducement Deu loant.
Od ses angles va li Salvere,
Grant joiё en funt de sa mere.
As apostres ad comandé
A destre part de la cité[vii]
Le cors a la Dame porter
E al sepulcre iloc poser.[viii]
[Les] treis virgines iloc estei[en]t
Ki avoc eus veillé aveient,
[f.105vb]
Le cors seintisme despoillerent,
A l'enterer l'aparillerent.[ix]
Tant le troverent blanc e cler[x]
Quë ens nel poënt esguarder,
Car tant i out de la blanccheur
E tant avoc de resplendur[xi]
K'eles le cors veer ne po[e]ient[xii]
Si le raguouent e teneient.[xiii]
Quant eles unt le cors lavé
E pus vestu e aturné,
En une bere le cucherent
E dunc aprés si esveillerent
Icil ki devant se dormeient,
Leverent sus, la bere veient.

---

[i] MS osteles. [ii] MS de aider averas. [iii] MS tei amai. [iv] MS iço. [vi] MS Michael. [vii] MS parte. [viii] MS posee. [ix] MS E a l'encerer. [x] MS clere. [xi] MS resplendisur. [xii] MS Ke eles. [xiii] MS E sil le.

373 "Mary, precious jewel, holiest virgin, mother, spouse, come away into everlasting life and the company of angels. I am your Son, and I am your Father; you are my daughter and also my mother. It is right, and I grant, that you should be together with me. You bore me and fed me, you suckled me and looked after me.

383 "When I deigned to come and live in the way of the world, to save the world, never could I find a woman, except you, whom I could enter into. You were my refuge and lodging, you received me very willingly; henceforth you shall be blessed, and crowned Queen of Heaven. I am King, you shall be Queen. Bounty shall be yours: you shall have the power to help all those whom you wish to."

395 When Our Lady had heard this, she bowed right down to the earth. She made her prayer most humbly, and begged Almighty God: "God, who has deigned to choose me and to commend your secrets to me, because you know that I loved you and I kept your commandment and did all that you wanted, receive my soul in Paradise." When she had ended her prayer, she turned away.

407 Then the soul came out of her body, and Jesus Christ received it. He commended it to Saint Michael, [and Saint Michael received it safely];[10] he and Saint Gabriel with him, who are the masters of God's angels.

413 The angels went round about, singing and praising God very sweetly. The Saviour went with his angels, and they made great joy of his mother. He commanded the apostles to take the body of the Lady to the south side of the city, and there place it in the sepulchre.

421 The three virgins were there, who had kept vigil with them. They undressed that most holy body, and prepared it for burial. They found it so white and shining they could not look at it, for in it was such whiteness, together with such splendour, that they could not see it where they [. . .][11] and held it.

431 When they had washed the body, and then dressed and prepared it, they laid it on a bier. After that, those who had been asleep before awoke; they got up and saw the bier.

[10] Not in MS: this is Ashford's v. 1536.

[11] Ashford "raguouent e bailloent" (v. 1566). The meaning of "raguouent" is uncertain; cf. *GL* II:80: "while it could be touched and bathed, it could not be seen."

[Q]uant unt fait l'apar[i]lement
[f.106ra]
Cum del porter al monument
Entr'eu[s] dïent e vunt querant[i]
Ki portera le raim devant
Ki ert venu de Paraïs.
Dunc seint Johan le raim ad pris.
A seint Pere le volt livrer,
'Tu dois', dist il, 'cest raim porter,[ii]
Car tu as sur nus la mestrie
E trestute la seignurie.
Tu dois del ciel lé clefs tenir,[iii]
Paradis clorë e ovrir,
Par tei deit hom aver entre[e]
La poüsté t'en est donee.'
E Seint Pere li respundi :
'Ami,' dist il, 'n'ert mie issi,
[f.106rb]
Tu es virgine de grant bunté,
Si es de grant auctorité,
Ki do[r]mis sur le piz Jhesu
La nuit que la traïsun fu.
E quant il en la crois fu mis,
Tu kë esteies sis amis,
Sa mere a regarder receus.
Virgines esteies, virgines fus.[iv]
Tu deis aler devant la bere
E porter le raim de lumere.
Nus autres le cors porterum
E cel autre mestre f[e]rum.'
Seint Johan issi l'otrïa
Cum seint Pere lë esgarda.
[D]unc ad seint Pere prist le co[rs],
De la meisun le port[a] hors,
Al mettre fors de la maisun
Dit un psaume ki si out nun :
[f.106va]
In exitu Israel de Egypto
Domus Jacob de populo suo [Ps. 113:1].
Quant la bere fu fors issu
Devers le ciel vint une nue,
Les environat e covri[v]
E tut entur si espandi.
Li apostres communement
Dedenz chanterent ducement,
Ensenble aveient grant clarté[vi]
Del raim kë ert devant porté.
Cil de Jerusalem oïrent[vii]
Le chant que li apostres firent,
Si issirent fors de la vile
Ke hom ke femme .xv. mile,
Ki [tres]tuz erent demandant
Ki ert ki feseit si duz chant.
Sempres fu venu ki lur dist
[f.106vb]
Ke Marie, le mere Crist,
Ert le jor a sa fin venue,
S'alme esteit ja del cors issue.
E li apostre issi chanterent[viii]
Ki al sepulcre le porterent.[ix]
Dunc unt la bere aperceue[x]
E la clarté dedenz veüe.
Dé Jueus [la] i out un maistre
Ki se començat a irestre,
Par mautalent e par grant ire
Començat as Jeüs a dire :

[iii] MS doies. [iv] MS e virgines f. [v] MS Ki les. [vi] MS Ensenblement. [vii] MS en oirent. [viii] MS apostres. [ix] MS K'al. [x] MS Adunc.

437 When they had made the preparations for carrying it to the tomb, they spoke among themselves, asking who would carry the branch in front of the bier, that had come from Paradise.

442 Then Saint John took the branch and wanted to give it to Saint Peter. "You," he said, "must carry this branch, for you are master over us and have lordship over all. You are to hold the keys of Heaven, to close and open Paradise: man shall have entry through you, for the power is given to you."

451 Then Saint Peter replied to him: "Friend," he said, "it shall not be thus. You are the virgin of great goodness, and so are of great authority — you who slept on Jesus' breast the night of the betrayal.

457 "And when he was put upon the Cross you, who were his friend, received his mother to look after. You were virgin, she was virgin. You must go before the bier and carry the branch of brightness. We others will carry the bier and do this other service."

465 Saint John agreed to what Saint Peter had decided.

467 Then Saint Peter took the body and carried it out of the house. At its placing outside the house, he said a Psalm that is called thus: *When Israel went out of Egypt, the house of Jacob from a people of strange language* . . . .[12]

473 When the bier had come out, a cloud came from the sky; it surrounded them and covered them and spread all about them. Inside it the apostles all sang sweetly in chorus. They were very bright all together, because of the branch that was carried in front.

481 The people of Jerusalem heard the song the apostles sang, and came out of the town: fifteen thousand men and women, all asking who it was making that sweet song.

487 Immediately one[13] arrived who told them that Mary, Christ's mother, had come to her death that day, that her soul had left her body. And the apostles who carried her to the sepulchre were singing like this.

493 Then they perceived the bier and saw the light in it. There was present a leader of the Jews, who became very angry; he began speaking to the Jews with malice and fury:

[12] Ps. 114 in *AV.*

[13] Some of the MSS say that Peter himself told them (Ashford, v. 1623).

'Venez od mei e si pernun
La bere e tut le cors ardrum,
Ceo est la mere al sudutur
Par ki nus sumus en freür.
Tuz les apostres ocirum,
Ke mes nul vivre ne lessum.'[i]
Es vus eus encontre venuz[ii]
Od trenchantz glaives e maçuz,[iii]
[f.107ra]
Mais ne lur poënt nul mal faire
Sur eus [est] verti le contraire,
Car Deus fist plusurs avogler
Ke il ne sorent u aler.
Cil ki out le mal dist devant,
Devant les autres vint curant
[E] ses dous mains mist a la bere,
Enpeinst avant e puis arere,
Tut vout abatre e aquasser
E le raim de paume porter,
Mais il failli a sun pensé,
Ne fist mie sa volunté,
Car ses mains furent [si] sachees[iv]
E a la berë afiche[e]s[v]
[Ke] tut li failli sa vertu,
Par les mains fud al lit pendu.
Il n'out es mains point de vigur,
[f.107rb]
Par tut le cors out grant dolur,
Ne pout ses mains arere aver,
Ne munt n'aval nes pout mover.
Començat sei a esmaër
E les apostres a preër.
Tuz les requist comunement,
E seint Pere meïmement,
Ke del lit ses mains departist
E amdous seins aver li feist[vi]
E si li rendist sa vertu.
Seint Pere li ad respundu :
'N'est mie [en] nostre poüsté
Ke tu par nus aiez santé
Si ne creies primes al fiz Deu[vii]
Ke Jüeus unt a tort dampné.'
Peres,' dist il, 'ben le creum
E sanz dutance le savum,
Ke cist Deu est [mult] pouestis,[viii]
[f.107va]
Reis e Sire de Paraïs.
Mais dïables nus unt supris
E nos quers en tenebris mis,
Ne lerrai mes ke jo nel di[e],
Jeo crei al fiz seint[e] Marie.'
Aprés ceo k'il dist tant 'jeo crei',
Si trest ses mains tant tost a sei,
E si estut desur ces piez,[ix]
Mais ses douz bras out mut blesez,
Kë il nes pout amunt porter
Ne ses mains a sun chef lever.
Dunc recomençat a preër
[f.107vb]
Les apostres kil deuissent aider.[x]
Dist seint Pere : 'Tu es guariz
Si tu creis iço ke tu dis.
Tuche a la bere tes deus mains,
Beise le lit, si serras seins,
Crei en Jesum, si tien sa lei,
Porte le raim de paume od tei,
Si tuche a iceus ke lur veue
Par pecché de nus unt perdu[e].
Si en Deu creient, si guarrunt,
Si nun, jamés ren ne verrunt.'

[i] MS vivere. [ii] MS Este vus. [iii] MS e od maçuz. [v] MS bere si a. [vi] MS amedous. [vii] MS creies. [viii] MS poutistis. [ix] MS peiez. [x] MS killi deuissent.

499 "Come with me. Let's take the bier and burn up the body. That's the mother of the deceiver — we're in trouble because of him. Let's kill all the apostles and leave not one alive."

505 Here they came against them, with sharp lances and clubs. But they could not do them any harm; on the contrary, it turned against them. For God struck many of them blind, so that they could not see where to go.

511 He who first spoke the evil came running ahead of the others and set both his hands to the bier, shoving forwards and then backwards. He wanted to tear it down and break it up, and take the palm branch, but he failed in his intention, and could not do his will.

519 For his hands were dragged forward and stuck to the bier, so all his strength failed and he hung from the litter by his hands.

523 He had no power in his hands, and he had great pain in all his body: he could not pull his hands away, nor move them either up or down. He began to be terrified, and prayed to the apostles.

529 He begged them all together, Saint Peter especially, to detach his hands from the litter and let him have them both back, healed, and to restore his strength to him.

534 Saint Peter replied to him: "It is not in our power to give you healing unless you first believe in the Son of God, whom the Jews wrongly condemned."

539 "Peter," he said, "we believed well, and knew without doubt, that this God is all-powerful, King and Lord of Paradise. But devils came upon us and cast our hearts into the shadows. But now I will no longer deny that I believe in the Son of Saint Mary."

547 As soon as he had said no more than "I believe," he drew his hands straight back to himself. He stood upon his feet, but both his arms were badly injured so that he could not raise them up, nor lift his hands to his face. So he began again to beg the apostles, that they must help him.

555 Saint Peter said, "You are healed if you believe what you say. Touch the bier with both your hands, kiss the bed — you shall be whole. Believe in Jesus and keep his law. Take the palm branch with you and touch those who lost their sight because of their sin against us. If they believe in God they shall be healed; if not, they will never see anything again."

Issi cum seint Pere lui dist,
Fust tut guariz e le raim prist.
A sa gent vint, si ad conté
[f.108ra]
Cum il poent aver sancté.
Si il en Deu unt lur creance,
Lur veue averunt sanz dutance.
Cunte lur le mal k'il senti
E coment out esté guari.
Asquans i out ke ce creërent,
Le raim baiserent, si guarierent.
Cil ki ne vudrient Deu prier
Ne le raim a lur oilz tucher,
Remistrent issi cum il erent,
Lumere unkes ne recovrerent.
Li apostre unt le cors porté[i]
Iloc u Deus l'out comandé,
Al val de Josaphat le mistrent
[f.108rb]
En un sepulcre bel assistrent.[ii]
Sempres fu le cors [si] levez,
Ne fu puis veu ne [fu] trovez.
Ne voil dire në afermer,[iii]
Ne en escrit nel pus trover,
Ke hom ne femme ki vesquit
Pus cel hure le cors veïst.
Li sepulcrë est ben mustrez,
Mais le cors ne fu pas trovez.
E li apostres furent mis
La u la nue les out pris,
En la guise e en la manere[iv]
Cum vindrent la, vindrint arere.[v]
Chescun fu en sa regïun
Pur faire predicatïon.[vi]
[f.108va]
Uncore pert, uncore dure
En Josaphat la sepulture
Ou le cors Nostre Dame fu
Ki ne pout estre puis veü.[vii]
Le jor meimes en fu porté
K[ë] al sepulcre fu posé.
Le cors ne pout l'em pus
trover,[viii]
Car Deu le fist resusciter.
Si nul demande ke jo crei[ix]
Del cors, il est al ciel par fei,
E l'alme par fei ensement,
De ço responderai breifment.
Jo crei k'ele est resuscité
E l'alme s'est al cors resemblé,
De li e[st] la char senz luxurie,[x]
Ben deit estre senz purreture.
Ne deit pas la char purrir
Ne par pureture perir
[f.108vb]
Dunt la char Dampnedeu fu fet[e],[xi]
Nee et conceue e traite.
De l'une char est l'autre ne[e],
L'une de l'autre est honore[e].
Cil ke le cors e l'alme fist
E l'un a l'autre ensemble mist
Puet bien le cors resusciter
E l'alme arere al cors poser,
E meïme[me]nt de sa mere
Dunt il esteit e fiz e pere.
Quant il mort pur nus suiffri
E al terz jor resurrexi,[xii]
Plusurs mors fist resusscitter,
Al vis apparer e parler.
Dunc dut sa mere quant li plut
Resusciter e quant il vout.

[i] MS apostres. [ii] MS s. mult bele. [iii] MS afermere. [iv] MS mamanere. [v] MS il vindrent. [vi] MS sa p. [vii] MS veue. [viii] MS trovere. [ix] MS nū … creie. [x] MS E lalme. [xii] MS terce.

565 As Saint Peter told him, he was entirely healed, and he took the branch. He went to his people and told them how they could receive healing. If they had faith in God, they would have their sight, without fail.

571 He told them the pain he had felt, and how he had been cured. There were some who believed this; they kissed the branch and were cured. Those who did not wish to pray to God, nor touch the branch to their eyes, remained just as they were and never recovered the light.

579 The apostles carried the body to where God had commanded. They placed it in the Vale of Josaphat; they put it fittingly into a sepulchre.

583 Then straightaway the body rose up and was never found or seen again. I cannot say or tell, nor can I find it written, that man or woman alive ever saw the body from that day to this. The sepulchre was to be seen, but the body was not found in it.

591 And the apostles were put back to where the cloud had taken them up; in the same wise, in the same fashion as they came, so they went back. Each one was in his place, to do his preaching. It is still to be seen,[14] it is still there, the sepulchre in Josaphat where the body of Our Lady was that can no longer be seen.

601 The very day it was placed in the sepulchre, it was carried away. The body can no longer be found there, because God brought it back to life.

605 If anybody asks what I believe about the body: it is in Heaven by faith, and the soul by faith also.[15] I shall reply briefly to this: I believe she was brought back to life, and the soul reunited with her body; her body is without any unchastity and must surely be free from corruption.

613 That flesh ought not to rot, nor perish by decay, from which was made and born, conceived and suckled, the flesh of the Lord God. From the one flesh was the other born, and the one is honoured by the other.

619 He who made body and soul, and put the one with the other, can very well raise up the flesh and put the soul back into the body. And especially that of his mother, to whom he was both Son and Father.

625 When he suffered death for us and rose up on the third day, he raised many dead people to life: they appeared, alive, and they talked. So he could raise his mother, when it pleased him and when he wanted to.[16]

---

[14] As in Mary's Lament (see p. 181 below), the writer invokes something that is "still there" to lend credence to his account.

[15] Ashford: "… en ciel par sei / E l'arme par sei …" (vv. 1742–43).

[16] Ashford: "Dunc dut il bien sa mere e pot / Resusciter desque lui plot" (vv. 1765–66).

Deus ad trestut en sa baillie,
[f.109ra]
Il ad la mort, il ad la vie,
Ciel e tere e ewe e mer.[i]
Dunc puet il bien resusciter
Cele ke li portat e nuri
E ki plus l'ama e servi
Ke hom ne femme de tut le mu[n]d[ii]
De tuz iceus ki esté unt.
[J]onas fu par sort mis en mer[iii]
K'avant dust une neif aler,[iv]
La baleine le transgluti,
Treis jors le tint, pus le rendi.
Al terz jor a terre le mist[v]
Par la vertu [de] Jhesu Crist.
[T]reis enfanz furent a arder mis
En un furneise tretut vifs.
Unkes nul d'els mal ne senti[vi]
[f.109rb]
Ne char ne quir ne blemi
Ne lur chevoil ne point lur dras
Ne n'out unques brue ne ars
Si ert le feu ardant entur
E cil erent en la chalur.
Deus ki tute rien furmat
E plusurs morz resuscitat
E Jonam en la mer salvat
E les enfanz al feu guardatz
Bien poet dunc resusciter
Sa merë e al ciel porter.
Or creum dunc comunement[vii]
Ke tut est al ciel hautement.
Or deprium la gloriüse,
La seinte virgine precïuse
Si veirement cum Deu l'out chere
K'ele oïe nostre priere[viii]
[f.109va]
E nus face la voie aver
Ke oilz del chef ne puet veër
Ne buche de hume reconter
N'oreille oïr ne quer penser[ix]
E pur la mort seinte Marie
Amen, amen, chescune en di[e].

[i] MS mere. [iii] MS mere. [iv] MS Ke avant. [v] MS terce. [vi] MS mal mal ne sentis. [vii] MS Ore. [viii] MS Ke ele … prierere. [ix] MS Ne oreille oireille.

631 God has everything in his power: he has life, he has death, heaven and earth, water and sea. So he can surely raise up her who bore and nurtured him, who loved and served him better than any man or woman who has ever been in the world.

639 Jonah, who once had to travel in a ship, was cast by lot into the sea; the whale swallowed him up. It held him for three days, then it gave him back. On the third day it put him onto the land, by the power of Jesus Christ.[17]

645 Three young men were placed alive into a furnace to be burned. None of them felt any pain, nor was their flesh or skin marked, nor their hair nor even their clothes. Nothing was the least bit scorched or burned, as the burning fire surrounded them and they were there in the heat.[18]

653 God who made everything, and who brought many dead to life, who saved Jonah in the sea and saved the young men in the fire, he can certainly bring his Mother back to life and take her up to Heaven.

659 Now let us all together believe that she is wholly, soul and body, on high in Heaven. Now let us pray to the glorious one, the precious holy Virgin, as truly as God holds her dear, that she will hear our prayer and show us the way, that the eyes in our head can never see, nor mouth of man tell, nor ear hear nor heart conceive — and for the death of Saint Mary let everybody say Amen, Amen.

[17] See Jonah, chapters 1–2. Jonah, emerging from the belly of the whale after three days, was considered to prefigure the resurrection of Jesus on the third day after his death — see Matt. 12:40.

[18] See Daniel 3:10–27.

Part III

The Passion

Chapter 6

Mary's Lament[1]

Introduction

The text is from Trinity College Dublin MS 374 (D.1.29) (s.xiii^2), ff.74ra–76vb,[2] corrected and completed from Cambridge, Emmanuel Coll., MS 106 (I.4.31) (s.xiv^m) (E in the footnotes and rubrics), ff.181r–190r. A prose lament, it is described in Dean and Boulton as being partly a dialogue between the Virgin and Jesus, but this is slightly misleading: it begins as a dialogue between the Lady and a (male) devotee, then Jesus' voice takes over, speaking to his Mother and to Saint John. After this, the voice is that of a narrator (who may be identical with the devotee, because of the final prayer). The Lament is based on Pseudo-Bernard's *Planctus*, and there are four manuscripts, one of which is probably continental; it is also a Passion narrative.[3]

It is notable that the Lady urges the devotee to write ("Si covent ke tu escrives . . ."). This is a highly-wrought, emotional piece, containing a good deal of direct speech; there is no Latin, and the Hebrew words from the Cross are translated (the audience, or user, is not expected to be very learned but will undoubtedly be stirred by the dramatic quality of the text). The account follows the Gospels quite closely, and mentions a legend according to which the Virgin's tears can still be seen on the stone.

The "still-there" topos, a favourite medieval device by which writers plead the truth of their account by indicating something that can still be seen (as witness that it really happened), has been discussed by Andrew King and Jacqueline Simpson.[4] No source has been found for this legend, although in the *Chronicle of Glastonbury Abbey* it was said they had "some of the stones and earth where Mary wept when she saw the Lord pierced by the lance, and her tears which flowed into the earth."[5] The *Apocryphal New Testament* may be among the chronicler's sources, although the legend does not appear there.

---

[1] D&B 955, prose, "Lament of the Virgin."

[2] See above, p. 74.

[3] D&B compares it with the previous item (954), a verse dialogue between "Bernard" and Mary (*PL* 182:1133–42); see *Plaintes*, ed. Tanquerey.

[4] King 2000, pp. 48–52, 161–62, and *passim*; and Simpson 2001 (chap. 5, "You Can See it There Still"). There is another example of what is "still there" in the Assumption: see p. 175 above.

[5] *Chronicle* (ed. Carley, trans. Townsend), chap. IX (pp. 24–25): *De Sancta Maria Matre Domini sunt hee reliquie.*

Text

[E f.181r: **Ici commencent les lamentations Nostre Dame**] [f.74ra] A Deu ! Ki me dorra tant des lermes que jeo puisse plurer nuit e jur deques li duz Jesu me deigne apparer en veillant ou en dormant pur conforter ma lasse de alme ? E vous, dames de Jerusalem, les beneites amies nostre Seignur, kar me aidez a plurer en priant e prier en plurant tant ke li duz Aignel, nostre duz e cher espus, s'apere a nus en sa grant beuté. Pensez, dames, devotement, recuillez ententivement en voz quors cume est amere chose al quor de sei deseverer de celui a ki vus estes espusees par le non[i] de chasteté. Attendez, dames, curez, virgnes, que vos havez haste[ii] a la duce reine e virgne ke porta li duz Jesu en ses beneurez flancs. C'est cele que le porta, c'est cele que le aleta de ces duz mameles, c'est cele ke par tut le siweit neis deskes a la croiz. Ha Deus ! Qu'est ceo que j'ai dit ? Le lessa ele dunc illuc ? Nenil, Deus ! Certes ele i fu tant cum ele pout plus demorer. Jeo crai veraiment qu'ele esteit ovec cele[s] dames dolentes que plorerent quant li duz Jesu,[iii] non pas cume sires del ciel e de la terre, mes cum plein [f.74rb] de tutes dolurs, dit ceste parole : 'O vus filles de Jerusalem, ne plorez pas sur mei, mes plurez sur vus e sur vos enfanz.'

[E ***Vox contemplationis ad beatam Dei genitricem***] Ma duce Dame de Parays, mere al duz Jesu Crist, si ceo est veir que jeo dis, Dame, jeo vus pri umblement ke vus me diez la verité e ne vus despleise mie que vostre serf parole si hardiement ové sa dame. E pur ceo, Dame, que jeo plus devotement e plus dignement puisse oir ceo ke vus dittez, jeo vus pri ke vus me donez aucunes des lermes ke vus eustes en sa passion.

[E ***Responsio virginis***] (*Ad quem illa*) O beu duz amis, ceo ke tu demandes si est comencement de tresgrant doel e de tresgrant plur, mes pur ceo que jeo sui glorifié ne puis plorer. Si covent ke tu escrives o tresgrant habunda[n]ce de lermes ceo que senti ové tresgrant dolur e od tresgrant angoisse.

[E ***Vox contemplationis***] Ma Dame de Paraïs, donez moi ceo que vus dites e fetes ceo ke jeo desir. Dame, dites ceo que vus pla[i]rra, vostre serf l'orra amiablement[iv] ceo ke vus deignerez dire. Ma duce Dame, kar me dites si vus esteietz en Jerusalem quant vostre duz fiz fu pris e lié.

---

[i] E 'le vou de ch.' [ii] E 'chasteté'. [iii] E 'J. amerjus'. [iv] E 'humblement'.

Translation

[Here begins the lament of Our Lady][1] Ah God! Who will grant me so many tears, that I may weep night and day until sweet Jesus deigns to appear, in my waking or my sleeping, to comfort my troubled soul?[2] And you, ladies of Jerusalem, the blessed friends of Our Lord, help me to weep in prayer and to pray in weeping, until the gentle Lamb, our sweet and dear Spouse, shall appear to us in his great beauty. Think in devotion, ladies, recollect intensely in your hearts, how bitter to the heart it is to be separated from him to whom you are wedded in the name of chastity. Wait, ladies; run, virgins; hasten to the sweet queen and virgin who carried gentle Jesus in her blessed womb. It is she who bore him, it is she who suckled him with her sweet breasts, it is she who followed him everywhere, even to the Cross. Ah, God! What have I said? Did she then leave him there? Oh, no, God! Truly, she was there until she could no longer stay. I believe truly that she was with those sorrowing ladies who wept when sweet Jesus, not as lord of heaven and earth but as filled with all sorrows, said these words: *Daughters of Jerusalem, weep not for me, but weep for yourselves, and for your children.*[3]

[A Voice in prayer to the Blessed One who bore God] My sweet Lady of Paradise, mother of gentle Jesus Christ, if what I say is true, Lady, I pray you humbly to tell me the truth. Do not be displeased that your servant speaks so boldly to his lady. And so that I may more devotedly and fittingly hear what you say, Lady, I beg you to give me some of the tears that you wept at his Passion.

[The response of the Virgin] (She speaks to him) O my dear friend, what you ask is the beginning of the greatest sorrow and weeping, but now that I am glorified I cannot weep. It behoves you to write, with a great outpouring of tears, about what I felt with the greatest sorrow and anguish.

[A Voice in prayer] My Lady of Paradise, give me what you say and do what I desire. Lady, speak as it pleases you; your servant will listen lovingly to whatever you deign to say. My precious Lady, tell me whether you were in Jerusalem when your gentle Son was seized and bound.

---

[1] According to this, the first part is spoken by the Lady herself, although the "I" changes partway down the paragraph.

[2] Cf. Jer. 9:1.

[3] Luke 23:28.

[E *Vox virginis respondentis*] (*Ad quem illa*) O beau duz amis, verraiment i esteie jeo, mes [f.74va] kant je oï que l'em le menot si vileinement, lors ne me poi tener que jeo n'i corusse, ausi anguissuse cume jeo esteie. Mes quant jeo le vi ferir o poinz e o paumes e escoupir[i] el visage e corune[r] d'espines, lors me failli sen e force, kar de la grant dolur que jeo aveie me failli la parole. Mes jeo n'esteie mie sule, kar mes sorru[r]s esteient ové mei tristes e dolentes e plureient mun duz enfant ausi cum s'il fust lur. Mes entre celes esteit une Magdalene[ii] que sur tutes ert plus dolente saunz mei. Mes quant Pilates comanda que li duz Aignel[iii] fust amené al turment, lors i out mult grant presse de gent qui le siweient. Li un le gaberent e se rieient, li autre li geterent la boue e les ordures a la teste e a la duce chere ou tut li angele de Parays se desirent a remirer.

Ha, lasse ! E jeo lui siweie si triste cum nule pout estre ovec celes que l'aveient siwi de Galilé, ki me sustindrent ausi cumme morte desques nus venimes la ou li larrun crucifierent mun duz fiz devant mei. Il me regardeit ausi ducement cum il saveit [f.74vb] en ki n'aveit si duçur non. Mes il se dolout plus, ço me semble, de ma dolur que de quancque l'em li feseit. Ha, lasse ! e jeo le regardeie cum anguissuse mere e vi cum il moriust de si leide mort e ke aider nel poeie. Lors me perneit une si grant dolur que quer ne poreit penser ne buche dire. E quel merveille, kar jeo vi ke le sanc de lui decureit de tutes parz a granz russeaus si ke le visage li esteit tut teint e cil qu'esteit avant li plus beaus q'unke fust semblout ja le plus leid. Lors veeie jeo la prophecie acomplie que Ysaïe dit : 'Nus veimes un home ke n'aveit beauté ne colur.' Certes ço me turmentoit trop grefment ke jeo vi que mun duz enfes, que jeo aveie porté en mes flauncs, me lesseit sule[iv] e esgarree. Ne ne me remaneit nul autre, kar jo n'aveie plus. E pur ceo ne poei jeo oblier ma dolur e la voiz m'esteit faillie, si ne poei fors gemir e suspirer quant jeo voleie parler, si me perneit une dolur que me rumpeit la parole. E quant jeo voleie crier, lors me veneit un anguisse ke me perceit le quer e une voiz [f.75ra] doleruse isseit hors que mustreit ben l'anguisse q'esteit dedenz. Ha, beaus quers amerus ! purquei ne crevez vus de pité quant la mestrie de parole avez perdue de compassion de mon enfant ?

[i] E 'escracher'. [ii] E 'Marie M.' [iii] E 'amerus'. [iv] MS sulee.

[The Voice of the Virgin answering] (She speaks to him) O my friend, truly I was there, and when I heard they were leading him so shamefully I could not help running there, so anguished was I. But when I saw them hitting him with fists and open hands, and spitting in his face, and crowning him with thorns, then my senses and my strength failed me; for the great sorrow I had, the words failed me. But I was not alone, for my sisters were with me, sad and sorrowful and mourning my sweet child as though he had been their own; among them was a Magdalene, who sorrowed more than all save only me. But when Pilate ordered the gentle Lamb to be led to the torment, then there was a very great crowd of people following him. Some mocked him and laughed, others threw mud and filth at his head, and at his sweet face wherein all the angels of Paradise desire to gaze as in if a mirror.

Ah, misery! And I followed him, grieving more than anybody could grieve, with the women who had followed him from Galilee, who supported me as they would a dead creature until we came to the place where the murderers crucified my gentle son before my eyes. He in whom there was nothing but sweetness looked at me as sweetly as he could — in whom was nothing but sweetness. But it seemed to me that he was more grieved at my sorrow than at what they were doing to him. Ah, misery! And I looked at him as a mother in anguish and saw how he had to die such an ugly death, and I could not help him. Then a terrible agony seized me, such that no heart could conceive nor mouth tell. And how marvellous! for I saw that his blood was running from all over him in great streams, so that his face was all dyed with it, and he who before was the most beautiful ever seen now seemed the ugliest. Then I saw fulfilled the prophecy of Isaiah: "We saw a man who had neither beauty nor colour."[4] Truly, it tortured me most grievously as I saw that my sweet son, whom I had carried in my body, was leaving me alone and lost. Nor was any other left to me, for I had no others. And therefore I could not forget my sorrow, and my voice failed me; I could only groan and sigh when I wanted to speak, for I was seized by a pain that shattered my words. And when I tried to cry out, then came a pain that pierced my heart and a voice came forth that showed the anguish within me. Ah, poor loving heart, why do you not break for pity, when you have lost the power of speech for compassion of my child?

[4] See Is. 53:2.

Amur si me feseit un poi parler enroement, kar jeo vi devant mei murir celui ke par amur morust e jeo defailli tute de la grant angoisse que me tuchoit al quor.[i] Il me regardeit ausi ducement cum un agneus e me voleit conforter, mes jeo ne poie nul confort receivre. Jeo plureie en disant e diseie en plorant :

'Beau fiz duz, beau fiz cher, beau fiz tresamerus, k'est ceo que vus sustrez,[ii] k'est ceo que vus fetes, q'est ceo ke jeo vei ? Ha, lasse, lasse ! Ki me tendra ke jeo ne more pur vus ? Ha, mort, mort ! Purquei moert mun duz fiz, purquei ne moert sa lasse de mere ové li ? O beau fiz, ke fra jeo ? M'amur duce, mun tendre fiz, ne me lessez pas aprés vus, mes treez mei aprés vus, si ke jeo more ovecke vus ? Beau fiz duz, vus morez trop cruelement sul, fetes tant ke vostre anguissuse mere more ovecke vus. Ma chere mort, ne me esparniez pas. Ore me plest aukes vostre venue. Tu[f.75rb]ez mei ovecke mun fiz. Fiz duz, tute ma joie e tute ma vie, tut mun confort, fai tant que jeo more ore endreit. Ha, duz fiz ! Reconussez vostre mere e oez sa preere. Certes c'est ben avenant que fiz oie sa mere si desconforté. Fiz duz, kar oiez vostre mere e me recevez ovecke vus en vostre passion, si ke nus qu'avom vesqui en une char e avom amé [en] un amur morum de une mort. O cheitive [o]uaille,[iii] purquei m'esparnez vus puis ke vus n'esparniez mun duz fiz ? Crucifiez mei ovec li ou mei tuez d'aucun autre mort, kar il ne me chaut de quele mort jeo more fors ke jeo morge orendreit, kar il n'est pas dreit qu'il morge sul. Vus me tollez tute ma joie e ma vie e ma esperance en tere, e purquei me lesse[z] v[u]s vivre en si grant dolur ? Ostez, ostez, pendez ceste lasse mere ovecke sun chier fiz. Certes meuz me vausist morir ke demener vie de mort. Ha, beu duz fiz, mun duz fiz, mun duz enfant ! Kar oiez la priere vostre mere ke tant est dolente. Ne seez pas a vostre tendre mere dur, q'avez tuzjurs esté deboneire a tuz. Recevez mei ovecke vus en vostre croiz si que jeo puisse vivre [f.75va] tuzjurs, mes ovecke vus e aprés la mort. Certes, ren ne me sereit si delitable cume morir entre voz braz en vostre croiz ne ren ne me poet plus grever que vivre aprés vostre mort. Ha, beu duz fiz, ha, dolente mere, ha lasse ! Tu esteies mi pere, tu esteies ma mere, tu esteies mun espus, tu esteies mi fiz, tu m'esteiez tut. Ore me tout l'em mun fiz, ore me tout l'em tut, kar ceo ert quanque jeo amai. Ha beau duz fiz, que frai jeo desoreenavant ? Beu sire, viverai jeo ? Beau duz sire, quei devendrai jeo ? Beau duz fiz, ou troverai jeo confort ?

[i] E adds: 'Ha ! loiaus qeor amureus. que ne crevez vous pas de pité quant la mestresce de parler avolt perdue sa parole par compassion de soen enfaunt.' [ii] E 'suffrez'. [iii] E has 'et diseit a Johan le Evangeliste'. These words seem to be misplaced: an anticipation, no doubt, of the reference to John below.

So love made me speak a little hoarsely, for I saw him who was dying for love dying before me, and I fainted away for the great anguish that went to my heart.[5] He looked at me as gently as a lamb and wanted to comfort me, but I could take no comfort. I wept saying, I said weeping:

"Sweetest son, dearest son, lovely and most loving son, what is taking you away? what are you doing? what am I seeing? Alas! ah, misery! Who will prevent me from dying for you? Ah, death, death! Why is my sweet son dying, why cannot his poor mother die with him? O dear son, what shall I do? My precious love, my tender son, do not leave me behind, but take me with you so that I may die with you. My beloved son, you die so cruelly alone, make your anguished mother die with you. My dear death — do not spare me. Now your coming pleases me somewhat — kill me with my son. Sweet son, all my joy and all my life, all my comfort, make it so that I die now at once. Ah, darling son! Recognize your mother and hear her prayer. Truly it is fitting that a son should hear his mother in such suffering. Dear son, hear your mother and receive her with you in your passion; we who have lived in one flesh and loved with one love, let us die with one death. O wretched sheep![6] Why spare me when you spare not my sweet son? Crucify me with him, or kill me with any other death; I care not what death I die as long as I die straight away, for it is not right for him to die alone. You bereave me of all my joy, all my life, all my hope on earth — why leave me to live in such terrible sorrow? Away! Away! Hang this wretched mother with her beloved son. Truly it is better for me to die than to live a living death. Ah, my lovely son, my dear son, my sweet child! Hear the prayer of your mother who is so sorrowful. Do not be harsh to your tender mother, you who have always been so meek to all. Take me with you onto your cross so that I may live for ever, but with you and after death. Truly, nothing would be so delightful as to die in your arms on your cross, nor would anything grieve me so much as to live after your death. Ah, dearest son! Ah, wretched mother! Alas! You were my father, you were my mother, you were my husband, you were my son, you were everything to me. Now they are taking away my son, they are taking away everything, for he was all that I loved. Ah, darling son, what shall I do from now on? Fair lord, shall I live? Beloved lord, what will become of me? Dearest son, where shall I find comfort?

[5] E adds: "Ah, loyal and loving heart! Why do you not break for pity, when the very Mistress of all speech was lost for words in compassion for her Child!"

[6] Here, the word "ouaille" suggests that the writer has misplaced a few lines — see footnote opposite.

Tresduz ami, ou troverai jeo aie ? Beau duz [fiz], jeo sai ben que vus poez fere quanque vus volez, mes s'il ne vus plet que jeo more o vus, jeo vus pri que vus me lessez aucun bonuré confort.'

[E ***Vox filii ad matrem suam***] Lors li dit li duz Aigneus, ausi angusseus[i] cum esteit en la croiz, et diseit a seint Johan[ii] le ewangeliste : 'Dame, veez ci vostre fiz. Ma duce mere, lesse vostre plorer e fetes grant joie, kar ore ai jeo trové le owaille que jeo ai tant quise e perdue. Un home mort, que tut li munde vive. Ma Dame, ceo que plest a Deu mun pere ne vus deit pas desplere. Ne plure plus, ma chere mere, [f.75vb] sachez que jeo ne vus larrai pas, einz serrai ovecke vus tuzjurs, kar si la mort ad en mei poer solunc la char, sachez ke la divinité dura tuzjurs. Dame, vus savez ben dunt jeo vinc, si ne vus devez pas curucer si jeo vois la dunt jeo vinc. Il est ben tens que jeo returne a celui ki m'enveia ça, e la ou jeo vois ore endreit vus n'i poez venir. Mes vus vendrez aprés, e endementers Johan ki est nostre nefs[iii] vus gardera e o vus remeindra en liu de fiz e vus serra leal confort.'

[E ***Vox filii ad beatum Johannem evangelistam***] Lors regarda a mun seignur seint Johan e si li dit : 'Veez ci ta mere. Jeo la te comand. Serf la e pren garde de lui. Gardez la cum ta mere, nun pas saunz plus ta mere, mes la mei e la tue.' Tant cum li duz Aigneaus parleit, ensi li deu ami ne cesserent de plurer ne ne poeient parler, kar dolur les martirizeit si qu'il ne poeient un mot dire. E ces deus beneurez virgnes oient lur ami parler en torment. Ne ne li poeient respondre de l'angoisse qu'il aveient de lui e esteient ausi cum morz, kar tuz li sens lur estoit failliz. Il oeient parler li duz amis qui morreit par [f.76ra] amur ne ne li poeient respundre ne ne saveient trover confort fors en plurer, kar li gleives lur aveit ja trespercé les quers. Quant li duz Aigneaus aveit comandé sa duce mere a mun seignur seint Johan, si cria e dit : 'Jeo ai tresgrant sei.'

---

[i] MS angussesus. [ii] MS croiz de S. J. (corrected from E). [iii] E 'vie'.

Sweetest friend, where shall I find help? My darling [son], I know you can do whatever you will, but if it is not your will that I die with you, I pray you to leave me some happy comfort."

[The voice of the Son to his Mother] Then the gentle Lamb spoke to her, so anguished as he was on the Cross, and said to Saint John the Evangelist: "Lady, see here your son.[7] Dearest mother, leave your weeping and have great joy, for now I have found the sheep that I had lost and so long sought. A man dies, so that all the world shall live. My Lady, what is pleasing to God my father must not be displeasing to you. Weep no more, my dear mother; know that I shall not leave you, rather I shall be with you always. Even if death has power over my flesh, know that godhead will endure for ever. Lady, you know where I came from, and so you must not be troubled if I go back whence I came. It is now time for me to return to him who sent me, and where I am going now, you cannot come there.[8] But you shall come after, and meanwhile John, who is our kinsman,[9] will look after you and stay with you as if he were your son; he will give you loyal comfort."

[The voice of the Son to blessed John the Evangelist] Then my lord looked at Saint John, and he said to him, "See here your mother.[10] I commend her to you. Serve her and take care of her. Watch over her as your mother, not only as your mother but as both mine and yours." While the gentle Lamb was speaking thus, the two friends never stopped weeping and could not talk, for sorrow tortured them so that they could not speak a word. And these two blessed virgins heard their friend speak in his torment. Nor could they answer him for the anguish they felt for him, and they were as if dead, for all their senses failed them. They heard the words of the beloved friend who was dying for love, but they could not answer him, nor could they find comfort except in tears, for the blade had pierced their hearts. When the gentle Lamb had commended his sweet mother to my lord Saint John, he cried out, saying "I am very thirsty."[11]

[7] John 19:26.

[8] Cf. John 13:33.

[9] See the table setting out Mary's family, p. 155 above (introduction to Assumption).

[10] John 19:27.

[11] John 19:28.

Lors li donerent li larun de vez vin egre ové fel a beivre. E quant il le senti, nel vout beivre. E lors si dit : 'Tut est acompli.' E escria en haute voiz : *Hely, hely, lama zabatani* [Matt. 27:46], c'est a dire 'Beau Sire Deu, purquei m'as tu deguerpi ?' Lors si rendi l'esperit. Lors trembla la tere e li solail enoscurist e les esteiles perdirent lur lumere, les peres fendirent. Allas ! Nus poums ben dire que nus avoms les quers plus durs ke pere que tute jur aum la remembrance e nen fesum point de force. Lors se turna la duce Dame vers la croiz e ne poeit parler, kar le grant doel qu'ele aveit li aveit si ferri le quer k'ele ne poeit estre,[i] einz chaï a tere paumee. Ele viveit en morant, ele moreit en vivant. Ne se delita fors en ceo qu'ele atendi ke l'em meist juz sun duz enfant de la croiz e ploreit en disant e diseit en plurant. 'Ha, beau [f.76rb] seignurs, rendez a ceste lasse de mere le cors de sun enfant. Vus en avez acompli tutes voz volentez. Al meins metez le jus tut mort, ceo me serra grant confort si jeo le puisse tenir tut mort.'

Quant la duce Dame se leva pur atucher a lui e ele n'i poeit avenir, si chet arere a tere. Lors si regardeit sun duz fiz qui pendeit en la croiz ducement cume celi que n'aveit fors dulçur. Lors se leva sus, si acola la croiz e baisa cele part la ou li sanc decureit, si ke de la grant dolur qu'ele i aveit rechaï ele pasmee a la tere. Mes amur la feseit relever e quideit atucher a sun ami, mes ele ne poeut avenir, kar amur quide fere ou il ne pot avenir. La chere que soleit estre si bele esteit ja tute pale, mes le sanc que chaieit des plaies sun duz fiz li rugisseit tut le visage.

Quant ele ne se poeit plus sustenir e beiseit la place ou li sanc de sun fiz decureit, endementers vint un nobles home qu'aveit a non Joseph, qu'esteit disciple al duz Jesu, mes ceo esteit en repost pur la pour des Gius. E si ala a Pilate e li pria qu'il li donast le precius cors Jesu. Quant Pilate l'out [f.76va] granté, si apella un sages home qu'ot a nun Nichodeme e fu ausi disciple nostre Seignur en repost. E vindrent la ou li Aigneaus ert crucifié e aporterent estrumentz de quei il pussent oster les clous e mettre le jus.

[i] E 'ne se pout sustenir'.

Then the scoundrels gave him a vessel with vinegar and gall to drink.[12] And when he tasted it, he did not wish to drink. And then he said "All has been fulfilled."[13] And he cried in a loud voice *Eli, Eli, lama sabachthani*, which is to say: "Dear Lord God, why have you forsaken me?" Then he rendered up his spirit. Then the earth trembled and the sun was darkened and the stars lost their light; the rocks split apart. Alas! We may well say that we have hearts harder than rock, for we have the memory every day and yet we do nothing. Then the sweet Lady turned towards the Cross and could not speak; the terrible suffering had so torn through her heart that she could not stand, and instead she fell fainting to the earth. She lived but was dying; dying, she was yet alive. She delighted in nothing, except that she waited for them to take her dear son down from the Cross. She wept saying, she said weeping: "Ah, my lords, give the body of the child back to this wretched mother. You have had all your will of him. At least take him down, quite dead as he is; it will be a great comfort to me if I can hold him in death."

When the gentle Lady rose to touch him, and she could not reach him, she fell back onto the ground. Then she looked at her gentle son, hanging on the Cross sweetly as one who was never anything but sweetness. Then she arose, embraced the Cross and kissed it where the blood ran down; for the great pain she suffered she fell again fainting to the earth. But love raised her up again, and she thought she could touch her darling, but she could not reach him; for love believes it can do, where it cannot. The face that used to be so beautiful was now all white, but the blood that fell from her dear son's wounds reddened her whole countenance.

When she could no longer stand, and was kissing the place where her son's blood ran, meanwhile there came a noble man whose name was Joseph, who was sweet Jesus' disciple, but he kept it secret for fear of the Jews. And he went to Pilate and begged him to give him Jesus' precious body. When Pilate agreed, he called a wise man named Nicodemus, who was also a disciple of Our Lord in secret.[14] And they came to where the Lamb had been crucified, bringing instruments with which to take out the nails and lift him down.

---

[12] See *Plaintes*, ed. Tanquerey, pp. 753–54: "le fel ovek le eysel tut ensement"; the vinegar has the property of spreading the gall quickly through the body, to maximize the pain (Appendix II, p. 161, "pur ly hastier a la mort").

[13] John 19:30.

[14] For Joseph of Arimathea and Nicodemus, see John 19:38–39. Nicodemus had visited Jesus and talked with him secretly (John 3), and later attempted to defend him (John 7:50–51). Joseph's gift of the tomb is also in the other Gospels.

Quant la beneite dame vit qu'il voleient oster sun enfant de la croiz, si se leva ausi cum s'ele fust resuscité e li revint un poi l'esperitz e lur aida aus[i] cum ele pout. Li uns osteit les clous des mains, li autre des piez, li autres sustindrent le cors e la duce virgne sustint les braz e les tret sur sun piz. Mes quant ele le pout tenir, lors le comença a beisir e acoler, e lors si recomença son doel si grant qu'ele fu tute pasmee ausi cume morte. Lors se mist ele au chief sun enfant e plureit si profundement qu'ele li aroseit tute la chere des lermes que chaierent des oilz. Lors se fereit ele de[i] ses mains e se pleigneit si amerement ke nul[ii] ne la poeit veer que ne plurast, s'il ne fust plus dur que pere. Lors criot ele si pitusement e si haut qui fu avis a ceus ki la virent q'unc mes si grant doel ne virent cume de li ne de ki il ussent si [f.76vb] grant pité. 'Ha, lasse ! lasse dolente mere ! Ha, tresduz fiz ! Pur [quei] vus unt cist larun de Gius crucifié si cruelement ? Ha, lasse ! Ore tenge mun enfant mort en mon gerun. Beau fiz, veez ci vostre triste mere. Quei fra vostre dolente mere aprés vostre mort ? Purquei me lessez vus vivre ? Ha, lasse ! doleruse mere ! Sur tutes autres q'unques enfant porterent, mult m'est faillie la grant joie que jeo aveie quant vus nasquistes. Mult m'est tost turné a grant dolur la grant joie que jeo aveie de vus, beau duz fiz. Ore ne sai mes que fere mes ke jeo me tue, kar aprés vostre mort ne porrai jeo vivre.' Endementers qu'ele diseit ço si le beseit ele le front e les oilz e le nes e plureit si parfundement ke sembleit qu'ele deveit tute fundrer[iii] en lermes e qu'ele moillout tut le cors sun enfant e la pere en ert tute moillé. Uncore dit l'em ke les lermes perent ben en la pere. Lors pensoit ele quel il aveit esté e coment ele l'aveit conceu saunz compaignie de home e enfanté sanz dolur. E diseit en suspirant 'Dites, dites cher fiz, dites m'amur duce, dites tute[iv] [E f.187v] ma vie, dites tute ma joye, dites tut mon confort, pur quei me lessés vous si dolente ? pur quei estes si enloigne de moi ? pur quei ne confortez vous vostre mere dolente ? Regardez, doucz Deus, ceste lasse de mere et eiez pité de moi.'

Ore, dire qui purra, ne qi savera penser, com la douce Dame ert anguisseuse ? Certes, jeo crei que nul ne purreit penser le dolur que ele sentoit, mes tute voirs sei ne desperoit ele mie, mes attendoit au tierce jour que il relevast. Ovesque la beneite Dame si aveient aschunes bones dames que ploreient, mes poi y aveit des dames que ne plorassent pur le grant doel que la beneite Dame fesoit. Certes, jeo crei que angles de paradis plorerent si ceo peust estre.

[i] MS des. [ii] MS nule. [iii] E 'fundre'. [iv] The Dublin MS breaks off here.

When the blessed Lady saw that they were going to take her child off the Cross, she got up as though coming back to life; her spirits returned to her a little, and she helped them as well as she could.[15] One pulled the nails from the hands, another from the feet, others supported the body, and the gentle virgin supported the arms and drew them to her breast. But as soon as she could hold him, she started to kiss and caress him; then her suffering began again so sharply that she fainted away as if dead. Then she sat by her child's head and wept so hard that she wetted his whole face with the tears that fell from her eyes. She beat at herself with her hands; she lamented so bitterly that none could see her without weeping, unless he were harder than stone. Then she cried so piteously and so loud that those who saw her thought they had never seen such great sorrow as hers, nor had they ever felt such great pity: "Alas! Poor sorrowing mother! Ah, sweetest son! Why have those murdering Jews crucified you so cruelly? Alas! Now let me hold my dead child in my lap. Darling son, behold your unhappy mother. What shall your poor mother do after your death? Why do you let me live? Alas! Sorrowful mother! Above all others who ever bore children, I have lost so much of the great joy I had when you were born. Swiftly it has all turned to bitter grief, that great joy I had of you, my dear son. Now I no longer know what to do, unless I kill myself, for I cannot live after your death." All the while she was saying this, she was kissing his forehead and eyes and nose, and was weeping so bitterly it seemed she must be melting in tears; she wetted her child's whole body, and the rocks were all wet. They say the tears can still be seen on the stone.[16] Then she thought about who he had been, and how she had conceived him without knowledge of a man and borne him without pain. And she said, sighing: "Speak, speak to me, dear son! Speak, my sweet love! Speak, my life and all my joy! Speak, my only comfort! Why do you leave me so wretched? Why are you so far from me? Why do you not console your unhappy mother? Dear Lord, look at your sorrowing mother, and take pity on me!"

Now, who can say or even conceive what anguish that sweet Lady felt? Truly, I believe nobody could imagine the agony she suffered: yet nevertheless she did not despair, but awaited the third day when he should arise. Some good women were there with the blessed Lady, weeping, but few of the women there were who did not weep for the bitter lament the blessed Lady made. Truly I believe the angels of Paradise wept, if that were possible.

[15] Cf. *Plaintes*, ed. Tanquerey, pp. 961ff.

[16] See above, p. 181.

A Deux! que fut cel angle ou archangle que ne ploreit cuntre nature la ou Deux, qi ne poeit morir, giseit mort cuntre nature? Qui fut si dur que ne ploreit qui veist le Saveur du munde si cruelement treiter, et veist la beneite Virge tute arusee de soen preciouse sang? Et qui est celui ou cele que veist cele seinte Dame si bo[f.188r]ne, si bele, tute douce, tute delitable, tormenté de si grant anguisse, pleine de si grant dolur, plorer si amerement? Certes, il n'y ad nul queor que peust suffrer a veer si grant anguisse come ele avoit, einz me merveillerei jeo si lui angle ne ploreient, neis en cele grant leessee lasus ou[i] dolur ne poet estre. Auxi com il poet estre que Deus morust pur la humanité qu'il prist, auxi pout il estre que lui angle doleuseient pur la mort lur Seignur.

Quant Joseph out mis jus le corps nostre Seignur, sicome le Evangile tesmoine, si l'enseveli et pus le mist en une tumbe tute novel qu'il aveit fet a soen eus demeigne. Dunques vindrent lui angle de paradis as femes au sepulcre lour Seignur et la douce Dame se demenoit si grant doleur leez le sepulcre endementers que Joseph et Nichodeme lui mistrent en sepulcre, et se voleit ensevelir ovesque lui. Dunques l'embraseit ele et le coleit et besoit si doucement come ele poeit et cria trop piteusement 'Ha, beaus seignurs amerus! Vous qui estes mes amis, eiez pité de moi, lessez moi unquore [f.188v] un poi mun duz Fiz, mon cher Amy, que jeo puisse unquore aschune horette veer sa douce chere et trover aschun confort. Héa, beaus seignurs! Ne l'ensevelez pas si tost, donetz lui moi, rendetz lui moi, pur Deu ottreiez le moy. Beaus douz seignurs, pur Deus rendés a ceste dolente mere soen enfaunt tuit seit il ore mort, suffrés unquore un petit que jeo le veye, car ceo me serra grant confort, et si vous le voletz tute voirs sevelir pur vostre cortesie, si me sevelés ové luy, car aprés lui n'averai jeo jamés ben.' Il le mistrent en la tumbe et la douce Dame le treist a sei. Cil le voleient ensevelir et ele le voleit retenir, et issi aveit entre eus une douce tencion. Il ploreient touz si forment qu'il n'y aveit nul que poet dire un soule mot. Il virent la douce Dame saunz nule confort et aveient greignur pité de la dolur de la Mere que de la mort lur Seignur. Par tut ou la tresdouce Virge passout, commensa sa dolur. Notez que nul que [la][ii] vist plorer ne se poeit tenir de plorer. Et issi a grant anguisse et ové tresgrantz suspirs et dolurs de la [f.189r] beneite Virge, ensevelirent il nostre Seingnur.

[i] MS en. [ii] MS Nō ne nul que.

Ah, God! What angel or archangel would not weep in spite of his nature, to see God, who cannot die, lying dead in spite of his Nature? Who so hard-hearted, not to weep at the sight of the Saviour of the world so cruelly treated, and of the blessed virgin all splashed with his precious blood? What man or woman, indeed, seeing that holy Lady so good and fair, so sweet and delightful, tormented with such agony and filled with such pain, crying so bitterly? Surely there is no heart that could bear to see the terrible anguish she suffered. So I would marvel if the angels were not weeping, even up there in the heavenly joy where no grief can be. Just as it is possible that God should die for the humanity he took upon himself, so may angels grieve for the death of their Lord.

When Joseph had brought down Our Lord's body, as the Gospel witnesses, he shrouded it and then placed it in a completely new tomb, that he had made for his own personal use. Then the angels of Paradise came to the women at the Lord's sepulchre, and our dear Lady raised a great lament beside the sepulchre when Joseph and Nicodemus laid him in it, and she wanted to be buried in the sepulchre with him. She embraced and caressed him, and kissed him as tenderly as she could, and she cried out piteously, "Ah, my dear loving lords, you who are my friends, have pity on me and leave me my dear Son, my sweet Friend, for a while, that I may see his lovely face for just a little longer, and seek comfort from it. Oh my dear lords, do not bury him so soon! Give him to me, give him back to me, for the love of God let me have him! Dear good lords, for God's sake give this grieving mother her child, even though he is now dead. Allow me a little longer to look at him, for this will be very comforting to me. And if you really wish to bury him so honourably, please bury me with him, for I shall never have any joy after he has gone." They laid him in the tomb, and the blessed Lady clutched him to her. They wished to bury him, and she wished to hold him, and there was a tender struggle between them. All were crying so bitterly that not one of them could say a single word. They saw their dear Lady inconsolable, and felt greater pity for the mother than for the death of their Lord. Wherever the sweet Virgin went, her grief burst out afresh; you can be sure that there was none who saw her weep who could help weeping too. And so, with bitter grief and deep sighs, and the lamenting of the blessed Virgin, they buried Our Lord.

Quant nostre Sire fust enseveli, dunc embraça la douce Dame la tumbe de cele part q'ele pout, si commensa ele a benestre soen douce enfaunt. Et la beneite Mere s'asist au tumbe et la besoit et la coleit ové tresgrant plenté des ameres lermes. Dunques vint mi sire seint Johan a qui nostre Sire l'aveit commaundé et ploreit taunt com cil qui ne sei poeit contenir ne sauler de plorer, et la leva en ploraunt, car ele esteit si tormenté des ameres gemissemenz, si lassé des aspres dolurs, si debatue des grantz plurs que ele n'avoit pez que la poeit sustenir. Lors, auxi com ele pout, ové l'aide des bones dames que ploreient, ovesque luy s'en entra en Jerusalem. Mes dunques recomensa la doel si grant come unques plus, car nul ne la vist que plorer ne covenist. Ele ploreit si durement et doluseit si amerement que de soen plorer moveit ele les autres maugré lur a plorer. Issi la menerent plorant jesques il vindrent a la mesun mun seignur seint Johan.

Quant ele vint leinz, dunques recommensa le doil tut [f.189v] de novel ne n'y aveit home ne femme que la poeit conforter. Dunques luy vint en memoire[i] tutz les poinz de la Passiun : une eure coment aveit esté crucifiez, une autre oure coment il l'aveient abeveretz, une autre coment il aveit esté feru au costé. Ele ploreit en criant et diseit en ploraunt : 'Ha, beau duz Jesu ! come l'em vous ad cruelement osciz ! Ha, douz Deux ! que est ceo, que jeo vei que celuy qui ciel et terre ne poeient comprendre si gist ore endreit en une tumbe de pere ? Ha, lasse dolente ! cil que esteit venu pur salu de tuit le munde, qui aveit pris char de mes flancs pur peccheurs reindre et esteit venu en terre pur eus, mes il ne le voleient unques receivre, einz luy feseient tutes les huntes, au derein le unt il osciz si come l'em pout huy ver.'

Ha ! Dame de gloire, Reigne de leesce, Funtaine de pité, Veine de misericorde, Pleine de sancté, Clarté dou ciel, Douçour de parais, Gloire des angles, Leesse des seinz, Pere precious des virgines, Dame tresbenuree, a vous commaunde [f.190r] jeo m'alme et moun corps, ma vie et ma mort et ma resurrection. Vous seiét beneite od vostre Fiz qui est et serra ovesques li Pere et li Seint Espirit un Deux *per secula seculorum*. Amen.

[i] MS mememoire.

When Our Lord was buried, the sweet Lady kissed the tomb all over, as far as she could reach, and she began to praise her beloved child. And the blessed Mother sat down by the tomb, and she kissed and embraced it with streams of bitter tears. Then came my lord Saint John, to whom Our Lord had commended her, and he wept as one who could not help himself nor even be sated with tears. And weeping, he raised her up, for she was so tortured with bitter groans, so wearied with bitter pain, so exhausted with long weeping that she could not hold herself upright. Then, as best she could, with the help of those good women who were weeping, she went into Jerusalem with him. And then the lamentation began again, so great as never before, for nobody could see her without being moved to tears. She cried so hard and grieved so bitterly that her weeping moved others, in spite of themselves, to weep too. Thus she was led, weeping, until they came to the house of my lord Saint John.

When she came in, her grief burst out afresh, and there was nobody, man or woman, who could console her. There came to her mind all the events of the Passion: one time how he had been crucified, another how they had given him to drink, yet again how he he had been stabbed through the side.[17] She wept, crying out, and weeping she said: "Ah, my beloved Jesus, how cruelly they killed you! Ah, sweet God, what is this, when I see that he whom neither heaven nor earth can comprehend is lying now in a tomb of stone? Ah, woe is me, he who came for the salvation of the whole world, who took flesh from my womb to redeem sinners and who came to earth for them, but they never wished to receive him and they did him every shame; at last they killed him, as can be seen today."

O Glorious Lady, Queen of Joy, Fountain of Pity, Heartspring of Mercy, Fullness of Sainthood, Heavenly Light, Sweetness of Paradise, Glory of Angels, the Joy of Saints, Precious Gem among virgins, most blessed Lady, I commend to you my soul and my body, my life and my death, and my resurrection. Glory be to you with your Son, who is and shall be with the Father and the Holy Spirit one God, "world without end." Amen.

---

[17] The word "oure" suggests the Hours of the Passion, and the meditations associated with them (see General Introduction, p. 11 above). An alternative meaning of the verb "abeveretz" (in the second phrase) is "poison."

Chapter 7

The Minstrels' Passion[1]

Introduction

This Passion narrative is from Cambridge, Trinity College MS B.14.39 (323) (s.xiii$^{3/4}$), ff.74ra–80vb. It is described in D&B as a homiletic narrative of the Passion in two Anglo-Norman redactions (four manuscripts listed), sometimes known as the *Passion des Jongleurs*. The Cambridge text has a Prologue that is not found in the many Continental manuscripts. It is presented as if to be recited aloud to an audience ("Listen, my lords"), though this may be simply a trick of the writer's, to enliven the text. No Latin is quoted, as though the audience might not understand it. The account follows the Gospels fairly closely, but the writer adds numerous illustrative and sometimes humorous details and (as we have seen elsewhere) some of the paraphrases are rather free.[2]

For comparison, see esp. *Northern Passion* (ed. Foster, vol. II of III): pp. 49–65 for list of manuscripts and discussion of sources of the French texts; pp. 102–25 for a version of the Anglo-Norman text (Cambridge, Trinity College MS O.2.14 (1118), ff.13ra–24va) — "nearer the ME Northern Passion of which the AN is a source." The Continental work was edited by Theben (*Die altfranzösischen ... "Passion"*); for the unique Prologue, see Burnam [*Passion Prologue*]; its relationship with the Clermont-Ferrand Passion's prologue is also discussed (the present text descends directly from the Clermont-Ferrand *Passio*). Readings from Burnam are added, in the prologue; readings from Foster's edition (F) are added in the main text.

---

[1] D&B 960, general heading "The Passion."

[2] Foster (in *Northern Passion*, II:47) suggests that among sources for Passion texts of this kind may be the "Gospel Harmonies," which wove all four Gospels into a continuous narrative (parallel passages from Gospels printed p. 59, note 6); see also *Preaching*, trans. Wenzel, p. xii.

Text

[f.74ra]
Seignurs, plaist vus escuter
Cum Deus wint en terre pur nus sauver.
Cet devum ducement oïr
Si nus a lu[i] volum venir.
Cet munde esteit tuz perduz
Que Deu n'i esteit ci venuz,
Ainz l'aümes tut adeisé,[i]
Deguerpi e deshonoré.
Quant li pius Deus nus visita,
Pur sa duçur, qui nus cria ;
En tere vint pur nostre amur,
Mut devum amer tel seignur.
Char prist de la vergine pucele,
Sa mere en fit, ele ert ancele.
Veez cum grant humilité
Quel duçur e quel pité
Que Deus hume pur nus dewint,
Enaprés mort en sustint.
Ne se poet plus enhumilier,
Tant le devum amer plus cher.
Trente deus aunz e un poi plus
Fu en cet cecle Crit Jesus
Pur ensample e pur doctriner
Cum nus devum a lu[i] aler
Par aumonies e orisuns
De alme, de cors afflictiuns.
Unques ne fit un sul pecché,
Pur lé noz fud crucifié.
Morz resuscitat, mundat leperoz,
Unke saindit a businus.[ii]
S'il le requit humblement,
Uncore le feit il ensement.
Cil qui sun essample suiverunt
E tent sa vie ja n'i faudrunt.
Ore escutét cum Deus vint en Jerusalem,
Ceo est la cité de Bethleem.
La cité vit si la gardat,
[f.74rb]
Dous disciples i enveat.
'Alét', dist il, 'en cel chastel.[iii]
Un anne e un asinel
Que vus [i] trovez m'amenét
Deliez, ja ren ne dutez.'
Cil alerent hastivement
Pur amur sun comandement,
Tant que li asnes fu amenez
E de lur dras aprestez.
Nostre Sire sur la sist
Cum li prophete l'orent dit.
Le jour devant u il ceo feit
Seint Lazre resusciter fit.
Cum ceo virent tote la gent
Que Jesu virent omnipotent,
Cil que les morz recuscitout,
Poez saver que grant joie en out.
Ascuns pristrent rames de paumers,
Li autres branches de olivers,
E li autre lur vestemenz
Estendeient lui de pavement.

[i] Burnam prints 'adossé'. [ii] These two lines are written at the top of the page and keyed to the main text. Burnam omits them, since he believes that they 'should not be considered as a part of the poem, but as a later addition by Scribe D [of the complete Trinity MS, as identified by Reichl].' [iii] MS chaltel.

Translation

1 My lords, be pleased to hear how God came to earth to save us. We must listen to this quietly, if we want to come to him. This world was utterly lost, had God not come here; but then we spurned him, abandoned and dishonoured him.

9 When our merciful God who created us so lovingly visited us, he came to earth for our sake. We ought to love such a Lord dearly. He took flesh from the virgin maiden; he made her his mother, who was his handmaiden.

15 Behold with what great humility, goodness, and pity, God became man for us; afterwards he suffered death. He could abase himself no further; so much the more dearly should we love him.

21 Thirty-two years and a little more was Christ Jesus in this world, to be an example to us and to teach us how we should go to him, by almsgiving, and by prayers of the soul and hardships of the body. He never committed a single sin — he was crucified for ours.

29 He raised the dead, he cleansed the leprous, he never [failed][1] the needy. If you pray humbly to him, he will still do so; those who follow his example and keep to his way will never fail.

35 Now hear how God came into Jerusalem, that is the city of Bethlehem. He saw the city and looked at it; he sent two disciples there.

39 "Go into that castle," he said. "Bring me the donkey and its young one that you will find there — untie them, do not be afraid." They went hastily, for love of his command, so that the donkeys were brought and their cloths prepared. Our Lord seated himself there, as the prophets had said.

49 The day before he did this, he raised up Saint Lazarus. All the people, having seen this, understood how all-powerful was Jesus, who could raise the dead to life; you can imagine how joyful they were. Some took branches of palm, others branches of olive, and others spread their garments on the road for him.

[1] The meaning of "saindit" (reading confirmed by Burnam) is uncertain.

Encuntre le Rey de majesté
S'en issirent de la cité,
A grant joie, a grant honur
Unt receü lur seignur.
E cil detriers e cil devant
Grant joie sunt fesant
E nis li petit enfanz
Vunt *osanna* par tut crianz.
Grant joie funt tut li fetheil,
Mais li feluns pristrent cunseil
Cumfaitement l'ocireient
Pur l'envie que il en aveient.
E li pius Deus que tut saveit,
Qui pur nus salver i veneit,
[f.74va]
De ses sainz ous prist a plurer
E de sun quor a suspirer.
Vai tei,' dit il, 'cité dolente,
Mut par as perdue ta entente
Qant tu ne cunuz tun seignur
Que wint morir pur tue amur.
Si tu saveies le turment
Que te vendrat hastivement,
Tu en aveies grant poür
E demenerés grant dolur,[i]
Kar hastivement venent li di
Que te saudrunt ti enimi,
Les tons beas murs abaterunt,
Pere sur autre n'i lerrunt ;
E tes enfanz que od tei sunt
A males peines ocirunt.
La tue gent pur male gent
Serrunt mené hastivement,
E ceo serrat li vengement
E de ma mort demustrement.'
Cum lur out tut acunté,
Aprés s'en alat a la cité.
Encuntre li se ovri la porte[ii]
Que mult esteit grant e forte.
Al temple entrat, justise i fit,
Sens ert li temple, ceo lur dit.
Les marchanz que il i [t]ruva
Od sun flel les engeta,
Le or e l'argent tut trebucha,
Qui il ert Deus ben lur mustra.
Aprés lur dit que sa mesum
Maisun deit estre de orisum.
Le jour al temple sermonout,
La nuit en Bethanie alout,[iii]
Sun ostel ert en Bethanie
En la maisun Marthe e Marie.
Lazarus lur frere esteit
Qui de la mort resurs esteit.
[f.74vb]
[O]re escutét tut ducement,
Gardét qui n'i ait parlement.
La passion Deu entendez,
Cument il fu pur nus penez.
Ne la poet oïr creature
Ke n'eit pité, ja tant n'ert dure,
Pur ceo qu'il eit entendement
Al Rei del cel omnipotent.
La lettr[ë]ure vus oïstes
Que cunte li ewangelistes.
Vos ne soutes que en munta,
Mais si Deu plait, vus l'orrés ja.

[i] MS demereies. [ii] MS overum. [iii] MS aluot.

59 They came out of the city, to meet the King of Majesty. They received their Lord with great joy and honour. Those behind and those before rejoiced with gladness, and even the little children went about crying "Hosanna!"

67 The faithful rejoiced; but the wicked men took counsel as to how they would kill him, because of the envy they felt. And merciful God who knows all, who had come here to save us, began to weep with his holy eyes and sigh from his heart.

75 "Woe unto you, O sorrowful city!" he said. "You have so lost your understanding, you do not know your Lord who comes to die for you. If you knew the torment that will soon fall upon you, you would feel great terror and make great lamentation. For the days will quickly come when your enemies will assault you; they will throw down your beautiful walls and leave not one stone upon another.

87 "And your children who are with you, they will slay them with cruel tortures. Your people will speedily be led away like criminals, and that will be the vengeance and the proof of my death." When he had said this, he went his way to the city.

95 The gates opened for him, that were so wide and strong. He entered the temple and wreaked judgement there; the temple was sacred, he told them. With his flail he drove out the merchants he found there; he sent all the gold and silver flying; thus he showed them that he was God. And he said his house ought to be a house of prayer.

105 That day he preached in the temple; that night he went to Bethany: his lodging was in Bethany, at the house of Martha and Mary. Lazarus was their brother, whom he had raised from death.[2]

111 Now listen quietly, and be sure not to chatter. Hear the Passion of God, how he was tormented for us. No creature, however hard-hearted he is, can hear this without pity; so let him understand about the Almighty King of Heaven.

119 You hear the account that the evangelists relate. You do not know how important it is but, God willing, you shall now hear it.

---

[2] The Prologue, together with Burnam's edition of it, ends here. F's French Passion begins with the next line.

La feste as Gius aprismot
— Ceo dit [li] liveres mot a mot —
Que Paschë esteit apelé,
Sur tote ren en eit gardé.
E li princes de cele lei
Que ne crurent en Deu le Rei
E li pruverë e li maistre
Querent mult, a destre e senestre,
Cument Jesu pusent prendre,
Par boidië en la croiz pendre.
Ches l'evesque sunt ensemblez
Que Caïphas fu apelez.
Ileoc un conseil unt tenu.
La parole fu de Jesu,
Cumfaitement le traïreint
Sanz la gent que mut cremeient,
E dïent tuz tut privément :
'Lassum aler tute la gent
Qui sunt venuz a ceste feste,
Vos i averez tost moleste.
Est issi ben ? Que vus semble ?'
Il otreient tuz ensemble.
Sis jorz aintz que la Pascha fu[i]
En Bethanie vint Jesu,
La u il de pité plura
Qant Lazarun resuscita,
[f.75ra]
En l'ostel Simun le leprus.
Saver poez ne fu pas suls,
Des disciples i ot asez,
Judas ne fu pas ubbliez.
Ileoc firent un grant manger,
Marthe fu a la apariler,
E un altre soror Marie,
Mut i out bele conpaignie.
Qant a la cene sunt asis,
Judas i fu, li enemis,[ii]
E Damnedeu, trestut nu pés ;[iii]
Marie en prit mut grant pitez,
Kar mult les aveit decrevez,
Mais ceo feseit humilitez.
Issi nus voleit il mustrer
Cum nus devum a lui aler.
La Magdelene l'ad purpensé
Cum le purreit servir a gré,
Par quei puit aver laisance[iv]
De ses pecchez dunt ad pesance,
Kar sicum li est avis
Fiz est al Rei de Paraïs,
Qui descendi del cel pur nus,
Il est nostre verai sucrus.
Ele aveit d'un cher ungnement
Un livere tut egalement,[v]
Forment cher e preciuus.
Pensat sei qu'au glorius[vi]
Le chef e les pez ungdereit,
Ben tod pur ceo merci aveit.
Desuz la table ele ert venue
Si que ele ne fu pas aparceue.
En sa main tint le ungnement
Que meuz valeit que or u argent.
As pez Jesu se lait aler,
Forment començat a plurer.
Grant suspirs gette del parfund,[vii]
Tuz ses pecchez en lermes vunt.

---

[i] MS sis ainz. [ii] MS sis e. [iii] MS damnenedeu. [iv] MS avec. [v] MS adds 'vel ohelement'; F has 'Une liure tot ovalment' (v. 62). [vi] MS quant g.

123 The Jews' festival was approaching — this is word for word what the book says — that was called Passover; it was celebrated above all things. And the princes of that creed, who did not believe in God the King, and the priests and the masters, asked around on every side how they could take Jesus by trickery and hang him on the Cross.

133 They assembled at the house of the bishop, who was called Caiaphas; they held a council there. The talk was all of Jesus: how they would deceitfully take him, without [trouble from] the people they were afraid of.

139 And they all said privately, "Let us allow all the people who have come to this feast to leave — you are going to have a lot of difficulties with them. Is this good? What do you think?" They all agreed.

145 Six days before the Passover, Jesus came to Bethany, there where he wept for pity when Lazarus arose to life, in the house of Simon the leper.

150 Let me tell you he was not alone: there were many disciples there, and Judas was not forgotten. They made a big meal; Martha was there to prepare it, and another sister, Mary — it was a very fine gathering.

157 When they were seated at the supper Judas his enemy was there, and the Lord God, whose feet were completely bare. Mary took great pity on him, for they were very cracked and sore,[3] but it was for humility: he wants to show us how we must come to him.

165 The Magdalene had wondered how she could do something to please him, so she could have relief from the sins that weighed upon her. For as she thought, he is Son of the King of Paradise, who came down from Heaven for us to be our true helper.

173 She had a whole pound of an expensive ointment, very costly and precious. She thought she would anoint the Glorious One, his head and his feet — she would surely deserve mercy for that.

179 She got under the table so that she would not be seen; in her hand she had the ointment worth more than gold or silver. She crept to the feet of Jesus and began to cry bitterly. She heaved great deep sighs, and her sins poured out with her tears.

---

[3] Love says (*Mirror*, p. 89 and note) this scene is evidence that Jesus habitually went barefoot. The passage is taken from his source (Pseudo-Bonaventure), and may reflect a Franciscan preoccupation.

Dolur aveit de ses pecch[e]z,
[f.75rb]
Od ses lermes laveit ses pez.
Od ses chevés les essua
E l'ugnement desus geta.
Le grant odor de l'ungnement
Empli la maisun e la gent.[i]
Li disciple ki l'unt veü
A mult grant dedeigne l'unt tenu.
Li traïtre Judas i fu
Qui ad sun sen perdu.
Sun fel quor ne poet suff[r]ir
[...][ii]
'Pur qui sufers cet gattement
De si precius ungnement ?
Ja vaut il ben tres cent deners[iii]
E plus asez, kar mult est chers.
Meuz vausit que fud donez
A povre gent que il fud gastez.'
Mais pur ceo nel dit Judas nent
Que cure eüst de povre gent,
Kar leres esteit e usure[r]s,
Sur tote ren amot deners.
'Diva,' fet Jesu, 'les ester Marie,[iv]
Ore ad tant fed que est m'amie.
Poveres averét assez,
Kui vos freez ben, si vus volez,
Mais mei n'averét vus lunge mie,
Jeo partirai de vostre conpaign[i]e.
Ceo que hele ad fed mut l'eim e pris.
Ainz que jeo sei aseviliz
Mun cors aromatizerat
De l'ungnement e meus li serrat.
Ore lui pardoin tuz ses pecchez,
Tuz les noveles e les welz.
Mut ad bon oevre fet en mai.
A wos le di par bone fei,
A memorie tenu serrat
Tuz jurs meis ceo que feit ad.[v]
Devant ma sepulture ad ceo fait,
[f.75va]
Mun cors ad uint, forment me plait.'
Judas Scarioht l'entent,
Pur poi qu'il de dol ne fent.
Entre ses dens dit belement
Si que nul fors Deu l'entent :
'Mal avét fed, je vus vendrai,
Ceste pecché restorerai
As feluns Gius, qui me durrunt
Des bons deners e vus prendrunt.'
Li traïtre plus n'i demore,
Aintz s'en turne en cel hure,
As princes wint e a la gent
Que Deu nen amouent nent.
'Dites mei,' fet il, 'a delivere,[vi]
Que me durrez se jo vos livre[vii]
Mun seignur que vus heét tant ?'
Il jurent en cuvenant
Trente deners. 'Guagét lé mei !'
'Nun le fium ben, par fei.'
Uns en i out que sout de vente,
Crent .i. dute que Judas ne se repente.[viii]
Mut tod trente deners li tent
E Judas volunters les prent.
Desoremés se penerat[ix]
Cum sun seignur traïrat.

---

[i] MS maisum. [ii] F 'Son seignor prist a demander' (v. 88). [iii] MS vuat. [iv] MS fet il J. [v] MS meuz. [vi] MS deliverer. [vii] MS d. a deliverer. [viii] F 'Vn en i out ki sauancist / Dunc duta que iudas se repentist' (vv. 135–36). [ix] MS deornemes.

187 She was sorrowful for her sins, and washed his feet with her tears. She wiped them with her hair, and poured on the ointment. Its strong scent filled the house and all the people. The disciples who saw it were very indignant.

195 The traitor Judas was there, he who had lost his senses. His wicked heart could not bear it, [F and he asked his Lord,] "Why do you allow this waste of such precious ointment? It must be worth three hundred pieces of silver, or even more — it is very expensive! Much better give the money to poor people than waste it so."

205 But Judas was not saying that because he cared about poor people. For he was a thief and a usurer, and loved nothing so much as money.

209 "Come now," said Jesus, "leave Mary alone; she has done enough to show that she is my friend. You will have enough poor people to do good to, if you want to. But you will not have me for much longer; I shall be leaving your company. I love and value what she has done. Before I am buried she will perfume my body with the ointment; it will be the better for it. Now I forgive her all her sins, the new ones and the old ones; this is a very good deed she has done for me. I assure you, what she has done will for ever be remembered. Before my burial she has done this: she has anointed my body and I am well pleased."

227 Judas Iscariot heard this, and he nearly burst for anger. He said softly, between his teeth, so that none but God should hear: "You have done ill. I shall sell you, and redeem this sin, to the wicked Jews who will take you and give me good money."

235 The traitor stayed no longer; he went away that same moment, and went to the princes, to those people abhorred of God. "Tell me quickly," he said, "what will you give me if I hand over my Lord to you, who hates you so much?" They swore to give him thirty silver pieces. "Promise me!" "Trust us, we will do it."

245 One of those there knew about business; he was afraid,[4] fearing that Judas would change his mind. Quickly he held out thirty pieces, and Judas took them eagerly. From now on he would plan how he was going to betray his Lord.

[4] "Crent .i. dute . . . "; the repetition is due to a gloss in the text (.i. means *id est*).

La Pasche vint e li jurs fu,
Li diciple Deu sunt venu,
Li enquerent : 'Sire, di nus :[i]
La nostre Pasche u tendirum nus ?'[ii]
Pere e Johan a apelét :[iii]
'A la cité m'en alez,
Un hume vus encont[r]erez
Euue portant, si li dirrez[iv]
Que ma Pasche voil en sa maisun,
Jeo e mi autre compainun,[v]
Manger tud privément.
Cil le vodrat tud ducement.
Ileoc freez apariler
[f.75vb]
Çoe ke nus averuns mester.'
Sicum il dit, si sunt turnez,
A la cité se sunt alez.
Trestut l'unt issi apressté
Cum Jesu lur out comandé.
E quant li jurz fu avesprez,
Nostre Sire s'en est turnez.
Venuz est en la maisuns,[vi]
Od lui ses duz conpaignuns.[vii]
Asis se sunt a cel manger,
Judas n'i fu pas derer.
Li nostre Sire mult l'amout,
Totes hures od lui manjout.
E li traïtres, que fesoit ?
Quant nostre Sire Deus beveit,
Emblout li en lei de glutun
Tut le plus bel de sun pessun.
Jesus ne fid nul sembland,
Ainz dormi sei en sun devant
Seint Johan ewangelistes,
Tut li meudre de ses ministres.

Tele chose i vit ne vuot escrire,
Kar lungue chose fu a dire.
'Frere,' dit Deus mult ducement,
'Ceo sachés vus veraiment,
Mult ai grant desirer
Hu[i] ced jour od vus manger.
Jeo ne mangerai mais od vus
Deque sei de mort rescus ;
Pur vus suffrir[ai] passiun
Que ne augez en perdiciun.'
Li nostre Sire ceo lur dit,
En ses baus mains le pain prist,
A sun Pere graces rend[viii]
Beneit le pain, si lur tent.
'Tenez,' fet il, 'si usez,
Ceo est mun cors que ci veez.
Mun cors mangez, mun sanc bevez,
[f.76ra]
Kar par ceo salvé serrez.
Li uns de vous me traïrat
E as Gius me liverat.
Tut est escrit la aventure
Del Fiz Marie en la escripture.'
Issi volt il tud enemplir
Quanc de lui est a venir.
'E nepurhoc mal avendra
Al traïtur que me traïra.
Meus li fu venu, par fei, assez
Qui il unques ne fud home nez.'
Quant li diciple l'unt oï,[ix]
Tut li menbre lur sunt fremi.
N'i ad celui que pour n'ad grand
E que sovent ne li demand,
'Sire,' ceo dit checun par sey,
'Si jeo sui ceo, dite[s] le mey.'

[i] MS de nus. [iii] MS ma a. [iv] MS portante. [v] MS a. autrea. [vi] MS maisums. [vii] MS a ses. [viii] MS sum. [ix] MS deable.

251 The day of the Passover arrived; God's disciples came and asked him, "Lord, tell us, where shall we spend our Passover?" He called Peter and John:

256 "Go to the city for me; you will meet a man carrying water. Tell him I want to have my Passover in his house, I and my other companions, to eat privately. He will agree courteously. Once there, prepare everything we shall need."

265 As he told them to, they set off and went to the city. They soon prepared everything as Jesus had commanded. And when evening had fallen Our Lord went there; he came to the house with his twelve companions.

273 They sat down to the meal, and Judas was not left out. Our Lord loved him well and always ate with him. So, what did the traitor do? While Our Lord was drinking, he greedily took all the choicest of the fish.

281 Jesus took no notice; Saint John the Evangelist, the very best of his ministers, was asleep on his breast. What did he dream of? I do not want to write it, for it would be too long to tell.[5]

287 "Brothers," said God softly, "please understand how much I want to eat with you now, on this day. I shall not eat with you again until I return from death. I shall suffer the Passion for you, so that you do not go down into perdition."

295 Our Lord said this to them. He took the bread in his beautiful hands, he gave thanks to his Father, blessed the bread and held it out to them.

299 "Take it," he said, "and eat it. This is my body you see here. Eat my body, drink my blood, for by this you will be saved. One of you will betray me and deliver me to the Jews. Everything that will happen to the Son of Mary is written in the Scripture."

307 Thus, he wanted to fulfil all the things that were to come to him. "And nevertheless evil will come to the traitor who is going to betray me. Better for him if he had never been born."

313 When the disciples heard this they trembled in all their limbs. There was not one of them who was not very frightened, and each kept asking, about himself: "Lord, if it is I, tell me."

[5] See Foster's Introduction (pp. 62–63) for this legend. God's speech, in the next line, may be "soft" in order not to wake John, who is dreaming the vision of Apocalypse (see the *Middle English Complaint*, pp. 176 & 205–6).

Quant Jesus ad ceo entendu
[...][i]
'Od mei mangue, od mei beit
Cil qui me traïr deit.'
E Judas lu[i] ad respondu :
'Su[i] jo dunc cil, maistre Jesu ?'
'Oïl,' dit il, 'ne larrai nent,[ii]
Ja l'as tu dit apertement !'
Ore laissent li diciple ester
De la traïsun demander.
Autre chose vunt enquerant,
Dund il erent plus dutant,
Quel de ceus greinur serreit.
Jesus a ceo lur responeit :
'Frere,' dit Deus, 'la riche gent,
Que li Enemis met a nent,
Icil quident estre le plus hald ;
Nu[n] sunt,' fed il, 'asét i faud.
Mais entre vus issi n'ert pas,
Li plus hald serrat li plus bas.
Cil qui plus s'en vodrat eshaucer
Sur tuz s'estot enhumilier
E tuz les estoverat servir
E sa volenté guerpir.
[f.76rb]
Jeo sui ici cum sergant
E serf a petit e a grant.
Jeo ne vinc pas pur seinurer
Ne pur maistré demener.
Mis duz Pere de lasus
M'enveiat pur ceo sa juz
E jo sui volunters ci venuz,
Ben sai que en croiz serrai penduz.
Aprés mei vus estout aler
Se vus al ciel volez munter.
Vus estes mi ami leaus,
Pur mei avét suffert grant maus.
Certes, jo vus guerdunerai
E mun cher Pere en prierai[iii]
Qui il vus rende guerdun,
Si frad, pas nel dutum.'
Ore unt li diciple cené
E des tables se sunt levé.
Deque de la table sunt levé,
Graces rendent, l'ure unt chanté.
Nostre Sire se leva,
Ignelement ses dras osta,
D'un mantel s'est avirunez,
I urent ja les pez lavez.
Ses dras a pris e aprestez
[...]
Mult belement entr'e[u]s seo sit,
Ore escutez qu'il lur dit,
Savét que fait a e demustré[iv]
Esample de grand humilité :
'Vus m'apelez maistre e seignur,[v]
Si faites ben e vostre honur,
Kar ceo est veir, ne mentez mie,
Par mai avrez durable vie.
Si jo me su[i] agenulez
Devant vus laver vus pez,[vi]
Ceste esample que jo vous laies
Issi de[vez] vus faire maies,
Li uns a l'autre ducement
Si[cum] jo ai fet apertement.
Dirrai', dit Deus, 'une ren,
[f.76va]
Veir serrat, ceo sai jo ben.
Mut vus verai esparpilez,
En ceste feye vos manquerez.

[i] F 'Mult douchement a respondu' (v. 228). [ii] F 'Ceo es tu verraiement' (v. 233). [iii] MS en frai. [iv] MS f. e ai d. [v] MS ma apelez. [vi] MS mis p.

319 When Jesus heard this [F he replied very gently], "He eats with me, he drinks with me, the one who is to betray me." And Judas said to him, "Am I he, master Jesus?" "Yes, I do not deny it," he said. "Now you have said it openly!"

327 Now the disciples left off asking about the betrayal. They began asking about something else, that they were more worried about: which of them should be the greatest.[6]

332 Jesus replied to this: "Brothers," said God, "the powerful people, whom the Devil brings to naught, here believe themselves the highest. But they are not," he said, "they fail. But among you it shall not be so: the highest shall be the lowest. He who most wishes to exalt himself must humble himself above all, and will have to serve all, forsaking his own will. I am here as a servant, and I serve both the small and the great.

345 "I did not come here to rule or to be master. My loving Father in Heaven sent me down here to serve, and I came here willingly. I know I shall be hung on the Cross. You will have to come after me if you want to go to Heaven. You are my faithful friends and you have suffered great hardship for me. Certainly I will reward you, and I will pray to my dear Father to reward you — he will do so, we cannot doubt it."

359 Now the disciples had eaten and risen from the table; they went up to the table and gave thanks and sang a prayer. Our Lord got up and quickly took off his clothes and wrapped himself in a cloak. [Although] they had already washed their feet,[7] he took cloths and prepared them. Gently he sat down among them — now hear what he said to them — learn what he did, showing an example of great humility.

373 "You call me master and lord — you do well, and it honours you. For it is true, if you do not fail you will receive eternal life through me. If I knelt before you to wash your feet, I am leaving you this example: you must do this henceforth for one another, courteously, as I have done openly. I shall tell you something," said God, "and it will come true, I know that. I shall see you all scattered; you will fail in this faith.[8]

[6] Luke 22:23–24: *And there was also a strife among them, which of them should be accounted the greatest.*

[7] F "A cels uoleit lauer les pez" (he wanted to wash their feet, v. 282).

[8] F reads 'En ceste nuit e esmaiez' (v. 314), "all scattered, this very night, and terrified."

Checun de vus me guerpirat[i]
De la pouur qu'il averat.
Trestut vus estoverat fuïr,
Kar poour averez de morir.
Jeo remaindrai entre la gent
Que ma vie ne aiment nent.
Deque li pastur est feruz
Li fuc dé berebiz est vencuz.
Jeo suffrai pur vus la mort,
Li Gius me ocirunt a tort.
Aprés ma mort me troverez
En Galilee u me querez.'
A seint Pere ne plout
De Damnedeu ceo qu'il out :
'Sire, que tu diz
Frei jo mult enviz.
Nent ne devum fuïr,
Ovoc tei me estoet morir.'[ii]
E Deus respund ducement :
'Ainz esterat tut autrement.
Ainz qui li chos chante, haut u bas,[iii]
Par tres feiz me nieras.'
Seint Pere li respund aprés :
'Ceste chose ne dites mes,
Pur anguse ne pur dolur
Ne renierai mun seignur.'
Li autre dient ensement
Qu'il nel reneirunt nent.[iv]
'Ore laisum', dit Deus, ester,
Kar autre chose voil demander.
Quant par le munde vus envoi[eie],
En povreté ne vus troveie.
Enveiai vus en mun sermun
Escrippe porter e burdum,
Faili vus nule furnesture
Ne covenable vesture ?'
[f.76vb]
'Nenil,' funt il, 'maistre Jesu,
Ainz avum asez [e]u.'
'Or vus dirrai que vus freez,
Checun de vus glaive prendrez,
Qui nul averat, sa cote vende,[v]
Bon glaive s'achate dunt se defende.'
Ileoc s'en uunt deus aportez.[vi]
'Ore en i ad,' fet Deus, 'Assez.'
Ileoc nen unt plus demorez,
Tut ensemble se sunt alez
Fors Judas que s'en est emblez
Qui de mal se est purpensez.
Venuz sunt en un verger
U esteient li oliver.
Munt Olivete out num li lius,
Deus i sout venir tut suls.
Este vus ileoc asemblez.
'Seignurs,' dit Deus, 'Ore en i asez.
Ne dormez pas, ainz veilez.
Merci criez de vus pecchez,
Que ne entrés en temptaciun[vii]
De male cogitaciun.'
Quant issi les out sermonez,
Un poi lunz de eus est alez.
Treis en ad oc sei menez,
Ceus que teneit as plus privez.
Li uns dé treis out num sein Pere,
Li autre Jacob e Johan sun frere.

[i] MS checum. [ii] MS me mestoet. [iv] MS Quil il ne r. [v] MS Quil. [vi] MS sent u. [vii] MS tepmtaciun.

387 "Each of you will forsake me because of the fear he feels. You will soon have to flee, for you will be afraid for your lives. I shall remain among the people who hate my life. As soon as the shepherd is struck down, the flock of sheep will be vanquished. I shall suffer death for you: the Jews will wrongly kill me. After my death you will find me, where you seek for me, in Galilee."

399 Saint Peter was not pleased at what he heard from the Lord God. "Lord, I shall do what you say very unwillingly! We must not flee; I must die with you!" And God replied gently, "But it shall be quite otherwise: before the cock crows, loud or soft, three times you will deny me."

409 Saint Peter answered him again: "Do not say those things! For no torture or pain will I deny my Lord!" And the others all said likewise, that they would not deny him.

415 "Now leave this," said God, "for I want to ask another thing. When I sent you out into the world, you did not find yourselves in poverty. I sent you to preach for me, to carry scrip and staff.[9] Did you lack any equipment or suitable clothes?" "No, master Jesus," they said, "we had enough of everything."

425 "Now I will tell you what to do. Every one of you take a sword; whoever has none must sell his coat and buy a good sword to defend himself." Two were brought there.

430 "Now there are some," said God. "That's enough." They stayed there no longer, and all together they departed — all except Judas, who had stolen away: he was planning evil.

435 They came into an orchard where there were olive trees. The place was called Mount of Olives; God had used to come here alone, now they are here all together. "My lords," said God, "now we are here, do not sleep, but watch. Ask mercy for your sins, nor fall into the temptation of bad thoughts."

445 When he had said this, he went apart from them a little way. He took three of them with him: those he held in greatest intimacy. One of the three was called Saint Peter, the others were James and John his brother.

[9] Luke says *sine sacculo* (*I sent you without purse, and scrip, and shoes* ..., Luke 22:35). Furthermore, we find Jesus' instructions earlier in the Gospel accounts: Matt. 10:10; Mark 6:8; Luke 9:3 (all in *AV*).

'Frere,' dit Deus, 'deque a la mort
Ert ma alme triste, sant confort.
Tenez vus od mei de dormir.'
[...]
Deus s'en est alugnét un petit,
Ore escutez qu'il ad dit.
Chaïr se lait as urisuns,
Sun Pere apele par ses nuns.
A genuz se est agenulez,
Ceo fet il pur nos pecchez.
'Pere,' fet il, 'ore crei jo ben
Que tu poez faire tun ren.
[f.77ra]
Si te plait, pas nel vodrai,
La mort, einz la trespasserei.
Mun cors ad pour de morir,
Ceste dolur [ne] voil suffrir,
Mais nepurhuc ma volenté
Ne seit pas feite, mes la dé.[i]
La tue volenté otrei,
Ore fais tut tun plaisir de mei.'[ii]
Issi se dementout li Sire
Qui sanz pecché ert e sanz ire.
Uns seinz angles est decenduz
Del cel qui li est aparuz.
Sun Seignur prist a conforter
De ce que il le veit dementer.
De la pour que Jesu out
[...] Gutes de sanc sa char suot
[...]
E desur la tere chaei[en]t.
Beau Sire, purquei suffriz
Si pur ceo nun qui vossis ?
Cel anguse e cel dolur,
Ceo esteit pur nostre amur,
Pur nus decunbrer del forfet
Qui li premerains home aveit fet.
Quant se levat de l'orisun
Jesus, que mult amer devum,
As diciples est venuz,
De dormir les trove vencuz.
'Diva,' dit Deus, 'purquei dormez ?
Un hure od mei veiller ne poez.
Judas ne dort ore nent,
Ainz me traïst a male gent.'
Quant Damnedeu issi parlout[iii]
Il veit Judas que traï l'out,[iv]
Ensemble od lui grand conpainie
De la gent ke Deu ne aiment mie.
Dé feluns Gius mut i out,
[f.77rb]
Li fel Judas les guiout.
Il ne veneient pas sanz armes,
Haches portent e gisarmes,
Si portent grants bastuns,
Lanternes cleres e branduns.
'Seignurs,' fet li fel Judas,
'Jesu ne connusez pas,
Celui que baiser me verrez,
Ceo est un maistre, celui prendrez,
Si le menez mut fermement[v]
Qui il ne vus eschape nent.'
Jesu ne out cure de fuïr
Qui de bon gré vult morir.
Entre ceus se met li Deus de nus :
'Diva,' fet il, 'que querez vus ?'
De ceo que Jesu lur dit
Une si grant poür lur prist,
Mais nepurquant il unt respondu :
'Pur Jesu sumes ici venuz.'
'Je sui ici,' Deus lur respont.

[i] 'dé' for 'té'. [ii] MS fait. [iii] MS se p. [iv] MS E veit. [v] MS formement.

451 "Brothers," said God, "My soul is now heavy as death, and comfortless. Keep awake with me. [F My flesh is afraid to die.]"[10] God withdrew from them a little; now hear what he said. He fell to praying, and called on his Father by his names. He knelt down on his knees — he did this for our sins.

461 "Father," he said, "I believe that you have power to do anything. Please, I do not wish to die when my death comes. My body is afraid of death — I do not want to suffer the pain. And yet, let not my will but yours be done. I submit to your will — do what you want with me." Thus the Lord spoke, lamenting: he who was without sin or wrath.

473 A holy angel came down from Heaven and appeared to him. He began to comfort his Lord, for he saw him in torment. Because of the terror he felt his flesh sweated drops of blood, [so large they ran down his body and][11] fell to the ground.

481 Fair Lord, why did you suffer, if you did not wish to do so? This anguish and pain, it was for love of us, to disburden us of the forfeit brought about by the first man.

487 When he rose from his prayer, Jesus, whom we ought to love so much, came to the disciples and found them all overcome by sleep. "Come now," said God, "why are you asleep? Can you not watch with me for an hour? Judas is not asleep now, he is betraying me to the wicked people."

495 While the Lord God was saying this, he saw Judas who had betrayed him, together with a crowd of those people who hate God. There were many wicked Jews, and the wicked Judas led them. They did not come unarmed: they carried axes and halberds, they carried sticks and bright lanterns and torches.

505 "Lords," said the wicked Judas, "you do not know Jesus. The one you see me kiss, that is a Master — take him. Hold him very firmly, lest he escape you."

511 Jesus, who meant to die with good grace, had no thought of running away. Our God placed himself among them.[12] "Look here," he said, "what do you want?" A great fear seized them at what Jesus said; nevertheless they replied, "We have come for Jesus." God answered them: "I am here."

---

[10] A line is missing here, see F: "Ma charn ad pour de morir" (v. 374).

[11] A line is missing here, see F: "Si grans qu'aval sa char corroient / et que desus terre cheoient" (vv. 399–400).

[12] F "Encuntrels uait li quel de nos" (v. 461); var. "A*n*trax ce mist ih*es*us po*r* noz."

Quant ceo out dit, autre vunt
E quant il furent relevé,
Tres feit lur ad demandé :
'Que querez vus, dite[s] le mei.'
'Jesum querum que se feit rei.'
'Ja l'avez mult ben oï,
Jeo sui Jesu, veez mai ci.'
Ore wint Judas, sil saluat,
En la face le baisat.
'Amis,' dit Deus, 'qu'as tu quis ?
Tu me baisez, si me traïz.'
A icest mot l'unt saisi
Li Gius qui de li n'unt merci.
E quant seint Pere od ceo veü,
De sa [e]spee ad un feru.
Maltus out nun, ben l'asena,
La destre oraille li copa.
[f.77va]
'Avoi,' di[t] Deus, 'Pere, ne faire,
Vous tu a tum Seignur deplaire ?[i]
Oste ta arme, sta en pais,
Ceste chose ne faite[s] mais,
Kar qui de glaive fert autru[i]
A glaive perrat le cors de lui.
Jeo n'ai cure de mai defendre,
De mun gré voil en la croiz pendre.
Kar sachez si jo volei,
La passiun ne suffreray,
Kar jeo averai a defendement
Angles, archangeles plus de cent,
Si jo volei, mais ne voil,
La mort suffrai sans orgoil.'
Ore oez grant bunté,
Essample de grant humilité.
Le oreille prist que ert coupee,
Al faus Gius l'ad resanee.[ii]
Ben demustre que Deus esteit
Par les miracles que feseit,
Mais li Gius de male vie
Tant erent plains de felunie
Qu'il diseient que tut ert fable
Quancque il feseit e par li diable.
Ore l'unt de tutes parz saysi
Li felun qui de lui n'unt merci.
Li diciple se sunt fui,
Checun sa part si l'unt guerpi.
En la maisun dan Chaïfas
Menerunt Jesu plus le pas.
Tresben le lient, pur nent,
Kar de fuir n'ad talent.
Il esteient tud d'une part,
Diseient qui il ert de male art,
Kar le Fiz Deu se feseit apeler,
'Que atenduns nus de li tuer ?'
[f.77vb]
Dous faus testimoines sunt levez,
De maldire se sunt penez :
'Oez, seignurs, que jeo li oï dire
— Que ja ne purrat dedire —
Que nostre temple destruereit,
Eintz tres jurs refet l'avereit.
Est il dunc si puisant ?
Salamon mit quarante anz.
Sil n'aveit plus feit ne dit,
Si est dreit que seit lapit.'
Tuz responent a une voiz :
'Deservi ad de pendre en croiz.'

[ii] MS As f.

520 When he had spoken, others arrived; when they came up he asked them three times: "What do you want? Tell me!" "We want Jesus who makes himself a king." "So I have heard — I am Jesus, see, here I am."

527 Then Judas came forward and greeted him, and kissed him in the face. "Friend," said God, "what have you done? You kiss me, and so you betray me."

531 At this word they seized him, those Jews who had no mercy on him. And when Saint Peter saw this, he struck one of them with his sword. His name was Maltus — he hit him hard, and cut off his right ear.

537 "Stop that!" said God. "Peter, you must not. Do you want to displease your Lord? Put up your sword and stand quietly. Never do that again! For whoever strikes another with a blade, his body shall perish by the blade. I do not care to defend myself; I desire, by my own will, to hang on the Cross. Understand that if I wanted, I would not suffer the Passion, for I could have angels in my defence, and a hundred archangels or more,[13] if I wished — but I do not. I shall endure death without pride."

551 Now hear of great goodness, an example of great humility. He took up the ear that had been severed, and he healed the wicked Jew. He showed he was God by the miracles he did, but the evil-living Jews were so full of wickedness that they said what he did was all lies and the Devil's work.

561 Now the felons who had no mercy seized him on all sides. The disciples fled; each in his turn abandoned him. They led Jesus directly to the house of Lord Caiaphas.

567 They bound him well, but for nothing, because he had no desire to flee. They all stood to one side, saying he was a magician because he called himself the Son of God. "What are we waiting for? Let us kill him!"

573 Two false witnesses got up and took pains to speak ill of him. "Listen, my lords, to what I heard him say, that he cannot deny: he would destroy our temple, and have it built up again within three days. Is he then so powerful? It took Solomon forty years.[14] If he never said or did more, it is right he should be stoned." They all replied with one voice, "He has deserved to hang on a cross!"

---

[13] See Matt. 26:53: *more than twelve legions.*

[14] See II Chron. 9:30 (in *LV*, II Paralip. 9:30).

Ore aveit sint Pere sun liu,
Juste les autres delé le fu,
Mais tant s'en est mustrez
Qui il ert sempres araisunez.
Cil qui se chafei[n]t envirun
Le conussent a la raisun.
Il li demandent : 'Dunt es tu
Des diciples al rei Jesu ?'
Peres respunt ignelement :
'Ceo que dites ne sai nent.'
Uns des Gius danz Caïphas,
Ver lui s'aprime quatre pas :
'Dunc ce vi jo,' feit il,
'Ensemble od lui en un curtil,
E si me ferit d'une espei[i]
Si que le oreille en oi copee
E tis maistre le me sana.'
Qui par ceo guarir quida
Il se comence a escundire,
A jurer, a maudire.
'Unques od lui certes ne fu
Ne jur ne nuit ensemble od lui.'
Seint Pere veit que n'i garrat,
D'iloc s'en turne, si s'en va.
[f.78ra]
Quant de la porte s'en isseit,
Une femme l'aparceit :
'Icit houme que de cenz fu,
Il est compainz, ço quit, Jesu.'
'Num est pas !' Un autre li dit,
'Quides qui il se maldeit ?'
'Tenés me dunc pur fole ?
Jo cunus ben a la parole,
Il est compai[n]z al Nazaren.'
Pere respont : 'Nu[n] su[i], par Deu.
Sachés que unches mes nel vi
For tant que ore le vei ici.'
Quant ceo out dit, li chosc chantat
E Jesu Peres regardat.
E sint Pere ore aparceit
De ceo que Jesu dit li aveit
Que ainceis que li chocs chanteit,
Treis fet le reniast.
Pere s'en ist hors a cel hure,[ii]
De quor suspire, des ouz plure,
Si grant deul ad ne seit que dire,[iii]
Asprement plure e suspire.
Ore laissum issi de sint Pere,
Si parlum de Deu, nostre Pere,
Qui est entre male gent
Qui l'acusent mult durement.
Si fust omicide u plain d'ire[iv]
U pire que home ne set dire,
Ne sai cument le hunirent
Plus laidement ne traïrent.
Il le pincent e reschinent li,
Enmi li vis l'unt escopi.
Li faus Gius, li culvert,
Le son bel vis l'unt cuvert.[v]
En la face ferent Jesu,
Puis dient : 'Qui ad ta[i] feru ?
Devinét tod, ne targét pas,
Si ço nun, tu comparras.'
Il ne responeit mot, li Sire,
[f.78rb]
Kar sanz orgoil ert e sanz ire,
Kar si vossit u deignat,
Tuz les arsit u devurat.

---

[i] MS feris. [ii] MS sentit h. [iv] MS p. oire. [v] MS decuvert.

585 Now, Saint Peter had a place next to the others near the fire, but he had shown himself enough so that before long he was addressed. Those warming themselves round about had reason to recognize him.

591 They asked him, "So, are you one of the disciples of King Jesus?" Peter replied immediately, "I have no idea what you are talking about."

595 One of the Jews of Lord Caiaphas took four steps towards him. "I saw you," he said, "with him in a garden. And then you struck me with a sword so that my ear was cut off, and your master healed it."

602 Because he thought he could protect himself, he began to deny, to swear, to blaspheme. "I was certainly never with him, neither day nor night was I with him."

607 Saint Peter saw that this could not save him, so he turned and went out. As he came through the door a woman caught sight of him. "That man who was inside, I believe he is a companion of Jesus." "It is not so," said he. Another said to her, "Do you believe his oaths?"

615 "Do you think me mad?" she said. "I know by his speech, he is a companion of the Nazarene." Peter replied, "No, I am not, by God! I tell you I never saw him before, except for seeing him here now."

621 When he had said this, the cock crowed, and Peter looked at Jesus. And now Saint Peter realised what Jesus had said to him, that before cock-crow he would deny him three times.

627 Peter went out then; his heart sighed and his eyes wept. He knew not what to say, and he wept and sighed bitterly.

631 Now let us leave off about Saint Peter, and talk of God, our Father, who is among the wicked men who accuse him so harshly; they were full of murder and anger, worse than anybody could say.

637 I cannot tell how they humiliated him — they could not have treated him more cruelly. They pinched and insulted him, they spat full in his face.

641 The false cowardly Jews covered his beautiful eyes, then struck him in the face, saying, "Who struck you? Hurry up and guess; quickly, or you will pay!"

647 Our Lord answered not a word, for he was without pride or anger. If he wished or deigned to, he could consume and burn them all up.

Devant Pilate l'unt amené,
Mut formement l'unt acusé.
'Sire,' funt il, 'nus ça menum
Faus prophete e un felun,
Tute deveie nostre gent
De la lei qu'il ne sent nent,
Dit qu'il est nostre seignurages,
Ben l'en deit faire huntages.
Sachét, nus avum, bel Sire,
Enz en quors grand dol e ire.
De ceo qui il dit est rei de nus,
Ja fud tuez ne fud pur vus.'
Issi l'acusent formement
Icele felunesse gent.
Ore veit Judas qui il est dannez
Quant si sires est a mort liverez
Par lui e par sa traïsun.
Les Gius ad mis a raisun :
'Seignurs,' fet il, 'pur Deu tenét
Tuz vus deners que ci veez.
Mult ai pecché e sanz mesure,
Ja n'averat Deus de mei cure,
Kar jo le ai traï e vendu
E del tut mescunu.'
Cil respunt : 'Que teint a nus ?
Tut le pecché seit sur vus.'
Quant ceo out Judas si a geté
[L'argent] el temple, s'en [est] emblé,[i]
Dese[s]pers si s'est penduz[ii]
De sa ceinture a un ceuz
De dol qui il ad, si est damnez
Pur ceo qui il est si desestperez,
Kar si il vossit sei tenir
E de sun pecché repentir,
Il eust merci e pardun
Cum nus avverum si nus volum.[iii]

[f.78va]

Ore laissum de Judas ester.
Il fit Jesu avant mener.[iv]
Pilate le mit a raisun[v]
E dit : 'Que ad forfeit cest hum ?
Jeo ne treus en lui nul enchaisun
Pur quei seit mis a dampnaciun.'
Pilate redit a nostre Sire :
'Poësté ai en ceste enpire
De vostre cors crucifier
U, si jo voil, de vus laisser.'
Jesu respunt mult ducement :
'Vus nent avez veraiment
Nule poësté de mei
Si duné ne fut de suverain rei.'
La femme Pilate vint avant
A sun seignur tut plorant :
'D'icet dreiturel ai mut sungé,
Qu'il est hume de grand bunté.
Pri vus, laisez, beu sire, ester
D'icest dreturel damner.'
Pilate dit : 'Kar laissum.'
'Par fei,' funt il, 'nu ne frum[vi]
Si tu Jesu laisses en pais,
Amis Cesar ne sarras mes,
Kar trestut cil que rei se funt
A nostre rei Cesar mesfunt.'
Quant Pilates out les paroles
Que les soens tenent pur foles,
L'ewe demande pur laver ;
Issi se quidout il sauver.

---

[i] MS E al t. [ii] MS sest si sest. [iii] MS cun. [iv] MS fil. [v] MS raisum. [vi] MS fet il.

651 They brought him before Pilate and accused him very harshly. "Lord," they said, "we bring here a false prophet and felon. He leads our people astray, away from the law he cares nothing about, and says he is sovereign over us — he must be made to suffer for it. Good sir, we declare we are heartily sorrowful and angry that he says he is king over us. If it were not for you, he would be dead already."

663 So these wicked people made their dreadful accusations. Then Judas saw that he was damned, and that his Lord was to be put to death because of him and his treason.

668 He began to speak to the Jews. "Lords," he said, "for God's sake take back all the silver pieces you see here. I have sinned greatly — immeasurably — never will God care for me, for I have betrayed and sold him, and misunderstood everything."

675 They said, "What is that to us? Let all the sin be upon you." When Judas heard that, he threw down the money in the temple and slunk out, and in despair he hanged himself with his belt from an elder-tree, because of his sorrow.

681 He was damned because of his despair, for had he wished to hold fast, and to repent of his sin, he would have received mercy and forgiveness, just as we shall if we desire it. Now let us leave Judas.

688 Pilate had Jesus led forward, and he questioned him. He said, "What has this man done wrong? I can find in him no reason why he should be condemned."

693 Pilate said to Our Lord, "In this empire, I have the power to crucify your body or, if you wish, to release you." Jesus replied very gently, "Truly you have no power over me unless it is given by the sovereign king."

701 Pilate's wife came forward to her lord, weeping: "I have dreamed so much about this righteous man, and that he is of great goodness. Dear lord, I beseech you to leave off condemning a righteous man."[15]

707 Pilate said, "Let us free him, then." "Faith!" they cried. "Let us not! If you leave Jesus in peace you will never more be Caesar's friend, for anybody who makes himself king does wrong to our king Caesar."[16]

713 When Pilate heard these words, that his own people thought mad, he called for water to wash in. Thus he thought he could save himself.

[15] Compare this passage with that in the Harley "Meditation" (see p. 238 below), where Pilate's wife is said to be "enticed" by the Devil, in order to prevent the Redemption.

[16] Caesar Augustus (63 BCE–CE 14) was succeeded by his stepson Tiberius (d. 37); see Luke 2:1, and e.g. Luke 3:1.

Devant eous tuz ses mai[n]z lava,
Enaprés a eous parla :
'Ci me delivere de sa mort
E de sanc jo n'i anost
D'icest home que vus blamez.'
Dunc ont checun escriez :[i]
'Li sanc e li pecché par dreit
Sur vus e sur vvos enfans seit.
[f.78vb]
Nul pecché net od lui, ceo sachez,
E trop par se feiz fort e sages.'
Pilate vult al pople plaire,
Lur volenté comande faire.
Barraban lur ad livré
E de Jesu ad comandé
Que il seit batuz e ledengez ;
Aprés seit crucifié.
Enmi la place l'amenerunt
Li faus Gius e se asemblerent,
De tuz ses dras l'unt despoillé,
A une esthache l'unt lié.
Li faus Gius, li mescreant,
Les mains li lient al devant
En corees que sunt noés ;
As chefs de bastuns encloes[ii]
La gloriuse char Jesu
Bateient il a grand vertu,
Mut le ferent asprement,
Chascun dit que il ne le sent,[iii]
Kar il ne vult crier merci
N'il ne gette brai ne cri.[iv]
Quant la char Deu unt batue,
Une purpre li unt vestue.
En sa destre li funt tenir
Un rosel pur escharnir.
Une corone li unt faite,
Ne fu de or ne d'argent purtraite.
D'aulbes espines fu overé,
Espessement enreorté.
La corone ert pungnante e menue,
Pur mal faire esteit mult ague.
[...]
Desus ferreint od un ees
Des plaies li funt vinz e dous,
Li sanc en saut en plusurs liuz,
Aval li vait par la face,
Tut cil s'en rient par la place.
'Seignurs,' fund il, 'fust en prendrum[v]
[f.79ra]
Dunt nus la sue croiz frum.'
Kar ja n'ert de bele uvre faite,[vi]
Ainz ert de une planche traite,[vii]
D'icel ruisel qui la purrit.[viii]
Mut ad lung tens que l'en li mit.
La plangche traistrent del taier,
Dous parz en firent od l'acir,
Si le firent en croz cheviler.
Unc [ne] manderent bon ovrer.[ix]

[i] MS sont. [ii] MS encloees. [iii] MS chaicun. 'n'ose' is written at the end of the line. [iv] MS braz. [vi] MS hure. [vii] MS de une de une. [viii] MS misel. [ix] MS mandat.

717 Before them all he washed his hands, and then he spoke to them: "This releases me from his death, and I clear myself[17] of the blood of this man you condemn."

722 Then each one cried, "Let the blood and the sin be rightly upon you and upon your children. No sin is born with him, you know, and he makes himself so strong and wise."

727 Pilate wanted to please the people and commanded their will to be done. He released Barabbas to them, and of Jesus he commanded that he was to be beaten and scorned and afterwards crucified.

733 The wicked Jews gathered together and led him into an open place; they took off all his clothes and tied him to a stake. The wicked cruel Jews tied his hands in front with knotted cords.

740 Using staves with nail-studded heads they beat Jesus' glorious flesh with great force — they beat him very cruelly. They all said he felt nothing, for he would not beg for mercy, nor did he cry or groan.

747 When they had beaten God's flesh they dressed him in purple; in his right hand they made him hold a reed, in mockery. They made him a crown: not of gold or finely-worked silver, but worked of hawthorn spines thickly twisted together.

755 The crown was thorny and tight — it was made small so as to hurt more. [Then they put it on his head.][18]

758 They pushed it down with a plank, and it made more than a score[19] of wounds that were sharp and painful to him. Blood sprang out in many places and ran down his face — everybody in the place laughed at him.

764 "My lords," they said, "let us fetch wood, and we shall make his Cross from it." It was never supposed to be of good workmanship, so they pulled a plank out of the stream where it was rotting; it was a long time since it had been put there.

769 They pulled this plank out of the mud, and split it in two with the steel; then they fashioned it into a cross — they called no skilled workman to do it.

[17] 'anost' (= enost?) is an incorrect rhyme.

[18] This line is added from F: "El chief la li mettent aprés" (v. 1089).

[19] In the text, "dous" is a rhyme-word; there is no special significance to the number 22.

Icet sainz fut que iloec fu pris,
Aportez fud de Parais.
Un fiz Adam l'en aportat,
Uns seinz angles li bailat.
Del pomer fu u crut la pomme
Que mit a mort li primer hume.
L'e[n] diseit ke Cipres od nun,
Trencher le fit dan Salomun.
E a nut il fit fere sa maisun,
Sis est uvres que nus entendun.
Sis lius ne poet estre trovez
U il fud mis ne alevez,
U il fud trop grand u trop petit,
Amunt fu porté e envis.
Par maltalent li carpenter
Le trebucherent en taier
'Meus vient', funt il, 'purer ci
Que estre al temple domini.
Fust reproché ore eez nun,
N'ert mais jur que ne marchun.'
Aprés lung tens i vint en la vile
Pur Salomon dame Sibille,
Par la planche n'osat passer,
Kar ne voleit l'ewe trubiler.
Aval s'e[n] vait lunz del passage,[i]
Ben l'aparceit, kar mult est sage,
Que la charn Deu i serrat lesé,
Enclina lé lui, par aval est passé.
[f.79rb]
Ore parlum de la grand dolur
Qui il suffri pur nostre amur.
Quant li Giu orent la croiz feite
Qui aveient de tair traite,
N'i ad celui que porter le vuot,
Checun dit 'a mei que cheout
Que jo li face tel servise ?'
Sur le [col] Jesu l'unt mise :
'Qui desure sustint la mort
Ben est dreit que il la port.'
En Golgatha en sun[t] venuz
Pur crucifier la char Jesu,
La croiz al Rei primes drecerent.
De ses cher dras le despoillerent,
Entre eus les partent li felum.
'Diva,' fet il, 'kar en getum,
Li ques de nus ait ces dras tuz.
Mut par frum ore que pruz.'
Sort un[t] getté sur les [draps] Crist.[ii]
Jeo ne sai a ques ben il a prit.

[ii] MS lescritz.

773 This holy wood,[20] that was taken from there, had been brought from Paradise. A son of Adam brought it, and it was given him by a holy angel. It was from the apple tree, where the apple grew that sent the first man to death; they say it is called Cypress.

780 Lord Solomon had it cut, and at night he had his house built, as we learn from his work. No position could be found for the wood, wherever it was laid or placed. Either it was too big, or too small.

786 It was taken up, with ill humour; the carpenters angrily tipped it into the mud. "Better let it rot there," they said, "than stay in the Lord's temple. Call it henceforth the Accursed Wood — we'll trample on it every day."

793 After many years, Lady Sibyl came to town to visit Solomon.[21] She dared not walk on the plank, for she did not wish to trouble the water. She went the long way round, for she could see, wise as she was, that the flesh of God would be placed upon it. She bowed towards it, and passed around downstream.

801 Now let us speak of the great agony he suffered for our love. When the Jews had made the Cross, that they had pulled out of the mud, there was nobody who would carry it.

806 They all said, "Why is it my turn, to do a job like that for him?" They loaded it onto Jesus' neck: "Whoever is going to die on there, it's right he should carry it."

811 They arrived at Golgotha, the place to crucify Jesus' body. First they raised up the Cross of the King. They stripped him of his fine robes, those felons, and divided them up.

816 "Come on!" cried one, "let's toss for them, to see which of us gets them all. That will be a fine thing to do." So they drew lots for Christ's robes — I don't know who was the lucky winner.

[20] See *GL* I:277–84 (68: The Finding of the Holy Cross). Lady Sibyl (below) is the Queen of Sheba in the Legend.

[21] The figure of (the) Sibyl is common in medieval literature as a pagan prophet of Christ; see e.g. *The Oxford Companion to Classical Literature*, s.v. Sibyl. See also *GL* I:40, for one of her prophecies.

Aprés dient il 'al fevre alez.'
'Nent,' il dient, 'al fevre alez.'[i]
A la forge venent tut dreit.[ii]
Quand Israel venir les veit,
Ses mains repost, si se est asis.
Ne frat nul, ceo m'e[s]t avis.
Al fevre dient la male gent
'Treis clous vu[s] fetes ignelement.
Jhesum vulum crucifier
Qui il ne puisse mes regner.'
'Seignurs,' fet il, 'jeo ai mal a[s] mains,
Mut ad lung tens que ne fui sains.'
'Quel mal est ceo ?' 'Al fu me quis,'
'Mustrés le nus,' 'Seignurs, ne puis.'
'Purquei, diable, ne poez ?'
'Tut ai les daiz emflez.'
'Par le grand Deu ja les mustrez,
[f.79va]
Vus estes morz si vus mentez.'
Il trait les mains, kar pour out,
Tute bullettés, cum Deu plot.
Sa male femme out le quor faus,
Si dit 'Tost vus ad pris cest maus.
N'ad uncore si mult petit nun
Que en[tre] mai e vus forgiun.
Ne remai[n]drat pur tun dehait
Que li treis clous ne seient fet.'
Le fer od les tanailes prit,
Desur le brese ardente le mit,
Le feu soffle od les dous fous,
Od le martel ad fet les clous.
E as Gius les ad liverez,
Cil les unt tuz portez.
Igne[l]pas unt Jesu pris,
Sus en la croiz dreit l'unt mis.
Enaprés ferent les clous
Que li percent parmi les os.
Longius le fert parmi le piz,
Ore est Jesu mut ben clofiz.
Li uns dé laruns pendeit a destre
E li autre a senestre.
En miliu fu li nostre maistre,
Li Reis de la gloire celeste.
Hure de terce tut dreit fu
Que en la croiz fu despendu.
Pur ceo fit Deus un orison
Que ne li firent si mal nun :
'Chere Pere, qui es al cel lamunt,
Pardunez lur ceo qu'il funt.'
A une dé croiz esteit Marie,
La sue mere esbaie,
Si fu Marie Cleophé
E Marie Magdaleiné.
[f.79vb]
E plusurs i esteient
Que la sue mere serveient,[iii]

[i] Dittography in both lines; see F, vv. 1227–28. [ii] MS Al la f. [iii] MS si veient.

821 Then they said, "To the blacksmith! Nay, to the blacksmith!" they cried.[22] So they went straight off to the forge. When Israel saw them coming, he rested his hands and sat down. He was going to do nothing, I think.

827 The wicked men said to the smith, "Hurry up and make three nails. We want to crucify Jesus, to stop him reigning any longer." "Lords," he said, "my hands are bad. They haven't been right for a long time."

833 "What's wrong with them?" "I scorched myself in the fire." "Show us, then." "No, my lords, I can't." "Why the hell not?" "My fingers are all swollen." "By the Great God, show us now! We'll kill you if you're lying!"

839 He stretched out his hands, for he was afraid: they were all blistered, by the will of God. His wicked wife, faithless woman, said, "This trouble came on you quickly! But it won't take much for you and me together to do the forging — all it needs now, to disgrace you, is not to do these three nails."

847 She took the iron in the tongs, and laid it on the burning coals. She blew up the fire with a pair of bellows, and with the hammer she made the nails.[23] She gave them to the Jews, who took them all away.

853 Straight away, they took Jesus and put him up on the Cross. Then they banged in the nails, that pierced between the bones. Longinus pierced him in the chest — and so Jesus was well and truly nailed up.

859 One of the thieves hung at his right, and the other at his left. In the middle was our Master, the King of celestial glory. It was just at the hour of Tierce that he was hung on the Cross.

865 So God made a prayer, notwithstanding how much pain they inflicted: "Dear Father, who is in Heaven above, forgive them for what they are doing."

869 At one of the crosses stood Mary, his horrified mother; Mary Cleophas was there too,[24] and Mary Magdalene. And there were several of those who served his mother.

[22] See F: "They asked 'Are the nails ready?' 'No!' 'Then off to the smith with you!'" (vv. 1227–28). The following story seems to have originated with this Passion, although it may have been suggested by a line about badly-made nails in an earlier Latin text (F, pp. 64–65).

[23] "Two bellows"; she would be unable to manage two pairs at once. However, there is an illustration of this scene in the Holkham Bible: two pairs are apparently rigged up so that they can be operated by one person (reproduced in Devonshire and Wood 1996, p. 107; *Northern Passion* is cited at p. 106).

[24] Mary's half-sister (see Mary's Family, p. 155 above).

Sur totes esteit pensantuse[i]
La sue mere glorieuse.
N'est merveile si ele est iree
Ne pur sun cher fiz enperee
Qui en sun ventre le porta[ii]
Par ki li munde sauvé serra.
Quant la dame en la croiz le vit,
Une si grand dolur le prit,
Dit ele 'Amis Jesu,
En cele croiz pens tu,[iii]
Ja es tu Deus de tote rent
E reis e sire de tuz bens.
Parlez od mei, beau fiz, amis,
Qui cel e tere e mere fesis.
Cument remaindrai aprés tei ?
Merci aiez, bel sire, de mei.'
'Merci,' dit Deus, 'pur ceo pene ci,
Que endurer ne voil issi.
Pur le puple voil suffrir passium
Qui il n'aut en perdiciun.
Mere, .i. autre fiz averas,[iv]
Pur ceo ne te larrai pas.
Veez Johan ensemble od tei,
Tis fis serrat en liu de mei.
Seint Johan ewangelistes
Est li meudre de mes ministres.[v]
Wardét ben, veici ta mere,
Issi li seiés amis e frere.
Ore seét desorenavant
Ensemble od lui, jeo cumand.'
'Sire, jo frai tut tun plaisir,
Grand doel ai qe te vei morir.'
Li faus Gius iloec esteient,

[f.80ra]
Devant lui passent e veient.
'C'est celi que le temple abaterat,
En treis jurz refeit le averat.'
Li maistre dient de la lei
'Que poet estre de ceo rei ?
Les autres fet resusciter,
Sei memes ne poet sauver.
Si est rei del pople Israel,
Descende sei — mut nus ert bel —
De cele croiz, ci le crerum tuz.
Mais nun fra, sicum jeo quit.'
Uns des laruns que ileoc pendeit
Deu ledengeout, si li diseit,
'Si tu es Deus e tu ren vaus,
Ore faite[s] nus dous saus.'
Sis conpains dit 'Tu as tord,
Il n'ad pas deservi la mort.
Mais nus avum ben deservie,
Kar mauveis ad esté nostre vie.
Tu ne creiz pas en Deu,
Pur ceo n'eez en croiz d'aiue.[vi]
Il ne soffre pas ceo qu'il deit,
Mes nus eimes a bon dreit,
Kar onques ne feimes si mal nun,
Si est ben dreit que mal avum.
Kar Deu ne mesfit unques ren,
Ainz fit a tuz autres ben.
Sire,' fet il, 'membrez tei
En tun regne pur Deu de mai.'
'Hui en cest jur,' fet Deus, 'amis,'
Serras od mei en Parais.'

[i] MS esteiet. [ii] MS len p. [iii] MS pent Jesu. [iv] MS li autre. [v] MS des m. [vi] MS ceo que.

875 Among them all she was in heavy mood, his glorious mother. It's no wonder she was in anguish, and terrified for her darling Son — she had carried in her body him who was to save the world.

881 When the lady saw him on the Cross, she was seized with great agony, crying, "Dearest Jesus, you are hanging on this cross — you are God of all beings, and King and Lord of all good things! Speak to me, dear son, friend, you who made heaven and earth and sea. How can I remain, after you are gone? Dear Lord, have mercy on me!"

891 God said, "It is for mercy that I suffer here, that I do not wish to stay here. I wish to suffer this passion, for the people, so that they shall not go into perdition. Mother, you shall have another son; I shall not leave you thus.

897 "See here John, who is with you — he shall be your son in my stead. Saint John the Evangelist is the best of those who serve me.

901 "[John], look well, see here your mother; be a friend and brother to her. From now on I command you to stay at her side." "Lord, I will do anything to please you. I am so desolate to see you dying!"

907 The false Jews were there too, passing before him, and looking. "That's the one who will knock the Temple down, and in three days he will have built it up again!"

911 The masters of the Law said, "What is it about this king? He can raise up others from death, but he can't save himself. If he is King of the people of Israel, let him fetch himself down — that will be good to see — from that cross. Then we'll all believe him. But he won't do it, I'm sure of that!"

919 One of the thieves hanging there insulted God, saying to him, "If you are God, and if you're worth anything, save the two of us now!"

923 His fellow said, "You are wrong! He hasn't deserved death, but we certainly have; our whole life has been wicked. You don't believe in God, and so you will get no help on the cross. He is suffering, but not because he must; we are here rightfully. We have never done anything but evil, so it's quite right for us to suffer evil now. But God never did any wrong; he did right to all others.[25]

935 "Lord," he said, "remember me, for God's sake, in your kingdom." "Today, this very day," said God, "you shall be in Paradise with me, my friend."

[25] F 'toz les iors b*ien*' (v. 1420).

Hure de midi fu obscure,
Li munde e tute creature,
Tenebres furent par le mund,
Trestute gent grand pour unt.
Tresque nune ad duré,
Tut li munt en oscur[t]é.
[f.80rb]
Tut li jur fu en nuz mué.
Li Giu se sunt amervilez,
Mut se merveillent li plusur
Dunt est venu tel tenebrur.
A mut pituse voiz s'escrie
Jesu, le fiz Marie,
E dit 'Helie, heli.'
Li faus Gius que l'unt oi,
'Il apele' funt il 'Helie
Qui lui venge faire aïe.'
'Jeo ai sei,' dit Deus, 'a beivre avez ?'
Funt li Gius 'ja n'i faudrez.'
N'aveit mie sei de liquor
Qui pur nus suffri tel dolur[i]
Sa sei esteit de nus sauver,
Les sons voleit de enfern geter.
Ceo ert la sei dunt se cunplaint,
Nul autre chose il n'aveit [plaint].[ii]
Ore escutez quel deablie
Que firent cele gent haïe.
Aisil pristrent e suie e fel,
Ben se gardent qui n'i out mel.
Un beivere li funt destemprer,
A grant merveille fu amer,
'Ne l'esparniez,' funt il, 'bevez,
Kar vus en averez asez.'
E il unt mis lur espie
Saver si vendreit Helie.
'Li prophete qu'il apelat
Ben tost de la croiz l'osterat.'
Or n'i vult Jesu plus ester,
De seit secle s'en volt aler.
Ore escutez qu'il a dit,
Jeo vus dirrai sulum l'escrit,
Cil ad dit 'Consummatum est',
Qui tote creature pest.
Lores enclina sun chef jus,
[f.80va]
Li esperit s'en vait lasus.
Del cors est li espirit volez,
Dreit en enfern est alez.
D'enfer brisa lé sereures[iii]
E derumpi tote[s] les clostures,
Hors en geta les sons amis
Qui li deable i aveit tramis.
Il les conduit a sun cher Pere
En la glorie la u il ere.
Joseph ab Arimathia
Vint a Pilate, si li preiat
Que li grantast le cors Jesu
Pur sun servise si li pleout.
Quant Pilate l'entendi,
De Joseph sun ami
De bon gre li granta
Quant que Joseph li rova.
Nicodemus i vint mut tost,
Od ses tanailes ostat les clous.
Joseph entre les braz le prit.
Jesu, que tut le munde fit,
Le seigneur de tut le munde,
Volupat en sindone munde,
En le sepulchre l'unt mis
Li riche reis de Parais.

---

[i] MS sulfri. [iii] MS sercures.

939 The hour of noon was dark, the world and everything in it; dark shadows filled the whole world, and many people were filled with terror. Until the hour of None the world endured utter darkness, the whole day was turned into night.

946 The Jews were astonished, and they marvelled where this darkness could have come from. In a piteous voice Jesus, Son of Mary, cried out, saying, "Eli! Eli!"

952 The false Jews who heard him said, "He's calling on Eli to come and help him."

955 "I am thirsty," said God, "have you anything to drink?" The Jews said, "There's plenty!" He wasn't thirsty for liquid, he who suffered such pain for us: his thirst was to save us, and to buy his own out of Hell. That was the thirst he complained of; he wanted nothing else.[26]

963 Now hear what devilry these hateful people did: they took vinegar and soot and gall — making sure to put no honey in it. They mixed him up quite a drink: it was unbelievably bitter.

967 "Don't leave a drop," they said, "drink up! You shall have as much as you like." And they posted their spies, to see whether Eli was coming: "That prophet he's calling will get him off the cross in no time!"

975 Now Jesus wanted to stay there no longer, and wished to go out of this world. Now, hear what he said — I'll tell you according to the Book — he who provides for every living creature said, "It is finished."

981 Then he bent down his head, and his spirit went away upwards. From the body, the spirit flew out and went directly to Hell.[27] He broke the locks of Hell and smashed all the gates; he cast out all his friends whom the Devil had sent there, and he led them to his dear Father, to the glory where he is.

991 Joseph of Arimathea came to Pilate, and begged him to let him have the body of Jesus, if it pleased him to reward his service. When Pilate heard this from his friend Joseph, he willingly granted all that Joseph asked him.

999 Nicodemus arrived quickly, and with his pincers he pulled out the nails. Joseph took him in his arms, Jesus, who made the whole world and who is Lord of the whole world; he wrapped him in a clean shroud and placed him in the sepulchre, the mighty King of Paradise.

---

26 For Jesus' thirst to save souls, cf. *FM*, pp. 566–67.

27 For the legend, see Tamburr 2007.

Li felun s'asemblerent,
Vindrent a Pilate si li demanderunt
Que le sepulchre gardast
Que houme Jesu n'en emblast,
Kar dunc, dient, serreit le error,
Hastivement rent pejur.
'Jeo vus command que'l gardez
Autresi ben cum vus savez.'
E cil qui veiler i deveient
Ignelepas si dormeient.
Al ters jur si leva sus
Nostre Sire, Rei Jesus.
A ses apostles s'aparut,
Quarante jurs od eus fu.
[f.80vb]
Si lur mustrat la novele lei
Puis les baisat checun par sei.
Issi nus puss'il sauver
E sa glorie amener. Amen.

1007 The wicked men gathered, and they came to Pilate and asked him to guard the sepulchre so that none should steal Jesus from it. For this, they said, would be a mishap that would quickly bring worse consequences. "I order you to guard it to the very best of your ability." And those who were supposed to be watching very quickly fell asleep.

1017 On the third day he rose again, our Lord King Jesus. He appeared to his apostles, and was with them for forty days. He showed them the New Law, and then he kissed each one of them. Thus may he save us, and bring us to his glory. Amen.

Part IV

Private Prayers

Chapter 8

Harley Prayers

Introduction

This selection, or series, of Anglo-Norman prayers from the famous MS Harley 2253 (c. 1330–40) illustrates on a small scale the variety of material in the whole manuscript.[1] One of the six distinguishable parts of the collection is this set of prayers in French, a few in Latin among them, for everyday use. The sequence begins on f.134r with a set of the names of the Angels and Archangels and the dangers for which remembrance of their name is efficacious, a list very similar to that in Oxford, Bodleian Library, MS Rawlinson C 814 (12654), f.1v (R in the footnotes).[2] D&B has several entries for these items from the Harley MS.[3] The contents of the series, presented in full with the exception of some Latin items, are as follows (the headings in the text below, in square brackets, are editorial):

952 (2): Names of Angels and Archangels, and what to pray for to each (f.134r).

455 (2): Psalms to say when one is in various kinds of trouble (f.134r).

Some but not all the Psalms, here and in St Maurice's list below, are penitential; the incipits are given untranslated in the manuscript, and it is not explained why these psalms in particular are prescribed. The Penitential Psalms usually number seven; note that several of the incipits are duplicated:[4]

1. Domine, ne in furore; Ps. 6 (6)
2. Beati quorum; Ps. 32 (31)
3. Domine, ne in furore; Ps. 38 (37)
4. Miserere mei; Ps. 51 (50)
5. Domine, exaudi; Ps. 102 (101)
6. De profundis; Ps. 130 (129)
7. Domine, exaudi; Ps. 143 (142)

[1] See the EETS facsimile edition (OS 255) for a description and list of contents; for discussion, see Fein 2000.

[2] See D&B 621 (in which the piece is addressed to "Bele file") and 621r.

[3] In the edition below, footnotes to each piece supply its D&B number, together with the article number from the facsimile.

[4] See General Introduction, p. 12 above (and p. 135 note 5, in Young Mary) for the Gradual Psalms. See also *Women's Books of Hours* (ed. Scott-Stokes, pp. 9–11). Psalm numbers are here given with the *AV* number first, followed by the *LV* number.

These seven psalms were sometimes matched with the seven Deadly Sins:[5] contra 1 *iram*, 2 *superbiam*, 3 *gulam*, 4 *luxuriam*, 5 *avaritiam*, 6 *invidiam*, 7 *acediam*. In the Efficacy of Prayers passage below, the "sixty days" formula includes number 6, "De Profundis." It is the only Penitential Psalm cited in our sequence, and there is no indication why the sin of envy should be an issue in this case.

869: Gloria (f.134v).

751: St Maurice's prayer (f.134v).[6]

699: A list of reasons for commemorating Friday (f.135r).

948 (and see 932): The saying of Masses — the special occasions, together with the number of candles and alms to offer (f.135r).

941: A prayer to the Three Kings: Jaspar, Melchior, Baltasar (f.135v).

The "wise men" are the subject of a substantial legend, and their names had medicinal properties. In *GL*, an account of them is found in the chapter on Epiphany (I:78–84). They are not called kings in the Gospel (Matt. 2:1–12); this, together with their names and the number three, is apocryphal.[7]

950 (and see 985): on the Efficacy of Prayers (f.136r).

456: Psalms to say for special purposes, ordained by St Hilary (ff.136v–137r).

As with the list of psalms above, it is not clear whether the whole psalm was to be said, or only the incipit.[8]

958: A Meditation of the Seven Hours, in prose (ff.138v–140r).

The last item, of the Seven Hours, is unusual in that it begins at Compline because Judas sold Jesus at this hour. The format is not original, but the treatment is: the text is not a translation.[9] The following note, about Pilate's Wife, is relevant to Passion narratives in our collection and elsewhere:

---

[5] See *The Anglo-Norman Lyric* (ed. Jeffrey and Levy), pp. 116ff.

[6] St Maurice's prayer is preceded by a prayer in Latin and and followed by another; translations are provided because they belong in the sequence.

[7] *ODCC*, s.v. *magi*. See also the *Liber de Diversis Medicinis*, ed. Ogden (pp. 42–43, & 99, for the names as a charm).

[8] For the use of psalms "for all manner of human needs," see Heinzer 2008 (p. 40); for whether the whole psalm was to be said, see ibid. p. 43 but also Sutherland 2008, pp. 78–79.

[9] See Boulton 1996–97 for a discussion of the piece, and for the Hours see General Introduction (Private Prayer) above.

When he [Pilate] *was set down on the judgement seat, his wife sent unto him, saying, Have thou nothing to do with that just man: for I have suffered many things this day in a dream because of him.*[10]

The short Gospel passage, about the woman interrupting men's business to tell her dream, invites dramatization and varying interpretation. It is ambiguous, because there is nothing to say whether the dream came from God or from the Devil.

In Passion narratives, the incident is treated in different ways: first, in the Meditation below, Pilate's wife appears because of the Devil's "enticing"; there is no suggestion that she is attempting to interfere with God's plan. In the Minstrels' Passion above (vv. 688–713) she comes forward to tell her dream, and she is given a speech of her own. This, together with the absence of anti-feminist comment, suggests the writer is sympathetic to her efforts to prevent the Crucifixion. In another Anglo-Norman Passion text,[11] the woman is given no speech of her own, and the writer takes the opportunity to explain that the dream was the work of the Devil. Preventing the Crucifixion would prevent the salvation of humankind, and here the Devil uses Woman as his agent, as he did in the Garden of Eden.[12] In the Gospel of Nicodemus,[13] the dream is interpreted as a clever trick on the part of Jesus the sorcerer to get himself reprieved! In this account, Pilate and his wife, named Procula, die as martyrs. Such a favourable view, says James, is characteristic of the East.[14] Medieval dream theory, which taught that dreams came from different sources, allowed dreams to be interpreted in widely different ways. The dramatic potential of Procula's dream was exploited in several mystery plays. Kolve gives a useful summary of the subject in *The Play Called Corpus Christi* (pp. 227–31). In one of the York Mystery Plays, the Devil comes on stage and explains exactly why he plans to abort the Crucifixion.[15]

---

[10] Matt. 27:19; the incident does not appear in the other Gospels.

[11] D&B 959, in prose (meditation before Tierce); an edition by Maureen Boulton is forthcoming.

[12] Such anti-feminism is found nowhere else in the *Merure* (Legge 1934).

[13] James, *Apocryphal New Testament*, p. 98 (Acts of Pilate, II).

[14] Ibid. pp. 154–55.

[15] ed. Smith, play XXX, pp. 270–91. A footnote discusses the wife's name.

Text

[Angels][i]

[f.134r] Quant vus levez le matyn, pensez de seint Michael e vus averez honour le jour.

Quaunt vus oyez toneyre, pensez de seint Gabriel e ren serrez grevez.

Quant vu mangerez ou beverez, pensez de seint Raphael e totes choses vus habounderount.

Quant vus irrez nul chemyn, pensez[ii] de seint Raguel e rien doterez.

Quant vus vendrez al jugement, pensez de seint Rachel e vus averez vostre volenté en bien.

Quant vus vendrez a feste, pensez de seint Pantesseron e vus serrez honorez.

Pensez de seint Abyel et de seint Brachiel quant vus vendrez devant prince ou seigneur e vus avendra bien.

Pensez de seint Uryel e de seint Tobye quant vus entrez en nef e vus passerez sauntz peryl.

[Psalms][iii]

Quy velt que Dieu sovyegne de ly, die troifoiz cest salme : *Usquequo Domine* [12:1].

Qui de rien se doute, die troizfoiz cest salme : *In te, Domine, speravi* [30:2].

Si vus volez estre deliveré del poer del deable, ditez le jour treyfoiz cest salme : *In te, Domine, speravi* [70:1].

[i] D&B 952 (2), facsimile 100. [ii] MS p. pensez. [iii] D&B 455 (2), facsimile 101.

Translation

[Angels]

When you rise in the morning, think of Saint Michael and you will have honour that day.

When you hear thunder, think of Saint Gabriel and you will come to no harm.

When you eat or drink, think of Saint Raphael and you will enjoy every plenty.

When you travel on any journey, think of Saint Raguel and you will have nothing to fear.

When you go to law, think of Saint Rachel[1] and you will get the good judgement you want.

When you come to a feast, think of Saint Pantesseron and you will be honoured.

Think of Saint Abyel[2] and of Saint Brachiel[3] when you come before prince or lord, and it will go well with you.

Think of Saint Uryel and of Saint Tobye when you go on board ship, and you will voyage without peril.[4]

[Psalms]

(The various psalms to be used in prayer are prescribed as follows:)

Whoever wishes God to remember him, say three times: *How long wilt thou forget me, O Lord?* [Ps. 13].

Whoever is afraid of anything, say three times: *In thee, O Lord, do I put my trust* [Ps. 31].

If you wish to be delivered from the power of the Devil, say: *In thee, O Lord, do I put my trust* [Ps. 71], three times in the day.[5]

---

1 R has "Barachiel."

2 R has "Tobiel."

3 R has "Barachiel."

4 Uriel is often counted among the Archangels, although it is Raphael (another Archangel) who appears in the Book of Tobit (Raguel is Sara's father); see General Introduction, p. 14 above, for medieval angelology.

5 For the distinction between the two psalms, 31 and 71, see below (p. 255, note 19). Here they are listed as if they are different psalms, and the second refers to the power of the Devil, as it does in the list below.

Quant vus devez aler la ou vus avez pour ou doute, dites ceste salme : *Iudica, Domine, nocentes me, expugna* etc [34:1].

Quant temptacion de votre char vus prent, ditez : *Iudica me Deus, et discerne* [42:1].

Quant vus levetz de vostre lit, dites : *Deus, in nomine tuo* [53:3].

Si vus estes en ascun adversité, dites sept foiz : *Exaudi, Deus, orationem meam (cum deprecor)* [63:2].

Si vus devez pleder ov votre enymy, dites : *Miserere mei, Deus, quoniam in te confidit*[i] [56:2].

Si vus devez combatre, ditez cest salme : *Eripe me de inimicis* [58:2].

Si vus seiez en pecchié, dites : *Deus misereatur nostri* [66:2].

Si vus estes environé de vos enimys, dites : *Exsurgat*[ii] *Deus* [67:2].

Quant vus estes en tribulatioun, dites : *Salvum me fac Deus, quoniam intraverunt* [68:2].

Quant vus volez rien comencer, dites : *Deus in adiutorium* [69:2].

Si vus volez qe Dieu receyve ta priere, ditez : *Deus venerunt gentes* [78:1].

Si vus estes en tribulacioun e volez estre delyvrez : *Domine, refugium* [89:1].

Si vus estes pris et mys en destresse, dites : *Domine, probasti* [138:2].

Cestes salmes avant nomez serrount ditez en genoillant ov grant devocioun e chescun a meynz troifoiz ou plus.

[Gloria][iii]

[f.134v] ***Gloria in excelsis deo* en fraunceis**

Joyous honour lasus en haut seit a Dampnedé
E pees en terre soit a gent de bone volenté.
Loé soit Sire Dieu, beneit e aoré.

[i] MS *conf'*. [ii] MS *Exurgat.* [iii] D&B 869, facsimile 102. This item is not set out as verse: the writing fills the page (a common way of saving space).

When you must go somewhere that makes you afraid or anxious, say: *Plead my cause, O Lord, with them that strive with me* [Ps. 35].

When you are assailed by fleshly temptation, say: *Judge me, O God, and plead my cause* [Ps. 43].

When you rise from your bed, say: *Save me, O God, by thy name* [Ps. 54].

If you are in any adversity, say seven times: *Hear my voice, O God, in my prayer* [Ps. 64].

If you must go to law, against your enemy, say : *Be merciful unto me, O God, be merciful unto me: for my soul trusteth in thee* [Ps. 57].

If you must fight, say: *Deliver me from mine enemies* [Ps. 59].

If you are in a state of sin, say: *God be merciful unto us, and bless us* [Ps. 67].

If you are surrounded by your enemies, say: *Let God arise* [Ps. 68].

When you are in tribulation, say: *Save me, O God; for the waters are come in unto my soul* [Ps. 69].

When you wish to begin anything, say: *Make haste, O God, to deliver me* [Ps. 70].

If you wish God to receive your prayer, say: *O God, the heathen are come into thine inheritance* [Ps. 79].

If you are in trouble and wish to be delivered, say: *Lord, thou hast been our dwelling place in all generations* [Ps. 90].

If you are taken and put in prison, say: *O Lord, thou hast searched me, and known me* [Ps. 139].

These psalms listed above are to be said kneeling with great devotion, and each one at least three times or more.[6]

[Gloria]

***Gloria in Excelsis Deo*, in French** Joyous honour there on high be to the Lord God, and peace on earth be to people of good will. Praised be the Lord God, blessed, and worshipped.

[6] A selection of four general prayers follows.

A joie Vus rendum graces pur votre grant bonté,
Sire Deu, Roy de Ciel, Piere de poesté
E Vus, Sire Jhesu Crist, le fitz Dieu benuré,
Fitz e Piere Tutpuissant, Aignel Dieu apelé,
Nos pecchiez nus pardonez e recevez a gre
Le preyeres que nus fesoms pur notre necessité,
Vus q'a destre seez le Piere en magesté,
Eyez merci de nus, Jhesu Crist, e pieté,
Que soul estes Sires, seint e trehauucé
Ov Dieu le Piere e Seint Espirit en joye, en deyté,
Quar ensi est sauntz fyn en herité.
Amen.

[*Confiteor*][i]

Confiteor tibi Deus omnia peccata mea quia tu, Deus, es sine peccato et obsecro te, Deus meus, Domine Jhesu Christe, Nazarene fili Dei vivi per passionem tuam et per lignum salutiffere crucis tue et per effusionem sancti sanguinis tui, in concedere remissionem omnium peccatorum meorum, peto, Domine, ut iudicas me secundum judicium indulgentie tue et per misericordiam tuam exoro, ut digneris inserere in me amorem tuum, suscita in me veram penitenciam et adiuva me, dele iniquitatem meam a conspectu tuo et ne avertas faciem tuam ab oratione mea, ne derelinquas me Deus meus, set confirma me in tua voluntate, doce me quod agere debeam, defende me Domine Deus meus contra omnes inimicos meos visibiles et invisibiles, defende me, Domine Jhesu Christe, contra jacula diabolica et contra angelos tartareos, suadentes et docentes me mala facere, Domine, ne discedas a me et ne derelinquas me, Domine Deus meus, et ne proicias me miserum famulum tuum, sed adiuva me, Domine Deus meus, et perfice in me doctrinam tuam et veram confessionem, quia tu es deus, Creator meus et Dominus meus, qui cum Patre, Filio et Spiritu Sancto vivis et regnas in secula seculorum, Amen.

[St Maurice][ii]

Icest oreysoun enveia Nostre Dame Seinte Marie a seint Moris, evesque de Parys, e ly comanda qu'il le aprist al pueple e qui chescun jour en bon devocion le dirra, hounte en le siecle ne avera ne de l'Enymy engyné serra, ne passioun en terre soffrera, ne femme d'enfant periera, ne mesaventure ne avendra, ne desconfés murra :

[i] Facsimile 103. [ii] D&B 751, facsimile 104.

We give you thanks with joy for your great goodness, Lord God, King of Heaven, Father of Power; and you Lord Jesus Christ, the blessed Son of God, Son and Father Omnipotent, called the Lamb of God. Forgive our sins and graciously receive the prayers we make in our need. You, Jesus Christ, who sit at the right hand of the Father in majesty, have mercy and pity on us, who are the only Lord, holy, and most high with God the Father and Holy Spirit in joy, in godhead, for thus is your kingdom without end. Amen.

[Confiteor]

I confess to you, God, all my sins, because you, O God, are without sin. And I beseech you, O my God, Lord Jesus Christ of Nazareth, Son of the Living God, through your Passion and through the salvific wood of your Cross, and through the outpouring of your holy Blood, offered in remission of all my sins, I beg you, O Lord, that you judge me according to the judgement of your indulgence, and your mercy, and I crave that you will vouchsafe to place your love within me. Arouse true repentance in me and help me, efface my iniquity from your sight, and turn not your face away from my prayer. O my God, do not abandon me, but strengthen me in your purposes, teach me to do what I ought. O my Lord God, protect me against all my enemies both visible and invisible; defend me, Lord Jesus Christ, against the darts of the devil and against the angels of hell, who are persuading and indoctrinating me to do evil. O Lord, do not leave me, and do not desert me, Lord my God. Do not cast out me, your miserable servant, but help me, O my Lord God; and perfect your doctrine and true confession in me. For you are God, my Creator and Lord, who with the Father, the Son, and the Holy Spirit, lives and reigns, world without end, Amen.

[St Maurice]

Our Lady Saint Mary sent this prayer to Saint Maurice, bishop of Paris, and commanded him to teach it to the people; and whoever said it daily with true devotion would never have shame in the world, would never be beguiled by the Enemy, nor suffer martyrdom on earth, nor — if woman — die in childbirth; nor would they undergo misfortune, nor die unconfessed:[7]

[7] This is a prayer of the Five Joys (cf. Thirteen Joys, above).

Gloriouse Dame, que le Fitz Dieu portastes e a ta benuré porture sanz conysaunce de houme conçustes sauntz dolour e sauve ta virginité le Fitz Dieu enfauntastes e de virginal let virginalment le letastes, Dame, si veroiement come cest voirs, e je fermement le croy, eyez en garde l'alme et le cors de moy. E pur celes noundisables joyes que le Fitz Dieu e le vostre vus fist quant il releva de mort e vewablement a vous apparust e que avyez quant il mounta en ciel veaunt vos eux e que avyez quant vynt tot festinauntz countre vous ov la court tote celestre, si vous assist al destre de ly e vus corona reigne de cel e de terre pur [f.135r] iceles seintisme joyes, je vus cry merci e requer qu'en totes mes bosoignes me vueillez counsiller e ayder moy e tous iceux pur queux prier vus doy, ma tredouce Dame, Virge Marie, Amen.

[Confession Prayer][i]

Rex seculorum et Domine Dominator qui me creasti, dona michi veram memoriam, veram penitenciam, et veram confessionem quam me oporteat et que tibi placeat. Da michi, Domine Jhesu Nazerene, veram cordis compunctionem et fontem lacrimarum quibus peccatorum meorum dissolvere vinculam et manum tuam que michi ad perseveranciam boni operis perducat nunc et in evum, Amen.

[Fridays][ii]

[f.135r] Um doit plus volentiers juner le vendredy qe nul autre jour de la simaigne, pur ce qe

a Vendredi entrerent les fitz Israel la Terre de Promission.
Vendredi morust Moises le prophete al mount de Alban.
Vendredy ocist David le prophete Golyas.
Vendredy fust decollez Helyas le prophete.
Vendredi fust decollés seint Johan le Baptistre.
Vendredy ocist Herodes cent millers e quaraunte quatre millers des Innocens e cele occisioun comença par Vendredi.

[i] Facsimile 105. [ii] D&B 699, facsimile 106.

"Glorious Lady, who bore the Son of God, and in your blessed pregnancy conceived without knowledge of a man; without pain, and with your virginity intact, you gave birth to the Son of God. Virgin, you suckled him with your virginal milk. Lady, if it is really true, and I steadfastly believe it, take my soul and my body into your care. And for that unutterable rapture, that your Son and God's gave you when he rose from death and appeared visibly to you, and that you had when he ascended to Heaven before your eyes, and that you had when he came hurrying towards you with all the celestial court; then he seated you at his right hand and crowned you Queen of heaven and of earth. For the sake of these holiest of joys, I ask your mercy and beg that in all my needs you will advise and help me, and all those for whom I should pray to you, my dearest Lady, Virgin Mary. Amen."

[Confession Prayer]

King of all Eternity and Lord of Lords, who created me, give me true recollection, true penitence, and true confession, as it behoves me and as it shall please you. Give unto me, Lord Jesus of Nazareth, true compunction of the heart, and a fountain of tears, by which the bonds of my sin may be dissolved; and give me your hand to lead me in perseverance of good works, now and for ever, Amen.

[Fridays]

One ought to fast more willingly on a Friday than on any other day of the week,[8] because

Friday the sons of Israel entered the Promised Land,
Friday the prophet Moses died on the Mount of Alban,
Friday the prophet David killed Goliath,
Friday the prophet Elyas was beheaded,[9]
Friday Saint John the Baptist was beheaded,
Friday Herod killed a hundred and forty-four thousand Innocents, and this killing began on a Friday.

[8] A similar list appears in *The Book of Brome* (ed. Smith; pp. 20–46, ll. 511–82). It is part of the catechism of *Adrian and Epotys*; similar dialogues have been dated by Paul Meyer to as far back as the sixth century. Versions may be consulted in *L'Enfant sage* (ed. Suchier), though the Harley version is not among those treated in this monograph; see pp. 164–75 for an excursus on the Friday material, pp. 169–72 for twelve French versions.

[9] sc. Elijah, who was taken up to Heaven in a whirlwind (II Kings 2:11–12). He returned, as prophesied (Mal. 4:5–6), in the person of John the Baptist (Matt. 11:14 & 17:9–13, Mark 9:9–13, Luke 1:17; in the Gospels he is called Elias).

Gabriel anuncia par Vendredi a Nostre Dame que Jhesu serreit nee de ly.
Vendredi fust seint Piere crucifié.
Vendredy fust Dieu crucifiez.
Vendredi trespassa Nostre Dame a cyel.
Vendredi fust seint Estevene lapidé e seint Paul decollé.
Vendredi Enoc e Elyas combaterount ov Antecrist.

[The Saying of Masses][i]

Quy est en tristour, prisone, poverte ou chiet en maladie face dire messes come desouz est escrit e yl serra ayde ; fface dire une messe de la Trinité par digmange e illumer treis chaundeles e doner treis almoignes as povres e offryr a la messe e ester ; lundy une messe de seint Michel e de tous angeles e archangles e illumer sept chaundeilles e doner sept almoignes, offryr e ester ; mardy de Seint Espirit e illumer sept chandeilles e doner sept almoignes, offryr e ester ; mesgredy de seint Johan le Baptistre e des Patriarches, illumer .iiii. chandeilles, doner .iiii. almoynes, offrir, ester ; jeovedy de seint Piere e des Apostles, illumer .xii. chandeilles e doner .xii. almoignes, offryr e ester ; vendredi de la Croys, illumer .v. chaundeilles, doner .v. almoignes, offryr e ester. Samady de Nostre Dame e de totes Virgines, illumer une chaundeille e doner une almoigne, e offryr e ester.

[f.135v] Cely que fra ces messes chaunter en le honour de Dieu e de seint Gyle yl avera ce qu'il en dreite fey demaundera. La primere serra de l'Anunciation Nostre Dame : *Rorate cely* ; la secounde de Noel : *Puer natus* ; la tierce : *Nos autem gloriari* ; la quarte de Pasche *Resurexi* ; la quinte de l'Ascencion : *Viri Galiley* ; la sisme de Pentecoste : *Spiritus Domini* ; la septisme de le Assumpcion de Nostre Dame : *Gaudeamus* etc.

[i] D&B 948 & 932, facsimile 107 & 108.

On a Friday, Gabriel announced to Our Lady that Jesus would
be born of her,
Friday Saint Peter was crucified,
Friday God was crucified,
Friday Our Lady passed away to Heaven,
Friday Saint Stephen was stoned and Saint Paul beheaded.
On a Friday shall Enoch and Elyas battle with Antichrist.

[The Saying of Masses]

Whoever is in sadness, prison, poverty, or who falls ill, let him have masses said as written below, and he shall be helped. Let him have a mass said for the Trinity on a Sunday, and light three candles, and give alms three times to the poor, and offer at the mass, and remain standing.[10] On Monday a mass for Saint Michael and All Angels, and light seven candles and give seven alms — offer, and stand. Tuesday, for the Holy Spirit, light seven candles and give seven alms — offer and stand. Wednesday, for Saint John the Baptist and the Patriarchs, light four candles, give four alms — offer, stand. Thursday, for Saint Peter and the Apostles, light twelve candles and give twelve alms — offer and stand. Friday of the Cross, light five candles, give five alms — offer and stand. Saturday, for Our Lady and all Virgins, light one candle and give alms once — offer and stand.[11]

Whoever has these masses sung in honour of God and of Saint Giles,[12] he will receive whatever he asks for in right faith. The first will be the Annunciation to Our Lady: "Drop down, dew from Heaven." The second, of Christmas: "A Boy is born." The third: "But it behoves us to glory . . . ." The fourth, of Easter: "I have arisen." The fifth, of the Ascension: "O men of Galilee." The sixth, of Pentecost: "the Spirit of the Lord." The seventh, of the Assumption of Our Lady: "Let us rejoice."[13]

---

[10] "offrir, e ester." It is not entirely clear what is meant by this repeated instruction.

[11] The significance of the numbers is as follows: 3 for the Trinity; 7 angels for seven churches (Rev. chapters 1–3); 7 gifts of the Holy Spirit; 4 is for John and 3 Patriarchs (Abraham, Isaac, Jacob); 12 Apostles; 5 Wounds of Christ. Thursday is for the Last Supper, Friday for the Passion; Saturday is sacred to the Virgin.

[12] D&B 932 begins with an explanation that Giles himself commended the masses to Charlemagne because of the sin he dared not confess (see the Giles legend in *GL,* II:147–49; though in *ODS* the emperor is said to be *not* Charlemagne). There may have been a tradition that such Masses were to be in honour of St Giles.

[13] *Rorate caeli* is the Introit for masses of the Virgin on Saturdays; *Puer natus* that for the third mass of Christmas Day; *Nos autem gloriari* that for Holy Thursday; *Resurrexi* that for Easter Day; *Viri Galilei* that for Ascension Day; *Spiritus Domini* that for Pentecost; and *Gaudeamus* that for the feast of the Assumption.

[Prayer to the Three Wise Men][i]

Je vus requer, Jaspar, Melchior e Baltazar, rois coronez, que Jhesum alastes querre quant il fust né de la Virge Marie, par icel douçour que vus vers ly ustes quant vus querre ly alastes e pur cele joye que vus ustes quant ly trovastes e vos douns ly offristes, que vus me consilez de ce dont je vus requer sicome Dieu vus oy e vos offrendres resçust. Verroi Dieu, auxi come lur offrendres reçustes, recevez huy ma oreisoun pur lur amour e auxi come l'estoille lur apparust en Orient que lur mena a vus al lu qu'il urent grantment desiré, auxi, Sire Dieu, aemplez mon desir, a leesse e joie, otreiez moi que je puisse avoir e vere ce que mon cuer desyre a la loenge Dieu e ma Dame Seinte Marie, Amen.

[The Efficacy of Prayers][ii]

[f.136r] Quy chescun jour denz seissaunte jours trente foiz *Veni creator spiritus qui Paraclitus* etc, trente foiz *Gloria in excelsis*, e trente foiz *De profundis* [Ps. 129] dirra, de la preiere qu'il fra dreitement a Dieu ja ne faudra.

[St Hilary's Psalms][iii]

[f.136v] Seint Hillere archeveque de Peyters ordina ces salmes pur prier a Dieu :

> Qui velt rien prier, a soy die ov devocion devaunt la Croys : *Ad te, Domine, levavi animam meam, Deus meus, in te confido* etc [24:2], et *Inclina, Domine, aurem tuam et exaudi me quoniam inops* etc [85:1].
>
> Quy est environee de ses enimis, die ov devocion cestes psaumes e il serra delyverez : *Exurgat Deus* [67:2], et *Deus laudem meam* [108:2].

[i] D&B 941, facsimile 108a. [ii] See D&B 950, and 985 for rubrics; facsimile 109a (109, an extract from John of Wales' *Communeloquium*, and 110, psalms in Latin, have not been transcribed). [iii] D&B 456, facsimile 111.

[Prayer to the Three Wise Men]

I pray to you, Jaspar, Melchior, and Baltasar, crowned kings, who went to seek Jesus when he was born of the Virgin Mary: by that sweetness you felt for him when you went to seek him and by that joy you felt when you found him and offered him your gifts, please counsel me in what I pray to you for, as God heard you and accepted your gifts. True God, as you accepted their gifts, please receive my prayer now for love of them. And, as the star in the East appeared to them to lead them to you in the place they had so greatly desired, so too, Lord God, fulfil my desire in happiness and joy; grant that I may have and see what my heart desires, to the glory of God and my Lady Saint Mary. Amen.

[The Efficacy of Prayers]

Whoever says, every day for sixty days, "Come, Holy Ghost" thirty times,[14] "Glory to God in the Highest" thirty times, *Out of the depths have I cried unto thee, O Lord*[15] thirty times; the prayer he makes directly to God shall never fail.

[St Hilary's Psalms]

Saint Hilary, archbishop of Poitiers,[16] ordained these psalms to be used in prayers to God:

> Whoever wants to ask anything, let him say *Unto thee, O Lord, do I lift up my soul. O my God, I trust in thee* [Ps. 25], and *Bow down thine ear, O Lord, hear me: for I am poor and needy* [Ps. 86], silently to himself with devotion before the Cross.
>
> Whoever is surrounded by his enemies, let him say these psalms with devotion: *Let God arise, let his enemies be scattered* [Ps. 68], and *Hold not thy peace, O God of my praise* [Ps. 109], and he shall be delivered.

[14] A hymn of Pentecost to the Holy Ghost (see *ODCC*, s.v. *Veni Creator*).

[15] Ps. 130 (129 in *LV*) is the 6th Penitential, and 11th Gradual, Psalm.

[16] Hilary (c. 315–c. 368) wrote Commentaries on the Psalms.

Si vus estes chey en bosoigne, eiez bone esperaunce en Dieu [e] dites *In te, Domine, speravi* [30:2] le primer. Si ascun vueille aler la ou il se doute, die treisfoiz ov devocion : *Iudica me, Deus, et discerne* etc [42:1], e ayle seurement.

Si vus estes molt en meseisse de cuer e volez que Dieus vus delyvre, diez a genoils ov lermes .vii. foiz : *Exaudi, Deus, orationem meam et ne despexeris* etc [63:2], *Miserere mei, Dominus, quoniam conculcavit* etc [55:2].

Si vus devez pleder ov vostre sovereine, priez Dieu humblement qu'il vus doint force e poer de acontrester vostre adversarie e ditez : *Miserere mei, Dominus, quoniam in te confidit* [56:2].

Quy deyve aler a bataille, die un ascun die pur ly : *Eripe me de inimicis meis, Deus meus, et ab insurgentibus* [58:2] ; *Exaudi, Deus, deprecationem meam, intende orationi mee* [60:2] ; *Exaudi, Deus, orationem meam cum deprecor* etc [63:2].

Quant vus levez le matyn dites *Deus in nomine tuo salvum me fac, Deus, repulisti* [53:3]. Treis *Pater Noster*, treis *Ave Maria*, e passerez cel jour sauntz encombraunce.

Qui ad volenté de peccher, prie Dieu devoutement qu'il ly doint repentaunce, e veroyment il serra delyvrez s'il die : *Deus misereatur* [66:2].

Quant vus alez vers vostre enymy ou ad vostre adversarie, dites ov devocioun : *Iudica, Domine, nocentes me* [34:1], e il ne avera poer de vus nuyre.

Quant vus avez de rien songié, alez l'endemain devant le crucifix en la eglise e dites : *Ad Dominum cum tribularer* [119:1], *Pater Noster*, *Ave Maria* e *Credo.*

Si ascun soit enprisonee, si se confesse bien e nettement e puis die ces psalmes, e si yl ne les puet dire, die ascun autre pur ly, mes [f.137r] qu'il soit bien e nettement confés, e pus le die quarauntefoiz : *Domine, probasti me* [138:2] ; *Eripe me, Domine, ab homine malo, a viro iniquo* etc [139:2].

If you have fallen into need, have good faith in God and say the first *In thee, O Lord, do I put my trust* [Ps. 31].[17] If anybody wishes to go anywhere that frightens them, say: *Judge me, O God, and plead my cause* [Ps. 43] with devotion three times, and go in safety.

If you are very troubled at heart and wish God to deliver you, say these — kneeling and with tears — seven times: *Hear my voice, O God, in my prayer: preserve my life from fear of the enemy* [Ps. 64], and *Be merciful unto me, O God: for man would swallow me up* [Ps. 56].

If you wish to go to law against your sovereign, pray God humbly to give you strength and power to win the case against your adversary, and say: *Be merciful unto me, O God ... for my soul trusteth in thee* [Ps. 57].

If a man must go into battle, let somebody say each day for him: *Deliver me from mine enemies* [Ps. 59], *Hear my cry, O God* [Ps. 61], *Hear my voice, O God* [Ps. 64].

When you rise in the morning, say: *Save me, O God, by thy name* [Ps. 54]. Say three Our Fathers, and three Hail Marys, and you will spend that day without any troubles.

Whoever feels the will to sin, let him pray God devoutly to give him repentance, and truly he will be delivered if he says *God be merciful unto us* [Ps. 67].

When you go towards your enemy or your adversary, say with devotion: *Plead my cause, O Lord, with them that strive with me* [Ps. 35], and he will have no power to harm you.

When you have dreamed of anything, go to the crucifix in the church next day and say: *In my distress I cried unto the Lord* [Ps. 120],[18] and Our Father, Hail Mary, and the Creed.

If anybody is imprisoned, let him be well and cleanly confessed, and then say these psalms. If he cannot say them, he may say others instead — so long as he is well and cleanly confessed. Then say forty times: *O Lord, thou hast searched me* [Ps. 139], and *Deliver me, O Lord, from the evil man* [Ps. 140].

---

[17] See note to Psalm 71 (p. 255, note 19) below; and p. 241, note 5, above.

[18] *Ad Dominum* is Gradual Psalm 1.

Si ascun vueille comencer ascune graunde chose, si prie l'eyde de Dieu e s'estende devant l'auter e die synk foiz : *Deus in adiutorium* [69:2].

Si ascun se doute que le deble eit poer de ly, die treifoiz cest salme : *In te, Domine, speravi* [70:1], le secounde.

Si ascun chose en defaute de siecle, die nueffoiz a genoils devant le Croys ov bon devocioun e Dieu ly aydera : *Deus venerunt gentes* [78:1].

Si ascun vuelle requere la merci de Dieu e qu'il otreye sa preyere e paremplisse soun desir en bien, die .x. foiz : *Ad te levavi oculos meos* [122:1] ; *Ad te, Domine, clamabo* [27:1] ; *Usquequo, Domine* [12:1].

Si ascun soit en anguisse ou tribulation, die par un digmange devant le cors Nostre Seigneur : *Domine, quid multiplicati* [3:2] ; *Salvum me fac* [11:2] ; *Deus (Domine) refugium* [45:2].

Si ascun soit grevement enmalady, die : *Domine refugium* [45:2], e il sentira aleggauncé.

En memoire de la passioun Jhesu Crist deit um dire ov bon devocioun : *Deus Deus meus, respice* [12:4], e a la elevacion : *Te Deum laudamus.*

[Meditation of the Hours][i]

[f.138v] Ici comence contemplacioun de la passioun Jhesu Crist e comence a comply pur ce que a cel oure Judas Scarioth ly vendy.

Quant vus dites comply, pensir devez mout ententivement coment Judas vendy Nostre Seigneur pur .xxx. deners e pur ce a tiel oure vus rendez coupable a Dieu priveement en vostre cuer e a prestre de bouche, si vus le poez avoir, de quanque vus avez le jour mesfait encountre les comaundementz Dieu.

[i] D&B 958, facsimile 115. The intervening items (a piece in Latin on plants, a set of questions to the dying in Latin, and a French and Latin verse "Against the King's taxes") have not been transcribed.

If anybody wants to undertake any great thing, let him pray for God's help and prostrate himself before the altar, and say *Make haste, O God, to deliver me* [Ps. 70], five times.

If anybody fears that the Devil has power over him, say the second *In thee, O Lord, do I put my trust* [Ps. 71], three times.[19]

If anything worldly is lacking, say: *O God, the heathen are come into thine inheritance* [Ps. 79], nine times before the Cross, with true devotion, and God will help him.

If anybody wants to ask for God's mercy, and that he will fulfil his desire for good, let him say ten times: *Unto thee I lift up mine eyes* [Ps. 123], *Unto thee will I cry, O Lord my rock* [Ps. 28], and *How long wilt thou forget me, O Lord?* [Ps. 13][20]

If anybody is in torment or tribulation, let him say, on a Sunday before the Body of Our Lord: *Lord, how are they increased that trouble me!* [Ps. 3], *Help, Lord; for the godly man ceaseth* [Ps. 12], and *God is our refuge and strength* [Ps. 46].

If anybody is seriously ill, say *God is our refuge and strength* [Ps. 46], and he will feel relief.

In memory of the Passion of Jesus Christ, one must say *Consider and hear me, O Lord my God* [Ps. 13], with great devotion, and at the Elevation of the Host: *We praise thee, O God: we acknowledge thee to be the Lord.*[21]

[Meditation of the Hours]

Here begins the Meditation on the Passion of Jesus Christ, starting with Compline because this is the Hour when Judas Iscariot sold him.

When you say Compline, you must think deeply about how Judas sold Our Lord for thirty pieces of silver; so at this hour admit your guilt to God privately in your heart, and aloud to a priest if available, of all that you have done against God's commandments that day.

---

[19] The writer distinguishes between two psalms (see p. 253, note to psalm 31 above) with the same opening words (see Kuczynski 2000, p. 149. This distinction suggests that the whole psalm was to be said). *LV* often counts the *heading* of a psalm as verse 1, which is why the first verse sometimes appears as verse 2 in the list opposite.

[20] The first, *Ad te levavi*, is Gradual Psalm 4.

[21] *Te Deum Laudamus* is not a psalm, but a hymn or Canticle.

E de ce que vus avetz en delit, en vanités e si vus eiez malement ou deshonestement parlé ou de vos yeux folement regardé e de quanqe vus quidez le jour par nul de vos synk sentz encountre la volenté de vostre Creatour avoir pecchié, si en requerez devoutement merci e pardoun e certeyne esperaunce eyez que vus averez ce que vus dreitement requerez en bounté eynssi qe vus soiez verroiement repentant e bien confés, quar ce dit Nostre Seigneur en le Ewangelye : 'Requerez e vus receverez.' Dites donque a cest comply einsi : 'Douz Sire, Jhesu Crist, je te renk graces qe a oure de comply estoiez trahy de Judas Scarioth e vendy pur .xxx. deners. Et aprés cest comply tu dys a trois de tes deciples "veilles et horez que vus ne entrez en temptatioun" e pus t'en alas tu un poy de tes deciples a la mountaunce de tant come um porroit rochier une piere e te cochas a la terre e prias trois foiz ton piere que cele passioun qu'adonque te fust en venant passast outre de toy, si ce [f.139r] pust estre, e donque apparust un aungle a toi et te counforta e tant come tu fus en t'oreysoun tu suas d'angoyse goutes de sang e dementiers dormirent tes desciples, mes tu soul ne dormys point jesque ataunt qe tu moruz en la Croys e pus dormys el sepulcre jesqe au jour de ta resurexioun e adonqe eveillas.'

A matines devez mout ententivement penser eynsi e dire : 'Je te renk graces, douz Seigneur Jhesu Crist, qe fus a matin par le tresoun Judas ton desciple pur nus pris, aprés fus lyé, despoillé, batu, buffeté, escharny, fausement acusé, de le orde salyve as Gyus soillé, de lur despitouse paroles ledengé, de tous tes desciples gerpi, tot soul lessé, de toun apostre refusé pur seigneur e toute cele nuyt vilement e crueument treité e defolé, dount je te mercy, tresdouz Seigneur, de tout moun cuer.'

A houre de prime dites : 'Je te renk graces, douz Sire Jhesu Crist, de ce qe a houre de prime fuz come lere lyé e mené a la court devant Pylat e a ly baillé pur estre a tort jugé e a tiel houre reporta Judas arere les .xxx. deners qu'il avoit resçu pur sa tresoun faire e tantost se pendy meismes de deol par deseperaunce. A ytel houre, tresdouz Seignur, te acuserent les Gyus a Pylat de trois choses : primes te surmistrent eux fausement que tu avoyez deffendu que l'em ne donast point truage au Roy Cesar en qui subiectioun eux estoient ; puis te surmistrent fausement que tu te fes roy pur tolyr a Cesar son regne terrien, aprés ce te accuserent de ce qe tu dys e voirs fu, que tu fuz le fitz Dieu.

And of what you have enjoyed, what vanities; and if you have spoken ill or dishonestly or used your eyes foolishly. And for all the sins you believe you have done through any of your five senses, against your Creator's will, you must pray devoutly for mercy and forgiveness. Have steadfast hope that you will receive bountifully what you pray for righteously, so long as you are truly repentant and fully confessed, for Our Lord says thus in the Gospel: *Ask, and it shall be given you.*[22] Then say, at this Compline: "Sweet Lord Jesus Christ, I give you thanks that at the hour of Compline you were betrayed by Judas Iscariot and sold for thirty pieces. And after this Compline you said to three of your disciples, 'Watch and pray, that you come not into temptation', and then you withdrew from your disciples a little way, about a stone's throw. And you lay down upon the earth and prayed three times to your Father, that this Passion you were about to undergo might pass away from you, if it might be so. And then an angel appeared to you and comforted you, and all the time you were in prayer you sweated drops of blood in your anguish. Meanwhile your disciples slept, but you alone did not sleep at all until you died on the Cross; then you slept in the sepulchre until the day of your resurrection, and you awoke."

At Matins, you must think very intently about this, saying: "I give you thanks, sweet Lord Jesus Christ, that at the matins hour you were taken for our sake, by the treason of your disciple Judas; then you were bound, stripped, beaten and buffeted, derided, falsely accused, soiled with the Jews' filthy spittle, slandered with their insolent words, abandoned by all your disciples and left all alone, denied as Lord by your apostles; all that night you were vilely, cruelly treated and spurned. For this I thank you, dear Lord, with all my heart."

At the hour of Prime, say: "I give you thanks, sweet Lord Jesus Christ, that at the hour of Prime you were fettered like a thief and led to the court before Pilate, and delivered to him to be falsely judged. And at such an hour did Judas bring back the thirty pieces that he obtained for doing treason; soon after, he hanged himself in sorrow and despair. At such an hour, dear Lord, the Jews accused you to Pilate of three things: first, they put it to you falsely that you had forbidden people to give any tribute to King Caesar, whose subjects they were. Then they falsely indicted you of making yourself king in order to take from Caesar his earthly kingdom; after that, they accused you of saying that you were the Son of God — and it was true.

[22] Matt. 7:7.

A icil houre fus tu envoyé e presenté de par Pylat a Herodes, si ne voloyes yleqe mot soner, dont l'em te tynt a fol e en escharnissement e moskerye te fist um vestir de une vesture blaunche come fol e tout ensi fus tu reenvoyé a Pylat.'

A houre de tierce dites : 'Je te renk graces, douz Seigneur Jhesu Crist, de ce qe tu soffris si debonayrement qe a houre de tierce les felouns Gyus crierent encountre toy si hydousement : "Crucifiez le, crucifiez le !" Adonque fus tu mené hors taunt come eus treterent de ta mort e countroverent la sentence de ta perdicioun. A icele [f.139v][i] maunda la femme Pilat a soun Seigneur qu'il ne s'entremeist mes de toy e ce par l'entisement de Deable que voloit desturber notre redemptioun pur laquiele tu deignas soffryr si dure passioun. A icel houre lava Pilat ses mayns e ne se voloit plus entremettre de toy e par ice se quida il fere net e quites qu'il ne fust coupable de ta mort. A icele houre fus tu lyé al pyler tot nu e tant batu de escourges qu'il n'y avoit lu en ton cors que ne fust dolerousement sanglant. A cele houre te vestirent d'un mauntel purpre e plyerent une coroune d'espynes e la mistrent sur ta teste e en moskaunt te saluerent e distrent : "Dieu, te salve, Roy des Gyus" e te ferirent en la teste e escrachierent en ta face e en genullaunt te ahorerent e pus te[ii] ousterent le mauntel de pourpre e te vestirent tes autres dras e te chacerent vers le mount de Calvarye pur pendre e crucifier. A cele houre te sywy ta douce mere ensemblement ové autres femes anguissousement plorauntz pur toy a quieles tu te tournas e prias qe eles ne plorassent pas pur toi. Cestes peynes e mout plus souffris tu pur nus entre tierce e mydy.'

A houre de mydy dites : 'Je te renk graces, douz Seigneur Jhesu Christ, qe a houre de midy estendis ton benet cors en la Croys e soffris tes mayns e tes piés de grosse clous si penousement trespersier e atachier en cele Croys en la quele furent quatre manere de fuist, qar le fuist qu'estoit dressié countremount fu de cedre, le traversein fu de palmer, e le soverein de tous, en le quel fust escrit en hebreu, gryu, e latyn, *Ihesu nazarenus rex iudeorum* [John 19:19], estoit d'olyue, e le fuist desouth que porta e soustint tous les autres estoit de cyprés. A icel houre requis tu notre tresmerciable Dieu ton piere qu'il pardonast as felouns Gyus ta mort tant cruele. A icel houre departirent ils tes dras mes la cote demora entiere pur la quele eux mistrent sort pur savoir a qui ele dust escheyer.

---

[i] MS a i. a icele. [ii] MS de.

At this hour you were sent, and presented on Pilate's behalf, to Herod; there, you would not utter a word, and so they took you for a madman. In scorn and mockery they had you clothed in a white robe, as a fool, and thus you were sent back to Pilate."

At the hour of Tierce, say: "I give you thanks, sweet Lord Jesus Christ, for your suffering so meekly when, at the hour of Tierce, the wicked Jews cried out hideously against you 'Crucify him! Crucify him!' Then you were led out while they planned your death and trumped up the sentence for your perdition. At this hour Pilate's wife sent to her lord, that he should have no more to do with you; this was through the enticing of the Devil, who wished to disrupt our Redemption, for which you deigned to suffer such a terrible Passion. At this hour, Pilate washed his hands, and wanted to have no more to do with you: by this he believed he could make himself clean and quit of guilt for your death. At this time you were bound naked to a pillar, and so beaten with scourges that there was no place on your body that was not pitifully bloodied. At this hour they put a purple robe on you, and wove a crown of thorns and put it on your head; mockingly they saluted you, saying, 'Hail to you, O God, King of the Jews.' And they beat you about the head and spat in your face, and kneeling they worshipped you. Then they took off the purple robe and dressed you in your other garments, and they drove you towards the Mount of Calvary to be hanged and crucified. At this hour your gentle mother followed you, together with other women, weeping bitterly for you; you turned to them and begged them not to weep for you. These torments, and many more, you suffered for us between Tierce and Midday."

At the hour of Midday,[23] say: "I give you thanks, sweet Lord Jesus Christ, that at the hour of Midday you stretched your blessed body on the Cross, and you suffered your hands and feet to be so painfully pierced with great nails, to fasten you to the Cross. In it were four kinds of wood:[24] for the timber raised vertically was of cedar, the cross-piece was palm-wood, and the top piece — on which was written in Hebrew, Greek, and Latin: *Jesus of Nazareth the King of the Jews* — was olive-wood; the timber below, that supported and sustained all the others, was cypress. At this hour you prayed to our all-merciful God your Father to forgive the wicked Jews for your cruel death. At this hour they shared out your clothes, but the robe remained whole, and so they drew lots to see who should get it.

---

[23] The hour of Sext is usually called "midi" in French (Nones is the ninth hour, not noon).

[24] On the four kinds of wood for the Cross, see Blake's extract from *The Golden Legend*, in *MERP* (esp. p. 153 and notes).

A icel houre te escrierent e blasfemerent, te escharnisoient e te despisoient les trespassauntz par le chemyn. A icel houre promis tu al laroun Paradys. A cele houre baillas tu ta tresseintisme mere a seint Johan l'Ewangeliste a garder. A cele houre devynt le solail obscur e tenebrous e jeske a haute nonne perdi sa clareté.'

A houre de nonne dites : 'Je te renk graces, douz Seignur Jhesu Crist, qe a houre de nonne levas un grant cry en la Croys la ou tu pendys e dys en Hebreu : "Dieux, Dieux, pur quoi m'as-tu guerpy ?" Ce ne dis tu pas [f.140r] pur ce que tu fussez de Dieu ton piere gerpy, qar ce ne fet mie a crere, mes pur ce que vis si poi des biencreauntz en toi de tous ceux pur qui redempcion e salu tu avoies souffert e uncore adonque soffris taunt de tormyntz e poynes, qar de tout le mound ne poeit um trover que en toi fermement crust a cel houre for qe votre beneitte mere e un soul laroun qe pendy prés de toi. Par quoi tu qui es fontaigne de vie te pleinsies adonqe que tu ustes seif e les enfruntz Giws te tendirent eysyl medlé ov fyel de quoi tu ne voleies beyvre. A quel houre tu dis : "Tout est acomply", qar donque fust fet e chevy quant que fust affere devant ta preciouse mort. Adonque crias tu a haute vois : *In manus tuas, Domine, commendo*[i] *Spiritum meum* [Luke 23:46]. Ensi rendis tu le espirit. A icel houre fendirent les peres e avynt grant terremeot, monumentz desclostrent e en issirent plusours cors des seintz. La coverture del temple fendy parmy. Pur queles merveilles e plusours autres que adonqe avindrent dit Centurio e le justes que ov ly erent : "verreiement le fitz Dieu estoit cesti." Adonqe vindrent le Guws e rompirent les jaunbes dé deus larouns que pendirent pres de toi d'une part e d'autre e lé vostres ne briserent il point, car ils te troverent mort. A cel houre [mes] un chivaler qe avoit a noun Longieus te vint ferir de une lance parmi le costie e tantost en issi sang e eawe pur nus rechater hors del poer del deable e laver nos almes de le ordure de pecchié.'

A houre de vespres dites : 'Je te renk graces, douz Sire Jhesu Crist, qe soffris qe Josep de Arymathie e Nichodemus les queux ne consentirent pas a ta mort venissent a houre de vespres en le honour de toi pur oustier ton seintisme cors de la Crois le queux par le congié de Pilat le pristrent ius de cele crois e le cochierent a terre e le oyndrent de myrre, e le envoluperent en vn drap delyé e le mistrent en sepulcre veant ta benette Mere qui estoit mout dolente pur toy.'

[i] MS *comendo.*

At this hour, those passing on the road called out and blasphemed; they mocked and despised you. At this hour you promised Paradise to the thief. At this hour you commended your most holy mother to Saint John the Evangelist, to look after her. At this hour the sun became dark and shadowed, and until the hour of Nones it lost its brightness."

At the hour of Nones, say: "I give you thanks, sweet Lord Jesus Christ, that at the hour of Nones you gave a great cry on the Cross as you hung there, and said in Hebrew 'God! God! Why have you forsaken me?' You did not say this because you had been forsaken by God your Father, for that is impossible to believe, but because you saw so few, among all those for whose redemption and salvation you had suffered and were even now suffering so many pains and torments, so few who truly believed in you. For at this hour nobody could be found in all the world who believed steadfastly in you, except for your blessed mother and a single thief who hung beside you. Therefore you, the fountain of life, complained you were thirsty; the ill-natured Jews offered you vinegar mixed with gall, and you did not wish to drink it. At this hour you said: 'All is finished,' for then everything was done and achieved that was to be done before your precious death. Then you cried in a loud voice: *Father, into thy hands I commend my spirit.* Thus you gave up the ghost. At this hour the rocks were riven and a great earthquake came; monuments broke open and many saints' bodies came forth. The veil of the temple was rent down the middle; because of these marvels, and several others that happened next, Centurio and the righteous men who were with him said: 'This was truly the Son of God.' Then the Jews came and broke the legs of the two thieves who hung on either side of you; they did not break yours, for they found you were dead. At this hour, again, a soldier by the name of Longeius[25] came to pierce you in the side with a lance, and straight away there came forth blood and water, to buy us back from the power of the Devil and to wash our souls from the filth of sin."

At the hour of Vespers, say: "I give you thanks, sweet Lord Jesus Christ, that you allowed Joseph of Arimathea and Nicodemus — these who did not consent to your death — to come at the hour of Vespers to honour you and to take your most holy body off the Cross. And they, with leave from Pilate, took it down from the Cross and laid it on the earth and anointed it with myrrh; they swathed it in a fine cloth and laid it in the sepulchre, in the presence of your blessed mother, who was mourning bitterly for you."

[25] Also known as Longinus: the centurion (Mark 15:39) was conflated with the soldier who pierced Jesus' side (John 19:34); see *MERP* (p. 71, footnote to "Wooing").

Chapter 9

A Woman's Prayer[1]

Introduction

The text printed below has hitherto escaped notice:[2] at first glance, MS Oxford, Bodleian Library, Douce 282 (SC 21856) (s.xiii^{m}), seems to consist of five Anglo-Norman sermons on the Book of Joshua, more or less derived from the first eight of Origen's homilies on Joshua in the translation of Rufinus.[3] However, the text of the sermons is interrupted by a set of misbound folios (56r–62v) bearing the incomplete text of a treatise on confession (*Ici comence la confessiun de pechez geir pur aver pardun*, inc. "[T]us icez [qu]i cest escrit orrunt u lirrunt, k'il le aient le plus en auctorité ..."), of which there are copies also in MSS London, BL Harley 273, Lambeth Palace Library 182, and Dublin, Trinity College 374. The confessional prayer by a female religious, which exists in only this manuscript, comes on ff.73r–77r (first line, the rest is blank), after the fifth of the sermons on Joshua and in the same hand.

As a piece of carefully-crafted devotional prose written for, and possibly by, a woman religious, it makes interesting use of contrast (*contentio*), ternary periods, and anaphora. Rhetorically intricate and very intense, it is perhaps inspired by the Good Friday *Improperia*;[4] it balances the speaker's own wickedness against the love of merciful Jesus. The speaker has nothing to give but her guilt-ridden self, but she proposes an exchange because Jesus is so merciful, and because he promised to share everything he bought (that is, us miserable humans) with his Father. Generically, the prayer is linked by its rhetorical patterning to the *Improperia*, but adapts its model freely. The sinner begins with a plea for mercy, but at first gives away little about the nature of her sins. She measures herself, dramatically, against Christ; later she talks of her body (and his) almost as though her sin were primarily sexual

[1] D&B 853, general heading "Prayers to God in Prose."

[2] E.g. in Sonet 1956; Sinclair 1978; also in Sinclair 1979, 1982, and 1987; Rézeau 1986.

[3] *Sermons on Joshua*, ed. Tony Hunt.

[4] Jesus reproaches mankind from the Cross (see Gray 1972, pp. 141–45). See also *FM*, pp. 224–29 (on Envy, Part III, xiii): several passages in this section are attributed to Bernard, but only one is traced to Bernard in the notes.

("cors … estendu en mortel pecché").[5] The *Improperia* were extremely well known: the form would have been familiar not only from the liturgy, and from preaching books, but also from poems and prayers based upon it.[6] The present author is unusual in that she reverses the dialogue, making herself the speaker instead of Christ.

[5] For comparison, see in the first instance *A Selection of Religious Lyrics*, ed. Gray, number 30; the note cites a passage from Caxton's *Golden Legend* (I:72–73, for Advent. In *GL*, I:203–14, the section is headed "Passion"). This dialogue with the crucified Christ was attributed to St Bernard.

[6] See Woolf 1968, chapter "Lyrics on the Passion" (authority and structure for such Complaints are provided by Lamentations 1:12; Micah 6:3; Isaiah 5:4).

Text

[f.73r] [B]eau Sire Pere, merci aez de ceste vostre cheitive ancele pecheresse pur amur de vostre duz Fiz, ke pur mei endura la mort par sa franchise sanz mes dessertes. Pur la sue amur [f.73v] vus pri ke vus me desliez des liens de pecché dunt jo sui tant destreinte, ke jo ne ne pus sanz la vostre aie neis moveir.[i] De celui faz mun messager ke a vostre destre set vestu de ma char, vostre duz Fiz, ke pur ço la prist, la sue duce merci, ke il par esprove seust nostre febleté e la mustrast a tuz noz besoignz. Il est vie e jo sui mortele. Ki[ii] purreie jo dunc a ma besoigne enveer fors celui ki ma[iii] char prist en terre e la sus au cel la porta e a vostre destre la sist pur mun advocat devenir e pur sei meimes[iv] offrir pur mei chescun jur ?

Beau duz Pere, esgardez mun advocat, veez le là juste mis a vostre destre, veez la mun eveske ke n'at mester de[v] offrir autri sanc pur ses prisuns, ke il en ad les piez e tut le cors mut largement teint del suen demeine. Esgardez, cher Sire, le sacrefise parfit e bien pleisant, la qui odur vus fu si suef e si plesant, quant pur mei fu offert en l'auter de la cruiz. Veez l'aignel blanc sanz tache, ki mot ne suna quant um li toli sa tuisun, ki fu buffeté en la face e eschopi en la chere e reproces suffri pur mei e gruz n'en fist. Mes pechez porta ke unkes pecché ne fist e mes pecchez sana par les suens plaies.

Tres piu Pere, regardez vostre duz Fiz, cum il fu cruelement treité pur mei. Regardez, duz Sire, ki ço est ki suefre, e pensez de celui e de cele pur ki il suefre. Duz Sire, merci, dun n'est ço le innocent, vostre duz Fiz, ke vus livrastes a mort pur mei cheitive rachater de la prisun al deable ? Dun n'est ço celui ki vie nus [f.74r] fist e duna, ki a la mort fu mené ausi cum berbiz devant le massecrer e a vus fu obedient pur mei desche a la mort ? Pensez, beau duz Sire, ke ço est vostre Fiz tutpuissant ke de mei n'aveit nul mester, e si li fistes[vi] vus a ma nature partir pur aver merci de mei. Veraiement ço est la vostre deité, beau duz Sire, ke pur pieté se vesti de la meie povre nature pur mei fere riche de la sue. Munta l'arbre de la croiz, rendi la pume emblee en Parais, fruit pur fruit, mes duz pur amer,[vii] vioge pur mortel. Enteuschez fumes par le premer, par le secund fumes gariz, la pume pendante emblai en l'arbre de Parais e vostre duz Fiz pur mun larrecin pendi en l'arbre de la croiz.

[i] MS mo m. [ii] MS La. [iii] MS ma ma. [iv] MS meines. [v] MS pur. [vi] MS fustes.
[vii] Apparently altered from amur.

Translation

Dear Lord, our Father, have mercy on this your wretched, sinful handmaiden for the love of your dear Son, who endured death for me through his generosity and without my deserving it. For his sake, I pray you to release me from the bonds of sin, whereby I am so restrained that I cannot even move without your help. I make him my messenger who sits at your right hand clothed in my flesh: your dear Son, who through his gentle mercy took it on for this, that he might know our frailty from experience and show mercy to all our needs. He is life, and I am mortal. Whom, then, can I send in my need, save him who put on my flesh on earth and who bore it up to Heaven, and sat there at your right hand to become my advocate and to offer himself for me every day?

Dear Father, look upon my Advocate, behold him seated there beside your right hand; see there my Bishop, who has no need to offer others' blood for his prisoners — he himself had his feet and his whole body plentifully dyed with his own. Look, dear Lord, upon the perfect and pleasing sacrifice, whose odour was so sweet and pleasant to you when it was offered for me on the altar of the Cross. See the spotless white Lamb, who was silent when they took his fleece, who was struck in the face and spat at, who suffered reproaches for me without complaint. He who never sinned bore my sins, and healed them through his wounds.

Merciful Father, look upon your beloved Son, who was cruelly treated for my sake. See, dear Lord, who it is who suffers; think of him, and of her for whom he suffers. Dear Lord, have mercy. Is this not the innocent one, your gentle Son, whom you delivered unto death to redeem me, a wretch, from the prison of the Devil? Is this not he, who made and gave life to us, who was led to his death like a sheep to the slaughter, and who — for me — was obedient to you even until death? Think, dearest Lord, that this is your omnipotent Son, who had no need of me, and you made him partake of my nature in order to have mercy on me. Truly, it is your great deity, dear Lord, who for pity put on my poor nature so as to make me rich in his nature. He mounted the tree of the Cross, and restored the apple stolen in Paradise, fruit for fruit: but sweet for bitter, and life-bringing for death-dealing. We were poisoned by the first; by the second we were healed. I stole the hanging apple from the tree of Paradise; your gentle Son, for my theft, was hanged on the tree of the Cross.

Beau duz Pere, levez l'oil de vostre grant hautesce sur l'oefre de pieté ke vostre duz Fiz ad fet. Esgardez cum tut sun cors est estendu pur le mien, ki suvent ad esté estendu en mortel pecché. Esgardez les beles meins sanz pecché, cum le sanc en eissi a grant radur, e pardunez les felunies ke mes meins unt ovrees. Veez sun dessarmé coste, cum cruelment il est de la lance percee. Lavez mei de la funtaine ke de ilokes eissi. Veez les beaus piez ke unkes n'esturent en veie de pecché mes tutdis alerent en la veie de voz cumandemenz, cum il sunt cruelement percez dé clous de fer. Beau Sire, pardunez mei les pecchez ke jo ai fait par mes piez, kar il duna pié pur pié. Sire, Rei del Ciel, pur vostre duz merci, fetes mei desore cure en la veie de voz cumandemenz, [f.74v] si ke jo a li puisse joindre mun esperit ke pur pieté se deigna de ma char vestir. Beau duz Pere, esgardez la teste de vostre duz enfant, cum ele pend enbrunc la u il suefre la mort pur mei. Regardez l'umanité k'il prist pur mei, cum ele est turmentee, e merci aiez de la dolente pur ki ele fu si menee. Ahi ! Sire, cum cel blanc piz est nu e cel coste ruge e ensangleté e cel beau ventre tendi e detrait, e cel real vut, cum il est pale e ces gentiz braz lungs, cum il refreidissent e celes gentiss quisses e celes beles jambes, cum povrement e dulurusement eles pendent e ces duz piez percez, cum il sunt arusez de cel precius sanc. Ahi ! duz Pere, esgardez tuz les menbres de vostre cher enfant, cum nul n'est quite de peine, e tut ço suffri pur mei.

Beau Sire, dunez li sun povre chatel ke il si cher achata, mun cheitif cors od tut les menbres a li servir desore e ma doleruse alme pur ki il duna la sue preciuse. Ço est cestui, duz Sire, ke vus ferites pur le pecché de vostre pueple, vostre duz Fiz ke vus tant amastes e tant amez, cil ki unkes mal ne fist e entre les feluns fu jugé cum fel. Ahi, tresduz enfant ! Ke avez vus forfait pur estre si jugé, ke avez vus mesfet pur estre si dejugé, ke avez vus feit pur si estre treité ? Quel cupe, quel felunie ? Ke fu acheisun de vostre mort e vostre dampnatiun ? Jo cheitive, jo sui l'achaisun. Jo sui la plaie de vostre dolur, jo sui la cupe de vostre mort, je sui la deserte de vostre occisiun e la venjance de vostre turment.

O quel jugement e cume merveillus ! [f.75r] Buche nel purreit dire ne quor penser. Le maveis fet le pecché e le [bon][i] le cumpere. Le cupable fet le forfet e l'innocent en est batu. Le felun fet le barat e le piu en est dampné. Ço ke le mauveis ad deservi soefre le bon. Ço ke le serf embla, si re[n]d le seignur.

[i] Blank space in the MS.

Dearest Father, lift up the eye of your great eminence to the work of pity your gentle Son has performed. See how his whole body is stretched out for mine, which has often been stretched out in mortal sin. See the fair hands without sin, how the blood came pouring out in streams, and forgive the wicked deeds my hands have done. See his unprotected side, how cruelly it is pierced with the lance. Wash me in the fountain that flowed from it. See the beautiful feet, that never stood in the path of sin but always went in the way of your commandments, how cruelly they are pierced with the iron nails. Dear Lord, forgive me the trespasses I have committed with my feet, for he gave foot for foot. Lord, King of Heaven, in your sweet mercy make me henceforth to hasten in the way of your commandments, so I may join my spirit to that of him who for pity deigned to put on my flesh. Dearest Father, see the head of your precious Child, how it hangs bowed down, there where he suffers death for me. See the humanity he took on for my sake, how it is tormented; and have mercy on the grieving one for whom it was so treated. Alas! Lord, how that white breast is bare and that side red and bloodied, and that fair belly stretched and racked, and that royal countenance — how pale it is — and the fine long arms, how cold they grow; and the fine thighs, beautiful legs, how wretchedly and painfully they hang down, and the gentle pierced feet, how they are sprinkled with that precious blood. Alas! dear Father, behold all the limbs of your beloved Child: how none is free of pain, and he suffered all this for me.

Dear Lord, give him this poor chattel of his that he bought so dear: my wretched body with all its limbs to serve him henceforth, and my sorrowful soul, for which he gave his own precious soul. This is he, dear Lord, whom you smote for the sin of your people, your gentle Son whom you so loved, whom you so love, he who never did wrong and was judged a criminal among criminals. Alas! sweet Child! How have you transgressed, to be so judged; what offence have you committed, to be so condemned; what have you done, to be so treated? What guilt, what felony? What was the reason for your death and your damnation? It is I, wretch that I am, who is the reason. I am the wound of your pain, I am the guilt of your death, I am the recompense of your slaughter and the vengeance of your torment.

O what judgement, and how wonderful! Mouth could not tell, nor heart conceive! The wicked commits the fault, and the good atones for it. The guilty commits the misdeed, and the innocent is beaten for it. The criminal performs the treachery, and the pious is condemned for it. What the wicked has deserved, the good suffers. Whatever the servant stole, the lord restores.

Ço ke hume out forfet, ço compere Deus. O Sire, Fiz Deu, e cher Ami, tant descendi bas la vostre humilité, ki purreit dire vostre grant pieté, vostre grant benignité, vostre grant compassiun ? Jo fis la felunie e vus en portates la peine. Jo cuntruvai la malice e vus endurez la peine e le turment. Jo m'enorguilli e vus vus enhumiliez. Jo m'engressi[i] de mes delices, e vus vus enmegristes par travailz e p[ar] junes. Jo fui inobediente e vus l'achatastes de la vie. Ma cuveitise me trest a la defendue pume, vostre charité trest al turment de la croiz. Jo me delitai en la duçur de la pume e vus pur ço gustastes l'amertume del fel. Jo tendi ma paume a la pume e vus ambesdous les voz a la peine des clous. Eve [a] ma male char mei surrist e me fet joie de mun mesfet, e la duce Marie doleruse[me]nt se deut de la vostre peine ke vus pur le men delit endurez.

Ore, Sire, Rei de Glorie, tut le mund veit cum ma maveisté est parant e cum la vostre pieté suspassant. Vencu avez e quessé par franchise quantke jo ai fet par felenie. Ore, men duz Rei, mun suef Seignur, mun cher Ami, li mien tresbeau Jesu, ma duçur, e li mien Deu, ke vus purrai jo rendre pur tuz les biens ke fet me avez ? Kar ne [f.75v] purreit pas estre en quor de hume trové le luer ke aferreit a tels desertes, ne purreit sen de hume purpenser luer resnable a soudre la misericorde Deu. Nepurquant, duz Sire, une chose pernez vus a gré, tut se[it] il petit, pur vostre grant povertè, ço est dolur de quor e lerme de l'oil e travail de cors pur mes pecchez e pur vostre honur e tuz les menbres clouficher de vostre pour, ke nul ne se estende desore fors en la croiz de vos cumandemenz. Meis ço ne puis jo aveir, duz Sire, si de vostre dun nun.

Beau Sire, ore le me dunez pur vostre grant pietè, a vostre oes, e a vus servir. E ke jo puisse la vostre duce amur si enclore en mun quor ke ren ne m'enducisse desore fors vus. Duz Sire, rens ne me pleise, rens ne me seit a delit fors vus sul. Duz Ami, merci vus cri, merci, merci, ke[ii] tute la joie de cest secle e tut le delit me seit vil e puiant sanz vus. Ço ke a vus desplest, ço puisse a mei desplere a tutdis. E le vostre pleisir si seit tutdis le men desir. Chascune[iii] joie me turn[e]t a ennui sanz vus e chascune tristur me seit delitable pur vus. Ma duce Esperance, merci vus cri pur tutes voz pietez, ke vus me pardunez mes mauveistez.

Ore pensez, Beau Sire, e ordenez la manere cume vus vudrez mes doleruses plaies saner, ke vus offre la plus chere chose ke jo aie. Ne me ai riens lessé, ne sai ke jo face plus, tute ma esp[er]ance vus ai enveé, mun Advocat, mun duz Ami, mun trescher Seignur.

[i] MS e men gressi. [ii] MS ke de. [iii] MS Clascune.

Whatever man did wrong, God atones for it. O Lord, Son of God, and dear Friend, so far did your humility descend — who can proclaim your great pity, your great goodness, your great compassion? I committed the sin, and you bore the punishment. I contrived the wrong, and you endure the pain and the torment. I grew proud, and you humiliated yourself. I grew fat on my pleasures, and you grew thin through travail and through fasting. I was disobedient, and you bought it with your life. My cupidity drew me to the forbidden apple; your charity drew you to the torment of the Cross. I delighted in the sweetness of the apple, and so you tasted the bitterness of gall. I held out my hand for the apple, and you held out both yours for the pain of the nails. Eve smiles on my wicked flesh and wishes me joy of my misdeed; holy Mary sorrowfully mourns the suffering that you endure on account of my delights.

Now, O Lord, King of Glory, all the world sees how manifest is my wickedness and how surpassing is your pity. By nobility, you have overcome and destroyed everything I did by wickedness. Now, my dear King, my gentle Lord, my beloved Friend, my own fairest Jesus, my Sweetness, and my own God, how can I repay all the good things you have done for me? For not in the heart of man could be found a fitting reward for such deeds, nor could the human mind conceive a proper fee to pay back the mercy of God. Nevertheless, dear Lord, be pleased to accept one thing, small though it be, for your great misery, that is sorrow of heart and tear of eye and travail of body for my sins and for your honour, and all my limbs nailed fast by fear of you, so that none shall henceforth stretch out save on the cross of your commandments. But I cannot have this, sweet Lord, except by your gift.

Dear Lord, now give me this in your great pity, for your profit and to serve you. And let me be able so to enclose your sweet love in my heart that nothing may henceforth soothe it except you. Dear Lord, let nothing please me, let nothing be delightful to me, save you alone. Dear Friend, I beg you mercy, mercy, mercy — that all the joy of this world, and all its delight, may be vile and stinking without you. Whatever displeases you, let it displease me for ever. And let your pleasure be for ever my desire. Let every joy turn to pain without you, and let every sadness be a delight to me for you. My sweet Hope, I give thanks for all your mercies, and for forgiving all my wickedness.

Now consider, dear Lord, and set forth the way you would wish to heal my painful wounds, for I offer you the dearest thing I own. I have left myself nothing, I know not what more to do; I have sent you all my hope, my Advocate, my gentle Friend, my dearest Lord.

Vostre beau Fiz, vestu de ma povre robe, pur vus mustrer de ki mes[f.76r]nee ad esté en cest cheitif secle. En cest cheitif secle aprist a plurer en berz e cluteaus afubler, feim e sei suffrir, lasser, e ensomeiller, liens e batures, buffez e escopisines, reproces suffri[r] e contrediz, curune d'espines porter, tuz ses menbres cloficher, fiel e eisil guster, mort suffrir pur obeir. Cest aprist il en ma trespovre curt. Beau Pere, pur fere vostre volenté, ore li rendez sun servise, cher Sire, kar il ad l'overaigne achevee ke vus li enjuinsistes. Sire, il n'at mester de requere[i] vostre regné a sun oes, kar ço est sun dreit e sun heritage. Mes veez ke il vus demande. 'Le voil', fet il, 'ke la u jo sui, la seit mun ministre.' E ke hume sache ques sunt ses ministres. Oez ke il dit : 'Ne vinc pas apeler les dreitureus, mes les pecchurs a penance.' Dunc li rendez mei, duz Sire, ke sui la plus cheitive des autres. Se nule deit merci deresner par pecché, ahi, lasse ! dunc dei jo aler devant tutes autres. E certes, Sire, usage est a chascune bone curt ke la u l'em prent enz les povres a l'aumosne, ke hume eslit les plus povres e les plus meseisez avant. Dunc m'en semble, e vus mames le veez, ke l'em de mei deit plus tost aveir pieté, ke jo sui la plus chaitive pein[e] querante e mendive ke unkes venist a vostre us. Mes ço me dune esperance, cher Sire, ke jo sui cele oeille ke deable vus out emblee e enparkee pur ki quere vus enveastes le bon Pastur, vostre cher Fiz, en terre, ke par travail de la mort me trest, tute ruignuse, morvuse e maubaillie [f.76v] de tutes parz de cele prisun. Ore m'ad lavé en sun chaut sanc e m'a reporté a vostre faude sur ses beles espaudles.

Ço est mun esperir, ço est tute me esperance, e tute ma fiance, duz Sire, kar jo sui vile de mei. Bien sai ke chere serrai tenue pur reverence de celi ki me porta. Char cher est ço ke ami dune, ja si petit ne seit, e meim[em]ent ço ki si cher custa. Dreiz est ke seie en despit pur ma malveisté, mes tut estuet oblier pur la sue grant charité ke tant cum Deus est avant de hume, tant est ma malice mendre de la sue bunté. Ke purreit le cheitif hume[ii] mesfere ke Deu ne quessast quant il vout hume devenir ? Quel orguil purreit si gros enfler ke si grant humilité n'abatereit ? Quel reaume de mort pureit si estre fort ne ferme ke le turment de la croiz del Fiz Deu ne treisist ? E certes, Sire, ki a dreit pesera[iii] le pecché de hume, la pieté del Fiz Deu si pesera[iv] cent mil plus dunc.

[i] MS requore. [ii] MS dume. [iii] MS pensera. [iv] MS p. la pietie c. m.

Your blessed Son is clad in my poor dress, to show you whose company he belonged to in this wretched world. In this wretched world he learned to weep in the cradle and to don rags, to bear hunger and thirst, to be tired, and sleep; to suffer fetters and beating, buffets and spitting, to endure reproach and opposition; to wear a crown of thorns and have all his limbs nailed through, to taste gall and vinegar, to suffer death out of obedience. That is what he learned in this very poor court of mine. Dear Father, to do your will, now return his service, Lord, for he has completed the task that you laid upon him. Lord, there is no need to beg you to let him have your kingdom to enjoy, for it is rightfully his inheritance. But see what he asks you: "I wish," he says, "that where I am, there should my servant be."[1] And let it be known who are his ministers. Hear what he says: "I came not to call the righteous to repentance, but the sinners."[2] So grant it me, dear Lord, for I am the most wretched of all. If any should claim mercy because of sin, alas, miserable! then I should go before all others. And truly, Lord, it is the custom at every noble court, that when the poor are brought in for alms, the poorest and most afflicted are chosen first. So it seems to me, and you see yourself, that I should be pitied the soonest, for I am the most wretched and beggarly, seeking penance, who ever came to your door. But it gives me hope, dear Lord, that I am the sheep that the Devil stole from you and impounded, for whom you sent the good Shepherd, your dear Son, to seek on earth, who by the anguish of death drew me, all pitifully scabbed and snotty, from all corners of that prison. Now he has washed me in his warm blood and brought me back to your fold on his fair shoulders.

That is my hope, that is all my trust, and all my faith, dear Lord, for I am worthless by myself. I know indeed that I shall be held dear for reverence of him who carried me. For what a friend gives is dear, however small it is, and especially what cost so dear. It is right that I ought to be despised for my wickedness, yet all should be forgotten for his great charity; for as God is far before all men, so far is my sin less than his goodness. What misdeed could miserable man do, that God did not wipe out when he chose to become man? What pride could puff up so high that such great humility could not bring low? What kingdom of death could be so strong and fast, that the Son of God's torment on the Cross could not subdue it? And truly, Lord, whoever correctly weighs the sin of man, the Son of God's compassion will weigh a hundred thousand times more.

[1] John 12:26.
[2] Matt. 9:13.

Ore dunc, beau duz Pere, mes mauveistez me pardunez pur le grant travailz vostre cher Fiz k'il pur mei endura. Dunez la meie cruelté a la sue duce pieté, ma purverseté a la sue duce mesure, ma felunie a sa deboneireté, mun orguil a sa humilité, ma duresce a sa benignité, ma inobedience al sue obedience,[i] ma amertume a sa duçur, la meie ire a sa suefté, la mei malice a la sue charité. Dunez mei tut a li e il me durra tut a Vus. E certes, Sire, a tort me avereit autre, quant si cher me[ii] achata. Ensurke[f.77r]tut quant vout a vus partir tuz ses purchaz ... [The rest of f.77r is blank].

[i] MS od odience. [ii] MS ma.

So now, fair sweet Father, forgive me my wickedness, for the sake of the great sufferings your dear Son endured for me. Give my cruelty to his gentle pity, my perversity to his gentle moderation, my crimes to his meekness, my pride to his humility, my hard-heartedness to his goodness, my disobedience to his obedience, my bitterness to his sweetness, my anger to his tenderness, my malice to his charity. Give me wholly to him, and he will give me wholly to you. And truly, Lord, it would be wrong for me to have anything else, when he bought me so dearly. Especially when he chose to share all his gains with you . . . .[3]

[3] Cf. II Cor. 1:7.

Part V

Vices and Confession

Chapter 10

Seven Deadly Sins[1]

Introduction

What was a standard treatise on the Seven Deadly Sins is found in Oxford, Bodleian Library MS Rawlinson C 46 (11912) (s.xiii^{2}), ff.300ra–vb and 322va–b, immediately preceding Honorius' *Elucidarium* on ff.301ra–322rb and following a set of definitions ff.291va–300ra.[2]

Prose treatises — on sins, commandments, articles of faith, sacraments — abound in varying redactions relating to confession and apparently composed for religious. Naturally, this sort of Guide overlaps with Guides to Confession (which may include the voices of priest and penitent). The present text contains only the Sins — breaking off apparently incomplete in Lecherie.[3] It describes the Sins, and the "branches" or sub-sins associated with each. These allow glimpses of daily life: pride in horses and harness, the wickedness of dancing, practising sorcery to get a girl, feeling bored in church, eating snacks so as to be able to drink more — the lazy teacher, the loud-mouth, and the busy-body.

The treatise proceeds in the third person ("ces sunt ..."); it is not a sermon but a guide-book, although we have added "you" here and there where appropriate.

[1] D&B 666, prose, "Treatises on Sins and Sacraments."

[2] See also Bodley 82 ff.50r–57v.

[3] See D&B 666 (six MSS are listed), but the account of the seventh sin is rounded off, like the others, with ways of erring in thought, word, and deed. However, there may have been a Conclusion to the treatise.

Text[i]

[f.300ra] Ces sunt les .vii. mortels pechez dunt li mund par est tut encumbrez : Orgoil, Envie, Ire, Peresce, Avarice, Glotonie, Lecherie. E chescun de ces ad mutes bronches. Kar **Orgoil**[ii] fait home estre de gros quer, hautein, despire les autres, desire hautesce e seignurie utre les autres. Orgoil est quant home quide de nul bein ke il eit ke ço seit de sei u qu'il eit de Deu par sa deserte u quant il se avente de aver ço ke il n'ad pas u quant il desire ke il n'eit per ne soverain. De Orgoil veint Ypocrisie, ço est feindre sei ço ke il n'est pas. Veineglorie fait pur los del secle. Avantance c'est avanter sei e ço ke il n'ad u de ço ke il ad. Inobedience ço est enreyfreté contre ces soverens. Irreverence est quant hom ne porte pas honur a ceus ke il deit. Perte de hunte ço est quant hom pert hunte e quant oblie afaitement. Estrif est a tuz purvers e contrarius. Despit ço est aviler sun preme pur bein ke il quide en sei. Surquiderie ço est enprendre chose utre poer u k'il se tient plus sage u meilur k'il est. Arrogance fet home vuler estre plus honuré ke a lui ne apent e si il n'est pas trop honuré, si en ad dedein. Jangle c'est aver trop paroles pur ço ke il quide plus valer ke un [f.300rb] autre e plus saver. Curiosité ço est entremettre sei de mutes choses pur sa pruesce u pur sun sen u pur mustrer sa valur pur sei eslever. Elatiun ço est aver le quor eslevé e hautein ke home ne volt suffrir de aver soverain ne per. Contumace ço est de aver le quor dur ke il ne volt faire ço ke il duit. Nunsuffrance ço est ke home ne volt suffrir ço ke lui greve u deplest. Home ad orgoil de quor pur force, pur beauté, pur pruesce, pur saver, pur richesce de honur, de hautesce par desir de veineglorie par dedein. Par elatiun de vertu de alme si s'enorgoilist home come si il est chastes, suffrables, si il est almoners e de autre beins. De buche peche l'en par orgoil, par avanter, par escharnisement, par entarier, par medire, par ledenger e par repruver. De fait peche l'en par orgoil mustrant sa pruesce pur los del secle u autre value. Par atiffure, par asceverure de robes, de chevaus, de harneis e de tels choses, de atiffure de chef u de chauceure, de quanke home ad delit de faire u de mustrer pur vaineglorie.

Envie Envie fet home aver le quor pesant de ço k'il veit autre melz valer de lui. De ço vent torment de quor, ço est doler de autrei bein. Mauveisse leesse ço est quant home est haité de autrei damage. Detraction ço est dire mal par detrés e a menuser autrei bein tant cum il poeit.

---

[i] The headwords are written in red, as is the first initial C, and the whole of the last folio.
[ii] In red.

Translation

These are the Seven Mortal Sins that beset everybody in the whole world: Pride, Envy, Anger, Sloth, Avarice, Greed, Lechery. And each of these has many branches. **Pride** makes a man arrogant, haughty, despising others, desiring high estate and lordship over others. Pride is when a man believes that any good he has is from himself, or that he has it from God by his own deserving; or when he boasts of having what he has not, or when he wishes to have no peer or sovereign. From Pride comes Hypocrisy, that is, to pretend to be what one is not. Vainglory acts for the world's praise. Ostentation is boasting — either of what you have not or of what you have. Disobedience is obstinacy towards your overlords. Irreverence is when one does not show honour to those to whom it is due. Shamelessness is when one loses shame and forgets proper behaviour. Strife is to be perverse and contradictory to everybody. Spite is to devalue one's neighbour because of the good one believes to be in oneself. Presumption is to take on what is beyond one's capacity, or to hold oneself wiser or better than one is. Arrogance makes a man wish to be more honoured than is proper for him; and if he is not over-praised, then he is contemptuous. The loud-mouth has too many words, because he thinks he is worth more, and wiser, than others. The busy-body undertakes many things because of his prowess or knowledge, or to show his valour so as to better himself. Haughtiness is to have a high and puffed-up attitude, so that one cannot bear to have overlord or peer. Contumacy is to have a hard heart, that does not wish to do what one ought. Impatience is when a man cannot endure anything that annoys or displeases him. One has pride in heart because of strength, beauty, prowess, wisdom, too much honour, haughtiness; in desire of vain glory, in disdain. The soul in its swollen virtue makes a man proud, as if he were chaste and patient, as if he gave alms or did other good works. One sins in pride of mouth by boasting, scoffing, getting irritated, slandering, lying, and accusing. In deeds, one may sin by pridefully displaying one's prowess or merit for the world's praise or other benefit. By dress, by excessive adornment of robes, horses, harness, and such things — by one's head-dress or one's footwear — whatever one enjoys doing or showing vaingloriously.

Envy Envy makes a man heavy-hearted when he sees another worthier than he is. From this comes the unquiet mind that is sorrow at others' good. Evil glee is when one is delighted at another's bad luck. Detraction is speaking evil behind somebody's back, and belittling others as much as one can.

Ingratitudine est metre en ubli les beins e les honurs ke l'em li ad fait k'il grez ne rend ne graces sicume il duist. Maleiçun ço est suheder u overer mal a sun preme. Acusatiun ço est acuser son preme pur lui empairer. Derisiun ço est escharnir e rire pur malice de son prome. Haunge ço est lung coruz par unt home desire autre grever. Descorde ço est quant home met mal entre la gent par maldire detrés. Envie fait home pecher de quor par doel aver de autrui bein e joie de autri mal par suspeciun e par male volenté. De buche peche li envius par detraction e par false pleinte e par semer descorde. De fet par faire[i] mal e damage e nusance a son prome e de mover plai a tort.

Ire [f.300va] Ire est une demesuree tempeste de quor. De ço vient impatience ke home ne poet suffrir ren ke li greve. Dedein de home semble eschar de ço ke n'est pas fait a sun talent. Tençun ço est dire par maltalent e ameres paroles. Ledenge ço est dire par male volenté tut led e le mal ke l'en set. Blasphemie ço est retter a Deu le mal ke lui chiet. Folehardiesse ço est emprendre folie de ferir, de nafrer e de ocire. Denaturesse ço est ublier pur un petit trepas mult bein ke l'en li ad fet. Malice ço est purparler mal u enginner sun prome. Gruz c'est medire a celee quant il ne volt u ne ose a overt. Hayne ço est ire aduree ke retret home de bein faire a autre e le entice de quere li mal oud grevance. Homicidie est quant home oscist autre u par sei u par autre e quant il met peine de aultre ocire par plai u par poyson u en nul autre manere. Ire fet home pecher de quor par desmesuree trublure, par haine, par rancor, par dedein. De buche par mesdire, par jurer, par tencer, par manacer, par repruver. De fait par ferir, par batre, par boter, par nafrer, par envenimer e par ocire.

Accidie [Accidie] trait le quor aval e le fait pesant e pereçus. De ço vent peresce, ço est amer udivesce e faindre sei malades u plus malades k'il est. Despurveance c'est quant hom ne se purveit de bein faire ne de mal eschivre. Petitesce de quor ço est quant home n'ose nul grant bein emprendre. Despeir de la bunté e de la merci Deu. Necgligence ke fait home negligent e ço ke il deit fere. Lachesce cum de chastier e de amonester, de aprendre e de reprendre en bone manere ceus k'il ad a guverner. Peresce de penance faire, de orer e de bein overer.

[i] MS par de f.

Ingratitude is forgetting goods and honours one has been given, so that one shows no gratitude or thanks as one should. Malice is wishing or doing evil to one's neighbour. Accusation is blaming one's neighbour so as to harm them. Derision is to mock or laugh maliciously at one's neighbour. Hate is the long-lived anger that makes one want to hurt others. Discord is when one stirs up ill feeling between people, by saying bad things behind their back. Envy makes a man sin in heart: by feeling sorrow for others' good and joy at others' ills, by suspicion, and by malevolence. The envious sin in word by detraction, false witness, and sowing discord. In deed, by doing harm and damage and nuisance to one's neighbour, and by bringing wrongful legal action.

Anger Anger is an immoderate violence of heart. Hence impatience, where one cannot stand anything inconvenient. A man's disdain is like mockery of anything not done to his liking. Quarrelling is saying hurtful and bitter words. Slandering is malevolently saying all the bad and ugly things one knows. Blasphemy is to blame God for everything that goes wrong. Rashness is to plunge madly into hitting, wounding, and killing. Hard-heartedness is forgetting all the good somebody has done you because of a little fault. Malice is plotting evil, or cheating one's neighbour. Grumbling is saying bad things privately when one neither wants nor dares to say them openly. Hate is a hardened anger that stops one doing good to others and tempts one to seek their harm wrongly. Homicide is when a man kills another; either himself or by another's agency, and when he strives to kill another by wounding, poison, or any other means. Anger makes one sin in heart by stormy thoughts, hate, rancour, disdain. In word: by speaking evil, swearing, quarrelling, threatening, accusing. In deed: by striking, beating, hitting, wounding, poisoning, or killing.

Sloth [Sloth] drags the heart downwards, and makes it heavy and lazy. From this comes laziness: this is loving idleness; and pretending to be ill, or iller than one is. Thoughtlessness is when one does not think about doing good or avoiding evil. Pusillanimity is when one dares not take on anything important. Despairing of God's goodness and mercy. Negligence, that makes one careless about what one ought to do. Cowardice: such as a reluctance to chastise and scold, or to teach and correct properly those one has to govern. Laziness in doing penance, saying prayers, and doing good.

Suspeciun c'est sucher mal de autres. Tritesce ço est quant home est anué de sa vie u de sun estat u de autre chose si k'il pert talant de bein faire. Par accidie peche l'en de quor quant il est trop dolent pur perte terriene u par desespeir u par ennui de sa vie e gruce contre Deu par enui de bein faire u de bein oir. De buche quant home maldit Deu u ore mal par ennui e quant trop se plaint de la volenté Deu. De fait par pesantime [f.300vb] e par perte de tens, par somuil quant home deust veiller, par mustrer tritesce en semblant e se sustret de ben faire.

Avarice [Avarice] est une desmesuree amur de terrien aver ke lie e destreint e englue le quor. De ço veint coveitise ke tut tens seit le home beer a plus aver e tant come home plus ad e il plus desire. Escharseté ço fait trop ferm tenir ço k'il ad contre raisun, ço est contre Deu e contre sun prome. Symonie c'est achater u vendre chose espiritele. Menceunge ço est dire faus a deceivre sun prome. Usure ço est vendre le tens pur guainer. Trecherie ço est deceivre sun prome en vente e en chat.[i] Larcin ço est embler autrui chose celeement. Sacrilege ço est rober u embler en Seinte Eglise u en seint liu come en Seint' Eglise u en cimetire u en abeie u de retenir dreitures de Seinte Eglise u detes u truvures u gages consentir a larcin u a trecherie u achater u de retenir chose ke est malement gayné a escient. Ravine e toute sicome funt robeors, malvez bailliz e malvez signurs. Parjurer pur gain aver pur dute de[ii] perte. Fausine cume de monee, des chartres u de sauls u de covenanz, fauls pleiz u de achesun de nuire pur coveitise de gain. Retenir ço ke[iii] l'en deit u sustrere partie. Avarice de quor est amur e coveitise de terrien aver le quel ke ço seit de aver u de saver e de autre chose e de penser gile pour autre deceivre u desirer autrui mort u damage pur gainer. De buche par[iv] faus serement e par mençunge, par faus testimonie u par trop preiser u blamer chose en vente u en chat. De fait par ravine, par toute, par larecin, par roberie, par usure, par symonie, par retenir servise a serganz a tort, par feintement servir e overer fausement, par pestre autrui blez u prez u pascure, par retenir chose engagee u prestee u trovee, par empeirer a escient chose engagee u prestee u baillé en garde. [...]

[f.322va][v] **Glotonie** Glotonie fait servir e obeir a mauveis talenz de la char. De ço venent delices de manger, de beivre e de quere diversitez pur paer sa lecherie.

[i] i.e. 'achat'. [ii] MS de de. [iii] MS ço ke ço ke. [iv] MS pur. [v] In red, to end.

Suspicion is supposing ill of others. Depression:[1] this is when one is weary of one's life, one's estate, or some other thing, so that one loses desire to do good. By sloth one sins in thought, if one is too upset at worldly loss, or in despair, or has lost interest in one's life and grumbles at God by being tired of doing or hearing good. In word: when one speaks ill of God or prays badly out of boredom, and when one complains too much about what God wants. In deed: by heaviness and by wasting time, by sleeping when one ought to wake, by looking miserable, and hanging back from doing good.

Avarice [Avarice] is an excessive love of earthly goods, that binds and restrains and clogs up the heart. From it comes covetousness, which is somebody always wanting to have more, and the more they have the more they want. Meanness makes one hold unreasonably onto what one has; this is against God and against one's neighbour. Simony is buying or selling spiritual things. Lying is to speak falsely so as to deceive one's neighbour. Usury is to sell time for gain.[2] Trickery is to cheat one's neighbour in sale or purchase. Robbery is secretly stealing other people's things. Sacrilege is to take or steal within the Holy Church, or in a sacred place such as a holy church, a graveyard, or an abbey; to keep back sacraments, debts, found objects, gages — consenting to robbery or trickery, or buying or keeping anything you know to have been wrongly acquired. Pillage and all such are what robbers, bad bailiffs, and wicked lords do. Forswearing to gain something, in fear of losing it. Forging, as: money, charters, seals, wills; false pleading in order to cause damage, because coveting gain. Holding back what one owes, or subtracting part of it. Avarice of heart is loving and coveting worldly things, whether it be goods or knowledge or anything else; thinking guilefully about cheating others, or desiring others' death or hurt for your own gain. In speech: by false oath and by lies, by false witness, by overly praising or dispraising goods in selling or buying. In deed: by pillage and stealing, thieving and robbing, usury or simony, wrongly holding back servants' pay, giving lazy service or working badly, pasturing [your beasts] on others' corn or meadows or pasture, by withholding anything promised or borrowed or found; by knowingly damaging anything promised, borrowed, or placed in safe-keeping.

Gluttony Greed makes you a slave, obedient to the evil desires of the flesh. It leads to delight in eating and drinking, and seeks diversity to satisfy its lust.

---

[1] For "sadness" (*accidia*), see General Introduction, p. 18 above.

[2] Or, "at interest." *Inter est* = the time *between* the one transaction and the other.

Trop ardante faim ke fet manger devant hure e tout june e abstinence. Trop grant talent de manger e de beivre ke fet surachater viande u beivre. Surfet ke fet trop lunge seer a manger e a beivere e le hanap trop aler e mesure ublier. Engruture ke fet devorer sanz bein mascher ke ne quide estre saul ne ne sofre sa viande defire e puis creve li home ke il n'ad talent ne poer de bein fere. Iveresce ke fet le sen trubler e tout le poer del cors. En engruture e en iveresce chet home suvent par autri preere e par estrif ki pura autre veintre u pur estre preisé de fole gent u par delit u par dreite glotonie. Glotonie fet home pecher de quor par grant desir, par grant talant, par grant delit de manger u de beivre e de trop enpenser u de griucer le quor quant il n'ad viande ne beivre a talent. De buche par trop jangler, par trop juer e tencer. De fet par trop manger e beivre trop hastivement, trop deliciusement, trop tost, par trop lung seer e trop mes aver e parmanger chose pur aver talent a beivre.

Lecherie [Lecherie] fet le quor fundre e decure[i] la u la volenté s'encline sanz guiement de raison. De ço vent fole largesce de doner e dependre. Blandiesce e losenge de paroles, oublesce e mençunge, joliveté ke fet home abandoner sun sen a folie e fet hom gay, de tut done a folie e utre poer e s'il plus ne pot, deliter fet en penser e de parler folie. Putage fet perdre hunte si ke l'en ne vult pur Deu ne pur home hunte lesser. Avo[f.322vb]tire fet home fauser la ley de mariage. Incest dunt l'en [n]'ad regard a parenté ne a affinité. Sacrilege par quei hom[ii] deshoneste seint liu u seint tens e peche en beneit u en beneite, peche contre nature ke home se entremet[iii] de ordure de sun cors contre nature e cest en meinte manere, ke hunte est a dire acheisun de lecherie e[iv] udivesce, trop manger, trop beivre, fole regardure, fous manier, beiser, cathiler, e gaiment parler, juius privez e fous dalier. Lecherie de quor est penser de ordure u delit, fole volenté, gelosie, consentir a folie u aider. De buche par blandir, requere folie par fol chant, paroles gayes, pramesses, mençunges e beisers. De fait par fornicaciun, par avotire, par incest, par denaturel peché, par soillure de char, par fous juis, par fole fiances, par conjurisons, sorceries, enchantemenz, atiffemenz e par fole contenance.

[i] MS deiure. [ii] MS hom len. [iii] MS entremẽt. [iv] MS ẽ.

Too fierce an appetite makes you eat before meal-times and takes away fasting and abstinence. Too great a desire to eat and drink makes you procure too much meat or drink. Surfeit makes you sit too long at table eating and drinking, the cup to pass too often, and moderation is forgotten. Sickness, that makes you devour without chewing properly, that never allows you to feel sated or food to be digested; then the glutton dies having neither desire nor capacity to do good. Drunkenness troubles the senses and takes strength from the body. A man often falls into illness and drunkenness through other people's urging, or through bragging as to who can consume the most, or to be admired by fools, or through appetite or downright greed. Gluttony makes a man sin in thought: by desire and fancy, by much pleasure in eating or drinking, thinking too much about food or being cross when the food and drink is not to one's liking. In speech: loud talking, gaming, quarrelling. In deed: eating too much and drinking too eagerly; with too much gusto or too early; sitting too long, having too many courses; eating something on purpose to increase thirst for drinking.

Lechery [Lechery] makes the heart melt and softens the brain, when the fancy wanders without reason's guidance. This causes foolish generosity in giving and spending. Blandishment and flattering words, forgetfulness and lying; jollity that makes a man forsake wisdom for silliness and makes him merry, and to give away everything madly and beyond his power, even if he can't give any more; and makes him think about pleasure and talk of folly. Debauchery makes him forget shamefastness, so that he wants neither for God's nor for anybody's sake to leave his shame. Adultery causes him to betray the law of matrimony. Incest is when one pays no heed to kinship or affinity.[3] Sacrilege, by which a man does shameful acts in a sacred place or time, or with a holy man or woman. A sin against nature, when a man does filthy carnal things unnaturally — and this in many ways — it is shameful to speak of the causes of lechery: idleness, over-eating, too much drinking, wanton looks and caresses, kissing, titillating, dirty talk, secret games and flirting. Lechery of the heart is thinking about dirty or exciting things, wanton desires, jealousy, consenting to foolishness or conniving at it. Of the mouth: flattery, encouraging lewdness by foolish songs, jolly talk, promises, lies, kisses. Of the deed: by fornication, adultery, incest, unnatural vice, pollution of the flesh, foolish games and engagements; by conjuring, sorcery, enchantments; by indecent dress and behaviour.

[3] All persons related by marriage or by godparenthood were prohibited.

Chapter 11

A Man's Confession[1]

Introduction

There are a number of Guides to Confession, mostly of the sort that priest or penitent might use as a check-list, and that could be read and thought about in advance. Such formulas vary in their introduction and treatment from one manuscript to another. This one, found in Oxford, Trinity College MS 7 (s.xv^{1}), ff.45v–47v, presents quite a contrast to others we examined for this volume. There are four manuscripts, but only the Oxford copy has the prologue warning the penitent to arrive in seemly fashion. This Guide is rather short, and follows the Seven Deadly Sins. It seems to be aimed at a particular kind of young man; further, he is expected to understand some Latin, but at one point the writer deliberately skims over a tricky passage ("cautilouse matiere").[2] The precincts of the church of "Seint Warie" are not identifiable; the name may be an incorrect spelling of "Marie," for the penitent is invited to declare himself sinful to Saint Mary in the first paragraph, which suggests this might be the name of the local church.[3] However, it more probably means "Sanctuary".[4] Although this text is short, each individual sin is if anything longer than in other Confessions, and much more personalized. The change of voice is interesting: the confessor instructs the penitent, and also tells him what to say. Unusually, the text is dated: 1389.

---

[1] D&B 658, prose, "Formulas for Confession."

[2] It is possible that "qe trop ne die" means the writer is reluctant to suggest "sins against nature."

[3] Ste Garie or Warie appears in Gautier de Coinci's *Miracle* "Dou Soller" (ed. Koenig), but Collet judges it to be a mistake (Collet 2000: there is no such saint).

[4] John Mirk's *Instructions*, ed. Peacock, contains reference to the "Seyntwary" or churchyard (p. 81, notes to line 330); the context (things to be confessed, and things not to be done in certain places) is similar to ours.

Text

[f.45v] ***De Confessione***[i] Homme qe se vout confesser il ne deyt pays venir au confessioun bruant ne saylant ne betant ne riant, mes il deyt humblement venir devant la chapelayn le chaperoun avalé e en jenul se mettra, la chere enbrunché. Dolent e mari deyt estre pur ces pecchés e dirra issint : Je me reng cupable a Deu, a Nostre Dame seint[e] Marie, a tous les seints de pays e a vous, sire chapelayn, qe estes ici lieu Dieu, en ceo qe j'ay pecché par orguyl.

Superbia Orguylous j'ay esté de ma beauté e de moun corps — de teste, de mayns, de pees, e de checun membre qe jeo ay. Orguylous j'ay esté de ma force, de ceo qe poi sourmonter mes proemes par lute, par lancer, par lever de peer, par sailer, e par plusours maners qe je ne say nomer. Orguylous j'ay esté de ceo qe Dieu me dona plus de grace qe a un autre, de sen, de saver ou de autres vertues ou de ceo qe jeo fu meutz oieu o meutz tenui o meutz oy ou plus avaunt apelé qe un de mes autres veysyns. Mout ay pecché par arrogaunce, par veine gloire, e par avantement de mal. Mout ay pecché par elacioun de ceo qe jeo me ay tenu meutz vaillaunt qe un autre en dit o en fet o de plus grant parenté e ensement de ceo qe ne ay pas esté si obessaunt a mes parens ne a mes soverayns come estre dusse.

Ira Jeo me reng cupable de ceo qe j'ay pecché par ire en ceo [f.46r] [qe] j'ay sovent offendu mes parens, en ceo qe j'ay mesdit a mes parens e de persone, en ce qe jeo ay tarié mes premes e curucé sanz lur deserte, en ceo qe j'ay porté coruce a mes premes dount jeo vodray qe mal lur fust avenu ou de corps ou de chateus — e donqe nometz cumbien de terme le curuce a duré, en ceo qe j'ay par estutye batu e defolé mes preomes — e donke nomét lequel il fust, clerks ou lay, et si clerk, lequel il fust dedeyns le ordre desu dekene ou noun, ou si ceo fust en vous defendant ou noun, ou dedeyns le purseynt de seynt Esglise ; s'il fust lay, lequel dedens seint warie ou dehors, ou en vous defendant ou noun, e si aprés le fet fustes a els acordé ou de acorder avyetz la voluntee.

Invidia Jeo me reng coupable de ceo qe j'ay pecché par envie, de ceo qe j'ay eu joye del esuuy mun preme e tristisse de soun [joie], en ceo qe ay envye de ceo qe un autre fust plus amé, plus preisé, plus richementz entecché ou meutz nory qe jeo ne fu, en ceo qe j'ay dit derere mun preme ceo qe ne voudray aver dit devant li par envie,[ii] e ceo est proprement apelé detractioun.

[i] All titles in this text, and the date at the end, are in red. [ii] MS devant par li.

Translation

On Confession A man who wishes to confess must not come to confession noisily — running, pushing and shoving, or laughing — but must come humbly before the chaplain, his hood lowered, and will get on his knees with his face cast down. He must be sorrowful and sad for his sins, and he will say this: "I acknowledge myself guilty to God, to Our Lady Saint Mary, to all the saints of the country, and to you my lord chaplain, who is here in the place of God, that I have sinned by pride.

Pride "I have been proud of my beauty and of my body: head, hands, feet, all the members that I have. I have been proud of my strength, that I can overcome my fellows in wrestling, throwing, weight-lifting, jumping, and in more ways than I can count. I have been proud that God gave more grace to me than to another, more sense, wisdom, and other virtues; or that I have been better [. . .],[1] better regarded, better heard of, or called forward more than any of my other fellows. I have sinned much by arrogance, vainglory, and evil vaunting. I have been very puffed up, holding myself more worthy than others in words or in deeds, or of higher parentage; and with that, I have not been as obedient to my parents or masters as I ought to be.

Anger "I declare myself guilty of sinning through anger, in that I have often offended my parents, in that I have spoken ill of my parents and of the priest. I have provoked and angered my fellows without their deserving it, in that I have mistreated them by wishing harm to come to them, either in body or in property." And then say how long the anger lasted — "that I arrogantly beat and trampled on my fellows" — and then say who it was: clerk or lay; and if a clerk, where he was placed in his order, above or below a deacon. And whether it was in self-defence or not, or whether in the precincts of Holy Church; and if he was a layman, whether it was within the sanctuary[2] or outside, whether you were defending yourself, and whether you made it up afterwards, or wanted to.

Envy "I declare myself guilty of sinning through envy: I have felt joy at the troubles of my fellow and sadness at his joy, I have envied another being better loved, more praised, more richly gifted, or better brought up than I was; because I have spoken behind somebody's back what I would not say in front of him, because of envy" — that is properly called detraction.

[1] The meaning of "oieu" is uncertain.

[2] or, St Warie (see note in Introduction, p. 287 above).

Accidia Jeo me reng cupable de ceo qe j'ay pecché par accidie, en ceo qe ay sovent esté parisous e sompnolent de matyn lever pur oyer mes matyns e ma messe e la parole Deu, en ceo qe n'ay pas profité a moy mesmes ne a autres ne al corps ne au alme come je puys aver fet par ma paresse, en ceo qe [f.46v] ay desiré trop mes eises[i] e de repos aver e de molement giscer, de mollement seer e de user lingetele trop dugé e trop delié e en atres maners plus qe ne say dire.

Gula Jeo me reng cupable de ceo qe j'ay pecché par glotonye e[n] mangaunt e en bevaunt trop egrement e acun fez estre hure, acun fez trop e outre mesoure — e dunke dites si unkes vus avynt qe vous avetz mangé taunt e ben qe vous ne le pussetz tenir dens vous sanz utrage fere e quant fethes et si ceo est par custume, en ceo qe sovent ay esté curyous e ententyf de fere aturnyr ma viande lecherement a bone sauces ou a bon especes[ii] — e dunke devetz dire si par glotonye avetz enfreynt lé junes qe sount establiez en seint' Esglise ou les junes qe par penaunce vous sunt enjoyntz — e devez entendre qe qanqe vous avez mangé e bien outre ceo qe votre nature puyt estre sustenue tot est espice de glotonye.

Avaricia Jeo me reng cupable en ceo qe j'ay pecché par avarice, en ceo qe j'ay pecché par trop coveiter les biens del secle — et devetz dire [si] par ma[v]eise covetyse de nuly avetz eu o tort ou par traisoun ou par torcivouse prises ou en nul autre manere e coment e en qele manere. En ceo qe ay esté trop averous de ceo qe n'ay pas esté apayé de ceo qe Dieu m'at envoyé, mes touz jours ay coveyt plus e plus, e en ceo qe j'ay quidé e entendu qe ceo qe jeo usse, tost me defaillist.

Luxuria [f.47r] Jeo me reng cupable par leccherie de moun cors — e du[n]ke devez dire qant femmes vous avetz pollué e qant fethes, e qante puceles ou femmes parjiisés[iii] avaunt ou femmes cursables ou femmes esposes ou vesves e si unqes lez feyztes dedens le purseint de seint' Eglise ou laquel vous l'avetz fet en jour de june ou en double feste, kar ceos sunt apelé les circumstaunces : *Quot quotiens quando cur ubique quomodo cum quo.*

---

[i] MS cises. [ii] MS esperes. [iii] MS piiises.

Sloth "I declare myself guilty of sinning by sloth, that I have often been lazy and sleepy about getting up in the morning to hear matins and the mass and the word of God. I have not benefited myself or others, either in body or in soul, as I could have done but for my laziness, in that I have desired ease and repose, and to lie soft, to sit soft, and to use linen too fine and delicate — and other things more than I can say.

Greed "I declare myself guilty of sinning by gluttony, in eating and drinking too eagerly and sometimes at the wrong time, sometimes too much and to excess."

And then say whether it ever happens that you eat so well and so much that you cannot keep it down without doing something disgusting, and when you did that, and whether it is habitual with you.

"And also that I have often carefully contrived to have my food luxuriously dressed up with fine sauces or good spices."

And then you must say whether in your greed you have broken the fasts established by Holy Church, or the fasts enjoined upon you as penance. And you must understand that when you have eaten more than your stomach can hold, that is a form of gluttony.

Avarice "I declare myself guilty of sinning through avarice: I have sinned by wanting too much of the world's goods."

And you must say whether you have had anything from anybody by wicked covetousness, or wrong, or treason, or wrongful possession, or in other ways — how and in what manner.

"And that I have been so greedy that I was not pleased with what God sent me, but every day I wanted more and more, and I believed and understood that if I used anything I would soon lose it.

Lust "I declare myself guilty of lechery in my body."

And then you must say how many women you polluted and when you did so — how many were virgins, or women who had been lain with before, or whether public women or married women or widows; or whether you ever did it in the precincts of Holy Church, or whether you did it on a fast day or a double feast day — for these are called the circumstances: *Quot quotiens quando cur ubique quomodo cum quo.*

Et iste circumstantia aggravant vel minuunt peccatum Ceo est une cautilouse matiere en seint Escripture, mes qe trop ne die, un mot entendetz. Checoun pollucioun[i] voluntarie qe ne feit naturelement espouse o vostre femme est mortel pecché. En ceo qe j'ay pecché par temptacioun de ma char, par maveise ardours de leccherye e par pollucioun en dormaunt e par tuz les maners qe j'ay pecché par lecherye de moun cors.

Contra precepta decalogi Jeo me reng cupable de ceo qe j'ay pecché e treyspassé contre les dys comandementz nostre Seignur, en ceo qe j'ay pecché par faus sermanss, par maveis suspecioun, par murmuracioun, par adulacion, par udivesse, par trop parler, en vanité, en vilanyes e folies ; en ceo qe j'ay despendu ma juvente plus en delices, e en jolyfté e en volageté que en le servise Dieu.

Per quinque sensus [f.47v] Jeo me reng cupable de ceo qe j'ay pecché par les cynk sens de moun corps : par vewe, par oyr, par odorer, par guster, par toucher, par aler, e par tuz lez membres de moun corps. Ore jugez[ii] vous mesmes si vous avetz plus pecché, ceo est asavoyr par faus temoyne, par fei faucement doné, par sacrilegie, par sorcerye ou en nule autre manere. E dunke dites issint : 'Jeo me rend[iii] coupable de touz mes pecchés qe icy ay nomé mortels e venialx e de tuz ceauz qe unqes fys puys qe jeo soy pechere e de mes pecchés obliés e de ceaus qe ne say par ma necgligense nomer e vous pry pur Dieu qe vous me assoilez e de ceo penaunce moy enjoynetz.'

Anno Domini M CCC lxxxix et anno regni regis Ricardi secundi etc.

[i] MS pollicioun. [ii] MS juger. [iii] MS reine.

Et iste circumstantia aggravant vel minuunt peccatum[3] This is a tricky subject in Holy Scripture, but so that I don't say too much I want you to understand one thing: all deliberate pollution, that does not unite you naturally with your wife, is mortal sin.

"And that I have sinned because of temptation in my flesh, by the evil ardour of lust, and by pollution in my sleep, and by all the ways I have committed lechery with my body.

Ten Commandments "I declare myself guilty of sinning and of breaking Our Lord's ten commandments, in that I have sinned by false oaths, by evil suspicion, by grumbling, by wrongful adulation, by laziness, by talking too much, in vanity, villainy, and folly; in that I have spent my youth more in luxury, and delight and flightiness, than in the service of God.

Five Senses "I declare myself guilty of sinning by my five bodily senses: sight, hearing, smelling, tasting, touching; as I go around, and in all my bodily members."

Now judge yourself, whether you have done any other sin: that is by false witness, swearing falsely, sacrilege, sorcery, or any other way. And then say this: "I declare myself guilty of all my sins that I have told here, mortal and venial, and of all I have ever done — because I am a sinner — and all I have forgotten, and those I cannot name because of my carelessness, and I beg you for the love of God to absolve me and give me penance."

"In the Year of Our Lord 1389, in the year of King Richard the Second's reign."

[3] The previous lines in Latin indicate that one must declare what, where, with whom, how many times, and so on; these circumstances aggravate or diminish the sin (*Et iste* . . . in red). This is a standard list: see Part V of *Ancrene Wisse* (trans. Savage and Watson, p. 165; note 27 gives a list of authorities). See also Millett 1999.

Chapter 12

On Penance[1]

Introduction

This rather longer Confession piece is from Oxford, Bodleian Library, MS Douce 282, with passages from London, Lambeth Palace MS 182 and Dublin, Trinity College MS 374 (D.1.29); see below. The treatise covers the three things necessary for penance (compunction, confession, and satisfaction) and is found in four manuscripts:

Dublin, Trinity College MS 374 (s.xiii^{2}),[2] ff.54va–58va.

London, BL, MS Harley 273 (s.xiii^{ex}), ff.103ra–110ra.

London, Lambeth Palace Library MS 182 (s.xiv^{1}), ff.201va–206rb. Lambeth lacks the introduction and makes a substantial cut in the presentation of compunction, confession, and satisfaction.

Oxford, Bodleian Library, MS Douce 282 (SC 21856) (s.xiii^{m}), ff.56r–62v. The text, though written in the same hand as the rest of the manuscript, is here misbound in a copy of five sermons on Joshua, and breaks off in the part on confession.

The Guide details why and how to confess; it continues with the seven deadly sins, the vices of the five senses, the meaning of "thought, word, and deed," and so on. It is of interest because it is so comprehensive (contrasting with the short Man's Confession), and because it is introduced as being based on the writings of a number of authorities, many of them British: Bartholomew of Exeter (d. 1184), Prior Clement of Llanthony (d. c. 1169); the prior Alexander is probably Alexander of Ashby, who lived 1148/1154–1208/1214; the prior Richard (of St Victor, d. 1173) may have been a native of Scotland. Master Escice has been identified as Hesychius — the others range from Gregory on down to Robert of Flemesbroc (probably Flamborough; if so, he is an identifiable authority).[3]

Its audience is comprehensive: it is addressed to all who hear or read; although nothing suggests whether a woman might use this treatise, except for

[1] D&B 672, prose, "Sermon on Penance."

[2] See p. 74, above.

[3] For Hesychius, see *ODCC*, pp. 768–69; for penitentials by Bartholomew of Exeter and Robert of Flamborough, see *Une Petite Sume*, ed. Hunt, p. 70; for Robert, see also the General Introduction (Sins and Confession), above.

the mention of vowing widowhood,[4] the adjectives seem to be all masculine. There are a number of Bible citations, but not in Latin — the only Latin names two well-known prayers. Of the authorities listed, five out of the fourteen are actually named in the text: Augustine, Peter Lombard, Bishop John (Chrysostom, c. 347–407), Bishop Bartholomew, Anselm. Other references are simply prefaced "it is written."

[4] See p. 307 below.

Text

[f.56r] **Ici comence la confessiun de pechez geir pur aver pardun**[i]

[T]uz icez ki cest escrit orrunt u lirrunt, k'il le aient le plus en auctorité e plus cher, sacent il de veir k'il est escepé des escriz de bons clers. Ices sunt saint Gregorie la pape, saint Aunsaume le arceveske, saint Augustin le eveske, saint Johan le eveske 'buche d'or', Bartholomeu le eveske, saint Bede le prestre, li abbés Ailred, li prior Clement, li prior Alisandre, le prior Ricard, Peres li Lumbard, Pere li Chantre de Paris, maistre Escice, maistre Robert de Flemesbroc e plusurs autres. Cest escrit enseigne quele fait veraie penitence e confessium e satisfactiun e quel bien ce seit de peché purement geir, e quel mal est de peché celer. Il enseigne queus sunt les maus ke meinen[t] home a dampnatiun e queles sunt les vertuz ke meinent home a sauvaciun. E il enseigne de confessiun faire. Si vus cest escrit mut usez, vus purrez les enfermetez de vostre alme bien sauver e par ceo vostre quor mut humilier e par tant mut profiter, ke vus puissez dunc vos pechez meuz geir devant iceo ke augez a confessiun. Icest escrit lisez voz[ii] suvent e ententivement.[iii]

[A] faire penitence sunt treis choses busuignables. Icestes sunt compunctiun, con[fe]ssiun, satisfactiun. Compunctiun encerche l'achesun de la maladie, la confessiun la demustre, satisfactiun [deg]uast. Com[f.56v]punctiun numbre les maus, confessiun les dampne, satisfactiun les amende. Compunciun truve la plaie, confessiun la uvere, satisfactiun la sane. Compunctiun aver sunt deus choses. Icestes sunt pour e esperance. Si vus dunc dutez Deu e est par[iv] compunctiun, esperez en lui, ke vus seez en lui reconcilié. Si vus dutez Deu pur ceo ke il puet [cors e alme] perdre al fu[v] de enfern, esperez en lui pur ceo k'il ne volt mie la mort del pecheor, mes ke il se converte e vive. Si vus dutez pur ceo ke Deu ne leist nient senz venjance, esperez en lui pur ceo k'il reindra Israel de tutes felunies. La satisfactiun est le echevement de l'enjuncte penitence u digne amendement de pechez. Sulum la quantité del peché deit estre la mesure de l'amendement, kar autre chose est la penitence meimes e autres choses fruitz de penitence.

[i] Red rubric. [ii] MS voez. [iii] D (f.54va) and L (f.201vb) begin here. [iv] MS e par est. [v] MS fin.

Translation

Here begins the confession — that is, telling sins to receive forgiveness

All those who hear or read this writing: so that they may hold it in greater authority and affection, let them know truly that it is excerpted from the writings of good clerks. These are Saint Gregory the pope, Saint Anselm the archbishop, Saint Augustine the bishop, Saint John "Golden Mouth" the bishop,[1] Bartholomew the bishop, Saint Bede the priest, the abbot Aelred, the prior Clement, the prior Alexander, the prior Richard, Peter the Lombard, Peter the Chanter of Paris,[2] Master Escice, Master Robert of Flamborough, and many others. This writing teaches what makes true penitence, confession, and satisfaction; how good it is to confess sin cleanly, and how bad it is to hide sin. It teaches which vices lead man to damnation, and which virtues lead man to salvation. And it teaches how to make confession. If you use this writing frequently, you will be able to heal the infirmities of your soul, and thereby humble your heart and do yourself much benefit because you will be able to confess your sins better, before you go to confession. Read and study this writing often and carefully.

To do penitence, three things are needed. These are compunction, confession, satisfaction. Compunction seeks the reason for the malady, confession shows it, satisfaction gets rid of it. Compunction numbers the vices, confession damns them, satisfaction mends them. Compunction finds the wound, confession opens it, satisfaction heals it. Having compunction means two things: these are fear and hope. So if you fear God and it is from compunction, have hope in him, that you may be reconciled with him. If you fear God because he can lose you body and soul in the fire of Hell, trust in him because he does not desire the death of the sinner, but that he should convert and live.[3] If you fear because God lets nothing pass without vengeance, trust in him because he will redeem Israel from all wickedness. Satisfaction is the performance of the penance[4] as instructed, and fitting amendment for sin. The measure of the amendment should be according to the quantity of the sin, for penitence itself is something different, and fruits of penitence different again.

---

1 St John Chrysostom.

2 See Baldwin 1970 (Peter was influential at Lateran IV).

3 Ez. 33:11.

4 "penitence"; sometimes one is written for the other, but they are distinct states in the soul of a sinner: penitence is contrition, and penance is satisfaction.

Penitence est dolur de ço ke est alé quant vus estes dolent del mal ke vus avez fait. Quant vus dunc reprovez e clamez vos maus, vus avez penitence. Quant vus par satisfactiun cumprez e amendez vos maus, vus avez fruit de penitence. Si vus desplest ço ke vus avez fait, vus estes repentant. Penitence est reproce del fait. Fruit de penitence est l'amendement del peché. Si en l'amendement est la afflictiun menur ke ne fuit le delit al peché, n'est mie digne le fruit de vostre penitence. Mes vus poez dire 'Coment puis jo saver quant ma penitence [f.57r] seit digne ?' Pur ço ke saver ne poez, pur ço est mester ke vus tuz jurz vus repentez. Asez poez faire, trop ne poez nient faire. Meuz est ke vus facez plus ke meins. Pur ço metez i entente ke vostre peché seit od fin e vostre devociun seit senz fin.[i]

Confessiun de buche est establie en Seinte Eglise pur treis acheisuns : la premiere achaisun est ke cil ki fuit einz orguillus eit humilité e hunte par le increpatiun e le chastiement del prestre, ke le pecheor ne rechece ; l'autre pur ço ke la confessiun de la buche est une tresgrande partie de satisfaciun, dunt saint Augustin dist 'Tant cum home est confés de plus prestres od esperance de pardun, tant serra il plus tost assous de ses pechez' ; la tierce acheisun est pur la cunisance del peché, kar suvent quida alcun devant la confessiun alcun peché venial estre criminal e greniur crime menur. De icest errur est il curé par la doctrine del prestre. Escripture parole de confessiun e dit 'Confessiun delivre l'alme de mort.' Confessiun ovre Parais. Dunc est confessiun esperance de salu. Il ne desert mie de estre justifié ki ne volt mie en sa vie sun peché geir. Icele confession delivre l'alme ke est fait od penitence. Veraie penitence est compunctiun e dolur de peché od plenere volenté de confessiun e de satisfactiun. Salomon dist 'Qui musce felunies, il ne serra pas adrecié.' [f.57v] Qui les geist e les leist il averat merci. Le peché ke fu en overaine mortel par confessiun est fait veniel, tut ne seit il aveire purgié. Si grant est la force de confessiun, ke si prestre vus faut, faites la vostre compaignun. Les cotidiens e legers pechez poez dire a vostre compaignun e les plus greinurs devez dire a vostre prestre. Mes quant prestre vus faut e vus estes en peril, vus devez les plus greinurs peche[z] dire a vostre compaignun.

[i] D (f.55ra) and L (f.202rb) end here and cut to the Decalogue.

Penitence is sorrow at what is past, when you are sorry for the wrong you have done. Thus when you reproach and proclaim your sins, you have penitence. When you pay and make amends for your sins, you have the fruit of penitence. If you are displeased with what you have done, you are repentant. Penitence reproaches the deed. The fruit of penitence is the amends for sin. If in the payment there is less pain than there was delight in the sin, the fruit of your penitence is not fitting. But you may say "How can I know when my penitence is worthy?" You cannot know, therefore it is needful for you to repent all the time. You can do enough; you can never do too much. It is better if you do too much, than too little. So make up your mind that your sin will have an end and your devotion will have no end.

Oral confession is established in Holy Church for three reasons: the first is that whoever was once proud should be humbled and shamed by the imprecations and chastisement of the priest, so that the sinner does not fall again. The next, because oral confession is a major part of satisfaction, of which Saint Augustine said, "So much as a man is confessed to more priests with hope of forgiveness, so much sooner will he be absolved of his sins."[5] The third reason is for the recognition of sin, for before confession one often believes some venial sin to be more serious and a graver sin less so. He is cured of this error by the priest's doctrine. Scripture tells of confession and says, "Confession delivers the soul from death."[6] Confession opens Paradise. So, confession is hope of salvation. He who does not wish to confess his sin in this life does not deserve a favourable judgement. This confession delivers the soul because it is done with penitence. True penitence is compunction and being sorry for sin, with full willingness to confession and satisfaction. Solomon says: "He who hides felonies shall not be restored to right."[7] He who confesses them and forsakes them shall receive mercy. A mortal deed when committed becomes venial by confession, even if not truly purged. So great is the power of confession, make it your companion even if you lack a priest. Daily sins, and light ones, you can tell your companion;[8] you must tell the graver ones to your priest. But when there is no priest and you are in peril, you must say the graver sins to your companion.

[5] Cf. *Preaching* (trans. Wenzel), p. 38: "Augustine" warns the penitent *not* to divide his confession among different priests; note 23 identifies the passage as from Pseudo-Augustine, *De vera et falsa poenitentia* 15 (*PL* 40:1125).

[6] Cf. Romans 10:9–10.

[7] Perhaps a garbled version of Ps. 32:5, or Prov. 28:13.

[8] Cf. *FM*, p. 469.

Plus aseuré chose est e les uns e les autres mustrer al prestre e de lui quere cunseil a ki est granté la poesté de lier e deslier. Si vus nul home ne avez a ki vus puissez voz pechez geir e en peril, la contriciun de quor sule suffist, kar la contriciun est la confessiun de quor. [S]achez de veir ke la generale confessiun purge e oste les venieus e les morteus pechez, ke vus ne savez nient e vudriez dire si vus les sussez. Vus estuit dunc chescun peché ke vus savez en vus lesser e geir, kar si vus retenez un mortel peché, tuz les autres sunt retenuz. Dementers dunc ke vus estes en mortel peché, tuz les biens ke vus faites ne vus poent mener a pardurable vie ne il ne vus valent a merite ne a remissiun de voz pechez, mes il valent a temporel bien e il vus funt plus cuvenable a la grace Deu receivre. Ne lessez mie de bien faire, tut seez vus en mortel peché, mes lessez le. En icest cas mut vus purrunt valer [f.58r] autrui biens e autrui preeres. Si vus dunc retenez la volunté de aucun peché u aucune chose ne savez en vus dunt tut venist il a memorie, vus ne friez mie de ço penitence. Si vus issi murissez, vus serriez dampné. Le peché taisir vient de orguil de quor. Pur ço ceile home sun peché k'il ne seit tenu defors itel quel il se fist devant Deu dedenz. Iço est funtaine de orguil, kar espece de orguil est ke home vult estre tenu a dreiturel ke est pecheor. Issi est il ateint k'il est ypochrite. U orguil regne u [y]pocrisie, humilité n'at liu. Senz humilité nul ne pot esperer pardun. La dunc u l'em taist la cunfession l'em ne deit esperer nul pardun del peché. Confession est testemoine de la concience ke crent Deu. Ki dute leaument Deu il n'at hunte de geir sun peché. Parfit poür tout e oste chescune hunte.

[V]us estoet suvent aler a confessiun, kar tant cum plus e plus purluignez la confession, tant serrez peur e plus perçus. Unkes ne quidez ke la generale confessiun puisse suffire si vus savez especialment vos pechez geir. Mes la generale confessiun de mutes choses est si aval mise ke par la conisance des generaus pechez. Si vus ententivement encerchez vostre consience, puissez plus legerement le especiale confessiun truver. Sachez ke vus devez tuz numeiment vos morteus pechez a un dire, ceo est a vostre prestre geir e a [f.58v] nul autre senz sun cungié si en peril de mort ne seit — en itel point dites le a ki ke vus poez aveir. Vus devez ensemblement od les pechez geir les circunstances des pechiez. Les circunstances des pechiez sunt liu e tens, la manere, e le numbre e iteles choses. L'en seut demander si ço suffist de une feiz geir chescun peché.

The sure thing is to show both the ones and the others to your priest, and ask advice from him, who has the power to bind and to unbind. If you have no one to whom you can confess when in peril, contrition of heart alone will suffice, for contrition is the heart's confession. Know truly that the general confession purges and takes away the venial and the mortal sins that you don't know about and would tell if you did. You need therefore to forsake and to disclose each sin that you know to be in you, for if you hold back one mortal sin all the others are held back. However, when you are in mortal sin, all the good deeds that you do cannot lead you to eternal life, nor do they count in your favour or in remission of your sins, but they count as temporal good and render you more fit to receive God's grace. Do not cease from doing good, even if you are in mortal sin, but abandon the sin. In this case, the virtues and prayers of others can be of great value to you. If you then remain willing towards a certain sin, or there is something in you you don't know that later comes back to your memory, you will not be doing penitence in this matter. If you die like this, you will be damned. Keeping quiet about sin comes from pride of heart. Therefore a man hides his sin, so as not to be seen outside as he is seen inside before God. This is the fount of pride, for it is a kind of pride when a man who is a sinner wants to be held as righteous. So he is judged to be a hypocrite. Where pride and hypocrisy hold sway, there is no place for humility. Without humility nobody can hope for forgiveness. So where one is silent in confession, one can hope for no forgiveness of sins. Confession is the testimony of the conscience that fears God. Whoever loyally fears God has no shame at confessing his sins. Perfect fear removes and takes away every shame.

You need to go to confession often, for if you delay confession more and more, the lazier and more fearful you will become. Never think the general confession is enough, if you know particular sins that you can confess. General confession, of many things, is of no value except for the recognition of general sins. If you search your conscience closely, you can more easily find the special confession. Know that you must tell forth your mortal sins by name to just one man, that is, confess to your priest and to none other without his leave unless you are in peril of death, in which case tell them to whomever you can get. Together with the sins, you must tell the circumstances of the sins. The circumstances are: place and time, manner, number, and such things. One might ask whether it is enough to confess each sin once.

Peres li Lumbard dist 'Ço suffist la u la crime est privee a sul Deu dire par le prestre e une feiz geir chescun pechié, kar sicum commun peché ad mester de commune remedie, issi est privee peché pur privé confessiun e privé satisfaciun purge.' Ne ceo n'est mestier ke ço ke nus avum une feiz gei ke nus autre feiz le dium, mes par lange de quor e nient de char devum a Deu assiduement geir.

[L]es autres dient ke tuteveis quant vus avez novel confessur ke vus devez tut iço ke vus avez einz a autre dit a lui derechief redire si vus vulez plener remedie de penitence aver. Pur ço devums issi faire k'il sace duner a vus penitence sulum les diverses acheisuns e les racines dé pechiez e k'il sache en avant tolir tutes les acheisuns des pechez, ke li pecheor ne rechece en peché. Icest est la plus aseuré manere, kar, cum il est devant dit, tant cum vus a plus prestres estes confés od esperance de pardun, tant averez plus astivement absolutiun de vostre peché. A vostre fin devez trestuz vos pechez geir. Quant dunc confession est a l'alme si [f.59r] busuignable cum la devez amer e user, kar de quant ke vus estes par veraie repentance e confessiun e satisfactiun purge en ceste vie en l'autre n'averez hunte ne dampnatiun. Verité dit en li evangile 'Ren n'est muscié ke ne seit demustré.' Mes ne dutez riens, kar saint Anseaume dit ke la cunisance e le record de voz pechez ne vus serrunt nient plus a his[d]our ne a hunte ke sunt ore a saint Pere u sainte Magdaleine lur pechez.

De ço dunt vus estes repentant e confés e ne avez mie ici vostre penitence fait e issi murrez, vus serrez par penitence de purgatorie purgé e puis sauvé. Mes pur ço ne metez mie a nunchaler de vus ici amender, kar saint Augustin dist ke cel feu de purgatorie ert plus dur ke nule peine ke l'em puisse en ceste vie ver u sentir. Ne despisez dunc nul peché, ke vus ici ne l'amendez, kar il est escrit 'Ki despit les petites choses, il dechet petit e petit.' L'autorité dit 'Nul peché n'est si veniel k'il ne devenge mortel s'il plest', ço est s'il est fait od suvenere e od grant delit. Ici ke ne vulez lesser ne ici geir ne amender mes ke ço ne seit fors un mortel peché e en iço murrez senz dute vus merra a pardurable dampnatiun.

Peter the Lombard says "It is sufficient, when a crime is private, to say it only to God through the priest and to confess each sin once. For as a public sin has need of a public remedy, so private sin is purged by private confession and satisfaction."[9] Nor is it necessary to say again what we have once confessed, but with the voice of the heart and not of the body we must confess assiduously to God.

Others say that whenever you have a new confessor, you must re-tell to him, all over again, all that you have already told to the other, if you want to have the full remedy of penitence. Therefore we must act so that he knows to give you penance according to the various reasons and roots of sin, and he knows in advance how to remove all the occasions of sin, lest the sinner fall back into sin. This is the surest way for, as was said before, if you confess to more priests in the hope of forgiveness, you will have absolution for your sin more quickly. At the end of your life, you must confess all your sins. So much, then, is confession necessary to the soul; you must love it and use it, for as much as you are purged in this life by true repentance and confession and satisfaction, so you will have neither shame nor damnation in the other. It is truly said in the Gospel: "Nothing is hidden that shall not be shown forth."[10] But fear nothing, for Saint Anselm says that the recognition and the record of your sins shall be no more terror and shame to you than are their sins, now, to Saint Peter or Saint Magdalene.

For those you repent and are confessed of, but for which you have not done your penance here: if you die thus you will be purged and saved by the penance of Purgatory. But do not therefore be careless about mending yourself here, for Saint Augustine says that that fire of Purgatory shall be fiercer than any pain one can see or feel in this life.[11] Do not therefore despise any sin, so that you do not amend it here, for it is written, "Whoever despises little things, he falls little by little."[12] The Authority says, "No sin is so venial that it cannot become mortal if it pleases"; that is, if it is done frequently and with great pleasure.[13] So, if you do not want to abandon it, nor confess and amend it, if it is a mortal sin and you die in it you will deserve eternal damnation without a doubt.

---

[9] See *PL* 192:884.

[10] Matt. 10:26; Mark 4:22; Luke 8:17, 12:2.

[11] See "Treatise on Job," ed. Taguchi, pp. 214–15 and note: the remark is attributed to Augustine in *FM* (pp. 412–15), where the reference is to Pseudo-Augustine, *De vera et falsa penitencia* 18.34 (*PL* 40:1127). See also a similar passage in the Pater Noster, p. 123 above.

[12] Ecclus. 19:1.

[13] The "Authority" may be the Cistercian Gunther of Pairis (in Alsace): see *PL* 212:120.

Li eveske Johan dit 'Si vus recordez ore de voz pechez e suvent devant Deu les pronunciez e pur eus preez, tost les purgerez. Si vus [f.59v] les ubliez, idunc recorderez de eus maugré vostre quant il serrunt publiez e demustrez en la veue de tuz vos amis e enemis e les sainz angeles.'

[S]achez dunc ke ço est la veraie e la fructuuse confessiun ke comence de la pour de Deu e de humilité ke ren ne ceile, ke rien ne se blandist quant il est issi ke nus devum rendre raisun al jor de jeuise de odives pensers e de osdives paroles. Sachez ke la confession deit estre treble e la compunctiun treble e la satisfactiun treble. La compunctiun deit estre nette e forte e ferme, nette ke ele seit senz mortel peché, ferme ke ele eit en purpos de garder sei de chescun mortel peché, forte ke ele entre en voiz de confessiun e en veraie satisfactiun. La confessiun deit estre humble e enterrine e nient partie. Humble est si ele geist les pechez od lur circunstances; entere ke ele geisse quant ke lui dunc suvient; nient partie ke ele ne seit par malveise hunte desturbé e celé a un e mustré[i] a un autre [c'est] a dire ke est tendre a ypocrisie e tuz jorz failir de merci. La satisfactiun deit estre d'einegré, descrete e digne; de einegré est ke home ne face enviz k'il deit faire pur la salu de s'alme; digne ke si grant seit la dolur en la penitence cume fu le delit al pechié. Saint Augustin dist 'Peché, quel k'il seit, petit u grant, il estuet k'il seit cumpré u de home repentant u de [f.60r] Deu veniant. Ki repent il peine sei meimes.'

[S]i vus vulez de vos pechez bien estre confés e vostre estat, quel il ad esté e quel il est ore, bien saver, vus estoet saveir e recorder e s[e]inte Escripture suvent e ententivement lisez e verez, kar chescune maladie de corage ad iloc sa medicine. Illuc purrez trover ke plest u desplest a Deu e cum vus estes a lui obedient u inobedient. Illoec purrez aprendre queus sunt les biens senz queus e les maus od queus nul home ne poet estre sauvé. Pernez dunc garde de ço ke Deu vus ad comandé, coment vus l'avez lessé e de ço k'il vus ad defendu, coment vus l'avez fait, e ço k'il vus ad granté, coment l'avez usé, e ço k'il vus ad amonesté, si vus l'avez enpris, coment vus l'avez tenu u par negligence lessé. E tutes icestes choses sicum vus avez pechié especialment geissez. [G]eissez dunc numeement e ententivement les pechiez ke avez fait e les benefices ke vus avez receu e la fei ke vus avez promis.

[i] MS estué.

Bishop John says, "If you recount your sins now, and pronounce them often before God and pray for them, you will purge them all. If you forget them, you will then recount them against your will, when they shall be published and demonstrated in the sight of all your friends and enemies and the holy angels."[14]

Know then that it is a true and fruitful confession that begins with fear of God and with humility that conceals nothing; that does not flatter itself since it is thus that we must give account of ourselves at the Day of Judgement, for idle thoughts and idle words. Know that confession must be treble, compunction treble, and satisfaction treble. Compunction must be clean and strong and firm: clean that it is without mortal sin, firm in its purpose to keep the self against every mortal sin, strong to enter the way of confession and true satisfaction. Confession must be humble and complete and not partial: humble if it confesses the sins with their circumstances, complete if it confesses everything it can remember, not partial if it is not spoiled by wrongful shame, nor hidden from one and shown to another. That is to say, it tends towards hypocrisy and always fails to receive mercy. Satisfaction must be wholehearted, discreet, and worthy: wholehearted in that one must not grudge what he must do to save his soul; worthy in that the pain of penance must be as the delight in the sin.[15] Saint Augustine says, "Sin, whether it is small or great, must be paid for, either by repenting of man or coming from God. Whoever repents must give himself pain."

If you want to be well confessed of your sins and of your state of soul — what it has been and what it is now — understand that you need to know and recall it, and see and read Holy Scripture often and thoroughly, for every sickness of heart has its cure there. In it you can find what pleases and displeases God, and how you can be obedient or disobedient to him. There you can learn what are the virtues without which, and the vices with which, no man can be saved. Pay attention, then, to what God has commanded you: what you have neglected and what he has forbidden; how you have acted, and how you have used what he has given you. And what he has admonished you: whether you have undertaken it and how you have held fast, or let go through negligence. And all these things, according to how you have sinned, confess especially. So, confess in detail and thoroughly the sins you have committed and the benefits you have received and the faith you have promised.

---

[14] Cf. *Lumere*, vv. 9865–74; there is no clear source identified for the passage (notes, in III:144, to vv. 9839ff & 9853, mention standard lists and priests' manuals).

[15] The third case, discretion, is omitted.

Acusez les pechiez, loeez le benfaitur, pronunciez la fei. Dotez pur les pechiez, pur les benefices rendez graces. Le covenant de la fei cunussez. Repensez tuz vos anz en amertume de vostre alme, encerchez tute vostre conscience, mustrez vostre vie a Deu. Geissez coment vus avez les dis comandemenz Deu trespassé, coment vus avez par les cinc sens de vostre cors, coment de la plenté del pé treskes al chief, dedenz e de[f.60v]fors, de tuz vos menbres en passiuns de malveis desirs avez usé. Coment par les privez e malveis esmeuentez de vostre alme avez Deu offendu. Geissez ke le covenant de baptesme e le aliance ke vus feistes a Deu en anfance e la promés ke vus feistes od le prestre en penitence e la professiun ke vus uverastes sollempnement en l'abit de religiun u de virginité u de viduité n'avez mie sous les[i] meins gardé[ii] e de quor e de buche e de overaine par omissiun defaillistes. Vus vus feinsistes e negligent fustes e tutes celes choses mespreistes. Geissez ke vus n'avez mie si bien vostre virginité ne vostre viduité ne vostre religiun ne vostre promesse ke vus avez a Deu fait n'avez mie si bien sous ne si bien teu ne si bien vescu cum vus pustes e deviez. Geissez ke si vus avez nul bien fait, ço ne vint pas de vus ne par vos merites.[iii]

[L]es dis cumandemenz Deu sunt icés Creez en Deu, ne jurez en vein par lui, feirez les festes, honorez pere e mere, ne ociez pas, ne faites mie fornicaciun, ne faites pas larecin, ne portez pas faus testimoine encuntre vostre prome, ne coveitez pas la femme vostre prome, ne coveitez pas la meisun vostre prome ne ke son seit.

[L]es set vices principaus sunt icés Orguil, envie, ire, tristesce del siecle u accidie, avarice, glutunie, lecherie. Nul peché criminel n'est pres[iv] ke [f.61r] ne seit un de icés u ke ne seit de alcun de icés. Pur iceo di jo pres pur iceo k'il sunt nus crimineus pechiez ke semble[nt][v] ke ne sunt mie cumpris dedenz ces set sicume male creance e ydolatrie. Icés set sunt apelez capitaus u principaus pechez ne mie pur ço k'il [seient greignurs de tuz autres, mes pur ço qu'il] sunt cumencement e nessance des autres pechez.

[L]e premer vice si est orguil. Icest nun de orguil a la fie est pris plus estreitement, a la fie plus largement. Sulum ço k'il est pris estreitement si est amur de sa propre hautesce. Sulum iceo k'il est pris plus largement si est apelé amur de sa propre volunté, ço est quant hume met sa volenté avant la volunté Deu. E chescun cel orguil est criminel peché. De orguil venent inobedience, jactance, ypochrisie, estrif, pertinaces, descordes, emprises de noveutez.

---

[i] MS mes. [ii] MS sous les m. lavez g. [iii] D (f.55ra) and L (f.202rb) resume, amplifying the following section on the Decalogue. [iv] DL 'pris'. [v] MS ke ne semble.

Blame the sins, praise the benefactor, pronounce the faith. Fear for the sins, give thanks for the benefits. Know the covenant of faith. Reflect all your days in bitterness of soul, search your conscience, show your life to God. Confess how you have broken God's ten commandments: how by the five senses of your body, how from the soles of your feet right up to your head, inwardly and outwardly, you have used all your members in passions of wicked desires. And how you have offended God in the secret and wicked movements of your soul. Confess how you have failed in the covenant of baptism, and the alliance you made with God in infancy, and the promise you made to the priest in penitence, and the profession you made solemnly in the habit of religion or of virginity or of widowhood — that you have not kept it under your hand — in heart or in word or in deed, by omission. You were lazy and negligent and did all those things awry. Confess that you have not known, held to, or lived your virginity nor your widowhood nor your religious vows nor the promise you made to God, as well as you could or should have done. Confess that if you have done something good it came neither from you nor through your merit.

The Ten Commandments of God are these Believe in God, do not swear by him in vain, keep the feasts, honour father and mother, do not kill, do not fornicate, do not rob, bear no false witness against your neighbour, do not covet your neighbour's wife, do not covet your neighbour's house nor anything that is his.

The Seven Principal Vices are these Pride, envy, anger, world-sadness or sloth, avarice, gluttony, lechery. No mortal sin exists that is not one of these or does not come from one of these. That is why I say it:[16] because there are mortal sins of ours that seem not to be included in the seven, such as bad faith and idolatry. These seven are called capital, or principal, not only because they are worse than all the others but because they are the beginning and birth of other sins.

The first vice is Pride. This name of pride is taken sometimes more narrowly, sometimes more widely. As taken narrowly, it is love of one's own status. As taken more widely, it is called love of one's own will: it is when a man sets his will against God's will. And every kind of pride is mortal sin. From pride come disobedience, boasting, hypocrisy, strife, obstinacy, discord, frivolity.

[16] The meaning of "pres" is uncertain in this context.

[L]e secund vice est envie. De orguil nest envie. Envie est hange de autrui bien. Envie est semblable a la teigne, kar ausi cume la teigne mangue sa mere, ço est le drap dunt ele est nee, issi turmente envie le corage la u ele nest.[i] De envie venent hanges, gruz, detractiun, hait de l'adversité de sun prosme, e turment de sa prosperité.

[L]e terz vice est ire. Ire est nient-resunable turment u trublement de corage. Quant ele turne a hange e a malice, si est criminel peché. De ire venent [f.61v] tencu[n]s, enflure de curage, leidenges, cri, indignaciun, blasphemies. Od cest ire nul dunc ne plest a Deu, kar il est dist 'Si vus offrez vostre dun devant l'auter e iloec vus recordez ke vostre frere ad aucune chose encuntre vus, lessez ilec vostre dun e alez [vus] acorder a vostre frere e puis offrez dun.'

[L]e quart vice est tristesce, la tristesce ke nest de l'envie del bien dedenz. Si iceste tristesce vent a si grant malice ke celui ki est triste desespeire de la misericorde De e pur ses mesaventures se deut k'il unkes fuit né, ço est criminel peché, ço est quant hume est triste k'il ne pot faire adulterie u autre criminel peché, ço est la tristesce ke fait la mort. La bone tristesce est en veraie penitence. De tristesce vient mal[ic]e e rancur, pusillinimité, desperaciun, paresce en tur les comandemenz Dampnedeu, vagatiun de corage entur iceles choses ke ne lest nient a faire.

[L]e quinte vice est coveitise. Avarice est desmesuree coveitise de aver, si ele est si grande ke hume cuveite aucunes choses a tort. Iceste cuveitise est defendue en la lei. De avarice venent traisuns, boisdies, decevance, parjures, inquietudines, violences, duresces encuntre misericorde.

[L]e sist vice est glutunie e desmesuré[ii] desir [f.62r] de manger u de beivre. Icele glutunie ke est od grant delit e od us hanté si est criminel peché. Iceste vice seut estre achaisun de mutz maus e pur ço le deit hom eschivre. De glutunie venent malveses, leesce, scurilité, immundice, mult parler, e duresce de engin.

[L]e setime vice est lecherie ke est plenere volunté de faire fornicaciun e chescune tele [vole]nte est criminel peché. Dunt il est dit en le evan[gelie] 'Qui veit[iii] femme a lui cuveiter il ad ja fait lecherie od lui en sun quor.'

[i] DL 'sa mece, c'est le drap, kaunt ele est noue, issi tormente le corage quant est noue envie.'
[ii] MS desmesuree. [iii] MS feit.

The second vice is Envy. Envy is born from pride. Envy is hate of others' good. Envy is like the clothes-moth, for as the worm eats its mother — that is, the cloth from which it is born — so envy torments the heart that bears it.[17] From envy come hate, grumbling, detraction, pleasure at one's neighbour's adversity and anguish at his prosperity.

The third vice is Anger. Anger is unreasonable anguish or trouble of heart. When it turns to hate and malice, that is mortal sin. From anger come quarrels, swelling of the heart, outrage, shouting, indignation, blasphemy. With this anger, nobody can please God, for it is said, "If you offer your gift before the altar, and you recall there that your brother has something against you, leave your offering there and go and make peace with your brother; then make your offering."[18]

The fourth vice is Sloth, or the sadness born of envy for inward good. This sadness comes with such malice that the sad person despairs of God's mercy, and because of his misdeeds he regrets that he was ever born, it is mortal sin; that is, when a man is sad that he cannot commit adultery or any other mortal sin, it is the sloth that brings death. Good sadness is in true penitence. From sloth come malice and rancour, pusillanimity, despair, laziness towards the Lord God's commandments, mental vacillation about things so that nothing is done.

The fifth vice is Covetousness. Avarice is excessive coveting of property, if it is so great that one covets some things wrongly. This covetousness is forbidden by the Law. From avarice come treasons, fraud, deception, false swearing, unquietness, violence, stubborn refusal of mercy.

The sixth vice is Gluttony and excessive desire to eat or to drink. This gluttony, if practised eagerly and habitually, is a mortal sin. This vice can be the occasion of many ills, therefore one must avoid it. From gluttony come wickedness, pleasures, scurrility, uncleanness, babbling, and obstinate guile.

The seventh vice is Lechery, which is wholehearted desire to commit fornication, and every such desire is mortal sin. So it is written in the Gospel: "Who looks at a woman and desires her has already done lechery with her in his heart."[19]

---

[17] DL expand the idea: the cloth is like a candle-wick; new envy torments the heart as if it were a newly-lighted candle.

[18] Matt. 5:23–24.

[19] Matt. 5:28.

De lecherie vent aveglesce de quor, despurveance, nunparmanableté, precipitaciun, amur de sei meimes, hange de Deu, amur de ces[t] siecle, hisdur e desperatiun del siecle ke est a venir. L'eveske Bartholomeu dist 'Chescun de icés set vices erraument ad les biens dunt[i] il est digne de salu.'[ii]

[L]i biens ke iço set vices destruient sunt set vertuz, ço est asaver humilité, charité, pacience, espi[ri]tuele leesce, tristesce del secle. Largesce avarice destruit, abstinence glutunie destruit, chasté destruit lecherie. Fornicaciun faire est dist en treis maneres. L'une [est] cultivement des ydles de Deu partir e les veines ydles cultiver cume Deu ; l'autre manere de faire fornicaciun est arere mettre l'amur de Deu ; la terce manere de fornicaciun est la charnele fornicaciun e est fait en en multes maneres, kar en quele manere ke unkes home encuntre le issure de ordure de lecherie se suil[f.62v]le, si est fornicaciun. De tutes icestes manieres de fornicaciun, ausi bien espiritueles cum charneles, si est dit par le psalmiste a Deu 'Vus destruirez tuz icés ki par fornicacion departent de vus.'

[Confession] [A] confessiun bien faire il estuet ke vus aiez le quor e puis confessiun de buche esluminé del Saint Espirit, e par iço contri[t]ion de quor, e puis confessiun de buche, e pus satisfaciun en overaigne, e ke vus eschivez [chescune] manere[iii] de peché, ke vus icestes choses aiez preez e faites preer Deu pur vus e pur tuz pecheurs ke Deu vus duinst si repentir e cunfessiun si pure e plenere e satisfactiun faire ke Deu seit paé vos pechez parduner. Preez ensement pur vostre cunfessur ke Deu le dui[n]st tele vie mener k'il seit sauuf e a vus par bone preere e par bone doctrine bone profiter. Devant la cunfessiun dunc lungement encerchez[iv] vostre curage ententivement en chescun hage, en chescun ordre, en chescun tens, en chescun liu, en chescun estat quele vie vus avez mené e cument vus avez peché. E[v] tut iço ke vus truverez en vus de mal purement geissez. Preez Deu devotement k'il vus face vos pechez plenerement venir a memorie e pur eus si duler e eus si geir e si parfitement hair e lesser k'il vus seient pardunez.

[i] MS dient. [ii] DL 'vices tolent le regne del ciel a sun fesur. Le prior Alisandre dit quiqunkes seit quite de ices set vices erralment od les bens dunt il est digne de salu.' [iii] MS materie. [iv] MS encercher. [v] MS En.

From lechery come blindness of heart, lack of foresight, instability, hot-headedness, love of self, hatred of God, love of this world, terror and despair of the world that is to come. The bishop Bartholomew says, "Each of these seven vices has exactly the virtues by which it is worthy to be saved."[20]

The good things that destroy these seven vices are Seven Virtues, that is to say: humility, charity, patience, spiritual lightness, sadness at the world.[21] Largesse destroys avarice, abstinence destroys gluttony, chastity destroys lechery. There are said to be three kinds of fornication. One is the cult of idols that separates us from God, and the cult of vain idols as if they were like God. The second way of doing fornication is to put away the love of God. The third kind of fornication is fornication of the flesh, and it is done in many ways, for in whatever form a man ever dirties himself with the issue of filth in lechery, that is fornication. Of all these kinds of fornication, both spiritual and corporeal, it is said by the Psalmist to God: "You shall destroy all those who by fornication depart from you."[22]

[Confession] To make a good confession, it is necessary to have your heart, and then your spoken confession, illumined by the Holy Spirit; by this contrition of heart, then by spoken confession, and then by satisfaction in deeds, you must avoid every kind of sin. You should have prayed about these things and had prayers said to God for you and for all sinners, so that God may grant you such repentance, and a confession so clean and full, and to do satisfaction, that God will be pleased to forgive your sins. Also pray for your confessor, that God may grant him to lead such life that he will be saved, and by good prayer and good doctrine to benefit you well. Before confession, then, search your conscience carefully at length: every age, every order, every time, every place, every estate; what life you have led, and how you have sinned. And simply confess everything bad you find in yourself. Devoutly pray God to make you remember your sins fully, and to sorrow for them and confess them, and hate and forsake them perfectly, that you may be forgiven.

---

[20] The passage in DL adds that sins rob the sinner of Heaven, and cites Prior Alexander instead of Bartholomew.

[21] As opposed to the *sin* of sadness, above. This is a list of eight virtues, unless "leesce" and "tristesce" are both remedies for Sloth.

[22] Ps. 73:27 (in *LV*, 72:27).

Preez Deu ententivement k'il ne soeffre le Diable vus desturber par hunte ne par pour ne par ubliance ne par hisdur de vos pechez plenerement [L f.204ra][i] geir, preez Deu pur vostre confessor, qu'il le vus face suef e affable e qu'il li doint volenté e saver de vus si conseiller cum vus avez mester. Pramettez a Deu que par si qu'il vus face venir en memorie voz pechez, vus les direz e nent nes celrez.

Si par pour ou par necgligence ou par hunte de voz pechez geir estes desturbé, pensez sovent e ententivement que si vus purement ne les geissez, quele hunte e hidur e pour vus averez al jur de juise quant tuz fez e paroles e pensers serrunt devant Deu e ses angeles e devant tuz homes apertement descovert, e cum dure chose ço ert estre turmenté od le Diable e ses angeles sanz fin e sanz entreval e sanz remedie. Melz est dunc devant un home aver hunte e estre salvé ke devant tut le munde estre dampné.

Sachez ben que nule chose confunde le Diable tant cum fet confession de peché, [f.204rb] kar pur ço ke le Diable sicum est sei meismes leid, issi est il en tuz ses fez leid e tres hidus, e pur ço tres grant honur li fet ki unques par celer ses pechez sa leidesce musce en son quer, k'ele ne seit veue dunt il nomement apele le coruce e le ire le Diable encontre sei. Qui unkes le met de son quer e coment il est leid e ord al prestre demustre[ii] confession, mes n'ait garde ki unques ço fet, car cum il plus renuncie le Diable tant paie il plus Deu, e tant cum il plus prise Deu car cum plus offend lui grevosement tant trove il vers Deu greignur grace. Ne ja n'ait pour e suffrir la grevose bataille de lui quant il ad en Deu tresfort refui.

Sachez ben de veir ke si vus volez penitence e confession fere profitablement vus estoet pardoner de quer a tuz iceus q'unt envers vus peché e a tuz iceus en ki vus avez peché pardun demander ; si vus ne poez a eus ateindre aez plenere volenté [f.204va] de ço fere, car verité dit en l'ewangele : 'Si vus ne pardonez a homes lur pechez ne vostre Pere celestien ne pardo[n]ra a vus les voz.' A chescun peché que vus est en ceste generale confession dites generalment e brevement, resteez iloc e dites especialment e plenerement 'Jeo ai en porpos de ces e de tuz autres pechez lesser', ou si vus volez, dites tut utre. E puis si dites especialment ke vus avez fet e pur quei e coment.

[i] The Douce text ends here. [ii] MS demustrer.

Pray God intently not to let the Devil distract you, by shame or fear or forgetfulness or horror, from confessing your sins fully. Pray to God for your confessor, that he will make it sweet and easy for you to speak, and to give him will and wisdom to counsel you as you have need. Promise God that if he will bring your sins to your memory, you will say them and not hide them.

If through fear or negligence or shame you are troubled when confessing your sins, think hard and often that if you do not confess them cleanly, what shame and horror and fear you will have at the Day of Judgement when all deeds and words and thoughts will be revealed openly before God and his angels and before all men, and what a hard thing it will be to be tormented by the Devil and his angels without end,[23] without respite, without remedy. It is better, therefore, to be shamed before one man and saved than to be damned before all the world.

Understand well that nothing confounds the Devil so much as confession of sins, for because the Devil himself is so ugly, so he is ugly and hideous in all his deeds. And so he does him a great favour, whoever hides his sins and conceals his ugliness in his heart, so that it will not be seen; thus he will especially call the anger and the fury of the Devil against him. Whoever displaces him from his heart and confesses to the priest how ugly and filthy he is: let him not be afraid to do this, for the more he renounces the Devil the more he pleases God, and the more he prizes God the more he grievously offends the Devil, and the more he finds good grace with God. He shall have no more fear, nor suffer the grievous battle with him when he has taken strong refuge in God.

Know truly that if you want to make penitence and confession profitably, you must heartily forgive all those who have sinned against you, and ask forgiveness of all those you have sinned against. If you cannot come to them, have full intention of doing so, for it is said truly in the Gospel: "If you do not forgive men their sins, your Heavenly Father will not forgive you yours."[24] For each of your sins, in general confession, speak generally and briefly. Stay there, and speak specifically and fully: "I intend to leave off these and all other sins," or say it differently if you wish. And then say specifically what you have done, and why and how.

[23] See Rev. 12:7–8.

[24] Matt. 6:15.

Quant vus venez dunc a confession, primes dites *Benedicite* e puis que il ben entende ço que vus volez dire, dites overtement, dites od suspirs e od gemissemenz, dites od lermes e od quer dolent ne aiez garde dites hardiement, dites a Deu e a son vicarie en iceste manere : 'Je geis a Deu e a vus, Pere, que jeo ai mult peché, en parole, en overaigne, en penser. Jeo ai peché mult grevosement. J'ai fet les set principaus e criminaus pecchez e ceus que de eus venent ke en dit, ke en fet, ke en pen[f.204vb]ser. Jeo ai peché par orguil, par veineglorie e par envie e par ire e par male tristesce, par avarice, par glotonie, par leccherie. Jeo ai trespassé les dis comandemenz. J'ai peché par cinc sens de mon cors, de la plante del pé desques al chef sum dedenz e dehors tuz mes membres en passiuns de malveis desirs ai malement usé. J'ai par les privez e malveis esmovemenz Dampnedeu offendu.

'Jeo geis ben que les bens ke j'ai par mon orguil ai cru qu'il vindrent de moy ou qu'il vindrent de Deu par mes merites ou jo quidai aver le ben en moy ke jo n'avei pas ou en despit des autres volei singulerment aver ço ke jeo n'avoie. Jeo ai mult peché par orguil. Jeo me ai enorguillé en prosperité, e ai esté grussant encontre Deu e homes en adversité ai esté. Jeo n'ai mie les graces que Deu m'ad donés ben usé cum jo dusse. Jeo n'ai mie esté entur charité n'entur les overaines de charité sicum jeo dusse, car jeo [f.205ra] ai esté a Deu e a mes prelaz e a mes parenz e a mes mestres e a mes seignur inobedient ; a ma volenté plus qu'a lur comandement[i] ne fui e si jeo lur comandement ou lur volenté fis enviz e od gruz e meins ben e meins purement le fis que jeo ne dusse. E si jeo volenters ou prestement ou plenerement de bon gré le fis, sovent pur ceo m'enorguilli e loe[n]ge ou aucune autre chose enquis.' Quel poet le frut de l'obedience fere menur ou tut tollir.

'Jeo ai mon prosme mult sovent corucé e envers eus mult corcé esté e en envie e en hange e par mon orguil e par male suspecion trop aperte e iceus ai mal volu, mal dit, mal fet e mal weité. Jeo ai d'eus malement sentu. Jeo ai de lur mal oir eu delit e joie. Jeo les ai en vile despit e de quer e de buche malement jugé. Jeo ai lur choses pur moy venger mal fet. Jeo ai le lur atort weté ke par juer ke par embler ke par enprunt ke par [f.205rb] trover e retenir si ai vers eus mult mespris. Jeo n'ai a eus sicum jeo dusse pardoné e pur ceo ai jeo grevement pecché.

---

[i] MS comandemente.

So when you come to confession, first say *Benedicite*[25] and then, so that he understands what you mean, say openly, say with sighs and groans, say with tears and with sorrowful heart — do not hesitate, say bravely — say to God and to his vicar in this manner: "I confess to God and to you, Father, that I have sinned very grievously. I have committed the seven principal and mortal sins, and those that come from them: in word, in deed, in thought. I have sinned by pride, vainglory, envy, anger, sloth, avarice, gluttony, lechery.[26] I have broken the ten commandments. I have sinned by the five senses of my body, from the sole of my foot to the top of my head, both inwardly and outwardly. I have wrongly used all my members in passions of evil desire. By my secret and wicked impulses I have offended the Lord God.

"I confess that the goodness I have, I have pridefully believed that it comes from myself, or from God because of my merits. Or I believed I had the goodness in me that I had not, or in despite of others wanted to have for myself what I had not. I have sinned much through pride. I have been arrogant in prosperity, and have been quarrelsome towards God and men in adversity. I have not used the graces God gave me properly as I should have. I have not undertaken charity nor works of charity as I should, for I have been disobedient to God, to my priests, to my parents and masters and lords; I have obeyed my will more than their command, and if I did their will or their command it was with envy and grumbling, and I did it less well and less purely than I should have. And if I did it willingly or quickly or thoroughly with good grace, I often took pride in that and sought praise or other things." Thus the fruit of obedience may be diminished or taken completely away.

"I have often angered my neighbours, and have often been angered with them; and in envy, hate, and through my pride and obvious suspicion have wished evil, spoken evil, done evil, and been on the lookout for evil. I have felt bad things about them. I have had delight and pleasure, hearing of their trouble. I have had them in vile contempt, and judged them wrongly in thought and word. I have done damage to their property, to revenge myself. I have wrongfully coveted what is theirs, by gambling, stealing, borrowing, finding and keeping — I have done them great wrong. I have not forgiven them as I ought, and in this I have sinned grievously.

---

25 "Benedicite" was used as a word of greeting.

26 There are apparently eight here; vainglory is usually considered to be a branch of pride, however.

'Jeo geis dunc ke jeo ai mult peché par lesser de fere les bens e par fere les maus en ceste manere e autres unt par moi peché, car mulz unt par moi mal fet e ben lessé. Jeo n'ai ben gardé virginité ne esposaille ne veduece. Jeo n'ai mie ben gardé ma casteté. Jeo ai encontre nature peché. Jeo ai peché par grosse ignorance e par simple [...], par mun poer, par ubliance, par necgligence. Jeo ai peché adecertes par precipitacion, par deliberacion, par ire, par malice. Jeo geis dunc que jeo ai mult peché en Deu e en homes e a Deu e a homes reque[r] pardon e pramet amendement. E a tuz iceus q'unt en mei peché jeo lur pardoins de quer. Jeo geis que j'ai lessé de fere les bens que jeo saveie e por[e]ie e devei[e] fere. Jeo despis e mis a nunchaler de aprendre lé bens ke furent [f.205va] a fere. Jeo geis que les bens[i] que j'ai fet furent menur e meins ben fet qu'il ne devereient e iceus par entente de vaineglorie ou par acune vice furent corrumpuz qu'il poent par dreit ou nent pleire ou despleire a Deu. Jo geis que j'ai fet les maus acient que jeo savoie e poeie e deveie eschivre par aie de Deu e de[ii] ses seinz ne conseil ne aie de home ne desirai ne demandai mes par duresse de quer hardiement pecchai. Jeo geis ke les bens que Deu me comanda a fere jeo les mis a nunchaler e despis le mal qu'il defendi volenters e hardiement le fis. Par malement user celes choses qu'il m'ad granté si ai mult peché. Iceles choses qu'il me monesta a fere, jeo les refusai ou si jo les empris a fere, jeo ne les gardai mie ben. Jeo geis dunc ben que j'ai en multes maneres Deu offendu en dit, en fet, e en penser. Jeo ai mult peché en parole cum par ribaudie, par hudives e foles e malveises e ame[f.205vb]res e leccheresses e vilaines e orguilluses e coveituses paroles, par enveisures e adecertes par estriver, par contredire, par manascer, par vanter, par veines e malveis contes e questions demander, par noveles conter e demander, par trop loer e trop blamer, par reprover, par leidenger, par losenger, par gruscer, par autres malement juger, par Diable trop nomer, par trop haut ou bas parler, par fous chaunz chaunter, par malveis conseil doner, en priveté descoverir, par folie e mal aprendre e enseingner, par malement parler, par malement enseiner, par maudire, par escomenger, par mentir, par autres dementir, par escharner, par veine desputeison, par detraction, par Deu e ses seinz blamer ou blasphemir, par faus dire, par faus testmoine porter, par pleider, par encuser, par descorde semer, par autres malement chalenger, par autres surnon apeler, par encontre autres od male volenté jurer, par malveis e fous escriz lire, [f.206ra] par enchantement dire, par choses nent descretement defendere ou comander par quei jeo fis autre pechez.

---

[i] MS rens. [ii] MS des.

"So I confess that I have sinned greatly by not doing good, and by doing wrong in this way. And others have sinned through me, for many have done wrong and forsaken good because of me. I have not respected virginity, wedlock, or widowhood. I have not kept chastity well. I have sinned against nature. I have sinned through gross ignorance and through stupidity, through fear, forgetfulness, and negligence. I have certainly sinned through rashness, deliberation, anger, and malice. Therefore I confess that I have sinned gravely against God and man, and from God and man I beg forgiveness, and promise amendment. And all those who have sinned against me, I forgive with my whole heart. I confess that I have left undone the good that I knew and could and should have done. I have despised, and neglected to learn of, the good that was to be done. I confess that the good things that I did were less and worse done than they should have been; and those were done from an impulse of vainglory, or were corrupted by some vice, so that rightly they could not at all please, or could displease, God. I confess that I have knowingly done those evils that I knew and could and should avoid with the help of God and his saints; nor did I desire or request the help or advice of men, but boldly sinned with a hard heart. I confess that the virtues God commanded me to do, I abandoned them in forgetfulness; willingly and boldly I did the evil although he forbade it. I have greatly sinned by using the things he granted me wrongly. I refused the things he ordered me to do or, if I undertook them, I did not keep to them. So I confess truly that in many ways I have offended God in word, deed, and thought. In word, I have sinned much: in ribaldry, by idle, foolish, bad, bitter, lecherous, ugly, prideful, and covetous words. By jesting, and certainly by striving, contradiction, threatening, boasting; by vain and wicked stories, and asking questions; by telling and asking about gossip, by too much praising and blaming, by reproving, insulting, flattering, grumbling; by judging others ill, by naming the Devil too much, by talking too loudly or too softly, by singing bad songs, by giving bad counsel, telling secrets, learning and teaching foolishly and badly, talking badly, teaching badly — by malediction, by cursing, by lying, breaking promises, derision, vain disputation, detraction, blaspheming or blaming God and his saints, false speaking, bearing false witness, pleading, accusing, sowing discord, challenging others wrongly, name-calling, swearing against others with evil intent, reading mad and wicked writings, practising magic; by forbidding or commanding things indiscreetly — by which I did other sins.

'Jeo ai plus grevosement par malveis pensers pecché, ke jo m'ai tant delité de mult pecchez, ke jeo consenti de fere les par overaignes e les fis les uns plus sovent e les uns plus relement,[i] mult pecchez purposai de fere, mes jeo les ne fis nent, mes ceo ne remist mie en moi, car jeo ne les soi mie fere ou jo ne les poeie nent fere e ço pesa moi e maugré soi a tuz iceus que me desturbent. Jeo geis que mulz pecchez me sunt chaü de memorie, mulz sunt mes privez pecchez, multes sunt les omissions, les bens que jeo fis poverement les fis, mult des fiez les fis nent covenablement a Deu, mult defiez rebotai la grace Deu. Jeo n'ai mie haï mal cum jeo duisse. De tutes icestes choses demand jeo pardon e sui[ii] apparaillé a confession fere e satisfaction de tuz les pecchez ke Deu me mettra en memorie [f.206rb] queus qu'il unkes seent. D'icés choses dunt j'ai issi dit e de mult des autres dun jo sui copable, que jeo ne sai dire e copable me sent, merci cri a Deu e a vus e copable me renc.'

Quant donc la confession est dite e l'amonestement fete e la penitence enjointe, devant ceo que vus departez, dites vostre *Confiteor* e demandez sa beneiçon e qu'il vus receive en ses bens e en ses oraisons.

[i] MS relevement. [ii] MS suei.

"I have sinned more grievously in evil thoughts: [I confess] that I so delighted in many sins that I consented to commit them through deeds; I did some more often and some more rarely. I intended to do many sins, but I did not do them. But that is not to my credit, for I did not know how to do them or was completely unable to do them, and that annoyed me, and I resented all those who prevented me. I confess that many sins have fallen from my memory: many are my secret sins, many are the omissions. The good I did, I did poorly; many times I did them unworthily to God. Many times I pushed away God's grace. I have not hated evil as I should. I ask forgiveness for all these things, and I am prepared to make confession and satisfaction for all the sins God will remind me of, whatever they are. For these things I have thus spoken of, and for many others that I am guilty of, which I don't know how to say and feel guilty about, I beg mercy from God and declare myself guilty to you."

So, when the confession is said and the admonishment done and the penance enjoined, before you leave say your *Confiteor*[27] and ask his blessing, and that he will include you in his good works and in his prayers.

[27] "Confiteor" is a standard Confession prayer; see, for example, p. 245 above.

Chapter 13

The Commandments[1]

Introduction

This treatise on making confession is based chiefly on the Decalogue. Confession guides may have varying structures; compare A Man's Confession (in this volume), which is based on the Seven Deadly Sins. The treatise survives in at least four Insular manuscripts; we present the Paris version (see below). It begins with the metaphor of confession as a robe which must fit well, so that we can appear appropriately dressed before Our Lord.[2] As well as the Ten Commandments, it discusses the seven Sins, the Commandments of the Gospel, fifteen Degrees of Charity, the Beatitudes. It ends with the "confession of praise" (not found in our other Confession pieces): a celebration of the happiness we feel once the confession is done.

The treatise is found in at least four Insular manuscripts:

C = Cambridge, Trinity College O.1.20 (s.xiii^{m}), ff.325r–330v (f.329 is blank). This important medical manuscript has been described in detail elsewhere.[3] The confessional treatise is the only non-medical work in the manuscript and is incomplete owing to the absence of at least one folio at the end.

L = London, Lambeth Palace MS Library 522 (s.xiv), ff.229r–244v. An extensive collection of religious and didactic pieces, mostly in verse and in Anglo-Norman, the whole described and partially edited by Robert Reinsch,[4] who simply refers to the Paris MS in connection with the present treatise.[5]

O = Oxford, St John's College 75 (s.xiv^{in}), ff.88va–90vb. The manuscript consists of penitential texts beginning with Raymond of Peñafort's *Summa de poenitentia* (ff.1ra–88rb),[6] then Martin of Braga's *Formula vitae honestae* (ff.91ra–92rb), Gregory's *Regula pastoralis* (ff.93ra–135ra), and a short, incomplete "Tractatus de carne superba

---

[1] D&B 667, prose, "Treatise on Confession."

[2] See Matt. 22:1–14.

[3] *Anglo-Norman Medicine* 1, ed. Hunt, pp. 17–21, with further texts from it edited in his *Anglo-Norman Medicine* 2.

[4] Reinsch 1880.

[5] Ibid. p. 78.

[6] I follow the refoliation of the MS which took place in February 1993.

que animam perdit" (inc. "Ad te manum meam extendo quem sentio in timore Dei tenere vexillum . . ."). At three points in the manuscript, vernacular items have been added: the confessional treatise on ff.88va–90vb, a form of confession (f.92va–b), and then, in a later fourteenth-century hand, an account of the Seven Deadly Sins and their subdivisions, in Anglo-Norman and Latin, introduced with a red rubric: *Ceo sunt les especes de orguyl vayne* [*glorie* . . .].

P = Paris, BNF, MS fr. 19525 (s.xiii^{m}), ff.82vb–86vb. A celebrated manuscript which contains saints' lives, didactic works, Adam of Exeter's Exposition of the Pater Noster (ff.72ra–82vb; another version of the Exposition is presented in this volume), and five Sermons on Joshua (ff.153rb–191rb).[7]

The edition below is based on the Paris MS, which is closely related to the Oxford MS. The Cambridge text is incomplete and is characterized by a number of earlier omissions which it shares with L (to which it is closely related). Short sections of the treatise are also found in MSS Lambeth Palace Library 182 (s.xiv^{1}), f.188va–b (= La), and Dublin, Trinity College 374 (s.xiii^{2}), ff.42vb–43rb (= D).

[7] *Sermons*, ed. Hunt.

Text

[f.82vb] Ki voldra bien e beau vestu aparer devant la face Jesu, il covient qu'il eit une robe ke ad a nun confession. Ki bien ceste robe use, ja n'avera guarde del Felun. Al comencement deit l'en prendre garde k'ele seit bien taillee, ke rien n'i ait que reprendre.

Ore donc issi devum comencier. Quanque remord la cunscience devum regeir humblement, purement e leaument : humblement par duçur[i] de quor, purement par cumfession de buche, leaument par satisfactiun de overaine. [C]eo est escrit en Job : 'Jeo sui ennuié de ma vie par amertume[ii] de quer. Jeo parlerai encuntre moi par cumfessiun de buche', ne mie escusant mei com Adam fist, mes acusant sicom l'Escripture enseigne. Li dreiturels se acuse al comencement de sa parole. Ore dunc al comencement se acuse le pecheur solumc les [set] vices criminals e cels qui de els naisent, [f.83ra] sicome dist seint Gregorie en un livre que l'em apele les *Morales*.[iii] Icés sunt les set vices principals : vaineglorie, envie, ire, tristesce, avarice, glutonie, lecherie.

De vaineglorie come de male racine nessent icestes males branches : vantance, quant home dit aucune chose pur estre preisé ; inobedience, quant hume ne deigne faire ceo ke l'em li comande ; ypocresie quant home semble bon dehors e si est ord e malveis par dedenz — itel ne entra pas devant la face Nostre Sire,[iv] sicome dit saint Job[v] — tençuns, descordes, emprises de noveleries. De envie nest hange, grundiller, detractiun, ceo est mesparler de riere, hait de mal sun prosme e doel de sun bien. De ire nessent tençuns, emfluere de queor, huntuses paroles, dedeing e blasphemes. De tristesce nest malice, rancur, esmaance[vi] de curage, desperance, negligence entor les comandemenz Deu, volage quer entor choses que sont defendues. De avarice nest traisun, parjures, mal repos, violences e duresces de quer encuntre misericorde. De glutunie nest vaine leesce, legerté, ordure, mult parler e fieble entendement. De leccherie nest avoeglesce de quor, nunraison, instabilité, fole haste, amur de sei memes, hange de Deu, amur del siecle present, hidur ou desesperance del siecle k'est a venir.

De ces set princi[f.83rb]pals vices les cinc sont espiritals e les dous sont charnals, c'est asaveir les cinc tuchent l'alme e les dous le cors.[vii] E tuz ensemble encumbrent le cors e l'alme.

---

[i] O 'dulur'. [ii] L 'amerture'. [iii] C '*Moraus*'. [iv] C 'n'avera part od nostre S.' [v] P also has 'saint Salomon' on f.85vb. [vi] CL 'manaces'. [vii] CL 'a l'alme et les dous al cors'.

Translation

Whoever wishes to appear properly and finely dressed before the face of Jesus must have a robe that is called confession. Whoever uses this robe well need never fear the Evil One. At the beginning one must take care that it is well tailored, so that it may be beyond reproach.

To begin with, when conscience pricks us we must confess humbly, straightforwardly, and loyally: humbly by gentleness of heart, straightforwardly by spoken confession, loyally by satisfaction in deeds. This is written in Job: "I am wearied of my life in bitterness of heart. I shall speak against myself in the confession of my mouth,"[1] not excusing myself as Adam did,[2] but accusing myself as Scripture teaches. The righteous man accuses himself from the moment he speaks. So now let the sinner accuse himself from the start, according to the seven criminal vices and those which are born from them, as Saint Gregory says in a book called the *Moralia*.[3] These are the seven principal vices: vainglory, envy, anger, sloth, avarice, gluttony, lechery.

From vainglory, as from an evil root, are born these evil branches: boasting, when a man says something in order to be praised; disobedience, when a man disdains to do what he is commanded to do; hypocrisy, when a man seems good outwardly but is inwardly filthy and wicked — such a man will not enter before the face of Our Lord, as Saint Job says[4] — quarrels, discord, seeking after novelty. From envy are born hate, grumbling, slander — that is, speaking evil behind people's backs — joy at one's neighbour's trouble and sorrow at his joy. From anger are born quarrels, swelling of the heart, shameful words, contempt, and blasphemies. From sloth are born malice, rancour, failure of courage, despair, neglect of God's commandments, a fickle heart concerning forbidden things. From avarice are born treason, lies, unquietness, violence, and hardness of heart towards mercy. From gluttony are born vain pleasure, frivolity, filth, much talking, and weak understanding. From lechery are born blindness of heart, unreasonableness, instability, hastiness, love of self, hatred of God, love of this world, fear or despair of the world to come.

Of these seven principal sins, five are spiritual and two carnal: that is to say, five concern the soul and two the body. All together they encumber the body and the soul.

---

[1] Job 10:1.

[2] See Gen. 3:9–12.

[3] See *PL* 75:896A and, for the account of the Deadly Sins, *PL* 76:621AB.

[4] Job 13:16.

Uncore fait asaveir que ces set issi sont entreliez, que chescun vient de autre, car vaineglorie engendre envie ; envie engendre ire ; de ire surt[i] tristesce ; tristesce, quant n'ad cumfort dedenz, quiert faus cumfort dehors e issi engendre avarice ; de glotonie nest leccherie. Deheez ait cele mere e tutes les fillees, car trop i ad mal engendreure quant nuli se puet a eles prendre qu'il ne parte soillé.

[E]naprés si ceste robe deit estre bien seante, si covient que l'en cerche la cunscience solonc les dis comandemenz de la lei que Deu dona a Moysen. Les treis partenent a l'amur Deu e les set partenent a l'amur de prosme.

Le premier comandement est itel : 'Tu auras Damnedeu tun Seignur e a lui sul serviras.' Ici pernez garde si vus avez leaument Deu aurré, si sur tutes choses li avez servi, si voz premesses li avez rendu, si les premesses de quer ou de buche en disant aucune chose ou fesant ou en pelerinage ou de[ii] mainte penance, e si ceo qu'en baptesme premistes avez rendu, c'est asaveir del tut[iii] refusé le Diable e ses overaingnes.

Le secund comandement est itel : 'Ne pernez pas le nun tun Seignur en vain.' Ici per[f.83va]nez garde se vus avez le nun tun Seignur de Crestien en vain, car seint Augustin dit issi 'Treschier freres, il ne vus suffist pas que vus avez receu le nun de Crestien, si vus ne fetes les overaignes de Crestien', car a celui profite de estre apelé Crestien ki tuz tens les comandemenz Jesu Crist retient en sun quer e en overaignes les parfait.[iv]

Le tierz comandement est itel : 'Gardez le Sabath', c'est le Samedi. Sabath signefie repos. Ici pernez garde si[v] vus avez eu pes de corage sicom aver deussez, e se vus avez laboré par jor de feste, [que l'en feste trop a custume][vi] encuntre le comandement de Sainte Iglise, ou vostre serf ou vostre ancele ou vostre boef ou vostre cheval avera laboré, e si encuntre vostre salu pecchastes par jur de feste que l'en fait trop a custume.

[i] MS suit. [ii] O 'en'. [iii] MS entun. [iv] C 'o. parfites'. [v] MS si si. [vi] Completed from C. L has 'labure t.'

Also you must know that the seven are linked, that each comes from another. For vainglory engenders envy, envy engenders anger, from anger comes forth sadness. Sadness or sloth, when it has no comfort within, seeks false comfort without and so engenders avarice; from gluttony lechery is born. Cursed be this mother and all her daughters, for there are many evil children that none can touch without going away defiled.

Next, if this robe is to be suitable, it is right to search one's conscience according to the Ten Commandments of the Law that God gave to Moses. Three pertain to the love of God, and seven pertain to the love of one's neighbour.

The First Commandment is this: "Thou shalt worship the Lord thy God and him alone shalt thou serve." Here, consider whether you have honoured God loyally: whether you have served him above all others, whether you have carried out your promises to him, either of heart or of mouth, or in saying or doing anything, or in pilgrimage or in many penances; and whether you have carried out what you promised in baptism: that is to say, rejecting the Devil and his works.

The Second Commandment is this: "Take not the name of thy Lord in vain." Here, see whether you have the name of your Lord, Christian, in vain, for Saint Augustine says: "Beloved brothers, it suffices not that you have received the name of Christian, if you do not do Christian works," for it profits him to be called Christian if at all times he keeps the commandments of Jesus Christ in his heart and perfects them in his deeds.[5]

The Third Commandment is this: "Keep the Sabbath," that is, Saturday.[6] "Sabbath" means rest. Here consider whether you have had the inner repose that you should have had, and whether you have worked on a feast day [C that is too often done] which is against Holy Church's commandment; or whether your servant or your maid or your ox or your horse has worked, and whether you have sinned against your salvation on a feast day, as is customarily too often done.

---

[5] The commonplace, originally from Augustine's *Tractatus 5 in epistolam Joannis ad Parthos*, was cited and used by many authors including King Alfred and Isidore of Seville (see Cross 1959).

[6] *sic.* Christians keep Sunday, Jews Saturday, as the day of rest. The word is from Hebrew, and the Bible calls it the sabbath day (Ex. 20:8–11). See *BVV*, p. 2, for the change from Saturday to Sunday.

Le quart comandement est itel : 'Honurez vostre pere e vostre mere.' Ici pernez garde si vus avez honuré vostre pere e vostre mere espiritauls e charnaus sicome vus deussez, e si vus lur avez maudit ou mesdit,[i] si de voz richesces lur avez [eidé] a lur bosoing, si vus avez lur comandement en bien tenu, si cunseil e aie volentiers lur avez doné.

Le quint comandement est itel : 'Vus ne freez[ii] pas homicide.' Ici gardez si vus home avez ocis de vostre propre main ou par cunseil doner u aie u favur u si espiritalment avez nul occis u par essample [u de manace u] de malveise parole u de [f.83vb] fesance u si vus avez fait aucun mortel pecchié par lequel vus meimes estes mort u si [en] vus ne remist pas ke ne feites un mortel pecchié u autre u si avez peu celui ke deveit murir de faim, car sicum dit seint Ambrosie 'Si vus nel pessez, vus le oscistes.'

Le sime comandement est itel : 'Vus ne frez pas leccherie.' Ici pernez garde si vus avez fait fornicaciun ou avolterie, si vus avez eu vostre cosine[iii] ou aucune autre de vostre parenté ou vostre comere ou cele que vus receustes[iv] al baptizier ou cele que vus avez receu al baptesme, si vus avez fait sacrilege, c'est asaveir si vus avez eu femme de religion ou femme ki fu en enceinte[v] e si vus fuistes ordiné[vi] e si vus avez fait lecherie encuntre nature sicome od madles u od bestes, si vus avez fait leccherie en maniere de chen u si femme l'ad fait a vus. Car sicum dit Methodie 'Ceo fu une acheison pur quei Deu envea le deluvie.' Uncore pernez garde si vus avez coneu femme tant com ele fu enceinte u puis ke aveit enfant avant ke fust purefié, si vus avez eu pucele ou vedve u si vus avez coneu [femme en tens de ses flurs].[vii]

[i] C 'mesfeit u maldit'. [ii] CL 'serrez'. [iii] C 'u si vostre cosine'. [iv] C 'recust'. [v] MS enointe. C has 'veveté'. [vi] O has in left-hand margin *Cave tibi ne nimis aperte circa hanc materiam loquaris.* [vii] These six words have been erased in the MS. C has 'sun flux'.

The Fourth Commandment is this: "Honour your father and your mother." Here, consider whether you have honoured your father and mother, both spiritual and natural, as you ought: whether you have cursed or slandered them, whether you have helped them in their need with your riches, whether you have kept their commandments well, whether you have willingly given them counsel and help.

The Fifth Commandment is this: "You shall not commit manslaughter." Here, consider whether you have killed any man by your own hand, or by giving advice or aid or favour; or whether you have killed anybody by example or by threats, or by evil words or deeds, or whether you have committed any mortal sin by which you will die, or there remains in you some mortal sin or other that you have done, or whether you have fed somebody who was dying of hunger. For as Saint Ambrose said, "If you do not feed him, you kill him."[7]

The Sixth Commandment is this: "You shall not commit lechery." Here, consider whether you have committed fornication or adultery, whether you have taken your cousin or any other of your relations, or your fellow-godparent,[8] or her whom you received at baptism, or her whom you have received at baptism.[9] Whether you have committed sacrilege: that is to say, whether you have taken a religious woman or a pregnant woman, or you are ordained;[10] or whether you have committed unnatural lechery such as with males or with animals, whether you have done it in the manner of dogs, or a woman has done it to you. For as Methodius says: "This was a reason why God sent the Flood."[11] And further, consider whether you have known a woman when she was pregnant, or, having had a child, she had not yet been purified; whether you have known a virgin or a widow, or whether you have known a woman at the time of her menstruation.

---

[7] See for example Ambrose, *De officiis* (ed. and trans. Davidson), vol. I, Bk. Two, 78 (pp. 310–13).

[8] "commere," cf. "god-sib" or gossip, with similar meaning: this refers to the "family" of godparents of any one child. If you are a woman, your "commere" is the other godmother (your "gossip"); if you are a man, your "commere" is likewise godmother to your godchild, and she is forbidden to you under the laws of incest whether she is a blood-relation (sib) or not.

[9] *sic.* The copyist has clearly written the same idea twice, and may have omitted to delete the repetition.

[10] The margin note in MS O reads: "Be careful not to speak of these matters too openly."

[11] Actually Pseudo-Methodius; see D'Evelyn 1918 for a general commentary and one of the many texts.

Uncore pernez garde si femme ad pecchié od autre home par vostre aide ou cunseil ou si vus avez beisé autre femme ke vus ne deussez.[i] De tuz ces poinz prenge garde la femme endreit sei si ele fait les ad.

Le setime co[f.84ra]mandement est itel : 'Vus ne frez pas larecin.' Ici pernez garde si vus avez rien cunquis a tort, ou par usure ou par ravine ou par larcin ou par trovure ou par fauses tailles ou par bosdie e iceo en diverses maneres sicom marchant pecchent quant il vendent choses e ceilent le mal qu'il i ad e dient le bien k'il n'i ad pas e se parjurent e mentent e vendent plus chier pur respit doner, peisent[ii] fausement e mesurent. Uncore pernez garde si vus avez fait arsun,[iii] ou de blez u de vinnes, u gardin estrepé ou coupé,[iv] u si vus avez esté faus juge u faus testimonie ou faus arbitre u faus assessor, si vus avez nuli encusé par quei mal lui avint u cunsel doné, u si vus avez soeffert ke aucun fust dampné a tort e vus peusez aver delivré, si vus avez [rien] receu de Giu u de larrun u de robur u de usurier u de symonial, si vus avez rien trové u aprenté ke n'avez rendu, si vus avez retenu louer de aucun de vos serganz, car nule de ces choses ne devez retenir. Uncore pernez garde si vus avez receu aucune chose de aucune persone ke ne deveit aveir rien propre, sicume de femmes espusés que rien ne deivent aver fors commun od lur barons, u de home de religiun ; se issi rien avez receu vus le devez rendre. Si rien avez cunquis par bataille, si [f.84rb] la bataille fu dreiturele de la vostre part, vus poez retenir ceo ke vus avez cumquis par le cungié le seignur de l'ost. Si vus ne l'avez pris de aucun povre u de gent de religiun, car donc le devez rendre. Pernez[v] garde si rien avez guainé par faus acunter, e si rien avez receu por leccherie faire, vus le devez rendre ne mie a la femme, mes dorras[vi] as povres.

Le utime comandement est itel : 'Vus ne dirrez pas faus testemoine.' Ici pernez garde de chescune maniere de mençunge, de parjurie, de feimentie, de parole udive, de parole enveisee, de parole dont vostre prosme out honte, de parole plaine de maldit, de parole plaine de blasphemie, de parole senz raison,[vii] de parole[viii] en laquele Diable est nomee, de parole orguillose e desdeignante, de parole par laquele est semé descord, de parole de leccherie e de foles chançunz. Ici pernez garde si vus avez dit, si vus avez honuré Deu de vostre buche e vostre quer fu loinz de Deu quant vus deistes vostre oreison, kar nus devum loer purement e vigorosement e od reverence, ne mie perçusement[ix] e en recoupant les paroles outressaillant.

---

[i] CL 'dusses u altrement thuché que ne dusses'. [ii] MS paient. [iii] C 'larcin'. [iv] C 'cep'. [v] MS perner. [vi] C 'doner'. [vii] C 'de parole od serment'. [viii] C 'de parole plein de maldit sanz reison'. [ix] O 'recusement ne en r.'

Also, consider whether a woman has sinned through your aid or counsel, or whether you have kissed[12] any woman you should not have. In all these points, let the woman examine her own situation, whether she has done those things.

The Seventh Commandment is this: "You shall not commit theft." Here, consider whether you have taken anything wrongly, by usury, by seizure, by theft, by finding and keeping, by false tallies, by fraud; and this in various manners, the way merchants sin when they sell things and hide what is bad about them and tell of the good where there is none. They swear and lie and sell too dear to give credit; they weigh and measure falsely. Also, consider whether you have set fire to wheat or vines, or torn up or cut gardens. Or whether you have been a false judge, false witness, false arbiter, or false assessor. Or if you have accused anybody or given counsel by which harm came to them. Or whether you have allowed anybody to be wrongly condemned, whom you could have freed; whether you have received anything from a Jew, a thief, a robber, a usurer, or from one who practises simony; whether you have found or taken anything you haven't given back; whether you have held back their pay from any of your servants — for you ought to keep none of those things. Also, consider whether you have received anything from any person who ought not to have property, such as married women who ought to have nothing except what is in common with their husbands, or men of religion. If you have received any such thing you ought to give it back. If you have won anything in battle, providing the battle was for the right on your side, you may keep what you have won with leave from the commander of the army, as long as you haven't taken it from poor people or religious, for then you must give it back. Consider whether you have gained anything by false accounting; or, if you have received anything for committing lechery, you must return it — not to the woman, but by giving it to the poor.

The Eighth Commandment is this: "You shall not speak false witness." Here, consider all forms of lie, perjury, hypocrisy, idle words, frivolous words, words that would cause shame to your neighbour, words full of malice, words full of blasphemy, unreasonable words, words where the Devil is named, prideful and contemptuous words, words that spread discord, words of lechery, and foolish songs. Here, consider whether you have spoken, honouring God with your mouth, while your heart was far from God when you said your prayer. For we should praise pure-heartedly, vigorously, and reverently, not lazily and leaving salient words out.

---

[12] As in modern French, "baiser" can have a second meaning = to have sex with. CL have "touched" here.

Ici pernez garde si vus avez lessé a receiver le cors Nostre Seignur quant le deussez receivre por ceo que ne voliez voz pecchiez lesser. E se vus le avez receu indignement u senz devocion, [f.84va] car en l'une e en l'autre maniere pecchastes vus mortelment. Pernez garde si vus avez eu mal suspezun u vus avez fait chose dont l'en peust aver de vus mal suspeçon, car l'un e l'autre est mal. Sicome dit seint Jeronime, 'Nus devum eschiwre tutes males suspeçons e ke l'en puisse resnablement feindre chose de male note encontre vus.' Uncore pernez guarde si vus avez jugié[i] de chose dont vus ne savez[ii] certeinté. Ceo defent l'Apostle, disant 'Vus ki estes, ki jugiez autri serf ?[iii] Se il esta, il esta a son seignor, se il chet, il chiet a son seignor.' Pensez si vus avez [esté] mult parlere en iglise u a mangier e remembre vus del riche home dont l'Evangile parole qui pur cele chose fu turmenté en sa lange.

Le novime comandement est itel : 'Vus ne coveiterez pas la chose vostre prosme.' Ici pernez garde de coveitise, ceo est de trop grant amur de chose cunquere, e de avarice, c'est trop grant amur de retenir, de ambiciun, ceo est trop grant amur de aver seignurie. Veez coment vus seez contenu en icés poinz. Coveitise en clers fait symonie, en chevaliers ravine, en burgeis usure e bodie, en glutons e hasardurs larcin. E por ceo que covei[ti]se e fol[iv] desir regne tant encontre[v] gent, si engendre udivesce. Ici tuchez de udiwesce, ceo est asaver ke vus avez gasté le [f.84vb] tens que presté vus fu pur penance faire en vanité. Pernez garde del tens passé, hastez a la compaignie des angles, suspirez a vostre heritage que vus avez perdu. Esveillez vostre teefve volunté, deplurez tant vostre malvesté cum vus avez espace. Ici tuchez si vus avez dormi en lit de argent u de yvoire u en tapiz u en noble coiltes de paile u en autre de trop grant pris, si vus avez mangié en vessel d'or u d'argent u en autre delit avez esté. Car tutes icés choses sunt de Egipte e ne apartienent nient a la Tere de Promissiun.[vi]

---

[i] CL 'esté jugé'. [ii] O 'saviet', L 'saviez'. [iii] C 'fet', L 'fait'. [iv] C 'pou'. [v] CL 'entre'. [vi] CL omit the passage from 'Esveillez' to 'Promissiun'.

Here, consider whether you have neglected to receive the Body of Our Lord when you ought to have done, because you didn't want to relinquish your sins; and whether you have received it unworthily or without devotion, for in either of these you were committing mortal sin. Consider whether you have had evil suspicion of anybody, or have done anything to cause anybody to be suspicious of you, for both are wrong. As Saint Jerome said, "We must avoid all evil suspicions, and whatever anybody may reasonably pretend as a bad thing against you."[13] Also consider whether you have given judgement in something you are not certain about. The Apostle forbids this, saying, "Who are you, to judge another's servant? If he stands, he stands by his lord; if he falls, he falls by his lord."[14] Consider whether you have been too talkative in church or at meals, and remember the rich man, of whom the Gospel says he was tormented in his tongue for that.[15]

The Ninth Commandment is this: "You shall not covet what is your neighbour's." Here, beware of covetousness, which is too great a love of gain; and avarice, which is too great a love of keeping things; ambition, which is too great a love of mastery. Look at how you have behaved in these things. Covetousness in clerks makes for simony, in knights pillage or rape, in burghers usury and fraud, in gluttons and gamesters theft. And because covetousness and vain desire are so common in people, this engenders idleness. Here, examine yourself for idleness, that is, whether you have wasted in vanity the time granted you in which to do penance. Consider the time that has passed, hasten towards the company of angels, yearn for the heritage you have lost. Waken your lukewarm will, weep for your sinfulness, while you have time to do so. Here, think about whether you have slept in a bed of silver or of ivory, or in tapestries or rich quilts of fine cloth, or in other stuff of very great price; whether you have eaten from vessels of gold or silver, or have been in other pleasures. For all these things are from Egypt,[16] and do not belong in the Promised Land.

---

[13] "Jeronime" in text. If Jeremiah is intended, the reference may be to Jer. 9:4–5. But cf. *PL* 23:355 & 26:780 (Jerome); and *PL* 30:399 (Pseudo-Jerome).

[14] Rom. 14:4.

[15] See Luke 16:19–25.

[16] In the Middle Ages, Egypt was considered the land of pagan luxury, which could be justifiably be plundered by the righteous because the pagans did not deserve their riches. This commonplace, found in Augustine's *On Christian Teaching*, usually refers to intellectual riches; see *De Doctrina* (ed. and trans. Green), Bk. II, 144–47 (pp. 124–27).

[L]e dime comandement est itel : 'Vus ne coveiterez pas la femme vostre prome.' Ici pernez garde de icele malveise eschele[i] par laquele l'en descent en enfern, dont le premier degré est delit, le secund cunsentement, le tierz overaine, le quart custume, le quint desperance. E pur ceo que l'en fait multes sorceries pur femmes comquere ici tuchez ces choses : si vus creustes as sorceries ou les feistes ou donastes essample ou cunsentistes, si vus gardastes les anz e les tens e la novele lune e enchantemenz e feistes force de un home encuntrer u autre sicum les fols dient 'Jeo aveie bon ou mal encuntrer al matin.' Ki fait cel mal, dit seint Agustin, 'Il perd le sacrement de baptesme.'

Enaprés per[f.85ra]nez garde si vus avez tenu les comandemenz de l'Evvangille, qui sont icels : 'donez e l'en durra a vus', 'relessez, e l'en relerra a vus', 'amez vos enemis', 'requerez pur cels ki vus pursiwent', 'suffreiz ke les petiz viengient a mei.' Ici prengent garde cil qui unt fiz u filles k'il nes recraent[ii] pas del servise Deu pur la vanité del siecle. E si vus lur avez apris lur dreite creance, uncore cerchez vostre cunscience si vus poez trover les pecchez que saint Pol numbre en une epistle k'il escrit as Romains en laquele il dit ke il i ad aucuns ke sunt repleni de tutes malvestiez, ceo est asaver de malice, de avarice, de fornicaciun, de felonie, de envie, de homicides, de tençun, de tricherie, de maligneté, de semence de descord, de detraction, de orgoil, de folies que sunt senz assez ;[iii] e ke ne sunt cumpaignables e senz misericorde e ke sont controvers[iv] de mal e ke ne sont pas obeisanz a lur pere e a lur mere e ke ne sont pas composez. Composé est cil ki religiousement se porte en vesture e en alure. Ici pernez garde si vus avez surfait de dras, si vostre robe est trop trainante e vostre chauceure trop estreite, si vus avez orguillouse ceinture u fermals ou anels ou ganz u seles[v] ou garlandesche d'or ou d'argent, car [f.85rb] par icés choses desire li home e est desiré. E si est li un e li autre grant pecchié e desirer e aver en volenté de estre desiré une chose. Sachez ke li Apostle dit ke ces pecchiez ke ci avum numbré ke cil qui tels funt sont digne de mort pardurable e ne mie sulement cil kis funt, mes ensenblement cil kis cunsentent as fesances. Vus cunsentez, vus ne [re]pernez pas le peccheur, mais par suffrance le noriscez en sa folie.

[i] MS (and C) exil. [ii] C 'garde que ont fiz u filles que il ne recreent'. [iii] om. (C). [iv] L 'controve'. [v] C 'sollers', L 'sodlers'.

The Tenth Commandment is this: "You shall not covet your neighbour's wife." Here, pay attention to that evil ladder by which one goes down into hell: whose first rung is desire, the second consent, the third deed, the fourth habit, and the fifth despair. And because people resort to many sorcerers' tricks to conquer women, think now on these things: whether you have believed in sorcery, or practised it, or set an example, or consented to it; whether you watched the seasons, the weather, the new moon, enchantment; whether you contrived a meeting with somebody, or suchlike, as fools say "I shall encounter something good — or bad — in the morning." Saint Augustine says, of whoever does this wickedness, "He loses the sacrament of baptism."[17]

Then, consider whether you have kept the Commandments of the Gospel, which are these: "Give, and it shall be given to you"; "Release, and it shall be released unto you"; "Love your enemies"; "Pray for those who persecute you"; "Let the little ones come to me."[18] And let those who have sons and daughters make sure they are not idle in the service of God for the world's vanity. And if you have taught them right belief, search again in your conscience in order to find those sins that Saint Paul enumerates in a letter he wrote to the Romans, in which he says there are those who are full of all kinds of wrongdoing: that is to say, of malice, avarice, fornication, felony, envy, murder, quarrelling, trickery, malignity, sowing discord, detraction, pride, follies which bring no reward; and [the children] are not sociable, lack mercy, invent wickedness, are disobedient to their father and mother, and are without gravity.[19] A grave person is one who behaves religiously in dress and in bearing. Now, consider whether you have too many clothes, whether your robe trails on the ground or your hose is too tight, whether you have ostentatious belts or buckles or rings or gloves or shoes, or garlands of gold or silver, for through these things a man desires and is desired. And both the one and the other is great sin: to desire and to wish to be desired are the same thing. Know that the Apostle says that those who commit such sins as we have listed here are worthy of everlasting death; and not only they who commit them but also they who consent to their being committed.[20] You consent when you do not reproach the sinner but, by allowing him, you nourish him in his folly.

---

[17] Cf. *FM* (pp. 582–85), which quotes Decretum 26, question 7; the note refers to Augustine as quoted in Gratian II.26.7.16 (1:1045–46).

[18] Luke 6:38 & 37 (*forgive, and ye shall be forgiven*); Matt. 5:44 & Luke 6:27; Mark 10:14 & Luke 18:16.

[19] Rom. 1:29–31.

[20] Rom. 1:32.

Enaprés pernés garde si vus estes en charité, car ki est dehors il est en male vie. Dont esgardez vostre vie, si vus i trovez les quince degrez de cherité lesquels li apostle recunte en une epistle en laquele il dit issi : 'Charité est suffrance e debonerté, charité n'ad pas envie, ne fait pas mal, n'est pas orgoilluse ne coveitouse, ne quiert pas sa loenge mes a Jesu Crist, n'est pas de legier curucé,[i] ne pense nul mal, ne esjoist[ii] pas de malveisté mes ad joie de verité, totes choses porte od suffrance, de nule rien n'ad suspeçun.' Cerche chescun sa cunscience ententivement e veie si il trove ces poinz. Si issi est, rendez graces a Deu e si autrement le trove, seit mult dolent, e nuit e jur, seit entur deçk'il les ait. Car 'Ki charité ne n'ad il li defailent tuz biens.' Enaprés pernét bone garde [f.85va] si vus avez fait les overaines de misericorde. Ceo est asaver si vus avez enseigné celui ke nul ou poi bien sout, si vus avez peu le fameilus, si vus avez doné a beivre a celui ki out sei, si vus avez vestu celui ki fu nu, si vus avez eschaufé celui ki [out freit, si avét herbergé celui ki] out mestier de hostel, si vus avez visité le malade, si vus avez enseveli le mort.

Aprés pernez garde si vus avez les vertuz que nostre Seignur enseigne en l'Evangile, car il dit issi : 'Cil sont benurez ki sont povre de espirit, car il sunt seignurs del regné Deu ; e benurez sont li deboneires, car il averont la tere ke senz fin dure ; e benurez sont cil qui plurent, car il serront cumfortez, e benurez sont cil ki coveitent dreiturreuté, car il averunt merci ; [e benurez sunt cil ki sunt merciables, que il avront merci ;] e benurez sunt cil ki unt [le] quer[iii] net, car il verrunt Deu ; e benurez sont [cil] ki sont les paisibles, car il serrunt apelez les fiz Deu ; e benurez sont cil qui soeffrent honte[iv] pur justice, car il averont le regné Deu.' Sachez ke si cestes vertuz avez e bien les gardez parfitement, benurez serrez, e si vus n'avez pas, faites a Deu vostre pleinte en confessiun, sis purrez recoverir. Uncore si vus eez nul bien empris e pus lessez,[v] car nul ne puet estre coruné ki bien n'ad chevé. E pernez garde [f.85vb] si aprés vostre pecchié avez esté haité que vus le feistes. De ceo dit seint Gregorie que nule rien ne desplest tant a Deu com orguil aprés pecchié.

---

[i] CL 'corage'. [ii] MS out. [iii] MS quert. [iv] MS (and C) e ont; L 'suffreite ont'. [v] C 'cesset que', L 'cessez'.

Next, take thought whether you are in charity, for whoever is not in charity is in wickedness of life. So examine your life, whether you find there the Fifteen Degrees of Charity that the Apostle names in a letter where he says this: "Charity is patience and meekness; charity envies not, does no harm, is neither proud nor covetous. It seeks not its own praise but that of Jesus Christ. It is not easily angered, it thinks no evil, it rejoices not in wickedness but rejoices in the truth. It bears all things with patience, and is suspicious of nothing."[21] Let everybody search his conscience diligently to see whether he finds these points. If it is so, give thanks to God. If he finds that it is not, let him be very sorrowful, both night and day, let him busy himself earnestly until he has them. For "Who has not charity, all virtues fail him."[22] Then, take good care that you have performed the Works of Mercy. That is, whether you have taught him who knew little or nothing, fed the hungry, given drink to him who thirsted, clothed the naked, warmed him who was cold, sheltered him who needed lodging, visited the sick, buried the dead.[23]

Then, consider whether you have the Blessings that Our Lord teaches in the Gospel, for he says this: "Blessed are those who are poor in heart, for they are lords of God's kingdom. And blessed are the meek, for they shall have the land that endures for ever. Blessed are those who weep, for they shall be comforted; and blessed are those who covet righteousness, for they shall receive mercy; and blessed are the merciful, who shall receive mercy. And blessed are the pure in heart, for they shall see God; and blessed are those who are peaceable, for they shall be called the sons of God. Blessed are those who suffer shame for the sake of justice, for they shall have the kingdom of God."[24] Know that if you have, and keep perfectly, these virtues, you shall be blessed. And if you have not, make your prayer and confession to God, and you can recover them. Also ask yourself whether you have begun any good thing and then let it fall, for none can be crowned who has achieved nothing good. And consider whether, after your sin, you were happy to have done it. On this matter, Saint Gregory says that nothing displeases God so much as pride after sin.[25]

---

[21] 1 Cor. 13:4–7.

[22] 1 Cor. 13:1–3. The "virtues" include knowledge, prophecy, and faith.

[23] Matt. 25:35–39. The Gospel lists six acts of mercy, and includes visiting prisoners. This author does not mention prisoners, but adds teaching the ignorant, warming the cold, and burying the dead (total eight).

[24] Matt. 5:3–10. The eight Beatitudes are not in quite the same order (2 and 3 are reversed), but they are all present.

[25] Cf. *PL* 76:345.

Uncore pernez garde que Damnedeu vus ad doné menbres pur lui servir, dunt veez bien si vus les eez mis en sun servise. Comencez al chief ou sunt les cinc[i] sens, ceo est asaver veue, oïe, odurer, guster, e le quint reest apelé tuchement, ceo apartient as mains. Veez bien si ces sens avez despendu al servise Deu u al servise al Diable. Enaprés pernez garde de chescun menbre jeskes as piez si vus les avez folement despenduz. Si vus repentez tant come vus espace avez e tut apertement a vostre cumfessur tutes voz villainies cuntez ne pur nule hunte[ii] ne laissez, car sicum dit seint Salomon 'Une hunte meinet li home a joie', ceo est icele ki l'en ad en disant son pecchié. Un autre hunte est ke le maine en enfern, celi ke li fait lesser a dire sun pecchié. Pensez estreitement de la grant hunte ke li peccheur averad al grant jugement quant li mond ses ledz pecchiez verra ke il ne poeit conoistre ici pur hunte a un sul home. Certes mult se tendra donc huni quant il orra diables encuntre li levier mult led cri e quant il serra [f.86ra] de la bele cumpaignie [Deu] sevré e as diables liveré, dunc serra il mult esgaré.

Ore pernez garde cum vus devez voz pecchiez dire en cumfessiun. Al comencement veez ki vus estes, si vus seez clerc u lai, de quele language, de quel age, de quele condicion, de quele science, de quel estat. Ceo est asaver le quel vus estes, haute persone u base, sicom evesqe ou prestre, car tutes icés choses agregent le pecché. Aprés veez quei ceo seit que vus avez pecchié, si en dit ou en fait ou en penser, ou devant gent ou priveement ; e par quei[iii] vus avez pecchié, car icés avez vus tué quant a l'alme ; e quantes feiz vus avez pecchié e par quele acheisun, si pur delit aveir ou l'en vus fist force e coment vus avez fait vostre pecchié, c'est asaveir en quele maniere e quant, si a jur de feste ou en vigile ou a jor de jeune. Quant sicum est ici escrit serrez cumfés, dunc aprimes vus gardez que vus ne recheez, car le drap que sovent chiet al tai, plus est ennuius de laver. Pur ceo fuiez occasiun de pecchier e si aventure avient que vus pecchiez, senz delai a cunfession alez, car bien savez ke si une femme amast un autre home ke sun espus e ele fust repentante e se volsist retraire mais son avultre nel vousist pas, si ele so[f.86rb]vent le acusast vers sun seignur, il en avereit poür de mes la requere. Autresi est il del Diable. Il ad hunte e poür quant il [est] acusé par confession a Nostre Seignur.

---

[i] MS quatre. [ii] O 'home'. [iii] MS queeus.

Also, reflect that the Lord God has given you members with which to serve him; therefore consider whether you have put them to work in his service. Begin at the head, where the Five Senses are: that is, sight, hearing, smell, taste; and the fifth is called touch, which belongs to the hands. See whether you have used these senses in the service of God or in the service of the Devil. Then consider every limb, down to the feet, and whether you have used them foolishly.[26] Repent while you have time, and openly tell your confessor all your wickednesses, nor leave out any for shame, for thus says Saint Solomon: "A shame leads a man to joy"[27] — that is, the one you feel when telling your sin. There is another shame, that leads one to Hell: the one which makes you neglect to say your sin. Think seriously about the great shame the sinner will have at the Great Judgement when the whole world will see his filthy sins, which he cannot for shame acknowledge here to just one man. He shall surely feel himself shamed when he hears the devils raising a horrible outcry against him; and when he is cut off from the fair company of God and delivered to the devils, then shall he be truly lost.

Now consider how you must say your sins in confession. At the beginning, consider who you are: whether clerk or lay; what is your language, age, condition, learning, and estate. That is to say: are you a highly placed person or lowly, such as a bishop or a priest, for all these things aggravate sin. Then consider how it is you have sinned: whether in word or deed or thought, in the presence of people or privately, and by whom you have sinned, for it is these you have killed in their soul. And how many times you have sinned and for what reason, whether to have pleasure or because somebody forced you to, and how you committed your sin, that is, in what way and when: whether on a feast day, or during a vigil, or on a fast day. When you have confessed as it is written here, first watch that you do not fall again, for the cloth that often falls in the mud becomes much more tiresome to wash. Therefore flee the opportunity to sin, and if it should so happen that you sin, go to confession without delay. For you know that if a woman loved a man other than her husband, and she were repentant and wished to draw back, but her seducer did not so wish; if she accused him at once to her husband, then he would be afraid to beg her further. So it is with the Devil. He has shame and fear when he is accused in confession to Our Lord.

---

[26] See Is. 1:6.

[27] Cf. Prov. 13:18.

Aprés ceste confessiun de pecchié vient une autre que mult est douce, si est apelé cunfessiun de loenge, quant li peccheur rend graces a sun seignur Jesu Crist ke de tuz mals l'ad deliveré. E quant celui qu'il deveit par dreit aver geté al fu de enfern ad ja apelé entre ses amis, quant de si hord liu l'ad pris e en si bel liu asis, e rend uncore grace de ceo k'il le garde, ke mes ne chiece en vil pecché, issi est le peccheur mult joius e haité e loe sun creatur nuit e jur. Ici pert il tote icele mauvaise savur k'il aveit avant del hord delit de sun pecchié, si entre en un grant douçur que vient de la misericorde e de la grace Dieu, dunt dit li prophete 'Gustez,' fait il, 'e veez come suef e dulz est li Sire. Cil est benuré ke met sa esperance en li.' Pur ceo vus, ki estes de peccheurs[i] sainz devenuz, dutez le Seignur, car il n'averunt ja falté[ii] de bien ke lui aiment e dutent, ces[iii] sunt les dous gardains que Deu ad mis pur garder ses[iv] amis, ceo est asaver amur e poür ; poür les fait fuir pecchié, amur vertu enbrascer, poür amoneste de enfern [f.86va] esloingner, amur fait force al ciel aproscier.

Ceste bone poür vient de treis choses ; ki en memorie les ad, ja senz poür ne serra. La premere est hidur de mort, ki vient a ure [nient] certeine ; la secunde est la grant destresce del grant jugement ou rien nule si dreit nun irrad avant ; la tierce chose est ke le feu d'enfern ja ne esteindera. Le autre gardein, c'est amur, vient ausi de treis choses, ceo est asaver que li home ait en ferme memorie coment Deu le cria pur estre parcener de sa grant joie e pur sa puissance e sun grant [s]aveir e sa grant deboneirté senz fin loer. Ceo est la Sainte Trinité, Pere e Fiz e Saint Espirit. La secunde chose est la gloriuse passiun Nostre Seignur k'il suffri pur sun serf de peine achater. Ki velt ceste duce chose parfitement penser ne purra ja feintement amer. La tierce chose est la grant debonairté nostre Seignur ke mustre aprés baptesme al peccheur ki tut ad ublié les dous granz biens ke avant avum nomé. Icest avient chescun jur, mes que li fols[v] serf refusé ait sun dulz Seignur tut li pardune. E aprés, si lealment le sert, le regné del Ciel franchement li done. Ki ces choses lealment recorde mult se penera de si bon seignur leaument amer.[vi]

---

[i] CL 'pechie'. [ii] CL 'defaute'. [iii] The text from here to the end of the section is found in MS Dublin, Trinity College 374 (s.xiii^2), ff.42vb–43rb, as part of a compendium which includes a series of meditations and Adam of Exeter's exposition of the Pater Noster (see above, p. 321). [iv] The text of C stops here. [v] L 'faus'. [vi] The Dublin text ends here.

After this confession of sins comes another that is very sweet. It is called the confession of praise, when the sinner gives thanks to his Lord Jesus Christ who has delivered him from all evil. And when he, who should by rights have thrown him into the fire of Hell, has called him to be among his friends, when he has taken him from such a vile place and put him in such a beautiful one, and he gives yet more thanks that he preserves him from falling ever again into filthy sin; so is the sinner very joyful and happy and praises his Creator night and day. Here he loses all that disgusting smell that he had before, from filthy delight in his sin, and enters into a great sweetness that comes from the mercy and grace of God, concerning which the Prophet says: "Taste," he says, "and see how soft and sweet is the Lord. He is blessed who puts his trust in him."[28] Therefore you, who have from sinners become saints, fear the Lord, for those who love and fear him will never lack his goodness. These are the two guardians that God has set to watch over his friends: that is to say, love and fear. Fear makes them flee sin, love makes them embrace virtue; fear warns them to keep away from Hell, love pushes them to approach Heaven.

This benign fear comes from three things. Whoever keeps them in mind will never be without fear. The first is terror of death, which comes nobody knows when. The second is the great fear of the Great Judgement, when no creature can go forward into Heaven but the righteous. The third thing is that the fire of Hell will never be extinguished. The other guardian, that is love, also comes from three things. That is, that man should keep steadfastly in mind how God created him to be a partner in his great joy, and for his power and great wisdom and great goodness praise him for ever. That is the Holy Trinity: Father, Son, and Holy Spirit. The second thing is the glorious Passion of Our Lord that he suffered to redeem his servants from pain. Whoever tries to think of this thing perfectly can never love half-heartedly. The third thing is the great goodness of Our Lord that he shows after baptism to the sinner who has completely forgotten the two great benefits that we have just named. This happens every day, but our gentle Lord pardons the foolish servant who has rejected him. And afterwards, if he serves him loyally, he freely gives him the Kingdom of Heaven. He who faithfully records these things will strive hard faithfully to love such a good Lord.

---

[28] Ps. 34:8 (33:9 in *LV*).

[f.86vb] Damnedeu par sa grant duçur e par la requeste de sa gloriuse Mere doinst a chescun peccheur e peccheresce de ses pecchez en icest siecle veraie repentance e verai confessiun e suffisant amendement, par quei puisse cel Seignur senz fin amer ki a ses amis rendrad cel loer ke lange ne puet recunter ne quer ne suffist a penser.[i] Amen.

[i] L adds 'Ceo doint Deu ke de cele compaignie seum ou n'a jamais si joie nun.'

May the Lord God, through his great sweetness and through the request of his glorious Mother, give to each sinner — man or woman — true repentance, true confession, and adequate satisfaction for their sins in this world, by which may he or she for ever love this Lord, who will give his friends such reward that tongue cannot tell nor heart suffice to imagine.[29] Amen.

[29] L adds "May God grant us to be among this company, where there is nought but joy for ever."

Part VI

Virtues and Rewards

Chapter 14

Three Vows

Introduction[1]

This three-part treatise (a prose sermon on the text of Paul's Epistle to the Romans 12:1) is found in Dublin, Trinity College MS 374 (D.1.29) (s.xiii^{2}), ff.69va–73rb;[2] no other manuscripts are listed. The piece is addressed to those who have dedicated themselves to God: these are almost certainly male, not female, readers, although it is not clear what kind of community is being addressed.[3] St Paul's Guide to Chastity, Poverty, and Silence is entitled a Sermon by D&B, but there is nothing to say "read ... or hear this," and no address to audience: merely the statement "treis choses sunt ...." The Preface refers to those (third person) committed to God; then, that the apostle speaks to us (first person) all. Only the Latin "fratres" passage is addressed to "vos" (second person). Besides the Bible, there are cited: Jerome, Benedict, the *Golden Legend* and *Vitas Patrum* (St Anthony and the Abbot), and Terence the "pagan."

The section on Silence discusses the sins of the tongue, which is lodged in a wet place and so easily slips into wrongdoing. It also explains how the soul, God's donkey, must be fastened to the hitching-post of silence in order to eat from God's manger. Then, like Samuel, it will be able to hear God's word. Both these ideas appear in the *Ancrene Wisse*, and both on the same page (as in our present text). However, the themes, together with a number of relevant Bible quotations, are arranged in a different order and so it is not likely that one text borrows directly from the other.[4]

---

[1] D&B 651, prose, "Sermon on Romans 12:1."

[2] For details, see the Introduction to Pater Noster, p. 74 above.

[3] One would expect monks to be able to read Latin, though many biblical quotations are translated or rather paraphrased into French.

[4] Savage and Watson note (in *AW* trans., p. 76; note 37 is on p. 352) that the whole passage is developed from Gregory's *Regula Pastoris* III:14 — also see Augustine, *Sermones* CLXXX.xi.12 (*PL* 38:978). See also Watson and Wogan-Browne 2004, for the *Compileison* and its relationship to *AW* (and Appendix, below).

Text

[Preface] [f.69va] Li Apostle parole a ceus ke a Deu se sunt pris e dit : *Obsecro vos per misericordiam Dei, fratres, ut exhibeatis corpora vestra hostiam viventem, sanctam,* [*Deo*] *placentem, racionabile obsequium vestrum* [Rom. 12:1]. Li Apostle dit a nus tuz : 'Jeo vus conjur par la misericorde Deu ke vus donez vos cors a ceo k'il vif sacrefise seient e a Deu pleisant e ke vostre service seit renable devant Deu.'

Treis choses sunt par unt la gent ki a Deu se sunt pris poent a lur prosme bon essample [f.69vb] doner e Deu paer e les seinz angles, c'est a saver s'il gardent la chasteté de cors e de pensé ke li Apostle apele *sanctimoniam*, c'est netté de fet e de pensé ; s'il vivent sanz propreté ; s'il se tenent en renable silence.

[Part 1] Iceste chasteté avant dite covent estre gardé en tuz les membres del cors, c'est asaver que nul des membres ne se besse a lecherie ne a felonie ne a legerté, kar un poet sun cors suiller ne mie sul par fornicacion, mes en chescune desordeinee contenement, ke nul des membres fet, sicum l'autorité dit : 'La mort entre par nos[i] fenestres', c'est le pecché entre a l'alme par les cinc sens del cors. Pur neent se fiera nul en chasteté de la char si le quer est corrumpu, ou de malice ou de fole volunté ou de malveis delit, kar al quer de l'home est tute la mort de l'alme ou tute la vie. De ceo dit Salomon en ses Proverbes : 'De tut vostre poer gardez vostre quer, kar de la vient la vie.' E Deu meismes dit : 'Del quor ist ceo que suille la gent', kar par bons desirs ou par malveis est l'alme salvé ou dampné. Mes [f.70ra] pur ceo ke de l'alme e de la char est une grant unité en la jointe de une persone, si fet a purveer ententivement que le delit de la char ne traie l'alme a sa consence e que hom ne doint tant de force a la char par unt ele munte en orguil e en prenge estrif a l'alme e deviengne dame de l'ostel ke par dreit deit estre ancele. Assez en i a el mund a ore que par descrecion e par fine religion a lur avis manguent assez e beivent e dorment aprés e quident estre en sure vie.

[i] MS vos.

Translation

[Preface] The Apostle speaks to those who have dedicated themselves to God, and says: *I beseech you therefore, brethren, by the mercies of God, that ye present your bodies a living sacrifice, holy, acceptable unto God, which is your reasonable service.* The Apostle says to us all: "I charge you, by the mercy of God, that you give your bodies to be a living sacrifice, pleasing to God; and may your service be fitting before God."

There are three things by which those dedicated to God may give good example to their neighbours, and by which they may please God and the holy angels: that is, if they keep the chastity in body and thought that the Apostle calls *holiness*,[1] that is purity in deed and thought; if they live without property; if they keep a fitting silence.

[Part 1] This chastity just mentioned must be kept in all members of the body: that is to say, none of the members should stoop to lechery, felony, or levity. For one can soil one's body not only by fornication but by any unseemly behaviour that any member does. Thus the Authority says: "Death enters by our windows,"[2] — that is, sin enters the soul by the five senses of the body. In vain may anybody trust in chastity of the flesh, if the heart is corrupted, either by malice or by stupid wilfulness, or by wicked pleasure: for in the heart of man is all the death of the soul, or all the life. Of this, Solomon says in his Proverbs: "Guard your heart with all your might, for thence cometh life."[3] And God himself says, "Whatever corrupts the people comes from the heart,"[4] for by good desires or wicked the soul is saved or damned. But because there is unity between the soul and the flesh when they are joined in a person, so one must watch carefully lest the delight of the flesh draw the soul's consent; and one must not give so much power to the flesh that it rises pridefully and quarrels with the soul and becomes lady of the house when it should properly be handmaiden. There are enough people in the world now who, by moral judgement and by fine religion, they think, eat well and drink, and sleep afterwards, believing themselves to be assured of life.

---

[1] See Heb. 12:14.

[2] Jer. 9:21. It is clear here that by "the Authority," Jeremiah is meant (not so with other cases).

[3] Prov. 4:23.

[4] Matt. 15:19.

Veient il qui ceo quident si la chaude char ne fet fumé e si le ventre plein ne fet pensé e si le lung dormir ne tout hure de hurer e talant de plorer e de ses pechez penser e le jugement Deu entreoblier. Seint Pol chastie sa char e le met[i] en servage de feim e de sei e de freit e de veilles e d'autres laburs assez e o tut ceo ne poet il sei deliverer de l'aguillun de la char. Jesu Crist meismes encontre sa bataille jeuna la quarenteine e en junant venqui le Diable pur nus enseigner a quel chef nus devom comencer si nous volums nos adversaries confundre. Dunc est plus seure chose a sivre teus [f.70rb] mestres que sote volenté.

Mult nus estoet estre pensifs e purveant si nus volums nos almes salver, kar n'ad nule si greve mort cum de l'alme ne nule si perilluse garde. Quel chose poet um plus tost aver fet ke tuer une alme ? Quel sete est plus tost forgé que peché ki poet neis governer son penser, enteimes de son fet ? Pur ceo ne deit nul someiller en peresce mes veiller ententivement e esforciblement entur son salu, kar 'nostre adverser li Diable ruist sicum leon e nus environe tut tens e quert k'il puisse devorer.' Mult est sa geule grant, tost ad fet de nus miettes cume nus sumes si Deu ne seit od nus. Il est esperit e parole esperitalment e sutilment a nostre esperit. E il amoneste a amer tutes choses passantes e perissantes pur fere nus passer les comandemenz Deu e perir en nos pechez. Ki est que ne deive duter si felon e si sutil enemi, ki nus forsclore ne poums de nus par mur ne par fosse ne par autre forscelesce ne nus nel poum tuer d'espé ne de autre arme ? De lui dit Deus a seint Job : 'Cum il est gluz e engrés sur nus. Il transglutera la fluie,' fet il, 'si ne [f.70va] se esmerveillera mie, si ad neis fiance que tut le flum Jordan li entre en la gule.' Par le fluie entendez tuz les paens e les mescreanz, par le flum Jordan tuz ceus ki sunt baptisez la ki seinteté[ii] li veil anteif redute ki tant fet de mal e tant ad esprové fleblés e changanbleté de home, ki li primer que Deus fist de sa bele main getta de Parays, dé duze conpaignuns ke Deus eslust en ravist l'un a Deus meismes, neis a li tempter estendi sa male main. Pur ceo vus di cest, que nul ne se fie en seinteté de sei ne en salveté de lui fors sul en la merci nostre Seignur.

[i] MS ment. [ii] MS s. quideus ki.

Do they not see, who think thus, that warm flesh leads to hot-headedness? does not a full belly make wicked thoughts? does not long sleeping rob them of time to pray, of desire to weep and think of their sins — and make them forget the judgement of God? Saint Paul chastened his flesh and enslaved it to hunger, thirst, cold, vigils, and many other labours; and with all this he could not free himself from the pricking of the flesh.[5] Jesus Christ himself during his battle fasted forty days, and while fasting overcame the Devil, to show us where to begin if we wish to confound our adversaries. To follow such masters is a surer way than to follow one's stupid desires.

We must be very thoughtful and watchful indeed if we wish to save our souls, for there is no more grievous death than that of the soul; and no safe-keeping more perilous. What could one do more quickly, than kill a soul? What arrow is more quickly forged than sin, that can govern even one's thoughts, even one's deeds? Therefore none must drowse in idleness, but must watch intently and strongly over their salvation, for "our adversary the Devil roars like a lion and surrounds us constantly, seeking whom he may devour."[6] Great is his maw; he will soon have made morsels of us, were God not with us. He is spirit, and he speaks spiritually and subtly to our spirit. He urges us to love all things passing and perishable, to make us neglect the commandments of God and perish in our sins. Who should not fear so wicked and so subtle an enemy, whom we cannot shut out from us by any wall or ditch or other fortress, nor kill by any sword or other weapon? Of him God said to Saint Job, "How ravenously and savagely he comes upon us. He will drink up the flood," said he, "he will not wonder, he is even confident that the entire River of Jordan can be engulfed in his mouth."[7] By the flood, understand all pagans and unbelievers; by the River of Jordan, all those who are baptized there, whose holiness the Ancient One fears — he who works so much ill and who has so proved the feebleness and fickleness of man; he who turned out of Paradise the first that God made with his fair hand; who, of the twelve companions chosen by God, ravished away one [Judas] from God himself; to whom he even extended his evil hand, to tempt him. Therefore I say this to you, that none should trust in his own sanctity nor in his salvation, but only in the mercy of Our Lord.

---

[5] Cf. II Cor. 11:27.

[6] I Peter 5:8.

[7] Job 40:23 (40:18 in *LV*).

Nus chaitis ki vivoms en cest reaum[e] de umbre de mort, en la enfermeté de la char, en liu de temptacion, travaillums en treis maneres, kar nus sumes legers a deceivere, e febles a ben fere, e freles a rester. Si nus volums juger entre ben e mal, ne savoms al chief venir ; si nus començom nul ben fere, tost defailloms ; si nus esforçums encuntre pecché, tost sumes abatuz e surmontez. Pur ceo est benuerez ki tuzjurs est pourus, ki ren ne se fie en sei, ki tuz regarde ses maus e ses fe[f.70vb]blesces e si nul ben ad en lui, dute qu'il ne seit corrumpu e nunplaisant a Deu. Aver fiance en sei n'est pas bone fei, mes cil est verraiment feel e de net quer ki de ren ne se creit ne de rens se fie en valur k'il eit, mes se tient si vil vessel defreint e deperdu. Cil ki issi perd s'alme, ki issi petit la prise, cil la garde a la vie pardurable.

[Part 2] Li secund chapitle est de lesser propreté. Dunc lessum nus tute ren e sivum le nu Jesu tuz nuz sicum li Apostle firent. Quant nus lessum pur lui ne mie sulement nos possessions ne la conpaignie de nos charneus amis mes neis de nos propre volentész, ke nus [ne] vivoms sulunc nostre avis, mes par ceus façoms nus overes qui en liu Deu nu sunt governurs. De cest governur dit nostre Sire : 'Ki vus oie, si oit mei e ki vus despit mei despit.' Neis s'il vivent malement e ben enseignent, si ne deit hom pas la science Deu despire pur vice de home. De ceus dit Deu meismes : 'Ço qu'il vus comandent ço facez ; sulunc lur overes ne fetes mie.' De iceste conversacion dit nostre Sire : 'Ki ne [f.71ra] guerpist pur mei quancqu'il ad ne porra[i] estre mon disciple', e 'Cil ki vient a mei e [ne] het pere e mere, freres e sorurs, femme e enfanz e neis s'alme pur mei ne porra estre mon disciple.' Cil het a dreit ses amis charneus ki pur amur ne pur compaignie de eus ren ne fet acuntre Deu ne ren ne lesse ke a Deu service apent. E cil het a dreit s'alme ki tutes ses volentez lesse pur la volenté Deu acomplir. Aillurs si dist Deus : 'Ki voldra venir aprés mei renie ses meismes e port sa croiz si me siwe', ausi cum s'il deist 'Ki me desire se despise, ki vout la mei volunté fere lest la sue, port sa croiz, soeffre peine. Sicum tuz mes membres furent en la croiz cloez, si seient les membres de mes disciples estreitement gardé de peché.'

[i] MS porrra.

We wretched ones who live in this realm of deathly shadow, in the instability of flesh, in the place of temptation, let us work in three ways: for we are easy to deceive, and weak in doing good, and frail in resisting [evil]. If we wish to judge between good and evil, we know not how to succeed; if we begin to do any good thing we quickly fail; if we steel ourselves against sin we are soon beaten and vanquished. Therefore he is blessed who is always afraid, who has no trust in himself, who examines all his ills and frailties and, if there is no good in him, fears that he is corrupt and unpleasing to God. To have faith in oneself is not good faith; but he who believes himself nothing and who trusts in the value of nothing, holding himself to be a dirty vessel, broken and lost, is truly faithful and clean of heart. He who thus loses his soul, who prizes it so little, it is he who keeps it unto eternal life.

[Part 2] The second chapter is to abandon property. So let us leave all things and follow the bare Jesus, all bare as the Apostles did.[8] When we forsake for him not only our possessions and the company of our worldly friends, but also even our own will, so that we live not according to our desire but do our works according to those who are our vicars of God. Of these vicars or governors Our Lord said, "Who hears you also hears me, and who despises you despises me."[9] Even if they live badly and teach well, men must not despise the knowledge of God because of human vice. Of them God himself says, "Whatever they command, do it; do not act according to their works."[10] Of this conversion to religious life, Our Lord said, "Whoever will not forsake for me what he has, cannot be my disciple," and "Whoever comes to me and hates not father, mother, brothers and sisters, wife and children, and even his own soul, cannot be my disciple."[11] A man rightly hates his worldly friends, if he will neither for their love nor for their company do anything against God, nor will neglect anything that pertains to the service of God. And he rightly hates his own soul, if he puts aside all his own will so as to accomplish the will of God. Elsewhere, God says thus: "He who wishes to come after me let him deny his own, carry his cross, and follow me"; likewise he says, "Who desires me despises himself; who wishes to do my will abandons his own, carries his cross, suffers pain.[12] Just as all my limbs were nailed to the Cross, so let the limbs of my disciples be strenuously kept from sin."

[8] See *PL* 22:1085 (Jerome).

[9] Luke 10:16.

[10] Matt. 23:3.

[11] Luke 14:33 & 26.

[12] Matt. 10:38: *And he that taketh not his cross, and followeth after me, is not worthy of me.* See also Luke 14:27.

Ben ad proprieté lessé qui tuz ses membres ad cloufiché *ut non extendant justi ad iniquitatem manus suas* [Ps. 124:3] *vel aliud aliquod membrum*. Pur ceo dist un sage home en le Ecclesiaste : 'Ne siwez pas voz coveitises mes de vostre volenté vus gardez cum de mort, kar si vus donez a vostre quer sun desir,' ceo dit, 'dunc fra il [f.71rb] vos enemis tuz joir sur vus.' Pur ço est sewre chose solunc le comandement Deu lesser nos choses, nus meismis, noz volentez a hune petite hurette, pur tut aver, quancque nus desiroms, pardurablement. Tutes lé richesces de cest mund e tutes les eises e tutes les delices nus dient a une voiz 'Volez vus nus aver ?' Dunc vus estuez desque en avant, si vus averez sanz fin en mult meillur estat ke nus ne sumes ore. Ci sumes cumme boschages qui les denz agacent, la serroms cume manne ki a chescun done savur de quanque il desire. Si ci vus pernez e[i] la vus perdez, pur ceo dit ben Salomon li sage : 'Honiz est la terre dunt enfes est rei e ou li princes manguent par matin.' Rei de la nostre terre, ço est de nostre cors. Resun e volenté : resun est rei sené, volenté est rei enfant. Dunc est hom le cors e l'alme ou volenté regne. Li prince qui manguent matin sunt les cinc sens del cors ke manguent matin quant talent lur prent en ceste siecle a tut lur poers e ren ne se estuent deskes a la ceine Deu.

Dunc serrunt confunduz li riche delicius quant cil qui pur Deu poveres furent [f.71va] en tere en bone pacience serrunt assis a haut deis de tute pleinté ke jamés ne faudera. Dunc si verrunt acomplie la science ke Davit dit en la psalme : *Divites eguerunt et esurierunt .i. egebunt e[t] esurient inquirentes autem dominum non minuentur omni bono* [Ps. 33:11], c'est ke 'Les riches serrunt poveres e famillus e cil poveres ki Deu quistrent en tere n'averunt defaute de nul ben.' Ne se espoent mie proudome s'il a[ii] aucune partie de aver terrien, s'il ben l'use en tele manere qu'il le voille autant a un autre ami Deu cum a sei ou plus, s'il ad greinur mester, n'est pas proprieté. Ki si ad aver, enz est sergant de comune e ki ben seit ço, dit l'autorité, bon gré se purchace.

---

[i] MS e ci e. [ii] MS si la.

He whose limbs are all nailed down has indeed forsaken property: *For the rod of the wicked shall not rest upon the lot of the righteous; lest the righteous put forth their hands unto iniquity.*[13] Therefore a wise man says in Ecclesiasticus, "Do not follow your desires, but guard yourself from your own will as from death; for if you give your heart its desire," he says, "that will cause all your enemies to rejoice over you."[14] Therefore it is a certain thing — to forsake our possessions, our selves, and our wants for a little space, according to God's commandment, so that we shall have everything we desire for ever. All the riches of this world, and all its comforts and all its delights, speak to us with one voice: "Do you want to have us?" Therefore reserve us to yourself henceforth, and you will receive us, without end, in a far better state than that we are now in. We are like rough plants that hurt the teeth; there we shall be like manna, which gives to each one the flavour of what they wish for. Here you take and there you will lose; thus it is well said by Solomon the wise: "The land where a child is king, and where princes eat in the morning, is put to shame."[15] King of our land — that is, of our body. Reason and desire: reason is the adult king and desire is the child king. So is man, the body and the soul, where desire reigns. The princes who eat in the morning are the five senses of the body, who eat in the morning when the fancy takes them in this world, with all their power, and do not reserve themselves for the banquet of God.

Then the rich and self-indulgent shall be confounded, when those who were poor and patient for God on earth shall be seated at the high table of all plenty that shall never fail. Then they shall see accomplished the knowledge that David speaks in the psalm: *The young lions do lack, and suffer hunger: but they that seek the Lord shall not want any good thing.*[16] This means "The rich shall be poor and needy, and those poor folk who seek God on earth shall lack for no good thing." Let no gentleman be anxious if he has some store of worldly goods; if he uses it well and in such a way that he would wish as much to another friend of God as to himself or more, if he has more need — that is not property. Whoever has goods is thereby a servant of the community; and whoever knows this well, says the Authority, buys grace for himself.

---

[13] Ps. 125:3 in *AV.* Our author adds, in Latin, "nor any other limb, either"; this is is not in the psalm, and may be a warning about chastity.

[14] Ecclus. 18:30–31.

[15] Eccles. 10:16.

[16] Ps. 34:10. "The young lions" are in the Hebrew (see *Tanakh*, psalm 34); the Latin version "interprets" the verse. See also Luke 1:53.

Mes ki a cele perfeccion sunt venuz qu'il mettent aver e sen e poer e quanque il unt a la comune des amis Deu, de ceus porra hom dire seurement ceo ke fu dit ja de la compaignie des apostles : *Multitudinis credencium erat cor unum et anima una ; nec quisquam illorum* [*que possidebat*] *aliquid suum* [*esse*] *dicebat, sed erant illis omnia comunia* [Act. 4:32], c'est 'La multitudine des creanz ke aveient [f.71vb] un quer e un alme ne nul ne apela ren le soen propre, mes tut lur estoet commun quanque il aveient.' Ki Deu quert de quer, tant sai jeo de verité qu'il n'ad autre propreté de tut le remanant del mund ou soen quor eit repos.

[Part 3] Le tierz chapitle est de renable silence. Mult parole seint Escripture en plusurs lius de los de silence e mult la prise Ysaïe e dit : 'Tute l'onur de justise e de dreiture si est silence.' E Jeremie redit : 'Bon est a entendre la misericorde Deu o silence.' Salomon si dit ke la mort e la vie de l'home si est en mains de sa langue. Ceo purvit seint Beneit quant il dist en sa rule : 'Tuz les tens del mund deivent les religius estudier. Greignur chose est a estudier a silence tenir qu'il n'est a tere, kar estudie si est un angoisse entente de curage a ascune chose fere.' Multes choses fesom nus par recusement ou neis a enviz, mes nule ren ne fesum nus o estudie si mult ne vienge de quor e de grant entente. Cum c'est grevose chose e profitable a garder la lange dit seint Jake l'apostle : 'En mult de choses pechum [f.72ra] trestuz,' ceo dit, 'mes cil est parfiz ki en parole ne peche.' La lange, fet il, si est en lu moiste e de leger esculurge de dreite veie. 'N'i ad beste el mund ne oisel si salvage ke nature d'ome ne puisse danter. Sule lange ne poet [danter] nul genre de salvagine.'[i] Pur quei ? 'Ke langue', ceo dit, 'si est un mal ke ne repose, plein de venim.' E quel chose est plus periluse de venim ? E quel chose fet plus a eschivre ? Sicum venim esteint la vie, issi destrut mult parler tut l'estat de religion.

[i] The MS reading seems to be corrupt: Jac. 3:8 has . . . *linguam autem nullus hominum domare potest.*

But whoever has achieved such perfection that they give goods and knowledge and power and everything they possess to the community of God's friends, of these it may surely be said, as was once said of the company of the Apostles: *The multitude of them that believed were of one heart and of one soul: neither said any of them that ought of the things which he possessed was his own; but they had all things common.* That is, "the many faithful people, who were one in heart and soul, and had nothing to call their own, but whatever they had was common to all." Whoever seeks God with his heart, I know truly that he has no other property than all the rest of the world where his heart may have repose.

[Part 3] The third chapter is about proper silence. Holy Scripture says much, in many places, in praise of silence, and Isaiah prizes it greatly, saying, "All the honour of justice and righteousness is silence."[17] And Jeremiah says further, "It is good to understand the mercy of God with silence."[18] Solomon says that the death and life of man is in the keeping of his tongue.[19] Saint Benedict provided for this when he said in his Rule: "At all hours of the day and night the religious must study. It is a greater thing to study in silence than it is to keep quiet, for to study is a painful effort of the will to achieve anything."[20] We do many things out of contrariety, or even against our will, but we undertake nothing by way of study unless it comes very much from the heart and from great determination. How painful a thing, and how profitable, it is to hold one's tongue, says the apostle James: "We all sin in many things," he says, "but he who sins not in word is perfect."[21] The tongue, he goes on, is set in a moist place and easily slips from the right way. "There is no beast or bird in the world so wild that man's nature cannot tame it. But no kind of wild beast can tame the tongue." Why? "Because the tongue," he says, "is an evil that knows no rest — full of poison."[22] And what is more dangerous than poison? And what is more to be avoided? Just as poison extinguishes life, so too much talking destroys the whole estate of religion.

---

[17] Is. 32:17.

[18] Lam. 3:26.

[19] Prov. 21:23; see also Prov. 18:21.

[20] See Appendix (p. 423, note 9) below.

[21] James 3:2: *For in many things we offend all. If any man offend not in word, the same is a perfect man, and able also to bridle the whole body* — though he does not in fact go on to say anything about the tongue being in a moist place (see notes about *Ancrene Wisse* in the introduction to this piece, above, and in the Appendix).

[22] James 3:7–8: *For every kind of beasts, and of birds, and of serpents, and of things in the sea, is tamed, and hath been tamed of mankind: But the tongue can no man tame; it is an unruly evil, full of deadly poison.* See note opposite: the author is paraphrasing more freely than usual (unless the text is corrupt).

Salomon dit en ses Proverbes : 'Ausi cum est de la cité sanz porte e sanz mur ou tuz poent entrer ki volent, ausi est de celui ki soen esperit ne poet restreindre de mult parler.' Ensement dit Deus par Moysen : 'vessel sanz covercle si ert suillé devant mei.' De ceo dit un abbé parfit in *Vitas Patrum* a seint Antoine de dous freres ke a li se furent acompaignez en chiminant : 'Avez bons freres trovez, danz abés', ceo li dit seint Antoigne. E il lui respondi 'Bons sunt veraiment, mes a lur maison e a lur estres la ou il mainent [f.72rb] ne i ad point de porte. Quicumque vout entrer en lur estable si enmeine lur hane.' Nostre alme si est le hane Deu. Tutes les fiez qu'ele en estudie de recorder ses pechez devant Deu, a penaunce fere, ou recorder la grace ke Deu a fet a home en terre ou a recorder les peines d'enfer dunt Deu par sa grace ad les soens rechatez, ou a remembrer de la joie de lasus ke Deu ad a soens par sa sule grace conquis e apparaillez e de ceo li rend graces a sen poer e a tutes celes fiez est nostre alme lié a la creche Deu pur manger. De cele creche meine hom la cheitive alme quant hom la deslie du chevestre de silence e la lesse cure par les cheines de veines paroles. Les paroles qu'ele ot si mue sa entente e si devient veine e voide de ceo qu'ele avoit avant par bone meditacion en son quor auné.

Ki est si parfit de nus ki puisse suideinement urer aprés ou penser de Deu que ren ne li veigne a runge ke desturbance li face de ceo qu'il ad dit ou oï avant. Ne sai si nul est teus, mes jeo n'ai pas cele grace. [f.72va] De autre part nus parloms o Deu o nos pensers ausi cume nus fesum par parole. Dunc ne poet estre ke cil ke mult entent a parler a gent k'il ne lesse cele manere avantdite a parler a Deu. Pur ceo e pur autres choses ad mester ke home se destreigne de mult parler a gent, ne mie sul des paroles hudives mes neis de celes que mult semblent necessaries a la feiz, kar sovent avent qu'om comence a parler de bosoignes e puis si descend hom a hudivesces. De hudivesces e detractions e malement juger a la feiz nos promes dunt nus un point ne savom par quele entente ou par quel besoing il les eient fet, lequel que les faiz de noz prosmes seient repernables ou nun, si est ceo mult perilluse chose a juger les par detriers, que Deu meismes dit 'Ne jugez nuli e vus ne serrez pas jugez, kar a meimes ke jugez autres serrez[i] vus jugez.'

[i] MS s. serrez.

Solomon says in his Proverbs, "As it is for the city without door or wall, where all may enter who will, so it is for him who cannot restrain his spirit from much talking."[23] God spoke thus through Moses: "A coverless vessel is unclean before me."[24] Of this, in the *Lives of the Fathers*,[25] a good abbot speaks to Saint Anthony, of two brothers who have become his travelling companions. "You have found good brothers, Lord Abbot," Saint Anthony said to him. And he replied: "Truly they are good, but in their house and in their place where they dwell there is no door. Whoever wants can enter their stable and take their donkey." Our soul is the donkey of God. All the times when it strives to recite its sins before God and to do penance, to remember the grace God has shown to man on earth, or the pains of Hell from which God by his grace has redeemed his own, or to recall the joy on high that God has in his own — whom he has by his grace alone won and apparelled — and to give thanks for that with all its might; and all these times our soul is fastened to God's manger, to eat. The wretched soul is taken away from this manger when it is unfastened from the hitching-post of silence and allowed to run in strings of vain words. The words it hears disturb its intention, and so it becomes vain and void of all it had gathered before through good meditation in the heart.

Who is so perfect among us, who can straight away pray afterwards, or think about God, that nothing comes remorsefully to make a disturbance in what he said or heard before? I do not know whether anybody is so, but I do not possess this gift. On the other hand, we talk to God with our thought just as we do with words. Thus, somebody who really wants to talk to people cannot but lose this way described above, of talking to God. For this and other reasons it is necessary for man to restrain himself from much talking with people: not only idle words, but also even those that seem very necessary at the time; for it often happens that one begins by speaking of necessities and then one falls into idle talk. Idleness and detraction and judging ill of our neighbours' deeds — when we know nothing of the intention or need for which they did them — that is, whether the deeds of our neighbours are blamable or not, so it is a dangerous thing, to judge behind others' backs, such that God himself said "Judge nobody, and you shall not be judged; for as much as you judge others, you shall yourselves be judged."[26]

[23] Prov. 25:28.

[24] Num. 19:15.

[25] For Anthony of Egypt (c. 251–356), see *GL* I:93–97 (at p. 95); the Latin edition (ed. Maggioni (XXI De Sancto Antonio), I:155–60, p. 158) refers further to Vit. Pat. V. iv. i.

[26] Matt. 7:1–2. See also Mark 4:24; Luke 6:37; Rom. 2:1.

Ne mie ke Deus face faus jugement sur ceus qui unt fausement jugé, mes ke Deu par sa grant dreiture vengera la fauseté de fous jugeurs qui les autres nicement jugent. Estre iceo si nus est grant mester ke nus amendum par silence le grant sur[f.72vb]fet de jaungle ke nus feimes al siecle devant nostre conversacion, kar il ad huit maneres de parler ou la gent mespernent sovent : parole fole, parole veine, parole hudive, parole escusante, parole nunchaste, parole fause, parole maldisante, parole tricheruse.

Fole parole est ke en dit par nunsavance a nuntens e a nunhure e la ou liu nent n'est. De ceo dit Salomon : 'Tens est de tere e tens est de parler.' E le Psalmiste requert e dit : 'Sire,' fet il, 'metez garde a ma buche e hus a mes leveres.' E aillurs dit : 'Homes ke multes paroles parolent ne poent fructifier en terre.'

Veine parole si est parole de vantance. De ceo dit le Psalmiste : 'Veines choses parole chescun a son prome', e aprés dit 'Deu destruira tutes leveres dubles e la haute parlante lange.'

Hudive parole est cele ke n'ad fes de nul profit ne de nulli bosoinge, dunt seinte Escripture dit : 'De chescune parole hudive que la gent parolent rendrunt il raison devant Deu al jugement.' E l'autorité dit : 'En mult parler ne poet hom faillir de peché.' Quancke passums ore nunchalusement e passums ultre e tenums a petit [f.73ra] ou a neent, tut serra al jugement plenerement e apertement devant Deu mustré e jugé. Dunc se deit chescun sage purver k'il ren ne die a son parlement qu'il puisse que ne apende a l'honur Deu ou a l'amendement de son prome ou a sa bosoingne de meme. E si autrement li chet, face sa confession, si se esgard autrefiez meuz.

It is not that God will falsely judge those who have judged falsely, but that God, by his great justice, will avenge the falsity of foolish judges who judge others foolishly. That being so, there is great need for us to atone by our silence for the surfeit of foolish jabbering that we created in the world before we entered religious life. For there are eight manners of talking, by which people often err: Foolish speech; Vain speech; Idle speech; Self-excusing speech; Unchaste speech; False speech; Evil-speaking or speaking ill of people; Treacherous speech.

Foolish speech is when one talks without knowing, out of season, out of turn, out of place. Of this says Solomon, "There is a season for keeping silence, and there is a season for talking."[27] And the Psalmist prays and says, "Lord, put a guard upon my mouth and a door upon my lips,"[28] and elsewhere says, "Men who speak many words cannot fructify on earth."[29]

Vain speech is boasting speech. Of this the Psalmist says, "Every man speaks vain words to his neighbour," and then says, "God will destroy all double-speaking tongues."[30]

Idle speech is the kind made neither for profit nor for necessity — of which Holy Scripture says, "For every idle word that people speak, they shall answer for it to God at the Judgement."[31] And the Authority says, "In much speaking, a man cannot fail to sin."[32] Whatever we now pass over carelessly, and pass beyond, thinking it little or nothing, at the Judgement it will all be fully and openly revealed and judged before God. So every wise man must know how to manage not to say anything in his speech, as far as he can, that does not pertain to the honour of God, to the bettering of one's neighbour, or to one's own necessity. And if it falls to him otherwise, he must make his confession and watch himself more carefully next time.

---

27 Eccles. 3:1–7.

28 Ps. 141:3 (140:3 in *LV*).

29 Ps. 140:11: *Let not an evil speaker be established in the earth* (139:12 in *LV*; *Vir linguosus* may be interpreted as much speaking *or* as evil speaking).

30 See Ps. 12:2–3 (11:3–4 in *LV*).

31 Matt. 12:36.

32 Prov. 10:19; the Authority is Solomon, considered to be the author of this book.

Parole escusante si est parole d'orguil e de malice. Par cele perdi Adam Paraïs, par cele volent les fous lur pechez escuser ou cuverir. Encuntre ceo dit le Psalmistre : 'Sire Deu,' fet il, '[N']ordinez mun quer en parole de malice a fere excusacions en pechez.'

Parole nunchaste si est orde parole e vilaine. Cele defent li Apostle en teu manere : 'Fornicacion ne suillure ne seit neis entre vous nomez, kar n'est pas signe que cil eient netteté de quor ki a custume parolent vilainement.'

Fause parole si est parole de neent e si poet hom a la fiez faus dire sanz mentir. Dire faus sanz mentir c'est quant hom quide veir dire e n'est pas veirs. Mentir si est dire faus a escient. De ceste dreine mençoinge dit le Psalmiste a Deu : 'Vus destruirez', fet il, 'tuz ceus qui parolent mençoinges.' [f.73rb] E aillurs dit l'autorité : 'La buche ke ment si tue l'alme e raisun.' Pur quei ? Kar Deus ki est verité si est vie de l'alme e quant om ment a escient, dunc lessum verité, c'est Deu, pur fause mençoinge qu'est la mort de l'alme.

Parole maldisante si est cele ke om dit pur grever son prosme, ou devant lui pur tarier e corucer ou detrés li en aucune detraction, dunt l'Apostle dit : 'Ne li mesdisant n'averunt le regne Deu.' E li Psalmistre dit a tele manere de gent ausi cum a un home : 'Vus feistes,' ceo dit, 'e parlez encontre vostre frere e meistes cupe encuntre le fiz vostre mere. Iceo fesiez,' dit Deu, 'e jeo me tu. Vus quidiez', ceo dit il, 'que jeo vus resemblasce a juger la gent a vostre foer. Nun, nun,' fet il, 'einz vus reprendrai, si vus mettrai vos fous jugementz devant le vis e ceo quant meins voldriez.'

Parole tricheruse si est parole duble, cele que l'em dit o duble quer pur[i] aucun deceivre. De ceus dit Davi : 'Les leveres tricheruses parolent en quor, c'est en duble quor.' E autre fiez dit : 'Destruiez', fet il, 'les duble leveres de vus meismes.'

[i] MS par.

Excusing speech means words of pride and of malice. By such did Adam lose Paradise; by such do the foolish try to cover or excuse their sins.[33] Against this the Psalmist says "Lord God," he says, "incline not my heart in words of malice to make excuses for sin."[34]

Unchaste speech is dirty, cheap talk. The Apostle forbids it, in this manner: "Let neither fornication nor filthiness be even named among you, for it is no sign of a clean heart in those who habitually say dirty things."[35]

False speech is speech of no value: one can speak falsely while at the same time not lying. To speak falsely without lying is when one thinks one is speaking truly and yet is not. Lying is knowingly speaking false. About this last lie, the Psalmist says to God, "You will destroy," he says, "all those who speak lies."[36] And elsewhere the Authority says, "The lying mouth kills both soul and reason."[37] Why? Because God who is truth is the soul's life, and when we lie knowingly we forsake truth, that is God, for the false lying that is the death of the soul.

Evil-speaking: this is what one says to grieve one's neighbour, either to his face so as to damage or anger him or behind his back in any kind of defamation, of which the Apostle says, "Nor shall the evil-speakers have the Kingdom of God."[38] And the Psalmist says to people of this kind, as to one man: "You act," he says, "and speak against your brother, and you put blame onto the son of your mother. You do this," says God, "and I am silent. You believe," he says, "that I am like you, judging people by your standards. No, no," he says, "rather I shall reprove you, and I shall put your foolish judgement before your face, and this when you shall least wish it."[39]

Treacherous speech is double speech: whatever one says with double heart to deceive anybody. Of these David says, "Treacherous lips speak in the heart — that is a double heart." And another time: "Destroy," he says, "the duplicity of your own lips."[40]

---

[33] See Gen. 3:12.

[34] Ps. 141:4 (140:4 in *LV*).

[35] See Col. 3:8.

[36] Ps. 5:6 (5:7 in *LV*).

[37] See Wisdom 1:11.

[38] Gal. 5:20–21.

[39] Ps. 50:20–21 (49:20–21 in *LV*).

[40] Ps. 12:2–3 (11:3 in *LV*): *They speak vanity every one with his neighbour: with flattering lips and a double heart do they speak*; and Prov. 4:24. Although the writer is still citing David, the second of these quotations is not a psalm.

Iceste pestilence dunt ai parlé e plus ke ne saverei dire ne ne pureie tute [f.73va] n'est de surparler. E par destresse de silence la pora hom ou de tut destrure ou mettre en teu point qu'ele ne porra guerres nuire. Pur ceo li ancien religius ki pur lur esprove demeine e par la grace de Deu aveient esprové le profit de religion e le peril avant tutes autres choses garderent silence, kar ben saveient e pur ceo plus se doteient ke la launge[i] si est en moiste liu e pur petit esculurge. Las ! chaitis ! Que from nus ki avoms le quor en la buche e ne mie la buche el quer e que avoms l'essperit es narilleis qui tut nostre esperit jetum de nus pur les autres aventer. *Qui iuxta illud comici pleni rimarum sumus et effluimus undique*, c'est, sicum dit un paen : 'Plein sumes de crevesces e si decurt de tute parz nostre ben, que ren ne nus poet remeindre.' E quei freums ? Terriums tut dis ? Nun. Mes il nus comande mult tere envers la gent pur parler a Deu sovent e pur oïr Deu parler a nus. De ceo dit Davi : 'Jo orrai ke Deu voldra parler en moi, kar il voldra parler de la pes de son pople.' Icele parole n'orrad pas li trop parlant e pur ceo ne porra il saver le conseil Deu, [f.73vb] quele pes il voldra fere a son pople. E ceo purra il duter que il ne seit pas de sun pople. Ore n'i ad dunc fors d'escuter que Deu voldra dire, sicum dit Samuel : 'Parlez, Sire,' fet il, 'que vostre serf vus escute.' Quant il avera dit son pleisir, si parlums a lui en confessions des maus que fet avoms e bone repentance pur pardon aver. Rendums li graces de tuz les bens qu'il nus ad fet au cors e a alme qu'il wouche sauf ses buntesz e de plus volenters nus face plus. Reparlums a lui en oraisuns, si li mustrum noz bosoignes. Requerum lui acordement qu'il nus pardoint nos trespas e k'il nus garde de peché e nus doint sa grace a fere son pleisir e nus meint a bone fin e a vie pardurable. Amen.

[Conclusion] E si[ii] le fesums e gardoms la chasteté de noz cors e de curage sicum avant est dit, dunc serrunt nos cors sacrifise vivant devant Deu. E si la proprité lessom, sicum dist est, si serrum seint e [a] Deu pleisant. Si nus gardum silence descrete de buche e de pensee, dunc ert renable nostre service devant Deu. Ore nus doint Deus grace e descretion a tut ço fere. Amen.

[i] MS lanūge. [ii] MS si si.

This pestilence I have spoken of, and more that I could not say, nor could I say it all, is not saying too much. By the restraint of silence one can destroy it altogether, or put it in such a place that it can do no harm. Therefore the religious of old, who by their own experience and by God's grace found the profit and the peril of religion, above all things kept silence; for they well knew, and so the more feared, that the tongue is in a moist place and can slip for the smallest thing. Alas! Wretches! What shall we do, whose heart is in our mouth instead of our mouth in our heart, and whose spirit is in our nostrils so that we cast our spirit out of us, to blow upon others. "Who, as the comic poet says, are full of cracks, and leak out everywhere" — that is, as a pagan says: "We are full of orifices, our goodness runs out of us from all parts, and nothing can remain in us."[41] What shall we do? Shall we keep silence for ever? No. But he commands much silence towards people, so as to speak often to God and hear God speak to us. Of this says David, "I shall hear that God wishes to speak to me, for he would speak of the peace of his people."[42] He who talks too much will not hear this word, and so will not know the counsel of God, nor what peace he wishes to make for his people. And so he could doubt it, that it was from his people. Now there is nothing else, but to listen to what God wishes to say, as Samuel says: "Speak, Lord," he says, "that your servant may hear you."[43] When he has spoken his will, then let us speak to him in confession of wrongs we have done, and in true repentance that we may have pardon. Let us give thanks to him for all the good he has done for us, body and soul, that he may vouchsafe his bounties and willingly give us more. Let us speak to him again in prayers, thus let us tell him our need. Let us pray to him for atonement, that he will forgive us our trespasses and keep us from sin, and give us his grace to do his pleasure, and lead us to a good end and everlasting life. Amen.

[Conclusion] And if we do this, and keep chastity in body and heart as is said above, so shall our bodies be a living sacrifice before God. And if we forsake property, as I have said, we shall be holy and pleasing to God. If we keep discreet silence in mouth and in thought, so shall our service be fitting before God. Now may God give us grace and discretion to achieve all this. Amen.

---

[41] The "pagan" is the Roman playwright Terence, whose work was well known in the Middle Ages. The line is ultimately from *Eunuchus* (ed. and trans. Sargeaunt, I.ii.25, pp. 244–45), and is here quoted by Bernard in his sermon *Dominica infra octavam assumptionis B. V. Mariae*, cap. XI (*PL* 183:435D).

[42] Ps. 85:8 (84:9 in *LV*).

[43] I Sam. 3:10 (I Reg. 3:10 in *LV*).

Chapter 15

The Beatitudes[1]

Introduction

In this Commentary on the Beatitudes, the focus is on virtue rather than on sin, complementing the confession material above. Oxford, Bodleian Library MS Bodley 654 (SC 27669) (s.xiii^{2}) contains the main text, ff.133v–140r; after the Pains of Purgatory.[2] The first part lists and describes the eight kinds of blessed people; it continues with discussion of three orders of salvation, advice for virgins, aspects of the holy life, and the five degrees of chastity. D&B entitles it "Ten Commandments" because it is Part 4 of the *Compileison* (D&B 644) on the Commandments. The text below is about a variety of virtues (not Commandments); chapter divisions show that it was part of a longer work.[3]

The Commentary is in the form of a sermon. We find the rhetorical "ore poez vus penser," and so on, with logical insistence on "because," "therefore." The French is sometimes given before the Latin quotations; sometimes the Latin is not given. As well as the Bible, the writer cites Bernard, Francis (c. 1181–1226), Gregory, Augustine, Jerome (c. 341–420), and Cecilia. He explains why we say the *Gloria* after psalms. He quantifies the three orders of salvation: 30, 60, 100. The state of virginity is 100, but there are six traps for a virgin. He cites the story of Pretextata, and sets out how to live a holy life: there are six things to keep to — the Latin is here paraphrased rather than translated. Finally, the degrees of chastity are gendered female, but stated to be "ausi ben en homes." The readers or users of this piece are clearly literate: much of the Latin is untranslated, and some of the paraphrases are very free. The writer expects readers to have a good knowledge of the Bible and of the Church Fathers.

---

[1] D&B 678, prose, "The Ten Commandments."

[2] See the next chapter in this volume (the folio numbers do not follow on immediately, because the Beatitudes are inside another text).

[3] See Appendix, below, for the *Compileison*.

Text

[f.133v] Nostre[i] Seignur Dampnedeu done sa beneson en le evangelie a ut manere de gens pur ut vertues qe il unt. E pur ceo checun home qe vult sa alme sauver e les benesons Deu vut aver e purchacer deit tote sa peine e tot sun poer mettre a ces ut vertues aver.

La premere vertue si est humilité. Dont asi cum orgul fu le comencement de toz pechez, ausi est humilité le comencement e la racine de totez vertues sanz laquele nule alme ne se put saver. E pur ceo dit nostre Sire en la premere beneson 'Beneit seent les umbles e toz qe doutent Deu, car lur est le regne du cel' : *Beati, inquid, pauperes spiritum quoniam ipsorum est regnum celorum* [Matt. 5:3]. Ore poez vus penser e demander quele est ceste humilité pur la quele Deu doune si haute beneson. A ceo vus dit seint Bernard issi : 'Humilité', fet il, 'est une vertue par laquele home conout verament ces defautes e se tent[ii] vil e de poi de value e desire[iii] sanz son peché estre tenu des autres en vilté.' E ceo devez mult coveiter, car de tant cum estes plus vil e plus vuz humiliez devant les gens en vostre quer, de tant estes vus plus precius devant Deu e de tant cum vus memes tenez plus precius e plus vus delitez de estre prisé [f.134r] e honuré en ceste vie, de tant en estes vus meins prisé de Deu e plus serrez deshonuré e honi en l'autre vie, sicum Deu dit en le evangelie : *Omnis qui se exaltat humiliabitur et qui se humiliat exaltabitur* [Luke 14:11].

E pur ceo vus lo jeo qe vus regardez vos defautes de cors e de alme. Si vus pensez quele chose veint hors de vostre bouche e hors de vos narils e hors de vos autres parties de vostre cors, vus ne veites unqes si vil femir cum vus portez entour, sicum dit seint Bernard : *Si inspicias quid per os et per nares tuos et per alios corporis meatus a te exiunt, nunquam vilius sterquilinium invenisti.*

[i] Red initial. The Latin passages in this text are written in slightly larger script. [ii] MS se tenent. [iii] MS desirer.

Translation

[I: Eight Virtues][1] Our Lord the Lord God gives his blessing in the Gospel to eight kinds of people, for eight virtues they possess. And therefore every man who wants to save his soul, and to receive and have the blessings of God, must put all his effort and pains to achieve those eight virtues.

[Humility] The first virtue, then, is humility. Because just as pride was the beginning of all sins, so humility is the beginning and root of all those virtues without which no soul may save itself. Therefore Our Lord says in the first Blessing: "Blessed be the humble, and all who fear God, for the heavenly kingdom is theirs": *Blessed are the poor in spirit, for theirs is the kingdom of heaven.* Now you may think, and ask, what is this humility for which God gives such high blessing. To you, Saint Bernard says this: "Humility," he says, "is a virtue by which a man truly knows his faults, and holds himself to be vile and valueless, and desires — aside from his sins — to be held as a vile thing by others."[2] And you must long for this very earnestly, for the more vile you are, and the more you humble yourself before people in your heart, the more precious you are before God; and the more you hold yourself to be precious, and the more you delight in being prized and honoured in this life, so much the less are you prized by God and will be more dishonoured and shamed in the other life, as God says in the Gospel: *For whosoever exalteth himself shall be abased; and he that humbleth himself shall be exalted.*

And therefore I advise you to look at your faults, of body and of soul. If you think about what kind of stuff comes out of your mouth and nose and out of other parts of your body, you will see there is nothing so disgusting as what you carry round with you, as Saint Bernard says: "If you look at what issues from your mouth and nose, and other motions of the body, never will you find manure more vile."[3]

---

[1] See Matt. 5:3–11.

[2] Cf. *Ancrene Wisse* (Part IV, ed. Hasenfratz, p. 291; trans. Savage and Watson, p. 150, note 112), where the notes cite Bernard's *De Grad. Hum.* cap. iv (*PL* 182:949).

[3] Cf. *Ancrene Wisse*: see notes in ed. Hasenfratz (p. 454), and trans. Savage and Watson (p. 384), that this is a commonplace of the *contempus mundi* tradition. They list a number of authorities, including Pseudo-Bernardine writings.

Quant a vostre alme, si vus regardez vus avez fet pechez mes ne savez si il vus sont pardoné ou noun ne vus ne savez en quel estat vus estes ne quele fin averez e pur ceo par devant Deu de tant vus humiliez le plus, car a icels qe sunt hombles done Deu sa grace e as orgulus tout il sa grace sicum dit seint Jake, car si home ust totes les graces e totes les vertues du mond e il fust pur ceo orgulus e emplé de quer e dedeignus e ust les autres en despit, il ust par ceo perdu totes vertues devant Deu.

Donc Deu dist en le evangelie : 'Deus homes', fet il, 'entrerent au temple a orer ; le un fu un farisen, ce est un home de religiun, e le autre fu un pupplican, ce est un pecheur home seculer. E le farisen dit a Deu : "Sire Deu, jeo vus reng graces qe jeo ne su pas sicum autre gens, lecheors, trecheors, robeors. Jeo june deus jours en la semeine, jeo doins mé dimes leaument de qanqe jeo ai, jeo vus reng graces, Sire Deu, qe jeo ne su mie cum autre genz ne cum ice pupplican." E le pupplican ne osa pas regarder ver mont mes regarda ver la terre e bati son pis e dit bas ses moz : "Deu eiez merci de moi pecheor", e se humilia. E le autre se avanta de ces benfez.' E nostre Seignur dit qe le pecheor aveit pardon de ces pechez e fu fet dreiturel e le autre perdi ses bens e si remit en son peché, car checun home dit 'Sire, qi se humilie sera enhaucé e checun qi se enhauce sera humilié.'

E entendez, sicum orgul fit les angeles deables, e de homes ausi qe sont les fiz Deu par bapteme fet les fiz du deable, ausi fet home[s] humilité les fiz Deu.

Ore devez saver qe qatre degrés sont de humilité par lesqueles home deit departer [f.134v] de la compainie dé diables. Le premere degré est aver le mond e le honur del mond en despit e tener sei vil. Le secunde degré est humilité de sei memes aver en despit e tener sei vil. Le terce est nul home ne jugge autre ne ne teigne nul autre plus vil de sei memes, mes tene sei plus vil de nul autre. Le quarte degré est humilité qe home eit en volunté e en desir de estre tenu des autres vil, ou si il seit vil tenu des autres, qe il en eit de ceo bone pacience qe il ne se greve vers les autres ne il memes pur ço seit grevé en son quer ne triste ne ennuié. E de tant cum home monte plus e crest en cest derein degré, de tant apruche il plus pres de Deu e plus est de Deu amé.

As for your soul, if you believe you have sinned but do not know whether the sins are forgiven or not, nor do you know what state you are in and what end you will have; for this reason the more you humble yourself before God the better, for God gives his grace to the humble and takes his grace from the proud, as Saint James says.[4] For if a man has all the graces and all the virtues in the world, and is for this reason proud and arrogant and disdainful, and has others in contempt, he has for this reason lost all virtues before God.

So God says in the Gospel: "Two men," he says, "went into the temple to pray. One was a Pharisee, that is, a man of religion, and the other was a publican, which is a sinful layman. And the Pharisee said to God, 'Lord God, I give you thanks that I am not like other people — lechers, traitors, robbers. I fast two days in the week, I give my tithes dutifully of everything I have. I give you thanks, Lord God, that I am nothing like other people, nor like this publican here.' And the publican did not dare to look upwards, but looked down to the earth and beat his breast and softly said these words: 'God have mercy on me, a sinner', and abased himself. And the other boasted of his good deeds." And Our Lord said the sinner had forgiveness for his sins and was made righteous, and the other lost his goodness and fell back into sin, for every man says, "Lord, whoever abases himself shall be exalted and whoever exalts himself shall be brought low."[5]

And listen, just as pride made angels into devils, and men also who are sons of God by baptism are made into sons of the Devil, so too does humility make men into sons of God.

[Four Degrees of Humility] Now you must learn that there are four steps of humility, by which man must escape from the company of devils. The first step is to have the world and its honour in contempt, and to hold oneself vile. The second step is the humility to have oneself in contempt and see oneself as vile. The third is: let no man judge another, nor see another as viler than himself, but see himself as viler than any other. The fourth step is the humility that one should wish and desire to be seen as vile by others. If he is seen as vile by others, let him have the patience not to be grieved at them, nor be grieved in himself about it in his heart, nor sad nor upset. And as much as a man grows and increases in this last degree, so much does he come closer to God and is more loved by God.

---

[4] James 4:6.

[5] Luke 18:10–14: ... *for every one that exalteth himself shall be abased; and he that humbleth himself shall be exalted* (where, however, Jesus is still speaking, not "every man").

Mes ore poez vus penser en vostre quer e dire issi : Coment put home tant humilier sei e vil tener qe est en bone vie cum en virginité, en chasteté, en charité e mult en a graces e vertues de cors e de alme ? Mes entendez ben qe tote graces e totes vertues sont les dons Deu. En home ne a ren de sei fors peché. Donqe celi qe a graces e vertues qe ne sont pas fors ausi cum du prest Dampnedeu, si il use malement il put pur ceo estre dampné. Car Deu a presté a home graces e sens a la meité du gain. Il vult qe home eit le pru e la merite a quere en ceste vie graces de Deu e a purchacer la joie pardurable. Mes Deus vult qe vus lui rendez sa partie des bens qe il vus a aphesté, ce est honur e grez e graces, sicum il dit en Ysaïe le prophete : *Gloriam meam alteri non dabo* [Is. 42:8 & 48:11], iceo dit Deu par le profete 'Jeo ne dorra[i] pas mon honur ne ma glorie a autri.'

Dont quant homo desire e se delite de estre prisé e honuré pur les bens qe Deus a mis en lui, il est desleals e emble e tout a Deu sa partie qe il dut aver du gain. E pur ceo est il digne de perdre sa partie, ce est adire sa merite. E pur ceo dit Deu en le evangelie dé gens qe junent e font amones e dient lur oreisons e font autre bens, si il desirent e se delitent en le honur du mond e pur ceo le font il, Deu dist qe il ount receu lur loer, ceo est le honur e le favor e le los du mond : *Amen dico vobis, receperunt mercedem suam* [Matt. 6:2 & 5], car icels ne averunt jamés autre loer de Deu fors la peine de enfern cum ypocrites, cum fauce genz qe Deu heet.

E pur ceo deit home hu[f.135r]milier e doter e purement pur Deu fere ben e a lui rendre graces e honur e dire en son quer : 'Sire Deu, ne donez pas a nus le honur des bens qe vus fetes a nus par vus, mes vostre noun seit parhonuré e neent le nostre.' *Non nobis, Domine, non nobis, sed nomini tuo da gloriam* [Ps. 113:9], ceo est la vertue de humilité, especiament de religion e de bone gens del secle. E pur ceo dist l'em a la fin dé salmes, sicum l'em dust dire aprés checun bon fet a Deu 'Glorie seit doné au Pere e au Fiz e au Seint Espirit' : *Gloria Patri et Filio et Spiritui Sancto*. Plusurs signes sont de humilité sicum vus si aprés orez. Un signe est par quey home put conustre si il a humilité e si il eime la compainie de ombles gens e eschue les orgulus. Un autre signe[i] est si home fet volunters chose la ou il a vilté quant aseche sanz peché. Un autre est si il eime poverté com povere dras ou povere viande.

---

[i] MS digneté.

But now you may wonder in your heart, and say this: How can a man so abase himself and hold himself vile when he is in virtuous life — in virginity, chastity, charity — and has many graces and virtues of body and soul? You must understand that all graces and all virtues are gifts of God. In a man there is nothing of his own but sin. So he who has graces and virtues — that are nothing if not lent by God — if he uses them badly he can be damned for that. For God has lent man graces and wits, so as to receive a share of the benefits. He wants man to have the wisdom and the merit to seek graces from God in this life, and to purchase everlasting joy. But God wants you to render up his share of the good things he has lent you, which is honour and goodwill and graces, as he says in Isaiah the prophet: *my glory will I not give to another*. God says this through the prophet: "I shall not give my honour, nor my glory, to others."

So when man desires and delights in being prized and honoured for the good things God has placed in him, he is disloyal; he keeps and hides from God his own share that he ought to have of the benefits. And for this he deserves to lose his share, his merit. Therefore God says in the Gospel, about people who fast and give alms and say their prayers and do other good things, if they desire and delight in the worldly honour and do them for its sake, God says they have received their recompense: that is, the honour and favour and praise of the world. *Verily I say unto you, They have their reward*, for these shall never have other recompense from God but the pains of Hell, as hypocrites, as false men whom God hates.

Therefore man must be humble and afraid, and do good purely for God, and render him thanks and honour, and say in his heart: "Lord God, do not give us the honour for the good you do for us through you, but let your name be glorified above all, not ours." *Not unto us, O Lord, not unto us, but unto thy name give glory, for thy mercy, and for thy truth's sake.*[6] This is the virtue of humility, especially among religious and the good people of the world. And this is why we say, at the end of psalms, as we ought to say after every good deed done for God, "Glory be given to God the Father and to the Son and to the Holy Spirit": *Glory be to the Father, and to the Son, and to the Holy Ghost.* There are many signs of humility, as you shall hear next. There is one sign by which a man can know whether he has humility: whether he loves the company of humble people and avoids the proud. Another sign is if a man willingly does a deed where there is vileness, when he perseveres without sin. Another is if he loves poverty, such as poor clothes or poor food.

---

[6] In *AV*, Ps. 115:1 (the Psalms are divided differently at this point).

Me le plus verai signe est quant home est de quer e de bouche pacient quant hom li mefet ou medit. Dont seint Franceis dist qe li home ne seet pas si il a humilité ou pacience, tant cum home fet ou dist solum sa volunté, mes quant l'em dit ou fet encontre reson. Tant cum il en a donke de humilité e de pacience, tant en a en li e neent plus. Icele fu la humilité Jesu Crist, car il respondi humblement a touz ses enemis e deboneremement. Il ne les maudist poynt ne les manasa, mes la ou il pendi en la croiz il pria pur eus e dist : 'Beu douz Pere, pardonez a cels qe me fount ceste peine e ceste hounte, car il ne sevunt ceo qe il font' : *Pater ignosce illis quia nesciunt quid faciunt* [Luke 23:34].

La secunde beneson si est ceste : 'Beneit seent cels qe sont deboneires', ces sont cele genz qe ne volent a nul home mal ne ne parlent ne ne font, mes ben font encontre le mal e venkent mal en autres par lur boneireté : *Beati mites quoniam ipsi possidebunt terram scilicet terram viventium* [Matt. 5:4]. Icels qe issi font ce qe Jesu Crist ensigna e comanda quant il dist 'Amez vos enemis e priez pur eus e donez vostre beneson e nul maleson a cels qe vus maudient e fetes ben a cels qe mal vus font' : *Diligite inimicos vestros et orate pro persequentibus et calumpniantibus vos* [Matt. 5:44]. [f.135v] *Benedicite et nolite maledicere* [Rom. 12:14].

La terce beneson est iceste : Benez seint cels qe plurunt pur lur pechez ou pur autres peines ou meseises ou pur le desir de la joie du cel aver. Car icels seront de Damnedeu confortez e solacez, car Deu memes promet a cels confort pardurable : *Beati inquit qui lugent quoniam ipsi consolabuntur* [Matt. 5:5]. Deu jeta un home hors de paradis ne mie pur fere isi paradis mes pur fere penance ou bone volunté. E cels qe ne volunt serunt mys aprés ceste vie ou en enfern ou en purgatorie la ou il front greve penance maugré lour. Ce est dunkes dreiture qe home qe perdi paradis par delit qe il suffre feim e seif e peine volunter' pur returner en paradis. Ceo fu le comencement de la predicacion Jesu Crist e de seint Johan le Baptist. Fetes penance e la joie du cel vus aprochera : *Agite inquid penitenciam*[i] *appropinquabit enim regnum celorum* [Matt. 3:2 & 4:17].

La quinte beneson est 'Benez seint les merciables, car Deu avera merci de eus' : *Beati misericordes, quoniam ipsi misericordiam consequentur* [Matt. 5:7]. Si nus voluns dunc aver la merci Deu, il nus covent aver merci des autres.

---

[i] MS *petuntenciam*.

But the truest sign is when a man is patient in heart and mouth when anybody acts or speaks against him. So, Saint Francis said that the man does not know whether he has humility or patience as long as he acts or speaks according to his desire, but when he acts or speaks according to reason. So as much as he has of humility and patience, so much he has in him and no more. This was the humility of Jesus Christ, for he replied humbly and courteously to all his enemies. He never cursed them or threatened them, but as he hung on the Cross he prayed for them and said, "Fair sweet Father, give pardon to those who inflict this pain and shame on me, for they don't know what they are doing": *Father, forgive them; for they know not what they do.*

[Meekness] The second Blessing is this: "Blessed be those who are gentle," that is, the people who wish evil to no man, neither do they do or speak it. But they do good against evil, and conquer evil in others by their meekness: *Blessed are the meek: for they shall inherit the earth.*[7] Thus they do what Jesus Christ taught and commanded when he said: "Love your enemies and pray for them; give your blessing, and not curses, to those who speak against you, and do good to those who do evil to you": *Love your enemies, bless them that curse you, do good to them that hate you, and pray for them which despitefully use you, and persecute you.*

[Tears] The third Blessing is this: Blessed be those who weep for their sins or for other pain or disease, or for the desire to have the joy of Heaven. For these shall be comforted and solaced by the Lord God, for God himself promises everlasting comfort to them: *Blessed are they that mourn: for they shall be comforted.*[8] God drove a man out of Paradise, not in order to make Paradise here but to do penance with good will. And those who will not, shall be thrown either into Hell or into Purgatory, where they shall do sore penance against their will. It is thus rightful that man, who lost Paradise through transgression, should suffer hunger and thirst and pain willingly so as to return to Paradise. This was the beginning of the teaching of Jesus Christ and of Saint John the Baptist: "Do penance, and the joy of Heaven shall come close to you"; *Repent ye: for the kingdom of heaven is at hand.*

[Mercy][9] The fifth Blessing is: "Blessed be the merciful, for God shall have mercy on them"; *Blessed are the merciful: for they shall obtain mercy.* So if we want to receive the mercy of God, we ought to have mercy on others.

---

[7] Matt. 5:5, not 5:4 as in *LV*.

[8] Matt. 5:4, not 5:5 as in *LV*.

[9] The fourth is missing; it would be Hunger and Thirst after Righteousness.

Car seint Jake li Apostle dit qe il avera jugement sanz merci qe ne at de autre merci. *Iudicium erit ei sine misericordia qui non fecerit misericordiam* [Jac. 2:13]. Ore devez vus saver qe Deu semblera e de mort en vie relevera en ors e en alme touz les homes e totes les femmes qe unqes aveint ou averont vie en ventre de lur mere e aparront devant Jesu Crist en cors e en alme en estat de l'age de trente aunz e les angelis departirent les mauveis des bons. E les bons esteront a destre de nostre Seignur e les mauveis a senestre. E adonc dira Jesu Crist a merciables : 'Venez mes beneiz frere e suers e si recevez joie ov mei sanz fin.' E il lur dira pur quey. E ce est pur ses overes de merci qe il feseint a lur prome. E si dirra issi : 'Jeo avoy feim e vus me pustes, e seif, e vus me donastes a beivere. Jeo fu nu e vus moi revestistes, e sanz hostel, e vus moi herbergastes. Jeo fu maladis, e vus me [f.136r] visitastes. Jeo fu en prison, e vus venistes a moy e mei eidastes.' E enaprés ce dira il a maveis tot le contrarie : 'Alez vus, maleite gent, en fu d'enfern[i] pardurable sanz fin qe est aparailé au deable e a toz ces cervans, car jeo avoi feim e seif ne manger ne beivere ne me donastis ne nul autre fez de merci ne me feites. E pur ceo serez vus sanz merci dampnez, car ceo qe vus donastes ou viastes a un dé meindres de mes freres ou de mes seurs qe poveres sunt, vus le feites a mei.'

E pur ceo deit checun home estre merciable as autres qe Deu eit merci de lui. E qe mult a, si en doine largement, e qe poi a doine volunteres ceo qe il put, e qe ren a a doner, si en eit au meins la bone volunté de doner e compassion, ce est a dire pité de autri peché e de autri meseise, e sa volunté serra counté devant Deu pur le fet. Car seinte Escripture dit qe quatre manere de homes averont la joie du ciel pur amone : ces qe unt ouel amur en Deu e a lur prome ; le riche home qe doune la meité de ces chateus par[ii] Deu, sicum fit Zacheus : *Ecce inquid dimidium bonorum meorum, domine, do pauperibus* [Luke 19:8] ; e li povere home qe doune un ferthin, sicum fit la povere vidue au temple de qi Deu dit qe ele dona plus qe toz les riches homes, car ele dona tot son vivere ; e li mult povere qe done un hanapé de ewe freide pur Deu : *Quicum[que] inquid dominus dederit calicem aque frigide tantum in nomine discipuli, amen dico vobis, non perdet mercedem suam* [Matt. 10:42].

[i] MS enefern. [ii] MS par (for 'pur').

For Saint James the Apostle said that whoever has no mercy on others shall receive judgement without mercy: *For he shall have judgment without mercy, that hath shewed no mercy.* Now you must know that God will gather up, and will raise from death to life, both body and soul, all the men and women who ever had or will have life from the belly of their mother. They shall appear before Jesus Christ as they were at thirty years old, and the angels shall separate the wicked from the good. And the good will be to the right of Our Lord, and the bad to the left. And then Jesus Christ will say to the merciful, "Come, my blessed brothers and sisters, and receive joy with me now without end." And he shall tell them why. And it is because of their works of mercy, that they did to their neighbours. And he shall say this: "I was hungry and you fed me; and thirsted, and you gave me to drink. I was naked and you clothed me; without lodging, and you sheltered me. I was sick, and you visited me; I was in prison, and you came to me and you helped me." And then he will say this, quite the opposite, to the wicked: "Go, wicked people, into the everlasting and endless fire of Hell that is prepared for the Devil and for all his servants, for I was hungry and thirsty and you gave me neither food nor drink, nor did you do any other work of mercy for me. And for this you shall be damned without mercy. For whatever you gave or denied to one of the least of my brothers or sisters, who are poor, you did for me."[10]

And therefore every man must be merciful to others, so that God will have mercy on him. And he who has much, let him give largely; he who has little, let him willingly give what he can; he who has nothing, let him at least have the good will to give, and compassion — that is to say, pity — for others' sin and for others' misfortune, and his will shall be counted for the deed before God. For Holy Scripture says that four kinds of men shall have the joy of Heaven for their alms: those who love God and their neighbour equally; the rich man who gives half of his goods for God, as did Zaccheus: *Behold, Lord, the half of my goods I give to the poor.* And the poor man who gives a farthing, as did the poor widow in the temple of God,[11] of whom God said she gave more than all the rich men, for she gave all she had; and the very poor who give a cup of cold water, for God: *And whosoever shall give to drink unto one of these little ones a cup of cold water only in the name of a disciple, verily I say unto you, he shall in no wise lose his reward.*

[10] Matt. 25:34–45.

[11] Mark 12:42. Note the English word "ferthin" here; the farthing was worth a quarter of one penny.

E celi qe ren ne a ne ren ne put doner, si il a bone volunté de doner, unde Gregorius : *Nunquam manus est vacua a munere si archa cordis repleta fuerint bona voluntate, quia non offertur deo dulcius bona voluntate.* Icés quatre manere de de gens seront en cel ouuelement reguerdonez.

La sime beneson est 'Benez seint toz cels qe unt le quer net, car il veront Deu apertement' : *Beati mundo corde quoniam ipsi Deum videbunt* [Matt. 5:8], celi qe a le quer net qe est sanz mortel peché de fet par oreison e par confession e qi a bone entente en toz ces fez a plere a Deu sanz veine glorie e sanz coveitise [f.136v] de estre guerdoné en ceste vie. De ceo pernez bone garde si vostre quer seit net ou non. Si noun, purge le sovent sicum seint Escripture vus aprent.

La setime beneson est 'Benez seint toz cels qe font pes la ou descord est, car il seront apellez les fiz Deu' : *Beati pacifici quoniam filii Dei vocabuntur* [Matt. 5:9]. E ausi sont il maudit qe desturbunt pes e font descord, car il sont les fiz au deable, sicum li seint Jesu Crist vint du cel en terre pur fere treble pes e quant il departi hors de cel mund, il fist son testament e lessa a toz ces disciplis, homes e femmes crestiens e dit 'Jeo deis de vus departer ore. E pur ceo vus done[i] jeo e vus devis e lesse en testament ma pes' : *Pacem meam do vobis, pacem reliquo vobis* [John 14:27]. Cels donc qe desturbunt le testament Deu, ce est pes, sont maleis e escumengez par dreit. Car si home seit escumengé qe desturbe testament de home, mut plus de assez est il escumengé qe desturbe le testament Deu.

La utime beneson est 'Benez seynt toz cels qe gu[e]re ou anguisse e tribulacion suffrent pur dreiture, car lur est le regné du cel' : *Beati qui persecutionem paciuntur propter justiciam, quoniam ipsorum est regnum celorum* [Matt. 5:10]. Ceste benesonz ount cels qe pur defendre verité e dreiture suffrent peine de male genz. Dont nostre Seignur aprés dit a cels : 'Quant genz vus heent e maudient e dient tote manere de mal encontre vus e metent sur vus pur l'amur de moy pur qui vus amez verité e dreiture, adonc poez vus aver joie de quer e de cors, car grant loer vus crest e vus est estué en cel pur vostre pacience' : *Beati inquid eritis cum vos oderint homines et cum persecuti vos fuerint et dixerint omne malum adversum vos mentientes propter me. Gaudete et exultate quoniam merces vestra copiosa est in celis* [Matt. 5:11–12].

[i] MS donc.

And he who has nothing and can give nothing, [it is enough] if he has good will to give, as Gregory says: "The hand is never empty of a gift, if the secret places of the heart are filled with good will, since nothing more pleasing than good will can be offered to God."[12] These four kinds of men shall, for this, be equally rewarded.

[A Clean Heart] The sixth Blessing is "Blessed be all those who have a clean heart, for they shall see God openly": *Blessed are the pure in heart: for they shall see God*; he has a pure heart who is without mortal sin in deed, by prayer and by confession, and who has good will in all these deeds to please God, without vain glory and without coveting reward in this life. Take good care whether your heart is pure or not. If not, purify it frequently, as Holy Scripture teaches you.

[Peace-Making] The seventh Blessing is "Blessed be all those who make peace where there is discord, for they shall be called the sons of God"; *Blessed are the peacemakers: for they shall be called the children of God.* And also they are accursed who trouble peace and make discord, for they are the sons of the Devil. So the holy Jesus Christ came from Heaven to earth to make a triple peace. And when he departed out of this world he made his testament and left it to all his disciples, Christian men and women, and said: "Now I must depart from you, and therefore I give you, I leave and bequeath my peace in testament to you"; *Peace I leave with you, my peace I give unto you.* Those who disturb God's testament, which is peace, are wicked and rightly cursed. For if one who destroys the testament of man is to be cursed, whoever destroys the testament of God is far more damnable.

[Suffering for Righteousness] The eighth Blessing is "Blessed be all those who suffer war or anguish or tribulation for righteousness, for theirs is the Kingdom of Heaven"; *Blessed are they which are persecuted for righteousness' sake: for theirs is the kingdom of heaven.* Those who suffer pain from wicked people, to defend truth and right, have this blessing. Our Lord then says to them: "When people hate and curse you, and say many bad things against you, and put upon you for my sake — for whom you love truth and right — then may you have joy in heart and body. For great reward for your patience is laid up for you, and increases, in Heaven"; *Blessed are ye, when men shall revile you, and persecute you, and shall say all manner of evil against you falsely, for my sake. Rejoice, and be exceeding glad: for great is your reward in heaven.*

[12] Cf. the Middle English *Pater Noster* (ed. Aarts p. 17, ll. 16–17; note on p. 105), and *BVV* (p. 217), where the saying is ascribed to Gregory; also see *FM* (p. 535), where the text cites Bernard but the note cites Ambrose (of Milan, 339–397).

E ausi doint il ceste beneson a cels qe suffrent les temptacions du mond e du Diable e de lur char demeyne e combatent e[n]contre eles e lé venkunt. E cels qe sont en labour corporel pur gayner lur vivere e lur estre[i] leuement a dreiture cum font gens de mester. E cels ou celes qe sunt en penaunce nut e jour cum en junes e en veilles e en oreisuns pur lur almes sauver.

Issi comence le quinte [f.137r] **chapitre de la conpelison dé dis comandemenz e parout dé .iii. ordres de savacion. Si en a treis perograf.**[ii] Je vus ai pardevant mustré qe a ut maneres de genz doune Deu sa beneson en le evangelie. Issi aprés vus parlerai dé treis ordres de salvacion, car qui en ces treis ordres ert trové, aseur put estre qe il ert savé e qe hors de ces treis ordres a sa fin sera trové, sanz fin sera dampné. Ore devez donc saver qe treis ordres sunt de savacion, ce est asaver espusaile e vidueté e virginité. E qui est hors de ces treis ordres trové, il sera sanz fin dampné.

E cels qe sont trové espouses e se gardent de mortel peché, si il eent en eus charité, il portent ausicum la bone terre trente manere de frut, sicum dit Deu en le evangelie par la parole Deu qe est en lur quer semé, ausicum la semense en la bone terre. Homes e femmes qe sunt viduez portent duble plus, ce est adire ceisante manere de frut. Mes virgines portent plus de frut, ce est adire cent duble, car icels e iceles[iii] qe sunt en pure virginité si sont pers a martirs e a prechurs en merite pardevant Deu. Virginité est parfite chasteté de cors e de volunté ou ferme purpos de garder sei en tele estat dekes la fin de sa vie. E tant precius est tel purpos qe se par force e de tort e contre sa volunté fust une puce corrumpue, ele nequedent sereit en les virgines coroné de Deu en cel si ele gardast aprés fermement en purpos de chasteté e de virginité. E cele pucele qe de son cors est sanz corrupcion de lecherie mes ele a desir e parfite volunté a consentir au delit de lecherie, ele pert sa virginité pardevant Deu, qe neit n'est[iv] sun quer.

[i] MS uestre. [ii] This heading is in red. [iii] MS ilceles. [iv] MS sont.

And he also gives this blessing to those who suffer the temptations of the world and the Devil, and those the flesh is heir to, and they fight against them and overcome them. And to those who are in physical labour to earn their living and being, properly and rightfully, as do craftsmen; and to those men and women who are in penance night and day, as in fasting, watching, and praying, to save their souls.

[II: Chapter 5: Three Orders of Salvation] Here begins the fifth chapter of the compilation[13] of the Ten Commandments, and tells of three orders of salvation. There are three paragraphs.[14] I have shown you, above, that in the Gospel God gives blessing to eight kinds of people. So next I shall tell you of the three orders of salvation. For whoever is found to be within these three orders can be sure of being saved; and whoever is found to be outside these three orders at his end, shall be damned without end. Now you must learn that the orders of salvation are three, that is: wedlock, widowhood, and virginity — and whoever is found to be outside these three orders shall be damned everlastingly.

Those found to be married and careful to avoid mortal sin, if there is charity in them, they bring forth — like the good fields — thirty kinds of fruit. Thus God says in the Gospel: by the word of God that is sown in their hearts, like the seed sown in good earth. Men and women who are widows bring forth more by two-fold: that is sixty kinds of fruit. But virgins bear the most fruit, that is a hundred two-fold,[15] for those — male and female — in pure virginity are the equal of martyrs and preachers before God. Virginity is perfect chastity of body and of thought, and steadfast purpose to keep oneself in that state until the end of one's life. This purpose is so precious that if a maiden is corrupted wrongfully and by force, against her will, she will nevertheless be among the virgins crowned by God in Heaven if she thereafter maintains herself steadfastly in that purpose of chastity and virginity. However, the virgin whose body is without defilement of lechery, but who desires and fully intends to consent to the pleasure of lechery, she loses her virginity in the sight of God, for her heart is not clean.

[13] This is the "fifth chapter" of a larger work; the *Compileison* is discussed in the Appendix, below.

[14] Here, the word is taken to mean "headings," because the material is not divisible into paragraphs.

[15] "cent duble" — the virgins' score is conventionally reckoned at one hundred (by analogy with the Parable of the Sower, Matt. 13:3–8; see also *MERP*, p. 47, on Holy Virginity).

Mes ele pust recoverer sa virginité par repentance de sa male volunté, mes si ele fust une fez par sa volunté descorrumpue del fet de lecherie, jamés ne poreit par penance ne par autre chose recoverer son pucelage. Dont pucele dust sovent penser le grant pris de virginité e par grant gelousie netement garder sey sicum vus poez ver en cest ensample. Si un home ust une pece de terre qe pust porter[i] [f.137v] cent sommes de blé e il par sa volunté la met en tel estat qe ele ne poreit jamés porter[ii] plus qe trente ou seissante a tout le plus, il en a sa terre mout enpiré. Ausi est li home ou la femme qe se font esposer e perdent lur virginité e morent en esposailes ou en vidueté. Mes seint Augustin dist qe la file pucele est meillur de sa mere marié e si eles seint amedeus humbles, eles seront en cel honurés, la file par sa virginité sera sicum une esteile lusante e clere, e la mere sicum une esteile oscure. Mes si la mere seit umble, ele avera lu en cel ov sa file pucele. E si ele seit orguluse, n'i avera nul lu fors ov le Diable qe de iluc chaït pur orgul. Dont pucele deit totes maneres des enginz de orgul de son cors e de son quer parfitement ouster.

Issi comence le setime chapitre de la [con]pelison des dis comandemenz e parout dé sis choses qe pucele deit doter. Si en a sis perografs.[iii] Jeo vus ai devant parlé dé treis ordres de savacion, ce est asaver d'esposayle, de vedueté, de virginité. Issi par la grace Deu vus tocherai les sis choses qe pucele deit doter.

Pucele qe vult sa alme saver, ele deit de sei orgul ouster e estre umble en quer e en parole e en overe, car ce est une dé sis choses qe pucele deit primes doter. Car li seint dit qe Deus ne ust pas esté paé de la virginité seinte Marie sanz humilité.

La secunde chose est qe pucele deit doter si est defaute de charité, car li seint dist qe, ausicum la lampe qe est sanz oile ne put lumere doner, ausi ne put pucelage sanz amur de Deu ne de son prome Deu paer.

---

[i] MS parter. [ii] MS parter. [iii] This heading is in red.

But she can recover her virginity by repenting of her wicked intention. But if once she is corrupted, consenting, by the deed of lechery, she can never recover her virginity by penance or by anything else. So a virgin must often think about the high price of virginity, and very jealously keep herself clean, as you can see by this example: if a man makes use of a piece of land that can produce a hundred measures of corn and he deliberately lets it get into such a state that it can never again produce thirty or sixty at the very most, he has greatly devalued his land. Such is the man or woman who gets married and loses their virginity and dies in wedlock or widowhood. But Saint Augustine says that the virgin daughter is better than her married mother, and if they are both humble they will be honoured in Heaven. The daughter will be like a clear shining star for her virginity, and the mother like a dim star. But if the mother is humble, she will have a place in Heaven with her virgin daughter. And if she is prideful, she will have no place but with the Devil, who fell from there by pride.[16] So virgins must thoroughly drive out all the snares of pride from their body and their heart.

[III: Chapter 7:[17] Six Perils for a Virgin] Here begins the seventh chapter of the compilation of the ten commandments, and tells of six things that a virgin must beware of. There are six paragraphs. I have told you before of the three orders of salvation, that is to say of wedlock, widowhood, virginity. Here, by the grace of God, I shall mention to you the six things of which a virgin must be fearful.

The virgin who wants to save her soul must drive out pride from herself and be humble in heart, in word, and in deed: for this is one of the six things a virgin must first of all beware of. For the saint says God would not have been pleased with Saint Mary's virginity without her humility.[18]

The second thing that a virgin must beware of is lack of charity, for the saint says that, as the lamp without oil cannot give light, so virginity without love of God and of one's neighbour cannot please God.[19]

---

16 See *PL* 39:1568.

17 There is no Chapter 6, though there is no break in the folio numbers.

18 This may be St Bernard; see Love's *Mirror*, p. 27 and note (on p. 243; the passage would be from his *Super "Missus Est"* IV). In *Preaching*, trans. Wenzel, p. 70, Bernard's *Super Missus est angelus* 1.5 is given (*PL* 183:59); see also *BVV*, pp. 255–56. However, the worthlessness of virginity without humility appears to be a medieval commonplace.

19 Cf. *FM*, pp. 194–95, but no source is indicated in the notes; this too may be a commonplace, given the Bible reference below.

Donc Deu dit en le evangelie dé dis virgines qe les cinc sages qe aveint oile en lur lampes, eles furent receus a la porte du cel e entrerent, e les cinc foles qe aveint lampes sanz oile furent rebotés e ne entrerent point. Par les lampes entendez bones overes. Defaute de oile signefie defaute de amur, ce est qe eles ne feseint pas purement pur Deu mes [pur] loange du secle aver, e pur cee furent eles dampnez e neqedent [f.138r] furent eles virgines e aveent bons fez.

La terce chose est qe pucele deit doter qe ele ne seit necligente e tene la amur de son Creator. E ce avent sovent pur ce qe pucele pense qe ele a poy peché, donc ele est meins fervent a penance fere. Mes ele deit encontre penser qe pur ce qe Deu la a hors de peché gardé plus qe autres qe unt vilement e grevement peché, tant la a Deu plus honuré, e pur ce deit ele plus Deu server qe les autres a qui Deu ne a mie tant de grace doné, qe ele ne seit pur sa necligence dampné ou sa virginité. Pensez e gardez qe tote la vie Jesu Crist fu en peine e en labur qe unqe peché ne fit. E si nasquid de une pucele e virgine fu de Deu. E sa vie fu en travail. Mult plus deit nostre vie estre en travail e en labur.

La quarte chose est qe pucele deit eschure est soilur de teche de peché, car la nape qe est mult blaunche e bele a regarder par petit put devener si soillé qe se sera leide chose a ver. Ausi est de le pucelage qe est soillé de peché de orgul e de veineglorie e de lecherouses pensez e de necligences e de autre peché. Dont celes qe unt lour virginité de cors e se sont en alme par corupcion de peché soylliés, eles resemblent les sarclus de mors qe sont dehors blankes e depeynz e si sont dedeinz plein de puneie e de venim de cors de mors. E pur ce a cele virgine mester qe vult sa bonté e alme garder, sovent la parole Deu oier e sovener sei des dis comandemens Deu qe sont en lu de merour a l'alme a regarder si l'em at fet encontre eus e tost par confession laver sei. Dont dit le seint : 'Si vus amez beuté de alme,'[i] fet il, 'amez confession.'

La quinte chose qe pucele deit doter si est duble quer. Sicum la pucele qe vult plere a Deu par chasteté e a[l] mond par ornemenz de dras e de guinples e de cuverchefs e de queintises.

[i] MS leuté de vostre a.

So God says in the Gospel of the ten virgins,[20] that the five wise ones who had oil in their lamps would be received at the gate of Heaven and enter in, and the five foolish ones whose lamps were without oil would be turned away and never enter there. By lamps, understand good works. Lack of oil means lack of love: that is, they do the works not purely for God but to have the praise of the world. For this they were damned, even though they were virgins and had done good works.

The third thing that a virgin must beware of is not to be negligent, and to keep hold of the love of her Creator. And it often happens, because a virgin thinks that she has sinned little, so she is less anxious to do penance. On the contrary, she ought to think that because God has kept her out of sin more than others who have sinned vilely and gravely, so God has honoured her more; therefore she ought to serve God more than those others to whom God has not given so much grace; so that she shall not be damned, with her virginity, for negligence. Think, and see that the whole life of Jesus Christ was in pain and labour, he who never did any sin. And he was born of a maiden, and was a virgin of God. And his life was in travail; so much more ought our life to be in travail and in labour.

The fourth thing that a virgin must avoid is soiling herself with taints of sin. For the cloth that is so white and fair to look on can become so soiled with the slightest thing that it will be an ugly thing to see. So it is with virginity, which is soiled with the sins of pride, vainglory, lecherous thoughts, negligence, and other sin. So those who have virginity of body, and who are soiled in their soul by the foulness of sin, they are like the sepulchres of the dead that are painted white outside and within are full of stench and the poison of dead bodies.[21] Therefore, the virgin who wants to keep her goodness and her soul needs to hear the word of God often, and to remember God's ten commandments which are set out and placed as a mirror for the soul to look into: to see whether one has acted against them and to wash oneself quickly by confession. So the saint says: "If you love beauty of soul," he says, "love confession."[22]

The fifth thing that a virgin must beware of is a double heart. Like the virgin who wants to please God by chastity, and please the world by ornaments of clothes and wimples and kerchiefs and fripperies.

---

[20] Matt 25:1–13.

[21] See Matt. 23:27. See also Acts 23:3: *God shall smite thee, thou whited wall.*

[22] See *BVV* p. 224: "And þ*er*fore seiþ seynt Bernard, 'Loue schrifte, ȝif þou wolte haue fairenesse. For schrifte is nouȝt, wiþ-oute fairenesse.'" See *PL* 182:258 (Bernard, *Ep.* 113.4; and cf. the passage on p. 387 below).

Dont seint Jerome conte qe une femme qe fu apellé Pretexta[ta] par le comandement de son baron atiffa sa file qe ele fu vestue e aorné a la guise de gentile femme seculere encontre la volunté de la pucele qe [f.138v] chastement sei voleit garder e la nut aprés vint un angel de cel e dit a la femme hidusement : 'Vus escumenge, femme. Pur quei fustes vus plus obedient a vostre baron qe a Deu e avez toché la teste de la pucele Deu de vos meins escumengés ? E pur ceo averez vus ore messaventure, qe vos meins ensecherunt ore endreit. E si vus ne repentez, vus e vostre baron e vos enfanz morez de male mort dedenz ces sis mois e irez en enfern.' E tout sicum il dit issi avint. E pur ceo sachez qe tant cum pucele se confourme a la manere du mund par tele manere de coveitises, de tant est ele le meins de Deu amé e prisé. Dont seint Jerome aprent une seinte pucele qe ele ne se acompaine pas a femmes qe [de] lur chevelures sont orguluses e de lur testes ne de manches estreites ne de ridees ne de gerlandesches ne de botons ne de tele vanités, mes qe ele se acompaine a celes qe sont sanz signe de orgul e simplement vestues.

La sime chose est qe pucele deit doter defaute de perseverance. Car li home qe esta, il deit doter e ver qe il ne chece. *Et hoc est quod dicit Apostolus : Qui stat, videat ne cadat* [I Cor. 10:12]. Car cele qe ben comence e pus fet malement ne sera pas coroné, mes cele qe est durable e perseverante en pucelage deke sa fin e en bones vertues, ele sera sauvé e devant tot le mund e de Deu au jugement honuré : *Qui enim perseveraverit usque in finem, hic salvus erit* [Matt. 10:22 & 24:13]. E pur ceo qe pucele deit aver en cel tant de digneté cum vus avez oï, pur ceo li Deable qe engeta Eve hors de Paradis par envie est en tour en totes maneres de fere la pucele perdre sa corone en cel par temtacions e par peché. E pur ceo deit ele estre sages e garnie e queinte e garder son quer e son cors en tote manere de seinteté qe ele puse dire cum fist seinte Cecilie : *Fiat domine cor meum et corpus meum immaculatum ut non confundar* [Ps. 118:80].

Sancti estote quoniam ego sanctus sum [Lev. 11:44]. Checun home qe vult a Deu aprocher e de Deu corone aver, il li covent par seinte vie a Deu sei acorder e en seinte vie perseverer. Donc nostre Sire dit en la autorité qe est [f.139r] issi devant mostré : 'Seez de seinte vie,' fet il, 'si vus volez a moi aprocher, car jeo su seint dé seinz.' Ore entendez ci qe sis choses sont qe gardent home en seinteté.

So Saint Jerome tells of a woman called Pretextata;[23] by her husband's command she decked out her daughter so that she was dressed and adorned in the fashion of a secular worldly gentlewoman, against the will of the maiden who wanted to keep herself chastely. And the next night an angel came from Heaven and spoke dreadfully to the wife: "Woman, I curse you! Why were you more obedient to your husband than to God, and touched the head of God's virgin with your detestable hands? For this you shall now suffer the mishap that your hands will shrivel up forthwith. And if you do not repent, you and your husband and children will die an evil death within these six months and go to Hell." And all he said came to pass. And therefore know that as much as a virgin conforms to the fashion of the world by this manner of covetousness, so much less is she loved and valued by God. So Saint Jerome taught a holy virgin that she must not go about with women who are proud of their hair and their head, nor of narrow sleeves or pleats, garlands or buttons or such vanities, but to accompany those who are without signs of pride, and simply dressed.

The sixth thing is that a virgin must beware lack of perseverance. For the man who stands must take care to see he does not fall. Thus saith the Apostle: *Wherefore let him that thinketh he standeth take heed lest he fall.* For she who begins well and then does badly will not be crowned; but she who is steadfast and persevering in virginity until death, and in good virtue, she shall be saved, and honoured before all the world and God at the Judgement: *he that endureth to the end shall be saved.* And because the virgin shall have so much dignity in Heaven as you have heard — for that, the Devil who drove Eve out of Paradise through envy is forever busy in every way to make the virgin lose her crown in Heaven, by temptations and by sin. And therefore she must be wise and ready and wily, and keep her heart and body in all the ways of holiness, so she can say with Saint Cecilia: *Let my heart be sound in thy statutes; that I be not ashamed.*[24]

[IV: Six Aspects of the Holy Life] *Ye shall therefore sanctify yourselves ... for I am holy.* Every man who wants to draw near to God and have a crown from God, he must accord himself to God through holy life, and persevere in holy life. So Our Lord says by the Authority that is shown here: "Be of holy life," he says, "if you wish to approach me, for I am the Holy of Holies."[25] Now hear what those six things are, that keep a man in holiness.

---

[23] Jerome, Ep. CVII, *PL* 22:872–73.

[24] In *AV*, Ps. 119:80. Cecilia (3rd century saint): see *GL* II:318–23.

[25] Lev. 11:44–45; the Authority is the word of God mediated by Moses and Aaron.

La premere chose si est oreison e devociun a Deu. Et hoc est quod dicit Augustinus : *Per orationes purissimas omnia nobis utilia tribuuntur et cuncta a nobis noxia effugantur*. Car tot pert home seinteté de vie si ceo ne seit par Deu gardé, sicum dit li prophete David : *Nisi dominus custodierit civitatem, frustra vigilat*[i] *qui custodit eam* [Ps. 126:1]. E pur ceo v[u]lt Deu de ceo sovent estre prié. E pur ceo cele pucele qe par necligence lest ses oreisons pert legerement sa seinteté e chet vilement en peché.

La secunde chose est sovenere confession, car li seint dit : 'Si vus amez beuté de alme, hauntez confession par quei la alme est de peché lavee.' E ceo poez vus ver en ces ensamples. Qe vult aver beles meins e nettes, il covent qe eles seent sovent lavez. E lingedrap devent mult soilé par petit quant il est longement deslavé.

La terce chose est oier sermon sovent, car ausicum le merur mustre a le home sa face, ausi nus mustrent les comandemens Deus nos teches e nos defautes qe il nus covent laver par penance. E ausicum le cors faut sanz recreacion de manger, ausi chet la alme en feblesse e en maladie sanz Escripture garder e sanz oier de Deu parler, *quia 'Non in solo pane vivit homo, sed in omni verbo quod procedit de ore Dei,' dicit Deus in evangelio* [Matt. 4:4].

La quarte chose est eschure male compainie, car celes qe sont en la voie vers Paradis ne se deivent pas acompainer a celes qe vunt vers enfern. Ne la pucele qe eime chasteté ne deit pas estre ov celes qe parlent de lavement de lecherie e de vanités, car, sicum David le prophete dit : 'Si vus seez en seinte compainie, vus garderez ben vostre seinteté e si vus seez ov malveis, vus la perderez' ; *Cum sancto sanctus eris et cum perverso perverteris* [Ps. 17:26–27].

La quinte chose est june e discipline e aspre vie, peine de cors e dure penance. Car ausicum sel garde la char de vernmine e de pureture, ausi garde aspre vie le home de temptacions de lecherie cum seif e feim suffrer e veiller e labourer.

---

[i] MS *vigiligat*.

The first thing is prayer and devotion to God, and this is what Augustine says: "By single-minded prayer, all that is profitable to us may be added unto us, and everything harmful to us may be banished."[26] For a man soon loses holiness of life if it is not guarded by God, as the prophet David says: *Except the Lord keep the city, the watchman waketh but in vain.*[27] And therefore God wishes us to say this prayer often. And therefore the virgin who neglects her prayers through carelessness easily loses her holiness and falls vilely into sin.

The second thing is to confess often, for the saint says "If you love beauty of soul, then you must frequent confession: thus the soul is cleansed of sin."[28] And you can see by these examples: Whoever wants to have beautiful clean hands must necessarily wash them often. And linen cloth becomes very dirty when left long unwashed.

The third thing is to hear sermons often. For as the mirror shows his face to a man, so God's commandments show us our stains and faults that we need to clean by penance. And just as the body fails without the refreshment of food, so the soul falls into weakness and sickness without seeing Scripture and without hearing talk of God, for *Man shall not live by bread alone, but by every word that proceedeth out of the mouth of God*, said God in the Gospel.

The fourth thing is to avoid bad company, for those who are on the road to Paradise ought not to accompany those who are going towards Hell. Nor should the virgin who loves chastity be with those who talk about the perfumes of lechery and of vanities, for as David the prophet says: "If you are in holy company you will preserve your holiness, and if you are with the wicked you will lose it"; *With the pure thou wilt shew thyself pure; and with the froward thou wilt shew thyself froward.*[29]

The fifth thing is fasting and discipline and a harsh life: bodily pain and severe penance. For as salt keeps the flesh from vermin and rottenness, so the harsh life — suffering thirst and hunger, and watching and working — keeps the man from temptations to lechery.

---

[26] This is unlikely to be Augustine: see *PL* 99:225A, and *PL* 40:1057 (the passage is marked "auctor incertus"). In Defensor's *Liber Scintillarum* (7th or 8th century), the passage is ascribed to Basil, a 4th century Father. Many MSS survive of this popular florilegium; however, the present author must have taken the passage from some other source in which it was attributed to Augustine (see MacCoull 2002).

[27] In *AV*, Ps. 127:1.

[28] The saint may be Bernard; see note to a similar passage, p. 383 above.

[29] In *AV*, Ps. 18:26.

La sime chose est ammone, car sicum dit li angele Raphael a Tobie : 'Ammone [f.139v] est de grant vertu, car ele delivere le home de mortel peché e de la mort de enfern e purge le home e ne le suffre pas entrer en oscurté ne en tenebris ne en soilur de peché, mes garde le home en seinteté e le fet en le cel entrer e la joie pardurable trover' ; *Elemosina inquid est que liberat a morte et purgat peccata et facit invenire misericordiam et vitam eternam* [Tob. 12:9].

Jeo vus ai devant dit e mustré queles sis choses gardent home en seinteté. Issi aprés vus tocherai par la grace Deu les cinc degrés de chasteté. Ore donke entendez qe cinc degrés e maneres sont de chasteté.

Le premere degré e le plus haut devant Deu si est virginité[i] de quer e de cors par vou promis a Deu ov ferme volunté de garder sei en netteté.

Le secunde degré si est en cele qe a ceste volunté de vivere en tele virginité, mes ele ne vult pas ceste virginité par promesse de bouche ne par vou sa volunté a Deu confermer.

Le terce degré si est en cele qe n'est pas uncore certeine ne purpensé si ele se vult marier ou vivere en virginité, mes cum Deu mettra en sa volunté, ce vodra ele fere e garder.

Le quarte degré est en cele qe de mariage ne de virginité ne a ausicum poi ou nent pensé, mes ce qe ele memes desira. Ce fra ele quant ele vodra de ceo penser.

Le quinte degré est de cele qe est uncore en virginité e a certain purpos de estre marié e de aver delit de sa char en esposailes, mes ele ne seet pas a qi ele se vult acoupler. Ceste n'est pas plus haute devant Deu, mes plus base qe bone femme qe est marié, car cele ne set pas qe ele vult aver. E la femme qe marié est ne quert autre fors celi a qi ele coplé.

[i] MS virginitete.

The sixth thing is alms, for as the angel Raphael said to Tobit, "Almsgiving is of great virtue, for it delivers a man from mortal sin and from the death of Hell, and purges the man, and will not let him go into darkness and shadows, nor into the filth of sin, but keeps the man in holiness and makes him enter Heaven and find everlasting joy"; *For alms doth deliver from death, and shall purge away all sin. Those that exercise alms and righteousness shall be filled with life.*

[V: Five Degrees of Chastity] I have told and shown you, above, what six things keep a man in holiness. Here next I shall mention, by the grace of God, the five degrees of chastity. So listen now, to what the five degrees and kinds of chastity are.

The first degree, and the highest before God, is virginity of heart and of body, promised by vow to God with steadfast desire to keep herself in cleanness.

The second degree is in her who has this desire to live in such virginity, but she does not wish to confirm her will in this virginity by spoken promise or vow to God.

The third degree is in her who is not yet certain, has not yet decided, whether to marry or live in virginity; but as God puts in her will, so she shall wish to do and maintain herself.

The fourth degree is in her who has not yet thought much or at all about marriage or virginity — but it will be what she herself desires. She will do it when she wishes to consider it.

The fifth degree is in her who is still a virgin and has a set purpose to be married and have fleshly delight in wedlock, but she does not know whom she wishes to be joined with. This one is no higher before God, but below the good woman who is married, for she does not know whom she wishes to have. And the woman who is married must seek no other than him to whom she is joined.

Memes ces cinc maneres de degrés sont en chasteté de vidueté, car cele vidue qe conferme de quer e de promesse a Deu par vou de bouche sa chasteté est plus haute devant Deu qe ne sont les autres qe ne volunt ceo voer. E ceste chasteté diverse ausi ben est en homes cum en femmes. Mes ce sachez, qe nul home ne nule femme put chasteté aver ne garder ne autre vertue purchacer sanz especiale grace de Deu. *Et hoc est quod dicitur* [f.140r] *a domino in evangelio : Sine me nichil potestis facere* [John 15:5] e pur ceo deit home e femme ententivement e sovent prier Deu de vertues dont il ou ele a mester a sa alme sauver e Deu li vult plus volunteres ottreer qe il ou ele vult demander. EXPLICIT.

These five kinds of degree are the same in chaste widowhood, for the widow who confirms her chastity in her heart, and in promise to God by spoken vow, is higher before God than those others who do not wish to vow this. And this chastity, of various kinds, is good in men as in women. But know this, that no man and no woman can have or keep chastity, nor acquire any other virtue, without special grace of God. And this is what it says of God in the Gospel: *For without me ye can do nothing*; and therefore man and woman must often and earnestly pray to God for the virtues they need to save their souls, and God will more willingly grant what they wish to ask for. *Explicit*.

Chapter 16

Purgatory[1]

Introduction

The present edition is from Oxford, Bodleian Library MS Bodley 654 (SC 27669) (s.xiii$^{2/4}$), ff.119r–125r, and also refers to MS Bodley 82 (s.xiv^{in}) (B82 in notes), ff.11v–28v.[2] The anonymous treatise draws on Anselm of Canterbury, Caesarius of Arles (c. 470–542), Honorius Augustodunensis;[3] and on a sermon by John of la Rochelle.[4] Composed in the thirteenth century, it resembles works in various languages inspired by the Fourth Lateran Council. There are seven manuscripts, and in two of these (not in the one presented here) it forms Part 3 of the *Compileison for the Religious Life*.[5] It was translated into Latin, and attributed to Robert Grosseteste in the fourteenth century.[6]

Robert Grosseteste, bishop of Lincoln 1235–1253, was one of the greatest writers and thinkers of his generation; philosopher, theologian, scientist — a useful summary of his intellectual achievements is found in McEvoy's *The Philosophy of Robert Grosseteste*.[7] Soon after his death, many dedicated disciples spent months and even years copying, collating, and disseminating his work. Furthermore, his thought was widely influential;[8] Matthew Paris describes him cordially in his *Historia Anglorum*, and all the epithets can be summed

---

[1] D&B 645, prose, *Les Peines de Purgatorie*, attributed to Robert Grosseteste.

[2] See also Relihan 1978, cited below *passim*; there is also a critical edition (unpublished) by Relihan, based on the Arundel MS.

[3] Early 12th century (self-styled "of Autun" but not identified).

[4] d. 1245, collaborated with Alexander of Hales. See Relihan 1978, pp. 159–60, who notes that he has been unable to find the specific source among John's sermons. A third of the work is based on a portion of Anselm's *De similitudinibus* (the last two chapters almost in their entirety); chapter 1 cites his *Meditatio ad concitandum timorem*; chapter 3 cites an identifiable sermon by Caesarius, although it is here attributed to Augustine.

[5] See Appendix, below; also see D&B 644, which deems that the Purgatory was apparently independent of the *Compileison*.

[6] For the work and its context (in several MSS), see Hunt 1985. See also Thomson 1940, pp. 136–37. Relihan 1978 discusses attribution and date; the *Peines* is a source for two Middle English works, *The Pricke of Conscience* and *A tretyse of gostly batayle*, especially the former (pp. 158 & 166–68).

[7] McEvoy 1982, pp. 445–52.

[8] See, for example, Hessenauer 1995.

up in one main point: the importance to Robert of the cure of souls.[9] He came of low birth, and Anglo-Norman was his native language.

Robert wrote a number of works in Latin and in Anglo-Norman; the best-known among the latter is *Le Chasteau d'Amour* (ten are listed in D&B's Index of Authors).[10] The attribution of our Purgatory to Robert is not very surprising, given his real concern with pastoral care; further, anonymous works have a tendency to become attached to well-known author-figures. His followers may have collected the piece and added it to the canon quite early, or it may indeed be by him, as several scholars maintain.[11]

The treatise (he calls it a "compilation") is headed section by section in careful detail, and reads like a spoken sermon: "Nous entendoms ... de parler a vus," and "Ore entendez ci touz communement e devoutement." However, the writer exhorts to meditation: "pensez ... pensez ententivement"; there is some use of the inexpressibility *topos*: "qe jeo ne vus sai numbrer"; he continues to use a personal tone: "car lur me semble ... or poez vus penser ... cher alme qe ceste escrit lirez." He addresses readers more than once — the text is intended also to be read privately, in spite of its sermon-like style. The audience was perhaps capable of understanding some Latin: it is notable that the Latin citations are not always translated exactly. It is addressed to "his" (unless written by a woman) brothers and sisters in God, and one might be tempted to correct "ses" to "mes," because the writer never uses the third person for himself again. But another manuscript of this text contains the same prologue, using an exactly parallel form of words.[12]

No anthology of medieval devotional literature would be complete without some fire and brimstone; the pains are described in uncomfortable detail, but it is notable that the corresponding glories that reward the saved souls

[9] Ibid. p. 377. Hessenauer further notes that respect for Robert led to his being regarded as "a sort of saint," although he was never canonized — hence the references to Saint Robert that are found in writings about him. Hessenauer, unlike McEvoy, lists the Purgatory among Robert's works. Thomson 1940 likewise confidently lists the Purgatory, both Latin and Anglo-Norman; it does not appear among his Spurious nor even Doubtful works.

[10] See McEvoy 2000, pp. 19–22, for details of his life; pp. 146–53 for his Anglo-Norman writings (in which the author dismisses the attribution of the Purgatory to Robert).

[11] Work is continuing on Robert's canon: Goering and Mantello identified and edited two more of his penitential texts ("Early Penitential Writings" and "Perambulauit Iudas") in the 1980s.

[12] MS Bodley 82 [f.11v]: "A ses tresch[e]rs freres e sors ...." See also Thomson 1940, pp. 136–37 (for the Latin version) & 158 (for the Anglo-Norman).

are also very vivid — making them more desirable, of course.[13] The notion of Purgatory — not to be confused with Hell, from which there is no deliverance — was an enormously fruitful subject for medieval literature and meditation.[14] Stories of journeys through Purgatory combined elements of hagiography, allegory, and romance. The present text is concerned with no such adventures, however edifying, but with the real fate of the souls after death who will emerge only when (if ever) their penance is completed.

[13] Thomson 1940 (p. 156) remarks that the *Peines* attempts to popularize or "visualize" religion.

[14] An account of Purgatory can be found in *GL*, under the heading All Souls (in Latin: *De commemoratione omnium fidelium defunctorum*); the chapter is more concerned with examples of intercession (which can reduce a soul's sentence in Purgatory) than with the pains and contrasting delights, as ours is. See also the General Introduction (Punishments and Rewards), above.

Text

[f.119r] **[Introduction]** ***In omnibus operibus tuis memorare novissima tua et in eternum non peccabis*** [Ecclus. 7:40].[i]

A ses cher freres e suers en Deu, a touz iceus ke ceste compilesoun lirunt,[ii] ou de autre lire l'orunt,[iii] saluz e sancté de alme e de cors en le douz Jesu Crist qe est nostre verei saveour.[iv] Nous entendoms par la grace nostre douz Seniur, solum[v] ceo qe nus le aums oÿ e apris en seinte Escripture, de parler a vus en iceste compilesoun de la peine de purgatorie a[l] savaciun de vos almes. Deu le vus ottreit issint fere par son beneit noun. Amen.[vi]

En ceste compileson donc, adeprimes, par la grace del Seint Espirit, vus moustrom pur quei homme deit sovent de quer penser de sa fin. Pus diroms de la peine de purgatorie. Aprés ce vus tocherom lé set peines [e] pur quel pechés les almes sunt en purgatorie penés. Aprés ceo vus diroms certeine e verai resoun pur quei vus devez enterement penser du grant jour de jugement. Pus aprés ce vus dirom de la grande peine de enfern. Au drein vus tocherom les glories qe le cors e lé almes sauvés en averunt e les confusiouns qe les dampnez averunt saunz fin. E aitaunt si finerom nostre sermon de purgatorie.

[Chapter 1]

[B82 f.12v] Ore entendez ci touz communement e devoutement. Oez ceo qe Salomon li sage dit en un livre qe il fit par la grace du ceint Espiriz ou il issi dit : 'En touz vos uveres,' fet il, 'pensez la fin de vostre vie e jamés peché ne frez.' Pensez dounc sovent qe vus morez e vus ne savez quant ne de quele mort ne en quel lu ne en quel tens ne en quel estat. E pur ceo, sicum dit seint Austin, toutdis seit vostre drein jour par devaunt vos eus de vostre quer. Quant vus levez donke de vostre lit, ne quedez pas vivre dekes a la nut ; quant vus alez cocher, ne quedez pas oveke la vie lever. Pensez dunke totes heures de la joie du cel e de la peine pardurable de enfern, e issi porez vus ben refreiner vostre cors e vostre quer de coveitises e de tote[s] mauveités. Pensez qe vostre cors, ja taunt ne le noricez, qe il ne devendra a la mort viaunde a verms e poreture e hidour a ver e la alme ov grant pour du cors partira. Car lé debles serunt la en present e les angeles a desputer de la vie de l'homme du comencement dekes a la fin. Les aungeles dirunt le ben e les debles le mal, qe ren ne sera oblié.

---

[i] Underlined in red (red line, not red script). [ii] B82 'lyrrunt', Latin *legerint.* The Latin is printed in Thomson 1940, p. 136. [iii] [*Sanctus Robertus lincolniensis*] *salutem et sanitatem.* [iv] *salvator* [*deinde indulgencie centum dies*]. B82 'n. v. salveor, Amen.' [v] *secundum quod audivimus de pena purgatorii.* [vi] B82 omits the ascription. The first sentence above and the paragraph below appear in red.

Translation

[Introduction] ***Whatsoever thou takest in hand, remember the end, and thou shalt never do amiss.***[1]

To his beloved brothers and sisters in God, to all those who read this compilation or hear it read by another, greetings, and health of soul and body in dear Jesus Christ who is our true Saviour. We intend to speak to you in this compilation, by the grace of our sweet Lord, according to what we have heard and learned in Holy Scripture, of the pains of Purgatory, to the salvation of your souls. May God grant you to do so by his blessed name. Amen.

So, in this compilation, by the grace of the Holy Spirit, we show you first of all why man ought often to think deeply about his death. Then we shall speak of the pain of Purgatory. After that, we shall deal with the seven pains, and which sins souls are tormented for in Purgatory. Then we shall give you true and certain reasons why you must think sincerely about the great Day of Judgement. Next, we shall speak of the great torment of Hell. Lastly, we shall treat of the glories that the souls and bodies of the saved shall have, and the destruction that the damned shall have without end. And so we shall finish our account of Purgatory.

[Chapter 1]

Now listen to this, all together and with devotion. Hear what the wise Solomon said in a book he made by the grace of the Holy Spirit, where he says: "In all your works," he says, "think about the end of your days and you shall never sin." Therefore give frequent thought to the death you will die: you do not know when or how or where, nor in what time or state of mind. And therefore, as Saint Augustine says, "Let your last day be ever before the eyes of your heart."[2] So when you rise from your bed, do not expect to live until nightfall; when you go to bed, do not expect to get up alive. Therefore be ever mindful of both the joy of Heaven and the everlasting pain of Hell, and so you will be able to restrain your body and heart from covetousness and from all vices. Think that your body, however well you feed it, will become food for worms and rottenness, and hideous to behold in death, and the soul will depart from the body in terror. For the devils will be present there, and the angels, to dispute the man's life from beginning to end. The angels will tell of the good, and the devils the bad, so that nothing shall be forgotten.

---

[1] In *AV*, Ecclus. 7:36. Robert translates "Solomon's" words, below.

[2] Cf. *A tretyse of gostly batayle*, ed. Horstman, p. 428; the notion may be from Pseudo-Augustine (*Liber de spiritu et anima*, xxxi, *PL* 40:800), or proverbial.

Totes les pensés a quels homme a concentu e totes les [f.119v] paroles qe home avera parlé serunt la examinés e les fez touz serunt moutrez, qe ren ne sera celé.

E ceo est ke Deu dit en le evvangelie : 'Nule chose ne est si privement musee qe ne sera moutré, ne si celé qe ne sera sue apert' : *Nichil absconditum quod non reveletur nec occultum quod non sciatur* [Matt. 10:26 ; Mark 4:22 ; Luke 8:17, 12:2]. E seint Anselme parout a l'alme e dit issi : 'Quei dirét[i] vus e quei frez vus quant reson serra demaundé de tote vostre vie, cum vus le avez mené dekes ataunt de tens cum vus poez de l'oyl cligner :[ii] *De omni verbo ocioso quod fuerint, homines reddent de eo rationem in die iudicii* [Matt. 12:36]. *Ibi etiam discutitur vita secretissima que est cordis.*' Adunke serez vus blamé e pené du tens qe vus averez despendu ou en par[o]le ou en cilence ou en labour ou en quiete, si vus ne eez eu entente e volunté a fere le pl[a]iser Deu si se ne seit amendé en ceste vie ? Estreitement sera vostre vie chargé dekes a la meindre pensé qe vus unkes avez pensé. Allas ! cum mouz de pechez qe vus ne poez ore veer ne remembrer vendrunt dunc avant apertement pur voir plus e par aventure plus a doter e plus oribles qe ces qe vus ore poez ver e mouz de choses qe vus quedez qe eles seint ore ben fetes apparunt a cel hore trop lede pechez. Dunke vus covent receivere solum vos fes ou peine ou joie. Car la alme qe ci est purgé de tote maners de peché morteus e de venials par penaunce e par oreisoun entra tantost ové les aungeles en la joie de Paradis.

Dé peines de purgatorie.[iii]

Mes icele alme qe ci a pris penaunce de morteus pechez e a la mort n'en a pas parfet sa penaunce cel alme ausi qe[iv] n'est pas purgé dé veniaus pechez, icestes deus maners des almes serunt en purgatorie ov gref peines par lé debles purgés e penés, la quele peine est plus dure e plus greve a sentir e a suffrer qe tote la peine qe lé martirs unt sufferte e plus grevouse qe tote les peines qe home poreit en ice mound sentir ou ver ou penser. La sera la alme en cele dure peine du Deables pené karaunte aunz pur la penaunce qe ele pout en karaunte jours issi legerement aver fet e pur karaunte jours en ice mond karaunte aunz la, sicum dit nostre [Seignur] per Ezechiel le prophete : *Diem pro anno dedi tibi* [Ez. 4:6]. E nekedent [f.120r] cele peine la ne fet rens a l'alme for purge peché. Car home nule merite ne nule joie en cele peine ne purchasera si il fut mil aunz en purgatorie.

---

[i] MS deret. [ii] MS digner. [iii] In red. [iv] MS ausi cum qe.

All the thoughts that a man has consented to, all the words he has spoken, shall be examined there; all his deeds shall be shown, so that nothing shall be hidden.

And this is what God says in the Gospel: "Nothing is so secretly hidden that it shall not be shown, nor so concealed that it shall not be openly known"; *For there is nothing hid, which shall not be manifested; neither was any thing kept secret, but that it should come abroad.* And Saint Anselm spoke to the soul, saying this: "What will you say and what will you do, when you are asked to justify your whole life, and how you have led it since you were first able to open your eyes? For *every idle word that men shall speak, they shall give account thereof in the day of judgement*; 'the secrets of the heart will there be broken open.'"[3] Then you will be blamed and punished for the time you have spent — in speech or silence, in labour or rest — if you have not had the intention or will to do what will please God, nor have improved yourself in this life. Your life will be examined closely, down to the least thought that you have ever thought. Alas! How many sins that you cannot now see or remember will then come forward openly, to be seen more clearly and perhaps more fearfully — and more horrible than those you can now see; and many things that you now think were well done will in that hour appear to be very ugly sins. Thus it will be proper for you to receive pain or joy, according to your deeds. For the soul that has been cleansed here, of all kinds of mortal and venial sins, by penance and prayer, shall enter straightaway into the joy of Paradise with the angels.

Of the pains of Purgatory.

But the soul that has undertaken penance here, for mortal sins, and at death has not completed its penance, and also the soul that is not cleansed of venial sins: these two kinds of soul shall be in Purgatory to be purged and punished with harsh pain by the devils. This pain is harsher and harder to feel and suffer than all the pain that martyrs have endured, and harsher than all the pains that one can feel or see or imagine in this world. There, the soul will be punished with this cruel Devil's pain for forty years, for a penance it could easily have completed, here, in forty days. Forty days in this world for forty years there, as Our Lord said by Ezekiel the Prophet: *I have appointed thee each day for a year.* And nevertheless, the pain suffered there does nothing for the soul except purge sin. For if a man were a thousand years in Purgatory he would earn neither merit nor joy through that pain.

[3] See Relihan 1978 in general for Anselm in this text.

Mes la peine qe home en iceste vie suffre ov bone volunté vaut a deus choses : a purger peché ci e pur checune peine avera home en cel especiale joie e ceo sera saunz nule fin, sicum dit frere Johan de la Rochele en un sermon des almes.

[Chapter 2] Issi comence le secunde chapitre de la compelison de purgatorie qe parout dé set peines par lé queles la alme est purgé e icest chapittre si en a set parografs.[i]

Je vus ai par devant moustré pur quei vus devez sovenerement penser de vostre fin e coment adounc tote vostre vie sera serché estreitement dekes a la meindre pensé, e enaprés queles deus maners des almes serunt en purgatorie penez. Issi aprés vus tocherum les peines especiales par lé queles la alme, quant ele departira du cors, est purgé. Ore entendez ben ci, vus qe cest escrit lesez, les set peines par les queles la alme est purgé quant ele departe hors de ceste vie.

La premere peine si est hidouse visiun de diables qe se moustrerunt apertement a l'alme en la mort, quant ele deit du cors departir ausi cum liouns cruels a chalanger e a raver la alme ouvekes eus ou en enfern ou en purgatorie pur ces pechez.

La secunde peine est de la grant doute del hidur qe la alme avera avaunt qe le jugement seit fini entre les angeles e lé deables de estre sauvé ou dampné, ausicum est quant home est entempesté en la mer e a grant doute de neer. Car tout eit la alme dreit fei e ferm esperaunce, nequedent Deu soffre qe la alme eit dounc cel pour pur purger sei de ces pechez.

La terce peine est le fu de purgatorie en lequel la alme si longement ardera dekes ele seit purgé de totes necligences e de totes maners de pechez. E autaunt ou plus qe li fu dunt l'em se chaufe ci est plus chaud qe n'est li ray du solail qe est lusaunt sur la terre, de taunt est li feu de purgatorie plus chaud qe le fu qe arde issi devant le gent. E ataunt cum il est plus fort isci mettere son pe nu en fu qe chaufe, ataunt plus fort sera a la alme de arder en cel fu nue quant ele sera de son cors ausicum tote despoilé.

[i] In red.

But pain that a man suffers with good grace in this life benefits him in two things: to purge sin here; and, for each pain, a man will receive especial joy in Heaven — and that will be everlasting, as Brother John of la Rochelle says in a sermon on souls.

[Chapter 2] Here begins the second chapter of the treatise on Purgatory, which tells of the seven pains that purge the soul, and this chapter therefore has seven divisions.[4]

I have shown you, above, why you must often think about your death, and then how your whole life is to be examined minutely, down to the smallest thought. And then, which two classes of soul will be punished in Purgatory. Hereafter, we shall expound to you the particular punishments by which the soul is purged when it leaves the body. Now, you who read this writing: understand well the seven punishments that cleanse the soul when it departs out of this life.

The first pain is the hideous sight of the devils, that show themselves openly to the soul in death when it must depart from the body: like cruel lions to persecute and ravage the soul that is among them, either in Hell or in Purgatory, for its sins.

The second pain is the great fear and horror that the soul will feel, before the judgement of the angels and the devils is completed — to be saved or damned — so it is when a man is storm-tossed in the sea and is in terror of drowning. For even if the soul has good faith and firm hope, nevertheless God allows the soul to feel this terror so as to cleanse itself of its sins.

The third is the fire of Purgatory, in which the soul will go on burning until it is purged of all negligence and all forms of sin. And as much, or more, as the fire we warm ourselves by is hotter than the ray of sunlight shining on earth, by so much is the fire of Purgatory hotter than the fire that burns here before us. And as it is harder, here, to put one's naked foot into burning fire, so much harsher will it be for the soul to burn naked in that fire, as it will have been stripped bare of its body.

[4] "parografs" seems to mean sections. Hunt refers to paragraphs, in quotation marks, in his discussion of the text (Hunt 1985, p. 8). It will be seen later that the author does not always keep to the promised divisions.

La quarte peyne sera maladie dont la alme serra [f.120v] pené, kar ausicum maladie issi en diverse manere greve le cors, ausi est la alme en purgatorie grevé e pené en sa manere de maladie pur peché, kar les uns sunt ausicum en parlesie pur accidie e pur peresse en le servise Deu, acuns sunt cum enjaunez pur envie, acuns sunt sicum en fevere pur ire, acuns sunt sicum en menesun e en flux pur lecherie de la quele il furent repentaunz, mes il ne parfirent pas parfitement lur penaunce en lur vie, acuns sunt cum en apostume e en ague pur orgul. Pensez dunc cum forte peyne sereit au cors de estre en une de ceste maladiez, ou karaunte aunz ou plus, ou deu jors ou treis, e pur ce poez vus entendre ke la alme est plus grevé de tele peine ke le cors, kar ausicum petite chose greve le oil plus qe le pé ou la mein, si est la alme pur sa tendre nature plus grevé e de meins qe ne est le cors.

La quinte peyne est qe les almes sont ausicum gens qe sont liez en prison, kar il sunt liez dé liens pur peché e enclos qe il ne pount hors vener deske lé lienz seint gastés e anentiz par le fu de purgatorie. Ne eles ne pount aprés ceste vie purchaser rens a eus deleverer, car eles ne pount ne menduier ne enpromter ne rens deservir, kar la n'est pas tens ne lu a merite deservir. Pensez dounc cum greve chose est as almes de estre cent aunz ou plus ou meins uncore en cele prison tormentez des diables e des peines avaunt nomez. Kar lé diables ount poer de tormenter les almes ausi longement cum eles unt teche ou semblaunce de peché, mes nent plus qe eles sunt de tot purchez.[i]

La sime peine est exil, kar les almes sunt exilés hors de ceste vie de lur amis saunz returner ne en lur pays, ceo est a dire en paradis entrer ne porunt, ne nule novele de nous ne unt, qe issi sumus en ceste vie taunt qe Deu face de nus sa volunté.

La setime peine est qe les almes sunt la ausicum en desert ou defaute est de tote choses dont eles se pount deliter. Ore sunt en freit, ore sunt en chaud, [or sunt] en si tresgrant plus[ii] ke nul home issi put penser. E si sunt en feim e en seif e en tote maners de defautes ové les peines avant nomez. E pur le grant desir qe eles ount a ver nostre Seinur plus sunt en une manere penez pur ceo qe eles ne pount lur desir aver qe des peines qe lur covent pur lur trespas suffrer.

---

[i] B82 'ke eles sunt de tutes purgez.' [ii] B82 'pluyes'.

The fourth pain will be the sickness that will punish the soul, for as various kinds of ailments afflict the body here, so in Purgatory the soul is pained in kind of illness according to its sin. For some are as if in palsy, because of sloth and laziness in the service of God, some are as if jaundiced with envy, others are as in fever with anger. Some have diarrhoea and flux, because of the lechery they repented of, but they did not completely finish their penance during this life; some are afflicted with rotting flesh and ague, because of pride. So imagine what a sore affliction it would be to the body to have one of those sicknesses for forty years or more, or even two or three days; by this you can understand that a soul is more vulnerable to such pain than a body. Just as a little thing hurts your eye more than your foot or hand; so the soul by its delicate nature is more hurt, and by less, than the body is.

The fifth is that the souls are like people chained in prison, for they are bound with the bonds of sin and shut up so that they can never come out until the bonds are consumed and eaten away by the fire of Purgatory. Nor can they, after this life, obtain any means of deliverance, for they cannot beg or borrow, nor get credit, for that is neither the time or place to acquire merit. Imagine, then, what a hard thing it is for souls to be tormented by devils and by the pains already mentioned in that prison for a hundred years, or less, or more. For the devils have power to torment souls for as long as they have any spot or shadow of sin, though no more once they are purged of everything.

The sixth is exile, for souls are exiled from this life, from their friends, with no return ever to their own land; this means they cannot enter Paradise nor hear any news of us, who are here in this life for as long as God does his will with us.

The seventh is that souls are there as if in the wilderness, where everything that could delight them is lacking. They are now in the cold, now in the heat, now in the fiercest rain anybody here could imagine. They are hungry and thirsty and in all kinds of deprivation, together with the pains already mentioned. And because of the fierce desire they feel to see Our Lord they suffer in yet another way, for they cannot have their desire but only the pains they must suffer for their misdeeds.[5]

---

[5] Relihan has been unable to identify the main source for our text among John of la Rochelle's writings, but states that this list of torments is from a sermon on All Souls (Relihan 1978, p. 159 note 9).

[Chapter 3] Issi comence le [f.121r] **terce chapitre de la compelison de purgatorie qe nus moustre pur quele peché les almes sunt en purgatorie penés, si en a deus perografs.**[i]

Je vus ai devaunt toché des peynes especiales par lé queles la alme, quant ele departe de son cors, est purgé. Issi aprés vus parleray des pechez pur les queles les almes sont en purgatorie penez. Deu nus doint issi fere qe il prenge a gré. Ore donk ci entendez pur quei les almes sont la si penez e les eschuez, qe la ne veignez.

Primes sont eles la penez pur ceo qe il ne parfirent pas ci lor penaunce dé graunz pechez qe sont morteus e nequedent il en furent dolens e veraiment confés de cels pechez. Pus sunt la peneez pur veniaus pechez e pur necligences pur ceo qe il ne se voleint de teu menues pechez en lur vie purger. E taunz sunt qe nul home en ceste vie ne les seet numbrer. Mes seint Augusti[n] nome acuns de cels pechez e dit issint : Quant vus mangez ou bevez plus qe vus ne avez mester, quant vus parlez plus qe mester ne sereit, quant vus estes en silence ou vus pussez ben fere e ayder de vostre parole e ne volez, quant vus parlez asprement a poveres pur ceo qe il demandent egrement[ii] du ben pur Deu, qaunt vus estes sein de cors e vus volez manger quant autres junent, quant par sompnolence e pesauntime de dormer home plus tard qe il ne dust veet a le eglise ou ses prier[e]s e ses hores tardivement ou[iii] en negligence dit, quant home en matrimonie quert delit charnel ov sa femme espouse saunz desir de engendrer enfaunz a le honur Deu, quant home tardivement visite les malades e seu[s] qe sunt enprisonez en cors, ou en la prison au Diable en alme par peché ou cels qe sont en purgatorie penez, les quels visiter par lermes e par oreison est grant amone, quant home ne met son leu poer a acorder cels qe sunt en descord, quant home parout asprement a son prosme quant il dust parler doucement, quant home prise la gent par losengerie plus qe ne dust tot dit il verité, quant home despent son tens en jaungle ou en udives paroles ou en veines pencés, ou en moster ou dehors, quant home se jure hastivement saunz purpens e pus ne pust son serment tener, quant home maudit legerement saunz coupe, quant home at suspeciun e quidaunce de mal la ou nul mal ne est.

---

[i] In red. [ii] MS engressement. [iii] MS t. e ou.

[Chapter 3] Here begins the third chapter of the treatise on Purgatory, that shows us which sins souls are punished for in Purgatory; there are two sections.

I have told you above of the special punishments by which the soul is purged when it leaves the body. Here, I shall next tell you of the sins that souls are punished for in Purgatory. God grant us to do here what will please him. So now hear why souls are so punished there, and of those who escape and never come there.[6]

First, they are punished there because they did not complete their penance here, for grave sins that were mortal, although they were sorry for them and had truly confessed those sins. Then, they are punished there for venial sins and for sins of omission, because they did not want to cleanse themselves of such small sins during their life. And there are so many that nobody in this world could count them. But Saint Augustine names some of these sins and says this:[7] When you eat or drink more than you need to, when you talk more than is necessary, when you keep silent where your words could do good or help somebody but you don't want to, when you speak sharply to the poor because they ask eagerly for alms in God's name, when you are in bodily health and wish to eat while others fast; when being drowsy and heavy with sleep one comes to church later than one should, or says one's prayers and hours late or negligently; when in marriage a man seeks carnal delight with his wedded wife without desiring to beget children for the honour of God; when one delays visiting the sick and those who are imprisoned in body, or in spirit imprisoned by the Devil because of sin, or those who are suffering in Purgatory. To visit these, by means of tears and prayers, is an act of great charity. Or when one does not loyally do all in one's power to reconcile those who are at discord; when one speaks sharply to one's neighbour when one ought to speak gently; when one praises people flatteringly rather than saying the truth; when one passes one's time in gossiping, in idle words or vain thoughts — either in church or outside — when one swears something hastily without thinking and then cannot keep one's promise; when one blames somebody casually without their guilt; when one has suspicions and believes evil to be where no evil is.

---

[6] There are not really two sections to this chapter. The writer means, perhaps, two kinds of sinner — but note he does not mention "those who never come there" in the following passage.

[7] Relihan cites the sermon, actually by Caesarius, on which this list of venial sins is based (Relihan 1978, p. 159 note 10).

Icés sunt menus pechez [f.121v] e plusurs tels qe nul home ne les put counter pur les quels la alme n'est pas digne a vener par devaunt Deu deskes ele seit de cels peché[s] purgez.

E pur ceo covent il qe nus en ceste vie fasom penaunce de tels pechez par nostre bone volunté. Ou si nostre Seignur nus enveit maladie ou greve perte ou perte de nos chateus ou de nos charneus amis ou autre tribulaciun amere, e donke si nus avumz bone pacience ausicum li bon enfaunt quant sun pere le chastie, si nus renduns graces a Deu e confessum nus de touz nos pechez solum nostre poer, donc nus purge Deu en ceste vie. E pur ceo covent il qe home seit sovent en lermes e en ureisuns e en junes e qe il face amone a son poer e les overes de merci a quere la merci Deu qe il pusse ov les angeles estre en alme en paradys saunz entrer en la peine de purgatorie quant le cors sera mis en tere a porrer e a estre viaunde a verms.

[Chapter 4] Isci comence le quarte chapittre de la compelison de purgatorie qe nus amoneste de penser sovent du jour de graunt jugement, si en a quatre parografs.[i]

Je vus ai devaunt parlé de pechez pur les queles les almes sunt en purgatorie penez. Ci aprés par la grace Deu vus toucheray brevement de le jour de graunt jugement qe vus par ceo pussez Deu doter e eschure encombrement de peché Deu vus doint par sa grace. Isci donc aprés pensez ententivement du drein jour quant Deu fra sun jugement de tote manere de gent e entendez coment le firmament e tot le mund sera plein de fu ardaunt e nostre Seignur Jesu vendra hors du cel apertement ov les aungeles e ov les archangeles, e les aungeles porterunt apertement la seinte croiz ou il fu pené e les clous e la launce dount il fu crucifié e percé e la coroune d'espines dont il fu coroné enco[n]tre pecheours qui lui saveint poi de gré e qe li unt morte[le]ment par lur peché corucé, ce est adire les signes de sa passion serunt mostré encontre pecheours cum les signes de ses plais e[ii] signe de la croiz e les anguisses e la mort e la manere de ses peines qe il suffri pur eus[iii] serunt [r]eprochez devaunt tot le mund encontre eus.

[i] In red. [ii] MS a. [iii] B82 'nus'.

These are the small sins, and there are so many like them that nobody can count them, for which the soul is not worthy to come before God until it is purged of them.

And therefore, in this life, it is proper for us to do penance for such sins with good will. Or, if Our Lord sends us sickness, or serious loss: loss of our chattels, or of our close friends, or other bitter tribulation; and if we then have great patience, like a good child when its father chastises it; if we give thanks to God and confess all our sins to the best of our ability, then God purifies us in this life. And so one ought often to be in tears, prayers, and fasting, to give alms and do the works of mercy as much as one can, to beg God's mercy, so one's soul may be in Paradise with the angels without going into the pain of Purgatory, when the body is put into the earth to rot and be food for worms.

[Chapter 4] Here begins the fourth chapter of the treatise on Purgatory, which admonishes us to think often of the day of great Judgement. There are four sections.[8]

I have told you, above, about the sins that souls are punished for in Purgatory. By the grace of God I shall tell you next, briefly, about the great Day of Judgement, so you may thereby be able to fear God and avoid the encumbrance of sin. God grant you this by his grace. So now, next, think intently about the Last Day, when God shall perform his judgement upon all sorts and conditions of people, and hear how the firmament and all the earth shall be filled with a burning fire. And Our Lord Jesus shall come openly out of Heaven with the angels and the archangels, and the angels shall carry — plainly for all to see — the Holy Cross where he was tormented, and the nails and the lance that crucified and pierced him, the crown of thorns he was crowned with, against the sinners who were ungrateful and mortally angered him by their sin. That is, the Signs of the Passion shall be shown against sinners as the signs of his wounds and the sign of the Cross, and the tortures and the death and the manner of pains he suffered for them shall be held in reproach against them before all the world.

8 Here again, the chapter does not divide into four. The seven torments mentioned below were enumerated in Robert's Chapter 2.

E un archangel dira haut de une bosine ce mot :[i] 'Vus touz qe estes [morz], levez de mort en vie e checun alme receive [f.122r] son cors.' Adonke en meindre tens qe home pout cligner[ii] de l'oil, ce est adire en un moment, en taunt de tens cum vostre mein torner poez, vendrunt touz cels qe unkes en ventre de lor mere vie aveint en cors e en alme qe nul ne pora tapir qe il ne venge avaunt e les pecheours serunt tremblans plein de pour e de hidur, kar nostre Sire Jesu Crist a mout de eus corucé enco[n]tre eus. E enfern aval sera overt a receivere lé malveis, la tere aval tremblera de terremote, kar ele ne vodra mes parter lé pecheours. Le mond environ sera tout ardaunt e les diables serunt en coste de eus e lor pechez serunt apertement devaunt eus e devaunt tot le mund e devaunt les aungeles e devaunt toz les diables moustrez. Le cel amont ferra les pecheurs de foudre e de toneire e il se vodrunt en la mer musser, mes la mer les gettera hors de sei sur la tere vilement. Nul liu les recevera fors soul enfern. E adonc dira nostre Seignur le hidous mot : 'Alez vus maleite gens en fu qe ardera pardurablement qe est aparaylé au diables e a lur servauns' ; *Ite, inquit, maledicti in ignem eternum qui paratus est diabolo et angelis eis* [Matt. 25:41].

Cel fu ne sera jamés esteint, kar tote la ewe qe est en tere ne pora pas esteindre de cel fu une estencele. E en cel fu ardrunt en cors e en alme saunz nule fin. E pur agreger lur peine il irunt hors de cel chaut e serunt baignés e plongez en eawe qe sera plus freide qe nule neif, sicum dist seinte Escripture en Job : *Ab aquis, inquid, nivium transibunt ad calorem nimium* [Job 24:19]. E Damnedeu dist memes en le evangelie qe lur vermine jamés ne mora : *Vermis eorum, inquid, non morietur et ignis eorum non extinguetur* [Mark 9:43 & 45]. E sicum dist Ysaïe le prophete : *Subter te, inquid, sternetur tinea et operimentum tuum vermes erunt* [Is. 14:11]. Par peine ci poez vus penser les peinez la. E par verms qe sont ci poez vus doter la vermine la, kar escrist est qe fu e vermine tormentera la char dé pecheurs saunz nule fin. Mes quele manere de vermine ? Nus ne trovum pas escrit apertement, mes pensez par la hidouse vermine qe vus poez issi ver la hidur qe la sera, kar il serunt sicum covert de serpens e de crepauz e de lisars e de autre male vermine qe serunt en liu de dras aliez a lechurs e a autre mauveis qe les mangerunt en lur membres [f.122v] e les penerunt ou il aveint delit encontre la volunté Deu en lur vies.

[i] MS moit. [ii] MS digner.

And an archangel shall cry aloud with a trumpet these words: "All you who are dead, arise from death to life, and let each soul receive back its body."[9] Then in less time than it takes to blink your eye, that is, in an instant — in as much time as it takes to wave your hand — all those ever born of woman, in body and soul, shall come forth. None shall be able to hide so as not to come forth, and the trembling sinners shall be filled with fear and terror, for Our Lord Jesus Christ is very wrathful against them. And Hell beneath shall be open to receive the wicked; the earth beneath shall shudder with earthquakes, for it no longer wants to carry sinners. The whole world over shall be burning, and the devils shall be beside them. And their sins shall be revealed openly before them, and to all the world, and to the angels and all the devils. The heavens above shall strike the sinners with lightning and thunder, and they shall strive to hide themselves in the sea, but the sea shall vomit them out horribly. No place will receive them, except only Hell. And then Our Lord will say these terrible words: "Go, you wicked people, into the fire that burns for ever, which is prepared for the devils and their servants"; *Depart from me, ye cursed, into everlasting fire, prepared for the devil and his angels.*

That fire shall never be quenched, for all the water that is on earth could not extinguish a single spark of that fire. And they shall burn, body and soul, in that fire without end. And to increase their torment they shall go out of that heat and be plunged and immersed into water that is colder than any snow, as the Holy Scripture says in Job: *Drought and heat consume the snow waters.* And the Lord God even in the Gospel says that the worms in them shall never die: *Where their worm dieth not, and the fire is not quenched.*[10] And so says Isaiah the Prophet: *the worm is spread under thee, and the worms cover thee.* By torment here, you may imagine the torments there. From the vermin that are here you may dread the vermin there, for it is written that fire and worms shall torment the flesh of sinners without end. But what kind of vermin? We do not find it written clearly, but think of the most disgusting vermin that you can see here, and so of the horrors that shall be there. For they shall be covered with snakes and toads, and lizards and other filthy vermin, that shall be bound, in place of clothes or sheets, onto lechers and other unrighteous; they shall gnaw at their limbs and afflict them in those places where they used to take pleasure, against God's will, during their lives.

---

[9] See I Cor. 15:52: *In a moment, in the twinkling of an eye, at the last trump: for the trumpet shall sound, and the dead shall be raised incorruptible, and we shall be changed.* The match is not exact, but the writer clearly has the "twinkling of an eye" in mind — and again, below. See earlier in this chapter of Corinthians, for the nature of these bodies.

[10] In *AV*, Mark 9:44 & 46.

E sicum dist li seint, la vermine vivera enz en la chaline d'enfern sicum lé pessuns vivunt en ewe. E saunz fin lermerunt cels qe la serunt. E sanz ceo uncore un sul home plora plus des lermes qe gutes[i] sunt de eawe en tot le mund qe acun fin unt. Mes aprés entendez la feim e la seif, car il ne averunt rens a manger e pur famine lur char demene[runt] cum gens devez devorunt. E sicum dist David le prophete : 'La mort lur pestera e lur manger sera' ; *Mors, inquid, depascet eos* [Ps. 48:15]. Car ausicum qe a feim desire a manger, ausi desirunt il la mort qe il tant haierunt ci jamés mes morer ne porunt. *Hinc est ilud in Apocalipsi : Desiderabunt mori et mors fugiet ab eis* [Apoc. 9:6]. Mult graunt seif averunt, car la flaume de fu mellé ov suffre puant e ov vent de tempestes beverunt, sicum dist le prophete David : *Ignis sulfur spiritus procellarum pars cillicis eorum* [Ps. 10:7]. E fel de draguns e venim de serpens sera lur vin :[ii] *Fel draconum vinum eorum et venenum aspidum insanabile* [Deut. 32:33]. E taunt averunt seif pur la grant chaline qe il sucherunt les testes de serpens pur attrere hors le venim, sicum li enfant suche la mamele de sa norice sicum Damnedeu par Job : *Capud, inquid, aspidum sugent* [Job 20:16]. Ceo dutent ben le glotuns penser e pur ceo sobreté amer.

Entendez plus qe tant averunt de dolur qe il ne porunt autre chose penser fors la peine qe lur covendra sanz fin suffrer. Jamés confort ne averunt ne esperaunce de estre delivers, car il saverunt ben qe il ount perdu la joie du cel pur la joie du mund qe il amerunt tant e cele joie unt il enterement perdu. E si verunt a compainus les diables hidus e checun harra autre e tencera a autre e checun gurra a se memes e se tuereit si il poet, car enfern serra plein de oscurté e de fumé e de puneise e de toz les mals qe home put penser. L'em dist en engleis : 3if hope nare herte te borste. Mes la serra le quer de home crevé si il porra. Car saunz fin viverunt e jamés relés de peines ne averunt. E pur ceo, vus cher alme qe ceste escrit lirez, pensez sanz feintise de les set peines e les eschuez e vus gardez net de pechez, car a tele cheitiveté vendrunt sanz fin e sanz esperaunce de eschaper, car jamés Deu ne verunt ne joie ne averunt.

[i] MS gugtes. [ii] MS vein.

As the saint says, the vermin shall live in the hot steamy fog of Hell as fish live in water.[11] And those who are there shall weep endlessly. And more than this, one man alone shall weep more tears than there are endless drops of water in all the world. But then, imagine the hunger and the thirst, for they shall have nothing to eat, and be so famished they shall devour their own flesh like madmen. And as David the Prophet said: "Death shall devour them and be their food"; *Death shall feed on them ....*[12] For as one who hungers desires to eat, so shall they desire death who here hated it so, but now they cannot die. Thus, in the Apocalypse: *And in those days shall men seek death, and shall not find it; and shall desire to die, and death shall flee from them.* They shall have a terrible thirst, for they drink the fiery flame mixed with reeking sulphur and the winds of tempest, as David the Prophet said: *Upon the wicked he shall rain snares, fire and brimstone, and an horrible tempest: this shall be the portion of their cup.*[13] The gall of dragons and the venom of serpents shall be their wine: *Their wine is the poison of dragons, and the cruel venom of asps.* They shall have such great thirst, for the heat, that they shall suck serpents' heads to draw out the poison as a child sucks its nurse's teat, as the Lord says through Job: *He shall suck the poison of asps.* Gluttons ought to take heed of this, and thereby love sobriety.

You must understand, too, that they shall have such agony they can think of nothing but the pains they must suffer without end. Never shall they have comfort, nor hope of deliverance, for they know they have lost the joy of Heaven in exchange for the joy of the world they so loved, and they have lost that joy utterly. They shall see hideous devils as their company, and each shall hate and quarrel with other; each shall attack himself and would kill himself if he could, for Hell is full of darkness, and smoke and stench and all the evils one can imagine. It is said in English: "Ʒif hope nare herte te borste."[14] But there, a man's heart would break if it could: for they shall live for ever and never be released from torment. And so you, dear soul who reads this writing, think bravely about the seven torments and avoid them, keeping yourself clean from sin; those who do not shall come to wretchedness without end and without hope of escape, for they shall never see God or have joy.

---

[11] See *PL* 172:1160 (Honorius); *PL* 184:792 (Bernard).

[12] In *AV*, Ps. 49:14.

[13] In *AV*, Ps. 11:6.

[14] This is a common proverb ("Without hope the heart will break"); see Hunt 1985, p. 8 and notes 25 & 26.

[Chapter 5] [f.123r] Isci comence le quinte chapitre de la compelison de purgator[i]e e parout dé set glories qe lé cors savez averunt quant il releverunt al jor de jugement de mort en vie e dé set confusions qe lé cors dampnez averunt, si at set parograths.[i]

Isci comence le quinte chapitre de la compelison de purgator[i]e e parout dé set glories qe lé cors savez averunt quant il releverunt al jor de jugement de mort en vie e dé set confusions qe lé cors dampnez averunt, si at set parograths.

Jeo vus ai devant toché du jor de grant jugement, si aprés par la grace Deu vus parlerai des glories qe les cors savez en averunt e dé confusions des cors dampnez. Ore donc entendez, chere alme, la joie qe les bons averunt qe serunt savez e metez leal peine par seinte vie a cele joie venir qe sanz fin dura, qe est si grande qe nul home ne la puet parcunter ne ver en ceste vie ne penser. Mes neqedent sicum[ii] seint Anselme escrit e dist, le cors dé bons savez avera set maneres de glories e la alme, ausi, set.

Le cors dé bons qe est ore si orde sera aprés la generale resurrecciun plus cler e plus lusant qe n'est ore le solail qant il est plus lusaunt. Mult sera bele asemblé quant touz lez savez serunt ensemble e checun avera tant de clarté. E lez pecheurs serunt plus neirs qe nul carbon e plus puanz qe nule caroine.

La secunde glorie qe le cors dé bons avera si sera justice, qe en tant de tens cum vus poez cligner[iii] de l'oil, pora le hom en cors e en alme voler de la terre deqes en cel e de l'un chef del munde dekes a l'autre chef. En quel lu qe il vodra pora il estre a sa volunté ausi legerement cum il pora penser, ausi legerement se pora il deqes la remuer sanz ren travailer, sicum le rai du solail en un moment pase hors de l'orient deqes en le occident. Mes les pecheurs en contrarie manere serunt tant chargez de peines e si pesanz serunt, qe il ne porunt mover pé ne mein ne nul menbre de lor cors. E ceo est que Deu dist en le evangelie sovent : *Ligatis manibus et pedibus mittite eos in tenebras exteriores*[iv] [Matt. 22:13].

La terce joie sera qe home glorifié sera si fort adonc, ja si fe[b]le ne seit ore, qe il pora mover e remuer totes les montaines du mond e totes les terres desouz cel a sa volunté si mester fust e nule ren ne li pora rester e nint plus ne travailera en ce qe il travaile ore en overer ses us e clore. Mes les pecheurs serunt si febles qe il ne porunt remuer ne ouster les vermes de lor eus.

[i] In red. [ii] 'dist' expuncted. [iii] MS digner. [iv] Underlined in red, as above.

[Chapter 5] Here begins the fifth chapter of the treatise on Purgatory,[15] and speaks of the seven glories that the bodies of the saved shall have when they arise from death to life at the Day of Judgement, and of the seven kinds of destruction that the bodies of the damned shall have. There are seven sections.

I have told you above about the Day of Great Judgement; by the grace of God I shall tell you next of the splendours the saved bodies shall then have, and the perdition of the damned bodies. Now, dear soul, hear of the joy that the good who are saved shall have, and strive faithfully to come to that endless joy by holy life; it is so great that none can see or finish telling of it, nor in this life imagine it. But nevertheless, as Saint Anselm writes and says, the bodies of the virtuous saved shall have seven kinds of glory; their souls, also seven.

The good man's body, that is here so disgusting, shall after the general resurrection be clearer and brighter than the sun when it shines most brightly. What a beautiful company, when all the saved shall be together and each shall be so bright! And the sinners shall be blacker than any coal and smellier than any carrion.

The second glory the saved shall have is justice; in the twinkling of an eye a man, body and soul, can fly from earth to heaven and from one end of the world to the other. Wherever he wants to be, he can come there at his pleasure, just as easily as thinking — so easily can he get there without any effort, as a ray of sunlight flashes in a moment out of the east as far as the west.[16] But sinners, on the other hand, shall be so loaded with pain and so heavy that they can move neither hand nor foot, nor any limb of their body. And this is what God says in the Gospel: *Bind him hand and foot, and take him away, and cast him into outer darkness.*

The third glory is that glorified man shall be so strong, be he never so feeble now, that he can move and remove all the mountains of the world and all the lands under heaven, at his will when need is, and nothing can resist him: it will be no more work for him than now it is work for him to open and close his eyes. But the sinners shall be so weak that they cannot move even to pluck the worms out of their eyes.

---

[15] The final two chapters are taken from Anselm's *De similitudinibus* (Relihan 1978, p. 160).

[16] There is a comparable passage about this and other glories in *AW* (*Anchoritic Spirituality*, trans. Savage and Watson, p. 83, note 69). See also *Sawles Warde* (ibid. p. 220), where the same source is cited in their note 23.

La quarte glorie sera franchise qe home glorifié ne sera en nule manere de miseise ne de servage, car il ne suffra rens for ceo qe lui plera ne nule chose [f.123v] ne lui pora desturber ne defendre de ceo qe il fere vodra, ne mur de fer ne de pere ne de terre ne closture ne element ne nule reen li pora rester qe il ne pora sanz travail parmi a sa volunté passer. Ne cele franchise jamés ne perdera. Mes les pecheurs qe en mortel peché ci sont mors serunt la en tant de servage qe il ne porunt ren fere de ce qe il vodrunt e il serunt destreint a fere e a soffrer quanqe est encontre lur volunté. Allas ! Allas ! qe il unqes furunt nez !

La quinte glorie sera saunté saunz maladie, car nule peine ne maladie ne corupciun ne pesantime jamés ne grevera le cors ne nule manere de dolur ne senterunt aprés ceo qe il sunt glorifiez, mes les pecheurs serunt tant grevé de diverse maladies pur lur peché, car sicum vus avez avant entendu de maladie de alme en purgator[i]e, ausi serunt il grevez en enfern en cors e en alme e se sera sanz nule fin e mout plus qe en purgatorie qe avera fin. E jamés par nule manere de medicine[i] santé ne porunt aver ne alegement receivere de lur anguisses ne de lur peines.

La sime glorie si sera delit qe home avera en toz sé sens e par dedens e par dehors autaunt ou plus qe home puet ou set desirer. Car ausicum le fer qe est tant eschaufé dedens e dehors issi qe se semble plus fu qe fer, ausi sera home glorifié de amur e de Deu repleni del[ii] espiritel joie e son delit. E ausicum le vessel qe est plungé en eawe e a ewe amont e aval e de tote pars e en coste e dedens e dehors e nent plus ne put receivere dedens sei qant il est plein, ausi sera de la joie dount home sera repleni qe il ne pora plus deserer.[iii] Ore pensez tot le contrarie en lé dampnez, car il serunt si repleniz de peines e de anguisses e dehors e dedens de fu ardant e de sulfre puant e de vermine e de peines plus de assez qe jeo ne vus sai numbrer.

La setime glorie est vie pardurable qe il ne porunt jamés morer. Mes il serunt ov nostre duz Seignur Jesu Crist ausi longement cum il sera Deu e home e se sera sanz fin. Ore en ceste vie si home puet vivere cent mil anz, au drein lui semble qe tote sa vie qe est passé ne est nul autre fors ausicum songe. Par peché pert home tant de joie e se purchase tant de peine, car tels qe[iv] serunt dampnez viverunt poi. Car lur me semble plus mort qe vie, car il serunt [f.124r] ausicum gens qe gesunt en traunces e jamés parfitement ne morunt.

[i] MS medicime. [ii] MS e des. [iii] B82 'puse plus desirer.' [iv] B82 'que teus que'.

The fourth glory shall be freedom: glorified man can be in no sort of discomfort or bondage. Nothing can afflict him unless he chooses, nor can anything hinder or prevent him doing what he wants to: no wall of iron, stone, or earth; no fence, no elemental force — nothing can resist him, that he cannot pass through effortlessly at will; nor shall he ever lose that freedom. But the sinners who died here in mortal sin shall there be in such bondage that they can do nothing they want to, and they shall be forced to do and endure whatever they do not choose. Alas! Alas, that they were ever born!

The fifth glory shall be health without sickness, for no hurt or ailment or corruption or heaviness can ever afflict the body, nor can they feel any sort of pain after they are glorified. But the sinners shall be afflicted by all sorts of sickness for their sins, for as you have already heard of the sickness of souls in Purgatory, so they shall be afflicted in Hell — soul and body — and it shall be without end, and much more than in Purgatory which shall have an end. And they can never have healing by any kind of medicine, nor obtain relief from their agonies or their punishment.

The sixth glory is the delight that a man shall have, in all his senses both inwardly and outwardly, as much or more than he can or knows how to desire. For, like iron that is here so heated within and without that it seems more fire than iron, so shall a man be glorified by love and filled by God with his spiritual joy and delight. And like a vessel plunged into water, having water from the bottom to the brim and all over, sides and inside and outside, that can hold no more inside itself, so full it is, so it shall be for the joy that shall so fill the man that he can desire no more.[17] Then think of the damned: quite the contrary, for they shall be filled so full of pain and anguish, inwardly and outwardly, of burning fire and stinking brimstone and vermin and more agonies than I know how to tell you.

The seventh glory is everlasting life, that they can never die. But they shall be with our blessed Lord Jesus Christ for as long as he is God and man, and that is for ever. If a man could now in this life live a hundred thousand years — at the last it seems to him that all his life past is nothing but a dream. By sin man loses so much joy and buys so much pain, for those who shall be damned live but little. For theirs, it seems to me, is more death than life, for they shall be like people who lie in a trance and never die completely.

[17] Cf. *A tretyse of gostly batayle*, ed. Horstman, p. 433.

[Chapter 6] Issi comence le sime chapitre de la compelison de purgatorie e parout dé set glories qe les almes savez averunt e des confusions dé dampnez, si a set perografs.[i]

Vus avez devant oï e entendu les set glories qe home avera en cors glorifié. Ore entendez les set glories qe partenent especiaument a l'alme.

La premere glorie sera qe la alme de home savera qanqe Deu a fet en cel e en terre e totes creatures. Car qant home vera la deseré face de nostre Seignur Dampnedeu, ren ne pora a lui estre celé. Car home vera la aperte reson de tote choses e pleine verité. La savera il de qanqe est alé e de qanqe est a vener. La savera checun de autre de quel pays e de qele gens il fu né e qanqe home at fet en sa vie. Mes ore poez vus penser e demander en icele manere : Sire, serunt mez pechez la su de cels qe seront savez dont jeo fu confés pur ceo qe ducent estre oustez e obliez ? E seint Anselme dist e vus respont : Qe vus rendez graces a Deu sanz fin pur touz les bens qe il vus at fet e toz icels qe ov vus serunt savez. Mes coment lui rendez vus graces de ceo qe il vus a vos pechez pardoné, si vus nen euses nule memorie de vos pechez ? Mes ceo ben entendez, qe nent plus de peine ne averez vus de cele memorie de vos pechez qe li home ne a qe jadis resut plaie dont il est parfitement e savement savé. E nent plus qe vus avez ore hunte de la chose qe vus feites quant vus fustes en bers, nent plus ne averez vus hunte de vus pechez qe vus sunt parfitement pardoné, e nent plus qe sein Pere a de ce qe il nia nostre Seignur ou Marie Magdalene de ceo qe ele pecha. Mes pur ceo qe Deu voleit par sa pité[ii] e saveit par son grant sen e pout par son grant poer pardoner si grant pechez e saner les plais dont home avoit deservi la mort pardurable de enfern, pur ceo amerez vus Deu le plus e plus le aorrez pur autri peché qe il a sané cum pur les vos. E issi dist David le prophete : 'Jeo chaunterai', fet il, 'les mercis nostre Seignur sanz nule fin' ; *Misericordias Deum in eternum cantabo* [Ps. 88:2]. Ceo ne porez pas fere si vus ne eusez vos mals en memorie des quels il vus a deliveré par sa pité. Pensez donc cum vus serez paee de cel saver qe vus averez par unt vus conoustrez toz les autres. Vus devez Deu [f.124v] amer le plus e cels a qi il a moustré sa merci. Mes cels qe serunt dampnez ne averunt saver, mes serunt ausicum gens devez pur la grant dolur e pur la grant peine de cors e de alme qe il averunt.

[i] Heading in red. [ii] Lacuna in B82.

[Chapter 6] Here begins the sixth chapter of the treatise on Purgatory, and tells of the seven glories that saved souls shall have, and the confusion of the damned. There are seven sections.

You have just heard and understood the seven glories that a man shall have in the glorified body. Now hear the seven glories that pertain especially to the soul.

The first glory is that the human soul shall know everything God has done, in heaven and earth and all creatures. For when man sees the beloved face of Our Lord God, nothing can be hidden from him. For man shall clearly see the reason for all things, and full truth. He shall know of what has passed and what is to come. There, each shall know of one another, of what land and what people they were born and all they have done in their life. But now you might think and ask this: "Lord, will my sins be known there by those who are saved? I confessed them, and therefore they ought to be taken away and forgotten." And Saint Anselm says in reply to you: "You must give thanks to God unceasingly for all the good he has done for you, and for those who are saved with you." But how do you give thanks to him for forgiving your sins, if you have no memory of your sins? But understand this: you will have no more pain in this memory of your sins than the man who once had a wound that is now perfectly and cleanly healed. And no more than you now feel shame at things you did when you were in the cradle, so no more will you feel shame at your sins that are now completely forgiven; no more than Saint Peter, that he denied Our Lord, or Mary Magdalene of what she sinned. But because God wanted in his pity — and could in his great wisdom, and might in his great power — to forgive such grave sins and heal the wounds for which man deserves eternal death in Hell, therefore love God more and more, and praise him for others' sins that he has healed as he did your own. And thus David the Prophet: "I shall sing," he says, "the mercies of Our Lord without end"; *I will sing of the mercies of the Lord for ever.*[18] You could not do this, unless you had memory of your sins from which in his pity he has delivered you. Think, then, of how pleased you will be with this wisdom you will have, by which you will recognize all the others. You ought to love God the more, and those to whom he has shown his mercy. But those who are damned shall have no wisdom, but shall be like people maddened by the great pain and agony that they suffer in body and soul.

[18] In *AV*, Ps. 89:1.

La secunde glorie sera verai amisté. Car checun amera ataunt autre ausi parfitement cum lui memes. Ausicum checun membre de cors desire ore ci naturement e eime la saunté e le ben de touz les autres menbres. Car nus touz serum[i] la ausicum un cors e diverse menbres e Jesu Crist sera nostre chef e nus amera atant e mult plus qe le chef amera ses menbres. E icele aliaunce de verai amisté ne sera jamés parmi le descord ne par autre chose amenusé ne chaungé. Mes Deu e touz les sauvez tant harront les dampnez qe le pere ne avera nule peté de son fiz dampné ne la mere de sa file dampné ne de nul autre sicum dist David le prophete : 'Li dreiturel home', fet il, 'avera joie e nule peté quant il verra la dreite venjaunce de Deu en les dampnez' ; *Letabitur justus cum viderit vindictam* [Ps. 57:11].

La terce glorie sera verai concord, car vus veez qe le un oil suit le autre quel part qe il se turne e le un ne se put turner sa ne la si le autre ne se torne autel acord sera entre Deu e touz ses seinz. Car qanqe la alme vodra le cors concentera. E qanqe Deu vodra, toz ses seinz acorderunt, e qanqe les seinz desiront, Deu le fra e checun sera si paé de sa joie e qe il ne la vodra pur greniur joie chaunger. E li meindre seint du cel amera autant la joie de seint Pere e de touz les autre seinz ausicum il memes eust iceles joies. Car il averunt tant de pes e de amur qe il serunt touz cum un cors e une alme. Mes les dampnez seront en taunt descord qe lur cors e lur alme jamés en nule chose acorderunt. Car le cors harra totdis la alme pur ce qe ele pensa encontre Deu e la alme harra totdis le cors e les menbres du cors pur ceo qe il firent chose encontre la volunté Deu.

La quarte glorie sera honur. Car toz serunt la honurez cum reis, cum emperours e cum les fiz e les files Deu, sicum dist David le prophete : 'Sire Deu,' fet il, 'vos amis sunt e serunt mult honuré sicum les fiz e les files Deu, mes lé dampnez serunt tant deshonuré qe il serunt en servage e en subjection a vermis e si serunt degetez en peine e en tote manere de vilté.'

[i] MS serunt.

The second glory shall be true friendship. For each will love every other as perfectly as he loves himself: as here each member of the body naturally desires and loves the health and the good of all the other members. For there we shall all be as one body and many members, and Jesus Christ shall be our head, and will love us as much and even more than a head loves its limbs.[19] And this togetherness of true friendship shall never be diminished or changed by discord or by anything else. But God and all the saved shall hate the damned so much that the father shall have no pity for his lost son, nor the mother for her lost daughter, nor any other, as David the Prophet said: "The righteous man" he says "shall have joy, not pity, when he sees the righteous vengeance of God upon the damned"; *The righteous shall rejoice when he seeth the vengeance.*[20]

The third glory shall be true concord, for you see that one eye follows the other whichever way it turns, and the one cannot turn here or there unless the other turns too, such accord shall there be between God and all his saints. For whatever the soul wishes, the body will consent. And whatever God wishes, all his saints will concur; whatever the saints wish, God will do; and every one will be so pleased with their joy they would not change it for any other. And the least saint in Heaven will love the joy of the Holy Father and of all the other saints as much as if he himself had these joys. For they will have so much peace and love that they will all be as one body and soul together. But the damned shall be in such discord, their bodies and souls shall never be in agreement about anything. For the body will always hate the soul because of its thoughts against God, and the soul will always hate the body and its members because of things they did against God's will.

The fourth glory shall be honour. For there, all shall be honoured like kings and emperors, as the sons and daughters of God, as David the Prophet said: "Lord God," he says, "your friends are and shall be greatly honoured as sons and daughters of God, but the damned shall be so dishonoured that they shall be in bondage and in subjection to worms, and shall be thrust down into punishment and all manner of vileness."[21]

---

[19] See I Cor. 12:12–27.

[20] In *AV*, Ps. 58:10.

[21] This could conceivably be a very free paraphrase of Ps. 149, or perhaps expanded from Ps. 82:6–7 (*... and all of you are children of the most High. But ye shall die like men ...*). See *Preaching*, trans. Wenzel, p. 234, for a passage which may be from a gloss of Augustine's on the latter psalm.

La quinte glorie si est poer, car il serunt si pussanz qe tote lur volunté parfete par tot. Car Deu qe est tot pussaunt sera a lur volunté en [f.125r] tote choses acordant. Mes les dampnez ren ne averunt de lur volunté e sicum est avant dist il serunt aforcez a fere qanqe est encontre lur volunté e se sera pur ceo qe il furent descordanz a la volunté Deu.

La sime glorie sera seurdé, car il serunt sanz pour e sanz doute de perdre lur joie. Ne sera pas la cum est ci. Car qi est ore rei ou emperour en cel cecle, il perdera sa digneté e le riche sa richesse ou tost ou tard, mes la digneté e la richesse celestiene qe une fez la sera entré jamés ne la perdera. Mes lé dampnez totdis averunt pour a suffrer plus de peines qe il ount. Car lé diables hidus hirunt e vendrunt desur eus sicum dist le livere de sein Job : *Vadent, inquid, et venient super eos oribiles* [Job 20:25].

La setime glorie sera parfite joie de ceo qe checun amera autre parfitement e avera autretant de joie de autri joie cum de sa joie demene qant il avera qanqe il vut deserer. Car tote les choses dount parfite joie put estre serunt la en une joie asemblés e cele joie averunt sanz fin toz les almes qe serunt savez. Mes en contrarie manere sera dé dampnez. Car tote les choses serunt en enfern dount peine pora estre asemblé a pener sanz fin seu qe serunt dampnez. De cele peines Deu nus defent par sa seinte peté. Amen.

The fifth glory shall be power, for they shall be so mighty that all their will shall be done perfectly. For God who is Almighty shall be at their will to grant them all things. But the damned shall have nothing of their own will, and as was said before they shall be forced to do what is against their will; this is because they were disobedient to God's will.

The sixth glory shall be safety, for they shall be without any anxiety or fear of losing their joy. It shall not be there as it is here. For whoever is king or emperor now in this world, he will lose his dignity, and the rich his riches, sooner or later; but the dignity and riches of Heaven, whoever has once entered there shall never lose them. But the damned will always have fear of suffering more pains than they already have. For the hideous devils will come and go upon them, as the book of Saint Job says: *terrors are upon him*.

The seventh glory shall be perfect joy, in that each will love others perfectly and have as much joy of others' joy as of his own joy, when he has as much as he can desire. For all the things in which perfect joy could be will be gathered there in one joy, and all the souls that are saved will have this joy for ever. But it shall be quite otherwise for the damned. For all the things which could give pain shall be gathered in Hell, to punish for ever those who are damned.

May God defend us from those pains, by his blessed pity. Amen.

Appendix

A note on the *Compileison* may be of interest to readers; it is linked to several of the texts in this volume: Purgatory, Beatitudes, Three Vows, and Pater Noster.[1]

The Purgatory in this volume has manuscript links with the *Compileison*;[2] note also that the Purgatory and the Beatitudes in this volume are from the same manuscript: Bodley 654 (see D&B 678: our Beatitudes are there entitled "Ten Commandments" because part of the *Compileison*). Further, a Pater Noster follows the *Compileison* in two of its manuscripts.[3]

The *Compileison* is of special interest in relation to our Three Vows text: one of the French versions of the *Ancrene Wisse*[4] is known as the *Compileison*. Later in this Appendix, we examine the passages, in various versions of the *Ancrene Wisse*,[5] that resemble a passage about proper Silence, in the Three Vows, in an effort to establish whether either work may have influenced the other.

One of Trethewey's manuscripts (Paris, BNF 6276) contains a commentary on the *Oratio dominica*, or Pater Noster, whose text differs substantially from Trethewey's base manuscript, which is Cambridge, Trinity College R.14.7. Paris 6276 is one of the MSS (Pa) for the Pater Noster by Adam of Exeter, and some readings are cited from it (see the Introduction to Pater Noster, above); Trethewey does not print it — his edition breaks off at the end of the *Compileison*.[6]

Trethewey offers a full description of the *Compileison* in his Introduction: it contains 1) The Deadly Sins, 2) Holy Penance, 3) The Pains of Purgatory, 4) The Ten Commandments, 5) The Life of Religious People; he also provides a

[1] For a general discussion of the *Compileison*, see esp. Watson and Wogan-Browne 2004; and see D&B 644, where cross-references are given.

[2] Compare D&B 644 with 645, for the manuscripts and the way their contents relate to one another; see Relihan 1978 for the *Compileison* and its relation to our Purgatory; see Watson and Wogan-Browne 2004, pp. 42–43 and notes 11 & 12 (their Appendix, pp. 56–59, sets out the "ordre" of the *Compileison* and how it relates to *Ancrene Wisse*).

[3] See below for the version by Adam presented in this volume; and see Watson and Wogan-Browne 2004, p. 50, where D&B 587 is cited as the other.

[4] *The French Text*, ed. Trethewey; see Watson and Wogan-Browne 2004, p. 47, for the way the *Compileison* relates to the Three Vows.

[5] Conventionally, the text edited by Tolkien (see below) is known as the *Ancrene Wisse*, and analogous versions of the text as *Ancrene Riwle* (*AW* and *AR*, respectively, below); the convention is not always adhered to strictly.

[6] For a description of the Paris MS, see his pp. xiv–xv.

table of the *Compileison*'s relation with other *AR* texts. Numbers 3 and 4 are not included in the edition because not based on *AR* material, but Trethewey tells us that number 3 is Robert Grosseteste's Purgatory, and that it was inserted wholesale into the *Compileison.*[7] It is to be noted that the *Compileison* survives in three manuscripts, and the Purgatory in seven — evidence that the latter circulated independently or with differing manuscript companions.

It is not certain whether either text, the Three Vows in this volume or the *Ancrene Wisse*, influenced the other. The only manuscript of Three Vows is s.xiii^{2}; the earliest manuscript of *AW* is c. 1220, although D&B says little about any known influences on our Three Vows text. The French *Ancrene Riwle* (according to D&B 643) is a fourteenth-century Anglo-Norman translation of a Middle English text of the end of the twelfth century (the latter evidently does not survive). It is possible that a late twelfth-century text might have influenced our writer.[8] This, however, does not allow much time for any influence to spread around. The relevant passages in both texts are about sins of speech, and about right silence, but the material is differently ordered (and treated), as follows:

The *AW* passage (in several versions, see below) begins with a quotation from Gregory, then cites Proverbs 18:21. Next come more proverbs, followed by a reference to God's donkey. Then James 1:26 is cited, followed by a passage about the tongue being in a moist place. More proverbs follow, and a further reference to Gregory.

The Three Vows passage begins with citations from Isaiah and Jerome, then comes Proverbs 18:21. Next, Benedict is cited, followed by James 3:2. The passage about the tongue in a moist place is between two citations from James (the next one is 3:7–8) as though it were to be found in James — but it is not. There are then more proverbs, a passage about Moses; the reference to God's donkey comes last. Furthermore, the Three Vows passage develops the donkey idea much more extensively than the *AW* passage does. One would guess that both writers were gleaning assorted references and ideas, on the topic of silence, out of florilegia.[9]

---

[7] Some of Robert Grosseteste's writings were addressed to Adam Rufus (of Oxford or of Exeter), the author of our Pater Noster. He was very attached to this Adam and mourned his death deeply; furthermore, one of his best friends was Adam Marsh (de Marisco), who was Adam Rufus' master. Relihan 1978 (p. 159 and note) discusses the *Compileison* as an aid to dating the Purgatory.

[8] See *Ancrene Riwle*, trans. Salu, p. xxiii, for a list of manuscripts.

[9] Abelard has a comparable passage in his Letter of Direction to Heloise: see *The Letters*, trans. Radice, pp. 133–35 (the reference to Benedict is to his *Rule*, chap. 42).

The *Gesta Romanorum* includes a piece on gluttony and drunkenness,[10] in which "Cesarius" declares that "the throat is the most intemperate and seductive part of the whole body." The footnote, citing Warton, supposes Cesarius to be either Caesarius of Heisterbach (a very prolific writer whose work might have been collected in florilegia), or Caesarius of Arles. In any case, the contexts are perhaps too different for this to be helpful.

The actual wording of the "tongue" passage in four of the many *Riwle* texts:

Ancrene Wisse[11] p. 40 (f.19a), 5–7: "ah þe tunge is slubbri for ha wadeð i wete. & slit lihtliche forð from lut word in to monie ...."

The Pepys version of *Ancrene Riwle*[12] p. 30 (p. 383a) 29–32: "Ac of þe tunge is mychel doute for it slydreþ al in wete. For oft we þenchen to speke bot lite, And after on woord glytt forþ anoþer liȝthlich ...."

The French *Ancrene Riwle* (D&B 643).[13] This is an Anglo-Norman translation of a Middle English text, end of twelfth century; there is one manuscript (BL Cotton Vitellius F vii)[14] — called AR C (for Cotton), pp. 62–63: [think before you speak] "mes la lange est si estrillante . pur ceo qele ... [estril]le legierement dun p[arole] desqes a plusours ..." (the gap in the manuscript, at just this point, is unfortunate).

The *Compileison for the Religious Life*, or *The French Text of the Ancrene Riwle* (D&B 644).[15] This incorporates parts of *AR*, but is unrelated to the previous text. Trethewey edits Trinity Coll. Cambridge MS R.14.7 (there are two other manuscripts — variants printed), called AR T (for Trinity), p. 184: [one intends to say little, but] "mes la langue est escri-liant e glascant. Car ele ueụt en moiste liu . e en moillie e escrille auant legerement . e glace de pou de moz en plusours ...."

In our Three Vows text, the passage about the tongue is in among references from James, as it is in the AR T passage.[16] The Proverbs quotation in

[10] Trans. Swan and Hooper, CLXXIX, pp. 345–47.

[11] EETS OS 249, ed. Tolkien.

[12] EETS OS 274, ed. Zettersten.

[13] EETS OS 219, ed. Herbert.

[14] See also *Ancrene Wisse* (*sic*), trans. White.

[15] EETS OS 240, ed. Trethewey.

[16] See *Ancrene Wisse*, ed. Millett, notes in vol. II, to Part 2 lines 380–441; the reference to the tongue may be from Augustine's commentary on Ps. 39:1 (38:2 in *LV*): *Non enim lingua frustra in udo est, nisi quia facile labitur* (frequently quoted by later writers).

our text is several lines further up: man's life and death in the hands of his tongue. In AR T, Solomon says "in multiloquio ... car deverite (de verité) escrille ele / e glace a fausete ..."; the James quotation in AR T is about "refrenens linguam suam"; in ours those three quotations are not about "refrenens." But, a little further down in ours, the passage about the donkey is from *Vitas Patrum*, the story of St Anthony, who says: ... there is no door, so "quicumque uout entrer ..." and may take the donkey. AR T has "in vitas patri sic legitur ... non habet ianuam. Q ... uult intrat et asinum soluit. Et beatus iacobus etc."

AR C is laid out in similar manner, but neither AR C nor AR T mentions St Anthony.

It is interesting that the particular motifs we have examined appear together on the same page in both texts, but the analysis given above shows it to be unlikely that one was copied across from the other; it is more likely that the writers were both using similar source-anthologies.

The translated text, with the reference to the donkey and to the slippery tongue, can be found on pp. 32–33 of Salu's *Ancrene Riwle* (p. 32 note 6 gives *PL* 73:864, for the donkey). The story is found in *GL*, but not in the *South English Legendary*.[17]

See also *Yorkshire Writers*, ed. Horstmann, I:317: "Þe tunges sleper, for it wades in wate[r], & glyddes lyghtly furthe fra faa wordes to many ...." The heading of this section is "Off thre maners ocupacions" (Anonymous Writings; MS Thornton). The passage contains references to the Epistle of James, and to Solomon, but there is no mention of St Anthony or God's donkey.

For further discussion of *AW*, see Watson 2003: (p. 197) it was a source for five compilations, including the Middle English *Pater Noster* (although the identifiable *AW* passage appears in our Three Vows, not our Pater Noster); (pp. 197–98) it was probably cited in Hilton's *Scale* and certainly in a version of Love's *Mirror* (although the footnote gives no page reference for the latter); (p. 200) an audience of semi-educated contemplatives, defined not so much by lack of Latinity as by lack of a *guarantee* of Latinity; (p. 204) as well as the ME *Pater*, two other works were written for solitaries or nuns. An early draft of the *Mirror* contains an allusion to part I of *AW*. Overall, the article argues that *AW* and its "descendants" are all interested in translating the ambitions of a solitary life into terms accessible to the devout laity.

---

[17] The donkey is in the Middle English *Gilte Legende* (I.20).

Primary Texts Cited

Adam Marsh, *The Letters of Adam Marsh*, vol. I, ed. and trans. C. H. Lawrence (Oxford, 2006).

Aelred of Rievaulx, *Opera Ascetica: De Institutione Inclusarum*, in *Aelredi Abbatis Rievallensis Opera Omnia,* vol. I, eds. A. Hoste and C. H. Talbot (Turnhout, 1971).

———, *Rule of Life for a Recluse*, trans. Mary Paul Macpherson, in *The Works of Aelred of Rievaulx*, vol. 1: *Treatises and Pastoral Prayer*, Cistercian Fathers Series 2 (1971; repr. Kalamazoo, 1982).

Alan of Lille, *Anticlaudianus*, trans. James J. Sheridan (Toronto, 1973).

Aldhelm: The Prose Works, trans. Michael Lapidge and Michael Herren (Ipswich, 1979).

King Alfred, "Preface to Gregory the Great's *Pastoral Care*," in *Alfred the Great: Asser's* Life of King Alfred *and other Contemporary Sources*, trans. Simon Keynes and Michael Lapidge (Harmondsworth, 1983).

Die altfranzösischen Achtsilbnerredaktion der "Passion", ed. Hermann Theben (Griefswald, 1909).

Ambrose, *De officiis*, ed. and trans. Ivor J. Davidson (2 vols., Oxford, 2001).

[Ancrene Riwle] *The French Text of the Ancrene Riwle*, ed. J. A. Herbert, EETS OS 219 (1944; repr. London, 1967).

[Ancrene Riwle] *The French Text of the Ancrene Riwle*, ed. W. H. Trethewey, EETS OS 240 (London, 1958).

Ancrene Riwle (The Corpus MS: *Ancrene Wisse*), trans. Mary Salu (1955; repr. Exeter, 1990).

Ancrene Wisse, ed. Robert Hasenfratz (Kalamazoo (TEAMS), 2000).

Ancrene Wisse, ed. J. R. R. Tolkien, EETS OS 249 (London, 1962).

Ancrene Wisse, trans. Savage and Watson, see *Anchoritic Spirituality.*

Ancrene Wisse: A Corrected Edition of the Text in Cambridge, Corpus Christi College, MS 402 with Variants from Other Manuscripts, ed. Bella Millett, EETS OS 325 & 326 (2 vols., Oxford, 2005 & 2006).

Ancrene Wisse: Guide for Anchoresses, trans. Hugh White (London, 1993).

Anchoritic Spirituality: Ancrene Wisse *and Associated Works*, trans. Anne Savage and Nicholas Watson (New York & Mahwah, NJ, 1991).

The Anglo-Norman Lyric: An Anthology, eds. David L. Jeffrey and Brian J. Levy (Toronto, 1990).

Anglo-Norman Medicine 1 & 2, ed. Tony Hunt (Cambridge, 1994, 1997).

The Apocryphal Gospels, trans. B. Harris Cowper (London, 1867).

The Apocryphal New Testament, ed. and trans. J. K. Elliott (Oxford, 1993).

The Apocryphal New Testament, trans. M. R. James (1924; repr. Oxford, 1926).

[Anselm] *The Prayers and Meditations of Saint Anselm with the* Proslogion, trans. Benedicta Ward (Harmondsworth, 1973).

Anselmi Opera Omnia, ed. F. S. Schmitt (6 vols., Edinburgh, 1946–61).

St Thomas Aquinas, *Summa Theologiæ*, ed. Blackfriars [Thomas Gilby and T. C. O'Brien] (61 vols., London, 1965).

Augustine, *Confessions*, vol. II (of 2), (facing-page) trans. William Watts, Loeb Classical Library (London & Cambridge, Mass., 1961).

———, *De Doctrina Christiana*, ed. and trans. R. P. H. Green (Oxford, 1995).

Bede's Ecclesiastical History of the English People, ed. and trans. B. Colgrave and R. A. B. Mynors (Oxford, 1969).

Bede, *Epistola ad Ecgbertum*, in *Venerabilis Baedae Opera* vol. I, ed. C. Plummer (2 vols., Oxford, 1896).

[*The Book of Brome*], *A Common-Place Book of the Fifteenth Century*, ed. Lucy Toulmin Smith (London, 1886).

[*BVV*] *The Book of Vices and Virtues*, ed. W. Nelson Francis, EETS OS 217 (London, 1942).

Carruthers, Mary J., and Jan M. Ziolkowski, eds., *The Medieval Craft of Memory: An Anthology of Texts and Pictures* (Philadelphia, 2002).

Chrétien de Troyes, *Le Roman de Perceval* ou *Le Conte du Graal*, ed. Keith Busby (Tübingen, 1993).

The Chronicle of Glastonbury Abbey, ed. James P. Carley, trans. David Townsend (1978; repr. Woodbridge, 1985).

Codex Apocryphus Novi Testamenti, vol. I, ed. J. C. Thilo (Leipzig, 1832).

Codex Apocryphus Novi Testamenti: The Uncanonical Gospels and Other Writings referring to the First Ages of Christianity, ed. J. A. Giles, Pt. 1 (London, 1852).

Councils & Synods, with other Documents relating to the English Church, vol. 1 (AD 871–1204), eds. D. Whitelock, M. Brett, and C. N. L. Brooke (2 vols., 1964, repr. Oxford, 1981).

Councils & Synods, with other Documents relating to the English Church, vol. II (AD 1205–1313), eds. F. M. Powicke and C. R. Cheney (2 vols., Oxford, 1964).

Decrees of the Ecumenical Councils, vol. I, ed. Norman P. Tanner (2 vols., London & Georgetown, 1989).

[Eadmer of Canterbury] trans. in Luigi Gambero, *Mary in the Middle Ages: the Blessed Virgin Mary in the Thought of Medieval Latin Theologians* (San Francisco, 2005).

The Early South English Legendary, ed. Carl Horstmann, EETS OS 87 (London, 1887).

[Edmund of Abingdon] *Mirour de Seinte Eglyse* (*St Edmund of Abingdon's* Speculum Ecclesiae), ed. A. D. Wilshere, ANTS 40 (London, 1982).

"Exhortation à l'amour divin: poème du XIIIe siècle," ed. F. J. Tanquerey, *Romania* 66 (1940–41), 321–54.

L'Enfant sage (Dialogue of Kaiser Hadrian and Child Epitus), ed. Walther Suchier (Dresden, 1910).

[*FM*] *Fasciculus Morum: A Fourteenth-Century Preacher's Handbook*, ed. and trans. Siegfried Wenzel (University Park & London, 1989).

Francis of Assisi: Early Documents, vol. 1, eds. Regis J. Armstrong, J. A. Wayne Hellman, and William J. Short (3 vols., New York, 1999).

Gautier de Coinci, *Les Miracles de Notre Dame*, ed. V. Frederic Koenig (4 vols., Geneva, 1955–70).

Gesta Romanorum, or Entertaining Moral Stories, trans. Charles Swan and Wynnard Hooper (1876; repr. New York, 1959).

Gilte Legende, vol. I, ed. Richard Hamer (with Vida Russell), EETS OS 327 (3 vols., Oxford, 2006).

The Good Wife taught her Daughter, The Good Wyfe wold a pylgremage, The Thewis of Gud Women, ed. T. F. Mustanoja (Helsinki, 1948).

[Gregory] Grégoire le Grand, *Dialogues*, ed. Adalbert de Vogüé, trans. Paul Antin (3 vols., Paris, 1978–80).

Guillaume le Clerc, *Le Besant de Dieu de Guillaume le Clerc de Normandie*, ed. P. Ruelle (Brussels, 1973).

[Harley 2253] *Facsimile of British Museum MS. Harley 2253*, ed. N. R. Ker, EETS OS 255 (London, 1965).

Herman de Valenciennes, *Li Romanz de Dieu et de sa mere d'Herman de Valenciennes chanoine et prêtre (XIIe siècle)*, ed. Ina Spiele (Leiden, 1975).

The Idea of the Vernacular: An Anthology of Middle English Literary Theory 1280–1520, eds. Jocelyn Wogan-Browne, Nicholas Watson, Andrew Taylor, and Ruth Evans (Exeter, 1999).

[*GL*] Jacobus de Voragine, *The Golden Legend: Readings on the Saints*, trans. William Granger Ryan (2 vols., 1993; repr. Princeton, 1995).

[*GL*, Jacobus] *Iacopo da Varazze: Legenda Aurea*, ed. Giovanni Paolo Maggioni (Florence, 1998).

The Letters of Abelard and Heloise, trans. Betty Radice, rev. M. T. Clanchy (1974; repr. London, 2003).

Liber de Diversis Medicinis, ed. Margaret Sinclair Ogden, EETS OS 207 (London, 1938).

Love, Nicholas, *The Mirror of the Blessed Life of Jesus Christ*, ed. Michael G. Sargent (Exeter, 2004).

[*Lumere*] *La Lumere as Lais*, by Pierre d'Abernon of Fetcham, ed. Glynn Hesketh, ANTS 54–55, 56–57, 58 (3 vols., London, 1996, 1998, 2000); vols. I & II, Text; vol. III, Introduction, Notes and Glossary.

Marie de France, *Saint Patrick's Purgatory*, ed. and trans. Michael J. Curley, Medieval and Renaissance Texts and Studies 94 (Tempe, Arizona: 1997).

The Middle English Prose Complaint of Our Lady and Gospel of Nicodemus, eds. C. William Marx and Jeanne F. Drennan (Heidelberg, 1987).

[*MERP*] *Middle English Religious Prose*, ed. N. F. Blake, York Medieval Texts (London, 1972).

The Northern Passion (vol. II), ed. F. A. Foster, EETS OS 147 (London, 1916).

Myrc [Mirk], *Instructions for Parish Priests*, ed. Edward Peacock, EETS OS 31 (London, 1868).

[*ODNB*] *The Oxford Dictionary of National Biography* (Oxford, 2004); online at: www.oxforddnb.com (individual entries are indicated in footnotes).

[*ODS*] *The Oxford Dictionary of Saints*, David Hugh Farmer, 3rd ed. (1978; repr. Oxford, 1992).

Orderic Vitalis, *The Ecclesiastical History of Orderic Vitalis*, ed. and trans. Marjorie Chibnall (6 vols., Oxford, 1969–80).

[*Passion Prologue*], ed. Bruce Burnam, "An unedited Anglo-Norman Prologue to the *Passion des Jongleurs* and its relation to the *Passio Christi* of Clermont-Ferrand," *MÆ* 60 (1991) 197–206.

Pastors and the Care of Souls in Medieval England, eds. John Shinners and William J. Dohar (Indiana, 1998).

Pater Noster (vernacular treatments), ed. Hans Robert Jauss, *Grundriss der romanischen Literaturen des Mittelalters* VI/2 (Heidelberg, 1970), pp. 23–25.

Þe Pater Noster of Richard Ermyte, a Late Middle English Exposition of the Lord's Prayer, ed. Florent Gérard Antoine Marie Aarts (The Hague, 1967).

[*PL*] *Patrologia Latina* (221 vols.), ed. J-P. Migne (Paris, 1844–64).

Peter of Cornwall, "The Vision of Ailsi," ed. and trans. R. Sharpe, *Cornish Studies* 13 (1985), 35–53.

Une Petite Sume de les Set Pechez Morteus (MS London BL Harley 4657), ed. Tony Hunt, in *Medieval French Textual Studies in Memory of T. B. W. Reid* (*Reid Memorial Volume*), ed. Ian Short, ANTS Occasional Publications 1 (London, 1984), pp. 65–98.

Plaintes de la Vierge en Anglo-Français (XIIIe et XIVe siècles), ed. F. J. Tanquerey (Paris, 1921).

Poem on the Assumption, ed. J. P. Strachey, Cambridge Anglo-Norman Texts (Cambridge, 1924).

Preaching in the Age of Chaucer: Selected Sermons in Translation, trans. Siegfried Wenzel (Washington, DC, 2008).

Richard de Saint-Victor, *Liber Exceptionum*, ed. J. Chatillon (Paris, 1958).

Richard Rolle of Hampole, ed. C. Horstman (2 vols., London, 1895–96).

Robert of Flamborough, *Liber Poenitentialis*, ed. J. J. Francis Firth, Studies & Texts 18 (Toronto, 1971).

[Robert Grosseteste] "The Early Penitential Writings of Robert Grosseteste," eds. Joseph Goering and F. A. C. Mantello, *Recherches de Théologie Ancienne et Médiévale* 54 (1987), 52–112.

Robert Grosseteste, *Hexaëmeron*, eds. Richard C. Dales and Servus Gieben (London, 1982).

———, *On the Six Days of Creation*, trans. C. F. J. Martin (Oxford, 1996).

"Robert Grosseteste at the Papal Curia, Lyons 1250: An Edition of the Documents," ed. Servus Gieben, *Collectanea Franciscana* 41 (1971), 349–93.

[———] "The Perambulauit Iudas (Speculum Confessionis) attributed to Robert Grosseteste," eds. Joseph Goering and Frank A. C. Mantello, *Revue Bénédictine* 96 (1986), 125–68.

Robert of Bridlington, *The Bridlington Dialogue: An Exposition of the Rule of St Augustine for the Life of the Clergy*, ed. and trans. by A Religious of the C.S.M.V. (London, 1960).

A Selection of Religious Lyrics, ed. Douglas Gray (Oxford, 1975).

Sermons on Joshua, ed. Tony Hunt, ANTS Plain Texts Series 12 & 13 (2 vols., London, 1998).

Tanakh = The Holy Scriptures (Philadelphia: The Jewish Publication Society, 1988).

Terence, *The Eunuch*, in The Loeb Classical Library, *Terence* (vol. I of II), (facing-page) trans. John Sargeaunt (1912; repr. London & Cambridge, Mass., 1959).

Thomas of Chobham, *Summa Confessorum*, ed. F. Broomfield, Analecta Mediaevalia Namurcensia 25 (Louvain & Paris, [1968]).

Thomas of Eccleston, *Fratris Thomae vulgo dicti de Eccleston Tractatus de adventu fratrum minorum in Angliam*, ed. A. G. Little (Manchester, 1951).

———, *The Coming of the Friars Minor to England and Germany being the Chronicles of Brother Thomas of Eccleston and Brother Jordan of Giano*, trans. E. Gurney Salter (London & Toronto, 1926).

[Treatise on Job] "A Middle English Penitential Treatise on Job 10:20–22, *Dimitte me, Domine*," ed. Mayumi Taguchi, *Mediaeval Studies* 67 (2005), 157–217.

A tretyse of gostly batayle, in *Richard Rolle* (vol. II) ed. Horstman, see above.

La Vie de Saint Laurent: An Anglo-Norman Poem of the Twelfth Century, ed. D. W. Russell, ANTS 34 (London, 1976).

Wace, *The Conception Notre Dame*, ed. William Ray Ashford (Chicago, 1933).

William of Malmesbury, *Gesta Pontificum Anglorum: The History of the English Bishops* (vol. 1), ed. and trans. M. Winterbottom, with R. M. Thomson (2 vols., Oxford, 2007).

William de Montibus: see Goering (study and texts), below.

Women's Books of Hours in England, ed. Charity Scott-Stokes, Library of Medieval Women (Cambridge, 2006).

Wulfstan, *The Homilies of Wulfstan*, ed. Dorothy Bethurum (1957; repr. Oxford, 1998).

York Mystery Plays, ed. Lucy Toulmin Smith (1885; repr. New York, 1963).

Yorkshire Writers: Richard Rolle of Hampole and his Followers, see *Richard Rolle*, ed. C. Horstman, above.

Secondary Texts Cited

Adam, B., *Katechetische Vaterunser-auslegungen: Texte und Untersuchungen zu deutschsprachigen Auslegungen des 14. und 15. Jahrhunderts* (Munich, 1976).

[*AND*] *The Anglo-Norman Dictionary*, eds. Louise W. Stone and William Rothwell, ANTS (7 fascicles, London, 1977–92).

[*AND*] *The Anglo-Norman Dictionary*, 2nd ed., eds. Stewart Gregory, William Rothwell, and David Trotter: I, A–C and II, D–E (MRHA 17: London, 2005); online at: `www.anglo-norman.net`

Ashley, Kathleen M., and Pamela Sheingorn, eds., *Interpreting Cultural Symbols: Saint Anne in Late Medieval Society* (Athens, Ga., & London, 1990).

Auerbach, Erich, *Literary Language and Its Public in Late Latin Antiquity and in the Middle Ages*, trans. Ralph Mannheim (New York, 1965; *Literatursprache und Publikum in der lateinischen Spätantike und im Mittelalter*, Berne, 1958).

Baldwin, John W., *Masters, Princes, and Merchants: the Social Views of Peter the Chanter and his Circle* (2 vols., Princeton, 1970).

Batt, Catherine, "'De celle mordure vient la mort dure': Perspectives on Puns and their Translation in Henry, Duke of Lancaster's *Le Livre des Seyntz Medicines*," in Olivier Bertrand and Jacqueline Jenkins eds., *The Medieval Translator* 10 (Turnhout, 2007), pp. 407–19.

Behm, U., *Bebilderte Vaterunser-Erklärungen des Mittelalters* (Baden-Baden, 1994).

Bloomfield, M. W., B-G. Guyot, D. R. Howard, and T. B. Kabealo, *Incipits of Latin Works on the Virtues and Vices, 1100–1500 AD: including a section of incipits of works on the Pater Noster* (Cambridge, Mass., 1979).

Bloomfield, Morton W., *The Seven Deadly Sins: An Introduction to the History of a Religious Concept with special reference to Medieval English Literature* (1952; repr. East Lansing, 1967).

Boulton, Maureen, "Le Langage de la dévotion affective en moyen français," *Le Moyen Français* 39–41 (1996–97), 53–63.

Boyle, Leonard, "The Fourth Lateran Council and Manuals of Popular Theology," in *The Popular Literature of Medieval England*, ed. Thomas J. Heffernan (Knoxville, 1985), pp. 30–43.

Cantini, G., "Adam de Marisco OFM, auctor spiritualis," *Antonianum* 23 (1948), 441–74.

Carruthers, Mary, "Sweetness," *Speculum* 81 (2006), 999-1013.

Clayton, Mary, *The Virgin Mary in Anglo-Saxon England* (Cambridge, 1990).

Collet, Olivier, *Glossaire et Index Critiques des œuvres d'attribution certaine de Gautier de Coinci* (Geneva, 2000).

Cross, J. E., "The Name and not the Deeds," *MLR* 54 (1959), Miscellaneous Notes page 6.

[D&B] Dean, Ruth, and Maureen Boulton, *Anglo-Norman Literature: A Guide to Texts and Manuscripts*, ANTS Occasional Publications 3 (London, 1999); see also Tony Hunt's review of this in *MÆ* 70 (2001), 340–43.

Dean, R. J., "Elizabeth, Abbess of Schönau, and Roger Ford," *Modern Philology* 41 (1944), 209–20.

———, "Manuscripts of St Elizabeth of Schönau in England," *MLR* 32 (1937), 62–71.

D'Evelyn, Charlotte, [Methodius] "The Middle English Metrical Version of the *Revelations* of Methodius; with a study of the influence of Methodius in Middle English Writings," *PMLA* 33, n.s. 26 (1918), 135–203.

Devonshire, Amanda, and Barbara Wood, eds., *Women in Industry and Technology* (London, 1996).

Dickinson, J. C., *The Shrine of Our Lady of Walsingham* (Cambridge, 1956).

Douie, D., "Adam 'De Marisco', an English Friar," *Durham University Journal* 32 (1940), 81–97.

Douie, Decima L., *Archbishop Pecham* (Oxford, 1952).

Dronke, Peter, "Laments of the *Maries*: From the Beginnings to the Mystery Plays," in *Festschrift Klaus von See: Studien zur europäischen Kulturtradition*, ed. Gerd Wolfgang Weber (Odense, 1988), pp. 89–116.

Duffy, Eamonn, *Marking the Hours: English People and their Prayers, 1240–1570* (New Haven & London, 2006).

———, "The Psalms and Lay Devotion in the Late Middle Ages," *BLR* 21:1 (April, 2008), 93–105.

———, *The Stripping of the Altars: Traditional Religion in England c1400–c1580* (New Haven, 1992).

Edwards, Graham Robert, "Purgatory: 'Birth' or Evolution?" *JEH* 36 (1985), 634–46.

Emden, A. B., *A Biographical Register of the University of Oxford to 1500 AD* (Oxford, 1957).

English Language Notes 44:1 (Spring / Summer 2006); contains a special section "Vernacular Theology and Medieval Studies," 77–137.

Esposito, Mario, "Inventaire des anciens mss français des bibliothèques de Dublin," *Revue des Bibliothèques* 24 (1914), 185–98.

Fein, Susanna, *Studies in the Harley Manuscript: The Scribes, Contents, and Social Contexts of British Library MS Harley 2253* (Kalamazoo, 2000).

Fleming, John V., *An Introduction to the Franciscan Literature of the Middle Ages* (Chicago, 1977).

Flint, Valerie, *The Rise of Magic in Early Medieval Europe* (Oxford, 1991).

Fulton, Rachel, *From Judgement to Passion: Devotion to Christ and the Virgin Mary, 800–1200* (New York, 2002).

Gambero, Luigi, *Mary in the Middle Ages*, see [Eadmer of Canterbury], above.

Giandrea, Mary Frances, *Episcopal Culture in Late Anglo-Saxon England* (Woodbridge, 2007).

Godden, Malcolm, "Did King Alfred write anything?" *MÆ* 76 (2007), 1–23.

Goering, Joseph, *William de Montibus (c. 1140–1213): The Schools and the Literature of Pastoral Care* (Toronto, 1992).

Gray, Douglas, *Themes and Images in the Medieval English Religious Lyric* (London, 1972).

Green, D. H., *Women Readers in the Middle Ages* (Cambridge, 2007).

Griffiths, Fiona J., *The Garden of Delights: Reform and Renaissance for Women in the Twelfth Century* (Philadelphia, 2007).

Hardison, O. B., *Christian Rite and Christian Drama in the Middle Ages* (Baltimore, 1965).

Heinimann, S., *Oratio dominica romanice: Das Vaterunser in den romanischen Sprachen von den Anfängen bis ins 16.Jahrhundert mit den griechischen und lateinischen Vorlagen . . .*, Beihefte zur *Zeitschrift für romanische Philologie* 219 (Tübingen, 1988).

———, "Il Paternostro in volgare francese: tradizione scritta e tradizione orale," in *Miscellanea di Studi in onore di Aurelio Roncaglia* 2 (Modena, 1989), pp. 663–72.

Heinzer, Felix, "Holy Text or Object of Display? Functions and Guises of the Psalter in the Middle Ages," *BLR* 21:1 (April, 2008), 37–47.

Hessenauer, Matthias, "The Impact of Grosseteste's Pastoral Care on Vernacular Religious Literature: *La Lumière as Lais* by Pierre de Peckham," *Instrumenta Patristica* 27 (1995), 377–91.

Howlett, David, *The English Origins of Old French Literature* (Dublin, 1996).

Humphreys, K. W., ed., *The Friars' Libraries* (London, 1990).

Hunt, Tony, "An Anglo-Norman Pater Noster," *Notes & Queries* 240 (1995), 16–18.

———, "Anecdota Anglo-Normannica," *Yearbook of English Studies* 15 (1985), 1–17.

James, M. R., *A Descriptive Catalogue of the Manuscripts in the Library of Lambeth Palace* 1 (5 parts in 1 vol., Cambridge, 1930).

———, *A Descriptive Catalogue of the Manuscripts in the Library of Pembroke College, Cambridge* (Cambridge, 1905).

Johnston, Alexandra F., "The Plays of the Religious Guilds of York: the Creed Play and the Pater Noster Play," *Speculum* 50 (1975), 55–90.

Keck, David, *Angels and Angelology in the Middle Ages* (New York & Oxford, 1998).

Kelly, J. N. D., *Early Christian Creeds*, 3rd ed. (1950; repr. London, 1972).

King, Andrew, The Faerie Queene *and Middle English Romance: The Matter of Just Memory* (Oxford, 2000).

Kolve, V. A., *The Play Called Corpus Christi* (Stanford, 1966).

Kuczynski, Michael P., "An 'Electric Stream': The Religious Contents," in Fein 2000 (q.v.), pp. 123–61.

Långfors, A., "Les Traductions et paraphrases du *Pater* en vers français du moyen âge: essai de bibliographie," *Neuphil. Mitt.* 14 (1912), 35–45.

Langlois, Ch-V., "C'est dou pere qui son filz enseigne . . . ," in *La Vie en France au moyen âge*, vol. 4 (Paris, 1928), pp. 47–65.

Legge, M. Dominica, *Anglo-Norman in the Cloisters* (Edinburgh, 1950).

———, *Anglo-Norman Literature and its Background* (Oxford, 1963).

———, "St Edmund on the 'Hours'," *MLR* 29 (1934), 72–74.

Le Goff, Jacques, *La Naissance du Purgatoire* (Paris, 1981); translated as *The Birth of Purgatory*, by Arthur Goldhammer (London, 1984).

Lerer, Seth, *Literacy and Power in Anglo-Saxon England* (Lincoln & London, 1991).

MacCoull, L. S. B., "More Sources for the *Liber Scintillarum* of Defensor of Ligugé,", *Revue Bénédictine* 112:3–4 (2002), 291–300.

Macy, Gary, "The Dogma of Transubstantiation in the Middle Ages," *JEH* 45 (1994), 11–41.

Mansfield, Mary C., *The Humiliation of Sinners: Public Penance in Thirteenth-Century France* (Ithaca & London, 1995).

Mayr-Harting, Henry, *Perception of Angels in History*: Inaugural Lecture delivered at the University of Oxford, 14th November 1977 (Oxford, 1998).

McEvoy, James, *The Philosophy of Robert Grosseteste* (Oxford, 1982).

———, *Robert Grosseteste* (Oxford, 2000).

McGuire, Brian Patrick, "Purgatory, the Communion of Saints, and Medieval Change," *Viator* 20 (1989), 61–84.

Meyer, P., "Légendes hagiographiques en français," *Histoire Littéraire de la France* 33 (1906), 328–458.

———, "Notice du MS. Egerton 2710 du Musée Britannique," *Bull. SATF* 15 (1889), 72–97.

———, "Trois nouveaux manuscrits des sermons français de Maurice de Sully," *Romania* 28 (1899), 245–68.

Millett, Bella, "*Ancrene Wisse* and the Book of Hours," in Denis Renevey and Christiana Whitehead eds., *Writing Religious Women: Female Spiritual and Textual Practices in Late Medieval England* (Cardiff, 2000), pp. 21–40.

Millett, Bella, "*Ancrene Wisse* and the conditions of confession," *English Studies* 80 (1999), 193–215.

Morawski, Joseph, ed., *Proverbes français antérieurs au XVe siècle* (Paris, 1925).

The Oxford Concise Companion to Classical Literature, eds. M. C. Howatson and Ian Chivers (1993; repr. Oxford & New York, 1996).

[*ODCC*] *The Oxford Dictionary of the Christian Church*, 3rd ed., ed. E. A. Livingstone (Oxford, 1997).

Pantin, W. A., *The English Church in the Fourteenth Century* (London, 1955).

Pelikan, Jaroslav, *The Christian Tradition: A History of the Development of Doctrine* (5 vols., Chicago & London, 1971–89).

Reames, S. L., *The* Legenda Aurea*: A Reexamination of its Paradoxical History* (Madison, 1985).

Reinsch, R., "Mittheilungen aus einer französischen Handschrift des Lambeth Palace zu London," *Archiv für das Studium der Neueren Sprachen* 63 (1880), 51–96.

Relihan, Robert J. Jr., "*Les Peines de Purgatoire*: The Anglo-Norman and Latin Manuscript Traditions," *Manuscripta* 21 (1978), 158–68.

Remley, Paul G., *Old English Biblical Verse: Studies in* Genesis, Exodus *and* Daniel (Cambridge, 1996).

Rézeau, P., *Répertoire d'incipit des prières français à la fin du moyen age. Addenda et corrigenda aux répertoires de Sonet et de Sinclair: nouveaux incipit* (Geneva, 1986).

Robson, C. A., *Maurice of Sully and the Medieval Vernacular Homily* (Oxford, 1952).

Rouse, R. H. & M. A., and R. A. B. Mynors, *Registrum Anglie de libris doctorum et auctorum veterum* (London, 1991).

Rubin, Miri, *Mother of God: A History of the Virgin Mary* (London, 2009).

Rudolph, Conrad, *The "Things of Greater Importance": Bernard of Clairvaux's* Apologia *and the Medieval Attitude towards Art* (Philadelphia, 1990).

Salminen, T. F., "An Anonymous French Religious Poem in the Fourteenth-Century MS Emmanuel College Cambridge I.4.31," *Neuphil. Mitt.* 41 (1940), 127–35.

Short, Ian, "Patrons and Polyglots: French Literature in Twelfth-Century England," *Anglo-Norman Studies* 14 (1992), 229–49.

Simpson, Jacqueline, *British Dragons*, 2nd ed. (1980; repr. Ware (Herts), 2001).

Sinclair, K. V., *French Devotional Texts of the Middle Ages: A Bibliographic Manuscript Guide* (Westport, Conn., 1979), and *First Supplement* (1982).

———, *Prières en ancien français* (Hamden, Conn., 1978).

———, *Prières en ancien français: additions et corrections aux articles 1–2374 du Répertoire de Sonet, Supplément*, Capricornia 7 (Townsville, Qld., 1987).

Skemer, Don C., *Binding Words: Textual Amulets in the Middle Ages* (University Park, Pa., 2006).

Sonet, J., *Répertoire d'incipit de prières en ancien français* (Geneva, 1956).

Southern, R. W., "The English Origins of the Miracles of the Virgin," *Mediaeval and Renaissance Studies* 4 (1958), 176–216.

———, *Robert Grosseteste: the Growth of an English Mind in Medieval Europe* (Oxford, 1986).

Sturges, Robert S., "Pseudo-Augustinian Writings," in *The Oxford Guide to the Historical Reception of Augustine* (forthcoming).

Sutherland, Annie, "English Psalms in the Middle Ages," *BLR* 21:1 (April, 2008), 75–92.

Tamburr, Karl, *The Harrowing of Hell in Medieval England* (Cambridge, 2007).

Tanner, Norman P., and Sethina Watson, "Least of the laity: the minimum requirements for a medieval Christian," *Journal of Medieval History* 32 (2006), 395–423.

Thomas, H. M., *The English and the Normans: Ethnic Hostility, Assimilation, and Identity, 1066–c. 1220* (Oxford, 2003).

Thomson, S. Harrison, *The Writings of Robert Grosseteste, Bishop of Lincoln 1235–1253* (Cambridge, 1940).

Trotter, D. A., "The Influence of Bible Commentaries on Old French Bible Translations," *MÆ* 56 (1987), 257–75.

Tubach, Frederic C., *Index Exemplorum: A Handbook of Medieval Religious Tales* (Helsinki, 1969).

Turville-Petre, Thorlac, *England the Nation: Language, Literature and National Identity, 1290–1340* (Oxford, 1996).

Vaughn, Sally, *St. Anselm and the handmaidens of God: A study of Anselm's correspondence with women* (Turnhout, 2002).

Vincent, Nicholas, "King Henry III and the Blessed Virgin Mary," in R. N. Swanson, ed., *The Church and Mary*, Studies in Church History 39 (Woodbridge, 2004), pp. 126–46.

Watson, Nicholas, "*Ancrene Wisse*, Religious Reform and the Late Middle Ages," in Yoko Wada ed., *A Companion to* Ancrene Wisse (Cambridge, 2003), 197–226.

———, and Jocelyn Wogan-Browne, "The French of England: the *Compileison*, *Ancrene Wisse*, and the idea of Anglo-Norman," *Journal of Romance Studies* 4:2 (Summer, 2004), 35–59.

Wenzel, Siegfried, *The Sin of Sloth* (Chapel Hill, 1967).

——— [Wenzel 1967a], "The Three Enemies of Man," *Mediaeval Studies* 29 (1967), 47–66.

Wogan-Browne, Jocelyn, "'Our Steward, St. Jerome': Theology and the Anglo-Norman Household," in Anneke B. Mulder-Bakker and Jocelyn Wogan-Browne eds., *Household, Women and Christianities in Late Antiquity and the Middle Ages* (Turnhout, 2005), pp. 149–57.

——— [Wogan-Browne 2005a], "Women's Formal and Informal Traditions of Biblical Knowledge in Anglo-Norman England," in Mathilde van Dijk and Renée Nip eds., *Saints, Scholars and Politicians: Gender as a Tool in Medieval Studies: Festschrift in honour of Anneke Mulder-Bakker on the Occasion of her Sixty-Fifth Birthday* (Turnhout, 2005), pp. 85–109.

Woolf, Rosemary, *The English Religious Lyric in the Middle Ages* (Oxford, 1968).

Zarnecki, George, "The Coronation of the Virgin on a Capital from Reading Abbey," *Journal of the Warburg and Courtauld Institutes* 13 (1950), 1–12.

Zink, M., *La Prédication en langue romane avant 1300* (Paris, 1976).

Index of Manuscripts Used

Numbers in parentheses refer to numbers given in printed catalogues of the libraries in question.

Index of Bible References

Numbers in italic type indicate references in texts, rather than in Introduction or Notes.

Index to Proper Names in Text

Names within, or prefacing, Bible quotations are not included.

Index to Introduction and Notes